13.50AA.
7

Between the idea
And the reality
Between the motion
And the act
Falls the Shadow

    *—T. S. Eliot,* The Hollow Men, *1925*

# French Communism
# in the Making, 1914-1924

ROBERT WOHL

Stanford University Press
Stanford, California
1966

Sources of photographs: 1, Collection Viollet; 2, 6, 12,
UPI; 3, 11, Bibliothèque Nationale; 5, 20, Dazy; 7, 8, 18,
22, Arbetarrörelsens Arkiv, Stockholm; 9, Hoover Institution; 10, 21, 23, Roger-Viollet; 17, 19, Musée Social; 24,
Keystone.

Stanford University Press
Stanford, California
© 1966 by the Board of Trustees of the
Leland Stanford Junior University
Printed in the United States of America
L.C. 66-15303

*Published with the assistance of the Ford Foundation*

# Preface

You see things; and you say "Why?"
But I dream things that never were; and I say
  "Why not?"
    —*George Bernard Shaw*, Back to Methuselah,
      *1921*

This book began with a question about the roots of the French political problem. Some may see my question as a reflection of the Cold War. I prefer to interpret it as a sign that the Cold War was coming to an end. At any rate, there can be no doubt about the political conditions that led me to my topic. In the middle 1950's, French democracy floundered helplessly between the extremes of the Right and the Left. Immobility was its operating principle; frustration, rage, and dark pessimism were its most visible fruits. If the Right was so successful in thwarting change, it was in great part because the Left was so divided. The key to the French political muddle, it was clear, lay in the French Communist Party—and the groups who voted for its candidates, participated in its demonstrations, and wrote long and learned essays justifying its existence. What did French workers, peasants, and intellectuals see in Communism, and why were they willing to overlook the obvious differences between Marxist theory and Russian practice? The answer to these questions was given by one of Simone de Beauvoir's characters. The Revolution would be made by the Soviet Union, Henri put it in *Les Mandarins,* or it would not be made at all. Hence the original orientation of my study. I wanted to know how French Left Wingers had come to identify their own hopes for improvement with the fate of the Russian Revolution.

This question seemed to call for a detailed analysis of the events of 1917–20. Yet the further I penetrated beneath the surface of the problem, the clearer it became that I would have to broaden the scope of my inquiry. I discovered, in the first place, that Communism had to be understood within a frame of reference different from the one with which I began. The PCF had not arisen in an ideological vacuum; nor was it enough to say it was a distant echo of the

Russian Revolution. Before 1914 there had been Socialism, revolutionary syndicalism, and too many varieties of anarchism to make naming them worthwhile. Moreover, under the eclectic leadership of Jean Jaurès, it seemed that the main bulk of these forces might be welded into a movement of Democratic Socialism. The working-class movement, Jaurès assured the Chamber in May 1907, had become parliamentary, so parliamentary that it was no longer possible to find in its motions the exact expression of its thought. Yet thirteen years later, on December 30, 1920, the delegates of Jaurès's own party assembled excitedly in the town of Tours and voted by a vast majority to join the Communist International. There had to be some connection between the PCF of 1920 and the SFIO of 1914. Thorez, I concluded, had somehow to be related to Jaurès. This explains my emphasis on the period before 1914. I need not apologize for having dragged the reader back into the muddy waters of the prewar period. From the standpoint of the present, what strikes the historian is not the menace of what emerged but the promise of what failed.

Second, I soon realized that 1920 was no more possible as an ending than 1917 had been as a beginning. Admiration for the Russian Revolution did not necessarily mean subordination to the Russian Communist Party. Nor, it turned out, had the domestication of the PCF been easy. For if the French were the most enthusiastic Bolsheviks of 1919, they were also the most rebellious Communists of 1922. Yet by 1924 the structure of the PCF had been transformed along Leninist lines, its first leaders, with a few exceptions, either excluded or deprived of influence, and their place taken by new men whose power was based not on their abilities or their popularity, but on their obedience to the leadership of the Russian Communist Party. How had the French Communists been brought to heel? What were those characteristics of French society which made the working-class movement susceptible to Communist control? Such questions inevitably led in the direction of comparison. Explaining what happened in France, I found, required knowing what happened in Russia, Germany, and Italy. French working-class leaders have always been aware that their movement differed from its counterparts in other European countries; I have endeavored to discover how and why.

Third, I came to the conclusion that the French working-class movement had to be studied in its relationship to the Russian Revolution. This relationship was one of cultural clash, as Franz Borkenau had early recognized and brilliantly explained: the Bolsheviks had tried to export Russian revolutionary methods to the West against the protests and resistance of Western Left Wingers. But it was also more than that, for neither the French working-class movement nor the Soviet regime stood still between 1917 and 1924. Both suffered a defeat; both adopted new techniques; both broke significantly with prewar patterns. And if it was true that the course of the Russian Revolution exercised a decisive influence upon the development of the PCF, it was also true that the impotence of the Western labor movement had had its influence upon the fate of the Soviet regime. What historical process linked events in France and events in Russia? Was there no larger explanation that would shed light on both developments? The search for an answer to these questions took me beyond the Left Wing, beyond the limits of the working-class movement itself, beyond France and Russia even, to a consideration of the ideological context within which all political movements operated in the early part of the century. Communism, I concluded, could only be understood in terms of a liberal crisis. The French Communist Party, in particular, had arisen because its prewar predecessors had failed. And their failure was, in turn, related to the holocaust of the First World War.

I ended, then, where others had begun. My work serves not to de-emphasize the importance of the War but to underline the havoc that it wrought and the men and movements that it buried. Communism was one of the many prices that Europe paid for its folly. Still, I would hope that all this stress on the large outlines of European history will not conceal the more ordinary human meaning of my story. When writing working-class history, there is an overwhelming tendency to speak in terms of abstractions—masses, ideologies, cost-of-living indexes, numbers of strikes and strikers, congress votes. The men who framed the ideas, led the strikes, and inspired the votes fade from sight and become pawns moved back and forth across graphs. The lack of reliable biographical materials and memoirs reinforces this tendency. I hope I have not neglected my graphs and my figures; the economic and social structure, I trust, will emerge quite clearly. But I am most of all anxious that the graphs and figures should come alive. The events that I describe concern not only the victory of one set of ideas over another, not only the passing of a social and economic system, but the triumphs and defeats of a group of men—for the most part, members of a single generation. I have sometimes judged these men harshly. This, I think, is the way that they would want it, for they judged harshly in their own time. They were not great men, but they fought for great ideas. And now their story deserves to be told.

I owe many debts of thanks. Of these I can mention only the most outstanding. Eugen Weber headed me down the path that led me to my topic. Cyril Black supervised the doctoral dissertation out of which the book developed; in the process, he managed to give me a taste for asking larger questions than historians are supposed to ask. If this book sometimes rises above mere narrative, it is very much his doing. Arno Mayer contributed numerous suggestions, some accepted, some rejected, but all informed by a deep knowledge of the subject. It was in answering his criticisms that I reached many of my conclusions. Kathleen Flanagan, my research assistant, was of more help than she herself suspected. Muriel Davison of Stanford University Press acted as a check on my exuberance and labored to prepare a bulky manuscript for publication. Nor should I forget the Ford Foundation, without whose financial aid the research for this book could never have been undertaken.

An American who approaches the study of French Communism must do so with misgivings. There is a gap between his world and the world of French working-class militants which books alone will not suffice to bridge. Moreover, suspicion of bourgeois intruders (not to mention fear of American hostility or incomprehension) makes the gathering of sources difficult. Assistance is thus not simply convenient; it is indispensable. Without it the student of Communism will never get beyond the outskirts of his subject. In my effort at understanding I have had the help of a number of persons, both here and in Europe, whose contribution cannot always be conveyed in footnotes. Alfred Rosmer, Boris Souvarine, Jules Humbert-Droz, C.-E. Labrousse, and André Frossard shared with me their memories and introduced me to some of the intricacies of French working-class politics. The Baroness Germaine de Rothschild opened doors that seemed securely bolted. Branko Lazitch and Milorad M. Drachkovitch provided me with hard-to-get biographical information, as did Jean Maitron, who also gave me access to the Monatte Archives before they were catalogued. Per Lind of the Arbetarrörelsens Arkiv, Agnes Peterson of the Hoover Institution, and Colette Chambelland of the Musée Social brought to my attention unusual materials that would otherwise have eluded me. Their unstinting willingness to help kept alive my sometimes flickering ideal of what a librarian should be.

There are others whose contribution is harder to summarize; yet they left their mark upon these pages. J. G. Bell of Stanford University Press harried me into presenting him with a substantially different—and I think better—manuscript than the one I had originally written. We did not always agree, but our disagreements had a way of improving the book. Annie Kriegel did so many things for me—intellectual, practical, and personal—that I hesitate to single out any one for emphasis. Perhaps the simplest thing would be to say that I learned more about French Communism at her home than anywhere else in Paris. My wife, Birgitta, submitted herself heroically to the ordeal of the index; she also encouraged me, caught me up short on my more outrageous generalizations, and reminded me that all books, even mine, must one day come to an end. Her high standards for scholarship were a constant guide. This book is dedicated to my mother. If today's deed is inseparable from yesterday's dream, if a commitment to craftsmanship is something that can be taught, if to inspire a book is to believe in it even when the author himself begins to doubt, then what follows is as much hers as mine.

R. W.

# Contents

*Eight pages of photographs follow p. 210*

# Abbreviations

| | |
|---|---|
| ARAC | Association Républicaine des Anciens Combattants |
| BP | Bureau Politique |
| CA | Comité Administratif |
| CAP | Comité Administratif Permanent |
| CD | Comité Directeur (Central Committee) |
| CGT | Confédération Générale du Travail |
| CGTU | Confédération Générale du Travail Unitaire |
| CCN | Comité Confédéral National |
| CN | Conseil National |
| CSR | Comité Syndicaliste Révolutionnaire |
| CYI | Communist Youth International |
| ECCI | Executive Committee of the Communist International |
| JC | Fédération des Jeunesses Communistes |
| KAPD | Kommunistische Arbeiterpartei Deutschlands (German Communist Workers Party) |
| KPD | Kommunistische Partei Deutschlands (German Communist Party) |
| NEP | New Economic Policy |
| PCF | Parti Communiste Français (French Communist Party) |
| POF | Parti Ouvrier Français |

PUP    Parti de l'Unité Prolétarienne

SFIO   Section Française de l'Internationale Ouvrière (French Socialist Party)

SPD    Sozialdemokratische Partei Deutschlands (German Social Democratic Party)

USPD   Unabhängige Sozialdemokratische Partei Deutschlands (Independent Social Democratic Party of Germany, or Independents)

French Communism in the Making, 1914–1924

## Chapter one

# The French Working-Class Movement before 1914

Ah! savez-vous ce dont nous souffrons le plus?
C'est qu'au fond, pour parler net, quand il s'agit
non pas de constater le mouvement général des
faits ou de prévoir le terme final de l'évolution,
mais quand il s'agit de déterminer la méthode
d'action du parti, l'action du parti, disons-le avec
le courage qui convient à un grand parti, trop
souvent, sous les mêmes mots, nous ne mettons
pas les mêmes idées.
—*Jean Jaurès, 1912*

Not only the bourgeoisie, with its banquets and its bonds, its solid francs and its even more solid families, regretted the good old days of pre-1914 France. To Socialists confronted with the schisms and impotence of the postwar decades, these seemed golden years of unity and comradeship, during which the party of Jean Jaurès and Jules Guesde appeared to be marching forward with all the momentum and inexorability of History itself. For syndicalists, the decade before 1914 emitted a no less sterling glow: these were the heroic years of the Confédération Générale du Travail, a rare moment in history when the forces of the working class were united, parties and politicians were banned from the unions, and "le grand soir" of the Revolution was a daily possibility rather than a dream. The historian must record such feelings; men live by myths, after all, and not by history. Still, he cannot help but suspect that in the years before '14 there lay the seeds of those troubles that came after. Were the schisms of 1920–21 implicit in the disagreements of 1905–14? Or did the War of 1914–18 come to smother the promising beginnings of a unified and democratic labor movement? The question is more than academic: an appreciation of what might have been is essential for a proper understanding of what is. The answer to such inquiries can only be sought in the evolution of the Socialist Party and the trade-union movement before 1914.

## GUESDISM

The French Socialist Party (Section Française de l'Internationale Ouvrière, or SFIO) was born at the Congress of Unity, held in Paris at the Salle du Globe in 1905. The terms of that unification had been very carefully weighed, and it is worth recalling them, for, like many married couples today, the party and its principles lived separate lives in more or less amicable isolation. The delegates to the Congress of Unity affirmed their common desire to found a party of class struggle and revolution, which, without neglecting the immediate reforms demanded by the working class, would always remain "a party of fundamental and unyielding opposition to the whole of the bourgeois class and to the State that is its instrument."[1] The commitment to revolutionary struggle is noteworthy chiefly because it marked the triumph of Jules Guesde's Social Democratic orthodoxy over the peculiarly French reformism of Jean Jaurès. The immediate impetus for unification and the terms on which it was achieved had not come from within France, but from the 1904 Congress of the Second International, in Amsterdam. Both Guesde and Jaurès had gone to Amsterdam to lay their case before the representatives of world Socialism. Despite Jaurès's impassioned eloquence, the decision had gone in favor of Guesde. The Dresden Resolution, which condemned the revisionist heresy, was to be applied in France. In the course of its deliberations, the Amsterdam Congress also found time to pass a unanimous motion calling for the unification of Socialist forces wherever they were divided. Both decisions were to influence profoundly the development of French Socialism. The first burdened the French Socialists with a program of German manufacture, which was, from the beginning, out of step with the party's practice and the social context within which it operated. The second had as its result the realization of Jaurès's long-standing dream of Socialist unity.

The Congress of Unity brought to an end 25 years of bickering and political infighting among the various groups vying for the leadership of the French Socialist movement. The countrymen of Babeuf, Saint-Simon, Fourier, Proudhon, and Blanqui, of course, might well have felt that they need yield to no one in their understanding of Socialism; their radical credentials extended back a century to the social whirlwind of 1789. As late as 1871, the Parisian lower classes reminded Europe that their fighting spirit still burned bright. But though the Commune was exhilarating while it lasted, its only practical effects had been to decimate the working-class movement and to discredit the two most popular revolutionary ideologies of the 1850's and 1860's: Proudhon's associationism and Blanqui's insurrectionism. It was true that many of Blanqui's disciples remained faithful to their imprisoned chief. They formed their own group, the Comité Révolutionnaire Central, and gave the French working-class movement more than their share of leaders, including Edouard Vaillant, Marcel Sembat, and Victor Griffuelhes. But Blanquism offered no key to the future: it had a symbol and rallying cry (Blanqui), a tradition (the insurrections of 1827, 1848, and 1871), and a goal (the dictatorship of the proletariat)—but no doctrine. Worst of all, it provided no sure link with the masses; and, if the defeat of the Commune contained any lesson for revolu-

[1] Numbered notes will be found at the back of the book, pp. 457–507.

tionaries it seemed to be that a Paris-based uprising by a minority of the working class was doomed to failure. An era of science, technology, and mass politics demanded new methods. Thus it was that French radicals, like the Russian Populists 15 years later, turned to the "scientific" Socialism of the Germans Karl Marx and Friedrich Engels.

The man who did more than any other to spread the new doctrine of Marxist Socialism in France was the radical journalist Jules Guesde.[2] Born in 1845 the son of a poor Parisian schoolteacher, Guesde had arrived at radicalism by the normal French route, being converted to atheism by Kant, to republicanism by Victor Hugo, and to radicalism by Proudhon. An article in defense of the Commune had brought him a heavy fine and a sentence of five years in prison, to which he had preferred the rigors and adventures of exile. While an exile in Switzerland, he flirted with the anarchists of the Jura and came into conflict with Marx. Conflict, however, gave way to admiration when Guesde decided that private property was an evil, and that economic and social problems could be solved only by collective ownership of the means of production. On returning to Paris in 1876, he studied Marx's writings and became acquainted with several German Socialists, in particular Karl Hirsch, a friend of Wilhelm Liebknecht. That same year he founded a radical newspaper, L'Egalité, in which he warned the workers against voting for republicans, who would inevitably betray them once they had passed through the doors of the Palais Bourbon, and called upon them to unify behind their own labor candidates.[3] The task of creating a proletarian party, which Guesde had set himself, was not an easy one. Not only were the workers intimidated by the memory of the suppression of the Commune, they were at that time attracted by the panaceas of republicanism, positivism, and cooperation. But Guesde's efforts, which Marx had followed anxiously from London, were crowned with success in 1879, when he persuaded the Third Workers' Congress at Marseille to declare against cooperation and in favor of collectivism and political action. Spurred on by this victory, Guesde crossed the Channel to London, where, together with Marx and Engels, he drew up a program for a new Workers' Party. The year was 1880.[4]

The newly formed Workers' Party (Parti des Travailleurs Socialistes de France) accepted the minimum program with which Marx, Engels, and Guesde had endowed it. But an important schism weakened the organization before it was able to get under way. It was to be expected that the anarchists and more timid radicals and syndicalists would leave the party once it was committed to the conquest of the State and the collectivization of property by political action; and this they did in 1880 at the Congress of Le Havre. However, even among the Socialists who remained, there were many, like Paul Brousse, Benoît Malon, and Gustave Rouanet, who found a lesson in revolutionary tactics from a German philosopher unpalatable. To them this minimum program, "born in Thames fogs," was "essentially anti-French" and too inflexible to be applied to the country at large.[5] The poor performance of the Socialists in the elections of 1881 (they received only 60,000 votes) convinced them that what was needed was a program of partial reforms. Moreover, the imperious manner of Guesde, whom the Socialist deputy Clovis Hugues christened "Torquemada en lorgnons," made obedience even less desirable. Condemned as anti-French, unrealistic, and dictatorial, it is not surprising that Guesde found himself in a minority at the Congress of St.-Etienne in 1882. The majority, under the leadership of Brousse, went on to found a new party, which was officially called the Fédération des Travailleurs Socialistes de France. However, Brousse's followers were more popularly known by Guesde's epithet for them—"Possibilists"—because of their emphasis on reform and municipal Socialism. The Guesdist minority withdrew to Roanne, where it founded the Parti Ouvrier Français (POF). This early split is significant chiefly for its exposure of a deep-seated aversion in French Socialists to foreign revolutionary doctrines, ideological homogeneity (especially at election time), and centralized organization. The French Communist Party would later be plagued by the same type of revolt.

The Guesdists were undaunted by this first schism. Under the leadership of Guesde and his brilliant second, Paul Lafargue, the POF established strongholds in the heavily industrialized North, in Lyon, Marseille, Roanne, Troyes, and in the Haute-Vienne, though Paris eluded their grasp.[6] The Socialist gospel as taught by Guesde was both simple and persuasive to a proletariat that felt alienated from the national community and exploited by its employers. The terrible abuses of the capitalist order, Guesde never tired of repeating, could be overcome only by "the expropriation of the capitalist class and the collective appropriation of the means of production and exchange."[7] Cooperation, trade unionism, pensions, social security, anti-clericalism, anti-militarism —none of these could eliminate the basic exploitation inherent in the capitalist system. In fact, any movement that distracted the worker from the struggle against capitalism was to be opposed as a dangerous diversion from the main task of revolution. Reforms were to be sought not because they could transform the capitalist order from within, as the Possibilists thought, but because the struggle for reform would heighten the workers' revolutionary consciousness.[8] To carry out the expropriation of the bourgeoisie, the working class would create a proletarian party, which would seize power through revolution. In order to be successful, this working-class party must be highly organized and disciplined. It must eschew no means in its struggle for political power. Thus far universal suffrage had been merely an "instrument of dupery," but it could be turned into an "instrument of emancipation" if the proletariat used it properly.[9] Electoral campaigns must be utilized as a forum for Socialist ideas, a unique opportunity to unmask the capitalist enemy and win new recruits.

Capitalist democracy was a sham, but the Republic was a necessary stage because under the Republic the class struggle was most naked and thus most directly experienced. Only a violent revolution could overthrow the bourgeoisie —Guesde did not believe that classes committed suicide—but revolution could be hastened through the use of the ballot box. Political power would be won by a minority led by an elite, and it was the task of this vanguard of the proletariat to seize the State machinery, to smash it, and to replace it with the dictatorship of the proletariat.[10]

Guesde believed that revolution was inevitable, and that the progress of science and industry which the bourgeoisie itself had set in motion was bringing it closer daily. In the mid-1880's the gaunt Marxist prophet seems to have thought the historic moment close at hand. In 1885, on the occasion of the clash of Russian and British imperialist ambitions in Afghanistan, Guesde wrote two curious articles, in which he predicted that the conflict of Russia and Britain, the two great bulwarks of reaction, would precipitate world revolution. Guesde made a distinction between progressive wars, which opened the way to revolution, and reactionary wars, which pitted people against people and substituted race hatred for class hatred. The British-Russian conflict would be of the first type, a "fruitful" war. On the other hand, if the Russians were stopped in Central Asia, the result would be revolution in Russia; and, delivered from the menace of Romanov guns, the German Social Democrats, too, would revolt, and the question of Alsace-Lorraine would then be resolved in the only feasible way—by the abolition of frontiers. If, on the other hand, Russia defeated Great Britain, the British Empire would revolt, and the last obstacle to revolution in England itself would be removed. Guesde concluded with an ode to the creative effects of war and cataclysm:

> Coule, coule, sang du soldat,
> Soldat du tzar ou de la reine
> Coule en ruisseau, coule en fontaine.
> C'est pour l'humanité, cette fois, que
> cette rasée sera féconde.[11]

I have not dwelt on these early views of Guesde for the joy of disinterring the bleached remnants of old ideas, but rather because this ideological cluster, with its emphasis on violent revolution, party discipline, and international revolution issuing out of war, is strongly reminiscent of the positions later associated with Bolshevism. Lenin himself would not have denied it. And it is not surprising that Grigorii Zinoviev could write admiringly of Guesde, or that Marcel Cachin, one of Guesde's disciples, could argue at the Congress of Tours that Bolshevism was merely Guesdism brought up to date.[12] Why, one wonders, if France had something resembling Leninism, did she have no Bolshevik Party? The simplest answer would be that Guesde was no Lenin.

The dreary dogmatism of the Frenchman was no match for the brilliant political improvisations of the Russian. A more profound answer, however, would be that France was not Russia. For if Guesde remained true to these early views, his party did not. We will return to this point later, but I wish to note here that there is a striking discontinuity between the Guesdism of the 1880's and the Communist Party that would be born at Tours.

### JAURESSIANISM

Ideological and organizational division remained the hallmark of French Socialism well into the 1890's. The second major schism occurred in Brousse's party, the Possibilists. By 1890 an important group within the party, led by the typesetter Jean Allemane, was seriously disturbed by an increasing *embourgeoisement* of the party's cadres and the tendency of party leaders and deputies to concentrate on narrowly electoral matters at the expense of political efforts on a national scale.[13] The party, they feared, was on the way to becoming simply a vote-getting machine. Allemane and his followers withdrew from the party in 1890, when they were defeated at the Congress of Châtellerault; and the next year they went on to form their own organization, the Parti Ouvrier Socialiste Révolutionnaire. The Allemanists believed that the emancipation of the proletariat had to be the work of the workers themselves. All their elected officeholders were under the direct supervision of a party committee of surveillance and, like the Communists later, were required to sign an undated letter of resignation and to contribute a substantial percentage of their government salary to the party treasury. The Allemanists also played an active role in the trade unions, where they often cooperated with the anarchists in their championship of the general strike and anti-militarism.[14] Suspicion of bourgeois Socialists and fear of the corrupting effects of political office found their fullest expression in the CGT and revolutionary syndicalism. But their influence was not confined to the unions: after 1905 Aristide Jobert, Robert Louzon, and the syndicalist Bourderon gave voice to these fears within the SFIO; they were always particularly strong in Paris; and they were to reappear in the Communist Party during its formative years.

Thus, by the mid-1890's there were in France at least four well-defined Socialist parties: the Guesdists, who emphasized the class struggle and the organization of the working class for both electoral campaigns and union activities; the Possibilists, who called for political action on the local level and the slow infiltration of the State from below; the Allemanists, who viewed parliament with suspicion and stressed the role of the working class in its own emancipation; and, finally, the Blanquists, who looked to the conspiratorial overthrow of the State and a dictatorship of the proletariat. There was, in addition, a fifth group of Socialists, known as the Independents, who, though few in number, were significant in electoral strength and influence. The Independent Socialists had first formed around Benoît Malon's *Revue Socialiste* and Jules Vallès's *Cri du Peuple*.[15] Though uncommitted to any doctrine (ideological flexibility was the essence of their position), they were united by their moderation, their faith in parliamentary methods, and their desire to base their views on the idealism typical of French revolutionary tradition rather than on the German materialism of Karl Marx. To many of the Independents, as Denis Brogan has observed, "Socialism meant little more than a generous hatred of bourgeois complacency and a vague dislike of the wage system."[16]

Despite their ideological ambiguity, the Independents soon demonstrated that their version of Socialism appealed to the masses. Of 48 Socialist deputies elected in 1893, 30 were Independents. In 1896, at the famous Socialist banquet of St.-Mandé, Alexandre Millerand presented a minimum program emphasizing gradual nationalization of the means of production, the conquest of political power by means of universal suffrage, and working-class internationalism; two years later the Independents organized themselves into the Fédération des Socialistes Indépendants de France. To have attended the school of Independent Socialism was, it turned out, if not a claim to orthodoxy within the working-class movement, at least a favorable credential for the premiership: three of the Independents, Aristide Briand, René Viviani, and Millerand himself, outgrew Socialism to become ardent defenders of that bourgeois Republic whose grave they had set out to dig. They will all appear again in this story. But the greatest of the Independents, and a man destined not only to remain faithful to Socialism, but to enrich and develop its doctrines, was Jean Jaurès.

It would be hard to imagine a Socialist temperamentally more different from Jules Guesde than Jaurès; yet together the two men shaped French Socialism and gave it its ideas and its style. Though like Jaurès a great orator and a mover of men, Guesde was a doctrinaire, a propagandist, an organizer, and, one suspects, at heart a disciplinarian. Guesde's mind was above all critical and analytic. When he looked at the world he saw not harmony and unity, but conflict and antagonism.[17] This outlook was, at least in part, a reflection of his own experience. Though of bourgeois origin, Guesde was a *déclassé*; a man of considerable culture, he had picked up all he knew in extensive reading and travel. For him the class struggle was a fact, not a theory. Jaurès, by contrast, was that extremely rare phenomenon in modern politics: the moralist, the philosopher, the poet become parliamentarian and party leader. This explains the contradictory judgments pronounced on Jaurès by both friends and enemies, some of whom, like Joseph Caillaux, considered him a thinker and a visionary rather than a politician; others of whom, like Georges Sorel, thought him a vulgar politician who was little better than a "cattle-dealer."[18] Judging Jaurès was further complicated by the fact that his mind operated according to a logic of its own: where others saw the clash of antagonistic principles, he saw unity.[19] His entire career was a tribute to his effort toward synthesis—of reform and revolution, of idealism and materialism, of individualism and collectivism, of nationalism and internationalism.

Guesde had adopted Socialism out of his conviction that it was the only alternative to a sick and evil society in the throes of dissolution, and out of his belief that the proletariat had to organize itself and capture the State in order to expropriate the capitalists. Guesde often seemed to be repeating by rote sterile and outmoded formulas learned in the 1870's. Jaurès was as open as Guesde was closed, as eclectic as Guesde was sectarian. His way to Socialism was both slower and more complex than Guesde's. For Jaurès, Socialism was a series of "discoveries and successive integrations."[20] In his first term as deputy, from 1885 to 1889, Jaurès was associated not with the Socialists but with the Opportunists. It was only in 1892-93 that the young professor of philosophy committed himself to collectivist Socialism; and even so there were many elements in Marxism to which he remained forever hostile.

Much of the difference in the Socialism of Guesde and Jaurès is explained by the fact that Jaurès came to Socialism not in the 1870's, when the memory of the Commune was still fresh and the workers excommunicated from the national community, but in the 1890's, when the Republic was firmly established and democracy a reality. Jaurès was himself the product of that Republic and that democracy. He was educated by the Republic and at the expense of the Republic; he became Vice-President of the Chamber of Deputies by way of an academic career, the usual ladder of advancement for intelligent sons of the petty bourgeoisie; he possessed, in its most perfect form, the French gift for clear but emotional oratory; and he had an intuitive respect for the values of those classes, scorned by Marx as reactionary, that constituted the social underpinning of the Third Republic: the peasant's attachment to the land, the artisan's satisfaction in a job well done, the desire of the petty bourgeois for capital and a *situation acquise*.[21]

Guesde believed that since capitalism was a universal phenomenon, the same policies were valid for all Socialist parties in all countries. Jaurès accepted Guesde's concept of "universal Socialism," but he felt that it had to be "adapted to our political and economic conditions, to the traditions, ideas, and spirit of our country." Just as there was a distinct French people within the human race, so there must be a distinctly French Socialism within the international Socialist movement.[22] Jaurès's attempt to synthesize international Socialism and French Socialism, Marxism and the French revolutionary tradition, provides one of the three major themes in the last 20 years of his life. The other two, his struggle for a unified party and his campaign for peace, in turn led him to an increasing emphasis on internationalism; for it was the International that assured him of a unified party, and it was from the action of international Socialism that he hoped to secure world peace.

Since French Socialism had its historical source in the republican movement, it is not surprising that Jaurès stressed continuity with the past. Socialism was to be not the negation but the completion of the bourgeois Republic, the extension of the Rights of Man from the political to the economic and social spheres. This veneration for the Republic and democracy shaped Jaurès's attitude toward revolution and reform. Though he never ruled out the possibility of a violent revolution, Jaurès clearly thought that it would be unnecessary and regrettable.[23] What Jaurès could never accept was the idea of revolution by a minority. A minority, no matter how intelligent or energetic, did not suffice to make a revolution; the task of holding power and constructing a new society was too great.[24] Socialism, then, would not be achieved by a sudden coup d'état, but rather by what Jaurès called "revolutionary evolution." What was "revolutionary evolution"? "As I understand it, it consists of introducing new forms of property into present-day society, forms that give this society the lie and go beyond it, that point to and prepare the way for the new order, and that by their inherent reach hasten the breakup of the old."[25]

Nonetheless, it would be incorrect to put down Jaurès as a simple reformist. In the great debate over revisionism opened by Eduard Bernstein, Jaurès agreed with neither the orthodox Marxists nor the revisionists. He disagreed with Bernstein because he believed that Socialism was necessarily revolutionary.[26] That revolution was the final goal must never be lost from view. Simple, day-to-day trade unionism was not enough. At the same time, Jaurès thought reforms were a means to revolution. They brought closer the final collapse of the old order. They were not "a bed of rest, but the camp bed on which the working class recouped its fighting strength."[27] Thus balanced between reformism and revolutionary fervor, Jaurès could claim that he stood for both "maximum reforms" from the Chamber and "maximum action" from the unions.[28]

Perhaps the most important element in Jaurès's Socialism was its moral idealism. Though fully aware of the material forces determining man's existence, Jaurès believed in the ability of men to shape their fate. For him—and this was where he departed from Marx—idealism and materialism were not antagonistic, but complementary.[29] Nor was historical idealism just an intellectual failing on the part of Jaurès; it was the wedge with which he opened a place in Socialism for the action of morality. For Jaurès, Socialism was not only inevitable, as Marx had said; it was also just. The victory of Socialism would thus not be the victory of a single class, the victory of the proletariat alone; it would be the victory of Humanity and Justice.[30]

This moral and humanitarian vision of the Socialist future was no doubt largely responsible for the popularity of Jauressianism. If Guesde was the prophet of the Socialist Revolution, preaching fire, brimstone, and eternal damnation, Jaurès was its poet, summoning believers and nonbelievers alike to heavenly reconciliation and social peace. The coming of Socialism, Jaurès said, would be "like a great religious revelation."[31] It would be "an ascension" for both the bourgeoisie and the proletariat. The sons of the bourgeoisie could enter the new order with pride.[32] The Socialists would not destroy private property; rather they would preserve, by a new organization of labor, "what is legitimate in personal property, and wipe out what is iniquitous and inhuman in it."[33] The Socialist Revolution, moreover, would be a revolution of art; it would summon "to the life of art and the life of beauty all human beings, whoever they might be; for the first time, our disinherited proletariat will know the sacred beauty of art."[34] Finally, the Socialist Revolution would be a revolution of liberty; it would be "the supreme affirmation of human rights." The authoritarianism of Louis Blanc and the anarchism of Proudhon would be reconciled in a Socialist society that was "at once one and diverse, organized and pluralist, disciplined and free."[35] Thus, the Socialist Revolution would be just, it would benefit all classes, it would be individualist as well as collectivist, it would fulfill the human personality, it would increase man's power over nature and his wealth, and it would give "man's efforts an intensity and effectiveness hitherto unknown."[36]

By the mid-1890's the spirit of sectarianism in the French Socialist movement seemed to be giving way to a widespread desire for unity. The factions were in decline. Brousse's party was no longer a force; the Possibilists' heyday had been the 1880's. Blanquism had always been more a mood than a program, and by 1895 that mood seemed a faint memory from the insurrectionary past, which came to life only during the yearly pilgrimages to the Mur des Fédérés. Allemanism, with its *ouvrièrisme,* its distrust of politicians and intellectuals, and its emphasis on the class struggle, was destined to find its outlet not in the Socialist movement but in revolutionary syndicalism.[a] In 1897 Allemane's party suffered a schism of its own, when its Parisian officeholders rebelled against the rigorous discipline to which they were subjected. The result of the split was a new group—the Alliance Communiste Révolutionnaire, a campaign committee rather than a party. Ideology no longer seemed the insurmountable barrier between the Guesdists and their Socialist rivals it had been 15 years before. In the early 1890's, the Guesdists had moved toward reformism, while Jaurès and the Blanquist Edouard Vaillant were now ready to accept much of Marxism, which, by Engels' death in 1895, was identified not with revolution and cataclysm, but with science, evolution, the organization of the proletariat, and the peaceful conquest of political power by universal suffrage.[37] As early as 1894 Guesde had remarked: "I can die now, since there is a man like Jaurès who will continue my work and bring it to fruition."[38] Organizational unity

[a] The Allemanists played an active role in the creation of the Fédération des Bourses du Travail. In 1900, out of 48 Bourses belonging to the federation, ten were controlled by the Allemanists. Pelloutier, *Histoire des Bourses du Travail* (1902), p. 151.

seemed called for, and negotiations for a merger of the competing groups were undertaken in 1896.

But the movement for unification was dealt a sudden setback by the entry of Alexandre Millerand into Waldeck-Rousseau's Ministry of Republican Defense in the aftermath of the Dreyfus case, and by Jaurès's participation in the Left Bloc during the premiership of Emile Combes. The Millerand affair forced the Socialists to confront the question of bourgeois allies and ministerialism. Should Socialists distinguish between progressive and reactionary elements in the bourgeoisie? Should they be party to the quarrels of the class they hoped to overthrow? Should a Socialist participate in a bourgeois government, as Millerand had done, in order to save Republican liberties? Jaurès answered all these questions in the affirmative: the Socialists were duty-bound to march alongside bourgeois defenders of the Republic; the proletariat would be responsible if the bourgeoisie committed an injustice that the working class might have prevented; moreover, the Socialists had nothing to fear from collaboration with the bourgeoisie. Guesde countered that such collaboration led straight to the abandonment of the class struggle, and that the campaign for Dreyfus had left the system that condemned Dreyfus intact, and therefore had not brought the proletariat one whit closer to collectivist society.[39]

For almost six years French Socialism was torn by the quarrel. The precious unity attained during the early 1890's was temporarily lost, as the Guesdists and Blanquists formed an anti-ministerial party and Jaurès and his followers a rival group. It was these two organizations, the Parti Socialiste de France and the Parti Socialiste Français, that the International intervened to unite at Amsterdam. The great debate over ministerialism, as we have seen, was decided by the German Social Democrats in Guesde's favor. Millerandism stood condemned and the Left Bloc banned. Thus, on the morrow of unity, Guesdism seemed to have won its final victory. Marx was safely installed as the god of the French Socialist movement after years of struggle. Or was he?

### THE SOCIALIST CONSENSUS

The unification of the two great Socialist factions in 1905 did not put an end to dissension in Socialist ranks. True, the Socialists remained faithful to their pact—or at least as faithful as might reasonably have been expected in a country where the second ballot made electoral bargains a political necessity as well as the better part of valor. They refused to vote for the budget; they supported the CGT in its constant skirmishes with the government; and they ceased all official cooperation with the Radicals, thus giving notice that they would eschew the illicit pleasures of government participation savored during the days of the Délégation des Gauches. No new Millerand arose to barter his Socialist soul for a minister's portfolio.[b] The issues of ministerialism and col-

[b] Briand and Viviani both refused to follow Jaurès into the new Unified Party.

laboration with the bourgeoisie, so bitterly debated from 1899 to 1904, now seemed dead, and Socialist orthodoxy assured.

But, although there was no real threat of schism during the years between unification and the War—the Socialists clung to their hard-won unity with almost religious passion—the leaders of the party were deeply divided over the major questions of the day, particularly over the anti-war campaign and relations with the CGT. These issues did not divide the party into the same reformist and revolutionary factions that had flourished before 1905—that split lingered on as a clash of temperaments, personalities, and sometimes doctrine. It was dwarfed, however, by the division between those who believed in some kind of drastic anti-governmental action in the event of war and those who thought such action impractical or dangerous, and by the conflict between those who sought a rapprochement with the revolutionary leaders of the CGT and those who wished to put the unions and their leaders in their place. The ironic result of these new preoccupations was that Guesde, who was skeptical of anti-militarism and hostile to revolutionary syndicalism, often seemed more conservative than Jaurès. In the great majority of cases, Jaurès succeeded in carrying the party with him, thanks in no small measure to the aid of the old Communard Edouard Vaillant, who lent the sanction of revolutionary tradition to Jaurès's compromises.[40] Thus, although the party had been modified on Guesde's terms, it was Jaurès who emerged as its leader in the years after 1905.

The changed alignment in the SFIO after 1905 was merely a reflection, and a pale one at that, of the change in the nation as a whole. The Moroccan crisis of that year opened up a period of brinksmanship, during which the clash of imperialist and national ambitions made peace as uncertain as the Kaiser's mood. In France the noisy militance of the CGT and the stubborn resistance of successive Radical governments pushed the social question to the fore. The orthodox Socialism of Guesde and Kautsky, with its smug certainty of victory, inflexible economic laws, and reliance on universal suffrage, seemed to many both outmoded and uninteresting in the aftermath of the "coup de Tanger."[41] The new generation thrilled not to the rallying cries of the Dreyfus case, not to democracy and science, but to the cults of aviation and revolution, of energy and spontaneity, of violence and discipline, of faith and intuition. The doctrinaire anti-clericalism of the Combes era was followed by a religious revival among the youth. Not that the young men of the time hungered after a life of contemplation or withdrawal. On the contrary. What they sought and found in Catholicism was a "faith capable of inspiring us to action and heightening our energies."[42] The Republic and democracy, their foundations still shaky, were under attack from both the revolutionary syndicalists on the Left and the royalists on the Right. These extremists offered the up-and-coming generation new mystiques, which had in common, if not their goals, at least an emphasis on the action of elites and the use of violence.[43] Such movements had their appeal for a disillusioned and skeptical nation that had begun to lose faith in the Republic and in democratic institutions. But, whatever the movement chosen, whether it was the revolutionary syndicalism of Sorel, the royalism of Charles Maurras, the Christian Socialism of Marc Sangnier, the Socialism of Jaurès, or the wild Futurism of the Italian Filippo Marinetti, this was a time for commitment. "Barking in the night," Romain Rolland wrote in evocation of the era's mood, "from one farm to another, in the midst of great forests, they took up one another's call without respite. The night was stormy. It wasn't easy to sleep in those days! The wind carted through the air the echo of so many injustices!!"[44]

The Socialist Party did not escape the ideological excitement of the period. In fact, during the years 1905–14, the party often seemed little more than a whirlpool of conflicting trends, held together by some magic force. Perhaps the best example of this doctrinal chaos was the discussion at the 1908 Congress of Toulouse of the question of reform. On the extreme Right was the unrepentant *blocard* J.-L. Breton, who warned the party against "the dangers of a policy of systematic isolation" and called for a return "to the republican and democratic traditions of French Socialism." On the extreme Left stood the former Allemanist Aristide Jobert (a colleague of Gustave Hervé on *La Guerre Sociale* and, like him, from the Federation of the Yonne), who represented an antiparliamentary and anti-militarist faction that had strong support in the Federation of the Seine. Jobert accused the party of being interested only in elections and the pork barrel. Instead of activity in the Assembly, to which he and his friends ascribed only "an importance of the thirty-sixth order," Jobert called upon the party to emphasize direct action: appeals to the people, a general strike, and insurrection. More difficult to classify was Hubert Lagardelle, a follower of Sorel who questioned the party's right to represent the proletariat, and saw for it a future as the bourgeois ally of revolutionary syndicalism. Guesde himself did not speak, but Paul Lafargue presented the orthodox Marxist interpretation—though with more revolutionary feeling than most Guesdist delegates were able to muster. For Lafargue, "parliamentarism was the regime of the lie," and, though the Guesdists favored sending deputies to the Chamber, it was not because this weakened the power of the capitalist government (the capitalist reaction was stronger than ever under Clemenceau), nor because the reforms they might help pass would establish Socialism step by step (the most useful reforms could not make the life of the working class bearable under the conditions of capitalism), but because the Chamber gave the party "a new battlefield, the most magnificent battlefield." And, towering above the extremes, trying to reconcile them all, were Vaillant and Jaurès, who paid homage to both reform and revolution, to both parliamentary activity and the general strike, to both Socialism and syndicalism. As Vaillant put it: "It is our wish that nothing standing for material, institutional, or intellectual progress be alien to the party, but that, on the contrary, it become part of the party's over-all program."[45]

Yet for all the din of congresses, the impassioned debates between Jauressians and Guesdists, and the sparkling repartee, there was at the center of this whirlpool of tendencies a deep consensus. That consensus consisted of a common commitment to parliamentary action and Republican defense, and a common desire to preserve the integrity of the party from the corruption of ministerialism and opportunism. The shared assumption was that if the SFIO preserved its own political purity, it could not help but fall heir to the bourgeois legacy. Though there were many ideas of how the revolution would come about, only a handful of syndicalists on the Left thought of the future Socialist regime as anything but the fulfillment of the Radical Republic.[46] This was as true of the Guesdists as it was of the Jauressians. Long before 1908, in fact, the distinction between Guesdists and Jauressians had begun to shrink. Both pursued a policy of reformism and cooperation with the leftist elements of the bourgeoisie, though the Guesdists were careful to deny it theoretically. The Guesdists' careful doctrinal distinctions hid the real consensus that underlay the party.

This is not to suggest that the SFIO harbored no factions. The Guesdists constituted an island of discontent: though recognizing Jaurès's virtues, they could not bring themselves to trust him. The insurrectionary anti-parliamentary, and syndicalist Left Wing (Hervé, Jobert, Lagardelle, André Morizet, Ernest Lafont) never failed to make its dissonant voice heard. Moreover, there were always on the Right awkward reformists like Alexandre Varenne and Albert Thomas to remind the revolutionaries that in fact they acted no differently from the moderates, and who called on the party "to say out loud what it always does in practice"—namely, that it would obey republican discipline and that it was a party of reform, in fact, "the best artisan of reforms."[47]

Still, the striking thing about this party was the breadth of its center and the weakness of its extremes. Those who threatened to escape from the consensus were drawn back by the magic force of Jaurès's ability to reconcile the irreconcilable. The Congress of Toulouse itself is the best example of the way the party framed its resolutions and its tactics. For, with one abstention (Breton's), the delegates unanimously approved a text that echoed the speeches of Jaurès and Vaillant almost verbatim. "Precisely because it is a party of revolution," this document read, the Socialist Party was "the party most basically committed to reform and the most active in its behalf."[48] The Guesdists could vote for this statement because it emphasized both the limits and the value of reform, the Left Wing because the general strike and insurrection had been recognized as legitimate weapons against the capitalist order; and even the Right could join in, because it was clearly stated that the party did not confuse true revolutionary movements with "skirmishes in which the workers hurled themselves at random against all the forces of the bourgeois State." Besides, what moderate did not have in his back pocket a revolutionary speech for appropriate occasions? And, to complete the story, it should be noted that the anti-parliamentarist Jobert went on to be elected to the Chamber in 1914.

What, one might ask, had happened to the militant Guesdism of the 1880's, the revolutionary Socialism that prefigured Lenin's Bolshevism in so many ways? Guesde still clung to his basic ideas: the inevitability of class struggle; the need for a social revolution to create a collectivist order; political power as the means to a revolutionary end; the use of universal suffrage to undermine the bourgeois State and to organize the workers. Even as late as 1907, Guesde insisted that he had never for a moment claimed that the proletariat must come to power legally. Elections were only a means of organizing the proletariat: "Ce sont ses grandes manœuvres."[49] But after 1893, though the doctrine remained the same, the emphasis in Guesdism changed. What Guesde would not admit was that organizing the proletariat and attempting to win public office had changed the very nature of the party and influenced the way its goals were seen.[50] Ultimately, the Guesdists were transformed by the political order they had set out to conquer; their success turned them into a party of reform. By 1897 the Guesdists had given up their anti-militarism, had modified their attitude toward private property in an attempt to win over the peasants and the petty bourgeoisie, and had begun to refer to themselves as the "party of order and social peace."[51] Why, then, did Guesde fight Jaurès so bitterly during the 1897–1904 period? For three reasons: first, because Guesde regarded Millerand's participation in the Waldeck-Rousseau cabinet as a breach of Socialist discipline; second, because he feared that the Socialists would be corrupted by associating with leftist elements in the bourgeoisie; and, perhaps most important of all, because Guesde's dogmatic temperament caused him to dislike Jaurès and fear the influence of his eclecticism on the working-class movement.[52]

Guesde's victory at Amsterdam in 1904 was not entirely pyrrhic, then, for the party did renounce collaboration with the Radicals. Jaurès accepted the decision of the International on this point, and Guesde had asked for nothing more. For that matter, the Guesdists themselves distinguished between Radicals and reactionaries at election time. But, this principle once established, it was Jaurès who gave the party its tone and its language, as the motion voted at Toulouse well shows. The short-term effect of the Dreyfus case and the Combes era had been to push the party in the direction of orthodoxy. The long-range effects were more profound and more lasting. Jaurès had succeeded in identifying Socialism not with a class, but with an ideal: Justice. And this, in turn, brought into the party a generation of young bourgeois intellectuals and professors who saw in Socialism the vanguard of democracy.[53] It was not the dogmatism of Guesde, or the insurrectionism of Hervé that dominated the party in the years before the War, but the soaring syntheses of Jaurès. As L.-O. Frossard, the first General Secretary of the French Communist Party, recalled his own conversion to Socialism: "I did not discover the doctrine right away. Jaurès flooded me with light. I was captured forever by the ideal he erected high up in the sky like a wonderful triumphal arch."[54]

### THE SFIO: A PROFILE

A political party is like an iceberg: ideology, that one-tenth which shows above, conceals the massive bulk of organizational and social forces that floats below. Though not to be discounted, ideology is more often a reflection of the latter than its determinant. And what lies beneath may help explain baffling contradictions on the surface. We have seen what the SFIO claimed to be and what it was; now let us look at the party's structure. How was it organized? How extensive was its support? What progress did it make in the ten years following unification? Who voted for its candidates? Who framed its policies? Finally, from which layers of society and from which occupations did it draw its voters and its leaders?[55]

There were three traditions upon which the party might have modeled its organization. There was, first, the example of the Guesdists, who had always stressed unity in doctrine and action. For Guesde there was one Socialist truth, whose principles never varied. The party must pursue the goal of Revolution as a centralized and disciplined body. Guesde's favorite analogy was with the army: the rank and file of the party were its troops, the leaders its general staff, party congresses an opportunity to review the troops; the Socialist divisions were to march off in good order to conquer the capitalist citadel; elections provided the best terrain for skirmishes with the enemy and the best opportunity to win new recruits from his ranks.[56] Second, there was the Allemanist tradition, providing for the close control of party deputies and city councilmen by a committee of surveillance. Finally, there was the precedent of the Independents, who, as their name suggests, clung zealously to both doctrinal and organizational autonomy. For them there could be no one doctrine and no one tactic, and organization was limited to a caucus in the Chamber and a campaign committee at election time, whose decisions were in no way binding. The resistance to organization of many Independents, one suspects of most, was based not on a specifically French predilection for liberty, as its partisans claimed, but rather on an awareness that today's class enemy might very well be tomorrow's ally. Jaurès differed basically from his fellow Independents in longing for a great, unified party that would gather in all Socialists. However, he believed that the party's doctrine and tactics could only emerge from the free clash of its members' opinions.[57]

The years of struggle directly preceding unification had gone far toward discrediting the Independent tradition. Jaurès had been sharply attacked by members of his own faction for defending Millerand against demands for his exclusion from the party.[58] In the Millerand case, and in others, independence had ended in class collaboration and ultimately in betrayal. The dangers of independence, then, were fresh in the minds of the men who had drawn up the new party's statutes. Moreover, there was the brilliant example of the German Social Democratic Party (SPD), the most powerful and most admired party in Europe[e] and a study in organization and discipline.

The statutes of the new party reflected Guesdist, Allemanist, and Independent influence as well as the experience of the struggle over Millerand. The revolutionaries got the firm commitment to the principles of class struggle and internationalism that they had wanted. They also got a certain measure of centralization. The basic unit of the party was to be the section, which corresponded to the administrative subdivision of the commune.[59] The various sections of a department formed a federation, administered by a federal committee. The party was governed by the decisions of a yearly national congress, to which the federations sent delegations in proportion to their own membership. In the interval between national congresses, the affairs of the party were administered by a National Council, which was composed of delegates from the federations (again in proportion to membership), representatives of the Socialist parliamentary Group (consisting of the party's deputies), and the Permanent Administrative Commission (CAP). The CAP had 22 members, including five paid officials—three secretaries and two treasurers—and was elected each year by the party congress. The revolutionaries' demand for institutionalized control over party deputies and journalists was also met. The deputies' delegation could comprise no more than a tenth of the National Council, and deputies could not belong to the CAP. The Group was required to submit an annual report to the party congress. Each deputy and city councilman was supposed to contribute ten francs per month (approximately $7) to the party treasury. All elected officeholders were to make themselves available to the party for public appearances. Every candidate for public office had to sign a pledge to respect the decisions of national and international congresses. Socialists accused of violating party regulations might, after a hearing, be expelled from the party. As for the press, every journalist would have absolute freedom of discussion in matters of doctrine and method, but was expected to abide by the decisions of national and international congresses in action. The National Council was supposed to control the party press, and could propose breaking off relations with any newspaper or review that did not follow the line laid down by party congresses.

It should be noted, however, that throughout these statutes there was a strong accent on federalism and individual rights. Thus the Independents, too, were satisfied, and the French dislike of centralization acknowledged. Each federation wrote its own statutes, selected its own candidates for public office, and

[e] By Guesde as by Lenin.

controlled its own members and press. A member of the party could be expelled only after a long and involved arbitration process, which included many opportunities for appeal. And the National Council was directed to exercise only "general political control" over the party press.

In theory, then, the party's organization was based on a subtle balancing of ideological homogeneity and intellectual freedom, of centralization and federalism, and leadership was divided among parliamentarians, paid officials, and delegates from the provinces. The statutes themselves were ambiguous; whether they were used to promote centralization and discipline or decentralization and free discussion depended on the men who administered them. These men, as it turned out, were willing to accept a minimum commitment to orthodoxy that was often violated in print and in action. The SFIO in the years before the War developed into an extremely loose structure, whose policies were set for the most part by a small group of parliamentarians, journalists, and intellectuals living in Paris. The attempt to subordinate the deputies to the party was only partly successful: no Socialist entered a bourgeois government, but the party's officeholders controlled as much as they were controlled. The party's leaders were all in the National Assembly, and what conflict arose tended to take the form of provincial rebellion against Parisian dominance, a problem, of course, that was not peculiar to the Socialist Party. The growing anachronism of the party statutes was recognized by the administrative reorganization of 1913, which ruled that deputies could enter the CAP provided they did not constitute more than a third of its membership; the force of this development was such that in 1914 more than half the men on the CAP either were deputies or soon would be.

With regard to control of the party press, it was the Jauressian conception which triumphed. Jaurès defended both the Left Wing and the Right against those who desired their exclusion; and it is a testimony to the ideological diversity of the unified party that it could find a place in its ranks and in the columns of its press for three such different men as the insurrectionalist and anti-patriot Gustave Hervé, the revolutionary syndicalist Victor Griffuelhes, and the reformist Albert Thomas. Both Guesde and Jaurès defended the right of the minority to be represented on the CAP when there was basic disagreement within the party on some major issue, as there was, for instance, in the case of the struggle against the danger of war.[d] It was thus that in 1920–21, during the

---

[d] Guesde stated at the Congress of Nancy that he favored proportional representation among the Socialists, even on the CAP. He took issue with Jaurès, however, for opening the columns of *L'Humanité* to non-Socialists like Griffuelhes. (SFIO, *4e Congrès national* [1907], p. 334.) At the Congress of Toulouse the following year, the Guesdists tried to expel the *Action Directe* group, led by Hervé and Jobert, which they considered non-Socialist. The point is that they were unsuccessful: Jobert and Hervé remained in the party.

great discussion on Bolshevism and the nature of the party, the tradition of the SFIO invoked in opposition to the new Bolshevik concept was the Jauressian tradition, the idea of "un parti de libre discussion et de libre critique." A party without free discussion, Jaurès had said in 1905, would be "a party of slavery."[60]

Even after unification, the Socialist Party did not succeed in becoming a mass party. Between 1905 and 1914 its membership rose more than two and a half times, increasing from 34,688 to 93,210.[e] However, a variety of circumstances prevented this growth from occasioning any facile optimism. First, these figures paled beside comparable figures for the German SPD, which by 1914 had more than a million members. Second, the SFIO's growth tended to come in spurts, during periods of hectic election campaigning. Third, the party's strength was not spread evenly throughout the country. In 1914 there were still departments where there was no Socialist federation and where the Socialist Party presented no candidates for office. The vast majority of party members came from the departments of the Nord, the Gard, the Haute-Vienne, the Aube, the Vaucluse, the Ardennes, the Pyrénées-Orientales, and the Seine. The north was a heavily industrialized area, but the south and Limousin were predominantly agricultural. During this period, the party maintained four dailies: *L'Humanité* in Paris, *Le Droit du Peuple* in Grenoble, *Le Populaire du Centre* in Limoges, and *Le Midi Socialiste* in Toulouse. The steady advance of *L'Humanité* under the editorship of Jaurès was heartening; by 1914 it was one of Paris's great papers. But the objective Socialist could not help but compare the 200,000 readers reached daily by his party press with the mass public across the Rhine, over two million strong, served by the SPD's 70 dailies.[61]

The Socialist electorate was more impressive. Even in 1906, the party had been a power in the Chamber. But in the eight years between 1906 and 1914, its vote jumped from 878,000 to 1,400,000, and its parliamentary Group from 54 to 101. Who voted for this party of class struggle?[62] Here one finds an interesting anomaly: much of the Socialist vote came not from workers, but from small proprietors, businessmen, government employees, and professional men. By 1914 Socialist propaganda had begun to penetrate the peasantry.[63] The Socialists, it seemed, were steadily encroaching on the electoral fiefs that had been the Radicals' preserve in the early years of the Third Republic.[64] But if the Socialists had succeeded in enlarging their electorate and winning the votes of the petty bourgeoisie, it was as defenders of the oppressed and the downtrodden, not as proponents of social revolution. As Georges Sorel caustically observed, "Parliamentary Socialism speaks as many languages as it has kinds of

---

[e] Much of this growth came in the election spring of 1914. At the end of 1913, the SFIO had only 72,765 members. Detailed membership figures were given at every National Congress in the Secretary's report and thereafter published in the official account of the congress's proceedings.

followers.... It is stopped by no contradiction, experience having shown that in the course of an election campaign, it is possible to bring together what in Marxist ideology are normally considered antagonistic forces. Besides, can't a deputy make himself useful to voters of every economic situation?"[1]

The leaders and militants of the party were very largely of bourgeois origin, and often intellectuals by training and profession. At the risk of simplification, one might describe the typical Socialist leader as a man whose parents were artisans, peasants, or white-collar workers, who had risen, by dint of his own efforts and the help of a state scholarship, to a position as journalist, lawyer, doctor, or schoolteacher.[65] In 1914, of the 27 leading militants only five were proletarian by either occupation or origin. Similarly, of the 76 Socialist deputies in the 1910–14 Chamber, eight were university professors, seven small farmers, seven journalists, seven lawyers, six doctors and pharmacists, five manufacturers and shopkeepers, one an engineer, one a chemist, and only 31 manual laborers and white-collar workers—and several of these were trade-union officials or civil servants.[66]

The fact that it was not led by workers and that it found voters in the bourgeoisie was in no way peculiar to the French Socialist Party. It was true, as Albert Thibaudet noted, that many leaders of the SFIO were trained as lawyers and professors;[67] and it is true that they gave the party its distinctly legalistic and academic stamp. Yet this argument from occupation is in the last analysis unsatisfactory. The vast majority of the leaders of the Second International were of bourgeois origin.[68] Lenin, after all, was trained as a lawyer; Zinoviev earned his living as a teacher; Trotsky and Mussolini were journalists. No, what distinguished the French Socialist Party was its commitment to the values of the bourgeois Republic. The French Socialists made no cult of the worker. Their aim was not to make proletarians of themselves, but to humanize both the bourgeoisie and the working class. Their ideals were the ideals of the bourgeoisie: thrift, security, craftsmanship, the family, justice. Here, then, was no red specter to frighten the bourgeoisie with; for nothing could be more orderly, more legal—or more bourgeois—than a Socialist congress, nothing more cour-

---

[1] Sorel, *Réflexions sur la violence*, 10th ed. (1946), pp. 54–55. Sorel pointed out that some Socialist candidates had separate electoral posters and platforms for the town and the country. Pierre Laval was a very good example of the kind of Socialist who could fit his speech and his posters to his audience. According to Henry Torrès, Laval covered the walls of Aubervilliers in 1914 with posters that appealed to the Socialist convictions of his voters in the following way: "Citizens, capitalism is disorder and suffering. It is iniquity in distribution.... Socialism is order and well-being. It is freedom and comfort shared by all members of the human family. My aim is to liberate labor from all exploitation and the citizens from all oppression." Laval was elected. (Henry Torrès, *Pierre Laval*, New York, 1941, p. 22.) Jacques Chastenet also remarks that the SFIO succeeded in penetrating the peasantry only by disguising itself "as left-wing Radicalism." (*Jours inquiets et jours sanglants, 1906–1918*, 1955, p. 150.) The question warrants further study.

teous than a Socialist interpellation in the Chamber. And to those sniping spokesmen of the syndicalist Left like Lagardelle, who accused the party of parading as a "class party" when it was really a "party of classes," Jaurès replied that the party had the right and the duty to look beyond the working class to all those shopkeepers, small farmers, and intellectuals who felt exploited.[69]

From the Marxist point of view, Jaurès may have seemed confused and even dangerous. But there is little question that, from the perspective of the French social and political situation, what he said made good sense. For in 1914, despite 14 years of what J. H. Clapham called an "industrial revolution" based on the expanded use of power, the proletariat still made up only two-fifths of the work force (39 per cent to be exact), while 44 per cent of all Frenchmen made their living in agriculture, 10 per cent in commerce, and 6 per cent in the civil service and the liberal professions.[70] Of far greater import for the future of a workers' party, however, was the fact that during the seven years from 1906 to 1913, an era of bitter class warfare, the industrial proletariat scarcely increased in size, while the bourgeoisie grew by one-sixth—from six to seven million.[71] For Socialists dedicated to democracy and universal suffrage, this was sobering news: it meant that a democratic social revolution could be made only with the aid and assent of the bourgeoisie.

### THE ORIGINS OF THE CGT

Like Janus, the French working-class movement faced in two directions: the Socialist Party looked toward the bourgeois Republic, while the federation of trade unions, the Confédération Générale du Travail, fixed its sights on the Revolution. In most European countries, notably in Germany and Great Britain, the trade unions had been satisfied to devote their attention to the daily task of representing the working class in its demands for economic reform, leaving political agitation and revolutionary threats to the Socialist parties. In France this division of labor had not occurred. The unions offered the working class not only an organization of resistance to the employer, but also an ideology. In Germany, Great Britain, and Russia, the day-to-day activities of the trade unions had led them in the direction of reformism. In France the Left wing of the labor movement found its outlet in the CGT; and though this band of revolutionaries probably never represented the attitude of the majority of organized workers (not to mention those outside the unions), it nevertheless gave French syndicalism its tone. Hervé, Jobert, and Lagardelle were merely tolerated in the SFIO; Griffuelhes, Emile Pouget, and Paul Delesalle made policy in the CGT.

Revolutionary syndicalism, the official doctrine of the CGT in the years before the War, took root between 1893 and 1905.[72] A curious mixture of the old and the new, of Proudhon and Marx, of industrial values and the revolt against the society brought by industrialism, its theory and practice emerged from an economic and social situation in which modern industry was in its infancy, the proletariat dispersed among small workshops, and the memory of revolution still alive.[73] Revolutionary syndicalism was the ideological offspring of a working class in the process of becoming a proletariat. Its doctrines were shaped in particular by three historical developments: the extreme sectarianism of the early Socialist movement; the growing disillusionment of the working class with parliamentary democracy and democratic Socialism that began to make itself felt after 1900; and, finally, the entry of the anarchists into the trade-union movement in the 1890's.

It was noted earlier that one of the great problems of the Socialist movement in the 25 years before 1905 had been its tendency toward division. A schism between the Guesdists and the Broussists in 1882; another split among Broussists in 1890, leading to the formation of the Allemanist party in 1891; the existence of competing movements such as the Blanquists and the Independents—all these divisions had their effect upon the development of the French trade-union movement. The result of rival Socialist appeals for trade-union support had been chaos. The first national federation of trade unions, the Fédération des Syndicats et Groupes Corporatifs (founded in 1886), fell almost immediately under the control of the Guesdists, who used its congresses as platforms for their own conceptions. The Fédération des Syndicats came to a dreary end in 1894, after splitting over the general strike, of which the Guesdists disapproved. From this experience working-class militants drew the conclusion that unity was impossible until the unions were independent of all political organizations.[74]

The years that followed bred disenchantment with the Republic. By 1905 the democratic and social Republic over which the Radicals had spilled so many fine words seemed no closer than it had 20 years before, when the unions had first been legalized. The Wilson affair, Panama, the Combes era—all these scandals, these persecutions, this *politique*—left in their wake a remnant of skepticism about the value of parliamentary democracy. One did not have to be an anarchist to agree with Proudhon that "Direct ou indirect, simple ou composé, le gouvernement du peuple sera toujours l'escamotage du peuple."[75] This skepticism extended to the Socialists, for though the worker voted for their candidates, he knew that the defections of Millerand, Briand, and Viviani would be followed by others.[g] True, Socialist pressure and a desire on the part of the bourgeoisie to blunt the edges of the class struggle had prompted some reforms: the ten-hour day for women, accident insurance, hygienic regulations, and, eventually, pensions. But reform had been piecemeal and grudging. Hours were still long, employment uncertain, housing conditions abysmal,

---

[g] Robert Michels noted that of the six Socialist deputies elected to the Chamber in 1893, only one remained faithful to the party until his death. The other five became "declared enemies" of the Socialist Party. *Political Parties* (Glencoe, Ill., 1958), p. 114.

existence in every way precarious. Clapham, certainly no prejudiced authority, could observe that "in the France of 1914 there was probably less 'practical Socialism,' less Socialist achievement in the broadest sense, than in any other country of Western Europe."[76] What evidence there is for the evaluation of living standards before 1914 suggests that although the French economy was booming and the national wealth steadily growing, the workers' share of the national income was actually shrinking.[77] It was the failure of the republican dream of class reconciliation which provided the backdrop for the social conflict of the decade before the War.[h]

The disunity of the Socialists, the betrayal of some of their most prominent leaders, the slowness of reform, the hard conditions of the workers' existence— all these factors help to explain why many workers turned in disgust from political action to trade unionism around 1900. But what they do not clarify is why this trade unionism took the unusual form of revolutionary syndicalism. Of course, the French proletariat had a revolutionary tradition lacking in more staid and stable countries. They were the heirs of Babeuf and Blanqui, of 1789 and the Commune. And the pull of tradition is never to be discounted in France. Yet revolutionary syndicalism was a basically new variant of this tradition. The missing element, the catalyst that turned trade unionism into revolutionary syndicalism, lay in the influence of the anarchists.

The early 1890's were the great age of anarchist terrorism and propaganda by the deed. But it became clear in France, as it had a decade earlier in Russia, that assassination and theft did not lead to revolution. As early as 1892 the anarchists began to infiltrate the unions.[78] Their aim, as one of them put it, was to wean the masses away from the Socialists, "who use the people today

---

[h] Take, for example, this song, which appeared in Pouget's *Almanach du Père Peinard* in 1899:

La République avait promis (bis)
De rendre les hommes tous amis (bis)
  Ell' disait: Liberté!
  Criait: Egalité!
  Voulait qu'on soit tous frères
A bas le son, à bas le son
  Voulait qu'on soit tous frères
A bas le son du canon!

La République avait juré (bis)
De faire la guerre aux curés (bis)
  Ell' devait dire adieu
  Aux églises, aux bons dieux
  Et nous rendre la terre
A bas le son, à bas le son,
  Et nous rendre la terre
A bas le son du canon!

La République avait promis (bis)
D'exterminer nos ennemis (bis)
  Nobles, riches et rois,
  Qui marchait sur nos droits
  Et viv'nt de nos misères
A bas le son, à bas le son,
  Et viv'nt de nos misères,
A bas le son du canon!

A ses promess's elle a menti (bis)
Ell' tourne le dos aux petits (bis)
  Ell' flirte avec les grands
  Couche avec les tyrans
  Et fusille nos frères,
A bas le son, à bas le son,
  Et fusille nos frères,
A bas le son du canon!

—Quoted in Jean Montreuil, *Histoire du mouvement ouvrier en France* (1946), pp. 214–15.

in order to advance their careers, and who, as masters tomorrow, would submit them to a heavier yoke than that of the bourgeoisie."[79] This process was further speeded up by the expulsion of the anarchists from the International in 1896. Chased from the International, hounded by the police, the anarchists took refuge in the unions, where they helped forge the theory and the practice of revolutionary syndicalism. Because of their political neutrality and their dedication, they soon were elected to positions of responsibility in the union movement.[80] Although the anarchists were not the only influence in the development of revolutionary syndicalism—Broussists, Blanquists, and Allemanists all played an important role—they left their imprint on the movement. They did not create the cry of revolt from which syndicalism issued, but they channeled it. And when syndicalist militants spoke of doing away with the State, warned against the danger of Socialists, hinted at a revolution in morals, and dreamed of a society of free producers, whether they knew it or not they were expressing themselves in the language of Proudhon and Kropotkin, a language that most of them had learned through prolonged and intimate contact with libertarian leaders.[81]

The CGT was founded in 1895, but the immediate results were meager. Only when the CGT merged with the Bourses du Travail (Federation of Labor Exchanges) in 1902 did it begin to wield real power among the workers. The key figure in the rapid growth of the labor exchanges was Fernand Pelloutier, whose short and tragic life streaked across the sky of the French labor movement like a comet.[82] A young man of strange and feverish appearance, fated to die at 33 of consumption and knowing it, totally dedicated to the workers' cause, Pelloutier moved from Guesdism to the Federation of Labor Exchanges, where, as Secretary from 1895 to 1900, he imbued French syndicalism with his ideals and his aspirations for the proletariat. Pelloutier believed, like many working-class leaders of the time, that the emancipation of the workers could only be effected by the workers themselves, and that independence from both the government and the Socialist parties was the prerequisite of working-class unity. His originality lay in his synthesis of anarchism and syndicalism, in his conviction that the means to the anarchist revolution was the labor exchange. Through the labor exchange, Pelloutier thought, the workers might build an anarchist society within the very citadel of the bourgeois State. When capitalism fell because of constant attack from within, the workers would be ready to replace it with their own institutions.[83] Pelloutier was convinced that, to free themselves, workers had first to be educated and enlightened; the working class, he insisted, had to raise itself spiritually. His definition of a revolutionary syndicalist remained the credo of an important segment of the CGT long after his death in 1900: "We are eternal rebels, men truly without god, without master, without country, the irreconcilable enemies of every form of despotism, whether moral or material, individual or collective—that is to say, of laws and dictatorships (including that of the proletariat)—and the passionate lovers of the cultivation of the self."[84]

Pelloutier did not live to see the union of the Federation of Labor Exchanges and the CGT in 1902 at Montpellier. Nevertheless, this new CGT was the organization which would carry on Pelloutier's legacy. It was the leaders of the new CGT—Griffuelhes, Pouget, Paul Delesalle, Alphonse Merrheim, Pierre Monatte—who hammered out the doctrines of revolutionary syndicalism in the decade before the War. The new CGT's organization was a strange combination of absolute centralization and absolute federalism.[i] Each union and labor exchange was independent of the Central and free to steer its own course; but, because of an undemocratic system of representation, the revolutionaries managed to win and keep control of both the Confederal Committee and the Confederal Bureau, against what was at the very least a strong minority of reformists and Guesdists.[85]

Unity and the growing social awareness of the twentieth century were a strong spur to growth. The CGT increased its membership steadily after the Montpellier congress, reaching 300,000 in 1906, 400,000 in 1908, and perhaps as many as 600,000 in 1914.[86] To be appreciated, however, this advance must be seen in perspective. The prewar CGT never attained either the huge memberships or the fat treasuries of the British and German trade-union federations. Its Confederal Bureau operated on a shoestring; and at the very height of its

---

[i] On second thought, not so strange; for the CGT's structure merely repeated, in an exaggerated form, the organizational pattern that recent French and American social scientists have found to be typical of French society as a whole. According to Stanley Hoffmann, the French style of authority tends to be neither democratic nor authoritarian. "It comes closer to a third model: the 'noninterventionist' style of authority, that is, not so much the blend as the coexistence of *limited* authoritarianism and *potential* insurrection against authority. What is most striking is the dislike of face-to-face discussions leading to compromises through participation of all parties involved in a problem. As in the authoritarian model, conflicts are referred to a higher central authority instead. However, the other essential aspect of this style is the sharp set of limits imposed on such authority: power is delegated to it so that the drama of face-to-face personal relations can be avoided but only in order that, and as long as, the exercise of power from above remains impersonal and curtailed both in scope (subject matter) and in intensity (means of action) by general rules, precedents, and inhibitions. Without such exercise of authority from above, the group or the society could hardly function—as in the authoritarian model—but the group does not display at all the solidarity found in that model, solidarity achieved through either common efforts to carry out the leader's orders or joint resistance to his commands. Since the only legitimate sources are the superior ones, but since the role of the leaders is also strictly limited, all associations below have an air of illegitimacy or conspiracy: this applies to peer groups in high school as well as to business associations or political parties." Stanley Hoffmann, "Paradoxes of the French Political Community," in *In Search of France* (Cambridge, Mass., 1963), pp. 8–9. See also Michel Crozier's brilliant essays "La France, terre de commandement," *Esprit*, December 1957, pp. 779–97, and "Le Citoyen," *Esprit*, February 1961, pp. 193–211.

militancy (1906–10) it probably represented less than 5 per cent of the workers eligible for union membership.[87]

Given the revolutionary syndicalists' numerical and financial weaknesses, it is all the more surprising that they should have been able to shake the foundations of bourgeois society before the War—but shake them they did. Strike after strike brought the CGT into conflict with the government, which, under the leadership of such former subversives as Clemenceau and Briand, was equally firm in its determination to maintain order. But, despite the staunchness of their government defenders, many bourgeois took the revolutionary manifestos of the CGT as the death knell of civilized society. In 1906, according to Eugen Weber, "Fear of a May Day uprising was widespread; housewives laid in stores sufficient to withstand a long siege, and then had to serve the accumulated macaroni and ham for weeks to protesting families."[88] And in 1909 the Nationalist deputy Cauthier de Clagny confessed that "One feels oneself slipping down a slope at the end of which one foresees an abyss.... Everything is disintegrating, everything is dissolving; all the foundations of the social edifice have been shaken loose; another jolt would be enough to bury us beneath the ruins."[89]

### SYNDICALIST DOCTRINE

The leaders of revolutionary syndicalism always denied that their movement had its origins in a doctrine. When asked whom he read, Victor Griffuelhes, the Secretary of the CGT, went out of his way to exclude Georges Sorel in favor of Dumas. Syndicalism, he claimed, was *the result of a long practice,* much more the creation of events than of such and such a man or men"; it was the product "of a life renewed and modified each day."[90] Griffuelhes was of course right, in the sense that revolutionary syndicalism did not emerge full blown from the head of any one man or the pages of any one book: its doctrines were the product of the reactions of many different men to the historical situation that I have sketched above. Its uniqueness as an ideology lay in the fact that it emerged out of a movement, out of a *practice,* as Griffuelhes put it, and not the other way around. Yet by 1906 revolutionary syndicalism had attracted to its banner such bourgeois intellectuals as Sorel, Lagardelle, and Edouard Berth, who were willing to supply the sophisticated theories that it lacked. Why?

To the intellectuals of these immediate prewar years, the practice of the CGT seemed extremely up to date. From certain points of view, it was. Joseph Schumpeter has written that "all revolutionary movements and ideologies that coexist at any given time always have a lot in common. They are the products of the same social process and must in many respects react in similar ways to similar necessities. Also, they cannot avoid borrowing from each other or splashing each other with their colors in their very squabbles."[91] Revolutionary syndicalism shared with Leninism a disdain for democracy and democratic Socialism, elitism, and a stress on violent revolution. The emphasis of its leaders on spontaneity and feeling and their dislike of intellectuals have led at least one historian to see in revolutionary syndicalism a French reflection of the wave of anti-rationalism that swept German and Italian youth in the decade before the War.[j] Like the Futurist Marinetti, the syndicalists thought that industrialism would bring with it a new culture and new values.[92] Another writer has found a similarity between the French General Staff's doctrine of the offensive and the syndicalist tactic of the general strike: they were both, he suggests, a "rationalization of weakness."[93] To close the circle, some Royalists dreamed of an alliance with the CGT, and Sorel was to make his way from syndicalism to Maurras to Lenin.[94]

Sorel's case of ideological homelessness was not the last. Other partisans of revolutionary syndicalism would drift away after the War, some to Communism, a few to fascism and corporatism, while still others would remain loyal to the old doctrines. The point is not that revolutionary syndicalism was a breeding ground for Communism and fascism—the great majority of syndicalists probably remained closer to Jaurès than to Sorel—but rather that it was a transitional ideology, a "mongrel creed," as Schumpeter called it, which seemed for a moment to reflect in its prism all the currents of the period.[95]

The core of syndicalism lay in its vision of the goal and the means by which the end might be achieved. The revolutionary syndicalists agreed with Marx that economic relationships were the dominant factor in human history, that the bourgeoisie and capitalism were doomed, and that the class struggle was inevitable. Since it was the economic factor in history that predominated, they argued, it was foolish to pursue the conquest of political power. While the Socialists worked to win control of the State and its administrative machinery in order to collectivize property, the revolutionary syndicalists wanted to smash the State and all its institutions. They believed that the movement of history was leading toward a stateless society, in which the basic units would be economic, not political—a loosely federated community of independent workshops that would be tied together in the same decentralized way as the labor exchanges and the unions in the CGT.

For syndicalists the class struggle was not only to be accepted, it was to be cultivated; for it was only in struggle with the bourgeoisie that the worker de-

[j] Carl Landauer, *European Socialism* (Berkeley, Calif., 1959), I, 354. It should be noted, however, that this anti-rationalism applied only to a segment of the French movement. A certain tendency represented by Pierre Monatte and Alphonse Merrheim never forgot Pelloutier's words: "The revolutionary mission of the enlightened proletariat is to pursue more methodically, more stubbornly than ever, the work of moral, administrative, and technical education necessary to make feasible a society of proud and free men." Quoted in Edouard Dolléans, *Histoire du mouvement ouvrier* (1946), II, 11.

veloped his self-consciousness and his will to revolution. Not that reforms were to be disdained; the syndicalists were well aware that men would rather work eight hours a day than ten. But these reforms were to be pursued not as an end—the workers' alienation could not be remedied within the framework of capitalism—but as a "springboard," "a pretext for action and agitation, a means of keeping minds alert."[96] There must be no reconciliation of classes. Democracy was as much a sham as any other form of capitalist government. In fact it was even worse, because it gave the illusion of equality. Reforms thus must be wrenched, not begged, from the bourgeoisie. The best way to carry on the class struggle was direct action: strikes, work stoppages, sabotage, and eventually the general strike. Direct action was preferable to political activity because it brought the worker face to face with his class enemy over economic issues, the real issues between them. Eventually the tempo of these struggles would rise, the economic conflict of today would become the conflagration of tomorrow, and the whole capitalist structure would collapse as the workers rose up in spontaneous anger and called a general strike: this would be the Revolution.[97]

The Revolution, it should be stressed, need not express the will of the majority. The leaders of the CGT were well aware that only a small percentage of the French proletariat shared their revolutionary aspirations. Out of their weakness they made a philosophy. Ideological precedents were not far to seek: both the anarchists and the Blanquists had put their faith in the revolutionary action of "an intelligent, conscious, and bold minority."[98] For the mass trade unions of Great Britain and Germany the revolutionary syndicalists had nothing but scorn. They were convinced that dedicated, courageous, and acutely class-conscious minorities could move and carry with them the inert masses. Their aim was not to assemble a huge army of industrial workers, which they could call out on strike as circumstances required, but rather to forge a battle-tested guerrilla band that could take the leadership of spontaneous mass movements; their tactic was not to engage in tests of strength with their class enemy, but rather to storm the capitalist fortress, calling strikes on the spur of the moment and calling them off just as quickly.[99]

The revolutionary syndicalists did not deny that their method was the "negation of the system of majorities,"[100] which they equated with the predominance of the unconscious mass.[101] As Alphonse Merrheim wrote in 1910, "It is not the voters, the passive people, who count, but the active ones. For the syndicalists, not the number but the will lays down the law."[102] Much to the displeasure of the reformists, whose unions were the largest, this principle was written into the statutes of the CGT. All unions had an equal voice in confederal deliberations, regardless of membership. One militant claimed after the Congress of Bourges in 1904 that the 27 members of the six weakest unions received equal representation with the 90,000 members of the six strongest.[103]

Thus revolutionary syndicalists distrusted intellectuals and politicians, put no store in parliamentary democracy, proclaimed their intention to destroy the State at the earliest possible opportunity, welcomed the class struggle, opposed any attempts at class reconciliation through reform, and, in their scorn for democratic method, put their faith in the action of minorities. Similar to Leninists in their elitism, revolutionary syndicalists differed from them markedly in their belief in spontaneity and in their conviction that syndicalism was the sharpest form of the class struggle. The originality of revolutionary syndicalism lay in its conviction that no real change was possible unless the workers created a whole new set of institutions to replace the bourgeois State, that the basis for this new culture could be found in the unions, and, finally, that the liberation of the workers could be brought about only by the workers themselves. This brings up the question of the relations between the CGT and the Socialist Party. For it should be clear by now that revolutionary syndicalism was violently opposed to the doctrine, practice, and social composition of the SFIO.

### THE PARTY AND THE UNIONS

Relations between the party and the unions were far from friendly, though accounts vary as to their actual degree of coolness. In 1907 a Socialist addressing other Socialists at a party congress called them "not cordial but, I would say as in diplomacy, correct."[104] The journalist Mermeix (Gabriel Terrail), in a book maliciously entitled *Le Syndicalisme contre le socialisme,* noted that the Socialist politician viewed syndicalism with as much alarm as the Conservative. The Conservative "fears it as a threat to his peace of mind, his property, and his social position"; the Socialist "fears its disobedience and the competition it gives him in working-class circles."[105] A third observer, this one a syndicalist, looking back on the period from the vantage point of 1922, concluded that from the time revolutionary syndicalism emerged as a political movement at the 1906 Congress of Amiens, "the labor movement in France had as its essential characteristic a perpetual conflict between these two elements—the aging father and the vigorous child, who had become enemies without daring to admit it to themselves."[106]

Many Socialists had hoped that after unification of the party in 1905, the CGT and the SFIO might be able to reach an understanding. These hopes were disappointed—at least in the short run. In 1906, at the CGT's famous Congress of Amiens, the confederation passed an almost unanimous resolution stating its aims as both the improvement of the worker's lot by reform and his "complete emancipation" by expropriation of the bourgeoisie. The position of the wage earner in a capitalist society made it incumbent on all workers to join a union, whatever their politics or philosophy. Members of the CGT were free to join any political or philosophical movement they chose, on the condition that they did not try to impose their ideas on other union members. The last and most controversial provision stated that as economic organizations, the unions need not concern themselves "with parties and sects, which are free to work toward a transformation of society outside [the unions] and alongside [them]."[107]

A compromise between the anarchists and the Guesdists, the so-called Charter of Amiens, was an ambiguous guide to future action. It was stated clearly that the CGT was to remain independent of political parties and "sects." But was this independence to be a true neutrality or a rivalry? The statement that "the union, which is today a defensive group, will one day be the unit of production and distribution, the basis of social reorganization" left more than a little doubt. Certainly, to many of the delegates who voted for the resolution, the "independence" of the CGT was merely the recognition of what Harvey Goldberg calls "an organizational necessity,"[108] i.e., the fact that it was impossible to enforce a single political line on an organization that included anarchists, Socialists, Catholics, and those unaffiliated to any political group. Among the revolutionary and anarchist ranks, however, some members interpreted the motion to mean that a new doctrine had been born. As one of them said in a phrase that would catch on and reverberate long after Amiens: "Syndicalism must stand as a theory alongside the anarchist and the Socialist theories. Besides, this doctrine is sufficient unto itself."[109] The following year, at the anarchist congress in Amsterdam, Pierre Monatte, of whom we shall hear a great deal later, went even further: the CGT *alone* represents the working class."[110] Despite the ambiguity of the resolution voted at Amiens and despite the angry protests of the Guesdists, this "syndicalist imperialism"[111] became the official doctrine of the CGT's leaders, accepted by revolutionaries and reformists alike, though for different reasons.[k] The confederal delegates could only applaud in agreement when Georges Dumoulin stepped forward at the Congress of Le Havre, in 1912, to assert what by then had become a cornerstone of syndicalist doctrine: "We consider ourselves Socialists as much as the members of the Socialist Party and more. . . . And we feel that we syndicalists are the heirs of the true Socialism."[112]

The Socialists, of course, could not remain indifferent to such pretensions. Both at the Congresses of Limoges and Nancy in 1906 and 1907 and again at the Congress of Lyon in 1912, major debates were held on the question of relations with the CGT. The problem was perplexing, especially for Socialists who were active in the unions. As one of them put it: "When I attend the section meetings of the Bourses [du Travail] as the representative of Bordeaux and Lille, I find myself among syndicalists. Should I bring Socialist ideas to this milieu? Should I keep quiet in union circles or go there as a Socialist?"[113]

[k] The revolutionaries because this freed them from the opportunism of bourgeois Socialists; the reformists because the CGT would no longer be dragged into purely political battles.

Throughout this period a small minority within the SFIO accepted the syndicalists' claim to represent the true Socialism. Lagardelle and his disciple Ernest Lafont, the elegant, cultured, and bourgeois attorney of the CGT, thought the party could do nothing better than accept its inferior status as the bourgeois ally of syndicalism. They agreed with such revolutionary syndicalists as Monatte, Merrheim, and Dumoulin that, as a doctrine, "Syndicalism is sufficient unto itself."[114] Lafont would later bring this heresy within the walls of the Communist temple. Few Socialists, however, wished to go this far, and, as on so many other questions, the party ended by voting on the motions of Guesde and Jaurès.

Nothing shows the difference in the temperaments and methods of Jaurès and Guesde better than their reactions to the syndicalist challenge. Guesde was as hostile to revolutionary syndicalism as the revolutionary syndicalists were to him.[1] Ever since the 1880's, Guesde had repeated endlessly that syndicalism could not bring the workers one step closer to emancipation because it did nothing to change the economic order that was at the source of their exploitation. Even when a strike ended in victory for the strikers, said Guesde, the employer remained an employer and the worker a worker. Syndicalism was thus necessarily reformist, just as political action was necessarily revolutionary. The Socialist Party was the only revolutionary party because it was the only party that undermined the principle of private property by attacking the State.[115] Nor would Guesde admit that the collectivist society of the future would be based on the union. This would be a crime against humanity. "No," he countered, "the production of the future will not be unionist production; it will be *la production humaine*."[116]

At the Congress of Limoges in 1906, Guesde proposed a party program based on a division of labor between the party and the CGT. First, the Socialists must join the unions and confront the syndicalists with the truth: that there could be no Revolution unless the party seized State power. They must penetrate the unions, Guesde said in a masterpiece of hairsplitting, "not to introduce politics into the unions, but to bring them the Socialist spirit."[117] Second, the party must try to enter into national agreements with the CGT; if such agreements were rejected by the CGT's Central, they must be sought with individual unions on the local level.[118] Guesde insisted all the while that he had no desire to declare war on the CGT, but everyone knew that war it would be if this motion were passed. Nevertheless, almost half the party voted for Guesde's policy.

It was the tolerance and tactical eclecticism of Jaurès and Vaillant, though, which triumphed—by a vote of 148 to 130 at Limoges, and by 167 to 141 at

---

[1] The Bourses du Travail had been founded as an anti-Guesdist federation of unions. The dominant figures in the early history of the Bourses had been Allemanists, Broussists, and Blanquists who were hostile to Guesde's POF. Jean Maitron, *Histoire du mouvement anarchiste en France, 1880–1914*, 2d ed. (1955), p. 279.

Nancy. When it came to the theory and practice of revolutionary syndicalism, Jaurès was torn. As one might expect, he disliked its undemocratic doctrine of minorities, its militant anti-patriotism, its tendency to view all issues through the prism of class, and, of course, its anti-parliamentarism.[119] Yet Jaurès's mind opened easily to new ideas, and he admired the élan of revolutionary syndicalism, its spontaneity, and the way it kept alive the workers' sense of exploitation.[120] Unlike Guesde, he had no desire to restrict the unions to purely reformist activities. The pretensions of the Charter of Amiens were to him a sign of the vitality of syndicalism. He was even willing to accept the general strike, provided it was not used to establish the dictatorship of a minority.

Jaurès and Vaillant were convinced that Socialism and syndicalism were both valid methods of struggle; and they believed that if the syndicalists were left to develop their organizations unbullied, they would eventually come to the Socialists of their own accord because of their common goals. Jaurès's motion was thus formulated in a spirit of reconciliation rather than opposition. He confined himself to observing that the basic harmony of the proletariat's political and economic goals would lead necessarily "without confusion, subordination, or defiance" to "free cooperation between the two bodies"; and he called upon all party members "to work to the best of their ability to dispel any misunderstanding between the CGT and the SFIO."[121]

This tactic of "libre coopération et libre entente" prevented open warfare between the CGT and the party, and made it possible for revolutionary syndicalists to stay in the SFIO and for Socialists to work in the unions. Jaurès and Vaillant turned out to be right. Relations between the party and the CGT did improve, to the extent that in July 1914 the syndicalist leaders were willing to enter into an Action Committee with the Socialists and even to defer to the arguments of Jaurès.[122] During the War the leaders of the two organizations consulted one another regularly. Such cooperation would have been unthinkable in 1906; it represented the triumph of Jaurès's policy. Moreover, if in 1906 and 1907 Jaurès contrived to appear more revolutionary than Guesde, it was at least in part because of his attitude toward the CGT. The true revolutionaries in the party undoubtedly voted for his motion and not for Guesde's.

But men's decisions do not always have the consequences that they foresee. If Guesde opposed the revolutionary syndicalists so consistently, it was because he saw them for the rivals of the Socialists that they really were. They threatened the development of the kind of party to which he had devoted over 25 years of his life. His apprehensions, it must be said, proved correct; for the Socialists could not relinquish the leadership of the working class to the syndicalists without changing the very nature of their party. This was, in fact, what happened. A division of labor developed, but it was the reverse of the one that Guesde had had in mind. The Socialists were cut off more and more from the proletariat. They watched the strikes of the syndicalists anxiously and defended them in the Chamber and in print, but they seldom participated in them.[m] Whether or not the syndicalists had been correct in asserting earlier that the party was merely the bourgeois ally of the proletariat, this soon became the case. The awkward relations between the party and the CGT caused the French working-class movement to develop a strange duality of doctrine. Many militants were active in both the party and the CGT. They solved what could have become a serious conflict of allegiance by splitting their ideological personalities: they were Socialists when in their sections and going to the polls and syndicalists when in their unions. This division of labor and ideological schizophrenia were not problems so long as the Socialist Party had no pretensions to a monopoly on the revolutionary elite. But when a party with such pretensions arose, as it did in 1921, the question was bound to be reopened.

### THE WORKING-CLASS MILIEUX

We have seen something of the leaders, ideologies, organization, and social composition of the SFIO and CGT and of the relations between them. If we ended our profile of the French working-class movement before 1914 with these remarks, the reader would have an incomplete basis for understanding what follows. It would be a little like going to France and seeing only Paris. Surrounding the SFIO and the CGT, cooperating with them, influencing them, were numerous groups with their own leadership, their own clientele, and their own climate of opinion. These groups might be viewed, as they are by Maurice Duverger, as "second powers," which control the activities and policies of political parties to some degree, but have no legal status.[123] Or one might speak of "constellations," the advantage of this approach being that it suggests the fields of force between which the working-class organizations were torn. I prefer the concept of "milieux," however, because it leads one to think in terms of the clusters of acquaintances and ideas, while at the same time indicating the fluid nature of these associations. Without giving my classification more universal value than it deserves, I should like to divide these milieux into two categories: those that lay to the left of the SFIO, what collectively might be called the Left Wing, and those that lay to its right, in the area of liberal ideology and bourgeois influence between the working-class movement and the Radical Party, namely the Masonic lodges and the Ligue des Droits de l'Homme et du Citoyen.

It has often been said that France suffers from a lack of intermediary asso-

---

[m] At Limoges in 1906, the Socialist deputy Groussier observed: "In the past we participated in strikes, but the situation has changed, and the CGT has always maintained that it did not want deputies interfering in strikes. . . . It is not so much the fear of insults as the fear of making things more difficult that dictates caution." SFIO, *3e Congrès national*, p. 43.

ciations between the individual and the State.[124] This is undoubtedly a precious observation. Without it we would understand France much less perfectly than we now do. However, like so many sociological concepts, the theory of organization needs to be sharpened by empirical and, above all, comparative study. It is essential, for instance, that we not confuse the very different cases of France and Russia, both of which can be said to suffer from a "poverty of group life." In Russia the need for defense against nomadic invaders, the vast spaces, and the low level of economic development had made it possible for the Muscovite princes to deprive all classes of their rights, their privileges, and even their personal freedom. A vacuum had developed between the individual and the State, and when that vacuum began to be filled at the end of the nineteenth century, the new societies that formed reflected the environment of police surveillance, infiltration, and popular apathy within which they struggled to achieve their goals. In these circumstances, it is not surprising that movements arose in Russia that regarded organization, discipline, dedication, and power as matters of life and death. In France, on the other hand, the decisive historical experience had been not the subjection of the nobility to the monarch, but its exclusion from positions of political and economic responsibility. The king governed through middle-class bureaucrats. Politics had become a game played by men who were in no danger of having to apply their ideas, and who could, furthermore, contemplate with equanimity the prospect of continued bureaucratic rule. For these reasons and others,[125] French groups tended to be characterized by extreme egalitarianism, indifference to organization, and a negative attitude toward authority. Their structure resembled that of the coterie rather than that of the army or the clan; their activities were more intellectual than social, and their existence was often precarious. All this does not mean, however, that they were any the less active.

Take, for example, the groups that went to make up the French Left Wing in the years before 1914. In addition to the regular meetings of Socialist sections, unions, and cooperatives, and the social services offered by the Bourses du Travail, there were countless lectures, study groups, and committees which were concentrated in the extremist milieux on the periphery of the CGT and the SFIO. In a given week during this period, one might find Pierre Laval haranguing the Jeunesses Socialistes Révolutionnaires of the Third Arrondissement "against military pensions and the aviation bond issue," or Berger discussing "sexual preservation" with the Study Group and Neo-Malthusians of the Eleventh and Twelfth Arrondissements; or one might attend the organizational meeting of the Anti-Parliamentary Committee of the Twentieth Arrondissement, or the dance sponsored by the Committee of the Red Cross and the Red Muse in honor of the anarchist prisoners of Russia. Or finally, if one's tastes ran in this direction, one might listen to the ubiquitous anarchist Sé-

bastien Faure speak on "Why I Entered Freemasonry; Why I Am in It; Why I Shall Stay in It." These are only a few of the events listed in *La Guerre Sociale* for a typical week in 1910.

Despite the hectic activities of such groups as the Jeunesses Socialistes and the Fédération Révolutionnaire Communiste, the favored *foyer* of the Left Wing was not so much the political organization as the newspaper or journal. Déclassés by birth or by choice, intellectuals by training or by aspiration, the majority of left-wingers earned either all or part of their living as journalists. The newspaper or review thus offered them both spiritual and material sustenance. Certainly there were journals for all tastes. Anarchists clustered around Jean Grave's *Les Temps Nouveaux* and *Le Libertaire*. Syndicalists found comrades of common mind at Monatte's *La Vie Ouvrière* and the CGT's *La Bataille Syndicaliste*. Intellectuals inclined toward syndicalism (like Sorel) preferred and were preferred by Lagardelle's *Le Mouvement Socialiste*. Socialists, syndicalists, and anarchists alike wrote for Hervé's *La Guerre Sociale* and Jobert's *L'Action Directe*.

These reviews were ephemeral, but, as in the case of French cabinets, their staffs were remarkably constant. The same names recurred constantly in the journals of the period. Denizens of a special realm that lay between the worlds of politics, the working-class movement, and literature, these men formed the nucleus of the Left Wing. Only their polemics and highly individual means of expression concealed the fact that they shared a common fund of ideas and attitudes, whose chief tenets were the superfluousness of parliaments, the hypocrisy of bourgeois society, the repressiveness of the nation, and the desirability of sweeping all these crumbling ruins aside in a gigantic social conflagration."[n] If all else failed, a Griffuelhes and an Hervé could at least agree on their dislike of Guesdists, whose parliamentarism, passivity, and patriotism they, along with all their friends, despised. How large was the Left Wing? According to Hervé, 300 persons frequented the meetings of the "insurrectionary Socialists" of the Seine.[126] Many hundreds more identified themselves with the anarchists or revolutionary syndicalists. The influence of the left-wing press was still greater. In 1910 Hervé claimed a circulation of 40,000 for his paper.

The members of these different groups were not all active in the same organizations. The anarchists met within the Fédération Communiste. The syndicalists preferred their labor exchange or their union. The Socialists lived an uneasy life in the SFIO. Yet there was an awareness among these men of the similarity of their ideas and their methods. At least twice during this period

[n] *La Guerre Sociale* for March 10–16, 1909, contained a statement of principles by the insurrectionist minority of the Federation of the Seine. The following will serve as a sample: "For us, the Socialist Party is a party of insurrection, and the modern form of insurrection is the general strike accompanied by military rebellion."

attempts were made to launch a left-wing party. In 1910 Hervé, Jobert, and Faure put forth the idea of a new party, but gave it up when their followers indicated their unwillingness to leave the old organizations.[o] The idea was raised again in 1912 by Charles-Albert and Jean Duchesne, who wrote a series of articles in La Guerre Sociale entitled "Toward the Revolutionary Party." Their proposals aroused a good deal of interest, and even such paladins of party unity as Jaurès, Albert Thomas, and Adrien Compère-Morel were drawn into the discussion. But this venture proved no more successful than its predecessor. Neither the syndicalists nor the anarchists were tempted by the idea of a political party. The CGT, wrote Griffuelhes, was the organization par excellence of the revolutionary. The business ended with a shower of new memberships in the SFIO, including that of Amédée Dunois, who was later to play a role of some importance in the founding of the French Communist Party.

Whereas the prevailing climate of the left-wing groups was anarcho-syndicalist, the dominant mood of the Masonic lodges and the Ligue des Droits de l'Homme et du Citoyen was positivist, anti-clerical, and republican.[127] The ostensible ends of the lodges were education, philanthropy, and philosophical and moral inquiry. Yet, as is well known, these offspring of the Enlightenment soon became the unofficial apparatus of the Radical Party, and, in an age of weak party organization, it is likely that their influence was often decisive in elections and in the organizing of political coalitions. The Ligue des Droits de l'Homme et du Citoyen had been founded in 1898, during the Dreyfus affair, to defend the principles of 1789 against the nationalists and the militarists. In 1912 it had 800 sections and 90,000 members, and it was a party to 8,000 cases a year, in 60 per cent of which it won some kind of redress for the plaintiff.[128]

Socialists played important roles in both these organizations during the period 1906–14. Masonic lodges first began to admit Socialists in the late 1880's.[129] The admittance of Socialists to these liberal milieux may be seen as both cause and effect of the reconciliation of Socialism with the bourgeois Republic. By 1912 five of the 33 members of the supreme council of the order (Mille, Arthur Groussier, Bachelet, Frédéric Brunet, Marcel Sembat) were Socialists. Numerous other important Socialists, such as Pierre Renaudel, Marcel Cachin, Jean Longuet, and Léon Blum, were brothers.[130] The President of the Ligue des Droits de l'Homme, Francis de Pressensé, was a Socialist. Though it was not uncommon for workers to belong to both the lodges and

---

[o] At a meeting of the insurrectionist Socialists of the Seine in March 1910, 36 members voted in favor of leaving the party immediately, 29 wanted to leave but at some unspecified future date, and six abstained. The Federation of the Yonne voted in favor of unity, and Hervé seized this opportunity to yield to discipline and thus save himself from the dangerous implications of his own extremism.

the Ligue, these were bourgeois organizations whose class nature both their functions and their fees assured.[131]

The issue of Socialist participation in these societies came up for debate at the SFIO's Congress of Lyon in 1912. The revolutionaries of the Seine, leading the attack, objected that Freemasonry was "the occult organization of Radicalism," the function of which was "to perpetuate the political domination by the bourgeoisie of the working class."[132] They moved that all Socialists be required to resign from these organizations within six months. The Guesdists, no less opposed but for once less dogmatic, merely observed that Socialists lost time in these organizations that might better be spent in educating and organizing the proletariat. The Masons replied that the lodges were not political associations but philosophical societies. Besides, they countered, they had been effective in spreading Socialist ideas to other Masons.[133] Sembat was one of the few Masons to meet the opposition head on. The discussions of the lodges, he admitted, satisfied a side of him that the party could not fulfill. "A whole portion of the human spirit lies uncultivated in present-day society, and can only be cultivated in the company of bourgeois. Well, then, in our lodges numerous workers and clerks and small shopkeepers can cultivate this part of their intelligence, which otherwise would lie fallow."[134]

As Sembat's remark makes clear, at stake in this debate was nothing less than the kind of party that the SFIO aspired to be. The left-wingers wanted a group of pure revolutionaries who would break all ties with the bourgeoisie. The Guesdists, by contrast, had as their goal a total party, which would absorb all the energies and satisfy all the social and intellectual needs of its members. It was Guesde's old dream of a mass organization of the proletariat within the citadel of capitalism. The defenders of Freemasonry and the Ligue did not want to isolate the party from the rest of society; they saw the SFIO as a political organization rather than a temple or a church. De Pressensé and Sembat both warned the party against becoming a closed sect, and their position won 1,505 votes, as against 927 for the Guesdists and 103 for the minority of the Seine. The majority's resolution reiterated the SFIO's indifference to the participation of its members in educational, philosophical, and moral groups that did not seek political power.[135]

We should now be prepared to understand the two characteristics of French Socialism which confounded and alarmed European revolutionary Marxists: the weakness of its Left Wing and the uncertainty of the boundary between Socialism and bourgeois liberalism. The first is easily explained when it is remembered that in France the energies of the Left Wing were drained off by anarchism and syndicalism. At the same time, contacts between Socialists and the progressive bourgeoisie were frequent, thanks to the existence of such societies as the Masonic lodges and the Ligue, not to mention daily association in the Chamber, in law courts, and in editorial offices. Many Socialists and liberals had similar backgrounds and mutual acquaintances. A man like Marcel Sembat had friendships throughout the spectrum of French politics and letters. Even anarchists like Faure and Victor Méric (the son of a senator) associated freely with bourgeois liberals. Only the syndicalists were committed to the isolation of classes; only they had a permanent link with the working masses; only they constituted the embryo of a true revolutionary party. Yet that party could not arise before 1914 because French syndicalists were opposed to political activity as such. Revolutionary Socialists like Hervé and Jobert were thus driven back beneath the umbrella of Socialist unity. It might be said, then, that the prerequisite for the formation of a "Communist Party" in France was the collapse of the Jauressian synthesis, the eclipse of revolutionary syndicalism, or both. Were there any signs of such developments in the years before 1914? This brings us to our final consideration: the direction of change in the French working-class movement on the eve of the First World War.

### THE DIRECTION OF CHANGE

Few historians have been satisfied with the statements of revolutionary determination which Socialists carried on their party cards. They have exposed, with merciless and perhaps overzealous logic, the widening gap between Socialist principles and Socialist practice during the decade following unification. Aaron Noland, for example, has concluded that by 1914 the SFIO had become a "constitutional party serving as the avant-garde of democracy."[136] To Milorad Drachkovitch the Socialists were an "integral part of the French Left," and belonged to "the same spiritual family as the Radicals."[137] Yet history is very much a matter of perspective. It is possible, as Max Weber pointed out, to study historical processes from various sides of the "causal chain."[138] Eugen Weber, in telling the story of the "nationalist revival" during the years between 1905 and 1914, has seen fit to emphasize the increasing militancy of the Socialists after 1905, or, at any rate, the distrust that an impression of such militancy inspired among Radicals and certain layers of the bourgeoisie which had formerly been open to democratic ideas.[139] B. W. Schaper writes that the integration of the French working class in all forms of social life was "hindered by a guilty conscience."[140] And let us not forget the "new insurgency" of Jaurès after 1905, which Harvey Goldberg has recently documented in an admirable biography.[141] So the picture is complex. Though reformist by tradition, by social composition, and by inclination, the SFIO continued to talk of revolution. If anything, a certain revolutionary conformism became de rigueur within the ranks of the party; those moderates who slipped from time to time and revealed their basic reformism quickly had their hands rapped by the guardians of Socialist orthodoxy. The moderates consequently kept quiet, with few exceptions. But Hervé and his friends babbled of insurrection to their hearts' content, and this gave the party an aura of revolutionary fervor which was, in fact, quite illusory.

It is within these limits that Jaurès's role must be understood. Jaurès took the orthodoxy of the Guesdists, the Left Wing's commitment to insurrection, and the reformism of the moderates, and welded these disparate pieces into one doctrine, conceding to each faction the minimum that its convictions and its pride would allow it to accept. The result was a synthesis, dissatisfying to intellectuals but powerful in its political appeal. The party spoke in terms of class; yet, as we have seen, it was not a class party, but a coalition of working-class, petty-bourgeois, and peasant elements led by intellectuals, teachers, lawyers, and bureaucrats. The party boasted of its internationalism, but its leaders traced their doctrine to French sources and never really felt at home with the theories of Marx. The party proclaimed its will to revolution; however, few of its members imagined for a moment a break with the existing parliamentary system, and all of them, revolutionaries and reformists alike, rushed to the defense of the government at the first sign of danger from the Right.

That these contradictory elements did not enter into conflict and bring crashing down the whole edifice of Socialist unity was due in part to the magic of Jaurès, and in even greater part to the nature of the period. The years 1905 to 1914 were golden years during which, though it was clear that the old century was dead, it was not yet certain what the new century would be like. This accounts for the aspect of contradiction: the new often mingled with the old. For Socialists these were years of expectation. Though the Radicals moved decisively to the Right after 1906, such men as Joseph Caillaux and Ferdinand Bouisson made it possible to hope that the liberal bourgeoisie had not turned their backs on social and economic reform. No Socialist, on the other hand, had yet grasped that social evolution was working against the possibility of a peaceful and democratic proletarian revolution, rather than in its favor. Precisely because it was eclectic, Jaurès's doctrine corresponded to the situation. Its emphasis on class conflict and revolutionary ends reflected the isolation of the Socialists and their confidence in the future, while its reformism and republicanism held out the possibility of alliance with the bourgeoisie. Revolutionaries and moderates thus could both find their place within the party.

Even before 1914 this marriage was not always a happy one. Jaurès's constant juggling of revolutionary words and reformist deeds was the source of what Drachkovitch calls "a chronic misunderstanding."[142] It would not do to make too much of this misunderstanding. Yet it was there, and it was bound to be there considering the wide base on which the party had been unified. The emphasis on revolution and class struggle lay at the root of the malaise that writer after writer sensed beneath the surface of the party. Many Socialists no doubt took the revolutionary slogans seriously; others did not, but were willing

to use them so long as it was understood that they were words and nothing
more; still others, such as Alexandre Varenne and Albert Thomas, wanted to
abandon them altogether. To most party members, however, such realism remained heresy.

Except for isolated minorities, then, the consensus held. But ideology is not
everything. And on the eve of the War, the SFIO faced other problems which
could not be spirited away by cleverly worded motions. The first had to do
with the problem of the State. The Charter of Unity defined the State as the
instrument of the "whole of the bourgeois class," and ruled that the attitude of
the party must be one of unyielding opposition. Guesde, who had inspired this
text, continued to maintain it to the letter. For him, those who wanted to
extend the power of "l'Etat-Gendarme de l'Etat Patron" by nationalizing industry were leading the working class to suicide.[143] Others, such as Albert
Thomas and Edgar Milhaud, saw in the concentration of industry, the progress
of municipal Socialism, and the development of State Socialism abroad unmistakable signs that new times required new tactics. For them the State in a
democracy was not always an "enemy to be downed" but "essentially a field
of battle where opposed classes meet."[144] There was no doubt where Jaurès
stood on this question: he had never accepted the Marxist concept of the class
State.[145] This raised the old question of coalitions with the liberal bourgeoisie
and even ministerialism. And if the attitude of the Radicals in 1914 did not encourage such speculations, no one could deny that a new turn of the political
wheel might bring them to the fore.[p]

The second issue was one of organization; and although it did not occasion
the same heated discussions, its implications went as deep. All parties agreed
that the numerical growth of the unified party had not come up to expectations.[146] By 1914 it was dimly realized by the few men who devoted themselves
to these questions that more intensive propaganda was not enough. What was
the solution? One answer was to improve the organization of the party, to
streamline its apparatus and strengthen its ties with the provinces. To this end
an administrative reorganization was carried out in 1913. Another response
was to extend the party's activities to peripheral groups, such as the Jeunesses
Socialistes, to whom, up to 1912, almost no attention had been devoted.[147] A
third was the old Guesdist hope of an alliance between the unions and
the party, and here there seemed to be real progress. Still a fourth was to appeal
to new social groups, such as the peasants and the oppressed nationalities in the

[p] The problem is not an academic one. In June 1914 Caillaux tempted Jaurès with the
prospect of a government of the Left, supported by Radicals and Socialists, in which Jaurès
would be Minister of Foreign Affairs. Jaurès promised Caillaux that despite the rule laid
down by the Congress of Amsterdam in 1904, his party would not "founder on the rocks
of scholasticism." Quoted in Harvey Goldberg, *The Life of Jean Jaurès* (Madison, Wis.,
1962), p. 454.

colonies. Neither group had been more than scratched by Socialist propaganda in 1914. The real problem was that the party had not yet made the transition from an elitist group to a mass party. To win the masses, it would be necessary to organize them, to broaden the scope of the party so that it would be more than a study group, a propaganda society, or an electoral committee. Few Socialists had envisaged such revolutionary techniques of organization before 1914; fewer yet would have found them attractive if they had.

There was a third issue that ranged unnoticed behind the other two: the problem of the International. Could the SFIO adapt itself to the peculiarities of the French situation, if need arose? Or was it, in fact, committed to follow the decisions of an International dominated by Central Europeans? It seemed that the question had been settled once and for all in 1904, at Amsterdam, but it was implicit in the dilemmas that faced the French party in 1914. How, for instance, would it be possible to embark on a bold program of reformism and even ministerialism within the framework of the International? The truth is that few French Socialists had thought these questions through. The regulations were ambiguous on the point of international discipline. The party statutes said that all members were bound to follow the decisions of both national and international congresses; but in 1911 Vaillant reminded his fellow Socialists that the function of the International Socialist Bureau was to coordinate, and not to direct, its national sections.[148] Jaurès's answer was that nationalism and internationalism were not contradictory, but complementary. Again, such a synthesis was possible only because of the peculiar outlines of the prewar period, during which the Socialists had not been confronted with the option of power and responsibility. When they were, it was inevitable that the principle of internationalism would be called into question.

The CGT, too, had its malaise and its crisis on the eve of the War. From 1906 to 1910, the federation had been in almost constant battle; its record of casualties, arrests, and defiance of government authority was one that any revolutionary organization might envy.[149] Moreover, the strikes of this era were not only militant, they were successful. Until 1909 the revolutionary syndicalists could have argued with cause that their tactics of storming the capitalist citadel were more effective than the moderation of British and German trade unions. However, after 1910 a new tendency set in: strikes began to meet with defeat and the incidence of strikes and the number of strikers began to decline.[150] The revolution that had seemed so close in May 1906 now receded from view, like a mirage. The signs of fatigue and of waning enthusiasm were unmistakable. Recruiting lagged despite prosperity, and some unions, like Merrheim's important metallurgical federation, were hard put to hold the members they had attracted earlier.[151] Within the CGT there was a widespread feeling that revolutionary syndicalism was in decline. Griffuelhes, who had left the secretariat but was as militant as ever, testified to the doldrums within syndicalist ranks in a series of articles he published in *Le Mouvement Socialiste* in January 1913: "There reigns in the world of syndicalism a deplorable state of mind and a profound ignorance of what needs to be done; a tendency toward extreme confusion prevails among our men; the syndicalist idea has lost some of its force and vitality."[152]

The decline in revolutionary fervor and the plateau in syndicalist recruiting coincided with an upsurge of reformism within the CGT. The reformists had always been strong in the Confederation, but the continuing refusal to adopt proportional representation at CGT congresses had made it possible for the revolutionaries consistently to outvote them. By 1914 that situation was changing. Contemporary observers noted that the confederal rank and file were turning toward reformist considerations at the outbreak of the War. And even the leaders of the CGT, the tried-and-true activists, were slipping away from their old intransigence. Writing in 1913, Jouhaux, the new confederal secretary, suggested a change in tactics for the CGT. "In place of those passing fits of anger and ferment, which most often manifest themselves in incoherence, syndicalists must substitute carefully planned and coordinated policies." The CGT, he argued, must be prepared to adapt itself to new conditions. "In our view, a movement that permitted itself to become frozen in a stance of immutability, without making allowances for transformations taking place around it, would be a movement without life, without influence, without a future."[153]

It was no accident that revolutionary syndicalism was losing its appeal on the eve of the War. The economic structure that made its doctrines possible and plausible was itself in the process of change. The soil from which syndicalism had sprung—the world of small workshops, feudal employers, a hostile State, and revolutionary memories—was being transformed by industrialization.[154] The workshop was giving way to the factory; the craftsman was being replaced by the unskilled laborer, who envisaged his union less as the embryo of a new society than as an agency for his own betterment. Perhaps most important of all, the capitalist adversary was adopting new techniques. Faced with the threat of confederal action, businessmen had begun to organize. Where unions had once joined battle with individual employers, they now confronted cartels and trusts. To defend themselves the workers, too, had to develop organizations through which they could influence the State. Such a shift in tactics could hardly be carried out in the name of the principles enshrined in the Charter of Amiens.

Thus, the French working-class movement was deeply divided in 1914. Two organizations—not quite hostile, but far from friendly—stood in uneasy balance, sometimes cooperating, sometimes in competition. Both the CGT and the SFIO were torn by internal contradictions. Both had minorities within their ranks that were opposed to the official policy. French Socialism had as its ambition not the destruction of the bourgeois Republic, but its renovation and fulfillment; in this sense, it was no longer revolutionary. Yet reformist goals were more easily declaimed than achieved: they required either a democratic majority or willing bourgeois allies. In 1914 the SFIO had no immediate prospects of either.

The CGT was the home of the revolutionary Left Wing. Its aim was to sweep away the system and to replace it with a new culture, a new code of values, a whole new set of social and economic relations among men. But the CGT, too, had its problems. It had never quite been able to make up its mind whether it was a union or a political party, an organization for the defense of the workers' interests or the basis upon which would be built a new society. "And its weakness," Alfred Rosmer commented, "lay precisely in the fact that it was something hybrid, at once a syndicalist organization and a political party, and more of a party than a syndicalist organization."[155] By the summer of 1914, every sign pointed to the fact that the CGT was on its way to becoming more of a union and less of a political party.

Both the SFIO and the CGT were burdened with ideologies that no longer corresponded either to the facts of the political, economic, and social environment in which they operated, or to their own practice. Under normal conditions their revolutionary illusions might have weathered the transition to democracy and could have coexisted more or less in harmony with reformist facts. But what these illusions could not survive was a war, a war that was bound to bring out all those tensions and contradictions which underlay both the CGT and the SFIO.

## Chapter two

# The Dilemmas of Sacred Union

Avec un Millerand prussien, avec un Millerand
italien, avec un Millerand français, avec un
Millerand anglais, il n'y a plus d'Internationale
ouvrière possible!
     —*Jules Guesde, at the Second International's*
     *Congress of Paris, 1900*

On June 28, 1914, Archduke Ferdinand of Austria was assassinated in the
Bosnian town of Sarajevo. Within two months the Powers were at war, Jaurès
lay dead, two Socialists sat in the French cabinet, and Europe had been turned
into a huge battlefield, drenched in rivers of blood. Despite long preparation,
the War came suddenly. Few had sought its outbreak. Few, however, feared
its implications. "What we need," the young Ilya Ehrenburg's Parisian baker
had told him, "is a good war; then everything will get straightened out."[1] The
long-awaited moment come, Frenchmen sang patriotic songs, chanted "On to
Berlin," and looted stores with foreign-sounding names. "No," wrote a young
French intellectual, "no one suddenly heard that slamming of a door which
closed itself behind us forever."[2]

A door slammed shut behind Socialism, too, that torrid summer. Old
quarrels were forgotten. New ones were born. And within two years of August
1914, impassable barriers separated men who had formerly belonged to the
same groups, voted for the same motions, and hated the same enemies. The
years 1905–14 had been a time of synthesis and gathering around the Center;
1914–20 was a time of disintegration and crystallization around the extremes.
And if the name of Jaurès was often mentioned, it was in memory of past
comradeship rather than in evocation of present union.

### THE QUESTION OF WAR

For all the suddenness of its outbreak, the War cannot be said to have caught
the French unprepared. The threat of war hung over Europe like an angry
storm cloud between 1905 and 1914, waiting for the lightning flash that would
discharge its ugly cargo of hate and devastation. During the Moroccan crisis

of 1905, Charles Péguy hurried off to buy his campaign equipment, convinced that the final confrontation was at hand. Within the space of a few hours, he wrote, a new epoch had opened for France and for the world.[3] War was avoided at Algeciras, and the uneasy peace was preserved. But for how long? "From one moment to the next, war was on the verge of breaking out. It was squelched, it burst out again. The slightest pretext served as fuel. The world felt itself at the mercy of an accident that would unleash the conflict. It waited. The most peace-loving people were oppressed by a feeling of inevitability."[4]

A great debate arose over the measures to be taken for French security. Ever since the revolutionary wars and the Jacobin dictatorship, the French Left had been identified with national defense. During the early years of the Third Republic, it had been the Left that had cried for *revanche* and the Right for peace at almost any price. But around the turn of the century, a basic reorientation took place. The Right was swept by a nationalist revival, and the Left moved toward pacifism, internationalism, and anti-militarism.[5] The passion of the debate and the terms on which it was conducted obscured the basic agreement between the Right and the Left on the need to defend the nation in case of aggression. "Better that war should come than to go on with this perpetual waiting," wrote one young nationalist.[6] "Peace is possible!" cried Jaurès. "Down with militarism! Down with war!" came the constant refrain from both Socialists and syndicalists. The national dialogue reached its climax with the struggle over the Three-Year Law, in which the Socialists joined with the left-wing Radicals to oppose any lengthening of military service. Fifteen years of anti-militarism left their mark on the thinking of the French working class. Once the War was over, echoes of speeches burning with anti-patriotism and internationalism came back to haunt the leaders of the Socialist Party and the CGT. Thus it is important to know exactly what was said during these years—even more important, to know what was meant, and what happened when the War actually came.

The Socialists were divided on the question of war, as on most things. On the extreme Left stood Hervé, the noisy and unpredictable schoolteacher from the Yonne. Guesde upheld what he thought to be the orthodox Marxist point of view. Finally, there was Jaurès, followed by a slim majority of the party, who offered a compromise motion embodying a little bit of both Hervé and Guesde.

Hervé's insurrectionism never won the support of more than a small minority of the party. Only the tolerance of Jaurès prevented his expulsion. Nevertheless, Hervé and Hervéism cannot be discounted. Many Frenchmen saw the SFIO through the haze of Hervé's anti-patriotism.[7] They had only to read their newspaper to get confirmation of their prejudices. "We hate our homelands," said Hervé. "We are anti-patriots."[8] Hervé's motion on war, presented at both the Congress of Limoges and the Congress of Nancy, repudi-

ated "the bourgeois and governmental patriotism that falsely affirms the existence of a community of interests among the inhabitants of the same country,"
and invited "all citizens to respond to any declaration of war, from whichever
side it may come, with a military strike and insurrection."[9] In 1914 Hervé became the most fervent of chauvinists, and in the 1930's he found a savior in
Marshal Pétain. It was Jaurès who paid for Hervé's extremism, which more
than one observer interpreted as "the peasant's old hate for military service"
rather than Socialist internationalism.[10]

The Guesdist argument carried more weight within party ranks; and, given
what happened in 1914, one might suppose that the reason for its popularity
was not so much its stern Marxist language as its hostility to anti-patriotism.
Guesde had begun his career as a flaming patriot at the time of the Commune.
Even in the early 1890's, he and his followers had disavowed anti-patriotism
and announced that "if attacked, France would have no more resolute defenders than the Socialists of the Parti Ouvrier, who are convinced of the
great role reserved for her in the approaching social Revolution."[11] To Guesde,
anti-militarism, anti-patriotism, and the threat of insurrection in case of war
were unsocialist and counterrevolutionary. As he explained with tired patience
at Limoges in 1906, wars could only be prevented by the achievement of Socialism; incitement to insurrection would only divert the working class from
its main goal, which was, of course, the conquest of the State. Insurrection was
both counterrevolutionary and impractical: counterrevolutionary because it
would weaken the most Socialist country; impractical because in a moment of
national emergency the common danger would make all other preoccupations
fade from view. Moreover, it was nonsense, Guesde insisted, to tell the worker
that he had no country. Since 1848, when universal suffrage had given him the
vote, he had the means of repossessing the nation and making it his own.
Internationalism was fine. But Socialism could only be achieved within the
borders of the nation. "Our duty," he urged, "is to make a revolution here at
home. The proletariat has no hold on German capitalism, but it has a hold on
French factories and French employers."[12] Noisy anti-patriotism of the Hervé
sort, Guesde thought, could only alienate the masses. "Ten more Socialists a
day will do more to prevent war than all the anti-militaristic hot air we've
been hearing."[13] Guesde's position, though never that of the majority, rallied
strong support, receiving 98 votes of a possible 254 at Limoges.

Jaurès, on the other hand, seeing complexity in this issue as in all others,
tried to reconcile patriotism and the struggle against war. His compromise
illustrates the nature and the limits of Socialist internationalism in France.
Jaurès never accepted the view that the workers had no country. That formula,
he wrote, though not entirely false, was only a partial truth. Not only was the
nation a fact, it had a "Socialist and human value."[14] The blatant anti-patriotism of the revolutionary syndicalists did not endanger the nation, but it did

constitute a "peril for the proletariat itself."[15] There was no necessary contradiction between internationalism and patriotism, just as there was no inevitable conflict between the interests of the French party and the policies of the International. As he concluded with a typically Jauressian twist, "A little internationalism takes [the worker] away from his country; a lot of internationalism brings him back to it."[16]

Jaurès's motion on war reflected his faith in the compatibility of internationalism and patriotism. It came in two parts. The opening clause assured the working class that it had not only the right but the "imperious duty" to join with the nation in safeguarding its independence against any aggressor. The second clause, however, affirmed the party's resolution to remain faithful to the decisions of the International, and urged the French proletariat to render these decisions effective by helping to organize, on both the national and international levels, a plan of action that, "depending on the circumstances, would put all the energy and all the effort of the working class and the Socialist Party behind the prevention and avoidance of war by all means, ranging from speeches in the Assembly, public agitation, and mass demonstrations to a general strike of the workers and insurrection."[17]

Whatever its equivocations, this resolution approved the use of the general strike and insurrection. The question was when to apply the first clause and when to apply the second. As might be expected, Guesde endorsed the first part of the motion, Hervé the second. For Jaurès, however, there was no contradiction. He believed that it was possible to distinguish between a defensive and an offensive war; and he saw the means for making this distinction in the willingness or refusal to submit to arbitration. If the French government attempted to wage imperialistic or aggressive war, then it would be the duty of Socialists to revolt. Otherwise, they would march in defense of their country. An optimist but not a utopian, Jaurès recognized that in the panic of a national emergency the working class might be deceived. In this case the proletariat would have both the right and the duty to overthrow its capitalist oppressors, establish the Socialist Republic, and defend the independence of the nation.[18] Underlying Jaurès's motion was his belief that peace was possible, though not inevitable, and his conviction that "decisive, heroic, determined, and carefully planned action" on the part of the Socialist Party might tip the balance between peace and war and save the proletariat from the "crime of mutual slaughter."[19]

If the Socialists nearly always hedged on the question of war and the general strike, lining their resolutions with escape clauses in order to rally a majority, the position of the CGT was stated in a way that left no room for doubt. At Amiens and again at Marseille in 1908, the CGT had proclaimed its unswerving opposition to the army and its refusal to support any war, no matter what the cause. The Congress of Amiens approved and recommended "all action tending toward anti-militarist and anti-patriotic propaganda," and asserted that this propaganda must become "ever more intense and daring."[20] The resolution adopted at Marseille, which was submitted by Merrheim, went even further. It reminded the worker that he had no country, and went on to declare that the workers must be educated on an international level so that, in the case of war between the Powers, they would respond to any mobilization order with a "revolutionary general strike."[21] The Marseille resolution remained the policy of the CGT right up to the outbreak of the War. Its implications were further elaborated by a special anti-war congress held in October 1912, which instructed the workers "that if, by folly or by calculation, the country in whose midst we are placed commits itself to a warlike adventure, in the face of our opposition and our warnings, the duty of all workers is to ignore the summons and rally to their class organizations, there to carry on the struggle against their only enemies: the capitalists."[22]

The common invocation of the general strike and insurrection should not conceal the fact that, in moving from the Socialists to the syndicalists, we have passed to a different world with different values. The revolutionary syndicalists made no attempt to reconcile internationalism with national defense. For those Socialists who made such an attempt, the CGT's leaders had nothing but scorn.[23] In their view, patriotism, like reform, was an attempt to deflect the working class from its main task of revolution. The syndicalist not only considered himself to have no country; he felt that he had been placed, through an accident of birth, in the country of his class enemy. When Lagardelle conducted his famous *enquête* in 1905, asking a series of militants whether or not the worker had a country, the response of Merrheim was typical: "No! The workers can have no country, for everything prevents them from having one."[24]

From 1900 to 1914 the syndicalists constantly opposed militarism, demonstrating in favor of Franco-German friendship when war threatened, flaunting before the bourgeoisie the threat of a general strike, and irritating the army with their *sou du soldat,* a small subsidy dispensed by the local labor exchanges to draftees quartered in the district. Hervéism, never more than a trickle of opposition in the party, had its real success in the CGT. And, despite the rising wave of reformism in the CGT by 1914, it is unlikely that the congress scheduled for that year would have seen any change in the Confederation's official policy toward war.

The threats of the CGT seem to have had their effect. In 1902 there had been 5,991 men classified as deserters or absent without leave; by 1907 that figure had risen to over 14,000; and at the end of 1911 the police were seeking 76,723 missing men, or the equivalent of two army corps.[25] To counter this threat of insurrection and subversion, the government had assembled, in its notorious Carnet B, a list of 2,501 of the most violent agitators, anti-militarists, and suspected spies, who were to be arrested immediately in the event of mobilization.

Even for the Socialists, the reaction of the syndicalists to a declaration of war represented a great unknown. Léon Blum's memory of the atmosphere preceding the outbreak of the War is one more example of the gap between the SFIO and the class of which they were supposed to be the avant-garde. "Do you remember revolutionary syndicalism? Do you remember what anxiety one felt then over the attitude of the mass of workers toward a mobilization order?"[26]

But even before 1914 some observers had understood the limits of this anti-patriotism. René Benjamin, a nationalist writer who took part in the maneuvers of 1908, predicted that fear of the gendarmes would frighten the workers out of their Hervéism when the mobilization came. The most ardent pacifists, he wrote, would be the first to leave for the front. "Anti-militarism is almost popular, a part of our workers' makeup; but anti-militarists are just poor chaps who will behave very well, provided they are marched up to the line of fire well in step."[27]

### THE COMING OF THE WAR

The assassination at Sarajevo did not immediately attract the attention of a public long accustomed to political murder and Balkan tension. The crisis was to smolder for over three weeks before finally bursting into the flame that would engulf all Europe. For the French the main distraction of that stifling summer was the trial of Madame Caillaux, which promised revelations both of passion and of politics. With such scandal in prospect, the communiqués from Vienna and Belgrade receded to back pages, where they received scant notice.

In the meantime, still unaware of the gravity of the situation, the Socialists met in congress at Paris on July 14–16 to determine their policy for the coming congress of the International at Vienna. The question at debate was whether or not to approve an amendment by Keir Hardie and Vaillant that recommended calling a general strike to prevent the outbreak of war. The arguments had all been heard before; what was new was the unmistakable suspicion of German intentions among the opponents of the general strike. Speaking for the Guesdists, Compère-Morel asked skeptically: "Why vote for motions that we would not put into effect?" Then he posed a question that could not help but embarrass his opponents: "If France were attacked, would you let her be crushed by staging a general strike?" Jaurès answered that he and his supporters were resolved to defend the nation if its independence were threatened. Nevertheless, he believed that the general strike could be used by the international working class before the outbreak of war in order to ensure peace and enforce arbitration. If the Socialists waited for the storm to break, it would be too late. Guesde retorted that to decree a universal general strike would mean delivering "German Socialist civilization to the hordes of the

Russian autocracy's army." Besides, he argued, even if the French succeeded in bringing off a general strike, which was unlikely, how could the International Socialist Bureau guarantee that the movement would be simultaneous in all countries? And if the Bureau did call this simultaneous general strike, he continued, the unequal state of Socialist and syndicalist organization in different countries would doom the most highly organized nation to defeat by the most barbarous. "And that," hammered Guesde, with his inflexible logic, "is a crime of high treason against Socialism."[28] Surprisingly, Guesde found support in Hervé, who had given up his insurrectionism on the ground that there would be no insurrectionists on the day of mobilization.

Nevertheless, the motion submitted by Jaurès was passed by a vote of 1,690 to 1,174, with 83 abstentions. This final resolution of the Socialists, passed just two weeks before the War began, makes plain the essential weakness of the Socialist position. The Socialists approved the principle of a universal general strike of the European working class. But it had been clear since the previous September, if not before, that the German Social Democrats neither would nor could participate in such an action.[29] The French Socialists had no power to unleash such a strike even in their own country; they could only suggest it. The CGT, leaving aside the question of its numerical weakness, was completely isolated internationally. The leaders of revolutionary syndicalism had tried in vain to get the Labor International to discuss the general strike. Under these circumstances, the manifesto of the Socialist Party could only be an incantation, a profession of hope—not an effective threat or a plan of action.

On July 23, Austria submitted her ultimatum to Serbia; that same day in Paris the Caillaux trial reached its dramatic peak. The crisis now erupted in all its seriousness. The SFIO and the CGT scheduled anti-war demonstrations and called for arbitration between Serbia and Austria. On July 27, Léon Jouhaux, the Secretary of the CGT, and Karl Legien, his German counterpart, met briefly in Brussels. The nature of the interview is still disputed, but the lack of communication seems to have been total.[30] On July 28 Austria declared war. The next day, Jaurès, accompanied by Guesde, Vaillant, Sembat, Jean Longuet, and Charles Rappoport, attended a meeting of the International Socialist Bureau in Brussels. Hugo Haase, representing the German SPD, said his party was determined to oppose the War, but Victor Adler could only confess the impotence of the Austrian Socialists before the tide of chauvinism. Haase and Jaurès embraced; rallies and demonstrations were promised; but of the general strike there was not a word. It was agreed that the International would meet in Paris on August 9.

Back in Paris the next evening, Jaurès led a Socialist delegation to see René Viviani, the Premier, who assured him that the French government was doing its best to indicate its desire for peace. That night, Jaurès and other Socialists met with a delegation of syndicalists to coordinate their peace campaigns. Preparations were made to form a joint action committee.[31] The syndicalists and Socialists planned a huge demonstration and continued to warn the government to beware of the wrath of the working class. "Guerre à la guerre!" cried the headlines of *La Bataille Syndicaliste,* the official CGT paper.

But this time the slide downhill toward war was not to be checked. Events seemed to have taken an inexorable turn as mobilization plans clanked into motion, and the initiative passed from the politicians to the general staffs. On July 31 Germany declared a state of "imminent danger of war," and demanded to know what France's attitude would be in the case of conflict with Russia; that evening Jaurès was assassinated by an unstable young man inflamed by articles in the right-wing press; the next day German mobilization was announced. In the space of a few hours the edifice built by decades of hard work and idealism crumbled, as the French workers docilely, sometimes even enthusiastically, marched off to war. As Ilya Ehrenburg remembered it:

Everyone ... had lost his head. One by one, the shops closed. People marched in the middle of the street shouting: "To Berlin! To Berlin!" They were not youths or groups of nationalists; no, everybody marched: old women, students, workers, bourgeois. They marched with flags and flowers and sang the *Marseillaise,* straining their voices. The whole of Paris abandoned its houses and rushed into the streets, saying good-bye, seeing people off, whistling, shouting. It was as though a human river had burst its banks and flooded the world. When at night I fell exhausted into my bed, the same shouts came in through the window: "To Berlin! To Berlin!"[32]

The new alignments were quickly formed. On August 1, Raymond Poincaré announced that there were no more parties, only Frenchmen resolved to defend their country; and on August 4, in his message to the Chamber and the Senate, he spoke of a "sacred union" that joined the sons of France "in a common indignation against the aggressor, and in a common patriotic faith." On that same day the Socialist deputies unanimously voted for the war credits requested by Poincaré. By the end of the month, Jules Guesde and Marcel Sembat had joined their bourgeois adversaries in the French cabinet.[a]

[a] Guesde's entry into the ministry, however, was not without complications. He accepted a cabinet appointment on the condition that the Socialists would be ministers without portfolio. This gesture would show that the Socialists were joining in the work of national defense, yet would also indicate that they did not intend to associate themselves with the administration of a capitalist government. While these negotiations were under way, Sembat accepted the Ministry of Public Works. Guesde was infuriated and informed Viviani that he was withdrawing from the government. Poincaré himself had to go to Guesde and argue with him for two hours before he agreed to withdraw his resignation. Zévaès, *Histoire du socialisme et du communisme en France de 1871 à 1947* (1947), pp. 357–58.

The whole question of Guesde's attitude toward the War and the Russian Revolution is an interesting one. From time to time, despite his social patriotism, the old revolutionary in him seems to have made its way to the surface. Charles Rappoport has recounted a curious anecdote about the train trip to Brussels for the last meeting of the International

The Socialists formulated their position on the War in a resolution passed by the Federation of the Seine on August 2. They would defend their country, the manifesto read, as they had always indicated they would do in the case of aggression. At the same time, however, they were pledged to preserve their ties with the International, so far as events allowed, and to maintain all reservations with regard to secret treaties whose contents were unknown to them.[33] In other words, the Socialists would march in defense of their country, but they would not give up their ideals. This resolution undoubtedly expressed the opinion of the overwhelming majority of the party at the outbreak of the War. The question at issue here was, could this distinction between national defense and identification with the government be maintained under the duress and psychological tension of a war of attrition? But then, in August everyone expected the War to be over by Christmas.

The retreat of the CGT was more abrupt, less orderly. The same day as the meeting of the Federation of the Seine, *La Bataille Syndicaliste* acknowledged that "events have overwhelmed us." "The workers did not all understand what sustained efforts were required to save mankind from the horrors of war." "Could we have demanded greater sacrifices from our comrades?" asked *La Bataille Syndicaliste*. "However much it costs us, we reply: 'No.' What we ask of everyone is an unshakable attachment to syndicalism, which must live through and survive the oncoming crisis." In the same issue, however, there was an article that set a very different tone. If war is inevitable, wrote the author, then let us make it a war to end all wars, to destroy militarism once and for all. "This monstrous crime that is going to plunge all Europe into barbarousness, into the abyss of mourning, and into ruins, let it be punished! Let thrones be overthrown, let crowns break! ... And let the name of the old Emperor Franz Joseph be cursed." It was this theme of crime and punishment, of victory and moral righteousness, not the theme of international solidarity, that would predominate in both the Socialist Party and the CGT during the early stages of the War.

### THE SHATTERED ILLUSION

Fifteen years of anti-militarism and talk of insurrection swept away in a few mad hours: how does one explain the rapidity with which the Socialists and

---

Socialist Bureau before the War broke out. Strangely silent during most of the trip, Guesde suddenly exclaimed: "I don't understand your fear of war. War is the mother of revolution." (Quoted in Goldberg, *The Life of Jean Jaurès*, p. 480.) Moreover, in 1915 Guesde wrote Marcel Deschamps that it was necessary to oppose the "fatal maneuvers" stemming from the desire of certain members of the party to transform the Sacred Union into permanent collaboration with the government. (André Marty Archives.) See also Alfred Rosmer, *Le Mouvement ouvrier pendant la guerre*, II (1959), 211, and p. 79 below.

syndicalists exchanged their red flags for tricolors and the *Internationale* for the *Marseillaise?* In the case of the Socialists, the answer is easy enough. They were both pacifists and patriots; their motions on war were attempts to reconcile national defense and internationalism. If Jaurès's motions continually defeated Guesde's, it was not because they called for insurrection, but because they recognized the need to defend the nation, and in addition offered a way of fighting against the menace of war.[b] When pacifism became impossible, as it did in August 1914, it was natural that patriotism should dominate the Socialist Party. Had not Jaurès himself stated at Brussels that the French government was practicing a policy of peace? At any rate, Jaurès's final attitude was ambiguous. Viviani, speaking at his funeral on August 4, claimed that on the night of his death Jaurès had congratulated him on the government's position and assured him that he could count on "everyone's aid."[34]

The Socialists had never concealed their patriotism; the leaders of the CGT, on the other hand, were bound by their own resolutions to call a general strike and raise the cry of insurrection. Why did the CGT collapse so quickly? Why did it not call a general strike? Fear of Carnet B certainly played an important role. The very night that Jaurès was assassinated, the Confederal Committee decided unanimously that it could not declare a general strike or an insurrection.[35] The syndicalist leaders agreed to support the policy of the party, which for them, of course, represented an important reversal of policy. Their fear of government action, it should be noted, was not without basis. Both Clemenceau and Messimy, the Minister of War, called for the application of Carnet B. "Give me the guillotine," Messimy had told Malvy, Minister of the Interior, "and I will guarantee you victory."[36] But Malvy had reason to believe that the syndicalists would prove loyal, and his information was correct. Eighty per cent of those listed in Carnet B volunteered for active service.[37]

However, the reasons for the collapse of the CGT go deeper. It was far too small in numbers and far too divided within itself to have taken any decisive action in 1914. Its ranks included acknowledged patriots as well as insurrectionists. As Georges Dumoulin later pointed out, the revolutionary syn-

---

[b] G. D. H. Cole comments quite rightly that "The Vaillant-Jaurès resolution recommended all means, without laying particular emphasis on any one. It did not so much recommend the general strike as refuse to rule it out." (*The Second International,* London, 1956, Part I, p. 66.) Many of those who opposed Guesde's motion did so because it encouraged a passive attitude toward the threat of war. See Pierre Renaudel's comments at the Congress of Nancy in SFIO, *4e Congrès national* [1907], pp. 251–52, 273. Among the coalition who voted for Jaurès's resolution were those who were skeptical of German intentions but wanted to put on record their own pacifism and internationalism. See, for example, Alexandre Varenne's remarks at the Congress of Nancy, *ibid.,* p. 208. At this congress Jaurès's motion was voted on in two parts. The vote on the first part (national defense) was 251 for, 23 against, and 30 abstentions; the vote on the second part (the general strike) was 169 for, 126 against, and 9 abstentions. *Ibid.,* pp. 315–19.

dicalists had been taken in by their own propaganda. "Our great manifestos served as banners for confederation strategy. We waved these flags to ward off harm and frighten away evil spirits."[38] The workers, at any rate, had always been more anti-militaristic than anti-patriotic.[39] Faced with a clear and present danger to their country, they rose to its defense. Desertions, which had been predicted at 13 per cent, were only one-tenth that figure. The leaders of the CGT had no choice but to yield to the evidence of their isolation. Had they attempted any other course, as Merrheim explained some five years later, "the working class ... would not have left to the police the job of shooting us; they would have shot us themselves."[40] In the hour of decision, the distinction between reformists and revolutionaries disappeared: there were only realists. "We were helpless, all of us," confessed Pierre Monatte. "The wave passed over, carrying us along with it."[41]

However, it was not the failure of the leaders of the SFIO and the CGT to stop the War, but the surrender of their principles, that was later held against them by their comrades. Already at Jaurès's funeral on August 4, in a moment of patriotic fervor and rhetorical flight, Jouhaux had allowed himself to cry: "All our hate for the savage imperialism that has led to this terrible crime!" It soon became evident that what he meant by "imperialism" was not the economic system that all the European States shared, but rather the Austrian and German monarchies. Taking their cue from such key utterances, Socialist and syndicalist journalists exchanged the language of class struggle for that of national unity. The War became a war to end all wars, a war of justice, a war of right. And when Guesde and Sembat entered the cabinet on August 26, the Socialist leadership published an interpretation of the War which, though by then familiar from the pages of L'Humanité, nevertheless rang strangely for a party that only seven years before had signed a resolution of the International declaring that wars were "inherent in the nature of capitalism" and would "only cease when capitalist economy is abolished."[42] "We can be certain," the Socialists declared, "that we are fighting not only for the existence of our country, not only for the grandeur of France, but for liberty, for the Republic, for civilization."[43]

In years to come, Socialists and syndicalists of leftist inclinations would ransack their brains for possible explanations of this shift. Was it weakness, ideological skepticism, or outright betrayal that caused these men to throw themselves into the war effort with so little concern for their prewar principles? The mystery seems less profound today. Men, we now recognize, are not motivated by ideas alone. Nor does their commitment to one goal prevent them from feeling the attraction of another. The fact that a man was a sans-patrie, as Dumoulin once protested, did not mean that he was against his country.[44] Moreover, the circumstances within which the War broke out made it easy to blame the conflict on German aggression. The French, after all, had done nothing to provoke war, while the Germans had blustered, rattled sabers, and issued threatening ultimatums. A question of national styles? Perhaps. But national styles create images that die hard. At any rate, contemporary documents indicate that few working-class militants had trouble reconciling their ideological convictions with their patriotism. As one syndicalist wrote to Jouhaux, "My conscience is clear, and I know the strength that comes from international comradeship; knowing what my pals expect of me, I've fought for the reconciliation of peoples and an end to war."[45]

Finally, is it too much to suggest that many Socialist and syndicalist leaders welcomed this opportunity to escape from the dilemmas that faced them on the eve of the War? Ideology committed the SFIO and CGT to irreconcilable class struggle. The attitude of the bourgeois parties before 1914 offered no alternative to opposition. Nonetheless, many Socialists and syndicalists no doubt felt the desire for integration into the national community that a few bold spirits like Thomas and Varenne expressed aloud. The enthusiasm with which men like Jouhaux and Sembat took up their new positions leads one to suspect that their thoughts went beyond the salvation of the *patrie*; that consciously or unconsciously they were anxious to abandon outmoded formulas, to come to terms with the problem of the State, and to break out of their isolation.

### THE EMERGENCE OF "SOCIAL CHAUVINISM"

Mobilization momentarily shattered the working-class organizations. Many party workers were called up immediately; the others quickly became absorbed in the everyday mechanics of life under a wartime regime. During the first chaotic weeks, Paris seemed like a deserted city. "The Grands Boulevards were empty; shop fronts were shuttered; buses, trams, cars, and horse cabs had disappeared. In their place flocks of sheep were herded across the Place de la Concorde on their way to the Gare de l'Est for shipment to the front."[46] Economic life ground to a standstill, and the patriotic enthusiasm of the first days was transformed into a grim determination to survive the first onslaughts of the Germans. In both the SFIO and the CGT the links between the center and the provinces were cut off amid the confusion of mobilization, and the central committees decided policy. The Socialist CAP created an executive committee to direct the party; it was composed of Guesde, Vaillant, Sembat, Compère-Morel, Alexandre Bracke-Desrousseaux, Louis Dubreuilh, Arthur Groussier, and Pierre Renaudel. With the exception of Dubreuilh, who was party Secretary, these men were all deputies. Compère-Morel, Groussier, Sembat, and Renaudel were in addition made responsible for editing *L'Humanité*.

Jaurès's death left the party without a leader. As Daniel Halévy wrote, the party "was Jaurès. It was his reflection. He created it. He kept it together."[47] Brousse had died in 1912. Allemane left the party in 1913. Neither Vaillant nor

Guesde was capable of taking Jaurès's place. Both were old and tired. Both threw themselves into the War with a wild chauvinism that soon discredited them with the party. Vaillant died in 1915. Guesde lived on until 1922, but he was sickly and increasingly tended to withdraw from party affairs. During this final period of his life, the Jacobinism of his youth seemed to have come back to drive out the Marxist orthodoxy of his mature years. Perhaps at heart he was always less a Marxist than a dogmatist. Sembat was a pleasure-loving man of the world; though widely liked, he had no claim to the leadership of the party. His sojourn at the Ministry of Public Works showed that he was more a journalist than an administrator.

It was Pierre Renaudel who stepped into this vacuum of power. Forty-two years old in 1914, an orator and journalist of talent and guile who had been active in Socialist ranks since the turn of the century, Renaudel came to dominate the party from his positions of influence as Director of *L'Humanité* and deputy from the Var. History has not recorded his success in love, but in politics, at least, the portly Socialist leader clearly had no luck. His efforts to imitate Jaurès's oratorical style and gestures ended in parody,[c] while the *nègre-blanc* motions at which he excelled earned him only the scorn of his comrades. For a brief period the center of gravity in a party stunned by war, he soon became the symbol of a collaboration with power that most militants preferred to forget. In 1920 he became one of the more conservative leaders of the new Socialist Party formed from the remnants of the old; and during the 1930's he was further discredited by getting involved in the movement to create a "Neo-Socialism."

Flanking Renaudel on his right and left were Albert Thomas and Jean Longuet, who were both to play important roles during the War. Thomas, the son of a butcher, was a graduate of the Ecole Normale Supérieure and a historian. No one better represented the new generation of Socialist leaders, educated in republican schools, drawn to the SFIO by Jaurès's democratic Socialism, and inclined to favor reformism. In May 1915 he entered the government as Under Secretary of State for Munitions, in which position he made himself a reputation as a first-rate administrator and the very incarnation of the Sacred Union. Rejected by the party after the War, he was to forge a brilliant career as head of the newly formed International Bureau of Labor. Jean Longuet was not to be so fortunate. The grandson of Marx, a Socialist of long standing, and a newly elected deputy, Longuet was a person of conscience and courage. Like Merrheim of the CGT, he suffered for these virtues; his attempt to honor his prewar principles made him a victim of a postwar generation that had no use for integrity when it did not lead to action.

[c] According to such diverse observers as Leon Trotsky, in *My Life* (New York, 1930), pp. 245–46, and Georges Bonnefous, in *Histoire politique de la Troisième République*, II (1957), 132.

In August 1914 there was a great consensus within the French working-class movement on the need to defend the nation against German aggression. During the last, critical days before the mobilization, the leaders of the working class assumed that the French government had done everything in its power to avoid war. The invasion of Belgium by Germany and the entry of Great Britain into the War on the side of France and Russia only further convinced the Socialist and syndicalist leaders that they were fighting a just war.[48] With Paris itself threatened, with the German army sweeping down through northern France like a scythe, there was no time for criticism or even for reflection. In that first month, Alfred Rosmer recalled, it was almost impossible to find anyone in Paris who would condemn the War. There was no Right, no Left, no Center—only one French nation united in arms against the invader. The anti-militaristic and anti-patriotic slogans of the years before the War seemed relics of a distant past.[49]

France was saved at the Marne, as the taxis of Paris sped off to carry reinforcements to the front in what Barbara Tuchman has called "the last gallantry of 1914, the last crusade of the old world." Then came the race for the sea, the fall of Antwerp, the battle at Ypres, and, with the coming of winter in November, the stabilization of the front. The war of movement had turned into the horror of trench warfare. Again to quote the eloquent words of Barbara Tuchman: "Running from Switzerland to the Channel like a gangrenous wound across French and Belgian territory, the trenches determined the war of position and attrition, the brutal, mud-filled, murderous insanity known as the Western Front that was to last for four more years."[50] The French spent 1915 trying to win back from the enemy the territory lost in the first month of war, while the Germans devoted their offensive efforts to the Eastern front. Marshal Joffre's tactic of *grignotage,* or nibbling away at the enemy, merely proved that what had been planned as a war of rapid offensives, and had begun as one, had turned into a contest of endurance in which a kilometer of wasteland might cost a river of blood.

Faced with the prospect of a long and costly war, the Socialist and syndicalist leaders devoted themselves all the more ardently to national defense. Sacred Union meant that the will of parties must temporarily be subordinated to the will of the nation. The working-class leaders accepted the full meaning of the phrase. The editorial writers of *L'Humanité* and *La Bataille* (the new title of *La Bataille Syndicaliste*) became masters at the art of *bourrage de crâne,* or making victory out of defeat. In their perpetual optimism they seldom presented a problem for the censor. Not content with supporting the war effort by abstaining from opposition, the Socialist and syndicalist leaders pushed toward a collaboration with power so close that in 1915 Merrheim would remark bitterly to Lenin, "The party, Jouhaux, and the government are three heads beneath the same cap."[51] This cooperation extended to war aims. There could be no question of peace, Guesde said at the first meeting of the Allied and Neutral

Socialists (in London in February 1915), until German imperialism was defeated. A French victory today was a precondition of a Socialist victory tomorrow.[52]

Moreover, in the fall of 1914, the Socialists broadened their conception of belligerency to include condemnation of the SPD. The last contact between French and German Socialists had taken place when Hermann Müller came to Paris on August 1 to consult with the French about their attitude toward voting for war credits. Though unable to speak definitively for his comrades, Müller had offered the opinion that the SPD deputies would either vote against or abstain on the war credits. "In my opinion," Müller said, "it's out of the question that we will vote for the war credits."[53] In fact, 14 of the 92 SPD deputies favored voting against the war credits; but they yielded to party discipline and voted with the majority.[54]

Alas, the fall of 1914 was no time for objectivity. The French Socialists made no attempt to understand the spirit in which the SPD had voted to support their government, or the fact that the Germans, too, might have felt their country endangered by a barbarous foreign power. To the French it was clear that the Germans had betrayed their Socialist principles; and they announced that once the War was over they intended to take the case before the tribunal of international Socialism. For the moment, however, all efforts must be devoted to winning the War by force of arms. And when the American Socialists undertook to piece together the fragments of the International and bring the belligerent Socialists together in a wartime conference in September 1914, Vaillant replied in a fit of chauvinism that there was no need to debate the responsibilities for the War since all intelligent and sincere Socialists were with the French. The others, he added petulantly, did not count.[55]

Thus, by September 1914, the Socialists had violated the two basic principles on which their unity had been built. By allowing two of their members to join a bourgeois government for purposes of national defense, the Socialists had given notice that they considered the class struggle temporarily adjourned. It followed quite logically that a government party could not associate with the enemy; and consequently internationalism, too, had to be put off until the War was over and France was safe. The CGT enthusiastically endorsed these policies.

### THE SPARK OF OPPOSITION

But there were a few Socialists and syndicalists for whom this final abdication was too much. In September they found their first champion. From Switzerland a French voice cried out in condemnation of the War. Placing himself "above the battle," Romain Rolland attacked the rulers of both France and Germany for their willingness to plunge European civilization into the horrors of war. The very title of Rolland's essay, "Au-dessus de la Mêlée," was a challenge to the policy of Sacred Union. "The worst enemy," wrote the author of *Jean-Christophe*, "is not across a border, but within each nation, and no nation has the courage to fight it. This enemy is the hundred-headed monster named imperialism, an arrogant and determined will to absorb everything, or subordinate everything, or crush everything, a will that tolerates no free eminence outside itself." Rolland called upon men of all countries to reject hate, to make a distinction between States and peoples, and to take up the struggle against the "octopus that is sucking the best blood of Europe."[56]

Nothing could have been less Marxist than this message of Christian brotherhood and love; yet it was in Rolland's Tolstoyan pacifism that the French opposition found its first ideological arms. Toward the end of October, a small group of internationalists began to form in Paris. Alfred Rosmer, Pierre Monatte, Henri Guilbeaux, Marcel Martinet, Amédée Dunois, Daniel Renoult, and the Russian Socialist Martov developed the habit of meeting weekly at the office of *La Vie Ouvrière*. Shortly afterward, Merrheim, Bourderon, and Leon Trotsky joined the group.[57] At first, all these disillusioned Socialists, syndicalists, anarchists, and left-wing intellectuals did was talk and exchange information; but in the bleak days of that first fall of the War, talk was itself a form of action—under the circumstances, the only one possible for men who opposed the War and blamed the capitalist powers equally for its outbreak.[58] Raymond Lefebvre, a young writer who was introduced to the group by Guilbeaux, has left a poignant memoir of those weekly meetings at the corner of the Granges-aux-Belles and the Quai de Jemappes: "We were content to poke sadly at the cold remains of the International; to draw up, with bitter memory, the enormous list of those who had fallen away; to predict, with useless clairvoyance, the length of a struggle in which civilization alone would be the vanquished."[59] For these men, Rolland's manifesto was a beacon in the night. "We were among those," Pierre Monatte would later write, "who spent whole nights copying this long and poignant cry of humanity."[60]

From this group came the first gesture of public opposition to the policy of Sacred Union. In October 1914, the Scandinavian Socialist parties had sounded out the CGT on the possibility of an international conference. At Jouhaux's suggestion, the administrative committee of the CGT had voted on December 6 to ignore the appeal, reiterating that Germany was responsible for the War and that it was up to the German workers to take the first steps to end the conflict. Monatte seized the opportunity created by this refusal to resign from the Confederal Committee. In his letter of resignation, which was circulated to the federations comprising the CGT, Monatte accused the CGT's leaders of having traded their syndicalist ideals for a new nationalist vocabulary:

The class-conscious workers of the belligerent nations cannot accept the slightest responsibility for this war; it rests entirely on the shoulders of the rulers of their countries. And far from discovering in the war reasons for drawing closer to them, it can only reinforce the workers' hatred of capitalism and the State. Today it is necessary, it is more than ever necessary, to maintain our independence jealously, and to hold resolutely to our ideals, which are our very reason for existence.[61]

The resignation of Monatte had not been the first sign of dissension in the Confederal Committee. Merrheim and Raoul Lenoir of the metallurgical workers' union both had been disturbed by the enthusiasm with which Jouhaux had pledged himself and the CGT to the Sacred Union and to the concept of a "war of liberation." The CGT, they feared, was losing its identity in its reckless patriotism. As Georges Dumoulin graphically put it in a letter to Jouhaux about this time: "Je pense que la C.G.T. est très bonne fille, s'est approchée trop près du lit gouvernemental et qu'elle a failli s'y coucher."[62] After the resignation (and immediate drafting) of Monatte,[63] Merrheim stayed on to represent the minority and fight against the policy of Sacred Union within the Confederal Committee. Merrheim made his Fédération des Métaux the spearhead in the campaign against the majority. On May 1, 1915, the Federation defied the censor and published a newsletter that mentioned Karl Liebknecht's speech to the Reichstag denouncing the War, reproduced an appeal for a collective peace movement by a group of German Socialists, and declared quite bluntly: *"This war is not our war."*[64] This was to be the slogan of the syndicalist opposition.

Merrheim found an ally in the federation of teachers' unions. Like so many of the unions, the Fédération des Syndicats d'Instituteurs almost disappeared as an organization between August 1, 1914, and June 1915. Its bureau was reduced to a Secretary, Hélène Brion, and a Treasurer, Fernand Loriot, both of whom were carried away by the wave of chauvinism. But in June 1915, two teachers from the provinces, Marie Mayoux and Louis Bouët, began a movement to win the federation to pacifism; and at the federation's annual congress in Paris on August 14, their views carried the day by a sizable majority. Brion and Loriot bowed to the majority and became active proponents of a negotiated peace. They joined Merrheim and Rosmer in distributing clandestine pacifist propaganda, and their journal, *L'Ecole,* became one of the few regularly appearing newspapers in which the syndicalist minority could find a forum. From August 1915 on, the leaders of the teachers' union were among the most dynamic workers in the anti-war movement, and later, after the Armistice, some of them played crucial roles in the creation of the Communist Party.

The strength of the syndicalist minority was first tested in the summer of 1915. At a conference of labor exchanges, unions, and federations held on August 15, 1915, the first such meeting since the outbreak of the War, Merrheim and Bourderon, supported by Loriot and Brion, submitted a resolution calling on the CGT to denounce the Sacred Union and return to its primary object, the class struggle.[65] This motion was overwhelmingly defeated by the majority's text approving the Sacred Union, and the very existence of the minority resolution was concealed. Nevertheless, it revealed a breach in the union movement that was to widen continually until it ended in the schism of the CGT in 1921.[66] The government was concerned enough to delegate Albert Thomas to persuade Merrheim to give up his policy of opposition.[67] Thomas failed, however, and throughout 1915 and 1916 the Fédération des Métaux continued to lead the opposition to the War within the CGT. Its journal, the *Union des Métaux,* urged the workers to demand peace, informed its readers of the Socialist and syndicalist movements in other European countries, and criticized the CGT's participation in the Allied Socialist congresses.

Nor did the SFIO remain immune to discontent over the forms that the Sacred Union was taking. As in the CGT, it was over the question of international relations with other Socialist parties that opposition first arose. Beginning in September 1914, the CAP had been confronted with various proposals for an international conference or gathering at which French and German Socialists would meet face to face: first by the American Socialist Party, then by the Scandinavians, and finally, in April and May 1915, by the Italians and the Swiss. The CAP, withdrawing further within the fortress of its own self-righteousness, had rejected all these offers.[68] The CAP's position was based on the assumption that the SPD had read itself out of the Socialist community by its acquiescence and participation in an imperialist foreign policy. But in the spring of 1915, new information threw this premise into doubt.[69] In May the Socialist parliamentary Group discovered the existence of the secret treaties ceding Constantinople to Russia. This revelation was followed by the news that the SPD's decision to vote for the war credits had not been unanimous.

The dissension within the party occasioned by these developments took the form of a provincial rebellion. As early as October 1914, René Nicod, Secretary of the Federation of the Ain, had published an open letter to Vaillant expressing his fears about the party's policies. "I would go so far as to say," he wrote, "that at this moment we are straying from the straight path of Socialist duty.... We must make greater efforts for peace; we must speak with the German Socialists."[70] Nicod was drafted. But the malaise in the party increased after the first of the year. On May 15, 1915, the Federation of the Haute-Vienne, an old Guesdist stronghold and one of the major centers of Socialist power, circulated to party members a manifesto questioning whether enough had been done to maintain a close liaison between the center and the federations. This was, of course, a thinly disguised blow at the parliamentary leadership. The manifesto, written by Paul Faure, went on to say that the Socialists of the Haute-Vienne did not think it was the proper role of the party "to push toward war to the bitter end, to adopt a bellicose stance, and to close its ears to all rumors of peace."[71] The circular made it especially clear that the Federation of the Haute-Vienne did not wish party leaders to discourage or disavow any peacemaking efforts on the part of foreign Socialist parties.

The Faure manifesto touched a responsive chord in the party, and undoubtedly expressed the afterthoughts that many members had had about the War and the role of the French Socialists in the Sacred Union. Three hundred thousand Frenchmen died in the first five months of fighting; another 600,000 were wounded, captured, or missing. Thousands more died every month (that very May, Joffre had paid for three miles of Artois soil with 400,000 casualties), and still there was no prospect of peace. How long could France stand such losses? Was it not the duty of the Socialists to do what they could to end the slaughter? It was now widely known that in Germany Karl Liebknecht was leading a Socialist opposition to the War, and that in Italy the majority of Socialists opposed Italian participation in the conflict. Was it not the role of the French to support their Socialist comrades, rather than to identify themselves with the policy of their own bourgeois government? Moreover, was the French government as innocent of all imperialistic designs as it had at first appeared? Many doubted it now that they knew of the secret treaties. After all, Jaurès himself, in his last speech on French soil, had assigned French imperialism its share of blame for the crisis. Had he not said that if war came, "All of us Socialists will be quick to dissociate ourselves from a crime committed by our rulers"?[72]

Out of these doubts was born the Socialist minority. In the provinces, the Federations of the Isère and the Rhone were quick to endorse the manifesto of the Haute-Vienne, while the Socialist daily in Limoges, the *Populaire du Centre,* began to act as a journal of opposition, though it was still inconsistent and timid in its criticism. In Paris, the deputies Jean Longuet, Pierre Laval, and Barthélemy Mayéras joined the opposition.[73] The response of the leadership (this was to become the traditional pattern) was first to ignore the challenge, and then, when this had become impossible, to call a special session of the National Council for July 14–15 to discuss the questions raised by the manifesto of the Haute-Vienne. The unanimous motion finally passed by the council made no concession to the minority. It endorsed once again the policy of Sacred Union and declared in a tone of ringing moral indignation, which had become de rigueur for all the SFIO's official utterances, that the War begun by Germany had to be fought to its logical conclusion, the final defeat of German militarism.[74]

### ZIMMERWALD: "LA FLAMME D'ESPOIR"

The first voices had risen in protest, the first gestures of discontent had been made. But the opposition, if one may even speak of an opposition at this point, was still weak to the point of nonexistence, painfully unsure of itself and what it stood for, and, worst of all, oppressed by a terrible sense of isolation. It was the Conference of Zimmerwald, appropriately held high above the European battlefields in the Swiss mountains near Berne in the first week of September 1915, that galvanized the dispersed elements of opposition in the party and the unions, and gave them a rallying cry, the skeleton of a program, and above all, perhaps, the assurance that they were not alone. The effects of Zimmerwald in France were complex: it both spurred on the growth of the opposition and divided it; it both frightened and inspired. One thing, however, was certain. A few determined men of different nationalities had come together and put on record their opposition to the War. With Zimmerwald the struggle against the War passed from individual rebellion to a new, more active stage of organized resistance.

Zimmerwald was the product, on an international level, of those questions and doubts that had given rise to an opposition in France during the first months of 1915.[75] As we have seen, the majority in the SFIO was firmly opposed to any resumption of relations with Socialists of the enemy camp. It believed that an international conference could take place only after responsibility for the War had been fixed and sanctions taken against the German Social Democrats for their complicity. The majorities of the Socialist parties in the other Allied countries held a similar view. The apparent willingness of German and Austrian Socialists to meet with their former Allied comrades only further hardened the hearts of the French against such contacts. For what was immoral from the point of view of the new Socialist ethics was inconsistent in the light of the new Socialist politics. How could a party committed heart and soul to national defense meet with representatives of a Power that occupied French soil and threatened the very existence of the *patrie*?

The Socialist parties of the neutral Powers, on the other hand, particularly the Scandinavians, the Swiss, and the Italians, could not accept this postponement of internationalism to the indefinite future. In December 1914, the Scandinavian parties met at Copenhagen and called on the International Socialist Bureau to convene a conference to discuss and thus hasten the peace; and in the first months of 1915, the Swiss Robert Grimm and the Italian Oddino Morgari came to Paris to try to temper the extremism of the SFIO. They were unsuccessful—the French leaders rejected out of hand any possibility of a meeting with German or Austrian Socialists. While in Paris, however, Grimm and Morgari made contact with the French and Russian internationalists, and upon arriving home they were able to report that, though isolated and small, a French minority did exist.

In the spring of 1915 the tempo of international contacts quickened. In February the Allied Socialists met in London; in April the Socialists of the Central Powers assembled in Vienna. These gatherings, far from being patriotic demonstrations, revealed the growing discontent with the policy of Sacred Union. At the end of April, a tiny conference of pacifist women met in

Switzerland. Louise Saumoneau, a courageous French schoolteacher, risked her profession and her liberty to attend.[d] A few days later, Willi Münzenberg presided over a conference of Socialist Youth, also in Switzerland. In May the Italian Socialists, encouraged by these signs of internationalism and frustrated by the inactivity of the International Socialist Bureau, voted to sponsor a conference of "all the parties, working-class organizations, and groups known to have remained faithful to the former principles and resolutions of the Labor International." Grimm and the Swiss party were charged with the details of its organization. Thus was born Zimmerwald.

The importance of a Socialist or syndicalist meeting cannot always be judged by the tenor of the resolutions that emerge from it. What is not said, what is said in private, the very fact of its occurrence, may be more significant than its public declarations. The importance of Zimmerwald was that it brought together revolutionary Socialists from all over Europe who opposed the War, including Frenchmen and Germans. The meeting itself was an act of defiance of the leaders of the European Socialist parties. From the historical point of view, Zimmerwald marked the first step in the process that led to the creation of the Third International. For it was at Zimmerwald that the Leninist Left made its international debut; and it was there that representatives of the French opposition first made contact with those ideas that only four years hence would divide them.

The French delegates to the conference were Alphonse Merrheim and the former Allemanist, Bourderon. They went to Zimmerwald as the representatives of the minority in the CGT. Merrheim, who himself was not a member of the SFIO, had attempted in vain to persuade one of the deputies from the Haute-Vienne to accompany him. Adrien Pressemane, one of the most internationalist of the deputies from Limoges, attended a meeting of the *La Vie Ouvrière* group and even expressed sympathy for its goals, but refused to participate in the conference itself because he feared it might precipitate a schism in the party.[76] The generation of Socialist leaders formed by Jaurès and Guesde obviously felt more at home in debates at the Palais Bourbon than in conspiratorial preparations for illegal conferences in Switzerland.[e] Merrheim and

---

[d] On returning to France, she was arrested and detained in the prison at St.-Lazare for seven weeks. See Kriegel, *Aux origines du communisme français, 1914–1920* (1964), I, 103.

[e] Trotsky tells an amusing story about the negotiations with the minority, which suggests the world of difference between French and Russian Socialism. In the summer of 1915 Morgari came to Paris to make preparations for the Zimmerwald Conference. He met with the *La Vie Ouvrière* group and a few Socialist deputies from the opposition at a sidewalk cafe on one of the Grands Boulevards. As long as the group restricted itself to professions of pacifism and exclamations about the need to resume international relations, everything went smoothly. But as soon as Morgari mentioned the need to obtain false passports, the Socialist deputies gulped down their coffee and made long faces, and one of them hurriedly called for the waiter and paid the check. This was the end of the meeting. "The

Bourderon therefore went to Zimmerwald alone, with the disapproval of both the party and the CGT. The mood of the two delegates may best be judged from the remarks Merrheim made before the congress of the teachers' federation on July 14, 1915. He and Bourderon, he said, were going to Zimmerwald in order to defend the Second International and preserve its unity "by calling it back to life."[77]

Merrheim was destined to play an important and controversial role in the events leading to the formation of the French Communist Party, and perhaps this is the appropriate place to say something about him and his background. Small, pale, with clear eyes and a tendency to slouch, Alphonse Merrheim was 44 years old in 1915.[78] A coppersmith by trade, he had been active in the union movement since 1891, eventually becoming Secretary of the Federation of Metal Workers, one of the largest and most aggressive CGT unions. Like Pelloutier, of whom he was the disciple and in many ways the heir, Merrheim was an anti-militarist and a fierce believer in the independence of the unions. Also like Pelloutier, he defined the revolution in terms of education and cultural transformation. In a period when threats of revolution were cheap and economic knowledge rare, Merrheim devoted himself to a study of French industry and the changes it was undergoing. Dedication to the working class and pessimism concerning its revolutionary consciousness were his outstanding characteristics. Despite the energy with which he discharged his duties (he is said to have worked 18 hours a day), he had little confidence in the internationalism of the French workers. In 1910-11 he published a study in *La Vie Ouvrière* predicting the coming of the War—at a time, it should be noted, when few Socialists and syndicalists really believed that war was a danger. Trotsky, never known for his generosity in judging others, dismissed Merrheim as a "cautious, slyly ingratiating, and calculating man."[79] But those French Socialists and syndicalists who worked with him and later fought him had a much higher estimation of his worth. L.-O. Frossard paid tribute to his sense of responsibility, and summed him up as "a brain, a man of character, a leader."[80] And Monatte, who never could understand his desertion of the extremist camp, wrote on Merrheim's death in 1925 that during the ten years before the War he had been "a model union official and syndicalist militant." "No one," he remarked, "did more than Merrheim to adapt the trade union movement to the struggle against modern, large-scale industry, . . . to take up and carry on Pelloutier's work, to put an end to mere talk and create a syndicalist organization conscious of its revolutionary role."[81]

Upon arriving in Berne, Merrheim was taken directly to Lenin, with whom he spent eight hours locked in discussion over the correct tactic to adopt at Zim-

___

ghost of Molière stalked across the *terrasse*," concluded Trotsky, "and, I think, the ghost of Rabelais, too." (*My Life,* p. 249.) Pierre Laval later told Henry Torrès that he had been the one who called for the check. It goes without saying that this was not his custom.

merwald. Lenin, convinced that there could be no middle ground between social chauvinism and social revolution, wanted Merrheim to agree to his formula of turning the imperialist war into a civil war between the proletariat and
the bourgeoisie. To Lenin, Zimmerwald already was significant only as the
first painful step toward building a new International. For Merrheim, Zimmerwald had a much more limited meaning. He saw it simply as the first
blow in the struggle against the War. The tough-minded little Frenchman had
no illusions about the ability of his small group to declare a general strike: "As
to a mass strike—oh! Comrade Lenin! I don't even know if I will be able to return to France and report what has happened at Zimmerwald! That's a long
way from being able to commit myself to saying to the French proletariat, 'Rise
against the War.' "[82]

The delegates were carted off to Zimmerwald in four stagecoaches, and, as
they jolted along the mountain road, they laughed at the thought that fifty
years after the founding of the First International it was still possible to squeeze
all the internationalists in Europe into four coaches. And yet, Trotsky recalled,
their mood was hopeful.[83] The French delegates generally sided with the moderate wing of the conference, but they made an excellent impression by signing
a joint Franco-German resolution declaring that "this war is not our war."[84]
Merrheim, moreover, delivered what Angelica Balabanova remembered as the
most ardent and impassioned of all the indictments of the War drawn up at
Zimmerwald.[85]

Nevertheless, when it came to the content of the manifesto that the conference would issue, Merrheim again clashed with Lenin, and in passing also
with Trotsky. To Lenin's demand that the declaration include some mention
of a new International, Merrheim replied that he and his group wanted to
limit themselves to action for peace. Our campaign is only beginning, he said,
addressing his remarks to Lenin. We have to deal with a disillusioned working
class, which has learned through bitter experience to believe in nothing. We
may succeed in winning over the proletariat, Merrheim added, but not if we
come before it with the old phrases that Hervé long ago emptied of all meaning. When Trotsky objected that Rosmer and Monatte thought differently,
Merrheim agreed that they believed a revolution would break out as a result
of the War; but he insisted that this revolution could not be decreed in a
formula. "A revolutionary movement can *only* arise out of the struggle for
peace. You, Comrade Lenin, are not governed by your longing for peace, but
by your wish to lay the foundations of a new International. This is what di-
vides us."[86]

The moderates triumphed. The manifesto, written by Trotsky with a mixture of passion and caution, stated that the responsibility for the War lay with
capitalist imperialism, called for action for peace, and attacked the leadership
of the various Socialist parties for their chauvinism and participation in the

War. As Merrheim had pointed out, this was the lowest common denominator that united the conference. What divided it—the question of the Third International and the turning of the imperialist war into a class war—was not mentioned.

Despite these conflicts of principle, Lenin and Zinoviev do not seem to have been unfavorably impressed by Merrheim and Bourderon. They ascribed their conservatism to the betrayal of the Socialist, syndicalist, and anarchist leaders, and to the fact that the enemy occupied a sixth of French territory. Their comments, written shortly after the conference, are interesting because of the confidence—for the moment, at least, quite unwarranted—with which these two Bolsheviks awaited the inevitable triumph of their own ideas in the French opposition:

The working class has been more successfully strangled in France than anywhere else.... The opposition in the French working class is only beginning. Unrest is everywhere. The best elements of the working-class movement are at the crossroads. A tremendous renaissance is beginning. Merrheim, a true son of the working class and its talented representative, is the incarnation of this new and profound process. From syndicalism he is moving toward Socialism, advancing cautiously while scouting its outskirts, without wanting to hear about Marxist theory (theory has been a bugaboo for many delegates), without yet agreeing to speak of the Third International![87]

The results of Zimmerwald in France at first seemed meager. The French Socialist press went out of its way to ignore it. *L'Humanité* published no résumé of the conference or its decisions. However, as the news leaked out, it became clear that Zimmerwald had expressed the unformulated thoughts of more than one Socialist and syndicalist. When Merrheim called a meeting of the Socialists of the Federation of the Seine to report on his mission, the members of the majority attended in force, and Renaudel himself rose to warn that Zimmerwald was the first step toward a split in the party, a prediction that proved only too accurate.[88] A few days later, the CAP made public a unanimous declaration reaffirming the necessity of an Allied victory and ordering the federations to avoid any appearance of sympathy with the Zimmerwald heresy.[89] This was the first public indication of anxiety about the spread of pacifist ideas, but in fact the party leaders had been worried for some time.[90] Nor did the CGT escape unscathed from the contagion of Zimmerwald. On December 12, 1915, 2,100 union members gathered at the CGT's Grande Salle and acclaimed a motion calling for an "energetic, persevering, and ardent campaign for the cessation of hostilities."[91]

The degree to which the rank and file of the party had become dissatisfied with the leadership's policy of class collaboration was revealed in December, at the first National Congress held since the coming of the War. The congress was scheduled to meet only from December 25 to 27, but the debates proceeded in such confusion that it was necessary to extend the meeting for another three days. The opposition had already proved its strength at the preliminary meetings of the Federation of the Seine, where one-third of the votes had gone against the leadership's policies.[92] This time the minority was determined not to fall into the trap of a common motion, as it had at the National Council of the previous July. The debates were stormy and marked by frequent incidents, some of a violent nature. Speakers were alternately applauded and howled down when they touched on the question of the War, and several times the *majoritaires* threatened to clear the galleries. On one such occasion the galleries replied by singing the *Internationale,* and the reaction was so tumultuous that the session had to be suspended for 15 minutes.[93]

Despite these obvious manifestations of disunion, however, the congress ended with one of those meaningless compromise resolutions that Socialist parliamentarians had long since mastered. The *majoritaires* appealed to the memory of Jaurès and the unity of the party; the *minoritaires* faltered and in their fatigue let themselves be taken in by the maneuver. Hubert Bourgin, bitterly disappointed because the final motion was not more patriotic, wrote in disgust: "It's a hash in which the most obvious bits have the colors of national defense but whose seasoning has a base of orthodox and mythological pacifism."[†] Bourgin's extreme chauvinism apart, it was clear that the outcome of the congress represented a victory for the majority and a defeat for the ideas of Zimmerwald. The motion was passed almost unanimously. Only 76 of the minority's votes held fast; they were registered in favor of Bourderon's resolution censoring the leadership of the CAP and the parliamentary Group and denouncing the voting of war credits.[94] The defeat can best be measured by the fact that the delegates of the Haute-Vienne voted with the majority. Embittered by this display of timidity, the Zimmerwaldians accused Longuet and his friends of having "stabbed in the back the German Socialist opposition, whose own behavior has been courageous and steadfast."[95]

### FROM ZIMMERWALD TO KIENTHAL

The Zimmerwaldians had no reason to despair. Instead of quashing the opposition in the party, the congress of December 1915 merely put up temporary dikes against it, dikes that must inevitably give way as the War dragged on its bloody course, as casualty lists grew and feelings of anger and guilt grew stronger among the rank and file. For the French, 1916 was the year of Ver-

---

[†] Hubert Bourgin, *Le Parti contre la patrie* (1924), p. 59. Resolutions like the one that emerged from this congress prompted Charles Rappoport to observe, "At any rate, in all the congresses, the resolutions, which for the most part went unread even in those rare cases when they were not unreadable, were only symbols. They indicated the road, the direction to be followed or avoided.... One turned to the left or the right without knowing the particulars of the road." *La Crise socialiste et sa solution* (1918), p. 3.

dun. The enthusiasm of 1914 had become a stolid acceptance of the horrible: as people are prone to do, the French were learning to live with war. Paris had regained its life, its glamour, and its sense of wickedness. The French *poilu* was still tough, still ready to kill and be killed when ordered. But constant *bourrage de crâne* and a leave behind the lines where life was easy and fortunes were being made had turned him into a cynic. "Eighteen months in the trenches," Alistair Horne writes, "had taken the edge off the fine ideologies of 1914."[96] For the opposition within the working-class movement, 1916 was a year of confused searching for an identity and a program. The fissures in the party and the CGT that were revealed in 1915 widened until both organizations were split into *majoritaires* and *minoritaires*. The two minorities, however, were not synonymous in program or method. Merrheim's syndicalist opposition had gone to Zimmerwald; Longuet and the Socialists of the Haute-Vienne had not. Moreover, the year 1916 saw the development of a division within the Socialist minority itself. From Zimmerwald on, it was increasingly evident that there were two oppositions and not one.

On the one hand there were the Zimmerwaldians, who disavowed the War and who wanted to return to the principles of prewar Socialism and syndicalism—as they were understood by the Left Wing. They did not think the party should participate in a capitalist government, whatever the circumstances; they opposed the voting of war credits; and they were willing to flout the authority of the International Socialist Bureau and their own party in order to re-establish connections with the other parties of the International, including the Germans and the Austrians. The Zimmerwaldian syndicalists, too, wished the CGT to refrain from all collaboration with the government. For both varieties of Zimmerwaldian, the key issue was internationalism, the willingness to put class before nation.

After the December congress, the Zimmerwaldians set out to organize themselves in a more coherent fashion. There already existed a Committee of International Action that had been created in November 1915. This committee, however, had been restricted to syndicalist activity alone.[97] In January 1916, Merrheim formed a Committee for the Resumption of International Relations, which brought together Socialists, syndicalists, anarchists, and a number of the Russian revolutionaries living in Paris. The nucleus of the Committee consisted of Merrheim, Bourderon, Loriot, Monatte, Rosmer, Rappoport, Louise Saumoneau, the anarcho-syndicalist Raymond Péricat, the left-wing schoolteachers Marie and François Mayoux, Trotsky, and Lozovsky.[98] The manifesto issued by the new Committee was careful to disavow any intention of competing with the CGT and the party; the Committee sought merely to fill the gap left by the moral collapse of the syndicalist and Socialist leadership.[99] But despite these disclaimers, it was inevitable that a group of this nature, which issued membership cards, which attacked the leadership of the

CGT and the party, and which was affiliated with the Zimmerwald movement internationally, would serve as a disruptive element within the larger organizations; and this was, in fact, what happened. This tiny committee, the direct heir of that group of internationalists who had met at the offices of *La Vie Ouvrière* in the fall of 1914, was one of the sources of the French Communist Party.

Following the traditional French pattern, the Committee for Resumption was divided into two sections, one to work in the SFIO, the other to agitate in the CGT. The Committee continued the newsletters on the War and the international situation which Alfred Rosmer had begun in the fall of 1915, and issued several pamphlets, including a report on the proceedings at Zimmerwald and an exchange of letters between Christian Rakovsky and Charles Gide on the origins of the War.[100] The conditions in which the Zimmerwaldians worked were extremely difficult. They were harassed from all sides. The government, always sensitive to pacifist ideas, banned their meetings and sent spies into their midst.[101] The majority in the party and the CGT refused to publish their articles and constantly distorted their views. Despite these difficulties, however, the Zimmerwaldians continued to gain ground. Toward the beginning of March 1916, Merrheim wrote optimistically to Robert Grimm in Switzerland that "our moral influence is growing and will soon make itself dramatically clear to the public."[102]

The Zimmerwaldians were not alone in their opposition; they were merely its extreme Left Wing. There was also the current that had emerged from the protest of the Haute-Vienne and that was commonly known as "the minority." The Zimmerwaldians and the minoritaires often joined forces to criticize the same policies, to applaud the same speakers, and to support the same motions. But it soon became clear that there was a very real difference between the two groupings. The minoritaires were more cautious in their criticisms; they accepted the view of the majority on the question of national defense and the necessity of voting the war credits; and, most important of all, they were obsessed with the need to maintain the unity of the party. Thus they often seemed to both the Socialist Right and the Socialist Left to wave like straws in the wind—first one way, then the other. As Jean Longuet, their leader and chief spokesman, explained in November 1915, at the meeting at which Merrheim had reported on his mission to Zimmerwald, they were groping toward a third position, one similar to that of the Kautsky-Bernstein-Haase group in Germany—what Lenin termed the Center. Longuet admitted that he admired the courage of Merrheim and Bourderon in going to Zimmerwald, but he thought the Conference itself premature and even dangerous.[103] Longuet and his friends were above all concerned that they not be considered defeatists or even doctrinaire pacifists.[104] At the December congress, they had voted with the majority against the Zimmerwaldians.

In the spring of 1916, however, the minority grew bolder, the result, at least in part, of pressure from the Left. It was no longer possible to maintain that the War had been a simple case of German aggression, or that the German Social Democrats had betrayed their principles en masse. In January Charles Gide and Mathias Morhardt formed a Société d'Etudes Documentaires et Critiques sur la Guerre, which included leading members of the Left.[105] At the same time, the minority learned the extent of the opposition in the SPD. They were able to read the speeches of Haase and Liebknecht to the Reichstag, and they no doubt blushed at their own timidity. They also discovered that it was the attitude of the SFIO that stood in the way of a meeting of the International. In March, Camille Huysmans, Secretary of the International Socialist Bureau, came to Paris, and the minoritaires met with him privately. They became convinced that it was necessary to convoke the International immediately if they did not want to see another Zimmerwald. As Raoul Verfeuil put it, "We must go to The Hague if we don't want others to go back to Zimmerwald."[106]

After Huysmans' trip to Paris, the majority summoned a National Council to denounce the peace campaign of the minority and the Socialists who had joined the Committee for Resumption. The Zimmerwaldians, on the other hand, hoped to force the minority to declare themselves on this occasion, and there is evidence that the minoritaires felt this pressure from the Left very keenly.[107] As late as December 1915, a motion to re-establish international relations with other Socialist parties had been defeated overwhelmingly by a national congress. By April 1916, the propaganda of the Zimmerwaldians and the hardships of the War had begun to tell. Over a third of the delegates voted against a resolution introduced by Renaudel stating that the resumption of international relations was unfeasible.[g] The Longuet-Pressemane motion, which demanded the re-establishment of relations among the sections of the International, received 960 out of 2,000 votes.[108]

The National Council of April 9, 1916, consummated the breach within the party between minoritaires and majoritaires. On May 1 the minority brought out its own journal, the *Populaire-Revue,* edited in Paris and published in Limoges, which immediately found a receptive audience. The majority responded some months later by creating the *Action Socialiste* to defend its point of view. The CAP and the parliamentary Group split definitively between minoritaires and majoritaires, and the two branches of the party began a fierce polemic.

Meanwhile, the representatives of the Zimmerwald movement, meeting at

[g] The vote was even closer than it seemed. Seven hundred of the majority's 1,987 votes were cast by delegates from occupied regions. These votes had been decided on in Paris by small groups of refugees; forty or fifty refugees had cast the votes for 12,000 party members. According to Longuet's calculations, the majority had assembled 1,300 regular and genuine votes as against 1,000 for the minority. *La Populaire-Revue,* May 14–20, 1916.

Berne in February, had decided to summon another international conference, which met at Kienthal, also in Switzerland, during the last week in April. The Committee for the Resumption of International Relations was not represented. Bourderon, Merrheim, and Marie Mayoux had been slated to go, but the government had denied them passports because of their involvement in pacifist propaganda.[109] However, three French delegates did attend, all of them minoritaires, all of them members of the parliamentary Group, and, interestingly enough, all of them schoolteachers or former schoolteachers: Pierre Brizon, Alexandre Blanc, and Jean Raffin-Dugens.[110]

The Kienthal Conference inaugurated a new era in international relations for the French Socialists. Before 1914 internationalism had meant songs, good fellowship, and debates, more often than not inconsequential, in which the French could claim to have played as radical a role as any of their fellow Socialists.[111] At Kienthal the French participants were subjected to a scathing interrogation by Russians, Poles, and Italians, and even were forced to endure the reproaches of a French journalist, Henri Guilbeaux, who prided himself on not belonging to the SFIO. It was the difference between a consultation and an indictment. From the French point of view, the major issue on the agenda was the question of national defense. Both the Left (the Leninists) and the Center (the Italians) were determined to wring from the minorities in the belligerent countries a definite commitment to vote against war credits. The great unknown was the attitude of the French. Without their cooperation, any demonstration by the Germans in favor of peace would almost certainly fail.

The French representatives could hardly have made a worse impression. Blanc and Raffin-Dugens left before the crucial debate. Brizon might have done better to leave himself; one participant recalled that in his off-hours he behaved like a traveling salesman, refusing to talk of anything but women.[112] When the debate on national defense came, Brizon insisted on speaking last, after Adolph Hoffman, the German delegate; by all accounts, his speech was embellished with so many frills and delivered in such a rhetorical manner that it alienated the entire audience.[113] "Comrades," Brizon is reported to have begun, "though I am an internationalist, I am still a Frenchman; therefore, I declare to you, I shall not utter one word, nor make any gesture, that might injure France—France, the land of the Re-vo-lu-ti-on."[114] When Brizon came to the question of war credits, he declared that the French delegates to the conference would certainly vote against them. But as he was being applauded, he quickly added that their vote depended on the military situation. This statement provoked a great protest; the excitable Italian Socialist leader Giacinto Serrati went so far as to grab Brizon by the collar and threaten him with a beating.[115]

Not surprisingly, there was little love lost between these French deputies and the Bolshevik delegation. To Brizon, whose Socialism was an unstable compound of concern for the underdog and revolutionary spirit, the Bolsheviks were "learned braggarts," and their demand that a new International be founded was a "betrayal of the old International."[116] Lenin and his supporters, for their part, were so disgusted with Brizon's shuffling between internationalism and patriotism that they drafted a declaration calling for his expulsion from the conference and condemning the policy of the French parliamentary minority as completely inconsistent with Socialism and the struggle against the War.[117] These three French deputies, however, were made of stronger stuff than their words had indicated. Before leaving Kienthal, Brizon drafted a manifesto proclaiming that only the triumph of Socialism could bring a lasting peace. "By all the means in your power," the manifesto urged the working class, "put an end to the world-wide butchery. Demand an immediate armistice! Peoples who are being ruined and killed, rise against the war!"[118] Furthermore, on returning home, the "pilgrims of Kienthal" did refuse to vote for war credits, at the cost of great personal abuse from the rest of the Chamber. Their fellow minoritaires did not follow suit.[119]

The majority reacted to Kienthal much as it had to Zimmerwald. After three days of deliberation, the CAP affirmed that the three French delegates had had no mandate to represent the party and invited their respective federations to take steps against them.[120] Despite the threat of punitive measures, the minority continued to gain. The majoritaires then called a National Council for August. Their tactic was to split the minoritaires from the Zimmerwaldians, and Renaudel insisted that the minoritaires opt for or against Kienthal. The minority refused: they would not condone Zimmerwald and Kienthal, but neither would they condemn them. The vote on the question of international relations showed that the balance of forces was still pretty much what it had been in April (1,081 vs. 1,836). The majoritaires emerged from this confrontation satisfied that they had checked the growth of the opposition.[121] But Brizon had the last word when he cried, in response to the accusations made against him and his fellow Kienthalians, "You bring us before the Socialist tribunal; but the Socialist Party isn't here; it's in the trenches, and its heart is at Zimmerwald and Kienthal."[122]

### TROTSKY AND THE COMMITTEE FOR RESUMPTION

We must return now to the evolution of the Committee for the Resumption of International Relations; for within that small and isolated body of extreme oppositionists were emerging conflicts of principle and tactics that foreshadow the later problems of the French Communist Party with the Comintern. These conflicts can best be seen in the clash between Merrheim and Bourderon on the one hand, and Trotsky and Lenin on the other. But, more profoundly, they reflect the difference between the French revolutionary experience and the Russian approach to the working-class movement.

Almost from the beginning of the War, the French opposition had been thrown into close contact with the Russian revolutionaries living in Paris.[123] In the early fall of 1914, the Menshevik Yulii Martov had published an article attacking Hervé's assertion that the Russian Socialists stood solidly behind the War. Monatte, encouraged by this ripple of opposition, had gone to see Martov, and through him had met the other Russian Socialists.[124] When Trotsky arrived in Paris from Austria in November, he immediately became friendly with Monatte and Rosmer, in whom he found kindred souls. It was Monatte who brought Trotsky to *La Vie Ouvrière* and who introduced him to Henri Guilbeaux, Merrheim, Bourderon, Louise Saumoneau, and Loriot.

The Russian revolutionary Socialists in Paris were gathered around *Nashe Slovo,* a small Russian-language newspaper that they published.[125] This daily, constantly short of funds and harassed by the censor, managed, thanks to the determination of its staff, to survive from 1914 to the outbreak of the Russian Revolution. In surviving, moreover, *Nashe Slovo* maintained a remarkably high standard of journalism at a time when the line between objectivity and subversion was often faintly drawn. In 1914 Lenin called its predecessor, *Golos,* "the best Socialist newspaper in Europe"; and Isaac Deutscher writes that in 1915 and 1916 *Nashe Slovo* was, after Lenin's *Sotsial-Demokrat,* "the most important laboratory of the revolution."[126] In addition to its co-directors, Trotsky and Martov, *Nashe Slovo* included among its contributors and correspondents such outstanding figures as Lozovsky, Rakovsky, Anatole Lunacharsky, Dmitrii Manuilsky, Karl Radek, Georgii Chicherin, Alexandra Kollontai, and Angelica Balabanova, all of whom were to play important roles under the Bolshevik regime.

The Russian Socialists grouped around *Nashe Slovo* were all internationalists; but they differed when it came to deciding on the form that opposition to the War should take.[127] Was the Second International discredited beyond all hope? Should a Third be created to take its place? Should the minorities that continued to support the War be condemned along with the social chauvinists? Finally, should the imperialist war be turned into a civil war? Lenin, of course, had answered all these questions affirmatively, and his articles were debated furiously by the editors of *Nashe Slovo* at their daily conferences in the print shop and the Café Rotonde.

Among Russian Social Democrats, as in all parties, the coming of the War had cut across the old prewar divisions, leaving on one side those who opposed the War and on the other those who supported it. Unlike many of his fellow Mensheviks, Martov remained an internationalist. Ilya Ehrenburg remembers meeting him several times at the room of a friend. "He was wretchedly unhappy over the collapse of the Second International. He coughed, went about in a threadbare overcoat, shivered with cold, and like Lapinski, tried to convince me—though in reality he was convincing himself—that the 'reckoning' was 'inevitable.' "[128]

Soon, however, the old factional quarrels revived. Martov was reluctant to condemn the Mensheviks who supported the War. "He was torn between his own conviction and the pull that the party he had founded exercised on him. He slid backwards and forwards, tried to patch up differences, and escaped from his dilemmas into the soothing atmosphere of the Parisian cafés."[129] Maverick Bolsheviks like Lozovsky, Manuilsky, and Lunacharsky felt the attraction of Lenin's revolutionary defeatism. Trotsky, always a loner, wavered between these two groups. He quibbled with Lenin's slogans. He refused to accept his defeatism. He was not sure that this was the propitious moment to announce a new International. He shrank from breaking with Martov, with whom he had old ties. Yet he could not deny that the Bolsheviks had for the most part remained internationalist, while his own faction had not. Under the impact of the War, the real differences between Lenin and Trotsky dwindled in importance.[130]

These debates had their echo in the ranks of the French opposition. We have already seen how Merrheim at Zimmerwald had refused to join Lenin in calling for a new International on the ground that the struggle for peace came first. Lenin did not allow this first failure to discourage him in his attempt to influence the French opposition. At the end of 1915 he sent to Paris Inessa Armand, a Bolshevik of long standing and a close personal friend, to act as his emissary within the French Zimmerwaldian movement. Thanks to the energy and efficiency of the police, we know the full extent of Inessa Armand's activity.[131] She took part in the formation of the Committee for the Resumption of International Relations. She distributed Lenin's pamphlet *Socialism and the War* and his letter to Savarov on the objectives and tasks of the opposition in France.[132] She addressed various groups of oppositionists on the point of view of the Zimmerwald Left, of which Lenin was the leader. She was in close contact with Socialist women's groups and the Jeunesses Socialistes, which received a visit in April 1916 from a young Swiss named Jules Humbert-Droz, who will play an important role in the later stages of this story.

But despite the dedication with which Inessa Armand handed out Lenin's articles and defended his views before the Committee for the Resumption of International Relations, she had no success in organizing a Leninist faction within the French Zimmerwaldian movement. Merrheim remained as opposed to such extremism as he had always been. His two concerns were to preserve the integrity and the isolation of the CGT (thus the constantly repeated phrase, "This war is not our war") and to end the War as soon as possible. As he put it, his efforts were devoted to limiting the effects and duration of the War "in so far as our meager forces allow us."[133]

Moreover, neither Merrheim nor Bourderon wanted to do anything that would undermine or split the existing working-class organizations. Like the minoritaires in the party, they too paid homage to the fetish of unity. The first manifesto of the Committee for Resumption underlined its provisional nature, as did later publications. When Inessa Armand suggested that the manifesto call for a new International and the transformation of the imperialist war into a class war, the members of the Committee objected violently. Merrheim, she reported to Lenin in January 1916, had told her that the Leninists were reminiscent of the old Guesdists in their extremism and lack of realism.[134] Inessa Armand's mission, in fact, had almost no effect; even Loriot, soon to be the leader of the French Leninists, later remarked that the French opposition had not been acquainted with Lenin's point of view at this time.[135] Lenin himself confirms this impression; on November 25, 1916, he wrote Inessa Armand a letter from Zurich, in which he complained that he had no contacts with the French: "I would have liked with all my heart to do something for the French Left Wing, but communications are still to be set up. Grisha [Belensky] writes at length, but letters absolutely devoid of sense; he pours out words, rehashes the same old stories, tells us nothing that makes any sense, nothing precise, with regard to the French Left Wing, and does not establish any kind of contact with them."[136]

However, if Lenin had no luck in influencing the French opposition from Switzerland, the same was not true of Trotsky, who, like Lozovsky, was a member of the Committee for Resumption and was linked by friendship to Monatte and Rosmer. From the initial organization of the Committee, Trotsky came into conflict with Merrheim and Bourderon.[137] Merrheim objected to admitting Trotsky to the Committee's executive commission and accused him of lacking tact; Trotsky reproached Merrheim for not having gone to Kienthal, and criticized the Committee in general for laxness in propaganda and organization. Trotsky continually prodded the Committee to take a more positive stand. In February 1916 he demanded that the Committee publish a brochure disavowing the patriotic Socialists. Again, in April, on the eve of the Socialist National Council, Trotsky declared that the Bourderon motion did not correspond to the Zimmerwaldian line. At the August National Council, the Zimmerwaldians, led by Brizon and Bourderon, abandoned their own motion and voted with the minority. Trotsky reacted by demanding that the Committee break definitively with the minoritaires.[138]

Trotsky's attitude toward the Longuet minority seems to have had psychological roots that went deeper than the political situation of the moment. If one can believe his autobiography, Trotsky decided while still a boy that his schoolmates could be divided into three groups: "the talebearers and the envious at one pole, the frank and courageous boys at the other, and the neutral, vacillating mass in the middle." "These three groups," he writes, "never quite disappeared during the years that followed. I met them again and again in my life, in the most varied circumstances."[139] By August 1916, Trotsky had come to the conclusion that Longuet and his friends could not be classed with the frank and the courageous. "In all fundamental questions," Trotsky argued in the resolution he submitted to the Committee at that time, "they [the minoritaires] go hand in hand with the present majority of the Socialist Party, and consequently with the parties of the imperialist bourgeoisie." In fact, Longuet was much worse than Renaudel and more dangerous than the outright social chauvinists, because he deceived the working class with his empty phrases and discredited the very idea of opposition. Renaudel, Trotsky said, needs Longuet as a screen, just as the government needs Renaudel in order to keep the country in the War. Thus, he concluded, we must constantly and everywhere expose Longuetism to the masses for what it is: an indispensable tool of the bourgeoisie.[140]

Trotsky's resolution was hotly debated by two sessions of the executive commission and two sittings of the Committee as a whole. The moderates, led by Bourderon, accused Trotsky of trying to split the SFIO and lead the opposition into a new International.[h] Invoking the tradition of syndicalist autonomy in reverse, Bourderon objected that syndicalists and anarchists had no business commenting on the internal affairs of the Socialist Party. The anarcho-syndicalist Raymond Péricat replied that they had all joined forces to fight nationalism in common. Otherwise, there was no reason for the Committee.[141]

This exchange was an important one in the light of both the past and the future of the French working-class movement. It raised the question of whether the War had not made irrelevant the old divisions between Socialists, syndicalists, and anarchists. Trotsky, for example, had already discovered that he had more in common with the Bolsheviks than with many of his former Menshevik allies. Would not the same realignment occur in France? Trotsky thought it would, and by the end of 1916 there were French Socialists, syndicalists, and anarchists who agreed with him.[142]

The debate ended with the approval of a text by Loriot that preserved the substance of Trotsky's resolution while moderating some of its language. Loriot went on to make a pamphlet from this motion, entitled *Les Socialistes*

[h] Kriegel, I, 138. It should be noted, however, that the moderates were not the only ones to oppose Trotsky's resolution. Lozovsky rejected it (1) because it assimilated the Longuetists to Jouhaux in the CGT, and thus blurred the differences between Longuet's group and the Right; (2) because it confused the objective results of the minoritaires' position (the deception of the masses) with their subjective intentions; and (3) because Lozovsky felt, like Bourderon, that it was a mistake to submit it to syndicalists and anarchists, who would vote for it not because they were revolutionary, but because they were anti-Socialist. (*Nashe Slovo*, 18.viii.16.) Lozovsky proposed, as a counter-policy, that the Zimmerwaldians treat the French Center as they did Kautsky's group in Germany: namely, criticize them and nudge them to the Left without denouncing them as counterrevolutionaries. (*Nashe Slovo*, 13.ix.16.) The difference between the two Russians was a basic one. For Trotsky the Center was already lost to the forces of counterrevolution; for Lozovsky, Longuetism was a transitional form in the liberation of the working class from patriotism. The question would arise again in 1919 and 1920.

*de Zimmerwald et la Guerre,* which stated the position of the Committee vis-à-vis the *minoritaires* much more forcefully than it had ever before been stated, and revealed very clearly Trotsky's influence on the thinking of the French opposition.[143] The regeneration of the old International, Loriot observed, seemed more and more unlikely. The unity of the SFIO was no more than a phantom. As for the minority, its members bore before the masses and history a large part of the responsibility for "the transformation of organized Socialism into a docile instrument of the imperialist bloc."[144] Their policy was contradictory and inconsistent to the point where they voted both for the resumption of international relations and for a government that made those international relations impossible, both for internationalism and for nationalism. "If the policies of the official majority of the Socialist Party undermine the future of French and international Socialism," wrote Loriot, "the policies of the minority threaten to compromise for good the *very idea* of opposition to governmental Socialism." There could be no greater condemnation. The rest of the pamphlet was devoted to proving "that national defense IS NOT SOCIALIST," and that "the proletariat's attitude toward the War could not be determined by the military or strategic position of the belligerent countries."[145] The pamphlet concluded that it was the duty of the working class to demand an end to the fighting and force the Socialist deputies to withdraw from the government and vote against the war credits.

Trotsky was expelled from France in September 1916 by the Briand government. By then, however, he had formulated many of the ideas and impressions that he would apply from Moscow during the first years of the French Communist Party. He had classified the Center of Longuet with the Right of Renaudel. He had insisted that it was a matter of life and death for the revolutionaries to distinguish themselves from this amorphous Center, which threatened to absorb and neutralize the real opposition. And, finally, he had glimpsed the possibility of a new grouping of revolutionaries, which would cut across the old boundaries and taboos and include Socialists, revolutionary syndicalists, and even anarchists.[146]

### A NEW CONSENSUS

Few syndicalists or Socialists, however, saw things as clearly and with as much assurance as Trotsky, who had the comfort of his Marxist method and absolute belief in the inevitability of revolution. When the anarchist Sébastien Faure inquired of his readers how many thought the CGT should remain independent of both the government and political parties (including the SFIO), he found 3,186 in favor of the complete independence of the syndicalist movement and only 32 friendly to a lasting liaison with the Socialist Party.[147] Needless to say, this was a far from balanced poll, yet it suggested what difficulties might confront any party that tried to enroll syndicalists and anarchists. Meanwhile, the line between the Zimmerwaldian and *minoritaire* Socialists tended to blur, much to the consternation of Trotsky, who railed from his exile in Cadiz that "opposition to Renaudel and Sembat still does not mean opposition to the capitalist government that is waging an imperialist war."[148] Loriot, who played an increasingly important role in the Zimmerwaldian camp, confessed to a correspondent in the provinces toward the end of November 1916 that he feared "certain Zimmerwaldians" would join Longuet's group at the approaching congress. "I am fighting," he wrote, "with all my energy against this surrender, which would strip the opposition of all significance."[149]

The National Congress of December 1916 revealed what progress the minority had made in the course of a year. The terrible losses at Verdun and the Somme, the defeat of Romania, the growing suspicion of French war aims, and the realization that the SFIO alone prevented a meeting of the International—all these had whittled away the near-unanimity of the previous year until the two factions were almost equal in strength.[150] The parliamentary Group was the scene of constant conflict between minoritaires and majoritaires. Just a few weeks before the congress met, Guesde and Sembat had left the government. But the policy of participation had been re-endorsed, and Albert Thomas had remained in the newly constituted Briand government as Minister of Armaments. At the congress, a series of votes on the agenda, the general policy of the party, international relations, and cabinet participation showed that the majority could count on a margin of less than 200 votes out of 3,000.[151] The rule of proportional representation was invoked, and the minority was given 11 of the 24 places on the new CAP. Pacifism was now respectable. "Granted that national defense is our duty," asked one delegate, "is that any reason for refusing to acknowledge another duty, that of unstinting effort to put an end to the present tragedy? Let us cooperate in national defense, but outside the government."[152] An increasing number of Socialists agreed with him.

The congress itself was marked by moments of great violence. "One would have sworn," reported one observer, "that it was all going to end in a fearsome brawl, so impossible did it seem to reconcile such contradictory points of view, such antagonistic feelings."[153] The majoritaires had invited to the Congress a delegation of patriotic Socialists from Allied countries, consisting of the Belgian Emile Vandervelde, the Englishmen Arthur Henderson and G. H. Roberts, the Russian Ilya Roubanovitch, and the Spaniard Martínez Barrio. Vandervelde, Roberts, and Henderson all held posts of responsibility in their respective governments and were known as unrelenting patriots. The arrival of the delegation caused the congress to break into a tumult, as the majoritaires cheered and the opposition booed. When Vandervelde rose to speak, the minoritaires responded by singing the *Internationale*.[154] "It's for that, then, that I've given so many years of my life," the embittered Guesde is supposed to have said as he left the congress hall.[155]

The minority felt itself on the verge of victory. As it turned out, its leaders were premature in their celebrations. The majority itself was in the process of transformation. A Center had formed around Albert Bedouce, the mayor of Toulouse, and Henri Sellier, which bridged the gap between majoritaires and minoritaires.[156] At the end of 1916, Marcel Cachin made the journey from chauvinism to pacifism; he would be followed by others. The extremists within the majority, for their part, already found Renaudel too tolerant of the pacifist Left.[157] A new majority, however, needed a new position; the slate had somehow to be wiped clean. How could the thunder of the minority be stolen without admitting that the policy of Sacred Union had been a tragic mistake—and thus that the men who had devised and administered it were tragically responsible? The answer to this awkward question was found in the strange phenomenon of Wilsonianism. For a brief moment the unity lost in 1915 seemed to be regained under the broad umbrella of Woodrow Wilson's diplomacy of peace. The National Congress voted almost unanimously to ask the Allied governments to respond favorably to Wilson's December 1916 offer of mediation, as did the Second National Conference of the CGT, which met in Paris on December 24–25. The leaders of both the minority and the majority in the SFIO and the CGT acclaimed Wilson's "peace without victory" speech of January 22, 1917. On the same occasion, the Socialist parliamentary Group drafted a manifesto appealing to the French government "to state clearly its agreement with Wilson's noble words of reason," and adopted as its own the American President's insistence on a peace without annexations or reparations.[158] These positions were ratified at the National Council of March 4 and 5; and it was indicative of the new mood of the majority that its resolution called on the Allied governments to announce their "formal and decisive approval" of Wilson's peace proposals.[159] International relations, however, were still to be postponed until the Germans had made clear their position with regard to the responsibilities for the War.

Meanwhile, the Committee for the Resumption of International Relations was undergoing its own crisis. As Loriot had feared, a number of Zimmerwaldians, including Bourderon and Raffin-Dugens, had broken discipline at the December congress and voted with the minority. Loriot drew from this experience the lesson that the Zimmerwaldians needed a different type of organization. "It is disastrous," he wrote to a friend, "that it should be this hesitant minority, without clearly defined ideas, that benefits from the revolt of the Socialist conscience."[160] Wilsonianism stretched to the breaking point the differences within the Committee between Rappoport and Loriot, who stood for doctrinal orthodoxy, and Bourderon and Raffin-Dugens, who favored a more tolerant attitude toward the minoritaires.[161] In February 1917, Merrheim, Bourderon, and Brizon joined a group of Socialists and syndicalists that included Jouhaux and Renaudel in sending a message of sympathy to Wilson. Loriot responded by accusing Merrheim and Bourderon of engaging "in platonic internationalism" and "placing themselves in the tow of Wilsonian-ism."[162] The result was a split in the Committee. Bourderon, Brizon, and Raffin-Dugens joined the Longuet minority. Merrheim withdrew from the Committee and concentrated his attention on the Federation of Metal Work-ers. The leadership of the Committee passed to Loriot, Rappoport, Louise Saumoneau, and François Mayoux, who gave it a more purely Socialist char-acter. The revolutionary and pacifist syndicalists who found Merrheim's lead-ership too timid followed Raymond Péricat in forming a Committee for the Defense of Syndicalism.[163]

Thus, by March 1917, all but the most extreme of majoritaires had aban-doned the policy of *guerre à l'outrance* adopted by the party in the dark hours of August 1914. Jacobinism and nationalism, discredited by the shedding of so much blood, would now yield increasingly to pacifism and internationalism. Those super-patriotic Socialists who resisted this trend would soon lose their influence in the party. The change in climate was shown by the blossoming of the pacifist press. Minoritaires and Zimmerwaldians could find an open forum for their views in such papers and reviews as *Le Populaire Socialiste-Interna-tionaliste, Le Journal du Peuple, La Vérité, Le Bonnet Rouge,* and, of course, *Le Populaire du Centre* and *L'Ecole de la Fédération,* which had been inter-nationalist ever since 1915. Sébastien Faure's *Ce Qu'il Faut Dire* was suppressed in 1917, but in January 1918 Brizon founded a weekly newspaper, *La Vague,* which specialized in printing letters from workers and soldiers and which soon became very popular with the masses.[164]

Certainly, there were still important differences between the minority and the majority. The majority refused to meet with enemy Socialists until the SPD acknowledged its guilt in supporting the War. The minority was eager to end the party's participation in the government. The steady growth of the minority's forces suggested that these issues would soon be settled in its favor. After the National Council of March 4–5, 1917, the minority formed a Commit-tee for the Defense of International Socialism to carry on and step up its cam-paign for the resumption of international relations.

Yet, even though these differences could call forth angry words and arouse bitter feelings, the fact remains that between majoritaires and minoritaires there existed a wide area of agreement. Few minoritaires denied that the party must support national defense by voting war credits. Few majoritaires re-jected Wilson's appeal for a peace without victory. After the March National Council, Bourgin remarked acidly, the party threw itself, "ears stopped up and eyes closed, into the Wilsonian adventure."[165] To a Russian Socialist like Trot-sky, at any rate, the differences between the minority and the majority seemed less important than their similarities. Longuet and his friends called them-selves internationalists, wrote Trotsky from Spain in late 1916, but in reality they followed the same policies as Renaudel. "They are with the 'nation,' with the State—not with the class in opposition to the State. They calm the conscience of the masses by their family opposition, their *opposition de boutique* ...in order to drag them along behind the cart of the official party, the party of the Renaudels and the Sembats."[166]

In the Committee for the Resumption of International Relations there remained a group of Socialists who refused to accept the principle of national defense, who called on the Socialist deputies to vote against the war credits, and who denounced Wilsonianism as an illusion. These Socialists denied that they were innovators. They had no policy, they insisted, except the doctrines of internationalism and social revolution adopted by the International before the outbreak of the War. They denounced the social patriots for having forced the working class to share the responsibility for the War.[167] But for all their ardor, they were a small and isolated group—in all, with their fellow syndicalists and anarchists, no more than a hundred militants, without any influence on the masses.[168] They hardly seemed a threat to the larger organizations that periodically denounced them for their "dangerous divisionism."

Yet history has up its sleeve an endless store of tricks. Before being expelled from France in October 1916, Trotsky addressed an open letter to Jules Guesde, in which he denounced him for participating in the bourgeois government that was driving from its territory a Russian revolutionary Socialist for a crime it knew he had not committed. You may console yourself, Trotsky wrote Guesde, in thinking that we are few; but we are more numerous than you suppose:

Get out of your armored car, Jules Guesde; step forth from the cage in which the capitalist State has shut you up, and look around a little. Perhaps for this one time fate will have pity on your sad old age, and you will be able to hear the dull noise of approaching events. We await these events; we summon them; we prepare the way for them. The fate of France would be terrible if the suffering of its working masses were not repaid by a great revenge—*our* revenge, Jules Guesde, in which there will be no place for you or yours.[169]

Trotsky's revenge came in Russia, not in France. On March 8, 1917, three days after the National Council of the SFIO had concluded its deliberations, bread riots broke out in Petrograd; within a week, a Soviet had been elected, the Tsar had abdicated, and a Provisional Government had taken office. Russian revolutionaries, scattered to the four corners of the globe, flocked home to take the leadership of the long-awaited revolution. Within four years, Guesde would leave the party he had helped to found, in which there was no longer room for him or his.

## Chapter three

# A New Sun in the East

La démocratie française—*qui ne l'est que de nom*
—retarde sur l'horloge du monde. Qu'elle aille
à Petrograd, comme Cachin, pour remettre sa
montre à l'heure!
        —*Romain Rolland, in a letter to Jean Gold-
        sky, May 29, 1917*

Wilson announced America's entry into the War on April 2, 1917. On April
16 Lenin arrived in Petrograd to proclaim his April Theses. That same day
General Robert Nivelle ordered his troops "over the top" in a suicidal offensive. How much of the history of the next forty-five years was anticipated in
these three events: liberal America, a world power; Bolshevik Russia, the eye
of world revolution; divided France, bled dry by her own victory. In 1917 and
1918 the names of Lenin and Wilson would be coupled.[1] What was the Russian
Revolution? The final triumph of democracy? The overthrow of capitalism?
The realization of the syndicalist utopia? The creation of a brutal party dictatorship? For years no one could be sure. The Russian Revolution became one
of those great and ambiguous human events in which all men see all things.
Few men, however, grasped that 1917 might spell the end of one epoch and
the beginning of another, or that Europe no longer had the power to decide
her own destinies.

In France the first inclination was to interpret the Revolution as the rejection of autocracy in favor of some form of democratic government. Russia, this
strange and incomprehensible land of Cossack barbarism and artistic sophisti-
cation, of Tolstoyan peasants and Dostoyevskian nihilists, was at last taking
her rightful place among her Western allies.[2] French democrats rejoiced at
the thought that the War would now assume the simple outlines of a struggle
between liberalism and imperialism. And, for that matter, what Frenchman,
no matter how reactionary, could remain indifferent to this clear evidence that
French democracy offered a model to other, more backward countries? But in
1917 such ideological enthusiasm and national pride had necessarily to give
way to more immediate preoccupations. For, above all, the news of revolution

in Petrograd brought thoughts of peace after a long, hard winter, during which determination had often been mingled with despair. It was this confusion of the issues of peace and revolution that gave events in Russia their explosive relevance. The attentions of Frenchmen, both bourgeois and proletarian, shifted anxiously to the East; French tongues grappled helplessly with unpronounceable Russian names. According to one leading minoritaire, news of the Revolution inspired among the masses "an unprecedented, almost delirious enthusiasm. In less than a week, the name of the weak and wordy Kerensky rose to the heights of popularity."[3]

### THE IMPACT OF THE FEBRUARY REVOLUTION

Frossard to the contrary, there were precedents for such enthusiasm. Before the War the Tsarist government had been viewed by all Socialists as the headquarters of European reaction, and its overthrow considered the first objective of revolutionary action.[4] The Russian Revolution of 1905 had been followed with intense interest by all sectors of the French working-class movement. Articles had poured forth from the press by the dozens, and, in contrast to so many other cases, enthusiasm had not been confined to newspapers alone. Meetings were held in Paris and the major provincial cities; protest marches were staged all over France; a fund-raising drive was launched; and the Russian Ambassador in Paris reported home to Petersburg that, "Everywhere, but mainly among the workers, meetings occur at which fiery speeches are delivered and resolutions against the Russian government are adopted, which are then sent to me."[5] The unity of the various Socialist sects was forged in the campaign against Tsarist brutality; and the first truly "international" action of the SFIO had been its response to the appeal of the International Socialist Bureau for a European-wide demonstration to honor the victims of Bloody Sunday. On a less partisan level, Anatole France, the party's leading literary sympathizer, founded a Society of Friends of the Russian People, which had a brief but brilliant success. If one can believe the account of Marcel Cohen, written many years after the fact, the reaction of the Parisian students was no less enthusiastic. At the Sorbonne, for example, a collection was organized; and radical students made the rounds of their professors soliciting contributions, with what results it is not known.[6]

Sympathy for the Russian Revolution had been made easier by personal contacts. Paul Lafargue seems to have been at home to Russian revolutionaries of all varieties, while Jaurès, Lucien Herr, and Jean Longuet were on warm, if not intimate, terms with the exiled leaders of the Socialist Revolutionary Party. Jaurès's relations with the Russian revolutionaries would merit study. It is one more example of the fact, too long ignored, that no European labor movement developed in isolation before 1914. Though too reformist for the most moderate of Russian Socialists, Jaurès knew them, sponsored their meetings, and followed their quarrels closely, going so far as to cite the Russian experience as an argument in favor of the Bloc des Gauches.[7] He also sensed that a Russian revolution might have repercussions of great importance in the West. What was happening in Russia, he wrote in June 1905, was the most important fact of history since the French Revolution. It was thus the duty of Socialists everywhere to devote all their energies to a "decisive effort" to liberate Russia; in so doing they would give impetus to democratic and working-class movements throughout the world.[8]

Still, it should be noted that if Jaurès was prescient in giving attention to events in Russia, he was considerably less so when it came to their interpretation. The Russian Revolution, he thought, was merely another link in the chain of the universal democratic revolution. What he expected from it was the overthrow of despotism, the end of privilege, and the transformation of the Russian alliance from an instrument of imperialism into a guarantee of peace and European equilibrium. In his eyes, the establishment of democracy in Russia had the certainty of an "irresistible event"; and undoubtedly he agreed with Herr that Russia would not resume "the normal course of her existence" until she had thrown off the yoke of autocratic government.[9]

So far as can be determined, these were the views of most French Socialists and syndicalists. No French working-class leader of any significance was inspired to analyze the Revolution and its failure in any great detail. Nor was there any parallel in France to the heated discussions that went on in Germany over the lessons of the Russian events.[10] This, of course, was what one would expect. What had the French, pacesetters in politics of all varieties, to learn from a people who were just now catching up? Even Hervé, a man whose leftist group was badly in need of new ideas, felt that the grandest ambition of the Russian revolutionary movement should be to attain those democratic liberties that already existed in France.[11]

In view of this tradition, it is not surprising that the Socialist parliamentary Group greeted the February Revolution of 1917 as the triumph of democratic institutions. But there was a new note added: a scarcely veiled concern for the effect the Revolution might have on the Russian war effort. The official declaration of the Group, issued on March 16, expressed the belief that revolutionary Russia would be a more trustworthy and valuable ally than autocratic Russia: "In moving thus toward her new destiny, Russia has tightened her alliance with the Western democracies, and she has joined the great movement that is leading the peoples of Europe, America, and Asia toward progress in political institutions and preparing the ground for the League of Nations."[12] Commenting on the Revolution, Renaudel emphasized that universal suffrage and racial equality would create a national unity that had been lacking under the old regime. "It is said," he wrote hopefully, "that everything that has happened in the streets of Petrograd has been carried out to the cry of 'Vive la

France!' "[13] The majoritaires in both the party and the CGT expressed the hope that the Russian events would set off similar movements in Germany.[14] But certain French Socialists allowed their concern over Russian intentions to show through in late March, when 16 of them signed a declaration by the deputy Barthélemy Mayéras, which pointed out "that an immediate and separate peace by Russia would be a peace against the French Republic."[15]

The reaction of the majoritaires to the Russian Revolution revealed the extent to which they had subordinated their Socialism to the war effort. But for other party members the February Revolution in Petrograd took on a different meaning. It fired their hopes for an immediate and honorable peace; it revived their faith in direct action; and it reinforced the hostility that many of them already felt for their leaders. The way in which enthusiasm for the Russian Revolution, the desire for peace, and resentment of the majoritaires could blend was demonstrated by a meeting on April 1, 1917, organized by the Ligue des Droits de l'Homme to honor the Revolution. The large hall was filled with an overflow crowd of 5,000. The historian Alphonse Aulard spoke on the parallel between the Russian and French Revolutions. The similarity he discovered—a common fighting spirit—was a tribute more to his patriotism than to his historical sense. Like our ancestors, he said, the Russians would show the Germans that a revolutionary people is invincible. While expressing the hope that the Russian Revolution would speed the end of the War, he could not refrain from adding that now was the time for the Germans to overthrow the Kaiser. Someone shouted "Down with the War!" Séverine, the veteran Socialist and champion of feminist causes, then told anecdotes about the heroines of the Russian revolutionary movement. The audience applauded warmly. However, when Vandervelde rose and began to criticize the German Socialists he was hooted down and booed for half an hour. There was a demonstration in favor of an immediate peace at any cost. Blows were exchanged. The uproar was so great that Renaudel and Jouhaux had to leave the meeting without giving the speeches they had prepared. The crowd was only calmed by the singing of Russian folk songs and the chanting of the *Internationale*. "The anger of the crowd," Jacques Mesnil observed in a letter to Romain Rolland, "was unleashed primarily against the renegade Socialists"—i.e. the majoritaires.[16] Though no one seemed to notice it, an important historical corner had been turned: the mystique of the Russian Revolution had become a weapon in the internal politics of the French working-class movement.

### THE CRISIS OF SPRING 1917

Ideas by themselves are like fireworks: they explode, light up the sky, then disappear—unless, that is, they become mixed with the social, economic, and psychological movements that make up the lifeblood of a people. If the Russian Revolution found a warm and lasting welcome in France, it was because the historical situation was propitious. Within two months of the tumultuous meeting just described, France found herself in the midst of the worst crisis of the War since August 1914. The winter of 1916–17 had been abnormally cold; coal was scarce; restaurants, groceries, and pastry shops had begun to ration their wares. In ordinary times, the effect of the tightening of belts is to weaken the unions; in the spring of 1917, because of the strong demand for labor, its result was just the opposite. After a long period of somnolence—indeed, virtual nonexistence—the syndicalist movement revived. Working-class salaries had lagged far behind inflated prices.[a] As early as 1916, Jouhaux had warned Albert Thomas that the Sacred Union was becoming a unilateral formula, which applied to the workers but not to their employers.[17] In 1916 there had been 314 strikes affecting 44,109 workers; in 1917 there would be 696 strikes, involving 293,810 workers. War-weariness increased the willingness to strike. The French had lost their confidence in an early victory, and the spontaneously organized syndicalist committees that sprouted everywhere in the first half of 1917—many of them with a high percentage of women members—had a way of passing rapidly from economic to political demands. Their battle cry was: "We want to know the real war aims."[b]

Merrheim, just one year earlier a lonely extremist acting in the cloak-and-dagger atmosphere of conspiratorial committee meetings, now became the darling of the Parisian workers. On May 1, his *Union des Métaux* defied the censor by publishing the Petrograd Soviet's appeal for peace. This was followed by another appeal, in which the Executive Committee of the Metal Workers' Federation advised its members "to participate in all demonstrations or actions intended to aid the proletarians of Russia and Germany in their efforts at liberation."[18] By the end of May, strikes had broken out among the metallurgical workers in Paris and in the basin of St.-Etienne, where the stoppage of work in the mines and the munitions factories was almost total.[19] In the capital, 10,000 seamstresses abandoned work; and during the months of May and June alone, 71 industries in Paris were affected by the wave of strikes. The strikers' demonstrations often turned into protests against the War and demands for peace. On June 4, Annamite troops were used against such a demonstration of strik-

[a] Between August 2, 1914, and December 31, 1916, the cost of living increased 45 per cent, while salaries rose 25 per cent in heavy industry, 22 per cent in light industry, and 16 per cent for women in light industry. Bernard Georges and Denise Tintant, *Léon Jouhaux, cinquante ans de syndicalisme* (1962), p. 164.

[b] Henri Barbé, "Souvenirs de militant et de dirigeant communiste" (ms. at the Hoover Institution), pp. 7–8. The workers were not alone in having lost their will to fight. On May 3, 1917, André Gide noted in his journal: "I believe less and less that a decision can be obtained by force of arms.... It is all very well to want to die, and to prefer dying to giving up one's honor. But it is absurd not to understand that men are dying." *Journal, 1889–1939* (1951), p. 626. See also the report of the German agent in Rotterdam of May 12, 1917, in the German Foreign Ministry archives, 4301/D1965054.

ing women in front of a factory at Courbevoie, and several of them were injured. Only the intervention of Malvy prevented Merrheim's arrest.[20]

These movements on the home front would not have assumed such a threatening nature if they had not coincided with a wave of mutinies in the Army. In February, Army intelligence had reported that morale was low. In their correspondence and their conversations soldiers repeatedly asked if "it would ever end." Others wrote, "We'll never have done with the Germans," and "We don't even know why we're fighting anymore."[21] Soldiers of peasant origin groaned that they were paying for the War with their lives while industrial workers enjoyed safety and high wages at home. About the same time General Nivelle, the new Commander-in-Chief, complained to the Minister of the Interior about the pacifist and anti-militarist tracts being distributed among the troops in ever-increasing numbers.[22] On April 3, the historian Elie Halévy described to a friend the spirit of unrest he had noticed among the soldiers who passed through the front-line hospital where he was working as a nurse: "I don't know what soldiers you have come across, weakened perhaps by loss of blood. I myself have seen only the rebelliously inclined who constantly seek some way of finishing this massacre and who, finding none, brood on violence."[23]

The failure of the Nivelle offensive of April 16 was the spark that lit this tinder. After five days of battle, there were over 30,000 dead and another 90,000 wounded, 5,000 of whom died at the front because of the absence of transportation to evacuate them.[24] On May 3, the Twenty-First Division refused to a man to go into battle. The leaders of this mutiny were quickly dealt with, but other units followed suit. On May 27, a battalion about to be sent to the front broke ranks and invaded railroad cars bound for Paris. The *gendarmerie* had to be used to quell the demonstration. Two days later, reserves stationed at Soissons began to riot, and two regiments went so far as to elect soldiers' councils and organize a march on the capital. Poincaré anxiously noted in his diary on May 30 that at Dormans some men had cried: "Down with war! Long live the Russian Revolution!"[25] The rumor spread to the front that civil war had broken out behind the lines, and that blood was being shed on the streets of Paris. According to Colonel Carré, the mutinies spread "like fire in dry prairie grass." Within a few days, "the rebellion had reached more than half our divisions, including even the elite corps, threatening the army with total disintegration."[26]

The mutinies in the Army and the strikes in the munitions industry were quietly suppressed, but the fright they gave the government was so severe that some generals favored executing whole battalions on the spot, without a trial, and in Paris the military governor, General Auguste Dubail, wanted to use troops to re-establish order.[27] To the Army and the Right in general, the mutinies and strikes were proof of the pernicious effects of an uncontrolled press, parliamentary missions to the front, and the subversion of foreign agents and pacifist agitators, who distributed their propaganda to the troops and preyed on soldiers on leave at railway stations.[28] General Pétain insisted that the press be more strictly censored, and that an end be put to pacifist activities. Malvy, the ill-starred Minister of the Interior, later claimed that the strikes of 1917 had economic causes, and denied that pacifist propaganda or foreign agitators had played an important role.[29] He was undoubtedly right. Yet these strikes did often turn into demonstrations against the War and the government, and the mutineers did look to the Russian Revolution for inspiration. In this sense, Poincaré, Clemenceau, and Pétain, too, were right in pointing to the increasing appearance of pacifist slogans.[30] The French, like the Russians and the Germans, were sick of war and eager to end it; it took great ingenuity and vigilance to keep them interested in killing and being killed.[31] By the end of May 1917, French workers and soldiers were ready to listen to pacifist agitators and read their tracts, whereas two years earlier they would have spurned them angrily.

### STOCKHOLM

The French Socialists, no matter what their previous policies, could not remain indifferent to the attraction of the Russian Revolution and the changing mood of the masses. The effect of the events of the spring of 1917 was to strengthen the position of the minority against the majority, as was shown dramatically at the May 27–28 meeting of the SFIO's National Council. On the agenda was the question of sending delegates to the proposed International Socialist Conference at Stockholm, which was sponsored by a joint Dutch-Scandinavian committee.[32] This, of course, was nothing less than the resumption of international relations which the minority had so long demanded and the majority so long dreaded. However, international relations now had the enthusiastic support of the Petrograd Soviet, which on May 27 had issued an appeal to the peoples of Europe for "concerted, decisive action in favor of peace" and for the "re-establishment and strengthening of international unity."

The more chauvinistic majoritaires responded to this talk of Stockholm and a negotiated peace by organizing a Comité Socialiste pour la Paix par le Droit. They argued that the proposed Conference would lead to a separate peace. The minoritaires, on the contrary, saw no danger of a separate peace. Longuet argued that the Russian Revolution would force the Allies to seek a peace based on the terms outlined by Wilson in his "peace without victory" speech.[33] Nevertheless, on April 26 the CAP decided by a vote of 13 to 11 to refuse the invitation to Stockholm, on the grounds that the Conference did not emanate from a proper source and that it would lead to attempts at a separate peace.[34]

Meanwhile, at the end of March a delegation of French Socialists, consisting of Marcel Cachin, Ernest Lafont, and Marius Moutet, had left for Petrograd, with the government's blessing, to revive the interest of the Russian Socialists in the pursuit of the War. Albert Thomas followed them in April. All four Socialists were members of the majority and until then opponents of any resumption of international relations, but Cachin, Lafont, and Moutet were in the process of abandoning their former chauvinism and moving toward the Center of the party.[35] The whole mission, it hardly need be said, was based on a total misunderstanding of the mood of the Russian Socialists. The French minority had objected to the quasi-governmental sponsorship of the mission, and for this reason Longuet had refused to form part of the delegation.[36]

In Petrograd, Albert Thomas attempted in vain to lecture the soviet about the need to defeat Prussian militarism, the dangers of Stockholm, and the ambiguities of the Petrograd peace formula, "Neither annexations nor indemnities."[37] The case of Cachin, Moutet, and Lafont was more dramatic. Instead of influencing the Russians, they were thrown on the defensive and forced to make concessions to the soviet. The three French deputies had to agree that Alsace-Lorraine would have its future settled by a plebiscite and not be returned automatically to France, as provided for in the secret treaties. According to Cachin's own testimony, they were submitted to a "brutal cross-examination" by the soviet, which accused them of being agents of French imperialism. At the same time, Kerensky seems to have convinced them that the fighting spirit of the Russian Army would be revived only if the French demonstrated their desire for peace by going to Stockholm.[38] It is hard to know which was more effective: the soviet's disapproval, Kerensky's logic, or the pacifist mood of the soldiers' meetings they addressed. At any rate, the three did not return the same men they had come. Having left patriotic Frenchmen, they came back "Russians."[39] Speaking to the French Ambassador, Maurice Paléologue, before leaving, Moutet admitted that he had changed his views about the War. "Fundamentally, the Russian Revolution is right. It is not so much a political as an international revolution. The bourgeois, capitalist, and imperialist classes have plunged the world into a frightful crisis they are now unable to overcome. Peace can only be brought about in accordance with the principles of the International."[40]

Missionaries whose flagging patriotic faith had not stood the test of confrontation, Cachin and Moutet rushed home from Petrograd to plead the case of the soviet before the National Council of May 27–28, when the mutinies in the Army and the strikes in Paris were reaching their height. The atmosphere was electric. Outside the Hôtel Moderne several hundred men and women were clustered. "To Stockholm!" they cried. "Bring our boys home!" "Peace!" At one point Renaudel appeared for a breath of fresh air. He was booed, blows were exchanged, and the disturbance persisted until the crowd was promised that the party would go to Stockholm.[41] The two travelers arrived in time for the afternoon session on May 27 and were immediately given the floor. Cachin spoke first and described the critical attitude they had encountered in Russia.

Everywhere they went they had been asked: "What are you going to do to put an end to the War?" If the French hoped to revive the morale of the Russian Army and prevent the Russians from meeting the Germans alone, argued Cachin and Moutet, they would have to go to Stockholm and force their government to formulate its war aims.[42] Delivered with enthusiasm and passion, this argument proved decisive. On the next day, Renaudel himself spoke in favor of a positive response. The majority and minority then joined forces to draft a motion that authorized sending a delegation to Stockholm, and sending Longuet and Renaudel on from Stockholm to Petrograd to discuss arrangements for a Socialist conference. A motion violently assailing the German and Austrian Socialists for their complicity in the War was withdrawn. Internationalism could no longer be denied.

### THE PASSPORTS ARE DENIED

The dramatic turnabout of the SFIO at the May 28 meeting of the National Council was very naturally seen, by both friends and enemies, as a victory for the minority and a defeat for the majority. *Le Populaire* claimed triumphantly that the party had now completely accepted the views of the minority, while *Le Temps* termed it a "total capitulation of the majoritaires to the revolutionary and internationalist minority." "Never before," wrote *Le Temps,* "has a mass party so lightly and thoughtlessly sacrificed the idea of the nation, and all concern for the nation's moral authority, to safeguard the mere appearance of political unity, a unity that is no longer to be found even in the party's official declarations."[43]

As usual, *Le Temps* exaggerated. The vote of May 28 was less a capitulation than a strategic retreat. The majoritaires, as Charles Rappoport pointed out, had voted to go to Stockholm "with their teeth clenched and their fingers crossed" ("la mort dans l'âme").[44] The majority had shifted their ground on the question of the resumption of international relations not because they had given up their patriotism—that, after all, was a part of their Socialism—but because, as Albert Thomas later admitted, "if we wanted to aid the Russian Revolution in its national defense effort and assure France the cooperation of the Russian Army, we had to agree to present our ideas and our cause at the Stockholm Conference."[45] Moreover, the majoritaires had no illusions about the possibility or desirability of an immediate peace; nor did they agree to go to Stockholm unconditionally. They would not consider attending the Stockholm Conference without assurance that the question of responsibility for the War could be raised, and the SPD arraigned before the tribunal of International Socialism and eventually punished "from an international point of view."[46] Quite obviously, this was not the kind of international conference the minority had so long been urging. Thus, when the Dutch-Scandinavian Committee sent out a questionnaire inquiring what issues the conference should discuss and under what conditions it should meet, the majority and minority again fell into conflict.

The Conference of Stockholm, however, despite the super-patriotic intentions of the majoritaires, was doomed to remain a project and not a fact because of the opposition of the Allied governments. Alexandre Ribot, the French Premier, was at first receptive to the idea of the conference, particularly when the majoritaires represented it as an opportunity to speak for the Allied cause.[47] But just at this moment came the wave of mutinies and strikes, and a shudder ran through conservative circles. The General Staff, in particular, feared for the morale of its troops. The constellation of Stockholm, mutinies, and strikes immediately evoked fearful thoughts of the Army's disintegration and of a Russian-style revolution in France.[48] On May 31, Poincaré asked General Pétain whether he could keep his Army in hand if French delegates met with Germans at an international Socialist conference. Pétain's answer, "uttered in a firm tone," was a simple "No." Deeply impressed, Paul Painlevé observed that after Pétain's statement it was impossible to approve passports for the Socialist delegation.[49]

Poincaré countered by pointing out that if the Russian front collapsed, the Germans would be able to send 75 divisions to the West. "Yes," Pétain said. "But the danger of an attack by 75 German divisions is distinctly less serious than the demoralization of our army."[50] This statement by Pétain, said Poincaré, convinced Ribot and Bourgeois. According to Ribot's account, the government felt that if they granted passports to the Socialist delegation, they would be held responsible for whatever happened at Stockholm. After the sudden turnabout of the National Council on May 28, the government had no reason to believe that the majoritaires would hold out against the minority once in the internationalist atmosphere of Stockholm.[51] On June 1, Ribot rose before the Chamber of Deputies to announce the government's decision. "The future peace," he said, "cannot be the work of a party, whatever party it might be. Today, the Socialists want to meet to discuss the war aims; tomorrow the Catholics of all countries would have the same rights. What would the role of governments be then? ... The peace to come can only be a French peace."[52]

At this juncture, Cachin requested and was granted the opportunity to address the Chamber in closed session concerning his trip to Russia. Under this guise, the Socialists succeeded in opening a full-dress debate, which linked the military implications of the Russian Revolution with the issue of French war aims, the question of passports, and the existence of widespread unrest in France. The Russian Army, Cachin assured his colleagues, was still formidable. However, to ensure its fighting spirit, the French government would have to renounce all annexationist war aims. Cachin urged the government to reconsider its stand on the passports for two reasons: first, by going to Stockholm, the French Socialists might play a decisive role in keeping Russia in the

War; second, the state of morale in France itself was bad, and evidence that the government was supporting a movement to end the War might improve it. Pierre Laval spoke in support of the second point. Quoting a correspondent at the front, he evoked the specter of the mutinies. Stockholm, he concluded, was the "polar star." Answering Cachin and Laval on June 5, Ribot made it clear that the government did not intend to change its policy. The Chamber, he said, must again make a show of unity; otherwise, France would be exposed to every kind of peril. "Weigh your decision carefully, gentlemen. Let no voice be missing from the vote. This I beg of you in the name of the government, in the name of France." Ribot's plea for national unity was all that was required to repulse the Socialist attack. The policy of the government was approved by a huge majority, which included 39 Socialist deputies, Renaudel among them.

The decision to withhold the Socialists' passports was crucial; it marked the first serious crack in the Sacred Union. Even Renaudel and Thomas had come to believe that it was essential to go to Stockholm, if only to condemn the German Social Democrats and demonstrate the willingness of the French to make peace. The government's refusal was worded in such a way that it cast doubt on the trustworthiness of the Socialists.[c] Moreover, after the secret sessions of June 1–5, it was increasingly difficult to maintain that the French government had no annexationist war aims. In the heat of the debate, Briand had admitted that the Allies had discussed the possibility of territorial concessions to France on the left bank of the Rhine and in Asia Minor.[53] In the Council of Ministers, Albert Thomas now spoke of the severe disagreements that were dividing his party, with even the best of the majoritaires being torn between their patriotism and their desire for party unity. He emphasized that if the Socialists were to continue to support the government, some concession on war aims would have to be made to Renaudel.[54] Thus the immediate effect of the government's denial of the delegates' passports was to force the majoritaires to face growing tension between their Socialism and their patriotism. Renaudel, for example, felt driven to criticize the President of the Republic in terms that Poincaré himself noted were "scarcely cordial."[55]

On the international stage, the failure of the Stockholm Conference was even more significant. Stockholm was an opportunity to reconcile the Right and the Center of the Socialist movement and to heal the wounds created at Zimmerwald and Kienthal. It was, as Daniel Ligou has remarked, "the Second International's last chance for survival."[56] The refusal of the Allied governments to

---

[c] "Pétain would most probably not have protested against the Stockholm meeting if he had not, at the same instant, had to deal with a wave of mutinies," writes Paul-Marie de la Gorce. "But his actual protest showed very clearly that the whole military hierarchy had established a connection between the dislocation that seemed to threaten the Army and the Socialist tendencies in favor of a negotiated peace." *The French Army, A Military-Political History* (New York, 1963), p. 130.

grant passports to their Socialists underlined the helplessness of the Socialist leadership and the bankruptcy of the policy of Sacred Union. The road that led to Moscow had now been opened.

The Sacred Union officially broke up in the fall of 1917, although it is clear that the majoritaires considered their separation from the government a prelude to later embraces rather than a divorce. Clemenceau had chosen as his prime target the young and popular Minister of the Interior, Louis Malvy. Accused by Clemenceau in the Chamber of having betrayed his country's interests, Malvy resigned on August 31; a week later, on September 7, Ribot and his cabinet followed suit. With Ribot adamantly opposed by both the Radicals and the Socialists, the succession fell to the brilliant mathematician Paul Painlevé. The Socialists were thus presented with an opportunity to reconsider their policy toward class collaboration. The minoritaires had long been demanding that the Socialists leave the government. "The ministerial experiment has lasted long enough," Longuet wrote on September 8. "Let's be ourselves."[57] The majoritaires, too, agreed on the timeliness of a withdrawal; but for different reasons. They hoped to provoke the formation of a cabinet that would carry on the War more vigorously and revise the war aims.[58] For the minoritaires it was a matter of principle, for the majoritaires a matter of personalities; but after a long debate the CAP decided that the new government would contain no Socialists. The great majority of the Socialist Group abstained on the vote of confidence, despite the fact that Painlevé, the new Premier, had publicly expressed regret at the refusal of the Socialists to join his cabinet. Thus the party seemed finally to be taking a more aggressive stance, and Longuet could rejoice that the party had at last reclaimed its independence.[59]

The ambiguities created by Stockholm, the Russian Revolution, and the departure from the government were much in evidence at the SFIO's National Congress of October 6–9, 1917, held at Bordeaux, possibly the most chaotic and disorganized of the wartime congresses. The minority came to Bordeaux with its usual program of peace, international relations, more precise peace aims, and nonparticipation in the government; but it was split down the middle on the question of the war credits, which Longuet and Pressemane could not bring themselves to reject.[60] For Longuet, true to the party's prewar traditions, internationalism and national defense were inseparable. The minoritaires would vote for war credits, he said, but they would not break with the Zimmerwaldians.[61] Renaudel, meanwhile, showed his new militancy by submitting a motion that called for sending delegates to Stockholm, supporting the war effort, participation in the government on certain conditions, and the revision of the Allies' war aims. This was a motion masterfully designed to still whatever doubts the majoritaires might have had and attract all waverers.

The results of this congress were what one might expect: the minority split into three parts over the question of the war credits, and the Renaudel motion

carried the day.[62] Longuet, musing over the results of the congress, saw little
to be encouraged about. The majority still outnumbered the minority by as
many votes as the previous year, despite the brief minoritaire success in May.[63]
As for the Zimmerwaldians, they were more isolated than ever. Louise Saumoneau's motion denouncing the war credits and the League of Nations received only a handful of votes.

### THE BOLSHEVIK REVOLUTION

The reaction of the French Socialists to the Bolshevik Revolution came in
stages: first surprise, then fear and anger at the thought of a separate peace,
and finally an attitude of watchful waiting that varied from cautious acceptance to thinly disguised hostility. The French could not have been expected
to greet the announcement of a coup d'état in Petrograd with rejoicing, or even
with premonitions of a new dawn for mankind; in the year of the Nivelle offensive and of Caporetto, any news was likely to be bad news and the unknown
was to be feared. Except in a few groups on the extreme Left, such as the Committee for the Resumption of International Relations, the names of Lenin
and Trotsky had been unknown until the February Revolution. During the
ten years that preceded the First World War, the Bolsheviks had been the least
influential and the most troublesome of all the Socialist parties in the International.[64] At the outbreak of the War, the International Socialist Bureau had
been on the verge of ordering the Bolsheviks to settle their differences with
the Mensheviks and create a unified party in Russia; and it is clear that the
French, uncompromising *unitaires* themselves, would have favored such an
ultimatum.[65] During the Congress of Copenhagen in 1910, Lenin had tried to
interest the Guesdists in an organization of the Left Wing within the Second
International, but the effort had been without success.[66] What contacts the
French did have with Russian Socialists tended to be with the Socialist Revolutionaries, whose representative, Roubanovitch, was well known in France. But
in general the Russian Socialists were dismissed by the French as terrible sectarians, whose Byzantine quarrels were to be avoided at all costs.[d]

Lenin had first come to the attention of the French public when he accepted
the Germans' offer to return him to Russia in a sealed coach; the Bolshevik

[d] In 1922 André Morizet thought back to the period before the War and marveled at the
way the Russian Socialists had been ignored: "But who among us paid attention before
the War to the representatives of Russian Socialism? We considered them negligible.
Indeed, we stayed away from them so as not to get involved in their terrible sectarian
quarrels. Hadn't Jaurès himself ordered the staff of *L'Humanité* not to accept their articles
except in the case of absolute necessity, aware as he was from long experience that printing
a line from any one of them inevitably entailed printing half a dozen annoying rectifica-
tions before the week was out." *Chez Lénine et Trotski* (1922), pp. 100–101. Alfred Rosmer makes almost exactly the same comment in his article on "Trotsky à Paris pendant
la première guerre mondiale," *La Révolution Prolétarienne*, October 1950, p. 289.

leader had enjoyed another brief spell of notoriety during the July uprising against the Provisional Government. Here was a man, most Frenchmen thought, who was both dangerous and a traitor: a fanatic revolutionary, he was also unsound on the question of the War. The impression he made upon French Socialists was no better. Cachin, who was to make a long career out of his attachment to Leninism, accused him of being either consciously or unconsciously a German agent.[67] Longuet was more sophisticated, but basically of the same opinion as Cachin. Lenin, he said, was neither a traitor nor an agent of the Wilhelmstrasse. But "his 'insurrectionism' and his fanatic doctrinairism can only lead to catastrophes for Russia and—whether he intends it to or not—serve German imperialism."[68] Even Rappoport, himself a Russian Socialist by origin and a member of the Left Wing, criticized Lenin for believing that a backward country like Russia could lead the way to social revolution. "The heroic example of Russia," he wrote with a typically Rappoportian twist, "can and must inspire us all. But, as in modern warfare, Revolution requires more than 'moral forces.' Russia alone would be powerless. It's not for the poor to give alms to the rich."[69] Rappoport was merely expressing the cultural disdain for barbaric Russia that so many French Socialists felt and would feel as they watched the Bolsheviks take the reins of the world revolutionary movement.

L'Humanité responded to the first news of the Bolshevik insurrection with caution: "Will this victory last? Will the maximalists, now masters of the capital, extend their rule to the rest of Russia?"[70] Only on November 19 would L'Humanité admit that the Bolsheviks seemed to be firmly in power. The lack of reliable information about events in Russia remained a serious obstacle to understanding throughout this early period. Communications between Russia and France were difficult because of the War and later because of the blockade. Not until the summer of 1920 would French Socialists be able to go to Russia to see the Bolshevik regime with their own eyes, and even then it would be a hazardous journey. Moreover, the censorship was especially stringent where it concerned news of the Russian Revolution because of the effect it might have on the morale of the Army.[71] What news of the Bolsheviks did seep through was distorted out of all recognition by the press; according to Boris Souvarine, there was no insult spared them, no crime or horror for which they were not held responsible.[72]

The first thought of the French Socialists was for the effect of the Bolshevik Revolution on the Russian war effort; they were more aware than most people of the uncertain state of Russian morale, and they knew that the Bolsheviks represented the spirit of Zimmerwald and Kienthal at its most extreme. When the Bolsheviks appealed to France for support of their peace policy in December 1917, the Socialist parliamentary Group, including the minoritaires, responded by urging the Russians not to conclude a separate peace. "Such a step," they argued, "would not only pave the way for a military victory of the Central Powers and a peace dictated on their terms; it would further serve—indeed, it already serves—the designs of the enemies of democracy and Socialism throughout the world, by allowing them to invoke the Russian Revolution as an example of disorganization and demoralization."[73]

This appeal only showed the abyss that separated the worlds of French and Russian Socialism. Trotsky, who was in no mood to accept a lecture on the principles of Socialism from the French, angrily reminded them that they had voted for the war credits and then had been denied permission to go to Stockholm. The leaders of the SFIO, he said, were themselves responsible for this humiliation because of their policy of Sacred Union; of all the Socialist parties, they were the least qualified to preach sermons to the Russians on the dangers of a separate peace. If the French did not want the Russians to make a separate peace, they should take part in the negotiations for a general peace and present their own conditions. Trotsky concluded, in language typical of this early era of revolutionary diplomacy, with an appeal to the French proletariat, over the heads of the Socialist leaders, to demand that its government participate in the peace negotiations.[e]

For all the unpleasantness of its language, Trotsky's rebuke could not be ignored; for what he was demanding was not a revolution, but merely that the Allied governments formulate their war aims and prove their will to peace. Such an appeal could easily be confused with Wilson's "peace without victory." Curiously enough, the early hostility of the French Socialists toward the Bolshevik Revolution was now tempered, if not dissipated, by the conflict in which they found themselves with their own government.

Clemenceau's return to power in mid-November had completed the process of the Socialists' estrangement from the government that had started with the denial of their passports. Clemenceau had not explicitly excluded the Socialists from the Sacred Union; but he made clear that he intended to fight defeatism

---

[e] Le Journal du Peuple, 5.i.18. The reaction of the workers, however, was not what Bolshevik mythology, with its arbitrary distinction between leaders and led, traitors and faithful, required. Temporarily, at least, the Bolsheviks became unpopular, and it was not until after the Armistice that the masses regained their original enthusiasm for the Russian Revolution. Victor Serge reports: "I worked in a printing shop on the Boulevard Port-Royal, and I had numerous contacts with the workers, both there and elsewhere. They, too, were exasperated by the unexpected turn that the Russian Revolution was taking. At first they had greeted it with heartfelt joy; then they got the idea that the 'maximalist' (as was said then) disturbances and demands were weakening the Russian army. I often heard it said (since people said it as soon as they discovered that I was Russian) that 'the Bolsheviks are bastards in the pay of Germany,' and that 'the Russians are all cowards.' I came close to getting myself beaten to death in a bistro for reading a Russian newspaper." (Mémoires d'un révolutionnaire, 1901–1941, 1951, p. 70.) Charles Rappoport had a similar experience. See the Rappoport memoirs in the Bibliothèque Nationale, p. 253.

wherever he might find it ("No more pacifist campaigns, no more German intrigues. Neither treason, nor half-treason. War. Nothing but war."), and he
held out no hope for the revision of war aims, a step that even the *majoritaires*
now believed essential. For all practical purposes, the program that Clemenceau set out to apply was that of the Action Française. He unleashed a reign of
terror against the pacifist movement which lasted throughout 1918 and which
extended from the anti-war propaganda of the schoolteachers Hélène Brion
and Lucie Colliard to the clandestine peace negotiations of Briand and Caillaux. The Socialists, who considered Clemenceau's election to the Premiership a provocation, henceforth found themselves in constant conflict with the
government, a new experience for many of them after three and a half years
of Sacred Union. On the vote of confidence, 64 Socialists voted against and the
rest abstained. When the Socialist deputies on December 28, 1917, demanded
a revision of the war aims and publication of the secret treaties, an obvious response to the radicalization of the Russian situation, the government imper-
iously refused. "Bitter campaigns," Eugen Weber writes, "in which *L'Homme
Enchaîné* and the *Action Française* had played the leading parts, had torn
down the fragile structure of party cooperation, and not all the king's horses
could put it together again."[1]

Meanwhile, the leaders of the party had conceived the idea of sending a mission, composed of Renaudel, Longuet, and Merrheim, to Petrograd to dissuade
the Bolsheviks from signing a separate peace. This was a revival of the Stockholm project under the duress of circumstance, with the difference that both
the *majoritaires* and the *minoritaires* hoped to exert pressure on the Bolsheviks to give up their monopoly of power.[9] Although the *minoritaires* did not
approve of Lenin or his methods, they felt that because the French government had sabotaged Stockholm, it was responsible for the Bolshevik Revolution and the collapse of the Kerensky government. If the French now had to
deal with Lenin and face the nightmare of a separate peace, argued Longuet,
it was their own fault.[74] On December 31, the Socialists sent a delegation to
Clemenceau to ask for passports. Clemenceau refused, with the time-honored
excuse that to grant the passports would be to give the mission the sanction of
the government. Furthermore, the French government could not take such a
serious step without consulting its Allies.[75] He might also have mentioned that
in the month of December the morale of the troops had dropped sharply, and

[1] Eugen Weber, *Action Française* (Stanford, Calif., 1962), p. 108. It seems, however, that
Clemenceau went out of his way to secure the collaboration of both the party and the
CGT. Three Socialist deputies accepted posts as Commissars in Clemenceau's government.
Jouhaux was offered a ministerial post by Clemenceau as the representative of the CGT,
but turned it down. Georges and Tintant, *Léon Jouhaux*, pp. 193–95.
[9] In late November a delegation of Russian Socialists, headed by the Menshevik Pavel
Axelrod, appeared before the CAP and argued for intervention in Russia by the International. This request naturally appealed to the minority. *Le Populaire du Centre*, 22.xi.17.

that on Christmas eve and Christmas Day there had been fraternization between German and French units at the front.

The Socialists were thus once more confronted with their own impotence; but somehow the pill was harder to swallow when administered by Clemenceau, whom they hated with a passion that had its roots in bitter memories. The parliamentary Group protested the denial of passports, and announced that although they would continue to vote for the war credits, they now had strong reservations about the government's policies. On January 11, a large number of Socialist deputies formally questioned the government on its Russian policy. Albert Thomas demanded that the government reply to the Russian peace offer and align its peace aims with Wilson's Fourteen Points. Stéphen Pichon, the Minister of Foreign Affairs, replied that the government refused "to rush into the hornet's nest of the Russian maximalist government, which locks up deputies to the Constituent Assembly who do not share its views and prevents this duly elected body from meeting."[76] Despite this clever appeal to their democratic sensibilities, 85 Socialist deputies refused the government their vote of confidence.

The incident was closed, but it was not without its aftermath. The minoritaires now began to defend the probity and good intentions of the Bolsheviks in their negotiations with the Germans against the slanders of the press.[77] Even the majoritaire Marcel Sembat reminded the government that the French Revolution, too, had seen its share of terrorism and dictatorship (although he quickly added that it was not his sympathy for Lenin and Trotsky, but his concern for France, for the Allies, and for "human justice" that made him urge the government to establish contact with the Bolsheviks).[78] Toward the end of January, an article by Mayéras anticipated the new attitude of the minoritaires; it was now obvious, he wrote, that what the French government abhorred in the Bolshevik regime was not so much its determination to leave the War as its desire to establish a Socialist and proletarian Republic.[79] Thus the minoritaires found themselves defending the Bolshevik Revolution less because of what it was—they knew very little as yet of what it was—than because of who opposed it.

### THE COMMITTEE FOR RESUMPTION AND THE BOLSHEVIK REVOLUTION

But what about the Zimmerwaldians and the Committee for the Resumption of International Relations? What had been their reaction to the development of the Russian Revolution? In mid-February 1918, Albert Thomas, writing in *L'Humanité,* formulated a question that troubled more than one Frenchman who viewed the activities of the pacifists with dismay. Was there a "maximalist" movement in France, Thomas asked. Reassuring those who feared subversion from within, Thomas replied that except for "a tiny minority" no one among the French masses desired to apply the Bolshevik formulas to France.[80] In substance, Thomas was right. But the very fact that he felt compelled to pose the question reveals the attraction the Russian Revolution could exert across international boundaries. Like the French Revolution, the Russian Revolution "had no territory of its own; indeed, its effect was to efface, in a way, all older frontiers. It brought men together, or divided them, in spite of laws, traditions, character, and language, turning enemies sometimes into compatriots, and kinsmen into strangers; or rather, it formed, above all particular nationalities, an intellectual common country of which men of all nations might become citizens."[81]

It has already been recounted how in January and February of 1917, the Committee for the Resumption of International Relations had suffered an internal crisis over what to do about national defense and how to respond to Wilson's peace offer. Merrheim, Bourderon, and Brizon had withdrawn from the Committee; Rappoport, Saumoneau, and Loriot had taken over the leadership. On the eve of the Russian Revolution, it seems, the Zimmerwald faction in the Socialist Party was losing its identity and merging imperceptibly with the minority. Marcel Martinet, the leftist poet and internationalist, observed in March, "Those here who identify themselves with Zimmerwald and Kienthal don't seem quite sure that they are following the right road." If the Zimmerwaldians had had more faith in their own convictions, Martinet continued, their influence would have been stronger and their actions would not have appeared so vain.[82] Loriot replied two weeks later that Martinet should distinguish between the Zimmerwaldians and "this amorphous opposition without a program and without strength that is grouped around *Le Populaire*."[83] But the existence of the misunderstanding suggests the difficulties that the French Left Wing was having in defining itself.

The members of the Committee for Resumption hailed the February Revolution with a manifesto, written by Loriot, which praised the Russian proletariat for redeeming the honor of international Socialism and announced that the Russian Revolution was only the first in a series of revolutions that would follow inevitably as a consequence of the War. The manifesto included a savage attack upon such patriotic Socialists as Hervé, Thomas, and Vandervelde. The majoritaires, it said, pretended to welcome the Russian Revolution; in fact, they were working behind the scenes to strangle it. They falsified what was happening inside Russia; they prevented the Russian revolutionaries from returning home; they accepted the war aims of the Allies. The manifesto ended with an appeal to follow the Russian example: "Everywhere rebellious peoples must rid themselves of their class governments and replace them with the delegates of workers and soldiers who have gone over to the people. The Russian Revolution is the signal for the universal revolution. And the universal revolution will assure the definitive success of the Russian Revolution."[84]

This manifesto, it should be noted, struck a new tone of revolutionary determination. Its terse sentences calling on the French proletariat to overthrow their government and come to the aid of the Russian Revolution suggest both the increased radicalism of the new leadership and the direct influence of Russian Socialists. Lozovsky, in fact, may have had a direct hand in its preparation. Only the most extreme Zimmerwaldians would have accepted its implications.

Of these the most important was Loriot. In April 1917 Loriot entered Switzerland illegally to confer with Robert Grimm and Angelica Balabanova about the Zimmerwaldian movement. While he was there he met Lenin, and approved his decision to cross Germany in a sealed car.[85] Up to that time he seems to have had only a vague idea of the Leninist position on the War. During 1917, however, under the impact of the Russian Revolution, Loriot grew more radical. This former schoolteacher, "of narrow and limited mind, an honest man, all of a piece, tall and thin, his protruding eyes set in a face framed by a grey beard,"[86] was anxious to escape from the ideological confusion that had plagued the French opposition throughout the War, and he was quick to seize on the lessons of the Russian Revolution. He had already been impressed by Trotsky's confidence in the revolution and by his intellectual aggressiveness in the Committee for Resumption; now he became an admirer of Lenin. On May 1, 1917, he wrote of the Third International as an established fact, and warned that there could be no compromise between Zimmerwald and patriotic Socialism. "The time of dangerous equivocation and of subtle, conciliatory formulas in which everyone finds the justification of his deeds is over. The time has come for definitions."[87]

Already at this point Loriot is said to have favored a split and the formation of a new, revolutionary party.[88] But he knew he was the only member of the Left Wing to hold this opinion; and thus he stayed on within the ranks of the SFIO to personify and further define the Zimmerwaldian point of view. At the National Council of February 18, 1918, the Zimmerwaldians refused to support the minoritaires' motion because of its ambiguity on the question of national defense. After an unsuccessful preliminary conference in which the two factions of the opposition tried to agree on a joint declaration, Loriot and François Mayoux presented their own resolution, which rejected all participation in bourgeois governments, instructed the party's deputies to vote against war credits, and called for an immediate armistice and the beginning of peace negotiations. The result of the split in the minority was that the Renaudel motion carried, even though for the first time the opposition had received a majority of the votes.[h]

When the minoritaires reproached the Zimmerwaldians for their "unfriend-

---

[h] The vote was: Renaudel, 1,461; Faure, 1,251; Loriot-Mayoux, 226. But later, when it was decided to vote simply for or against the Renaudel motion, the majoritaires still managed to summon a majority of the votes. The final count was: for Renaudel, 1,548; opposed, 1,415; abstaining, 9. *Ecole de la Fédération*, 2.iii.18, pp. 185–87.

ly political attitude," Loriot replied with a series of articles in which he argued
that the real conflict in the party was not between minoritaires and majoritaires, but between those two groups on the one hand and Zimmerwald on the
other. The conflict between minoritaires and majoritaires, he insisted, had always been superficial. For the leaders of the two factions, at least, it had been
more a struggle for personal influence than for different policies. Every time
the leaders had got together behind the din of noisy congresses to discuss the
questions raised by the War, they had easily agreed on a common policy.
Sooner or later, Loriot concluded, the two factions would merge.[89] Six weeks
later Loriot tried to define more fully the difference between his own position
and the "essentially bourgeois" conception of the minoritaires. For the minority, argued Loriot, a refusal to vote for war credits was a weapon to be used
against one bourgeois government in order to replace it with another. "We do
not intend to grant the credits to any bourgeois government. We regard the
refusal to vote for them as a form of protest by the still oppressed working class,
a protest not against a ministry, not against the way the War is being conducted, but against war itself and the capitalist system."[90] Yet if Loriot agreed
with Lenin that the minoritaires were "essentially bourgeois" and that there
must be a new organization to group the Socialists who were still loyal to the
revolutionary doctrines of the Second International, he could not accept Lenin's revolutionary defeatism, which he saw, as he explained later, "as a call for
revolution over the corpses of twenty million workers."[91] If Loriot was a
Leninist, then, he was only half a Leninist; and the half of Leninism that he
accepted in 1917 and 1918 was the half that coincided with the revolutionary
doctrines of the Second International, which he felt had been trampled in the
dust by the majoritaires and the minoritaires in their espousal of national defense.

It is interesting to find, moreover, that even the members of the Left Wing
were not at first united in their reaction to the Bolshevik insurrection and the
new Soviet regime. Loriot, it is true, spoke of the realization of the Socialist
program in Russia by the Bolsheviks.[92] But Rappoport, who was more familiar
with the history and methods of Bolshevism, denied that the Bolshevik coup
d'état could be considered a Socialist revolution, and wrote of Lenin's triumph
as "a dead end."[93] When Lenin dissolved the Constituent Assembly, Rappoport
spoke of the "horrible vacuum" Lenin had created around himself, and he concluded with an observation that showed considerable insight into the nature of
the Bolshevik Revolution. "Yes," he wrote, "Lenin loves the people and the
revolution. But he loves them the way a nationalist loves his country: he
murders and ruins them. Lenin is the nationalist of the social revolution."[94]
Merrheim, much like Longuet, defended the probity of Trotsky and the Bolsheviks, and blamed the French government for the situation in Russia. He
held that it was necessary to reserve judgment on the Bolsheviks because of the

isolation imposed on them by the Allies.[95] And even the manifesto with which the Committee for Resumption greeted the Bolshevik Revolution showed a certain reserve. It approved the revolutionary steps of the Bolsheviks and congratulated them on their energy. But it went on to point out that the Bolsheviks had benefited from a particularly favorable situation that did not exist in the other belligerent countries, and it concluded: "Whatever efforts a minority may make to arouse the masses, a revolutionary situation is created by a cluster of factors, some of which escape its influence." There was certainly the hint here, perhaps added at the insistence of Rappoport, that the Jacobin heresies of Bolshevism were inapplicable in France. The manifesto ended with an appeal to the revolutionary spontaneity of the masses: "The duty of the proletarians of all countries is, therefore, by a mass action against their oppressors, either to take power themselves in order to conclude a peace, or to exert irresistible pressure on their rulers to accept the Russian proposals."[96]

### REVOLUTIONARY PACIFISM AT ST.-ETIENNE

The Socialists of the Committee for Resumption had no means of putting this program into action. Its very language suggested an apology for their own weakness rather than a threat to the government. Nevertheless, there was one outburst of revolutionary pacifism in France in the spring of 1918 that deserves mention, if only because it further indicates the nature and limitations of the French opposition.

Merrheim had taken on the leadership of the opposition in the CGT from the very beginning of the War. At the confederal congresses of 1915 and 1916, he had submitted motions stating that "this war is not our war," and that "all governments are engaged in a war of conquest." But through it all he had adhered to the idea of maintaining a loyal opposition *within* the CGT, and he had denounced the policy of revolutionary defeatism and schism.[97] His leadership of the syndicalist opposition had not gone unchallenged; a number of dissenters, inspired by anarchist ideas and annoyed by Merrheim's conservatism, had seceded from the syndicalist section of the Committee for Resumption and formed a Committee of Syndicalist Defense in 1917. This new opposition group was composed of anarcho-syndicalists like Péricat, Hubert, Lepetit, and Andrieux, who thought that the Committee for Resumption "spent too much time talking and not enough acting." Though Merrheim at first joined the Committee of Syndicalist Defense, he soon found himself opposed to its extremism, which he considered irresponsible and a threat to the unity of the CGT.

In December 1917, the CGT met in conference at Clermont-Ferrand and passed almost unanimously a motion condemning the Sacred Union as a mockery and declaring its support for the peace terms of President Wilson and the Russian Revolution.[98] The atmosphere in which the conference met was uncertain and confused, because of the return to power of Clemenceau in France and the Bolshevik coup d'état in Russia. "At that time," recalled Merrheim a year and a half later, "the morale of the population was in a frightful state; all France anxiously awaited a tremendous military effort by Germany."[99] The debates were bitter, as the quarrels of the War were revived, but the leaders of the minority—Merrheim, Bourderon, and Péricat—finally acceded to a resolution of unanimity, on the condition that the leaders of the CGT change their policies and play a more active part in the opposition to the government.[100]

These hopes were not fulfilled; as the first months of 1918 slipped by with no signs of a more vigorous stand, the syndicalist opposition grew more and more discontented with the leadership's policies. In March, Péricat announced: "Peace must be obtained at any cost.... We must organize a large movement in the near future to force the government to conclude an immediate armistice."[101] The Conference of Clermont-Ferrand had agreed that a confederal congress should be convened after consultation with the unions. The CGT leadership, however, was not eager for this confrontation, which promised a full-dress discussion of its wartime policies; Péricat's Committee of Syndicalist Defense used Jouhaux's delaying action as the occasion for a demonstration against his policies. Despite Merrheim's opposition, the representatives of 200 minoritaire unions met at St.-Etienne on May 19, 1918. With Georges Dumoulin presiding, the angry delegates quickly passed motions condemning the timidity of the confederal leadership and calling for peace negotiations and an immediate armistice.[102]

Meanwhile a wave of strikes had broken out in the Loire basin. The center of the unrest was the industrial complex of St.-Etienne. Though the strikes had their origin in a shortage of foodstuffs and ill-feeling between employers and workers, they seem very quickly to have turned into demonstrations against the War. The workers seized control of factories and entire municipalities. Soldiers sent to suppress the strikes fraternized with the strikers.[103] On the initiative of the Committee of Syndicalist Defense, the congress of the syndicalist minority voted to support the strike wave. Its leaders, Péricat and Andrieux, invoked the Bolshevik experience, and attempted to extend the Loire strikes into a general political strike by the French proletariat against the War.[104]

The industrial unrest in the Loire coincided with a massive wave of strikes among the metallurgical workers of Paris. One hundred and eighty thousand metallurgical workers defied Merrheim and walked off the job to protest the sending of younger workers to the front. The rumor spread that the strikers would be replaced by Americans. Fear of the draft, however, was hardly a suitable issue for a mass strike when the Germans were marching on Paris; and a more ideological slogan was sought and found in the appeal to the government to announce its war aims. For the first time in the armament factories at St.-Denis, an industrial suburb of Paris, workers acclaimed the Russian Revolution and the Soviets.[105]

The strikes in the Loire and in Paris were suppressed. The leaders of the Committee of Syndicalist Defense were arrested; hundreds of syndicalist delegates were sent to the front and dispersed in the provinces; there is even some evidence that Clemenceau deliberately allowed the strikes to spread in order to have a pretext for moving against the centers of pacifist agitation.[106] Merrheim considered the strikes ill-advised and even dangerous; but he defended Péricat and his fellow syndicalists against charges of defeatism and intelligence with the enemy, and urged Clemenceau and a group of 180 deputies of the Left to ponder the extent of the malaise that had led the French proletariat to such rebelliousness at a moment of national emergency. "It is time," he said, "to speak to the working class, or you will see in France the same sort of events that led in Russia to the peace of Brest-Litovsk."[107]

Clemenceau could easily afford to ignore such warnings. Not that the Sacred Union survived the War unblemished. France, like Russia and Germany, had her internal unrest, her pacifists, her strikes, and her mutinies. In the unrest in the Loire in May 1918, France even experienced a ripple of revolutionary pacifism. Such evidence of discontent left bitter scars, and convinced conservative circles that the nation was being subverted from within and tainted by Bolshevik contagion.[108] But from the point of view of the working-class organizations, the events of the spring of 1918 merely showed that insurrectionism was no more possible in the France of 1918 than it had been in the France of August 1914. The Zimmerwaldian leaders themselves realized this: both Merrheim and Loriot opposed the strikes of the Loire and the tactics of Péricat. The fact was that revolutionary defeatism was a peculiarly Russian slogan, one that had no relevance in France, where the great majority of the nation remained united in its determination to drive the invader from native soil. If the Bolsheviks succeeded in winning power in Russia, it was not because their propaganda had undermined the war effort, but because the great majority of the Russian people had lost interest in pursuing a war that they had never understood and whose aims meant very little to them. The French, on the other hand, had been educated in the religion of the nation. The difference between Loriot and Lenin was the difference between France and Russia, between democracy and autocracy, between, as Jaurès would have put it, a nation in which the proletariat had a stake and a society in which the great majority of the population was alienated from the government.

### THE MINORITAIRES TRIUMPH

Now let us return to the final episodes in the struggle between the minoritaires and the majoritaires. The Socialist majority had managed to carry the day once more at the National Council of February 17–18, 1918, but then only barely and with the aid of the Zimmerwaldians, who insisted on presenting a separate motion. Writing on the aftermath of the council, Renaudel explained that the majority had reaffirmed its position on war credits because it did not want to shake the "moral solidity" of the country by some "useless act."[109] Many Socialists, however, had lost faith in the policy of cooperation with the government after the repeated humiliations of December and January and the refusal of the French government to reply positively to President Wilson's peace proposals. Frossard asked if perhaps a refusal to vote for war credits were not the most effective weapon against such a reactionary government, a government that endangered the best interests of the country. "We want to cry 'Watch out!' to the people of France."[110] Paul Mistral, another moderate, pointed out that the government was not merely reactionary; it had been inefficient in its conduct of the War, its diplomacy had been bad, and it had lost Russia through its own incompetence. Now, he concluded, the only solution was to act through the International.[111]

In April 1918 the old quarrel between the minoritaires and the majoritaires flared up once more in all its violence when 40 Socialist deputies signed a declaration approving a statement by the Swedish Socialist Hjalmar Branting, to the effect that the German SPD had barred itself from membership in the International by its betrayal of the principle of self-determination.[‡] The minority reacted bitterly to this declaration because it felt that the majoritaires had reneged on their agreement of the previous year to attend an international conference. Their quarrel was further deepened by the question of intervention in Russia, which came to the fore in the summer of 1918. In mid-July Kerensky appeared before the Confederal Committee of the CGT and drew up an indictment against the Bolsheviks and their Revolution, which he characterized as the triumph of anarchy.[112] In the discussion period following Kerensky's speech, Charles Dumas, a Socialist close to the majoritaire leadership, remarked that the French people felt betrayed by the Treaty of Brest-Litovsk; he left no doubt that the French public, even that part with "advanced republican ideas," would support intervention in Russia.[113]

Victory for the minority and their internationalist interpretation of Socialism finally came at the National Council of July 28, 1918. At the front the tide of battle had already turned; the German *Friedenssturm* had been repelled, and the second battle of the Marne, like the first, had been decided in favor of the

---

‡ On April 11, 1918, the SPD newspaper, *Vorwärts,* had written: "The only solution to the inextricable situation in which the world now flounders is the total victory of the German armies." Branting replied in the Swedish *Social-Demokraten*: "Obviously a party that thus betrays the right of peoples to self-determination excludes itself from the International." Forty Socialist deputies in France stated their agreement with Branting in a declaration which observed: "Today the mask has been discarded; the old party scorns hypocrisy." (Branting Archives.) Albert Thomas later joined the 40.

Allies. The minority felt that the improvement of the military situation had again made an international conference possible.[114] Longuet submitted a motion in the name of the minoritaires calling for the denial of war credits to the Clemenceau government (while admitting the importance of national defense), and repeated the belief of the French party in the importance and the feasibility of an international Socialist conference.[115] Renaudel's resolution, though condemning the reactionary policy of Clemenceau, reaffirmed the need for a final and lasting victory, and approved the voting of war credits for this purpose.[116] At issue was the whole question of the wartime leadership of the majority, whom the minoritaires accused of having consciously violated "the letter and the spirit of the decisions of party congresses and statutes," and of advocating "a Socialism based on class collaboration and the repudiation of internationalist principles."[117]

But most important of all the questions dividing the minority from the majority by July 1918 was intervention in Russia. The majoritaires, as Dumas had indicated, could not forgive the Bolsheviks for Brest-Litovsk and for the nearly successful May offensive, which had brought Paris within range of German guns. Renaudel's motion approved the principle of intervention with the qualification that it be carried out with "the greatest circumspection" and that it not contribute to counterrevolution. It was only too evident, however, that the majoritaires were not concerned with revolution or counterrevolution. Not so the minoritaires, for whom the right to rebellion was sacred: they rejected intervention unless it was called for by the Russian people themselves. The most dramatic incident of the council came when Longuet explained the position of the minority:

*Longuet:* We are against any military action that is not carried out with the consent of the Soviet government, which has the support of the Russian masses.
*Albert Thomas:* Admit that you favor the Bolsheviks.
*Longuet:* We do not want to impose a government on a country by force. If Kerensky and his friends were called back to power tomorrow, we would be equally opposed to an intervention on behalf of the Bolsheviks.[118]

This exchange sums up the minoritaires' attitude toward the Bolshevik Revolution at this stage. As Renoult wrote a few weeks earlier, they were neither Bolsheviks nor anti-Bolsheviks; nor did they want to become a party to the conflicts that divided the Russians, although they would defend the Russians' right to solve their problems in their own way.[119] In other words, the minoritaires wished to apply to the Russian Revolution the same policy of self-determination that Wilson had suggested as the basis for a lasting peace.

The minoritaires at last had their victory. The Longuet-Mistral motion was adopted by 1,544 votes to 1,172 for Renaudel and a mere 152 for Loriot's declaration of revolutionary principles. The minoritaires had discovered that defense of the Russian Revolution could have its rewards. For the minoritaires, however, this was an end and not a beginning. They saw no danger as yet from the Left, whose attempts at self-definition they regarded with the good-natured tolerance of men who had grown up in a party that included both Gustave Hervé and Albert Thomas. As *Le Populaire* remarked in its summary of the National Council: "With it ended the phase of War Socialism: the phase of Peace Socialism has now begun!"[120]

The CGT avoided this final confrontation between minoritaires and majoritaires, partly because its leaders were more willing to take up an attitude of opposition toward the government, but primarily because the leaders of the minority were concerned to preserve the unity of their organizations and had no desire to pursue a policy of adventure. The last war congress of the CGT, which met in Paris in the second week of July 1918, was not without its moments of violence. The minoritaires unburdened their consciences and accused the leadership of betraying the syndicalist movement to the principle of class collaboration. Bourderon, Dumoulin, and Merrheim delivered long speeches justifying their position during the War and recounting their opposition to the Sacred Union.[121] The still serious military situation, however, acted as a check on radicalism; the tide had not yet turned, and the German Army was less than 80 kilometers from Paris. In the end, a commission that included members of both factions drew up a compromise resolution that avoided the sticky issue of judging the past, indirectly denounced Péricat's Committee of Syndicalist Defense, condemned any Allied intervention in Russia that did not have the support of the Russian people, and announced its support for peace as defined by Wilson, by the Russian Revolution, "and even by Zimmerwald." Thus, the majoritaires of the CGT, unlike their Socialist counterparts, were willing to denounce the Russian intervention and accept Zimmerwald; the minoritaires were agreeable to abandoning Péricat; and this no doubt was the price of unity. After impassioned pleas by Dumoulin and Merrheim, the motion was adopted by a vote of 908 to 253, with 46 abstentions.[122]

There has long been a debate about Merrheim's role in the opposition to the War. In May 1918 he intervened to help settle the strikes in the Loire and in the Paris munitions factories. At the congress of his own federation in July 1918, he was repeatedly attacked for his caution. He was accused of demoralizing the strikers, of falling into the trap of "republican defense," and of cooperating with the government to choke off the strikes.[123] The syndicalist opposition, and particularly his own comrades from *La Vie Ouvrière*, could never forgive him for his reconciliation with Jouhaux, which was first broached at Clermont-Ferrand and later sealed at the Congress of Paris. His increasing hostility to the Bolshevik Revolution in 1919 and 1920 opened a permanent breach between him and his former comrades. "Merrheim," Monatte remarked bitterly in 1919, "does not want to make the revolutionary leap. Like a horse before a jump, Merrheim stops and draws back."[124] As was to be the pattern in such things, the Communists came to consider Merrheim the worst of traitors, despite his heroic conduct during the early days of the War, when few men dared to raise their voices in opposition.

Monatte later suggested that Merrheim may have been corrupted by his contact with the forces of the bourgeois Left. But this explanation reveals more about Monatte's own commitment to the ideology of revolutionary syndicalism than it does about Merrheim.*j* The fact is that Merrheim did not change; the conditions in which he acted changed. Merrheim's basic conception of revolutionary syndicalism was the same as Pelloutier's: the need to educate the working class and preserve its isolation so that when the moment came, it could take over from the bourgeoisie. His interpretation of the social revolution was moral, not political; his greatest fear was premature revolution, and what he abhorred above all things was the sort of syndicalist bluff that he felt was a tradition in France.[125] Merrheim had fought the War because he had diagnosed it as the product of capitalism; he had opposed the Sacred Union because he had wanted to save the integrity of the working class. But there was a deep strain of pessimism in him that made him oppose the mass movements of 1917–20. Unlike his former comrades—perhaps the difference of temperament is the real key here—he did not believe that the proletariat was sufficiently developed to seize power.[126] It was therefore no accident that Merrheim had clashed with Trotsky or that he had enjoyed excellent relations with Martov: he was in a sense a French Menshevik.[k] And it was ultimately his pessimism and his hostility to Jacobinism (and its Russian variant, permanent revolution) that led him to reconcile with the majority.

The wartime policies of the SFIO came up for a final review at the National Congress of October 6–9, 1918. The Allied victory was now certain; in late September the German will had broken, and Allied armies were advancing on all fronts. The majoritaires, no doubt with the CGT congress in mind, were anxious to forget old quarrels and end the War in unity. Clemenceau's persecution of the Left made such a rapprochement easier than it might otherwise have been. Renaudel, at his cleverest, quoted Loriot on the basic similarity between the majority and the minority and the inevitability of their merger.[127]

The minoritaires, however, insisted that the past be liquidated and the

---

*j* "Why is it that Merrheim, who had passed the sternest tests, suddenly weakened? I have racked my brains to find an explanation.... For my part, I attribute his withdrawal to his circle of friends, to Paul Meunier, Dulat, Horschiller. Through men like this the bourgeoisie corrupted him without his knowing it. A working-class militant who runs around with intelligent bourgeois, even if they are honest, ceases to see problems from the point of view of class; he no longer sees with the eyes of a worker." *La Révolution Prolétarienne,* November 1925, p. 12.

*k* That Merrheim was a syndicalist and Martov a Socialist is only a measure of the difference between the French and Russian working-class movements.

majority's wartime policies repudiated.[128] As the Left applauded frenetically and shouted "Vive la République des Soviets!" Longuet read a letter from Jacques Sadoul in Russia to Romain Rolland condemning the majoritaires for their complicity in the intervention.[129] One observer thought that this display of devotion to the Russian Revolution was the price the minoritaires had to pay for the support of the Zimmerwaldians, who did not push their own motion.[130] It seems unlikely that the minority needed much persuading. The final balloting confirmed the July triumph of the minoritaires by a margin of over 300 votes. To the bitter end the minoritaires remained faithful to the stand the party had taken in its prewar congresses. Yet never had extremists been less extreme; not even four years of *bourrage de crâne*, Clemenceau, and disillusionment with French war aims could bring the minoritaires to repudiate the principle of national defense. Their motion did not condemn the Sacred Union but the way in which it had been conducted.

After the crucial vote, the mood was one of reconciliation. Renaudel lost his position as editor of *L'Humanité,* but he was replaced by Cachin, a repentant social-patriot with an infallible instinct for finding the majority. Frossard, a talented young minoritaire, became General Secretary. Even Loriot got his reward, to show that no one had hard feelings (or that no one took him seriously); he was made party Treasurer, to the great consternation of some of his extremist friends, who regarded a paid post in the party as the beginning of corruption.[131] The composition of the new CAP respected the principle of proportional representation. On it were eight ex-minoritaires (Longuet, Faure, Maurice Délépine, Frossard, Grandvallet, Paul Louis, Maurice Maurin, Raoul Verfeuil), three ex-Zimmerwaldians (Bourderon, Loriot, Saumoneau), one centrist (Sembat), and ten ex-majoritaires (Thomas, Bracke, Renaudel, Dubreuilh, Ernest Poisson, Louis Camélinat, Pierre Dormoy, Jean-Baptiste Lebas, Gaston Lévy, J.-B. Séverac). The Zimmerwaldian *Journal du Peuple* expressed in its headlines the satisfaction of most Socialists on the aftermath of the October congress: "THE SOCIALIST PARTY RETURNS TO SOCIALISM! RESURRECTION!"

### THE WAR AND THE FRENCH WORKING-CLASS MOVEMENT

Thus the French working-class organizations emerged shaken but intact from the experience of four years of war. The CGT had divided into majoritaires (Jouhaux), minoritaires (Merrheim), and a small guerrilla band of ultra-leftists (the Committee of Syndicalist Defense) who made their influence felt at the end of the War, if only in a negative way. The polemics between minoritaires and majoritaires had been bitter, but Merrheim's passion for unity prevented the breach from becoming irreparable. The Socialist Party weathered the crisis of the War less successfully, perhaps because it had been less ideologically homogeneous. It also broke up into three factions, though the lines of division did not exactly parallel those of the CGT. On the Right were the majoritaires (Renaudel, Thomas), who believed that the War should be carried on until Germany was unconditionally defeated. Since the Sacred Union was the basis for successful national defense, they argued, collaboration with the government must be continued until victory had been won. In the Center were the minoritaires (Longuet, Faure), who felt that the war effort must be supported so long as Germany threatened France, but that international relations among Socialists should be reestablished as soon as possible, and every effort made to negotiate a peace according to the principles announced by President Wilson and the Russian Revolution. For all their opposition to the majority, the Socialist minoritaires, with the exception of the "pilgrims of Kienthal," continued to vote for war credits and to support the French government. Finally, on the Left was a third group, the Zimmerwaldians (Loriot, Saumoneau), organized in the Committee for the Resumption of International Relations. The Zimmerwaldians rejected the Sacred Union, asserted that "this war is not our war," refused to agree that the Central Powers alone were responsible for the War, and were opposed to voting for war credits.

This difference between the minoritaires and the Zimmerwaldians went deeper than a simple agreement about the origins of the War. It derived from the very nature of the French working-class movement. The minoritaires were Socialists of the traditional French variety, while the Zimmerwaldians stemmed from the prewar Left Wing. The difference was one of temperament, of personal relations, and of ideology. The ambiguities and indecisiveness of the minority in trying to reconcile patriotism and internationalism were basically the legacy of Jaurès, who had always insisted that love of country and Socialism were not contradictory but complementary. The Zimmerwaldian tendency had originally sprung from the *Vie Ouvrière–Nashe Slovo* group; and throughout its existence, and even after it was absorbed into the French Communist Party, it bore the marks of this dual parentage—revolutionary syndicalism on the one hand, Russian Socialism on the other. It was no mere chance that the leaders of the Zimmerwaldian Left in the SFIO were either revolutionary syndicalists (Bourderon, Mayoux) or men marked by Russian Socialism (Rappoport), or both (Loriot); for, as Alfred Rosmer has pointed out, France differed from Germany in that the Left Wing of the working-class movement was "almost entirely outside the party," and that it "exercised its influence and acted through the CGT."[132]

The minoritaires and the Zimmerwaldians, therefore, represented two different temperaments, two different traditions, two different approaches to the problem of the War. From the comparative point of view, however, it is perhaps even more enlightening to emphasize the moderation of both tendencies of the French opposition. The French opposition was basically a pacifist and not a revolutionary movement. France had no Lenin, no Liebknecht, not even a Bordiga.[133] Inessa Armand's letters to Lenin are eloquent testimony to the frustrations she suffered in trying to spread Leninist ideas in the Committee for Resumption while Merrheim was at its head. Moreover, in his resistance to Lenin's view of the War, Merrheim was not alone. Loriot himself admitted that he had never adopted the Leninist position during the War; and Rapoport, dismissing Lenin's views as "nationalism in reverse," said that all Socialists agreed in considering them absurd.[134]

Of course, there was good reason why the French opposition could not go beyond pacifism: until the last weeks of the War, German soldiers trampled French soil, and, despite fifteen years of anti-patriotic propaganda, it was impossible to persuade the French worker or peasant that he had no stake in the survival of the nation. Or, for that matter, his leaders. As Jaurès had written in 1911, the Socialists and syndicalists did not really mean what they said when they asserted that the worker had no country. The War merely brought to the surface the great national differences that lay beneath the phrases of the common ideology to which the parties of the Second International did homage. If the Russians were the most revolutionary of all Socialists in their reaction to the War and the least taken in by the appeal to Sacred Union, it was because they were, of all European Socialists, the most alienated from their own government and their own society. The French Socialists, on the other hand, represented a coalition of workers, peasants, and petty bourgeois who were already deeply integrated into the social, political, and cultural life of the Third Republic. The Sacred Union was the expression of that integration, accepted with enthusiasm by some, deplored by others, but a reality with which all working-class leaders had to reckon.[135]

The threat of German victory was not the only limitation on the French opposition. Also deterring it from Leninism, or any variant of Leninism, was the weight of tradition. The French oppositionists were basically concerned with returning to the past. They regarded the War as an interruption, not as a breakthrough to the future. Longuet wanted to return to the delicate Jauressian synthesis of the prewar period; Merrheim wanted to return to pure revolutionary syndicalism; even Loriot and the Socialists of the Committee for Resumption thought of themselves as restoring to its rightful place the orthodoxy of the Second International.[136] The extent of this commitment to tradition is shown by the fact that all but a few members of the Zimmerwaldian group continued to pay their respects to the old dogmas of working-class unity and trade-union autonomy.

By October 1918 a handful of Socialists, syndicalists, and anarchists had come around to Lenin's idea that there must be a regrouping of revolutionary forces in a Third International.[137] The War, they argued, had drawn a new line of demarcation in the working-class movement, between the internationalists and the patriots, or, as Alfred Rosmer would put it somewhat later, between those who had gone to Zimmerwald and those who had not. The old labels had not offered any security against defection to the bourgeoisie under the stress of war. Socialists, syndicalists, and anarchists had supported the Sacred Union. Socialists, syndicalists, and anarchists had joined together in the Committee for the Resumption of International Relations to struggle against the War. Now it was necessary to form a Third International composed of those militants who had remained true to the old ideals.

Such a program, however, required schism in the party and in the CGT, and few Socialists or syndicalists wished to go that far. In both the SFIO and the CGT there was a tendency toward reconciliation at the end of the War. The refusal of Merrheim and Dumoulin to sacrifice Jouhaux to the anger of their vengeful comrades and to force a confrontation left the CGT minority confused and without leaders. The conflict between majoritaires and minoritaires in the party, it is true, did not end on such a peaceful note. The Socialist minoritaires demanded and got their pound of flesh; the wartime leadership of the social patriots was repudiated.[1] But, this satisfaction of principle achieved, most minoritaires were anxious to forgive and forget—provided that the majority would follow the official policies laid down by the congress of October 1918.[138] Only the Kienthalian deputy Alexandre Blanc introduced a threatening note. "If today's majoritaires do as they have promised and lead the party back to the International," he wrote on October 15, 1918, "so much the better for the party. We will help them. But if they weaken, we will fight them with the same toughness that they showed in fighting yesterday's majoritaires."[139]

But to which International should the party return: the International of Renaudel and Vandervelde, or the International of Lenin and Trotsky? This was the question that within a few months would undermine the party's unity and torment the new majority's leaders.

[1] On October 24, 1918, Charles Dumas wrote to Branting: "Vous avez vu le vote du Congrès français. C'est le triomphe de la stupidité intégrale. La minorité triomphe matériellement à l'heure précise où la majorité triomphe moralement par la victoire. Et pour comble la minorité pacifiste se rallie d'enthousiasme à Wilson, dont le programme de capitulation complète de l'Allemagne n'est que la réalisation d'un 'jusqu'auboutisme' que les plus ardents majoritaires n'osaient murmurer que tout bas." Branting Archives.

## Chapter four

# The Revolution in Search of Its Leaders

-Alors faudra continuer à s'battre après la
guerre?
-Oui, p't'êt. . . .
-T'en veux encore, toi!
-Oui, parce que j'n'en veux plus! grogna-t-on.
-Et pas contre des étrangers, p't'êt, i'faudra
s'battre?
-P't'êt, oui.
  *—Soldiers speaking in the trenches.*
  *Henri Barbusse,* Le Feu

The Armistice opened the Pandora's box of anger, hope, and frustration that
had been repressed by the War and by the urgent need to drive the invader
from French soil. The stability of the old bourgeois world of pre-1914 France
had been dealt a stunning blow. Eight million men had been mobilized; five
million had been either killed or wounded; 10 per cent of the active male population was dead; 600,000 had been invalided. Nearly 7 per cent of the richest
and most industrialized part of the country had been devastated, while the national wealth had been reduced by a quarter. Inflation was rampant. By September 1920, the franc, that most unvarying of all the gauges of bourgeois
virtue, had fallen to less than a fifth of its prewar purchasing power. There
were almost four times as many francs in circulation as there had been in 1913.[1]

The psychological damage was even more profound. The experience of war
had called the old social and political values into question. Money was now
being made and spent with an abandon that made the *situation acquise* seem
like a relic of another era. An unmistakable scent of decadence wafted above
the old, exhausted Europe. Tristan Tzara came to Paris and proclaimed the
religion of Dada: "the protest with the fists of all one's being in destructive action"; "the absolute, indisputable belief in every god that is the immediate
product of spontaneity"; the "elegant and unprejudiced leap from one harmony to the other sphere."[2] People spoke of nothing but sport and speed, cock-
tails and jazz, Charlot and Mistinguett—and Revolution.

In pre-1914 Europe, revolution had been a doctrine and a dream, a myth by
which small groups of dedicated men lived and died; in 1919 it was a mood
that pervaded all layers of society. Four years of suffering had awakened the
urge for regeneration, for change and innovation. Four years of danger, of

discipline, but seldom of routine, made the return to normal painful. Four years of promises and propaganda about "la guerre du droit" and "the war to end all wars" had created both great cynicism and great expectations: cynicism about the "eternal lie of the leaders," expectations of a world in which such holocausts would be impossible. The old words, as D. H. Lawrence put it, had been "cancelled out" for that generation. "Honor," "glory," and even "democracy" had a spurious ring; and in the mouths of men like Poincaré these resonant syllables seemed to hide hideous grins, the product of mountains of corpses. Hemingway's comment that "there were many words that you could not stand to hear" sums up the disillusionment of a whole generation of Europeans.[a]

Such disillusion could lead to nihilism and opportunism, and quite often did. But it could also inspire a search for new mystiques. Many bourgeois, as well as workers, had come to believe that some kind of radical social change was inevitable.[b] The War itself had tended to break down social barriers and to create a new comradeship among those who had been at the front. Some hoped that this alliance of fighting men would be continued after the War; in such a league of veterans they placed their hopes for a new world.[3] The idea was that a revolutionary and internationalist Sacred Union might succeed where Poincaré's had failed. The vague and faintly radical imagery of Wilsonianism appealed to this mood; the fiery rhetoric of Bolshevism appealed to it even more strongly. For the ideology of the Russian Revolution exploited simultaneously the urge to destruction, the desire for regeneration, and the disgust with the old bourgeois society that was, in the eyes of many, responsible for the disaster of the War.

Despite the Allies' intervention and the civil war, the Bolsheviks' regime survived. On July 10, 1918, they established a Russian Socialist Federated Soviet Republic that claimed to put all central and local authority in the hands of the laboring masses and their representatives in the soviets. The Bolshevik leaders called upon exploited peoples everywhere to follow their example, and to overthrow world capitalism and imperialism and replace them with the dictatorship of the people's soviets. On November 8, 1918, at the Sixth Congress of Soviets, Lenin announced that the imperialists of the Anglo-French-

[a] I might as readily quote Barbusse, who wrote in 1920: "The most beautiful words were soiled through such use; and the word 'victory' itself was drummed into us in such a disgusting way that even now, we cannot hear it without a feeling of nausea." *Der Schimmer im Abgrund* (Leipzig, 1920), p. 15.

[b] On March 3, 1918, André Gide noted in his diary: "Lucien Maury, with whom I had lunch in Paris the other day, is extremely worried about the wave of Socialism that he feels mounting up, and that he expects to submerge the world we know as soon as people are sure the war is over. He believes that revolution is inevitable and sees no way to prevent it." *Journal, 1889–1939* (1951), p. 648.

American group "are making ready to build a Chinese wall to protect themselves from Bolshevism, like a quarantine against the plague." No matter, concluded Lenin: "The bacillus of Bolshevism will pass through the wall and infect the workers of all countries."[4]

In the spring of 1919 both friends and enemies of the old order thought that Europe was on the eve of revolution. Toward the end of March, Colonel House confided to his diary that "Bolshevism is gaining everywhere.... We are sitting upon an open powder magazine and some day a spark may ignite it."[5] A few days later, Lloyd George warned Clemenceau, in a secret memorandum, "The whole of Europe is filled with the spirit of revolution. There is a deep sense not only of discontent, but of anger and revolt among the workmen against prewar conditions. The whole existing order, in its political, social, and economic aspects is questioned by the masses of the population from one end of Europe to the other."[6] Less than a week later, there were Soviet republics in Hungary and Bavaria and mutinies in the French fleet in the Black Sea, and Lenin could announce that "this will be our last difficult July, and next July we shall greet the victory of the International Soviet Republic."[7] "We already hear," exulted Zinoviev, "the cracking of the buildings of the old captalist Europe about to collapse."[8]

Would the "bacillus of Bolshevism" infect France? It seemed in 1919 and 1920 as if it had. Soviets were established in Paris; papers entitled *Le Communiste* and *Le Bolcheviste* made spectacular, if short-lived, appearances; the names of Lenin and Trotsky became everyday words with which to frighten little bourgeois children and urge on proletarian crowds; and in September 1919, at the Lyon congress of the CGT, Pierre Monatte could assert, without fear of contradiction, that there was then one great question confronting the labor movement that caused all others to pale in significance: the question of the Russian Revolution.[9] Within a few months of the Armistice, the leaders of the SFIO and the CGT found themselves faced with a radically new situation. Their policy of Sacred Union was discredited. Their organizations were invaded by a huge army of restless and angry recruits, for whom the old Socialist and syndicalist traditions had little meaning. The economic crisis had unleashed a wave of strikes that often turned into demonstrations against the government. The old International was in disrepute, and a new International had arisen to challenge it for the allegiance of the masses. Finally, a constantly growing circle of agitators had seized upon the doctrines of Bolshevism and were calling for the modernization of the traditional ideologies of both the party and the CGT. The rapidity with which events marched was such that within the year both Longuet and Merrheim, the leaders of the wartime opposition, would find themselves denounced by Moscow and its partisans as traitors who had gone over to the bourgeoisie.

### THE RADICALIZATION OF THE WORKING CLASS

The French workers had, as a whole, borne the rigors of the War with resignation, and sometimes even with heroism. They had served and died in the trenches; they had been shuttled back and forth between the front and strategic war industries; they had seen their economic position steadily worsen as slowly rising wages failed to keep pace with the cost of living. Their leaders had been in the forefront of the war effort. Not that there had not been movements of dissatisfaction and revolt; there had been. But these movements had been limited, and as long as France was in danger, as she decidedly was after the Treaty of Brest-Litovsk and the launching of the German offensive in the spring of 1918, national unity was somehow maintained and many voices who were normally inclined to criticize the government kept silent.

The reason the Socialist and syndicalist leaders gave for the policy of Sacred Union, both to themselves and to their followers, was that by helping to win the War the working class would earn the right to help make the peace, and to rebuild France in the light of their own doctrines. A French victory today, Jules Guesde had said in 1915, would be "the beginning as well as the precondition of a Socialist victory tomorrow."[e] A syndicalist militant, writing to Jouhaux that same summer, had urged him to see that the CGT remained faithful to the Sacred Union, so that after the hostilities were over it could claim payment on the debt to the working class contracted by the bourgeois parties.[10]

By the spring of 1919 it appeared that this policy of class reconciliation had been a mistake. The call to class conflict had been sounded even before the end of the War, first with the repeated refusal of passports for delegates to international Socialist congresses, then even more distinctly in August 1918, with the prosecution and conviction of Malvy, the former Minister of the Interior, for his toleration of the pacifist movement. On the Left this verdict was considered an indictment of the working class. From the Malvy case, *Le Populaire,* the new Parisian daily of the minoritaires, drew the lesson that "the capitalist regime is rotten to the bone, and that the working class and Socialism must more than ever remain on their terrain of class and opposition."[11] Merrheim saw in the Malvy verdict a vindication of his opposition to the policy of Sacred Union.[12] And the majoritaires of the CGT and minoritaires of the United Trade Unions of the Seine met to draw up a joint manifesto, which contained a scarcely veiled threat to the established order: "We are astounded and outraged to learn of the High Court's verdict, a verdict that is a blow against the working class [and that] casts doubts on its intentions and its deeds. This we

---

[e] See pp. 57–58 above.

cannot accept. After four years of sacrifice and self-denial, we have the right to expect a more informed understanding of our needs and aspirations."[13] For Socialists like Albert Thomas, who had carefully cultivated the alliance between the working class and the government, this break spelled frustration and the end of their effective influence in the party.[14]

To the breach between the government and the working class inspired by the anti-pacifist campaigns of Clemenceau at home was added the provocation of French intervention in Russia. The Armistice marked an important change in the attitude of the working-class movement toward Russia. For if it had been possible to believe in the summer of 1918 that the government was sending troops to the Ukraine merely in order to defend the country, it was only too clear after the Armistice that the government was opposing the Bolsheviks not because they were agents of German imperialism, but because they were revolutionaries and Socialists. On December 29, 1918, the Foreign Minister, Stéphen Pichon, admitted to the Chamber that the French government was working toward the encirclement and destruction of the Bolshevik regime. When he pointed out in justification of the government's policy that the Bolshevik government ruled by terror and that thousands of people had been shot by the Bolsheviks without a trial, a Socialist deputy interjected that "in 1793, we did the same thing." Few Socialists were convinced by Pichon's argument that the existence of a Bolshevik Russia constituted a threat to French security because of the opening it might give German expansionism.

Intervention in Russia became all the more unpopular because it was associated with the slow pace of demobilization and the government's resistance to a Wilsonian peace. The equation between domestic and foreign affairs seemed more and more obvious: a bourgeois and imperialistic government was doing everything in its power to destroy in Russia what the Socialist Party represented in France. Even those Socialists of the Right and Center who looked upon the methods of Bolshevism with distaste were now faced with a dilemma. The French Socialist Party had always insisted on the right to revolution, even though the majority of its members had no intention of making one. Were not the Bolsheviks now exercising that right? Besides, did not the Russian people have the Wilsonian right to self-determination? Even a convinced majoritaire like the classicist Bracke felt driven to protest against the policy of intervention, which now seemed mistaken not only to revolutionaries but to men of the Left in general. It was humiliating, Bracke wrote, that France, Republican France, should find herself in the first rank of the enemies of the Russian Revolution. What was the "democracy" the Allies claimed to represent if it did not include under the right to self-determination the right to revolution?[15]

Reaction at home and counterrevolutionary intervention abroad pushed the Socialist and syndicalist leaders toward the Left, made them assume a more revolutionary and uncompromising stance, and caused them to rue their honeymoon with the government. But if the leaders of the labor movement were swinging toward the Left, they still lagged behind their followers. As in Russia in 1917, the general staff of the revolutionary forces now found themselves running to keep up with their troops. For many the transition from Sacred Union to revolutionary opposition was too abrupt, and they were left behind in the radical turmoil of 1919 and 1920.

Socialist and syndicalist leaders accustomed to representing a small and dedicated elite of militants now found themselves with a mass movement on their hands. With the ending of the War, both the CGT and the SFIO were invaded by an onrush of new recruits. The rise in membership began in 1918, while the War was still in progress, but it reached its peak in 1920. In the fifteen months following the Armistice, about a million and a half new members joined the CGT. By January 1920, the CGT counted close to two million members, more than three times the prewar figure.[d] The progress in certain unions was even more striking. The Federation of Railroad Workers went from 30,000 to 320,000 in a few months. Merrheim's Federation of Metal Workers rose from 7,501 in 1912 to 204,280 by the end of 1918.[16] The growth of the SFIO was almost as spectacular. In 1914, at the height of its prewar power, the party had had only 93,210 members. The War decimated its ranks, and in 1918 it claimed only 34,063 members. In 1919, however, that number rose to 133,277, and by the Congress of Tours in December 1920, the party had a membership of 179,787. It was these new recruits who were at the root of the splits in the SFIO and the CGT in 1920 and 1921.

Moreover, not only had the dimensions of the working-class movement exploded; the very nature and ambitions of the working class had undergone a transformation. This was not the semi-proletariat, semi-artisanat that Jaurès had stirred at the turn of the century with his ringing phrases about Humanity and Republican Defense. The years of war had wrought a dramatic change in the economy, producing a "second industrial revolution," as David Thomson has called it, "violently carried through in the worst conditions."[17] Paris had become a major industrial center, and the social and economic bases for the Red Belt of Parisian suburbs had been laid. In response to wartime needs, there had been a shift from textiles to metallurgy, the effect of which can best be seen in the expansion of the metalworkers' union. As Gordon Wright has remarked, "This change meant not merely new products, but a new kind of labor force—more concentrated, more unskilled, more inclined to radical-

---

[d] The official government figure was 1,580,967. Roger Picard, *Le Mouvement syndical durant la Guerre* (1927), p. 86. The National Confederal Committee of January 1920 claimed 2,400,000 members. Paul Louis, *Le Syndicalisme français d'Amiens à St.-Etienne* (1924), p. 190.

ism."[18] In order to make up the labor shortage during the War, thousands of women and young boys had been introduced to heavy industry, and many of them stayed on after the Armistice.[19] Peasants had been brought to the factories; in some cases, factories had been taken to the peasants (where they would be safe from German advance and assured of a labor supply). Another source of unskilled labor had been found in foreign immigration: the hiring of Poles, Italians, and Spaniards helped maintain the flow of Frenchmen to the trenches. This astonishing mixture of sexes, age groups, social backgrounds, and nationalities had been crowded into factories, trained in a matter of days, and subjected to the timing techniques and piece rates of the Taylor System. As different from the French craftsmen of the 1890's as the automobile was from the horse and buggy, this new labor force gave France its first experience of mass syndicalism.[e]

The thousands of new recruits and seasoned militants who flocked into working-class organizations after the War were no doubt driven by a variety of motives. Some were revolutionaries, who had come back from the trenches haunted and embittered by the experience of the War and anxious to take prompt revenge on the regime they held responsible for their suffering. Others were reformists, closer in spirit to Wilson than to Lenin. Still others, probably the majority in the CGT, were merely interested in a fuller belly and a shorter workday. Whatever the motives of these new adherents to syndicalism, economic, psychological, and ideological factors acted in 1919 and 1920 to weld them together, and to produce a powerful movement of unrest that for a brief moment had the look of revolution. Galloping inflation had forced the cost of living to an exorbitant level. The index of wholesale prices, which had stood at 118 in 1914, reached 392 in 1918 and 412 in 1919, and then zoomed to 589 in 1920.[20] In the first six months of 1919 alone, the franc lost half its value in relation to the dollar. The necessities of life were either unobtainable or so expensive they were hard to manage on a worker's salary. Moreover, all around there were signs of newfound affluence and a flourishing black market that defied government efforts to control it. Not surprisingly, the workers grumbled at the growing gap between prices and wages, talked of profiteers who had grown rich on their blood, and threatened a reckoning. In 1918 there had been 499 strikes with 176,187 participants; in 1919 there were 2,206 strikes with 1,160,718 participants.

[e] Michel Collinet, *Essai sur la condition ouvrière* (1951), p. 68. A few examples will suffice to show how dramatic the change had been. The Delaunay-Belleville automobile factory in St.-Denis had employed 1,800 workers before the War; by the end of 1917 it employed 28,000 workers. The Hotchkiss factory had employed 1,500 people before 1914; by 1918 it had over three times that number. St.-Denis itself had grown from 50,000 to 70,000 inhabitants in three and a half years. Henri Barbé, "Souvenirs de militant et de dirigeant communiste" (ms. at the Hoover Institution), pp. 1–2.

These strikes were ordinarily triggered by disputes over wages and working conditions, or by the struggle for the eight-hour day; but it was the characteristic of this period that such movements had a way of turning into protests against the government and the bourgeois order. Inflation, profiteering, the slow rate of demobilization, the refusal of an amnesty for political prisoners, intervention in the affairs of other countries—to a French worker all this seemed to indicate a clear-cut pattern of reaction for which the government, and not events, was held accountable. Dissatisfaction with the government was accompanied by a corresponding enthusiasm for the Russian Revolution, "cette grande lueur à l'Est," as Jules Romains called it.[21] Brest-Litovsk and the danger of a separate peace had now been forgotten, and the Soviet regime symbolized a society in which the workers were not exploited, there were no war profiteers, and there had been a true peace without victory. The Bolsheviks were exposing bourgeois democracy for the sham that it was, and that was an enterprise which could only endear them to French workers embittered by constant *bourrage de crâne*. Besides, had not the workers' own leaders been telling them the same thing for years? Most of all, the workers loved the Russian Revolution for its enemies. As a friend put it to Alexandre Blanc: I know nothing of Bolshevism. I have neither the leisure nor the means to study it. But my landlord, my boss, and my neighbor—each of whom is more greedy and reactionary than the next—speak badly of it. Therefore it must be doing something worthwhile.[22] It was in this spirit that the French workers, alienated from their own government by the past as well as by the present, often turned to its avowed enemy for their slogans in 1919 and 1920.

One final remark about the nature of this new working-class movement is in order. Great strikes called to cries of "Vive la Révolution Russe!" and "Vive les Soviets!" could cast terror into bourgeois hearts, and give the old ladies who inhabited the Faubourg Saint-Germain the impression that France stood on the brink of a new 1789. Yet the strength of the syndicalist movement of 1919–20—its numbers and its ideological bent—was also its weakness. For one thing, the heterogeneous coalition of revolutionaries, reformists, and angry masses responded to different stimuli. A quick reform pushed through the Chamber, a concession on wages, an hour chopped from the workday, and the strike that yesterday seemed to constitute an embryo of social revolution dissolved into thin air. For another, the new recruits had no staying power; though quick to attack, they were also quick to surrender. A whiff of determined resistance on the part of the government or their employers sent them scurrying out of their unions. Finally, the ideology that motivated these masses was too vague to be effective. In the minds of most workers, admiration for the Bolshevik Revolution was happily commingled with Wilsonianism and the traditional ideologies of Socialism and syndicalism; and events were to show that it was one thing to applaud Lenin and Trotsky, another to follow their example. Small wonder that the events of 1919–20 would leave the working-class leaders with the impression that they had been deserted by their troops, while the militant rank and file would remain convinced that it had been betrayed by its captains.

The Socialist minoritaires interpreted their victory at the National Congress of October 1918 as a condemnation of War Socialism, a mandate to return to the traditional internationalist Socialism of the pre-1914 period, and, finally, an expression of support for the Russian Revolution and the Soviet Republic.[23] Renaudel and Loriot had both taunted the minoritaires with the ambiguity of their program and the indecisiveness of their opposition. Renaudel had even argued that had the minoritaires been entrusted with the destinies of the party, their actions would not have differed from his and those of his followers.[24] And there was force in his logic—for, as we have seen, the minoritaires could never bring themselves to break with the idea of national defense. Throughout the War, however, from the manifesto of the Haute-Vienne to the National Congress of October 1918, there was one idea to which the minority clung with almost religious devotion. That was the need for, and the efficacy of, a meeting of the International, so that the War might be ended through the combined pressure on their governments of the Socialist parties of all the belligerent countries.[25]

It was therefore natural, once the War was ended, for one of the first goals of the party's new leadership to be the reconstruction of the Second International. The leaders of the new majority were aware that War Socialism, Zimmerwald, Stockholm, and intervention in Russia had put serious strains on the unity of the International; they themselves believed that War Socialism must be repudiated and certain elements purged; they had heard some echoes of the Bolsheviks' hostility to the leaders of the Second International. Nevertheless, the new majoritaires were convinced that the old wounds could be healed, and they hoped to act as a bridge between Zimmerwald and the old International, between the Left Wing and the old majority. Daniel Renoult, for example, writing in January 1919, objected to a statement in Le Temps that the Second International was dead. He admitted that it still faced a period of difficulties and conflicts. "But its strength, drawn from the inner recesses of the working masses," he wrote optimistically, "is indestructible."[26]

The first postwar meeting of the International, held in Berne from February 3 to 10, 1919, showed how misplaced this optimism had been. The ostensible purpose of the Berne Conference was to present the Versailles negotiators with the Socialists' recommendations for a lasting peace, and to settle the question of the Socialists' responsibilities for the outbreak of the War. The French neo-majoritaires hoped that Berne would lay the foundations for a new and revived International. From the beginning, however, the shadow of the Bolshevik Revolution hung over the proceedings at Berne and prevented any reconciliation of the estranged factions. The Left Wing of the international Socialist movement—the Bolsheviks, the German Spartacists, the Bulgarian "Narrow" Social Democrats, and the Socialist parties of Italy, Switzerland, Serbia, and Romania—boycotted the conference on principle, because of the participation of the patriotic Socialists and the "hangmen" of the German Revolution.[f] This left the French neo-majority and their Centrist counterparts in the other Socialist parties to face the Right, who naturally enough contrived to dominate the conference's work and to give it a decidedly anti-Bolshevik character.

The French delegation was headed by Longuet and Renaudel, and represented the majority and minority factions according to their relative strength within the party, the ex-minoritaires of course being the more numerous. Loriot had also agreed to join the delegation—not because he thought the conference would or should accomplish its aim of reconstructing the International, but because he hoped to make contact with the Bolsheviks, and because he believed that from the tactical point of view the Berne Conference would provide an excellent opportunity to proclaim a new International.[27] Even before the conference opened, the French delegation was severely split. "We went to Berne, majoritaires and minoritaires, as if we already formed two different delegations," recalled Frossard.[28]

Despite the efforts of the French neo-majoritaires to avoid, or at least postpone, the issue, the conference decided to vote on the question of the Bolshevik dictatorship of the proletariat. The French Right made no secret of its distaste for the Bolshevik Revolution and its principles. Led by Renaudel, it followed the majority of the conference in supporting a resolution introduced by Hjalmar Branting, the head of the Swedish Social Democratic Party, which condemned the Bolshevik Revolution as nothing more than "capitalism with many shareholders."[29] Forced to state its position, the French neo-majority produced a series of resolutions on the Bolshevik Revolution that varied from the enthusiasm of Loriot, Paul Faure, and Verfeuil to the more reserved attitude of Pressemane. Finally, the majority of the French delegation (minus Loriot) joined with the Spanish, Dutch, and Norwegians in voting for a Centrist resolution that praised the Russian Revolution in general terms and withheld judgment until a closer inspection could be made. The Adler-Longuet motion stated very well the dilemma of the Center's position toward the Bol-

---

[f] Merle Fainsod, *International Socialism and the War* (Cambridge, Mass., 1935), pp. 219–20. In January 1919, Karl Liebknecht and Rosa Luxemburg were shot during an uprising in Berlin. At the same time, the leaders of the SPD made it clear that they preferred a Western orientation.

sheviks. The leaders of the Center were not yet sure they agreed with everything the Bolsheviks stood for; but at the same time, they dared not reject any part of the Russian Revolution for fear they would become "the victims of the class-motivated maneuvers and slanders of bourgeois governments."[30] Loriot would have none of such sophistry. He made a separate statement, in which he accused many of the delegates to the conference of having come to Berne to justify their "governmental, nationalist, and chauvinist War Neo-Socialism." "We have no intention," he said, "of being either the dupes or the accomplices of this anti-Socialist and counterrevolutionary activity. The appearance of life that one is trying to give the Second International is an illusion."[31]

Despite the clash with the Right occasioned by the question of the Bolshevik dictatorship, the French neo-majority came back from Berne still optimistic about the possibilities of rebuilding on the ruins left by the War, Zimmerwald, and the Russian Revolution. Amédée Dunois expressed the opinion that the Zimmerwaldian sections would return when they saw that the International had restored prewar Socialist orthodoxy to its place of honor.[32] Cachin was almost enthusiastic. Berne, he wrote, had not put an end to the party's controversies. "But such as it was, it lacked neither dignity, nor grandeur, nor a certain utility. In opposition to the wild statements now coming from Paris, it has given voice to necessary words of moderation and wisdom, which tomorrow will be translated into acts."[33]

Meanwhile, on January 24, 1919, just a few days before the beginning of the Berne Conference, the Bolsheviks had issued an appeal for an international gathering of the revolutionary Left. The revolution seemed about to spread to Germany. A German Communist Party had been formed at the end of December. Despite the brutal murder of Karl Liebknecht and Rosa Luxemburg, Bolshevik hopes for revolution in Germany remained undimmed.[34] The creation of a Third International, of course, had been a central plank in Lenin's revolutionary program ever since August 1914. But in January 1919, with Russia blockaded from the West and Central and Eastern Europe in flames, the Bolsheviks could not hope to assemble a representative congress in Moscow. Their main concern was to proclaim the formation of a new Communist International, which would prevent the revival of the old International in Berne.[35] The invitation to the conference, drafted by Trotsky, stated in simple, direct sentences the aims and tactics on which the new International would be based. The task of the proletariat, the invitation read, was to seize State power immediately, to destroy the State apparatus of the bourgeoisie, and to replace it with the dictatorship of the proletariat:

Not false bourgeois democracy—that hypocritical form of the rule of the financial oligarchy—with its purely formal equality, but proletarian democracy, which gives the working masses the opportunity to make a reality of their freedom; not par-

liamentarism, but self-government of these masses by their elected organs; not capitalist bureaucracy, but organs of administration created by the masses themselves,
with the masses really taking part in the government of the country and in socialist
reconstruction—this should be the type of proletarian State. Its concrete form is
given in the regime of Soviets or of similar organs.[36]

The basic method of struggle for the overthrow of the bourgeoisie by the
proletariat was to be mass action, including "open, armed conflict" with the
bourgeoisie. Three tendencies were distinguished among the parties of the
old Socialist International: the social chauvinists, who were to be fought un-
sparingly; the Center (Kautsky), from which it was necessary to attract the
revolutionary elements; and the revolutionary elements of the Left, who were
to form the basis of the new International. It was emphasized that organizational separation from the Centrist tendency was at a certain historical moment
"absolutely essential." On the other hand, it was necessary to join forces with
the revolutionary elements outside the Socialist parties who stood for the dictatorship of the proletariat; chief among these were the syndicalists. The isolation of the Bolsheviks from the outside world was underlined by the vagueness
of their invitation to the "groups and organizations within the French socialist
and syndicalist movement which by and large support Loriot."[37]

At the congress, which sat in Moscow from March 2 to 19, 1919, it was decided over the protests of the German Spartacist delegate to found a Third,
Communist International. With Loriot unable to attend, France was represented by Henri Guilbeaux and Jacques Sadoul, two Frenchmen then living in
Moscow who had rallied to the Bolshevik Revolution, neither of whom had
the authorization or mandate of the SFIO or the Committee for Resumption.
Guilbeaux represented the French Zimmerwaldian Left (with which he was
not in contact), and Sadoul the French Communist group in Russia. In his address to the Congress, Sadoul emphasized the embryonic state of the French
Communist movement. Nine-tenths of the Socialists, he claimed, were hostile
to the Bolshevik Revolution. "In fact, comrades," he concluded, "at the present
time I see no revolutionary leaders within the Socialist Party."[38] Zinoviev, the
new President of the International, thanked Paul Faure and Loriot for their
efforts to defend the Bolsheviks against the majority at the Berne Conference,
which was condemned as "an attempt to galvanize the corpse of the Second
International."[39]

The First Congress of the Comintern was notable not for its debates, which
were without color, but for the resolutions that emerged from it, which stated
the principles and tactics of the new International. The resolution on the Berne
Conference again underlined that "an organizational split with the Center is
an absolute necessity. It is the task of the Communists of each separate country to define the moment of this split in accordance with the stage of development that their movement has attained."[40] An appeal to the workers of the

world proclaimed that "the honor, independence, and most elementary interests of the proletariat of all countries" demanded that they force their governments, by revolutionary means if necessary, to renounce all intervention in
Russian affairs.[41] The manifesto of the congress, addressed to the proletariat
of the entire world and once more written by Trotsky, stated that the most important task of "the class-conscious and honest workers of all countries" was to
create and strengthen Soviets of workers', soldiers', and peasants' deputies,
through which the working class, once it had come to power, would be able to
manage its economic and cultural life, as it now did in Russia.[42] These texts
developed what were to be the three basic themes in the relations of the Bolsheviks with the Western proletariat during 1919: the necessity to break with
the Socialist moderates, to fight the intervention, and to emulate the Bolsheviks by forming Soviets. Of the role of the party there was as yet no word.

Hence, at the very time that the new French majority was harboring hopes
that the revolutionary Left could be wooed back to the old International, the
Bolsheviks were creating a new international organization and proclaiming
the historical necessity of a split. These first documents of the Third International, written in the fever of revolution and shot through with scorn for all
those Socialists who sought to avoid the choice between the dictatorship of the
proletariat and bourgeois democracy, called for nothing less than a radical realignment of the international working-class movement. In French terms, they
implied the regrouping of revolutionary Socialists, syndicalists, and even anarchists in a new Communist organization, that same regrouping which had
already taken place in embryo in the Committee for Resumption during the
War. Such a realignment, though it ran counter to French tradition, was made
the more plausible by the emphasis of the Bolsheviks on anti-parliamentarism,
proletarian dictatorship, internationalism, hostility to the old Socialist parties,
and Soviets. For what was this regime of Soviets except the old syndicalist
dream of a society of free producers? And what were these Bolsheviks, except
the Russian equivalent of the French revolutionary syndicalists? Such questions would occur to more than one syndicalist and anarchist in 1919 and 1920.

The creation of the Third International called into question the very existence of the SFIO. According to the new classification introduced by the Bolsheviks, the French majority (Longuet, Faure, Pressemane, Frossard, Cachin,
Renoult, Dunois) seemed to fall in the category of the Center, which Trotsky
had defined in his invitation to the congress as "consisting of those elements
who are always vacillating, incapable of a firm line of conduct, and at times
downright treacherous."[43] How would the French majority react to Bolshevism? Would the Center stay in the old International? Would it be drawn
inevitably to the Third? Or would it disintegrate under the strain of the two
extremes, as the Bolsheviks had said it would? For the moment, the French
majority still had faith that the Second International could be made workable

for all factions. In late March 1919, Paul Faure expressed his disappointment that the Italians had decided to leave the Second International and join the Third. "Why not first wage an energetic battle in the very midst of the International during its next congress? To obtain a majority was by no means impossible. We could then have headed in the right direction, a tested organization with solid cadres, and conducted whatever purges would have proved necessary."[44] But Faure had to concede that if the Italians and the Russians stayed out of the Second International and other sections were led to follow suit, the reconstruction of the old International would be impossible. Thus, within a month, the situation of the SFIO had radically changed, and the prospects for the old International were much dimmer than the Center had at first thought.

### THE EXTRAORDINARY NATIONAL CONGRESS OF APRIL 1919

The French working-class leaders had at first greeted the Bolshevik Revolution with reservations, and even with hostility. Some had approved the idea of intervention. But as they entered into conflict with their own government in the spring of 1919, they warmed correspondingly to the defense of the Soviet regime. They discovered, for one thing, that the Russian Revolution was popular among the masses who were flooding into their organizations. Moreover, they were sincerely ashamed of the fact that their own government was in the forefront of reaction. Those Socialists of the Right, like Renaudel and Thomas, who continued to condemn the Bolsheviks for violating Socialist orthodoxy, found themselves booed and hissed from Socialist platforms. The Zimmerwaldians, meanwhile, sensed a great surge of popular support for their extremist views and their identification with the Soviet Republic.[45]

Confronted with these two extremes, the leaders of the Center attempted to tread a narrow line between defense of the Bolshevik Revolution and acceptance of its doctrines. They opposed intervention, both on principle and on the ground that it did not accord with the interests of France. Throughout 1918 and 1919, the pages of *Le Populaire* and *L'Humanité* teemed with condemnations of the policy of intervention and expressions of support for the Bolsheviks. In the Chamber of Deputies, the Socialists of the Center continually sniped at the Clemenceau government for its Russian policy and warned of the unsettling effect that it was having on the working class.[46] In criticizing the intervention, however, they invoked the Declaration of the Rights of Man and Wilson's Fourteen Points, rather than the *Communist Manifesto*. They spoke as democrats, as Jacobins, as Wilsonians, not as Socialists and certainly not as embryonic Bolsheviks. It was probably Renoult who best expressed the attitude of the majority of the party toward the Bolshevik Revolution. We consider the Russian Revolution as a whole, Renoult wrote in mid-February, just as Clemenceau considers the French Revolution. We love it and serve it with all our strength because it represents the greatest effort of liberation that the working class has ever attempted. That does not mean, however, he continued, that we seek to universalize its methods or to extend to France acts that are the product of a peculiar social and political milieu. Not in the least. We merely say that in taking power, the Russian people was forced to establish a dictatorship in order to carry out a social revolution. In other conditions, he concluded, the Russian peasants and workers might have been able to accomplish their social revolution by means of a political assembly, as the French bourgeoisie had done in 1789.[47]

An Extraordinary National Congress was summoned by the Socialists for April 20–22, 1919, to adopt a platform for the coming elections and discuss the questions raised by the Berne Conference and the disintegration of the Second International. The wave of unrest unleashed by the Armistice and the Bolshevik Revolution was, at this moment, reaching its height. A Soviet Republic had been proclaimed in Budapest on March 21; Bavaria followed suit in the first week of April. Serious mutinies occurred in the French Black Sea fleet in April, and French military units had to be evacuated from Odessa when they refused to march against the Bolsheviks.[48] Within France, the level of discontent was quickly mounting. The working class grumbled at the slow pace of demobilization and the economic squeeze. On March 23–24, the Confederal Committee adopted a resolution stating that it was "the unanimous will of the working class" to win the eight-hour day. Five days later, the last remnants of the Sacred Union collapsed when Raoul Villain, Jaurès's assassin, was acquitted "in the name of victory," despite the testimony of a long string of distinguished witnesses to Jaurès's patriotism. The Federation of the Seine immediately issued a manifesto protesting this decision as a "class verdict" and a "gesture of civil war."[49] To compound the affront, the anarchist Emile Cottin, who had tried unsuccessfully to murder Clemenceau in February, was condemned to death,[g] and the Chamber of Deputies voted funds for the continuation of intervention in Russia. These events sparked a series of demonstrations and strikes, which lasted throughout the months of May and June. In March and April alone, almost 100,000 workers went out on strike, as opposed to 30,000 during the same months of the previous year. On April 6, over 100,000 persons answered a Socialist call to protest the acquittal of Jaurès's murderer.[50] The Chamber, frightened by the aroused temper of the workers, hastily pushed through a bill granting the working class the eight-hour day.

The Extraordinary National Congress of April was remarkable both for the radical temper it revealed among the rank and file and for the desire of the leaders to avoid the questions raised by the Bolshevik Revolution and the Third International. The preliminary debates at the Federation of the Seine

[g] Cottin was reprieved by Clemenceau and released from prison ten years later.

had uncovered unsuspected depths of emotion, as one speaker after another had risen to detail his grievances against the leaders of the party and to express his impatience for a policy of action. Guesde, Thomas, and Sembat were criticized for their participation in a bourgeois government, and one delegate suggested that had Lenin and Trotsky been in their places, things would have worked out differently.[51] Le Temps noted righteously that "as a result of the outbidding that is at the basis of all revolutionary politics," the Zimmerwaldian extremists, who had declared themselves partisans of the Third International, constituted an ever greater threat to the ex-minoritaires. "There is no longer a place for majoritaires of the Varenne, Thomas, or even Renaudel type," commented Le Temps, "in this ferociously revolutionary milieu, in which Longuet passes for a reactionary and Mayéras appears shy or shrinking."[52]

Le Temps was quite astute in noting the phenomenon of radicalization, but as usual its explanation left something to be desired. It was not merely the dynamic of revolutionary parties that had caused the party's Parisian members to move toward the Left; the very constitution of the party had changed since the beginning of the War. The struggle between minoritaires and majoritaires had given new life to the sections; many militants who before 1914 had found outlets for their energies in other forms of activity—in syndicalism or anarchism, for example—had now begun to take an active role in the party's affairs. Socialism benefited from the vogue of the Russian Revolution. Who could say that what had happened in Russia would not be repeated in France? The younger members the SFIO had lacked before the War now enrolled in droves. Many of these enthusiasts of 1919 and 1920 no doubt came to the party out of snobbism or careerism; Socialism, of course, had always been prey to such recruits. The agitated atmosphere of 1919 encouraged the belief that revolution was imminent. But what distinguished this generation of Socialists from its predecessor, which had entered the party after the Dreyfus case, was its hatred for the War and its hostility toward the Socialist leaders who had pledged the party to the Sacred Union. "They came to us overflowing with the frightening bitterness of those tragic years," Frossard recalled in 1930. "The War had marked them cruelly and the odor of death still lingered on their martyred flesh. The spirit of rebellion breathed in them. They returned from the great slaughter mutilated or bruised, eager for prompt revenge. They blamed the regime: it had made them suffer, and they wanted to overthrow it."[53]

In April 1919, however, the new militants were still disorganized and their influence confined to Paris, so that the Center easily managed to dominate the national congress and give it a moderate tone. The party's electoral program, presented in the name of the CAP and written by the mild-mannered and bookish Léon Blum, was a restatement of the canons of prewar French Socialism, which in its very traditionalism represented a rebuke to the Bolsheviks for attempting to give their own methods universal validity. No document could have demonstrated more convincingly that the Jauressian synthesis was designed for a period of peaceful social evolution, and not for a period of war and revolution. "The Socialist Party," read the Program, "does not confuse revolution and violence. . . . It has always turned the workers away from premature movements and impulsive demonstrations." But, at the same time, "the Socialist Party would not run away from any opportunities with which the bourgeoisie's own mistakes presented it." On the question of the dictatorship of the proletariat, the Program was firm: "The duration of this period of transition must be as brief as circumstances permit." And, though the French Socialists stressed that they were loyal defenders of the Russian Revolution, they did not hide their preference for democratic institutions: "The experiences of Russia and Germany and the difficulties that they must overcome make it clear what the most favorable conditions for the success of Revolution are: . . . the prior existence in every country of democratic institutions and traditions."

The accent throughout the Program was on reform rather than revolution. Revolution would be accepted, but it would certainly not be precipitated. It was emphasized that although the passage to Socialism had been accomplished by violence in Russia, in France it might very well be realized by the gradual improvement of the existing order. Blum returned to the inspiration of the Toulouse compromise of 1908 to point out that the party worked for the revolution when it fought for reform, when it sought to democratize public institutions, and when it helped increase the productive capacity of the nation. Even before the triumph of Socialism, it was possible to introduce to the world "increasing order and increasing liberty, and every step in this direction lays the foundation for and hastens the historic moment of the proletariat."[h]

In the debates at the congress, Loriot condemned the Program because it did not recognize that the existing situation was a revolutionary one and because it spoke in terms of reform rather than revolution. The duty of Socialists, he said, was not to follow the masses, but to precede them. Blum replied with a conciliatory speech that stressed the inseparability of democracy and Socialism. The dictatorship of the proletariat he dismissed as nothing more than "the organized transition between the old regime and the new." "One might call it a rule of professional technique."[54] Blum's spiriting away of the entire problem of democracy and dictatorship was so warmly received by the congress

[h] *L'Humanité*, 11.iv.19. The Program ended with a concrete list of reforms, which included the calling of a Constituent Assembly; universal suffrage for men and women; proportional representation; a single Assembly; administrative decentralization; nationalization of the great centralized industries; a graduated income tax; a capital levy for the rebuilding of the country; social security; a shortening of the workday; a minimum wage; and the exploitation for the common good of natural resources and the transport industries.

that it was decided to publish his speech separately as a statement of the party's principles. The Program was similarly approved by a large majority of the congress, which included both Longuet and Thomas.

For the first time, the question of adherence to the Third International was broached. There were three points of view. A small minority, led by Loriot, wanted the party to proclaim its adherence to the Communist International immediately. The former majority wished merely to remain in the old International, with which it found no fault. A third group, consisting mainly of the old minoritaires, wanted to stay in the Second International on the condition that it be oriented more decisively to the Left. Speaking for this Centrist group, Longuet declared that he and his friends wanted to indicate by their motion their determination to preserve their ties with their Russian, Italian, and Swiss comrades.[55] When put to a vote, the Longuet resolution narrowly defeated the motion of the former majority. Loriot's plea for immediate adherence won only 270 mandates out of a total of over 2,000.

Despite the overwhelming defeat of Loriot's motion, the April congress marked an important step in the radicalization of the party and the movement toward the Third International. Longuet's motion approved the conduct of the French delegation at Berne, and expressed the hope that the parties of the Left would attend the next congress of the Second International. This, as Loriot remarked, was pure illusion.[56] Moreover, the Longuet motion attempted to satisfy the Left Wing by calling for the emulation of the Russian, Hungarian, and German proletariats and by demanding purges, both in the International and in the individual parties. By passing this motion, the delegates to the congress registered their disapproval of Socialist tactics during the War. The demand for sweeping purges was indicative of the new spirit within the party. From April 1919 to December 1920, the question of adherence to the Third International would be the central issue of Socialist politics in France. *Le Temps,* with its customary disdain for motions that emerged from Socialist assemblies, pointed out the fragility of the compromise that was reached at the April congress. The majority, wrote *Le Temps,* "has voted in favor of remaining in the Second International only on the condition that it unhesitatingly prepare the way to the Third.... Parallel action by the two Internationals first, their merger later, in conditions that will guarantee the preponderance of extremist influence—such is the real significance of this decision."[57]

### VARIETIES OF BOLSHEVISM

At Berne and again at the April congress, the leaders of the Socialist majority strove to avoid the awkward problem of judging the tactics of the Bolshevik Revolution. They could repeat with Daniel Renoult that they were neither Bolsheviks nor anti-Bolsheviks. The leaders of the Left Wing showed no such reticence. 1919 was a year for extremism, in politics as in morals and literature. Both Bolshevism and anti-Bolshevism were in style; both were products of the crisis of European society brought on by the War. In 1919 there were as many varieties of Bolshevism as there were left-wing groups. Ideological proliferation was facilitated by the cloud of ambiguity and ignorance with which the Bolshevik Revolution was surrounded. Even after the Armistice, all news about the soviets and the revolutionary agitation in Central Europe was carefully censored. The word "soviet" was not permitted, and the censors were instructed to delete, whenever possible, the expression "workers' and soldiers' councils."[58] The Allied blockade made travel to Russia an impossibility. Under such conditions, the imagination was free to define Bolshevism as it liked. It must be said that the Bolsheviks themselves did not encourage careful theoretical distinctions. While on the one hand they tightened the links that bound their party, on the other they issued theses, manifestos, and programs in praise of soviet democracy. The result was an ideological confusion so profound that for one brief, mad moment, left-wing Socialists, syndicalists, anarchists, and intellectuals were all convinced that they had found the essence of their own convictions in the strange new doctrine of Bolshevism.

### The Committee of the Third International

The Zimmerwaldian current in the party emerged from the War in a position of extreme weakness. Brizon's pacifism, phrased in terms more reminiscent of the Jacquerie than of Marx, had occasioned a mightier response among the masses than either Loriot's attempt at ideological consistency or Longuet's efforts to reconcile internationalism and national defense. The circulation of Brizon's weekly paper, *La Vague,* which specialized in letters from workers, soldiers, and peasants, leaped to 8,000 soon after its founding at the beginning of 1918; André Marty claimed that its influence within the Army and the Navy was enormous, with one copy sometimes passing through a hundred hands.[59] Loriot and his partisans, on the other hand, seemed to fall into the trap of the minority at the end of the War. At the Socialist congress of October 1918, it had been Longuet who had been the most vociferous defender of the Russian Revolution. The Zimmerwaldians ended up voting with the minoritaires against the former majority at the insistence of the provincial delegates, even though Loriot himself admitted that the Left was unable to detach the minority from the bonds that tied it to the nationalists.[60] Once the War was over, the ostensible reason for the Committee for Resumption no longer existed. The minoritaires were anxious to forgive and forget the mistakes of the War, both those of the Right and those of the Left. For them the War was a bad dream, to be forgotten as soon as possible. Writing to a provincial correspondent in late January 1919, Loriot confessed that although he was encouraged by the reception given the Zimmerwaldians by the rank and file, he remained "somewhat skeptical about the realization of our hopes in the near future."[61] A police report mentions an attendance of only some twenty persons at a meeting the Committee held on February 7, 1919.[62]

A different man might easily have given up. But Loriot persisted doggedly in his belief that it was necessary to purge the party, to bring its ideology up to date, and to set it on the path laid out by the Bolshevik Revolution. The homogeneity of the minority, he wrote in November 1918, was only an illusion, which would disappear at the first breath of revolution.[63] The next month the bearded and long-limbed schoolteacher appeared before the Federal Council of the Federation of the Seine to state that "Socialism has written its name in letters of fire above the entire universe with this one word: Bolshevism."[64] In January 1919, responding to an article by Bracke, Loriot insisted that Bolshevism was not a peculiarly Russian phenomenon, arguing that "in its essential principles it exists everywhere, and that it alone represents the power of renovation, of production, and of human progress that Socialism contains, for it *is* Socialism."[65] At the April congress of 1919, the Zimmerwaldian vote split, certain Leftists approving Blum's Program, others voting against. Loriot and Saumoneau refused to respond to a Centrist plea for unanimity, and sustained their own motion, which denounced reformism, parliamentarism, Wilsonianism, and the League of Nations as illusions, and which called for the total seizure of power by the proletariat.[i] When the spokesmen of the Center accused Loriot of intransigence, he explained that he and his followers had not voted for Blum's Program "because we are revolutionaries and Communists, and *it* is not."[66] The Program spoke of social revolution and the dictatorship of the proletariat, said Loriot, but it spoke of them as if they were something theoretical and abstract, eventualities to be accepted at some remote future date. The sponsors of this motion, he continued, reason as if there had never been a war, as if it were 1914 and not 1919. At the present time, such an attitude was counterrevolutionary. "What we object to in this cold academic report—chockfull, by the way, of innuendos and omissions—is not that it is contrary to doctrine, but that it is an anachronism."[j]

The creation of the Third International breathed new life into the Zimmer-

---

[i] The motion read: "Only revolution can bring a full and rapid answer to the problems of social reorganization. It alone can deliver Humanity from the nightmare of war, and, by making production the basis of society, give work a new vitality and freedom by making speculation, the cause of inflation, impossible." Comité pour la Reprise des Relations Internationales, *Programme (Congrès des 20, 21 et 22 avril 1919)* (1919), no pagination. Loriot and Saumoneau were almost alone within the SFIO in condemning Wilsonianism.
[j] *La Vie Ouvrière*, 30.iv.19. In 1927, after he had broken with the Communist Party, Loriot explained that he had opposed Blum's Program not because he thought reforms were useless, but because he felt that in a revolutionary period it was "an anachronism and a threat to the proletariat" to try to perfect the existing regime. In elaborating this program of reforms, said Loriot, the party had let it be understood that it would not support a spontaneous movement of the masses against the established order. The party "thus was posing conditions for the Revolution." In 1919 Loriot considered this attitude non-Marxist because true historical materialism "knows no premature revolution." *La Révolution Prolétarienne*, 1.iv.27.

wald faction and gave it a reason for being. The Committee for Resumption announced for immediate adherence to the Third International, and defended this position at the April congress of the SFIO. On May 8, 1919, the Committee for Resumption, meeting with Péricat's Committee of Syndicalist Defense and other anarchist and semi-anarchist elements, decided to transform itself into a Committee for the Third International (Comité pour la 3ᵉ Internationale). The composition of the new committee was heavily anarchist and syndicalist. Alfred Rosmer, Péricat, Loriot, and Saumoneau were its secretaries.[67] At the first meeting, Loriot and Saumoneau made it clear that the purpose of the group was not to foment a split in the party or the CGT, but rather "to propagandize in all the revolutionary parties on behalf of this new International."[68] The members of the Committee were required to remain in the groups to which they already belonged, to the great disgust of certain anarchists and syndicalists, such as Péricat, who were in favor of splitting off immediately and forming a Communist Party.

### La Vie Ouvrière

As 1919 passed, the Committee for the Third International tended to concentrate its attentions more on the SFIO and less on the CGT, the result in part of Loriot's feeling that the Longuetist tendency in the party was closer to the Third International than the CGT's leadership. The Zimmerwaldian syndicalists, meanwhile, set out to organize their own opposition group within the CGT. In mid-April 1919, a circular announced the reappearance of the prewar *Vie Ouvrière,* under the editorship of Pierre Monatte and Alfred Rosmer. The members of the inner circle of *La Vie Ouvrière* (Monatte, Rosmer, Louzon, Gaston Monmousseau, Pierre Sémard, Guillaume Verdier, Maurice Chambelland) did not cut themselves off from the activities of the Committee for the Third International or the fate of the Socialist Party. On the contrary, the peculiarity of the *Vie Ouvrière* group was precisely that it now considered the Socialist Party important, whereas before the War it had dismissed it as irrelevant to the needs and aspirations of the working class. According to Monatte, *La Vie Ouvrière* stood somewhat outside both the party and the CGT. The group of *La Vie Ouvrière,* he claimed, was "an alloy of syndicalism and Bolshevism."[69] It published articles by Socialists, syndicalists, and anarchists, and later disseminated the materials of the Amsterdam Bureau of the Third International, and, of course, of the Committee for the Third International, for which it was at first one of the principal channels of communication.

The evolution of Rosmer's and Monatte's thinking suggests the tremendous impact that the four years from 1914 to 1918, four years of war and revolution, had had upon the traditional ideologies of the French working-class movement. Before 1914 Monatte and Rosmer had been revolutionary syndicalists, extremely hostile to all forms of Socialism and zealous defenders of the autonomy of the unions against both party and government interference. During the War their internationalism and pacifism had brought them into contact with Trotsky and Lozovsky, who influenced both of them deeply. These two Russian revolutionaries, one a wayward Menshevik, the other a wayward Bolshevik, represented a type of Socialism that Rosmer and Monatte had never seen. They ran for no offices, sought no votes, were true internationalists, and talked of making a revolution as if they meant it."[70] The first circular of *La Vie Ouvrière* acknowledged the editors' debt to Trotsky. Significantly, his name was linked with that of Romain Rolland: "Rolland and Trotsky: these two men have saved us from disgust and despair; they have preserved our reasons for living and revived our confidence in Humanity and Revolution."[71]

The revolutionary syndicalists of *La Vie Ouvrière* responded immediately to the Bolsheviks' appeal for a new grouping of revolutionaries in a Third International. Their position was that although the principles of revolutionary syndicalism remained valid, they must be revised and brought up to date on the basis of the experience of the War and the Russian Revolution. "The War," Alfred Rosmer wrote in the first issue of *La Vie Ouvrière,* "has been the great test; it has established a new classification. On one side the traitors, the Socialist defaulters, who, when faced with revolution, become aware of the fact that they are only simple democrats; on the other side, the revolutionaries. There cannot be, in effect, two Internationals." The new International would be a continuation of the Zimmerwald movement. In it would gather all those who had resisted the collapse of European Socialism and syndicalism, and had gone to Zimmerwald and Kienthal.[72]

The War had thus drawn a new line of demarcation in the working-class movement. It had also shown the weaknesses in the traditional ideology of revolutionary syndicalism. According to *La Vie Ouvrière,* the syndicalists had been mistaken to fight simultaneously against both capitalism and the State; the conception of revolution based upon the union had been a chimera. The Bolshevik Revolution, on the other hand, had revealed a new kind of Socialism, which syndicalists could accept. "Everywhere in the world electoral Socialism gives way to revolutionary Socialism. The Russian Revolution brings Socialism back to life."[73]

This realignment of French syndicalism, however, was only accomplished at the price of a considerable distortion of Russian realities. The group around *La Vie Ouvrière* saw in the Bolshevik Revolution a confirmation of their own ideology of revolutionary syndicalism. In January 1918, Jacques Sadoul had written a letter to France pointing out the syndicalist nature of the Russian Revolution and the Soviet regime. The Bolsheviks, he claimed, treated the worker not as a citizen but as a producer; and in the system of soviets authority flowed from the people to the elected assembly, and not vice versa as in a parliamentary regime.[74] The editors of *La Vie Ouvrière* seem to have been deeply impressed by Sadoul's testimony, and they confessed that from the beginning they had been struck by the similarities between French syndicalism and the institutions and methods of the Russian Revolution. "Is the Soviet something so different from the local federation of unions?" Monatte asked in May. "Is the federal Republic of Soviets something so different from what a federal syndicalist Republic might be?"[75] Verdier went so far as to suggest that Lenin and Trotsky had studied revolutionary syndicalism while spending their exile in France. "We have at the present hour," said Verdier in September 1919, "a practical school that derives its inspiration from Proudhon: it's the Russian Revolution."[76] Moreover, many revolutionary syndicalists saw the Russian Revolution as the vindication of their traditional tactics of direct action and the general strike. The general strike, *La Vie Ouvrière* concluded, was more appropriate as a "revolutionary tool" than ever. Had the Russian Revolution not begun with a strike of the textile workers that grew into a general strike of all the Petrograd workers?[77] If there were differences between the Bolsheviks and the French syndicalists, in the spring of 1919 they seemed less important than the similarities. As one reader of *La Vie Ouvrière* put it, " 'Bolchevick' and 'democrat' seem to me at the present time to be the two terms in opposition, the two 'tendencies' between which the working-class movement must choose."[78]

### The Realignment of the Syndicalist Minority

In the spring of 1919, the revolutionary syndicalists of *La Vie Ouvrière,* like their Socialist and anarchist allies in the Committee for the Third International, thought that revolution was "proche, inévitable, fatale, aux quatre coins de l'Europe."[79] The events of May and June 1919 only further confirmed them in this belief. The majoritaire-dominated Confederal Committee of the CGT had summoned the working class to stage a massive work stoppage on May 1, to demonstrate its power, its moderation, and its determination to obtain the eight-hour day. The CGT's appeal had emphasized the need to avoid all incidents and to carry out the demonstration in an atmosphere of calm. The minoritaire United Trade Unions of the Seine countered by calling out its members for street demonstrations. On May 1, despite the fact that Clemenceau had explicitly forbidden demonstrations in the streets, thousands of workers turned out to express their disapproval of the government. There were numerous clashes between the demonstrators and the police and Garde Républicaine at the Place de la Concorde and on the Grands Boulevards. Paving stones were ripped from the streets and thrown at the police; barricades were raised; buses were overturned. Near the Gare de Lyon, Léon Jouhaux was beaten as he stooped to help a woman who had fallen. Paul Poncet, a Socialist deputy, was struck by a saber. At the Place de l'Opéra a nineteen-year-old electrician named Charles Lorne was shot and killed. That night and the next day the mood among the syndicalists was tense. Certain minoritaires raised the question of a general strike and—who could know?—perhaps even revolution. The provinces, however, had been quiet, and even some minoritaires feared that to call a general strike would be to walk into the trap set by the government. With the minoritaires divided and the situation uncertain, the voices of moderation triumphed; the CGT contented itself with a protest and the announcement that Jouhaux would resign from the Peace Conference, in which he had been participating as a technical adviser to the French delegation.[80]

The movement of unrest continued. In May there were 330 strikes with 215,200 participants, in June 590 strikes with 501,000 participants. On May 8, more than 100,000 persons attended the funeral of Charles Lorne, in a quiet and solemn protest against the government's brutality. On May 25 the working class made its annual pilgrimage to the Mur des Fédérés at Père Lachaise cemetery, to pay its respects to the Communards of 1871. L'Humanité noted that the workers shouted as their slogans: "Vive les marins de Sébastopol! Vive la Révolution Russe! Vive les soviets!"[81] At the beginning of June, the miners of the Pas-de-Calais and the metallurgical workers and mechanics of the Seine region went out on strike after a dispute with their employers over the application of the new eight-hour law. The strike movement gained momentum in early June, and employees of the métro and other transport workers walked out in support of the miners and metallurgists. From the beginning, the strike of the metalworkers took the form of a protest against Merrheim and the Federation's leadership, whom they accused of being "sold out to the bosses, to the government, to the Comité des Forges."[82] "Day after day, the committee rooms of the various syndicalist organizations were invaded by excited mobs, who treated the leaders to all manner of abuse and even, on one occasion, carried them off bodily to be exposed in public to the insults of an infuriated crowd."[83] As the movement progressed, it passed out of the hands of the original strike committee and into the hands of a spontaneous Action Committee, which attempted to abandon the original economic demands and call a general strike, and eventually to proclaim a revolution that would deliver the country into the hands of the CGT.[84] Excited by the march of events, Cachin compared the national mood to the one described by Taine in his Origins of Contemporary France. "For those of us who have the leisure," Cachin counseled, "no book could be more instructive."[85] La Vie Ouvrière was confident that France was on the eve of revolution: "Where are we going? Where are we going?" Monatte asked on June 11. "From discontent to discontent, from strike to strike, from a semi-economic and semi-political strike to a purely political strike. We're going straight to the bankruptcy of the bourgeoisie, that is, to the Revolution."[86]

The strike of the Parisian metalworkers ended in complete defeat; but the efforts of the revolutionary forces shifted to another terrain. At the end of April, the Soviet Commissar of Foreign Affairs, Chicherin, had appealed to the workers of the Allied countries to help put an end to intervention and the blockade: "It is none other than your rulers who are keeping civil war alive among us by giving help to the brutal counterrevolutionaries, and creating hunger and unemployment by the criminal blockade of Soviet Russia."[87] The minoritaires insisted that this appeal be answered with more than manifestos and newspaper articles. This pressure from within the CGT was paralleled in the case of the SFIO by the demand of the Italian Socialist Party that it give some kind of proof of its internationalism and sympathy for the Russian Revolution. The means chosen was a general strike in protest against intervention in Russia and Hungary. The leadership of both the CGT and the party assented to the proposal, though, one can surmise, without enthusiasm. Longuet assured the Italians of French support; and on July 14, the representatives of the French and Italian CGT's met and made concrete arrangements for a 24-hour strike to be held on July 21, 1919.[88] The Socialists supported the demonstration. The British Labour Party refused to commit itself to a strike; however, it agreed to hold demonstrations against intervention. In France, at the insistence of the majoritaires, the strike was directed toward both economic and political objectives: in favor of demobilization, an amnesty for all political prisoners, and the re-establishment of constitutional liberties, and against the high cost of living and intervention in Russia and Hungary.[89] There is no doubt that the motives of the majoritaires and the minoritaires were at variance. The feeling of Jouhaux and his supporters seems to have been that the strike would be a good opportunity to demonstrate the strength and determination of the working class. For the minoritaires, by contrast, it was the prelude to revolution, "the beginning," as Alfred Rosmer put it, "of an action that we must then carry through to the end."[90]

In France the strike did not take place. On the night of July 18, the leaders of the CGT were called in by Clemenceau, who promised them that if the movement was called off, the government would speed up demobilization, decree a partial amnesty, and take stronger steps to hold down the cost of living.[91] Consultation with the unions, meanwhile, had shown that the strike had little chance of success—or so the majoritaires said. At any rate, the very day before the movement was to have begun, the leadership of the CGT canceled it. The failure of the strike gave rise to bitter recriminations between majoritaires and minoritaires. The latter claimed that the majority had never accepted the strike wholeheartedly, and that in May and June it had allowed a revolutionary situation to slip by; the former replied that the wildcat strikes of May and June had demoralized the working class, and that the criticisms of the minoritaires had undercut the confederal leadership.[92] Both the Italians and the Bolsheviks blamed the French Socialist and syndicalist leaders for the failure of the strike.

The conciliators of the French Center, Zinoviev charged, were responsible for the collapse of the Hungarian Republic. From Hungary the President of the Comintern drew the lesson that "from now on, no concession to opportunism must be made. We must understand that old, official Social Democracy is our worst enemy."[93]

Minoritaires confronted majoritaires at the Congress of Lyon, held from September 15 to 21, 1919, the first postwar congress of the CGT. The realignment of factions that had begun at the Congress of Paris in July 1918 was now complete. Merrheim, Dumoulin, and Bourderon had rejoined Jouhaux; Monatte, Péricat, Monmousseau, and Joseph Tommasi were the new leaders of the minority. The leaders of the CGT had worked out a Minimum Program, which combined the immediate goal of reform with the long-term ideal of a society of free producers, the traditional goal of revolutionary syndicalism. "We must orient ourselves," read the Program, "toward positive action, and be capable not only of making street riots but of taking in hand the administration of production." "To carry out reforms, even partial ones, does not mean giving up our ideals; on the contrary, it means preparing for and sketching out in rough outline the new order toward which we are headed."[94] For the minoritaires this was heresy. They denounced the participation of the CGT in the reformist Amsterdam International of Labor Unions (founded in July 1919) and the Washington Conference; asserted that the majority had lost its faith in revolution; and accused the CGT leadership of having broken with the traditional principles of syndicalism by establishing new relationships with the government.[95]

What had happened, in effect, was that both the majority and the minority had revised their concept of syndicalism in the light of the War and the Russian Revolution. Both factions were now willing to cooperate with political parties. The majority often consulted with the leaders of the SFIO. The minority wanted to take the CGT into the Third International. Both factions had also changed their attitude toward the State and toward political action. The minoritaires wanted to follow the example of the Bolsheviks, and seize power in order to establish a dictatorship of the proletariat. The majoritaires wished to continue the social and economic relations with the State they had developed during the War. It was true that the minoritaires accepted Bolshevism because they saw reflected in it the image of their own anarcho-syndicalism. That illusion would be shattered with the increased knowledge of the party dictatorship that came in 1920. But even then, an important part of the original minoritaire coalition would remain true to its original enthusiasm for the Bolshevik Revolution and break for good with the old anarcho-syndicalism. For better or for worse, the revolutionary syndicalism of pre-1914 France was dead; and if the Minimum Program of the CGT resembled the Program of the party, it was because the syndicalist majority had moved closer to Jauressian reformism and away from the insurrectionism of the heroic age.

Where the majority and the minority differed most markedly, in fact, was in their definitions of revolution. The majoritaires, influenced perhaps by the engineers and civil servants who had recently joined the CGT, no longer believed that violent revolution was desirable. For Jouhaux the revolution was not "the catastrophic act that brings about the collapse of the system," but "*the slow process of evolution that little by little eats away at this system.*" The revolution, he said, must be constructive and not destructive; it must lead to greater production, not to famine; it must be economic and not political.[96] The minority, on the other hand, had accepted the Bolshevik concept of revolution as the seizure of power. Under the impact of the War and the Russian Revolution, the alliance between Proudhonist economic organization and Blanquist insurrectionism characteristic of prewar revolutionary syndicalism had thus broken down into its separate parts. The Proudhonist strand found its contemporary expression in the new reformism, the Blanquist tendency in Bolshevism. The principle of selection, however, that divided minoritaires from majoritaires was not by any means simply a matter of ideology or tradition. Blanquism, after all, is fundamentally a temperament and not an ideology; and it was the spectacle of the Bolshevik Revolution that forced the syndicalists to choose between "constructive syndicalism" and the "anarchy" of revolution. Men of revolutionary temperament, like Monatte and Monmousseau, went to Bolshevism. The more cautious and pessimistic, like Bourderon and Merrheim, turned to the reformism implicit in Pelloutier's stress on education and organization.

With the help of Merrheim and Bourderon, the majority was once more able to repulse the attack of the minoritaires. The policies of the leadership were approved by a vote of 1,393 to 588, with 42 abstentions. At Monatte's initiative the minority set out to organize its forces. In October a committee of 26 minority unions was formed; Monatte, Tommasi, Péricat, and Monmousseau were its leaders. This provisional committee later became the Comité Syndicaliste Révolutionnaire (CSR), which acted as a nucleus in the CGT around which the revolutionaries could gather and coordinate their plans.[97] The members of the CSR were handicapped, however, by the unity of the CGT leadership and also by divisions within their own ranks. In comparison with Loriot's group in the party, the syndicalist minority was still only in the first stages of growth at the end of 1919. In December 1919, Monatte confessed to the left-wing schoolteacher Louis Bouët that the syndicalist minority as yet "has difficulty sticking together."[98]

*Anarchists, Intellectuals, and Exiles*

The Socialists of the Left Wing worked through the Committee for the Third International, and tried to influence their party to join the new International. Loriot continually resisted the idea of a split, for as time went by his hopes of bringing the whole party into the Communist International rose. The syndicalist partisans of Moscow were more dispersed. The great majority belonged to the CSR; a specific faction was grouped around *La Vie Ouvrière*; in addition, a number of the most important militants of *La Vie Ouvrière* (for example, Monatte, Rosmer, and Monmousseau) also belonged to the Committee for the Third International. From these three positions, the group controlling *La Vie Ouvrière* worked for the adherence of the French unions to the Third International and the return of the CGT to its former principles. It was, however, typical of the confusion of 1919 and the divisions within the French working-class movement that there were still other groups on the Left, which accepted neither the revolutionary Socialism of Loriot nor the revolutionary syndicalism of Rosmer and Monatte. These minuscule clusters of militants objected particularly to the idea of trying to capture the old organizations, which they regarded as thoroughly rotten and beyond hope of repair. Their program was to split off immediately from the CGT and SFIO, to form a new Communist Party, and to make a revolution. After an exhaustive study of these groups, based on private archives, Annie Kriegel has christened them the "Ultra-Left," and has portrayed them as a strange child of syndicalist anarchism and Bolshevism.[99]

Raymond Péricat and several of his followers had taken part in the creation of the Committee for the Third International; Péricat, in fact, had been named one of its four secretaries. But on the very day the Committee was formed, he and his group, the Comité de la Défense Syndicaliste, had decided in favor of the creation of a Communist Party. At the beginning of June 1919, the new party, which officially called itself Parti Communiste, Section Française de l'Internationale, published a manifesto and a set of by-laws. The language of these documents was a curious mixture of traditional French anarchism and Russian Bolshevism. The State was to be overthrown by a general strike of the masses. All bourgeois laws were to be repealed and the civil service abolished. In the new Communist society, there would be no State, no set family structure, no enslavement of women. The free schools would bear as their motto the old anarchist rallying cry "Neither God nor master!" Pelloutier's association of free producers had now become soviets: "All for all, without frontiers, without rivalry between one province and another, one city and another, one set of fields and another; but a simple division into corporations administering themselves as the members of a confederation do, naming their representatives, 'their soviets,' which will have to maintain close contact with the soviets of other corporations, French and foreign, and which will meet in a central soviet."[100]

The manifesto spoke of "union and mutual aid, among the differing groups in the Third International, for the struggle against capitalism," and with true anarchist fervor opposed any kind of coercion or idolatry, their goal a "Regime

of liberty, freed from militarism, from religious dogmas, and from the prejudices of the Nation, with a single constraint—humanity."[101] Above all, the new
party would be anti-parliamentary. As a later appeal put it, parliamentarism
had created a caste of irresponsible and irremovable rulers; in the Soviet regime, democracy would be direct and workers would govern themselves: "The
idol of Authority will be reduced to dust; its cult and its priests will be treated
with universal hatred and scorn. Governments of the lie will be replaced by a
system of intelligent management of workers' interests by their temporary
delegates."[102]

The anarchists of the Parti Communiste had hoped that the agitation of the
spring and early summer of 1919 would end in revolution. At the end of June,
Péricat's paper, L'Internationale, had appealed to the French proletariat and
peasantry to form soviets with desperate urgency: "No more pantomimes, no
more speeches—deeds!"[103] But of course the revolution had not come, and the
Parti Communiste soon found itself in difficulties. Loriot flatly refused to
secede from the Socialist Party and merge his group with the Parti Communiste. The government forbade the meetings of Péricat's group, its correspondence was seized, and it was vilified in the press. Its paper, L'Internationale,
was in constant financial straits; finally, in September 1919, it disappeared.
With no revolution at hand, sectarian logic took hold, and the Parti Communiste's handful of militants fell to quarreling among themselves. In late December 1919 it split into two groups, a Fédération Communiste des Soviets and a
Parti Communiste.

The split of the "Ultra-Left" at the end of 1919 was an almost ludicrous example of the divisive tendencies in the French working-class movement. One
militant explained later that the difference between the Parti Communiste and
the Fédération Communiste des Soviets lay in the fact that the former worked
for the education of the proletarian elite, whereas the latter devoted itself to
the education of the proletarian masses.[104] But the fact was, of course, that
neither attained any influence on the masses, or, with very few exceptions,
on the elite.[105] The essence of both the Parti Communiste and the Fédération
Communiste des Soviets was their opposition to parliamentary Socialism, and
their mistaken belief that the Russian soviets fulfilled the anarchist and syndicalist dream of decentralization and autonomy. By the end of 1920, these
anarchist militants had discovered that they had nothing in common with the
Bolsheviks; and in 1921 and 1922 they became the bitterest enemies of the
Communist Party.

The Committee for the Third International, La Vie Ouvrière, the CSR, the
Parti Communiste, and the Fédération Communiste des Soviets were by no
means the only French groups attracted to Bolshevism in 1919. In October the
first issue of the review Clarté appeared under the editorship of Henri Barbusse, and announced as its program "We want to make a revolution in

men's minds."[106] *Clarté* opposed class privilege, and sought to substitute a human ideal for the patriotic ideal, a regime of reason and sincerity for a regime of money and hate, and international organization for national organization. Its international central committee included such well-known intellectuals as Georges Duhamel, Anatole France, Jules Romains, Vicente Blasco-Ibáñez, Upton Sinclair, H. G. Wells, and Stefan Zweig. *Clarté* was closely associated with the leftist veterans' organization, the Association Républicaine des Anciens Combattants (ARAC), and though neither was Bolshevik as such, both devoted themselves to the defense of the Russian Revolution and favored the cause of the Third International.[107] Raymond Lefebvre and Paul Vaillant-Couturier formed the link between *Clarté,* the ARAC, and the Committee for the Third International; Barbusse became increasingly sympathetic to Bolshevism, until he finally entered the French Communist Party in 1923.

Meanwhile, a French Communist group had been formed in Moscow in October 1918.[108] From October 1918 to March 1919, the group published a weekly newspaper called *La Troisième Internationale,* the goals of which were stated to be "the enlightenment of the workers of France, Belgium, and Switzerland about the Russian Revolution; agitation among French soldiers at the front in Russia; the organization of the French, Belgian, and Swiss workers living in Russia."[109] The French group in Moscow played almost no role in the origins of the French Communist Party, but it did produce a noted Communist martyr (Jeanne Labourbe), a famous Russian scholar (Pierre Pascal), two public figures who attained some notoriety in France for their Bolshevik sympathies (Henri Guilbeaux and Jacques Sadoul), and a future leader of French Communism (Suzanne Girault). Relations among revolutionaries in exile are always difficult, and the French group in Moscow was no exception. Victor Serge, who often went to its meetings in 1920 and 1921, called it a "little nest of vipers," and he remarks that "the quarrels, hatreds, denunciations, and counter-denunciations" of Guilbeaux and Sadoul demoralized the group, and ended up attracting the attention of the Cheka.[110]

### Two Swallows: Converts to Bolshevism

The creation of a Third International, the stylishness of Bolshevism, and the revolutionary atmosphere of April, May, and June 1919 all combined to attract new recruits to the Zimmerwaldian opposition. In August, Louise Saumoneau and Péricat resigned as secretaries of the Committee for the Third International and were replaced by Pierre Monatte and the anarchist Marcel Vergeat. Charles Rappoport, Raymond Lefebvre, Paul Vaillant-Couturier, Boris Souvarine, Albert Treint, Victor Méric, and the colorful poet-critic Georges Pioch strengthened the position of the Committee within the Socialist Party, and gave the Committee itself a more Socialist tinge. These men followed very different paths to Communism, and it would be a mistake to try to force them under any one rubric. We have already seen how Loriot, Monatte, and Rosmer made their way to Bolshevism (or what they thought of as Bolshevism) by a combination of internationalism, personal contacts, and ideological background. The process of conversion might be summed up in the following way: their internationalism alienated them from the existing labor organizations after the outbreak of the War; personal contact with men like Trotsky, Lozovsky, and Lenin introduced them to a new kind of Socialism; finally, their syndicalism prepared them to accept this new and revolutionary interpretation of Socialism. In the case of Péricat and Vergeat, enthusiasm for the Soviet regime was the result of a temporary misunderstanding of the relationship between Bolshevism and anarchism. Rappoport came to Bolshevism grudgingly, out of fidelity to the logic of his prewar Socialism—which, by the way, proves him to be one of the few Guesdists who took Guesde's views seriously in the decade before the War. Méric and Pioch were bourgeois journalists who inhabited that semi-anarchist, semi-intellectual world to the left of the party. They were drawn to Bolshevism partly because it was fashionable, partly out of ideological confusion, and partly because of what *Le Temps* would call "the outbidding at the basis of all revolutionary politics." All these men had a background of extremist political views; together their histories show how the Russian Revolution acted on the prewar ideological traditions that competed for the allegiance of the French Left Wing. Lefebvre and Souvarine represent a different case: they were younger men, what one might call the first and most ardent swallows of a new ideological summer. What fascinated them in Bolshevism was not what was venerable, but what was new. Their case bears study in some detail; for their development demonstrates the impact that the Russian Revolution was having on important elements of the younger generation, elements that Bolshevism would have to attract if it hoped to entrench itself in France.

A sensitive and religious young writer of conservative bourgeois origin,[k] Raymond Lefebvre had not joined the SFIO before the War because he had been repelled by the empty rhetoric and careerism so prevalent among its members.[111] As was typical of his generation, Lefebvre had passed through the mill of ideological enthusiasms: for a time a nationalist and an admirer of Charles Maurras, he had felt the attraction of Marc Sangnier's Christian Socialism, inquired into the doctrines of revolutionary syndicalism, and had finally fallen under the spell of Jaurès's internationalism. Each of these movements had a side that appealed to the young Lefebvre: the first, an emphasis on the need for French revival; the second, a call to Christian charity; the third, an activism and a tie with the masses (always cherished by intellectuals); the last, a paci-

[k] Lefebvre was 29 years old in 1919.

fism and a rejection of selfish nationalism. Taken separately, none satisfied him. The struggle against the War brought Lefebvre the cause he had been seeking. In the fall of 1914, he came into contact with the group of *La Vie Ouvrière*. That winter, the young intellectual was drafted and sent to the front, where he served with distinction as a stretcher-bearer. Wounded at Verdun, he returned home a different man than he had left. Where before there had been enthusiasm and flirtation, now there was passion and commitment. Most important, Lefebvre had become convinced that only revolution could save Europe from decadence. Back in Paris, he threw himself into a round of feverish activity, joining the Socialist Party, founding the Association Républicaine des Anciens Combattants with Paul Vaillant-Couturier and Georges Bruyère, and helping Henri Barbusse and other intellectuals of the Left to launch the review *Clarté*.[112]

At first nothing seemed to distinguish Lefebvre from other Socialists except, perhaps, his literary inclinations and the earnestness with which he pleaded his internationalist views. A supporter of the minority within the party, he was one of those new recruits responsible for pushing the SFIO leftward in 1917 and 1918. What little he knew about the Committee for Resumption he did not like. Loriot he found too sectarian, too doctrinaire, too Marxist.[113] Wilsonianism was more to his taste; and in April 1918 he joined the Coalition Républicaine, convinced that once the Germans were defeated, all good republicans should band together to make sure the reactionary French government respected and adhered to Wilson's formula of an honorable peace. All this is what one would expect from a Jauressian Socialist who had remained faithful to his internationalist ideas, and for whom the lines dividing Socialism from the bourgeois Left were vague. But Lefebvre was both more extreme and more open to outside influences than the minoritaires, like Longuet, Pressemane, and Faure, with whom he first associated. And in the summer of 1919, under the impact of French events and Bolshevik ideas, he made the transition to the Committee for the Third International. Lefebvre's conversion to Bolshevism was important; it was one of the first signs of the incipient crumbling of the Center. But most important for our purposes at the moment are those characteristics of the Third International and the Soviet regime which attracted a young French Socialist like Lefebvre. These he presented in a pamphlet which he wrote for *La Vie Ouvrière* in September 1919, entitled *L'Internationale des Soviets*.

Let no one say, wrote Lefebvre, that the difference between the two Internationals was a mere question of numbers or even of personalities, and not of principles. "In men, tactics, doctrine [the two Internationals] have nothing in common."[114] The Second was parliamentary, democratic, national. "The other, conceived in the terror of 1915, in the noise of autumn offensives, is the daughter of war. It has the ardent and sad vehemence of those who have known the field of battle, and who have learned European languages while listening to the cries of soldiers." This new International was animated by hatred for the parliamentarians who had betrayed it. It despised the democratic regime that permitted war profiteers to cloak their operations with the mantle of legality. And, above all, it hated war, the army, and the nation. "Finally," said Lefebvre, "it knows what one calls a Revolution, and not from the brochures of Guesde or the quartos of Kautsky." The Third International worked out its doctrines in the field. Its program was written amidst the cheers and boos of a soviet, without anyone's bothering to ask whether it was maximum or minimum. "Its leaders are the workers, the soldiers, and the peasants of Europe. It is a coalition of recovered victims, the revolutionary dictatorship. It exists."[115]

Lefebvre's pamphlet was permeated with a scorn for parliamentary democracy. "Democracy," he wrote, "is the uncertain regime of the popular will surprised every four years in its sleep."[116] The soviet, by contrast, insisted Lefebvre, with some imagination, was more democratic. The delegate to the soviet left his town for days, not for years, and hence he acted with "an honesty, a conscientiousness in the small things, a promptness, and a faithfulness to the popular will that the present democracies have rarely known, even at their peak—and, above all, a youngness of heart."[117] The people, wrote Lefebvre, were tired of worshiping at the feet of their deputies, who, almost without exception, had betrayed them at the beginning of the War, and would do so again given the opportunity. For Lefebvre the choice between the two Internationals was simple: "Soviet or Parliament? Democracy or Communism . . .? Elections or Revolution? Alliance with the bourgeois Left or with anarcho-syndicalism?"[118]

Boris Souvarine (born Boris Lifchitz) followed a slightly different path to Bolshevism. Only 25 years old in 1919, Souvarine had already established himself in the publications of the Left Wing as a journalist with a gift for the resounding phrase and as something of an expert on Russian affairs, a circumstance which he owed in part to his birth (he was born in Kiev and was a naturalized French citizen), but even more to the fact that he had taken advantage of his four years as a librarian in the French Army to learn the Russian language. Discharged in 1916, Souvarine, like Lefebvre, had joined the Socialist Party and associated with the minoritaires. In March 1917 he wrote the first analyses of the Russian Revolution for *Le Journal du Peuple*. Even in these early articles, Souvarine expressed a great admiration for the Russian Socialists, although he did not approve of Lenin. In June 1917 he pointed out that the disunity of the Russian Socialists had turned out to be a source of strength, whereas the unity of the French and the Germans had proved to be a source of weakness: " 'Make Socialists,' Vandervelde used to say, 'and not voters.' The French have made voters, the Russians have made Socialists. The first have made unity; the second have made a Revolution. *Ceci vaut bien cela.*"[119]

In 1917 the young Souvarine entered into a polemic with no less redoubtable an adversary than Lenin himself. Souvarine wrote an open letter "To our friends in Switzerland," in which he criticized Lenin for his attacks on Longuet and Trotsky. Souvarine defended the minoritaires and their position that national defense was compatible with Socialism. Lenin replied just before leaving for Petrograd to proclaim his April Theses. He explained patiently to Souvarine that it was necessary to distinguish between revolutionary and reactionary wars. The true Socialist was for national defense in a revolutionary war, but not in a reactionary war. Souvarine had objected to Lenin's idea of a new International because it would be handicapped by its numerical weakness. Lenin scoffed at the young Frenchman's timidity: "Numerical weakness? But since when have revolutionaries determined their policies according to whether they were in the minority or the majority? ... And how could people who, after two years of great world crisis, give diametrically opposed answers on the paramount question of the present-day tactics of the proletariat, in good conscience work side by side in the same party?"[120]

Souvarine was to echo these words many times; but it was not until 1919 that he emerged as one of the leading propagandists and enthusiasts of Bolshevism in France. In 1919 he wrote two pamphlets on the Bolsheviks, one entitled *Eloge des Bolcheviks,* the other *La Troisième Internationale.* In *Eloge des Bolcheviks,* Souvarine sketched the history of the Bolshevik Revolution, listed the accomplishments of the Communists in their two short years of rule, and emphasized the advantages of a Soviet regime over parliamentary democracy. In his pamphlet on the Third International, he dwelt on the betrayal of the leaders of the Second International. They had done more than merely cast overboard all traces of Socialism, wrote Souvarine: *"They have passed over to the camp of our class enemies."*[121] At this time Souvarine could still appreciate the minoritaires, whom he described as "rather hesitant Socialists, obsessed with noble scruples and having an imperfect understanding of the duties of a Socialist."[122] The great weakness of the Second International, Souvarine insisted, had been its reliance on legal, parliamentary methods; it made the ballot and parliament the essential weapons of the proletariat, relegating mass action to a secondary position. Actually, election campaigns and parliamentary debates should only be occasions for spreading Socialist ideas.[123] What he was saying, of course, was only a restatement of what Guesde had said in 1880. It is a measure of the evolution of French Socialism, as well as of French democracy, that in 1919 it was necessary to learn this lesson from Russian prophets.

Lefebvre and Souvarine represented a precious contribution to the forces of the Bolshevist Left Wing. To the orthodoxy of Loriot, the dedication of Rosmer, the working-class contacts of Monatte, and the wit and erudition of Rappoport, they added their youth, their energy, and the brilliance of their pens. What did these gifted young bourgeois see in Bolshevism? Not so much the resurrection of old working-class ideologies, in which they had no real stake, as something radically new: an activist faith that would never be satisfied with half-measures, half-reforms, or half-revolutions; a Socialism that would emphasize principles rather than numbers; a new and intriguing kind of democracy, in which parliaments would be replaced by soviets and deputies by workers; an international league of revolutionaries who would not hesitate to use violence to create the kind of society in which there would be no more violence; and perhaps (who could deny it?) the opportunity to play in France the roles that Lenin and Trotsky had played in Russia.

### TWO DISAPPOINTMENTS

Tossed about on this sea of unrest and ideological turbulence, the Socialist Center tried to steer a course between the extremes of both Left and Right, between the Bolshevism of Loriot and the anti-Bolshevism of Renaudel. However, the task of moderation was made increasingly difficult by the radical mood produced by the Bolshevik Revolution and the hostility of the French government to Socialist proposals for social, economic, and political reforms. The effect of the Bolshevik Revolution on the French political spectrum was such that the Right moved further right, the Left moved further left, and the moderates temporarily joined the Right to protect the established social order against the contagion of Bolshevism, which all right-minded men were united in regarding as an invention of German malevolence, designed especially to plague France.[124] Almost despite themselves, the leaders of the Socialist Center were forced leftward as the atmosphere of class tension heightened. In July, Cachin, always an accurate barometer of the mood of the Center, criticized the inaction of the International Socialist Bureau. "In the French section," he wrote, "complaints are multiplying." And in August, Faure railed against the members of the Permanent Commission of the Second International, meeting in Lucerne, for their attacks on the Bolsheviks. "At the present time, to palaver about Democracy in such a way as to contrast it to the policies of the Russian and Hungarian revolutions is to act wrongly; it's to make us the moral and political accomplices of world reaction, which is at war with the working class of Russia and Hungary."[125]

Meanwhile, in May, the provisions of the Versailles Peace Treaty had become known. The Socialists, to an incredible degree, had put their faith in the statesmanship and high principles of President Wilson. Wilsonianism had been the chief means by which the Socialist leaders had bridged "the chasm between their general principles and the reality of war."[126] Wilson's peace proposals, moreover, had helped soften the conflicts within the SFIO and the CGT, and had strengthened the Center at the expense of both extremes. The increasing estrangement of the working-class organizations from their own government had only increased their commitment to Wilsonianism. And it can be said without exaggeration that on the international level, the program of the SFIO's majority was nothing but Wilson's honorable peace and the League of Nations dressed up in Socialist language.

When the details of the Peace Treaty were made public, the disappointment of the Socialists and syndicalists was bitter. "What a cruel disillusionment for the peoples of the world!" wrote Paul Mistral. "At the same time, what a lesson! In order to lead us to the worst of sacrifices, they spoke of 'la Guerre du Droit' and of a peace of justice and disarmament. The peace treaty drawn up by the Entente is the negation of everything that we had hoped for."[127] Renoult pointed out that Wilson's defeat had shown that bourgeois idealism, no matter how sincere, would always prove incapable of solving the problems confronting the world.[128] The outcry of the moderates was most poignant. "We have been repudiated," Léon Blum wrote on July 19, 1919. "The tacit pact that dictated all our actions for five years has been broken. . . . And, despite the claims of conscience, one almost comes to doubt that we chose rightly among our duties."[129]

Since the elections had been postponed until November 1919, a new Socialist congress met in Paris from September 11 to 14 to reconsider the party's electoral program and debate its tactics. The question of "general policy" was not discussed explicitly, and there was no vote on adherence to the Third International. Nevertheless, these issues were at the heart of the debates. The month before, in response to an article by Renaudel on the crisis in the party, Loriot had reiterated that before the party could agree on a program of action, it must choose either for or against Bolshevism, either for or against the proletarian revolution, either for or against the Third International.[130] Renaudel, on the other hand, had made it clear that he would leave the party rather than become a member of the Third International.[131] The great concern of the leaders of the Center was to preserve the unity of the party and present a united front at the elections. During the weeks preceding the congress, the pages of *L'Humanité* and *Le Populaire* had been filled with articles on the crisis in the party's ranks. On the day of the congress's opening, Frossard warned that the party would pay dearly if it failed to resolve its differences: "The working class would leave us to our Byzantinism, and there would be good days ahead for the mob of exploiters."[132]

The congress was turbulent. On the third day of the assembly, wrote Dunois, "The awe-inspiring deadly word of schism already seemed to run through the heated, stifling hall."[133] The Right objected to running on a platform of solidarity with the Russian Revolution. The Left and Center insisted. The Left, moreover, attempted to pass a motion purging the 11 deputies who had twice voted for war credits after the Armistice had been signed and who had abstained in the vote on the Peace Treaty. Finally a compromise was reached. The April electoral program was reapproved by a large majority and the congress reprimanded, but did not expel, the 11 controversial deputies.

The congress agreed almost unanimously that in the coming elections it would compete as the party of revolution and make no electoral alliances of any kind. Commenting on the congress the next day, Paul Faure admitted that principles had been sacrificed to unity, and hurried to reassure the Left that although there had been no mention of the Russian Revolution in the final resolutions, it continued to be a major concern of his faction. "To defend Lenin," he wrote, "is more honorable than to be identified with the ignoble business of international reaction, in which our bourgeoisie plays a leading role."[134] But the Left emerged from the congress embittered, and skeptical of the good faith of the Center. Alexandre Blanc observed that the split of the party was now a fact, and that this would appear dramatically during the electoral campaign. "Wouldn't a good divorce be better than a bad marriage?" he asked.[135]

The Socialist leaders approached the elections of November 1919 with great hopes, estimating that at the very least they would elect a group of deputies large enough to put through a program of bold social and economic legislation.[136] They had reason to hope, on the basis of the increase in their membership and the response to their demonstrations, that there had been an important shift in public opinion toward Socialism and its policies. It turned out that they had badly misinterpreted the mood of the nation. The majority of the French had watched the strikes and demonstrations of the spring and summer of 1919 with increasing concern. Fed on a daily diet of stories of atrocities and misery in Russia, the French middle classes were easily convinced that the specter of Bolshevism hung over France itself, and that any concession to the working class would be class suicide. After all, had it not been concessions to the Social Democrats that had brought the advent of Bolshevism in Russia in 1917? Many bourgeois thought so.[137] It was perhaps *Le Temps* which best summed up the attitude toward Bolshevism of judicious Frenchmen: "The danger of Bolshevism in France is real. One shouldn't inflate it: that would be an exaggeration. One shouldn't ignore it: that would be blindness. One shouldn't make light of it: that would be gullibility. Against this real peril, the country's healthy forces must unite."[138]

The campaign was carefully planned. Running against the Socialists was the Bloc National, which banded together Republicans of all shades. The purpose of the Bloc National was to continue the Sacred Union forged by the War, to enforce the Treaty of Versailles, to reconcile the Catholics to the Republic, and, most important for the moment, to defend "civilization against Bolshevism, which is only one form of the German peril and the very negation of all social progress."[139] Clemenceau set the tone for the election in a speech at Strasbourg on November 3, when he declared that "Between them [the Bolshevists] and us, it's a question of force."[140] So that no Frenchman could underestimate the danger that faced him, Ernest Billet, one of the backers of the

Bloc National, covered the walls of France with a poster portraying a hairy and voracious Bolshevik with a knife between his teeth.

The Socialists, by contrast, conducted a quite restrained campaign, in which they followed closely the program and the regulations adopted at their last two congresses. In general, the federations observed discipline and avoided electoral alliances with other progressive Republicans of the Left.[141] The great majority of the provincial federations protested against the accusation of extremism and violence and made no mention of Bolshevism or the Russian Revolution. The Socialist campaign was at its most radical in the Department of the Seine. The militants of the third district of the Seine ran at the head of their list Jacques Sadoul, who had been sentenced to death by the government for deserting to the Bolsheviks while on a military mission to Russia.[1] *L'Humanité* used the occasion offered by the anniversary of the Bolshevik coup d'état on November 7 to proclaim the party's solidarity with the Soviet regime. But even so, it should be noted that the furthest the Socialist candidates would go was to suggest that they were supporters of the Russian Revolution and against French intervention in Russia. They never for a moment hinted that they would like to import Bolshevism into France, and they based their support of the Russian Revolution on the right of all peoples to self-determination.[142] The tone of the Socialist campaign was too pro-Bolshevik for the moderates; the attitude toward Bolshevism was too detached and noncommittal for the extreme Left. This compromise was the price of unity, for in Paris radicals like Lefebvre and Vaillant-Couturier ran side by side with moderates like Sembat.

The Parisian electorate did not enter into these fine distinctions: it seems to have voted for or against the Russian Revolution.[143] A strike of the printers' union deprived Paris of newspapers during the week before the elections, and this may have hurt the Socialists, who appear to have conducted their campaign in disorganization. At any rate, the defeat of the Socialists was predetermined by their own decision not to enter into any electoral alliances, for the new electoral system, a modified form of proportional representation, favored combinations. Though the Socialists received 23 per cent of the total vote (1,728,000), they succeeded in electing only 11.1 per cent of the deputies (68).[144] They lost 33 seats in old France alone, along with all the seats previously held by the German Social Democrats in Alsace. Guesde, Cachin, Sembat, Bracke, Albert Thomas, and Varenne were re-elected, but several of the minoritaires' leading spokesmen—Barabant, Albert Bedouce, Brizon, Longuet, and Raffin-Dugens—failed to hold their seats. Among the newly elected Socialist deputies were Léon Blum, Paul Vaillant-Couturier, Joseph Paul-Boncour, Pierre Dormoy, and René Nicod.

---

[1] Sadoul was sentenced *in absentia* on November 8, 1919—just in time for the elections.

The results of the elections only further exacerbated the crisis that already threatened the unity of the party. Frossard, the new General Secretary, pointed out with pride that the party had gained at least 218,426 votes since 1914, not counting Alsace-Lorraine, but he did not deny that the results were disappointing, especially since the party had presented candidates in many districts in which there had been no Socialist candidates in 1914.[145] Since the electoral campaign had been carried out on the basis of a compromise between Right and Left, each extreme could blame the defeat on the other. Renaudel insisted that the party had done so poorly because it had associated itself with the Russian Revolution.[146] The Left asserted the contrary. But, most important of all, the position of the Center was subjected to further strains. The Bolshevik critique of parliamentary democracy now seemed justified: the techniques of universal suffrage appeared to have been used to cheat the party of its due. Even for moderates, the lesson of the elections seemed to be that moderation was impossible.[147]

### THE BIRTH OF RECONSTRUCTION

The publication of the Peace Treaty and the elections cut the ground out from under those Socialists who had attempted to continue the Jauressian tradition of belief in revolution through democracy. The development of the international situation made it clear that the Second International was a structure damaged beyond repair. By December 1919 the antagonism between the leaders of the Second and the Third Internationals had reached a pitch that allowed for no retreat, and the parties of international Socialism were drawn irresistibly to one side or the other. The Third International had definitely gained the allegiance of the Italian Socialist Party, the Swedish Left Socialists, the Norwegian Labor Party, and the British Socialist Party. It had temporarily lost the Swiss, who reversed their earlier decision in favor of adherence, and who now put forward a proposal to reconstruct the Second International on a more revolutionary basis. The British Labour Party, the German Majority Socialists, the Belgian Socialist Party, and the majority of the Scandinavian parties were firmly behind the Second International. The Austrian and American Socialist parties were as yet undecided.[148] For the French majority, the decisive turn came when the German Independents (USPD), the party closest to their own views, voted at their Leipzig congress to leave the Second International. While rejecting immediate membership in the Comintern, the USPD declared that "an effective proletarian International should be formed by uniting our party with the Third International and with social-revolutionary parties of other countries."[149]

The decision of the German Independents had immediate repercussions on the attitude of the French Center. The leaders of the Center were now forced to give up their hope of reviving the Second International, especially since their

followers were demanding a more definite orientation to the Left.[m] Longuet
and his friends, however, continued to resist the attraction of the Third International. They fastened onto the idea, thrown out by the Swiss, of "reconstructing" the old International on a more revolutionary basis. On December
23, Faure considered the decision of the London commission to postpone the
Geneva conference of the Second International until July and termed it the
"death sentence of the Second International." He suggested that the Swiss party
call a meeting of all the parties that either belonged to the Third International,
had left the Second without having joined the Third, or belonged to the Second
International but wanted to reconstitute the unity of the Left.[150] On December
28, the leaders of the Center formed a group for the purpose of reconstructing
the International. Its members included Longuet, Faure, Frossard, Renoult,
Dunois, Mayéras, Morizet, Tommasi, Verfeuil, Paul Louis, and Louis Sellier.
And the following day, Faure announced the Center's new position on the
Third International. The Center, he said, now wanted to join the Third International; but it wanted to do so on its own terms, without giving up any of
its beliefs or traditions, and without breaking the unity of the party.[151]

Another National Congress was called for the end of February, to reconsider
the question of the International. The pages of *L'Humanité, Le Populaire,* and
*Le Journal du Peuple* were opened to the debate over the international orientation of the party. The Right had taken hope in the disintegration of the Center
under the impact of the Bolshevik Revolution. Its leaders pointed to the excesses of the Russian Revolution and called for unity: "Let us not lose our heads
every time a backward people quickens its progress toward stages that others
have left behind," wrote Adrien Marquet.[152] The Left viewed the Center's new
position suspiciously. Boris Souvarine rejoiced at the readiness of the Center to
leave the Second International in order to join the Third. But he went on to
ask why did the Reconstructors feel they had to wait, why did they engage in
all these maneuvers? Souvarine insisted that anyone who was not for the Third
International was against it; and he explained that the Left opposed the Reconstructors because they sought to avoid the necessary changes in the party and
"to build with materials of inferior quality."[153]

Longuet now found himself under constant attack from the Left. And the

[m] About this time Longuet wrote Camille Huysmans, explaining the reason for the new
policy of the French Center: "I must confess that ever since I returned from London I've
done my best to persuade our friends to stay with the idea of an entente among the left-
wing parties of the Second International—the people who have left it and those elements
in the Third International who want to get together—leaving in abeyance for the time
being the question of resigning from the Second. But I have come to realize that this solution would not have satisfied many of our friends who might have joined the supporters
of immediate adherence to the Third International, who have been much in evidence since
the decision of the USPD at Leipzig." Quoted from Annie Kriegel, *Aux origines du Communisme français, 1914–1920* (1964), I, 341.

barbs of the French Bolshevists took on added sting when it became clear that they had the full support of the Russians. In September 1919, Trotsky addressed a letter to Loriot, Monatte, Rosmer, and Péricat reminding them that there was no essential difference between Longuet and Renaudel.[154] The implication was that Longuet was a counterrevolutionary. On January 9, 1920, *La Vie Ouvrière* published a letter from Lenin to Loriot, in which the Bolshevik leader referred to Longuet as a "refined opportunist" and blamed him for the failure of the strike of July 21. Lenin warned Loriot that the French Communists would have to endure a long struggle with Socialist politicians of Longuet's type, and he encouraged them to be firm. "The more forceful and firm the Communists' attitude," he wrote, "the quicker will be their complete victory."[155] Longuet, outraged and hurt, recalled his defense of the Russian Revolution "when there were more blows to receive than compliments to reap," and accused Loriot and his friends of the Left Wing of misinforming the Bolsheviks "in a secret correspondence, a clandestine diplomacy with Moscow."[156] The same day that Lenin's letter appeared, Longuet wrote to Moscow to assure Lenin that he did not hold him responsible for his language because he realized it had been based on inadequate information about French affairs. Longuet simply could not accept the fact that for Lenin and Trotsky he was a counterrevolutionary. Ask Keremer (Viktor Taratuta) or Litvinov, he wrote Lenin, and they will set you straight. After all that *Le Populaire* has done for the Russian Revolution, he concluded, "it is really painful to see you not only favoring over us people who have never done anything useful for you, but in addition helping them in their feeble and futile campaigns."[157]

### THE CONGRESS OF STRASBOURG

The National Congress of the SFIO met at the Palais des Fêtes in Strasbourg from February 25 to 29, 1920. Ironically, it was the same hall in which Clemenceau had scourged Bolshevism just a few months before. To add to the drama of the setting, a general strike of railroad workers broke out on the day the congress opened. There were three motions before the congress: that of the Committee for the Reconstruction of the International, which demanded that the party leave the Second International and enter into negotiations with the German Independents for the reconstruction with the Bolsheviks of a new International; the motion of the *Vie Socialiste* group, the former majoritaires, which reiterated the party's allegiance to the Second International and condemned Bolshevism; and that of the Committee for the Third International, which called for immediate adherence to the Third International, the overthrow of the capitalist State, and its replacement by a proletarian government, in which soviets would replace parliament.[158] The meetings of the Federation of the Seine, at which the Loriot motion in favor of immediate adherence had been passed by a large majority, seemed to indicate that the congress might follow suit." But Loriot himself did not think that the Left would be able to summon up a majority for its motion at Strasbourg.[159]

Strasbourg was the first congress at which the Left was able to provide real opposition to the Center and challenge its leadership of the party. It was in a sense the second stage of the radicalization that had begun with the manifesto of the Haute-Vienne. The Right now hid conveniently behind the coattails of the Center, and in the end the majoritaires of *La Vie Socialiste* voted for the Reconstructors' motion, even though they had no intention of associating with Bolsheviks in a new revolutionary International. Two questions ran through all the debates: that of national defense, which looked back to the conduct of the Socialists, both majoritaires and minoritaires, during the War; and the challenge of the Third International, which looked forward to the future policies of the party.

The discussion of these questions revealed the growing gap between the Center and the Left. The leaders of the former minority were again and again criticized by provincial delegates for their timidity during the War.[160] Paul Faure, addressing the partisans of the Third International, remarked that "with every word you speak, there is a deeper abyss between you and us."[161] Raymond Lefebvre referred explicitly to this crisis of understanding when, during an impassioned speech, he cried to Renaudel: "Vous êtes trop bien portant pour comprendre la France mutilée."[162] The clash between the Center and the Left also took the form of a disagreement over the possibilities for revolution in France. The Center insisted that the situation was not revolutionary, and that the Left represented an updated form of Hervéism. The Left replied that revolution could not be predicted, and that it was necessary to be prepared for it at all times.[163] The difference was much the same as in the CGT. The Center feared a revolution of bloodshed and anarchy; the Left was prepared to follow the Bolsheviks and ride out the whirlwind of revolution. Later in the year, the French Communists would applaud Trotsky's argument in *Terror and Communism* that just as "one learns to ride on horse-back only when sitting on the horse," so one learns how to make a revolution only after having seized State power.[164] Lefebvre and his friends were determined not to allow the horse of revolution to slip by when the opportunity came.

Perhaps the most dramatic moment of the Congress came when Renaudel read excerpts from Lenin's works, and presented his doctrine of revolutionary defeatism: "I demand," Renaudel said, "that regardless of the faction to which he belongs, the French Socialist who is ready to say that we should have contributed to the defeat of France stand! (*Très bien! Applause. Noise.*)" There was a long moment of silence. Raffin-Dugens interjected that for the doctrine to apply it was necessary to have defeat on both sides. Then, suddenly, Loriot

---

" The vote was 9,930 for Loriot, 5,988 for Faure, and 616 for Renaudel.

rose from his bench: "Je me lève, moi. (*Applause on the Left.*) For my part, I accept this thesis in its entirety, and if during the War we hesitated to make it ours, it was not because we were against defeat, but because we thought that the blood of twenty million workers was too high a price to pay for the proletarian revolution that would inevitably have ensued! (*Applause.*)"[165] At these words, according to Frossard, "a long tremor of amazement ran through the assembly."[166]

Despite the liveliness of the debate, the Congress of Strasbourg was chiefly characterized by its refusal to pronounce definitively on either the past or the future. The orators of the Center still managed to dominate the congress and impose their point of view. The question of national defense was not resolved. The furthest the congress would go was to proclaim that the parties interested in reconstructing the International "will, in the first place, have to condemn, as the International at Moscow has done, collaboration of any kind with the bourgeoisie, and especially the ministerial coalitions that operated in most European countries during the War."[167] There were no purges, and the Center repeatedly objected to Moscow's demand for hostages. The attitude toward the Third International was one of enthusiasm. Frossard assured the party in his report on the international situation that the prospects for an international conference of Reconstructors were excellent. Paul Faure declared, in what was probably the most applauded speech of the congress, that the Center did not want to be separated from the Bolsheviks and the German Independents. But, he added, for the benefit of the Committee for the Third International, neither did they intend to engage in a policy of adventure: "For the Revolution, and for the preparation of the Revolution, yes; but don't count on us for an abortive adventure in which the sacred blood of the working class would flow once more."[168]

The party still found this language acceptable. The congress voted by a huge majority to follow the German Independents and leave the Second International, while rejecting the Loriot motion for immediate adherence in favor of Longuet's resolution of reconstruction by a margin of 3,000 to 1,621. It was impossible, read Longuet's motion, to judge in detail or with finality all the work and deeds of the Russian Revolution. "But the French Socialist Party, the ally, it goes without saying, of all movements to emancipate the proletariat, does not consider any of the fundamental declarations of the Moscow International in contradiction with the essential principles of Socialism."[169] The CAP was instructed to enter into negotiations with the Third International, the German Independents, and the Swiss and Italian Socialist parties, in order to prepare a conference for a final regrouping of "all those parties resolved to continue to act on the basis of the traditional principles of Socialism."[170]

The delegates returned to Paris in a special train authorized by the strike committee of Strasbourg and draped with red flags. Their spirits were high.

However, to the objective observer it was clear that the decisions at Strasbourg had merely put off the final question that had been plaguing the French party for a year now: whether or not to go to Moscow, whether or not to accept the Bolshevik interpretation of Socialism. The Left was not displeased by the results of the congress. They well understood the spirit in which the Reconstructors' motion had been passed.[171] As for the Centrists, they assumed an optimism in public that they could hardly feel in private, and suggested that they would be able to get along better with the Russians than with their French followers. "I'm not at all sure that Lenin is with the most Leninist members of the French party," wrote Faure. "We saw that in Italy. The disciples are sometimes the worst enemies of the apostle."[172] But the most interesting and incisive analysis of the congress was made by a visiting Dutch Communist, Henrietta Roland-Holst. Roland-Holst observed that the development of the Communist group within the Left was still in its infancy. What united the various currents of the Left was less their agreement on a positive strategy for the future than their condemnation of the policies of the past, and their hatred for the social-patriots—Sembat, Thomas, Renaudel, Bracke, and their friends. It was this negative unity which underlay the growing strength of the Left. Roland-Holst's comment anticipated the conflicts that would plague the anomalous coalition of the Left during the first few years of the French Communist Party.

Chapter five

# The French Go to Moscow

Sie sind der Meinung, diese Herrschaften aus
dem Lager der Reformisten, sie kommen in die
Kommunistischen Internationale, wie man in ein
Gasthaus kommt.
—*Grigorii Zinoviev, at the Second World
Congress of the Comintern*

During 1919 the French working class had floundered, striking out blindly
against the social order, with ferocity but without direction. The French bourgeoisie, by contrast, seemed for a moment to have lost its nerve. By 1920 the
working-class movement had found revolutionary leaders, but the revolutionary wave had reached its peak everywhere in Europe and had begun to
recede. In France the forces of social conservation had caught their breath and
were ready to pass to the counterattack. The result was a violent clash between
the working class and the State, which ended in the rout of the CGT and the
discrediting of the concept of spontaneous revolution. It was in the backwash
of this defeat that the French Socialist Party went to Moscow.

### THE LEFT WING AFTER STRASBOURG

In the working-class movement, the coming of the new year was marked by
the increasing strength and confidence of the Left Wing. During 1919 there
had been great pressure within the Committee for the Third International to
leave the old organizations and form a new, truly Communist party, which
would immediately proclaim its adherence to the Third International. As late
as January 1920, Souvarine called upon Socialists, syndicalists, and anarchists
"to burn the old labels" and develop a new doctrine that would satisfy all revolutionaries.[1] Such a regrouping of the Left Wing assumed that the traditional
organizations and ideologies were so corrupted by the experience of the War
that they were beyond all hope of renovation. Loriot and Monatte had always
opposed this policy of abandonment. What happened at Strasbourg proved
them right. Both the Committee and the CSR were growing; both were extending their influence into the provinces. Within a matter of months, the

Communists would have a majority in the SFIO. Before long the minoritaires would control the CGT. Why should the Left Wing renounce the patrimony that would soon be theirs?[2]

These considerations were reflected in the reorganization of the Committee carried out in March 1920. The anarchists Péricat, Henri Sirolle, and Emile Chauvelon were replaced. Louise Saumoneau, upset by the insulting tone the polemics against Longuet were taking, left the Committee and moved toward the Reconstructors. Charles Rappoport and Boris Souvarine were elected to the Executive Commission. Loriot became the General Secretary in charge of the Committee; Monatte and Souvarine were appointed his assistants, the former entrusted with domestic affairs, the latter with international communications. Despite the presence of Monatte and Rosmer, the Committee began to take on an overwhelmingly Socialist character.

For the first time, reliable communications with the Bolsheviks were established. Up to the spring of 1920, the French, like the Germans and Italians, had received only intermittent, isolated messages from the Bolsheviks.[3] Lenin had managed to transmit his letter to Loriot; Trotsky had gotten through a letter to Monatte concerning Longuet; Zinoviev had sent a message to the Socialist Party for the Congress of Strasbourg; Guilbeaux had addressed a radiogram to Loriot at the end of February. But these were regarded as personal communications, and not in any sense as directives.[4] The few attempts at more direct contacts had failed. Manuilsky, temporarily in France under the pretext of carrying out a Red Cross mission for the repatriation of prisoners of war, had been forced to leave the country before he could enter into contact with the Committee.[5] No French delegate had attended the conference of the Third International held in Amsterdam on February 3–9, 1920. The French Communists had as yet received no subsidies from Moscow.

All this changed after Strasbourg. Souvarine established contact with the Bolsheviks through the West European Bureau in Berlin, through the Secretariat in Amsterdam, through Switzerland, and perhaps through Copenhagen, where Litvinov was then residing.[6] Henrietta Roland-Holst was able to attend the Congress of Strasbourg as an observer and unofficial representative of the Comintern, although she did not have the awesome prestige that later Bolshevik delegates would have. Soon thereafter, a Russian agent by the name of Diogott entered France illegally from Italy.[a] With the aid of subsidies fur-

[a] Vladimir Diogott, V "svobodnom" podpole (Vospominaniya o podpolnoi rabote za granitsei v 1919–1921 godakh) (Moscow, 1923), pp. 32–46. Diogott had several interesting comments to make on the leaders of the French Left Wing. Almost immediately upon arriving in Paris, the Bolshevik agent had a rendezvous with Lefebvre at the department store "Aux Magasins du Louvre." Diogott was very impressed by Lefebvre and noted that he looked more like a Russian nihilist than a French intellectual. Lefebvre met the Russian with open arms. "I am happy to see the first representative of the Russian Revolution," he is supposed to have said. "The working class of France feels and acknowledges its guilt

nished by Diogott, Souvarine was able to establish the *Bulletin Communiste,* a weekly theoretical journal that was to act as the voice of the Communist faction in the Socialist Party.[7] For the first time, the writings of the Bolsheviks on such questions as parliamentarism, the trade unions, and the role of the party became available to the militants of the French working-class movement. Preparations were made to send a delegation of French Communists to the Second World Congress of the Comintern.

Prospects for victory, reorganization, and contacts with the Bolsheviks brought more demands for revolutionary purity, not fewer. After Strasbourg the polemics of the Communists against the leaders of the Center lost all pretense of comradeship. Loriot thanked Faure and Pressemane for having shown by their speeches at the congress that they had nothing in common with the Third International. He now openly classed them with the party's Right, a step he had always hesitated to take.[8] The change was most dramatic in the case of those Socialists who had formerly been bound to the minority by friendship and the common struggle against the social-patriots. In the summer of 1919, Raymond Lefebvre had dedicated his pamphlet on *L'Internationale des Soviets* to Longuet and Délépine. But toward the end of April 1920, he complained of the maneuvers and hesitations of the Reconstructors, and concluded sadly that "everything and every day makes us fear that those who stood with us in the fight against the War during the War no longer agree with us on the methods, nor even completely on the objectives, of the new war."[9] Souvarine followed very much the same line of development. An early contributor to *Le Populaire,* he had written Lenin in 1917 to defend the *minoritaires* against what he felt were unjustified attacks. As late as September 1919, he saw fit to praise a speech by Longuet before the Chamber that Trotsky later condemned as the height of opportunism.[10] Under the influence of the Russian Revolution, however, Souvarine's admiration for the leaders of the Center gave way to scorn. After Strasbourg he wrote an article for a Swiss Communist journal in which he sought to demonstrate that there was no real difference between Faure and Renaudel. "The Right and the Center inevitably had to merge," he concluded, "for their theories are identical."[11] Loriot had been saying nothing else since 1916; but Souvarine, with the fervor of the convert, announced these truths as if he had discovered them. At any rate, for him as for Loriot and Lefebvre, the

---

before the Russian Revolution." Lefebvre assured Diogott that the French proletariat would do its duty (p. 32). The young Frenchman took the Russian to Victor Méric's house, where he met other Communists and discussed the overthrow of the French government in the immunity the Third Republic extended to its parliamentary representatives. To a Bolshevik like Diogott, these French Communists seemed like mere children when it came to conspiratorial work (p. 33). The Russian came away convinced that Loriot could no longer lead the French Communists. His nervousness, Diogott wrote, showed in every gesture (p. 34).

lines defining the party had to be redrawn in such a way that they excluded the Blums, the Faures, and even the Longuets; if carried out, this program would mean a Socialist Party oriented further to the Left than any France had seen since the early days of Guesde's Parti Ouvrier Français.

### THE "CIVIC BATTLE OF THE MARNE"

1920 began with the future of the French economy and of French society still in doubt. As Pierre Monatte pointed out, the debts incurred during the War, both financial and moral, had yet to be settled.[12] The French bourgeoisie, for its part, showed no desire to acknowledge either. Millerand, who formed a new government at the end of January 1920, called upon the nation to "produce more, consume less." "We owe the country, which expects its governors to be worthy of it, the example of a freely granted and firmly practiced discipline."[13] The leaders of the CGT understood the need for France to go to work; and with their new ambitions and their new sense of responsibility for an economy that they now felt sure of inheriting, they were ready to cooperate in the task of social reconstruction. However, they in turn had to deal with an opposition on their Left that was becoming increasingly vociferous; and their dilemma was made all the more difficult because they had nothing to show for their policy of class collaboration except promises and a government more reactionary than the one it had replaced. The minoritaires, meanwhile, continued to believe in the immediacy of revolution. And the complexity of the situation was such that their support within the organization grew as the possibilities for successful revolutionary action receded.[14] An unbending bourgeoisie, a syndicalist movement divided in its objectives, a vanishing revolutionary situation—this was the backdrop for the great wave of strikes which shook France in the spring of 1920 and which finally made it clear that France was not going to follow the example of Russia, Hungary, or even Germany.

The first round of conflict came in February.[15] The protagonist was the burgeoning Railroad Workers' Federation, which had more than doubled in size since 1918 and which was rent within by a fierce battle between majoritaires and minoritaires. On February 19, a railroad worker on the minoritaire Paris-Lyon-Marseille (PLM) line, Companaud, was laid off for 48 hours for absenting himself without permission to attend a meeting of his union's administrative council. The incident itself was minor; but a successful strike in January at Périgueux encouraged the union to press for a confrontation with the company. The company was not averse to a test; it was alarmed at the stepped-up tempo of workers' demands and hoped to discredit the union. An attempt at mediation by the government was unsuccessful, and a strike was called on February 23. The PLM company responded with a lockout. The strike, which was spontaneous, spread rapidly to the rest of the PLM line, and on February 28 a general railway strike was called. Though convinced that the time for such a movement had not been well chosen, the Administrative Commission of the CGT decided to support the railroad workers, and preparations were made for a general transport strike to begin on March 1.

On February 29, however, after Millerand had intervened, an agreement was reached between the companies and the union, which granted the railroad workers the wage increases they had asked for, prohibited sanctions on the strikers, and provided the basis for a discussion of the future of the railway system as a whole. The majoritaires considered the strike a great victory, or at least they gave that impression. But neither the railroad companies nor the minoritaires were satisfied. *La Vie Ouvrière* cried that it was a surrender, not a victory, and charged that the leadership of the Railroad Workers' Federation had given in just when the CGT was getting ready to enter the strike and extend it to other industries,[16] while the companies interpreted Millerand's compromise in such a way that a number of strikers lost their jobs. In the meantime, the government had given notice that it would not stand by as a spectator while the railroad workers paralyzed the nation's transportation network. Indicating to the Chamber that this was a political movement, "and to give it its real name, a revolutionary one," Millerand announced that the government would take every possible step to defeat such a strike, including calling up into the army the workers on certain sections of the PLM. The Chamber approved this policy by a huge majority.[17]

Such threats only further excited the minoritaires. Before proceeding to make a revolution, however, they had to unseat the majority. Opportunities for a confrontation were offered by the numerous network assemblies that preceded the national meeting of the Railroad Workers' Federation. In congress after congress, minoritaires defeated the majority and passed motions calling for a more audacious policy. When the National Congress met on April 22, the minoritaires' victory was assured. The new leader of the union was Gaston Monmousseau. A former anarchist who had been drawn to syndicalism by the struggle against the War,[18] Monmousseau cared little for questions of hours and wages. His program was political: to set up the "occasion" that would stampede the masses into revolutionary action. At his urging, the congress voted on April 25 to call a general strike if the men who had been laid off were not reinstated immediately. The companies, of course, had no intention of yielding. Nor could the railway union look to the government for support. Queried in San Remo about his position, Millerand wired back a lecture on the politics of liberalism. In a democracy founded on law, he pontificated, no personal or group consideration could authorize a citizen or an association to act against the public interest. The government would not intervene.[19]

During the next five days the excitement of the railway workers was transformed into a syndicalist movement of national proportions. Anxious to gain the support of the CGT for their strike, the leaders of the Railroad Workers' Federation entered into contact with the Administrative Commission. However, owing to the pressure of time and a series of misunderstandings that we cannot go into here, the railway union announced its strike for May 1, before winning the support of the Administrative Commission; and when the Commission met on April 28, it found itself faced with a fait accompli. Sensitive to accusations of cowardice and timidity, the CGT leaders voted to support the strike; but there is no doubt that they were from the beginning disgruntled and pessimistic about its chances of success. At Jouhaux's insistence, it was decided to base the strike on the defense of syndicalist rights and the nationalization of the railroads, the mines, and the electrical industry.[20] The minoritaires, however, interpreted the strike as the beginning of the long-awaited social revolution, and this gave the movement an extremist flavor that the government was quick to exploit. It was the tragic finale of the "dialogue des sourds" in which the two factions had been engaged since 1915. The most that Jouhaux's group hoped for from the strike was the rationalization of French capitalism and a demonstration of confederal strength, while the minoritaires dreamed aloud of a social upheaval that would end with the installation of "the direct power of workers', peasants', and soldiers' unions."[b]

The moment for a great strike was badly chosen. The continual unrest of the past year had turned public opinion against the working class.[c] The Right, fresh from its victory in the November elections, agitated for the dissolution of

[b] Verdier in *La Vie Ouvrière*, 30.iv.20. A week later, when the strike was already under way, Marius Hanot of the Fédération Communiste des Soviets repeated the same theme: "The moment French syndicalism has been waiting for has arrived.... The working class has decided to go all out; for it, the general strike now being planned can be a question of life or death. The period we are entering is grave, moving, crucial. Our course is set: general strike, insurrection, revolution. Then we will deserve a Communist system." *Le Soviet*, 9.v.20.

[c] Jules Romains has captured very well what was probably the mood of the majority of the country at the time: "The workers, for their part, could tell themselves that as a class, it was they who had won the war. While the peasants and the white-collar brigade were getting themselves killed for five sous a day, they were turning out artillery shells, in safety, for 50 francs a day. In the end they had been given not the purple heart but the eight-hour day, which they doubtless preferred. Their wages rose constantly, while the salaries of professional men stayed put, and the income of the coupon-clippers vanished into thin air. Never had they had their hands on so much money. Never had they seen so many bourgeois so envious of their earnings, of their amusements, of their fun. But they seem fidgety. As soon as their old needs are satisfied they discover new ones. And nothing's worse for a man's peace of mind than to be constantly discovering new needs. It's like an itchy skin rash. They've been inoculated with discontent; they carry it in their veins like a chronic disease. Today they know they can no longer be satisfied. If by chance they felt content, they'd feel like cowards or traitors; they'd be ashamed to face their friends." *Cette Grande Lueur à l'Est* (1941), p. 24.

the CGT. Talk of a Bolshevik conspiracy in France antagonized the Radical milieux that might otherwise have been well disposed toward a purely economic movement. Gone were the days when Clemenceau flirted with the syndicalists and talked of the degeneration of the bourgeoisie. Millerand's government was resolved to teach the unions a lesson: namely that the debts contracted at the time of the Sacred Union were not collectable, at least not now. The companies, for their part, pushed on with the struggle. They had no cause for concern. Since mid-March they had had an agreement with the government on the steps to be taken in the event of a strike. In anticipation of violence, they had organized "civic unions," proto-fascist groups modeled after similar bodies in Germany and Spain.[21] Most serious of all for the outcome of the strike, the syndicalists themselves were uncertain. Consultation with the unions showed an apathetic tendency among the masses.[22]

The stratagem seized upon by Jouhaux was to launch a series of strike waves, one following another as in battle order. The aim was to exhaust the store of raw materials available to industry by calling out the transport employees, while at the same time keeping the majority of workers on their jobs to show the strength and discipline of the CGT and the government's powerlessness.[23] The general strike of May 1 went successfully enough. As a first reinforcement of the railway workers, the CGT ordered out the miners, the seamen, and the dockers. On May 7, the Confederation called out 400,000 metalworkers, and on May 10, workers in the building trades, the automobile and aviation industry, the navigation industry, and the transport industry. They were followed in turn by the miners of the Pas-de-Calais and the Nord. These strike orders were obeyed, but not without doubts and desertions. The electrical technicians, for example, had had to be called out before the transport workers could be persuaded to stand fast.[24]

The government fought back with all the means at its disposal, and clearly had public opinion behind it. Despite hectic efforts to explain the need for nationalization of the great public-service industries, the CGT's program does not seem to have been understood by either its own militants or the public at large.[25] Aided by the bourgeois press, the authorities sought to give the impression that the CGT was trying to starve Paris. The leaders of the Railroad Workers' Union were arrested, along with leading members of various left-wing groups, and an attempt was made to show that the strike itself was the work of Bolshevik subversion and foreign conspirators.[26] This was not so; but then as now people were ready to accept what they suspected already, and this rumor corresponded to their picture of a world infested by anti-French conspiracies. There was no question of compromise. For the Right this "civic battle of the Marne," as it was called, was the necessary complement to the victory over Germany and it was necessary to go "jusqu'au bout." The companies announced that there would be no negotiations until the workers returned to their jobs, and the government initiated legal proceedings against the CGT. As the Radical Minister of the Interior, Théodore Steeg, explained on May 20, the government sought to establish the principle that a deliberate attempt to disrupt a country's life and throw it into ruin was not only a political act, but a common crime.[27]

The outcome of the strike was the total defeat of the CGT. The students of the Grandes Ecoles helped maintain service on the railway lines and the métro. The defection of the workers on the North and East networks prevented the success of the railroad strike. Traffic never dropped below 52 per cent of normal; after May 6, the morale of the strikers fell continually. The calling out of the gas workers and the cabinetmakers on May 13 was merely the movement's dying gasp. On May 21, an extraordinary meeting of the Confederal Committee voted to call off the strike. The next day the great majority of workers went back to their jobs; on May 28, the railway workers gave up the struggle which they had at first elected to carry on alone.

### THE CONSEQUENCES OF THE MAY STRIKE

The effects of the May strike on the working-class movement are hard to over-emphasize. Twenty-two thousand railway workers lost their jobs. Of 100 men employed by the railroads in 1920, 40 went on strike; five of these were fired, and only two or three of these five had returned to their posts in 1936.[28] Moreover, the reaction against violence and revolutionary propaganda that followed the strike was reflected in a general decline in union membership. The CGT, which had claimed 2,500,000 members at the beginning of 1920, had only half that number by the end of the year, and less than 600,000 by the spring of 1921.[29] Both the majoritaires and the minoritaires suffered from the defeat, though in different ways. The attitude of the bourgeoisie hardened, and the leaders of the CGT were no longer able to exact concessions from the government. Their Minimum Program, which had been based on the assumption that the working class was powerful enough to demand its share in the management of the nation's economic life, now seemed a chimera; employers took advantage of the new situation and the economic crisis to cut wages and renege on the eight-hour day; and the Confederation itself was hounded with the threat of dissolution.[d] In the case of the minoritaires, hopes for a cataclysmic general strike, which would proceed from economic demands to insurrection to revolution, were dashed, at least temporarily. The strike of May 1920 marked the effective end of the wave of unrest that had shaken the French social order for over a year. The working class subsided into quiescence; the following year, May 1

---

[d] The government went so far as to obtain a court order dissolving the CGT, but it was never enforced. Bernard Georges and Denise Tintant, *Léon Jouhaux, cinquante ans de syndicalisme* (1962), p. 399.

passed practically unnoticed by the nation at large, a "bitter experience for those who remember May 1, 1919."[30]

Naturally enough, both minoritaires and majoritaires blamed the failure of the strike on their opponents. The minoritaires insisted that the CGT leadership had sabotaged the strike by not calling a general strike as soon as it became apparent that the wave strategy was ineffective. The majoritaires countered that this would not have overcome the main difficulty, the defection of the workers on the North and East networks, and they blamed the minoritaires for talking of revolution and ruining what chance of success the strike had had.[31] Both were right. From the point of view of revolutionary syndicalism, the majoritaires were skeptics and pessimists. From the point of view of constructive syndicalism, the minoritaires were nuisances and reactionaries. The result of these recriminations was to hasten the split of the CGT.

The Communist Left Wing, too, was impressed by the events of May 1920. Monatte, Loriot, Souvarine, Monmousseau, and a number of anarchists from the Parti Communiste and the Fédération des Soviets were arrested by Millerand in early May. They were charged with having broken the laws against "anarchist intrigues," and with having plotted against the security of the State. Ironically, neither the Committee for the Third International, nor the CSR, nor the Parti Communiste, nor the Fédération des Soviets had had any real part in the preparation of the strike. They had not even encouraged it.[32] It is true that Monmousseau, the leader of the strike in its early stages, belonged to the Committee for the Third International. But he had precipitated the movement not on the orders of the Committee or of Moscow, as Le Temps claimed, but as a member of his railroad union.[33] Nothing could have shown better the impotence and disorganization of the French working-class movement. Such young extremists as Boris Souvarine had no real contact with working-class organizations.[34] Even men like Monatte and Rosmer had very little direct influence on the unions. Intellectuals like Souvarine were even slightly flattered that the government had considered them dangerous enough to be worth imprisoning; they thought that Armageddon was at hand.

The obvious lesson of the strike of May 1920 was that the French working-class movement had to abandon its romantic dreams of spontaneous revolution and organize. Raymond Lefebvre, precocious as always, pointed the moral. As early as the end of April, Lefebvre had argued in favor of a party that would unite all revolutionaries, whether they were Socialists, syndicalists, or anarchists.[35] In June, just before leaving for Moscow for the Second World Congress of the Comintern, a trip from which he was never to return, the ardent young militant wrote an article emphasizing the need for a disciplined party to take the head of spontaneous revolutionary movements. Certainly, Lefebvre wrote, one can't simply decree the Revolution for a set date. Mass movements are born, unfold, and strike like forces of nature. But their success or failure depends on whether or not there is a class organization to guide them:

Today's large-scale social movements cannot be planned in a day or a month. They require method, dedication, and systematic and carefully considered violence, which must be farsighted, calculated, and precise. They also require a faith that has never been dirtied in the mud of class collaboration. Finally, they require an iron determination that never weakens in the midst of action, that never yields to camaraderie, that never compromises with failure of nerve, so that when a movement unexpectedly arises, everything is ready.[36]

It was clear to Lefebvre that the method, the faith, and the determination he sought were to be found only in Moscow. Many others agreed, though few yet understood the organizational revolution that Moscow's method implied.

Whoever has followed the history of the French working-class movement from the height of its militance in 1919 to the nadir of its impotence in 1921 will inevitably ask why France's postwar revolution failed. The question is a difficult one, which cannot be dismissed by brandishing a set of statistics. Revolutions are like brush fires; they burst into flame from a single spark, and though one may explain why they have happened, it is extremely difficult to say why they have not. The most one can do is to observe whether or not inflammable materials were present.

By Marxist standards, the French proletariat was ready. The salaried working class constituted nearly one-half the active population; it was cultured; it had a long revolutionary tradition; it had a high degree of class consciousness.[37] The War had put this working class in motion and called the old order into question. To understand why the French proletariat did not make a revolution, one can turn with profit to Lenin, a man who in both word and deed was a specialist in the art of rebellion. In 1920 Lenin listed four conditions for a successful revolution. First and most important, Lenin wrote, the vanguard of the working class must be ideologically won over to Communism. Second, the class forces hostile to the proletariat must be confused and at loggerheads with one another. Third, petty-bourgeois democracy must have disgraced itself and demonstrated its bankruptcy. Finally, there must be a mass mood among the proletariat "in favor of supporting the most determined, unreservedly bold, revolutionary action against the bourgeoisie." "Then, indeed," concluded Lenin, "revolution is ripe; then, indeed, if we have correctly gauged all the conditions outlined above and if we have chosen the moment rightly, our victory is assured."[38]

Of these four prerequisites for revolution, France satisfied only the fourth, and that merely for a brief moment in the spring and early summer of 1919. When the situation was potentially revolutionary, that is in May and June 1919, there were no Communist leaders to take direction of the movement. The men at the head of both the SFIO and the CGT were committed to gradual change and rejected the Blanquism of the Bolsheviks as inapplicable to a highly developed country such as France. By 1920 Communist leaders existed, but they had no organization and no link with the masses. Nor were the class forces that were hostile to the proletariat in conflict with one another and therefore neutralized. The Bolshevik scare itself helped to weld them together. The Bloc National was the concrete manifestation of this union. The very victory of the Bolsheviks in Russia, the coming to power of Communists in Hungary and Bavaria, and unrest in Germany served to prevent the reproduction of the same type of revolutionary situation in countries that were able to observe the experience of their neighbors.

Most important of all, perhaps, the leaders of the bourgeoisie were not confused; on the contrary, both Clemenceau and Millerand acted with great confidence and firmness in the two moments of greatest crisis, in May 1919 and May 1920. In a period where bourgeois leaders everywhere had lost confidence in their own values and the destinies of their own class, the French bourgeoisie was still able to produce statesmen of iron will. A historian of the Austro-Hungarian Empire has observed that the age required men "hewn out of gnarled wood."[39] Clemenceau and Millerand were such men. Their confidence and their will derived in part from their own natures, in part from Republican tradition, but in greatest part from the fact that France had won the War. The victory was proof for French liberal politicians that the War had been just and that French institutions were sound. True, some Frenchmen had lost their faith in parliamentary democracy. But events showed that they were not the majority, and the elections of 1924 would bring the petty-bourgeois Cartel to power. Democracy would not lose its value as a mystique for the petty bourgeoisie until the economic crisis of the 1930's.

Finally, one wonders to what extent the mass mood of 1919 would have supported a "most determined, unreservedly bold, revolutionary action against the bourgeoisie." It is possible that resolute leaders of Lenin's and Trotsky's caliber might have carried the masses with them in a mighty assault against the bourgeois State. But it should be remembered that if thousands turned out to protest Villain's acquittal and to demonstrate on May 1, thousands more came out to watch the victory march of the French Army on July 14, 1919. How many were present at both? Side by side, these two events suggest the complexity of the situation in France. There was uneasiness; there was anger at the men who had taken France into the War; there was exaltation in victory; there was the expectation of radical change; but there was no revolution.

THE BOLSHEVIKS AND FRANCE

The Strasbourg Congress had decided two things in its long and stormy deliberations: first, to establish contact with the Bolsheviks and to make an inquiry into the nature of the Russian Revolution; and second, to send representatives to the Swiss, the Italians, and the German Independents to prepare for a conference on the reconstruction of the International on a revolutionary basis. As it turned out, only the mission to the Russians was of any importance. In the spring, Paul Faure was dispatched to Switzerland, Daniel Renoult to Italy, Mistral to Germany, and Longuet to the British Labour Party. Cachin and Frossard were chosen to make the trip to Moscow over the protests of Renaudel, who insisted on the right to be included in the delegation.[e] The overture to the Italians met with an outright refusal; the leaders of the PSI still remembered the abortive strike of July 21, and they had no illusions about the French party's revolutionary spirit. The Swiss were open to the idea of a conference, but the German Independents had sent their own delegation to Russia and refused to enter into negotiations until their representatives returned.[40] The English reaffirmed their intention of remaining in the Second International. It was the attitude of the Germans that was decisive; without them Reconstruction had no meaning. Thus the efforts to reconstruct the International were frustrated for the moment; and in the summer of 1920 all eyes turned to Moscow, where the Bolsheviks had convoked the Second World Congress of their Communist International.

Heretofore we have considered the attitude of the French toward events in Russia. We must now inquire into the reciprocal attitudes of the Bolsheviks. With what preconceived ideas did they approach their first contacts with the French Socialists? What importance did they ascribe to France? What goals did they pursue there? What kind of a party did they want? What men had they chosen to lead it?

Russian radicals had traditionally been divided in their feelings toward France: like the Russia of Blok's poem "The Scythians," they gazed into that most Western of Western countries "with hatred, and with love." The Bolsheviks constituted no exception.[41] For them, France was the historic land of enlightenment and revolution. It was in Paris that Marx had formulated his theories of revolution, as indeed it was in France that Socialism had been born. There was not a Bolshevik leader who had not studied in detail the history of the French revolutionary movement, as there was not one who did not have in his heart a special place for the French working class, the nameless heroes of 1793, 1848, and 1871, the predecessors of the Bolsheviks themselves. Everything—revolutionary past, culture, economic development—pointed to the fact that France was destined to play a central role in the world revolution. No trip to Europe was complete without a visit to Paris, the shrine of revolution.

Such pilgrimages, however, invariably proved disappointing. The land of grasping bourgeois dynasties, mean-minded shopkeepers, chauvinistic workers, anarchist intellectuals, and Socialist leaders who deserted regularly to the bourgeoisie, the France of the Third Republic represented everything the Bolsheviks execrated. How was this paradox of a revolutionary past and a bourgeois

[e] *L'Humanité*, 10.vi.20. The French delegation had at first been supposed to include Longuet, but Frossard took his place at the last minute.

present to be resolved? For most Bolsheviks it was simple. The French bourgeoisie, the cleverest and most cultured in Europe, had deceived the proletariat, while at the same time buying off the better-paid workers with the profits of imperialism. Schools, churches, masonic lodges, newspapers, movies, and plays were used to give the worker the illusion that he shared in the Republic. Still, such deceptions would not have succeeded had the French proletariat possessed revolutionary leaders armed with the proper Marxist theories. Instead, they had been saddled with irresponsible agitators like Hervé, dogmatists like Guesde, and reformists like Jaurès, who for all his idealism had never been able to rise above bourgeois pacifism. Under the leadership of Jaurès, the SFIO had become the most parliamentary party in Europe, and its reformism had either tied the workers to the coattails of Radicalism or turned them in disgust toward anarchism or revolutionary syndicalism. The War had revealed the basic opportunism of the French working-class organizations: Hervé, Guesde, the Jauressians, Jouhaux, and the anarchists had all foundered in the most sordid chauvinism. Having sunk furthest into the pit of social patriotism, the French labor organizations were the slowest to revive and purge themselves. All this might have been foreseen before the War; it was the inevitable result of the absence of a revolutionary party.

This appreciation of the French situation may have varied in its details from one Bolshevik leader to another. Lenin and Zinoviev, who had no personal knowledge of the French working-class movement, might have emphasized the lack of theory and organization;[1] Trotsky and Lozovsky might have pointed to the immense reserves of revolutionary energy in the unions and among the anarchists. But all would have agreed that the main body of the

[1] The time has come to re-evaluate Lenin's understanding of the Western labor movement. Many Western Communists who had the opportunity to talk with Lenin carried away the impression that he had a profound grasp of the nature and problems of the working-class movement in the West. (See, for example, Rosmer, *Moscou sous Lénine,* 1953, p. 70.) Nothing could be less true. An analysis of Lenin's *Works* would show that he misunderstood the German Social Democratic Party, was uninterested in the French working-class movement, and was almost completely ignorant of Italy and Spain. The fact is that Lenin was interested in the Western labor movement only insofar as it offered arguments that might be used in his polemics with other Russian Socialists.

Though it is true that the Bolshevik leader lived in Paris for over three and a half years (from December 1908 to July 1912), and though it is probably true, as Ilya Ehrenburg has written, that he "followed French political life attentively, studied its history, its economics, knew the living conditions of the French workers" (*People and Life, 1891–1921,* New York, 1962, p. 69), we know from his wife that he had almost no contacts with the leaders of the French working-class movement, including the militants of the Left Wing. Even Rosmer had to admit that few Socialists or syndicalists knew Lenin during his exile in Paris. ("Trotsky à Paris pendant la première guerre mondiale," *La Révolution Prolétarienne,* October 1950, p. 289.) The only Socialist whom we know Lenin met is Paul Lafargue. These remarks about Lenin apply equally well to Zinoviev.

French proletariat was basically sound. It was the leadership, the all-important organizing center, which was ailing. What was needed was a radical overhauling, which would remove the defective engine and replace it with a powerful new revolutionary motor.

It was taken for granted by the Bolsheviks throughout 1919 that this new leadership could only come from the ranks of the Left Wing. The First Congress of the Comintern, it will be remembered, had resolved that an organizational split between the Left and the Center was, at a certain point, an "absolute necessity." In French terms this meant that Loriot's group had to break with both Renaudel and Longuet (not to mention Thomas), join with those anarchists and syndicalists who accepted the Third International (Péricat, Rosmer, Monatte), and form a Communist Party. This policy was formulated at the time when the Bolsheviks were most isolated and their hopes for world revolution brightest: it assumed that a clash to the death between capitalism and Socialism was not only inevitable, but imminent. The optimism of the Bolshevik leaders reached such heights that Zinoviev, writing in April 1919, could predict that by the time his article appeared, the three existing Soviet Republics might very well have become six or more. "Old Europe," he observed excitedly, "rolls at a dizzy pace toward the proletarian revolution."[42] Never had the Bolsheviks distinguished more carefully between the two Frances; never had they seemed more justified. Bourgeois France, the France of Clemenceau, was in the forefront of intervention in Russia. Soviet Russia had no more determined enemy.[43] Proletarian France, on the other hand, had at last shaken off its somnolence and was on the move. It would rise up and overthrow its rulers; at the very least, it would save Soviet Russia from imperialist intervention. Walled off from the outside world and starved for news, the Bolsheviks grasped at every rumor to show that their ideas were gaining in Europe. Lenin reported proudly that in France strikes were called to cries of "Vive les soviets!" and that in Paris there were two "Communist newspapers," Péricat's *L'Internationale* and Georges Anquetil's *Le Titre Censuré!!!*[44] One we know as anarchist; the other was suspected by the Left Wing of being subsidized by the police. So great was the isolation of the Bolsheviks, so precarious their contacts with the West.

Isolation, however, did not breed doubt. Nor did it make the Soviet leaders hesitate to apply their own tactics to the West. The events of the summer of 1919 only further convinced the Bolsheviks that their policy of revolutionary purity was correct. From the defeat of the German Revolution, the fall of the Hungarian Soviet Republic, and the failure of the July strike against intervention, they drew the lesson that any cooperation with the leaders of the old Social Democratic parties was impossible, and indeed dangerous.[45] The Social Democrats had betrayed the revolution once; they would do so again. Bolshevik demands for the secession of Loriot's group from the SFIO and the formation of an "autonomous Communist organization" grew more insistent.[46] Trotsky took time from his own military duties to dash off a letter to the French Communists in September 1919, warning them that they must break with Longuet. "In the epoch in which we live," concluded Trotsky, "it is better to have declared enemies than doubtful friends." This is the theme repeated over and over again in the Bolshevik theses, manifestos, and articles of this period.[47]

The Bolsheviks, then, seemed to be committed to an immediate break with the Center. We have already noted the personal attack that Lenin made on Longuet on the eve of the Strasbourg Congress, to which the Centrist leader reacted in injured pride. Yet it seems that a subtle but marked change took place in the attitude of the Bolsheviks around the turn of the year, and especially with the birth of Reconstruction. In early February 1920, the Executive Committee of the Comintern addressed a letter to the German Independents, stating that it would be "highly desirable to enter into negotiations with the parties which declare themselves ready for a final break with the Second International."[48] This letter requested the representatives of these parties to come to Russia. A later declaration of the Western European Secretariat in Amsterdam announced that the Third International would welcome negotiations with the French Socialist Party as soon as it had broken definitively with Renaudel and Thomas.[49] Consequent letters to the German Independent Party and the invitation to the Second World Congress showed that the Bolsheviks were now anxious to enter into negotiations with the representatives of the Center parties of France and Germany.[50]

How does one explain this shift in the attitude of the Bolsheviks? In 1919, when the Revolution seemed just around the bend, the Bolsheviks had emphasized their solidarity with all groups of the Left Wing, with anarchists and syndicalists as well as Socialists. But by the spring of 1920, it had become clear that the Revolution was not imminent. The wave of spontaneous social conflict unleashed by the War had subsided; everywhere the bourgeoisie was passing to the counteroffensive. The Bolsheviks now switched their focus to "protracted revolution."[51] The split in the German Communist Party in October 1919 and the formation of the anti-parliamentary KAPD in April 1920 were the immediate impetus for the re-evaluation of Bolshevik tactics. But these events had implications that went far beyond the boundaries of Germany. Leninism was composed of two elements: revolutionary activism and a theory of organization. The latter might lead to the former, but in 1919 Lenin had emphasized the first. And this is what Bolshevism had meant to the Europeans who had flocked to its banner—this and a vision of some kind of direct democracy. Lenin's devotion to revolutionary spontaneity had made possible the rapprochement with the anarchists and syndicalists. But this was nothing more than a flirtation and a remarkably un-Leninist one at that. Throughout his career Lenin had always opposed anarchism and revolutionary syndicalism as dangers for the proletariat.[52] Now, with the revolution postponed, he returned to his earlier emphasis on organization, discipline, and revolutionary theory. His enthusiasm for the anarchists diminished, and he suddenly became acutely aware of the dangers of the ultra-leftist deviation.

The result of these new preoccupations was Lenin's essay *"Left-Wing" Communism: An Infantile Disorder*. In *"Left-Wing" Communism*, Lenin observed that the movement to the Left in Germany had strengthened the Independent Socialist Party (USPD) rather than the ultra-leftist KAPD. This new turn in the situation made it all the more necessary to win over the revolutionary elements of the USPD.

> The German Independent Social Democratic Party is obviously not homogeneous. Alongside the old opportunist leaders . . . there has arisen in this party a Left proletarian wing which is growing with remarkable rapidity. . . . This proletarian wing has already proposed . . . immediate and unconditional affiliation with the Third International. To fear a "compromise" with this wing of the party is positively ridiculous. On the contrary, it is *the duty* of Communists to seek *and to find* a suitable form of compromise with them, such a compromise as, on the one hand, would facilitate and accelerate the necessary complete fusion with this wing, and, on the other, would in no way hamper the Communists in their ideological and political struggle against the opportunist Right Wing.[53]

The Bolsheviks adopted a similar strategy with regard to the SFIO, though perhaps with greater misgivings. They considered the French party more reactionary, on the whole, than the USPD, which had separated from its Right. The Scheidemanns and Noskes of French Socialism, they noted with concern, were still in the SFIO.[54] They dismissed Longuet as a counterrevolutionary who was moving toward the Right. They feared that the Centrist leaders, sensing the mood of the masses, might attempt to escape from their dilemma by recognizing the dictatorship of the proletariat verbally while remaining in fact committed to their old ways.[55] On the other hand, they realized that there were many revolutionary elements within the SFIO who were sympathetic to the Russian Revolution; and they now had reason to believe that it might be possible to win the majorities of these large parties and thus get an immediate mass following in France. Reluctance to break with these Centrist elements was reinforced by reports from France testifying to the Left Wing's weakness and lack of ideological homogeneity.[g] These circumstances dictated

---

[g] See Trotsky, *Kommunisticheskoe dvizhenie vo Frantsii* (Moscow, 1923), pp. 51–55. It seems likely that the Bolshevik leaders were uncertain of their policy toward the German Independents and the French Socialists in the months preceding the opening of the Second World Congress. They still played with the idea of a split from the old organizations. Alfred Rosmer, who had made his way to Moscow through a disturbed and embattled Europe in order to take part in the work of the Second Congress, relates that, in June, Lenin spoke to him of the necessity for the Zimmerwaldian minority to leave the

to the Bolsheviks the need to deal with the leaders of the French majority. However, the Soviet leaders were understandably anxious not to dilute the revolutionary nature of the International by admitting opportunistic elements. How were you to steal the army without taking the general staff? One way might be to formulate conditions of admission in such a way that they would bar the way to Socialists of Longuet's type, while leaving the gates of the International open to the masses who until then had mistakenly followed their reformist leaders. It was with these devious designs that the Bolsheviks made ready to negotiate with the representatives of the SFIO.

### CACHIN'S AND FROSSARD'S "CHEMIN DES DAMES"

It was significant that the two men chosen by the Socialist leaders to represent them at the negotiations with the Bolsheviks in Moscow were Marcel Cachin and L.-O. Frossard. Longuet and Faure were Centrists out of principle; Cachin and Frossard were Centrists out of political agility. Cachin, as was noted earlier, had been to Russia once before, in the spring of 1917. Until then he had been a majoritaire and a social-patriot of the deepest conviction; in 1915, as an agent for the French government, he had tried to persuade the Italian Socialists to enter the War on the side of the Entente. Legend has it that it was Cachin who handed Mussolini the French subsidies that enabled him to start his own newspaper and shift from anti-patriotism to violent nationalism. Once in Russia, however, and under attack from the Soviets for his conduct during the War, Cachin had broken; he returned home a dedicated Centrist. It had been

---

party in order to form a French Communist Party. "They have waited too long already," Lenin said. Rosmer replied that the leaders of the French minority felt differently, and that although many of them had been anxious to leave the party in the past, they had come to feel since Strasbourg that they might rapidly win the majority in the party. "If that's the case," he remarked, "I've made a mistake in my thesis; ask the Secretariat of the International for a copy and send me the modifications you suggest." Rosmer, *Moscou sous Lénine*, pp. 69–70.

It is only fair to add, however, that Rosmer told me in conversation (February 13, 1961) that the Russians realized the weakness of the French Left Wing; that their policy in Germany and France was to win the majority of the party; and that they never seriously considered basing themselves on the Left. This last statement is certainly exaggerated. On the very eve of the Second Congress, Trotsky wrote an article calling on the Loriot group in the party and the Monatte-Rosmer clique in the unions to set up an independent, centralized party with its own daily newspapers. Trotsky, *Kommunisticheskoe dvizhenie*, pp. 51.–55.

We must conclude, it seems to me, that the Bolsheviks moved slowly, haltingly, hesitantly, but decisively, toward a new tactical position in the spring and summer of 1920. Implicit in that new position was the admission that the International sketched out in 1919 no longer corresponded to the situation. For a similar view, see James W. Hulse, *The Forming of the Communist International* (Stanford, Calif., 1964), and Donald Urquidi, "The Origins of the Italian Communist Party, 1918–1921" (unpublished doctoral dissertation, Columbia University, 1962).

his speech which persuaded the National Council to reverse its stand and send a delegation to Stockholm. Between 1917 and 1920 he made himself the champion of the Russian Revolution in the Chamber, though he always qualified his enthusiasm for its principles, to such an extent that one would have thought him a Wilsonian rather than a Bolshevik—and indeed he was.[56]

"Sturdy, jolly, an indefatigable speaker both in private and in public, the possessor of a deep and sonorous laugh, quick to shake hands, subject to enthusiasms,"[57] Cachin already had behind him a long career as a Socialist municipal councillor, propagandist, journalist, and deputy, and before him an even longer career as a Communist leader. A former Guesdist, Cachin worshiped the working class with the unqualified devotion of a bygone era. He was not unintelligent or without personal courage, as his later career demonstrated. But all his intellectual ability was channeled into articles and speeches that were more noteworthy for their rhetorical effect than for their logic; and his physical courage in the struggle against the class enemy was tempered by a fear of being isolated from the working class, and by a tendency to be carried away by abrupt enthusiasms that made him the most undependable of allies in an intraparty struggle. He is a perfect example of a generation of French Socialists who attached more importance to words than to deeds, to sentiment than to Marxist theory. He was never happier than amidst an acclaiming crowd of workers, at the tribune of the Chamber delivering a burning speech in defense of the Russian Revolution, or in the committee room of a Socialist Congress searching for a compromise that would reconcile the irreconcilable. He was never more unhappy than when forced to discuss a question of principle or to take an unpopular position.

Frossard represents a more interesting case. No figure of the interwar period has been more securely consigned to the dustbin of history. Yet one wonders whether he was not more unlucky than unworthy. At any rate, his career, too, has its value as a prototype. Unlike Cachin, Frossard had been a minoritaire throughout the War, and had been rewarded for his services and talent by being made General Secretary of the party after the victory of the Center in 1918. He, like so many other Socialists of his generation, had been drawn to Socialism not by doctrine but by the oratory of Jaurès. For him, Socialism was a religion and a mystique. He was a man destined to be precocious in all things, even in death: he began his career as a militant at the age of 16; he was graduated from the Ecole Normale two years later; he was only 28 when he became General Secretary of the SFIO; and he died in 1946 at the age of 56—not, however, before he had held a ministerial portfolio and tarnished his already soiled reputation by collaborating with Vichy. All those who came into contact with him testified to his abilities. He had exceptional administrative gifts, a prodigious memory, and a golden voice that could move a crowd to tears or laughter. Unlike most Socialist leaders, he also had roots in the syndicalist movement. But he was a politician through and through and was famous for his powers of compromise and maneuver rather than for his devotion to doctrine. "I took to politics like a duck to water," he wrote many years later in summing up his career.[58] And he was to reach his heights and ruin his own career in trying to persuade the French (and the Russians) that Bolshevism was nothing but Jauressianism à la sauce tartare.

Cachin and Frossard did not go to Moscow as supplicants. They went as representatives of a large and proud party with a long and glorious tradition of revolutionary struggle. They had two charges: to establish contact with the Bolsheviks and the authorized organs of the Third International, and to learn what they could about the achievements of the Soviet regime. The delegates were also instructed by the CAP to complain to Lenin about Bolshevik attacks on certain leading Centrists, such as Longuet; to ask what importance the International ascribed to "the so-called French Communist parties" that were seeking to divide the French working class; and to set forth the terms on which the French would consider joining the Third International, one of the main ones being that the party would not be required to expel anyone.[59]

The French delegation, however, was far from being as noncommittal as its instructions suggested. Frossard left for Moscow convinced that the SFIO had no choice but to join the Third International.[60] The evolution of the international situation and the enthusiasm of the French workers for the Bolshevik Revolution had persuaded him that this was the only solution. Thus, for Frossard, even before he got to Russia, it was not a question of whether or not the French would join the Third International, but rather of the conditions on which they would join. Cachin was more hostile to the Bolsheviks. According to Frossard, while passing through Berlin Cachin had sought out Georg Ledebour, the moderate leader of the German Independents, and promised him he would tell Lenin that Russian methods were not suited to the West. But the taste of revolution and the smell of Russian air had magical effects upon Cachin. "As we drew near the Russian border ten days later, he was overcome by an irresistible attraction toward Communism."[61] "It seems to me impossible," he confided to Frossard, "that we should not join the Third International. These Germans don't know up from down."

When the French arrived in Moscow, on June 16, 1920, no one was there to meet them. They immediately had occasion to envy the deference with which the Italians, who had preceded them to Moscow in a special train, were treated; Frossard felt that their reception had been carefully prepared to show them the difference between real Communists and social patriots. "C'est le purgatoire, si l'on veut, avant le paradis."[62] It is just as likely that it was simply Russian inefficiency and lack of organization. They were finally discovered in their hotel that night by Viktor Taratuta and Jacques Sadoul, who apologized to them profusely for the inconvenience they had suffered. The tactic the Bolsheviks used on them throughout their visit was the alternation of hot and cold showers, of the carrot and the stick. Taratuta, Sadoul, and Pierre Pascal escorted them around Moscow and flooded them with facts and figures about the regime, its aims and its accomplishments. But at the same time they were subjected to such constant attacks and reproaches, from the most humble members of the Soviet up to the members of the Politburo, that a malicious Swiss Communist would sum up their trip as a "Chemin des Dames."[63]

When the two Centrist delegates visited the French group, the irascible Guilbeaux took advantage of the occasion to accuse Cachin of being a chauvinist and a social patriot. On June 18 they were invited to appear before a session of the Moscow Soviet. Given the opportunity to address the Russian workers, Cachin warmed to his audience, and in a flight of rhetoric that inspired a great round of applause, begged forgiveness for the crimes of the French bourgeoisie. Kamenev and Bukharin replied by praising Loriot and Monatte, and listing the "crimes" of the French Socialists, Cachin and Frossard included.[64] The next day Cachin and Frossard appeared before the Executive Committee of the Comintern (ECCI). After they had presented their own reports, in which they protested that they had done everything possible to defend the Russian Revolution and stated that the French party could not allow expulsions to be imposed on them from the outside, they were subjected to a scathing interrogation by Radek, Zinoviev, Lozovsky, Chablin, Serrati, John Reed, Sadoul, and Bukharin. Bukharin so wounded Cachin's pride by accusing him of chauvinism and treason at the beginning of the War that he burst out crying. Bukharin concluded by demanding bluntly: "Do you condemn the party's treasonous attitude during the War?" The French delegates tried to answer these questions as best they could, while replying to Bukharin that the dignity of their party did not allow them to respond to his insults.[65]

It was Lenin who delivered the principal speech, a fact that indicates the importance the Russians ascribed to the French party. Lenin first attacked the German Independents. Then he turned to the French and their reformist allies. Addressing Cachin and Frossard in thickly accented French, he repeated several times in a good-natured but no doubt ominous tone: "Here in Russia, we shoot reformists." Lenin attacked the French not for having failed to make a revolution, but for having failed to prepare for one. Holding L'Humanité open before him, the Bolshevik leader flailed the Socialist daily for its lack of unity. The job of the party's journal, he said, must be one of education, of explanation, of popularization of the ideas that would guide the workers toward their liberation. Lenin did not seek to hide the profound differences separating the Russians and the French: between the opportunistic policies of the SFIO and the Third International's concept of the dictatorship of the proletariat, there was an "abyss." But Lenin emphasized that there was nothing in the Bolsheviks' methods that the French could not learn. The

Bolshevik Revolution, he said, resembled the French Revolution both in its application at home and in its foreign policy.[66]

The interview was closed. Lenin instructed the ECCI to answer the questions the French had formulated. As Frossard noted, Lenin had been hard but he had not burned his bridges behind him. He had made it clear that the Bolsheviks wanted the French in the Third International. The French, in turn, jumped at the bait. Frossard reacted unfavorably to the discipline and brutality of the Bolsheviks, but as a politician he knew that life often blunts the sharpest edges. What was important was to keep the allegiance of the masses, and, for the moment at least, the masses were with the Third International.[67] On June 26 he wrote in his travel diary: "With regard to our personal adherence to the Communist International, it is now only a question of hours. *Le courant nous emporte*."[68]

### THE SECOND WORLD CONGRESS

Cachin and Frossard had left Paris on May 31, the day before the invitation to the Second World Congress of the Comintern was issued. Thus, officially they had neither the intention nor the authority to remain in Russia to participate in the debates of the congress. The Bolsheviks, however, were particularly anxious that the French should stay; they no doubt felt that the atmosphere of the congress would soften their resistance. Lenin sent Kamenev to ask the French to remain, and Bukharin, Radek, Sadoul, and Taratuta seconded his plea. On June 29, the Executive Committee officially invited them to take part in the congress with a consulting vote, despite the objections of Guilbeaux and the Dutch Communist David Wijnkoop. The French wired home to their party for permission to stay. Permission was granted by a National Council meeting of July 4, 1920, which, however, rejected a motion submitted by the Committee of the Third International for immediate adherence to the Comintern.[69]

Meanwhile, also on June 29, Cachin appeared before the ECCI to reply to its indictment. The French, he said, agreed that the Revolution could come only through violence; the SFIO had not defended the Bolshevik Revolution with sufficient vigor; now he and Frossard would return home to prepare the French proletariat to imitate the Russians; more specifically, they would unite with the adherents of Bolshevism in France to ensure that the SFIO joined the Third International. Reconstruction, Cachin admitted, was absurd.[70]

These matters settled, Cachin and Frossard journeyed down the Volga River with thirty other delegates, including Rákosi, Wijnkoop, Serrati, Ludovico D'Aragona, and Angel Pestaña. Lozovsky and Angelica Balabanova were the party's guides. It was later charged by dissident Russian Socialists that Cachin and Frossard had been taken for a tour *à la Potemkin,* that their time was spent at official banquets, official factories, official pioneer camps, and that they had had no contact with real workers.[71] This was certainly true. How could it have been otherwise when the two French delegates did not know the language, were burdened with a busy itinerary established by their hosts, and depended upon chance encounters with Russians knowing French for what glimpses they got into everyday life? How different is it today?

At any rate, the two men reacted very differently to the Russian climate of revolution. Frossard was not charmed by Russian customs, nor by the food, which he found inadequate in both quality and quantity. More than once he envied the Italians the canned foodstuffs they had had the foresight to bring, and on July 6 he fell sick. For all his discomfort, he seems to have seen the Soviet regime pretty much for what it was. He was depressed by its living standards, impressed by the immensity of its propaganda effort, convinced that behind the revolutionary phrases there existed good sense and a states-manlike commitment to order. Cachin, on the other hand, was the stuff of which *illuminés* are made: every morning he awoke a little more Bolshevik, a little less Reconstructor.

What the two men did agree on, however, was the necessity of joining the Third International. The question was when, how, and on what terms. The Russians were obviously anxious that they join as soon as possible. Toward this end they pursued their game of threats and inducements. On July 15, just before the congress was to begin, the ECCI presented them with a false radio message stating that the National Council had voted to join the Third International by a small majority. Taratuta assured them that the adherence of the French party was not going to excite anyone in Russia; at the same time he sent a radiogram to Paris summarizing and even exaggerating the statements Cachin and Frossard had made to the ECCI. The French were in a quandary: should they immediately inform the party of their decision to adhere or should they wait? After a thoughtful discussion, they resolved to wait. But then they were suddenly presented with the news that Renaudel had written an article announcing their "abrupt return" to France. This decided them. The die was now cast. After carefully weighing every word, they dispatched a telegram to France stating that the conditions of admission to the International had now been formulated and that "personally we consider adherence necessary."[72]

The First Congress of the Comintern had been more a gesture of intent than an act of organization. Like so many of the actions of the Bolsheviks in 1919, it was a reaction to an event in the West, in this case the attempt of the Socialists to reconstruct the Second International at Berne. But the First Congress had left the basic questions of the working-class movement unanswered, or at least answered only vaguely. It had emphasized the coming revolution, the need to create soviets, the struggle against the opportunists in both the Right and Center of the working-class movement, and it had appealed to all revolutionary elements, whether they were Socialist, anarchist, or syndicalist. The very ambiguity of what the Third International stood for increased its popularity. In March 1920 such disparate individuals as the Italian moderate Socialists Costantino Lazzari and Claudio Treves, the French writer Barbusse, the Dutch left Communist Roland-Holst, the French Centrists Dunois and Verfeuil, the syndicalist Calzan, and the anarchist Emile Chauvelon could announce for adherence.[73] The relationship of the unions to the Comintern had been left particularly vague. At the end of July, Loriot himself, in a letter to an anarchist schoolteacher, admitted that the situation was extremely complex. The Third International, he wrote, was neither a Socialist nor a syndicalist International: it was a Communist International. He supposed that syndicalist organizations would be able to join; but he admitted that this question was still obscure, and he expressed the hope that the Second Congress would throw some light on these questions.[74]

The composition of the French delegation to the Second Congress illustrates the eclecticism of the moment. Flanking Cachin and Frossard were numerous members of the Left Wing, whose comradeship they almost certainly would have preferred to do without. Hardly a shade of postwar radicalism went unrepresented. Raymond Lefebvre and Alfred Rosmer had made their way to Russia separately as delegates of the Committee for the Third International; Vergeat and Lepetit (Bertho) were present as observers for the syndicalist minority; Mauricius (Mauriskoff) fulfilled the same function for the Parti Communiste; Guilbeaux and Sadoul participated actively as representatives of the French group in Moscow; while even the revolutionary students' organization had managed to send a delegate by the name of Goldenberg. To add a further note of confusion, Ernest Lafont, whose left-wing sympathies were beginning to revive after a long period of Centrism, appeared in Petrograd sometime in July.

The congress met in an atmosphere of feverish enthusiasm. The Russian Army was sweeping through Poland toward Warsaw; and a map had been set up in the congress hall to show the daily progress of the Red vanguard, which, it was hoped, would now carry the Revolution into the heart of Europe on its bayonets.[75] The congress held its first meetings in Petrograd, where Lenin delivered the opening report and attempted to show with the aid of Lord Keynes that the capitalist crisis had brought about a revolutionary era, and that the main obstacle to revolution was the opportunism of the reformist Socialist leaders. The theme of the Second Congress, however, was not to be spontaneous revolution or the need to create soviets, as had been the case in the First. All the Bolshevik leaders stressed the importance of discipline and the conscious preparation of the revolutionary struggle. The delegates were handed Lenin's *"Left-Wing" Communism* and Trotsky's *Terror and Communism* on their arrival. In both these books there was an emphasis on organization, discipline, and the need to bend theory to the imperatives of seizing and holding State power. No longer were deviations on the parliamentary and trade-union questions to be allowed.

The great innovation of the congress was the emphasis it placed on the role of the party. The soviets, the Bolsheviks now insisted, could not replace the party. Zinoviev sounded the keynote of the congress when he announced that "the Communist Party forms the motive power, the most important part—the head, the brains of the soviets. . . . The party should be the guiding spirit of the soviets, the trade unions, the schools, the cooperatives, and all organizations formed by the working class."[76] The Communists were not to withdraw from the trade unions; they were to penetrate them and win them over from within. They were not to boycott elections; they were to use them to discredit the parliamentary regime.

The Bolshevik delegation dominated the congress from one end to the other. The Bolsheviks continually stressed that they did not expect reverence for the Russian Revolution. The Communist International was not a Russian but a world organization, and the Bolsheviks were merely disciplined soldiers in the ranks of the world revolutionary movement.[77] But the failure of the revolutionary movement in the West and the brilliant success of the Bolsheviks in consolidating their revolution made equality difficult. Serrati expressed this only too accurately when he pointed out that Lenin was the leader of the Russian Revolution while he was only the head of a tiny Communist Party.[78] As E. H. Carr has remarked, whatever the ostensible purpose of the Second Congress, its historical result "was to establish Russian leadership of the Comintern on an impregnable basis."[79]

Cachin and Frossard followed the debates as closely as they could, but their role tended to be passive rather than active. They had to stand by while they were treated to further abuse. Zinoviev, in his report on the French situation, took the SFIO to task for its tradition of social pacifism and its Wilsonianism.[80] Although Lenin criticized the Ultra-Left in Italy, Holland, Germany, and England, he made it clear that in France the main enemy was opportunism. Trotsky went out of his way to indicate his solidarity with the revolutionary syndicalists, despite their theoretical differences. I can talk things over with Rosmer, he said, but what do I have in common with Renaudel?[81] On one occasion, Zinoviev scourged Frossard directly for an article he had written suggesting that in the Third International the various parties would be free to determine their tactics as they pleased: "So you see, they have the idea that the Communist International is a good hotel, where representatives of different countries will sing the *Internationale* and pay one another compliments. Then everyone will go his separate way and continue the old practices. We will never permit the accursed practices of the Second International."[82]

Discussing *L'Humanité,* Zinoviev scoffed at the idea of proportional representation for the views of the various factions: "It is a kind of provocation: eight drops of aqua destillata, three drops of poison, and then, as an antidote, four drops of milk. (*Applause.*) This cannot go on."[83] On the subject of Longuet, Zinoviev was evasive. He categorically rejected any idea of comradeship with the leaders of the Center, including Kautsky, Hilferding, and Longuet. But he cleverly left the door open: "The French tell us Longuet will probably change his mind now, he will change his views. If he accepts our point of view, so much the better; we will welcome him, if he is sincere and earnest."[84]

The real action of the congress for the French delegation took place in the corridors. The French were anxious to return home. They emphasized to Zinoviev and Kamenev that they could not accept conditions that required the party to expel specific persons. Zinoviev seemed to agree. But on July 26, the exuberant President of the Comintern handed them a reply to their questions concerning the terms of admission to the Third International that was so stiff it "dumbfounded" them.[85] Included in the Russian memorandum, which reproached the French for their timidity and opportunism, and condemned Longuet, Faure, and Pressemane by name, were nine conditions for French admission to the Third International. Frossard and Cachin reacted violently. Rakovsky and other Bolsheviks attempted to calm their fears. According to Frossard, Cachin gave in, but he (Frossard) maintained his opposition. He had been told by Wilhelm Dittmann and Artur Crispien, the delegates of the USPD, that the Congress intended to make the conditions of admission still more stringent, that the party would be required to expel Longuet, and that it would have to give two-thirds of the places on the new Central Committee to Loriot and his friends. Zinoviev once more attempted to dissuade Frossard from his opposition. He insisted that the Bolsheviks were not after the expulsion of Longuet, but were merely concerned about the reformist policies that he symbolized. As for the two-thirds, that was "merely a wish."

Frossard later suggested that he gave in against his better instincts. He felt, he said, that it was his duty to stand by the Russian Revolution. Besides, it was the party that would decide and not Cachin and himself, who were simply its agents. His aim was to preserve as much party unity as possible. "Our plan was to keep the maximum, to save everything that circumstances permitted us to save. We remained with the working class, at the side of the world's first Socialist revolution."[86] The last sentence gives the key to his decision. The working class stood with the Bolsheviks; the Socialist leaders had no choice but to follow. For all his maneuvers, Frossard had been outwitted by the Bolsheviks. Having already telegraphed home his decision, he knew very well that he could not change his mind without playing into the hands of the Right.

The French question, meanwhile, was having reverberations in the congress. On July 28, Cachin read a declaration, signed by himself and Frossard, accepting the International's demands and promising to work for a stronger, more centralized, and more revolutionary party. He insisted, however, that Longuet, had he been there, would have done the same.[87] "We shall henceforth break conclusively with the past," he said, "and advance resolutely to deeds, the judgment of which we shall leave to the Communist International." Cachin's judiciously worded statement did little to satisfy the more radical members of the congress, who were anxious to bar the Center before passing on to the Revolution they were certain was close at hand. Nicola Bombacci, Guilbeaux, Bordiga, Wijnkoop, Lozovsky, Rakovsky, Münzenberg, and Lefebvre all spoke against admitting the Center.[h] Lefebvre pointed out how thoroughly corrupt the Socialist parliamentary Group was, how the majority had lost the support of the masses, and how parliamentarism had been discredited. He warned against the danger of admitting the SFIO without a thoroughgoing purge. The conversion of Cachin and Frossard, he urged, was only a conversion of individuals. With their long opportunist past, they would lead the French party on the basis of a minimum program. The Left must remain pitiless and unyielding; the masses, he guaranteed, would follow.[88]

It was typical of the new turn in Bolshevik policy that Zinoviev felt compelled to defend the policy of the ECCI against these enraged revolutionary purists. Zinoviev admitted that he considered the declaration of Cachin and Frossard "a sort of retreat," in relation to their earlier statements.[89] He insisted, however, that it was necessary to deal with the representatives of the Center in order not to lose the French workers for the Communist International. "How would we be able to explain to them that we had not negotiated with Cachin and Frossard?"[90] He pointed out, moreover, that the ECCI had sent a letter to the French workers, on the very day the French delegates left for Moscow, in which it denounced Longuet as a social pacifist and compared Renaudel and Thomas to the "dog" Noske.[i] But even these remarks did not reassure the Left, and Lenin's original Eighteen Theses were increased to 21. According to the Twenty-One Conditions, the German Independents and the French Center had to call extraordinary congresses within four months, and those Socialists who rejected the conditions had to be expelled. In his Theses, Lenin had not set a time limit. The revised conditions were at least in part a reaction to the treatment that the Bolsheviks had accorded the Center.[91]

Cachin and Frossard were blissfully unaware of these developments. They

[h] Bombacci was soon to become a fascist.
[i] Gustav Noske was a German Social Democrat who, as Minister of War, acted to suppress the Spartacist movement in Germany in 1918–19. He was known throughout the international Communist movement as one of the hangmen of the German revolution and one of the murderers of Rosa Luxemburg and Karl Liebknecht.

had one last meeting with Lenin on July 28 and left for France the next day, eight days before the congress was to end and a full week before the Twenty-One Conditions were ratified. Lenin was absorbed in the Polish campaign, and mused to them about the chances of the Revolution's bursting out of Poland to infect Germany, Hungary, the Balkans, and Italy. After an hour and a half of conversation, the two Frenchmen promised to send after them a larger delegation to Russia. Lenin urged them to make sure it included some workers. And also Jean Longuet, they countered, who they were confident would be with the International. According to Frossard, Lenin smiled skeptically and said: "I doubt it." He repeated, however, that personalities had no importance; and they left him on that note.[92]

As Cachin and Frossard traveled home, they might very well have mused on the accomplishments of their mission. True, the Bolsheviks had handed out some rude blows. After all, they were revolutionaries engaged in a life-and-death struggle for the mastery of a huge State, and—who could tell?—perhaps all of Europe. But underneath their bluntness, these Bolsheviks had shown themselves to be sensible and hardheaded negotiators. It was clear they wanted as large a majority as possible in France, and they had even talked of concessions to the peculiarities of the French situation. They had not demanded that the French make a revolution, merely that they build up their organization and prepare for one. Perhaps a dose of Bolshevik resoluteness and ardor would not hurt the tired old French party. Perhaps a new age demanded new methods.

### AT THE CIRQUE DE PARIS

Cachin and Frossard arrived in Paris on August 12, after an uneventful trip by way of Reval and Stockholm. At Petrograd they halted their journey while Cachin, who was already beginning to feel himself a veteran of Russian visits, showed Frossard the Winter Palace and what still remained of the painting collections at the Hermitage. André le Troquer, who met the two French delegates at the Gare du Nord, found Frossard was "still a little reticent, but Marcel Cachin was enthusiastic, resolutely decided." "From Marcel Cachin's first words," recalled Le Troquer many years later, "I was struck by the unexpected extension ... that he gave to Karl Marx's formula: 'Force is the great midwife of History.' "[j]

---

[j] *Journal Officiel de la République Française, Débats, Assemblée Nationale,* 18.ii.58. Not all the French delegates to the Second Congress fared as well as Cachin and Frossard. Ernest Lafont, who had come to the congress on his own initiative, was expelled from Russian territory on Trotsky's orders. Oddly enough, Lafont later joined the new Communist Party, though he soon found it confining. Mauricius, the delegate of the Parti Communiste, was detained until the other delegates had returned home, at Rosmer's insistence. Rosmer suspected him of being a police agent. Henri Guilbeaux, *Du Kremlin au Cherche-Midi* (1933), pp. 243–44. For the more gruesome fate of Lefebvre, Lepetit, and Vergeat, see pp. 196–97 below.

The next night Cachin and Frossard reported on their trip at a mass meeting held in the Cirque de Paris. It had been decided in advance that they would not touch on the question of adherence to the Third International, but merely recount what they had seen. This distinction required an objectivity of which Cachin was no longer capable. And what doubts Frossard might have had vanished when he saw the audience and sensed its mood. Over 10,000 spectators, many of them workers, crowded into the vast amphitheater. The meeting began at eight and lasted three hours. By a quarter after eight there was not a free seat in the Cirque, and men and women were huddled together anxiously under the electric lights, waiting for the reports of the two travelers. "We never saw a more attentive, a more vibrant, a more enthusiastic audience," wrote *L'Humanité*'s correspondent.[93] Frossard, who was a veteran of thousands of campaign meetings, recalled that none of them "left with me such a moving and imperishable memory."[94] When Cachin and Frossard finally managed to make their way through the crowd onto the stage, they were greeted with shouts of "Vive Cachin! Vive Frossard! Vive Jaurès! Vive Lénine! Vive Sadoul! Vive les Soviets!" The crowd chanted the *Internationale* in unison.

This was no moment for reportage. What the crowd wanted was a myth. The two French delegates rose to the occasion. Frossard, the first speaker, began by asserting that the Russian Revolution was "the most terrific event of the century."[95] Paraphrasing Jaurès, he then pointed out the bond between the French revolutionary tradition and the Russian Revolution, which Lenin had been at such great pains to emphasize during their visit: "They [the Russians] are faithful to this action of the past 'as the river is faithful to its source in flowing toward the sea.' It's because they have drive and momentum that they go forward, that they act, and that they are the true heirs of our revolutionary tradition; they have taken up the flame while we have only kept the ashes!"

With the audience hanging on his every word, Frossard went on to emphasize the influence of the Bolsheviks and their popularity within the country. "It's a new world that is getting to its feet there in the East, already trembling and overflowing with life." Frossard dwelt particularly on the proletarian basis of Bolshevik power and the importance of the unions, which he described as "the pillar of Soviet society." And finally, he explained how the Soviet workers were aware that France was at the head of the anti-Russian alliance, and how they were asked everywhere they went: "But what is the Parisian proletariat doing?" "Comrade workers," he concluded, "it is not a question of asking you to make a revolution tomorrow, nor, if you make it, of slavishly copying the Russian soviets. It's a question today of demonstrating, in some way other than in words, our solidarity with the Russian proletariat."

Cachin spoke next, and as usual his speech was highly emotional. "What joy," he sighed, "for an old Socialist, who has dreamed for thirty years of seeing a society in which labor is not exploited, to set foot in Russia, where labor alone has power and all the power." The important thing, emphasized Cachin, was that Russia was a Socialist State in which the bourgeoisie had been driven from their positions of entrenched power; all other considerations must pale before this fact of Soviet power.

A Republic without a bourgeoisie, where the workers and peasants alone command, that is what kind of a regime it is. Try to imagine the consequences of such an act of affirmation! You can question the means by which the idea is applied. You can criticize, reason, find fault, judge peremptorily and severely from the safety of your armchair! You will not have altered the fact, the enormous fact, unique in the history of the world.

From August 15 to September 25, 1920, Cachin and Frossard toured France, explaining their Russian trip and advocating adherence to the Third International. At the same time, they published a series of articles in *L'Humanité* describing different facets of Soviet society: the trade unions, the position of the intellectuals, the educational system, the Soviet courts, the function of the Communist Party. Throughout their travels and articles, they defended the undemocratic nature of the Soviet regime, and scolded the French Socialists for their carping criticism of the Bolsheviks. After all, the Bolsheviks had made *their* revolution. This was what had given the Russian Revolution its great, worldwide prestige. The Russians had dispossessed the possessors.[96] "When a French Socialist meets such men," wrote Cachin, who spoke from experience on this matter, "he has everything to learn from them. He has lessons to take; he has none to give."[97] It is true that the Bolsheviks often treated the French Socialists with violence and bitterness, Cachin wrote. But they were justified in their excesses by the fact that they were in the midst of the battle to create Socialism.

If they often express themselves bitterly and violently, it's because they are involved in the most intense and most decisive of battles. They offer us the example of men of implacable energy; within their own country they have destroyed the old bourgeois world; they are reconstructing the life of their nation on a new basis; they are building Socialism over there as we must build it ourselves in our own country.[98]

Only *amour-propre* could prevent the French Socialists from recognizing their achievements and following their example.

These points—the strength and influence of the Soviet regime (indeed the very fact of its existence!), the connection between the Russian Revolution and the French revolutionary tradition, the need for the French proletariat to make a gesture of solidarity with their Russian brothers, who had been shot at with French guns by French soldiers—were to be the main themes of Cachin and Frossard in their campaign for the Third International. They did not ask the French workers to make a revolution; nor did they ask them to adopt Bolshevik methods or institutions. And, in their haste to excuse the Bolsheviks for the violence of their language and the bitterness of their attacks on the French Socialist leaders, they suggested that it was in bad taste to criticize men who had actually made a revolution. This attitude, inculcated in the French workers by the Socialist leaders at an early stage, together with the immediate popularity that the Russian Revolution already enjoyed and the distrust the French militants felt for their wartime leaders, provided the basis for the influence the Bolsheviks were later able to exert on the French working-class movement.

### THE DISINTEGRATION OF THE CENTER

The telegram Cachin and Frossard had sent from Moscow and their statements on their return opened a great debate within the party that lasted until the Congress of Tours. The Right (Renaudel, Thomas) had announced from the beginning that to go to Moscow would mean a split. They now had the added authority of Guesde, who remained untouched by the enthusiasm of Cachin, once one of his favorite pupils. For the old dogmatist, the Bolsheviks remained the assassins of Plekhanov, and it was absurd to think of building Socialism "in Europe's most backward country, intellectually, politically, economically."[99] Two visits to his retreat on the Rue Singer in Passy failed to shake his opposition. The most Cachin and Frossard could wring from him was the affirmation "Il faut monter la garde autour de la Révolution russe!"[100] The real question, however, was what would the Center do, what position would the majority of the party take? Here it is necessary to make a distinction between the leaders and the rank and file. The leadership of the Center splintered into three parts. The Left Center followed Cachin and Frossard, Longuet and Faure tried to remain uncommitted, and the Right Center rejoined the Right.

The reaction of Daniel Renoult was typical of the response of those elements among the Reconstructors who all along had interpreted Reconstruction as a prelude to joining the Third International. Renoult applauded the telegram from Moscow, and interpreted it to mean that the SFIO could now enter the Third International with a clear conscience. If two men as prudent and as well known for their spirit of compromise as Cachin and Frossard had approved adherence, then the Bolsheviks must not have presented any condition that was unacceptable to the French party. This new turn of events, Renoult went on, had made the anticipated Congress of Reconstruction both impractical and unnecessary. The spirit of the Strasbourg resolution had not been fulfilled. Even if a Congress of Reconstruction were to be held, it should not take place until *after* the next congress of the party; and Renoult was confident that the party would vote for adherence to the Third International by a large majority at such a congress.[101]

A few days later, the same commentator suggested in what mood enlightened Centrists now contemplated membership in the Third International.

Joining Moscow's International, said Renoult, would not have the terrible results that many Socialists had predicted. But it would have one very important effect: it would make the party revolutionary. The last remnants of War Socialism would be rooted out; the party, reinvigorated by the spirit of revolutionary Russia, would abandon its vacillating and timid policies; the actions of the CAP and the parliamentary Group would be coordinated, which would finally make it possible to give the party effective leadership.[102] As for the Nine Conditions, Renoult saw nothing in them that was in contradiction with the historical principles of Socialism. Besides, it was not a question of trying to impose on everyone a rigorously uniform interpretation. Nor would those men who had forged certain methods or "rules of action" in fifteen or twenty years of Socialist struggle be forced to give up all that overnight. "All those who accept these Conditions in general," concluded Renoult, "will have the right and the duty to vote for adherence to the Third International."[103]

In their first statements, Cachin and Frossard did everything possible to suggest that this was the proper interpretation of the Nine Conditions. They knew that adherence to the Third International would mean a split in the party; but they wanted the schism to be as far to the Right as possible and they were particularly anxious to salvage the Longuet-Faure wing of the party.[104] Cachin insisted that there was really only one condition: "to break decisively with class collaboration, to act like Socialists, to prepare for the coming revolution. The rest is a question of form, that is to say, secondary."[105] Frossard, at a meeting of the Federation of the Seine held in early September, emphasized that during the negotiations in Moscow, expulsion had never been considered a necessary condition for admittance to the Comintern: " 'What we ask of you,' Bukharin made clear, 'is that you fight with the greatest possible energy against opportunism and social reformism. We're not asking you to give up your Socialist unity'—that is to say," added Frossard, "our unity among real Socialists."[106] Frossard assured this gathering that there were only nine conditions. The unity of French syndicalism, he guaranteed, was in no way endangered by the Comintern. Cachin concluded by sugaring the pill of the conditions still further: "Lorsqu'à tête reposée, chacun de vous lira le texte des neufs conditions, qui nous sont proposées, il en retiendra l'esprit plus que la lettre."[107]

Not all the leaders of the Center, however, were so taken with the Comintern, nor did they lose their heads over the statements of Cachin and Frossard. Longuet and Faure were at first extremely reserved in their comments. On August 30 *Le Populaire* published the Eighteen Theses that Lenin had prepared before the congress, and on September 2 it published the text of the Twenty-One Conditions, taken from the German paper *Die Freiheit*. On examining these conditions, Faure found that those pertaining to the unions, the expelling of Longuet, and the predominance of the Left in the central organs of the party were unacceptable.[108] If Moscow put these conditions on the

French party's membership in the Third International, Faure wrote, then for his part, no matter how strong his wish to join, he had to reject the terms.[109] Longuet was at first more cautious. He admitted that the bonds between the sections of the old International had been too loose. But two days later he declared that the Twenty-One Conditions were "absolutely unacceptable."[110] Divided profoundly on this question, the Committee for the Reconstruction of the International quickly disintegrated. On September 23, Renoult, Dunois, Paul Louis, Tommasi, Ferdinand Faure, Frossard, and C.-E. Labrousse resigned from the Committee.

Frossard and Cachin were caught in a dilemma by the question of the conditions. Frossard later claimed that he had learned of the Twenty-One Conditions only toward the end of September, during a meeting in Lille.[k] He accused the Bolsheviks of having deliberately deceived him and Cachin. As the reader will suspect, the truth was more complex. Frossard himself admitted that he knew the conditions were being augmented when he left the congress. He had heard from Crispien that Longuet might be barred by name, and that the Left might be awarded two-thirds of the places on the Central Committee of the new party. He had no doubt hoped to be able to deal with these ticklish questions when they arose. On the other hand, the Bolsheviks themselves had been pushed by the Left to raise the conditions of admission. The result was a chaos of conditions. For a brief moment in the fall of 1920 there were four sets of conditions: the Eighteen Theses of Lenin; the Nine Conditions brought back by Cachin and Frossard; the Ten Conditions in the letter of the ECCI to the French proletariat;[l] and the Twenty-One Conditions published by *Die Freiheit* and later by *Le Populaire*. The first reaction of Frossard and Cachin was to insist that the Twenty-One Conditions did not apply to France. But a letter from Serrati, published by *Le Populaire* on October 2, made it clear that the conditions were applicable everywhere, with no exceptions. On October 8 the conditions were finally published in *L'Humanité,* and five days later Frossard publicly acknowledged them—adding, however, that they were only a general guide to revolutionary action, to be followed to the extent circumstances permitted.

---

[k] Frossard, *De Jaurès à Lénine* (1930), p. 165. See also his *La Décomposition du Communisme* (n.d.), p. 12: "The Nine Conditions we were acquainted with at Moscow had become Twenty-One by the time we arrived in Paris. But what could we do? We had begun our campaign. They knew that we were in too deep to turn back. Even if we had wanted to, the defeat of the Red Army after its march on Warsaw would have prevented us from doing so. It was thus with halting steps and a far from easy mind that we laid the groundwork for the Congress of Tours."

[l] The Tenth Condition, which was added to the letter of the Executive, was the one requiring the Center to come to terms with the Left. See *Der Zweite Weltkongress der Kommunistischen Internationale an der französische Proletariat* (Berlin, 1920), and André Pierre, *Le 2ᵉ Congrès de l'Internationale Communiste* (1920). Pierre was a Centrist.

The announcement of the Twenty-One Conditions further exacerbated the tensions within the party, and frustrated the efforts of Cachin and Frossard to keep the split in the party as far to the Right as possible. Pressemane analyzed the Twenty-One Conditions and found them completely unacceptable. Meanwhile, Léon Blum had emerged as the leading spokesman of the Right. Toward the end of October he published a series of articles in *L'Humanité,* in which he argued against adherence to the Third International. The real question at issue, insisted Blum, was not the defense of the Russian Revolution, or even whether the Revolution had failed or succeeded. Nor was it a question of revolution versus reform. Reformism, Blum asserted, was dead in France. The real issue was whether or not the principles and methods of Moscow had universal value. What were opposed were two different concepts of revolution: the French and the Bolshevik.[111]

Blum then went on in succeeding articles to contrast the democratic basis of the existing party with the autocratic tendencies of Bolshevism: "I refuse to reconstruct the party in the image of the old-time Carbonari or Freemasons. I refuse to subject it to a compulsory discipline that proceeds from the top down. I refuse to think of it as some kind of vast secret society. And if it is absolutely necessary to choose, I still prefer what is to what is being offered us."[112] Blum accused the Communists of being unduly preoccupied with the seizure of power. Such a doctrine, he argued, might lead to premature attempts at insurrection, or at best to seizures of power in circumstances such that the period of the dictatorship of the proletariat would last too long.[113]

Blum's attempt to come to grips with Bolshevism illustrates the dilemma faced by European democratic Socialism after the War and the Russian Revolution. Blum argued that one could love the Russian Revolution dearly, be committed to its defense, yet reject Bolshevism *in France.* Yet this was precisely the kind of intellectual evasion which the Bolsheviks refused to permit. And in a world torn by strife, in which the bourgeoisie seemed lined up on one side and the proletariat on the other, it was the arguments of the Bolsheviks that were the more convincing to men of revolutionary convictions. As Daniel Renoult said: "The Third International and the Russian Revolution are indissolubly united. For us," he went on, "Russia is not just *any country.* ... It is the common homeland of all Socialists; its cause is *ours*; its suffering makes our heart bleed."[114]

### THE REACTION OF THE LEFT WING

The Committee for the Third International and the Left Wing in general were no more pleased by the conversion of Cachin and Frossard than the Right.[115] During the months preceding the return of the two French representatives, the leaders of the Left Wing had become more and more violent in their attacks on the Reconstructors. The onslaught had been led by Souvarine, who found in the vitriolic language of the Bolsheviks a fit model for his own style. By mid-July he had concluded that the policy of the Center was "in fact that of class collaboration, dressed in a revolutionary mask"; and that its line was "even more dangerous than avowed reformism, for it deceives the proletariat, makes it vulnerable to cruel disappointments, and discredits Socialism."[116] The distinction between tactical error and political betrayal had been abandoned altogether in true Leninist fashion. "It's not two, ten, or twenty members who are traitors; it's the entire majority," he announced on July 22.[117]

The first reaction of Souvarine to the conversion of the Centrist delegates was to suggest that the ECCI had overestimated their value. Besides, Souvarine thought it was unlikely that the statements of Cachin and Frossard would be acceptable to their Centrist friends, even to Daniel Renoult and Paul Louis.[118] But even if the Reconstructors did intend to follow their delegates and seek admission to the Third International, Souvarine warned them that their lives would not be easy. The situation, he observed, was now turning in favor of the Committee. Its task was far from finished. It would live on in order to make sure that the resolutions of the Communist International were carried out to the letter. And the Committee had no intention of allowing the policies for which it had fought so stubbornly to be applied by men who yesterday had been its enemies.[119]

These threats hid bitter disappointment and an unwillingness to distinguish between policies and men. Nevertheless, for the moment Souvarine and his friends had no choice but to cooperate with Cachin and Frossard, who had come back to France invested with the authority of the Third International. The Left Wing was still weak; its leaders were in prison; they expected to be there for some time to come. Souvarine criticized the timidity of the statements made by the French delegates to the ECCI; but he added that the Committee would welcome any sincere aid from Cachin and Frossard; and in September he noted that, since returning, they had been faithful to their commitments.[120] As for Longuet and his friends, he pointed out that they had not been expelled in the Conditions. However, they would bar themselves if they continued to oppose Communist propaganda. The Communist International, wrote Souvarine, was a group for the defense of the proletariat, and not a parliament. "To those who say that they cannot accept the expulsions required by the Communist International, we reply that the Communist International is even less able to accept members who would be fatal to it. The Communist Hercules makes no claim of cleansing the Augean stables of the Second International and of parties gone rotten through electoralism and opportunism. It has built its own house, which is also a clean house, and it is not open to whoever wants to enter."[121]

Despite the biting words which continued to issue from Souvarine's pen, he and his fellow members of the Committee joined with Cachin, Frossard, and those who followed them to draw up a common motion for the Congress of Tours. Souvarine was its principal author; Amédée Dunois and Paul Louis contributed the sections on the unions. Even a Bolshevik, no matter how devoted, had to admit that the bourgeois democracy of the Third Republic offered certain advantages. One was the treatment it gave political prisoners. You could write articles (so long as they were signed with a pseudonym), edit a Communist journal, receive visitors, plan strategy for the overthrow of the government, publish a series of books by Lenin, or mastermind a campaign to bring the SFIO into the Communist International. Souvarine did all these things; and in 1920 and early 1921 the Santé became a sort of second headquarters for the party.[122]

The motion drafted by Souvarine and accepted by Cachin and Frossard was not a simple restatement of the Twenty-One Conditions—which even the members of the Left Wing regarded as impossible—but an attempt to adapt the Conditions to the French situation.[123] There were three major modifications. Souvarine's text specifically stated that the representatives of the Center alluded to in Condition Seven (Longuet and friends) should be excepted from exclusion, as provided in Condition Twenty; and that these exceptions should also hold for the delegates to the congress who voted against the motion of the Left but were willing to accept the decisions of the congress. This concession was a sop to the Center. It had the sanction of Zinoviev himself, who had met with Renoult in October, at the Congress of the German Independents at Halle, and agreed that not only would Longuet's forces be permitted to stay in the party if they submitted to the majority, but they would also receive one-third of the places on the party's ruling bodies.[124] Second, the section on the unions rejected the tactic of burrowing from within (*noyautage*) adopted by the Second Congress, and stated that though the unions and the party would "coordinate their action, one organization would not be subject to the other." Finally, the new party would continue to call itself "Parti Socialiste, Section Française de l'Internationale Communiste," and not "Parti Communiste."[125] These were all major concessions on the part of the Comintern. If adhered to, they would have implied a policy that acknowledged national differences. What they meant in reality was that the Bolsheviks were willing to yield the form to gain the substance. The important thing was to cast the net as widely as possible.

If the Socialists of the Committee for the Third International were momentarily taken aback by the decision of the Comintern to deal with the delegates of the Center, one can imagine the reaction of the syndicalists and anarchists, for whom the SFIO was the traditional enemy and parliamentarism a blight on revolutionary virtue. We will consider the response of the revolutionary syndicalists in detail at a later point. For the moment, suffice it to say that the policies of the Comintern threw them into disarray; and though they remained uncommitted in public, they did not hesitate to reveal their concern in private. As for the militants of the Ultra-Left, they regarded the events leading up to the formation of the French Communist Party with unconcealed hostility. Mauriskoff, of the Parti Communiste, accused Souvarine of wanting to create a mass party that would include the Center.[126] *Le Communiste,* the journal of the Fédération Communiste des Soviets, reacted unfavorably to the parliamentarism of Communist tactics. In early September, Mauriskoff wrote in a fit of pique, "If in Moscow they still don't want 'to recognize' us, we shall remain 'Communists.' "[127] In October the Parti Communiste broke with both the Committee for the Third International and the syndicalist minority because they refused to leave their organizations. But a Communist Party, no matter how extremist and violent, had no reason for being outside the Moscow International. The last issue of *Le Communiste* appeared on December 12, 1920, just before the opening of the Congress of Tours. Other Ultra-Leftists of Socialist leanings resolved to carry on the struggle for revolutionary purity from within the new party. To them the reconciliation of the Left and the Center smelled of deals, parliamentarism, and corruption. And thus it was that one of the motions at Tours, submitted in the name of Heine and Leroy and opposed by the Left, called for a "pure and simple" acceptance of the Twenty-One Conditions.

### THE TWENTY-SECOND CONDITION

As the campaign for the Third International approached its climax, battle lines hardened. The great bulk of the party, it was obvious, would follow Cachin and Frossard and go to Moscow. The Left had little choice but to accept these tardy conversions to Bolshevism, even if grudgingly and with suspicion. The Right, it was just as clear, would split from the majority rather than enter the Third International; and, in any case, it was a departure agreed to by both sides, for the Comintern would not accept them. In early December this Right took more precise form when Vincent Auriol, Marius Moutet, Blum, Bracke, Mayéras, Paul-Boncour, and Pressemane formed a Committee of Socialist Resistance.[128] The organization of the Right revealed the final disintegration of the Longuet majority. Its Left followed Cachin, Frossard, and Renoult to union with the Committee for the Third International. Its Right joined Blum and Paul-Boncour on the Committee of Socialist Resistance.

This much was foreseeable; Frossard had accepted the inevitability of a split with the Right and a portion of the Center as far back as June. The burning question, however, involved the fate of Longuet and his circle. Would Longuet accept the Twenty-One Conditions and swallow his pride? Or would he move toward a bloc with the Right? The last phase of the campaign for the Third International turned into a battle for Longuet's soul. The leaders of the Left

Center, particularly Frossard and Renoult, clung to Longuet with the desperation of men neck-deep in quicksand, who hold on for dear life to the last solid branch on firm ground. They brandished their agreement with Zinoviev at Halle, and pointed to the motion of the Left which specifically demanded Longuet's exemption from the clause in the conditions expelling him.[129] They spoke of the special treatment the International was according him. They asked him to make that single step in their direction which would save the party's revolutionary unity.

The Bolsheviks, though, approached the matter of Longuet in a quite different spirit. They had indulged Renoult's whim with good-natured condescension because they were anxious to win as large a party as possible in France. However, they did not think for a minute that Longuet would actually agree to enter the Third International. Nor did they intend to let him. Ever since the fall of 1919, Russian propaganda had been designed to make it impossible for Longuet to go to Moscow. The Twenty-One Conditions were merely one of the instruments for achieving the desired purpose. "What would you do if the Hilferding-Dittmann-Crispien group accepted your Twenty-One Conditions?" Zinoviev was once asked. "We would find a Twenty-Second," he replied.[m]

The Twenty-Second Condition was the willingness to accept humiliation. Less than a week after concluding the agreement with Renoult at Halle, Zinoviev addressed an appeal to the French workers that was intended to back Longuet and his friends against the wall. French comrades, the message ran, the Communist International is ready to come to an understanding with you about any matter of detail or organization. The only condition that the Communist International insists upon as an "absolute ultimatum" is a complete break with the reformists and the expulsion of all those who will not accept the dictatorship of the proletariat. "All the rest is only of secondary importance." Then the crucial paragraph: "With a pistol at their throat, you must insist on an answer from Longuet and his followers, and depending on their answer, and on whether or not they accept the Communist International's theses and conditions in good faith and agree to apply them wholeheartedly, in fact and not only in words, a final decision on them will be made."[130]

Frossard made light of "Zinoviev's pistol," and went so far as to state at a

[m] Ruth Fischer, *Stalin and German Communism* (Cambridge, Mass., 1948), p. 143. Zinoviev talked quite frankly about the Russian position the next summer, at the Third World Congress. The Bolsheviks agreed to Renoult's demands at Halle, he explained, not because they had decided to accept Longuet and his friends, but because the Communist wing was weak and its leaders were in prison. The tactic of the Executive Committee was to continually prod and humiliate Longuet, while demonstrating to the French working class that the Comintern was willing to compromise. *Protokoll des III Kongresses der Kommunistischen Internationale, Moskau, 22. Juni bis 12. Juli, 1921* (Hamburg, 1921), pp. 192–94.

meeting of the Federation of the Seine that he had never consented, nor would he ever consent, to the exclusion of Longuet, which he would consider "as an indignity and a dishonor."[131] But his reassurances did little to erase the memory of Zinoviev's clumsy threats or the sting of Souvarine's insults. *Le Populaire* had occasion almost every day in December to complain of attacks against the Reconstructors by the Committee for the Third International, especially Souvarine, of whom the least that can be said is that he was overzealous and oversuccessful in assimilating the Bolshevik style of polemic. In early December, Souvarine made it clear that the Left accorded an extremely limited significance to the agreement made with Zinoviev at Halle:

The Committee for the Third International, in asking the Executive Committee of the International to apply the clause on exceptions to the exclusion of Centrists, in no way intended to assure impunity to the Longuets who act against the interests of the proletariat every day; nor does it intend to permit them to pursue their counter-revolutionary activity in the party.[132]

Souvarine followed this article with another, a few days later, in which he implied vague threats even if the Center did accept the Conditions and was thus allowed in the new Communist Party. The so-called "Left" Reconstructors, he wrote, had shown by their attitude that they had nothing in common with the Communists. Whatever their attitude after the Congress of Tours, the Left would refuse to collaborate with them in the central organs of the party. If Longuet and his friends accepted the decision of the Congress and Moscow's Theses, Souvarine granted, then they would be able to stay in the party. They would even be given the chance to rehabilitate themselves. But they would have to prove themselves before they could expect to be entrusted with positions of responsibility. And Souvarine ended with a vicious personal attack on Longuet: "If Longuet imagines that he is thinking when he dreams, that he is speaking when he rambles, and that he is writing when he scribbles over paper, we will not be cruel enough to deprive him of his last illusions; but no one will contest the right of the party's majority to send an evil-doing mediocrity off to practice his evil deeds somewhere else."[133]

Longuet meanwhile searched for a middle course between the determined resistance of the Right and the boundless enthusiasm of the Left; but his discomfort and doubts were clear. He and Faure prepared a separate motion for the Congress of Tours which asked the Third International to admit the SFIO, but rejected the Conditions bearing on clandestine organization, expulsions for infractions of discipline, periodic purges, the subordination of the unions to the party, the ending of proportional representation in the party's ruling bodies and newspapers, and the changing of the party's name.[134] The Longuet-Faure motion accepted the concept of the dictatorship of the proletariat, acknowledged that parliament was of limited value as a means of social transformation, and went at least as far as the motion of the Left on the question of the relationship between the party and the unions, demanding a firm entente between the CAP and the CGT. What divided the two motions in fact was not doctrine (the Longuet-Faure resolution only repeated the reservations of the Left and added its objection to clandestine activity), but the Reconstructors' insistence that the party preserve its national autonomy and not be dictated to from Moscow. As Longuet wrote at the end of November, he and his friends had also formulated one condition sine qua non: that the freedom to express oneself within the party was not to be infringed upon. The party was not to be forced to undergo "the imbecilic and fatal surgery that certain people are demanding."[135]

To Socialists eager for a revolutionary gesture, these words of wisdom seemed like unnecessary and even suspicious quibbling. As the opening of the Congress neared, the gap between Longuet and the partisans of the Third International widened. Rumors of a conspiracy against the party's unity were rife; and when Faure attended a meeting of the Committee of Socialist Resistance, Frossard lost no time in exploiting his act against the Center and in favor of adherence. On December 5–7, 1920, the representatives of the European Center met in Berne to set a date for a Socialist international congress to be held at Vienna in February 1921. This was the origin of the so-called Second-and-a-Half International. The Centrists criticized the Third International for its attempt to impose Bolshevik tactics on all countries, and asserted the need for national autonomy and flexible methods. On December 11, *Le Populaire* came out strongly in favor of the Berne Conference. What a difference, wrote Longuet, between its declarations and "Zinoviev's frenetic imprecations."[136]

Longuet's increasing estrangement from Moscow may well have been hastened by news just received from northern Europe. On December 1, *L'Humanité* had announced the disappearance of Raymond Lefebvre and his traveling companions, the syndicalists Lepetit and Vergeat. The official Communist version, based on reports from Stockholm, was that the three Frenchmen had perished while trying to run the Allied blockade. Eager to return home from their extended stay in "the land of soviets," the three were said to have set off across the White Sea in a small sailboat. A violent storm had come up, and the group was never heard from again. The Communist interpretation, of course, assumed that the three Frenchmen had been anxious to return to France to reveal the glories of the Russian Revolution. Other commentators were more suspicious. *Le Libertaire,* for example, did not hesitate to suggest that Lefebvre, Vergeat, and Lepetit had been the victims of Bolshevik intrigue. The two syndicalists, it turned out, had written letters home expressing their disillusionment with the Russian Revolution. Might not the Bolsheviks have acted to prevent the return of such unenthusiastic observers to France? Many anarchists thought so, and Longuet and his friends were perhaps not immune to suspicions of this sort themselves.[137]

At any rate, by the middle of December the outcome of the Socialists' congress was no longer in doubt. Preliminary voting in the federations had revealed the existence of a "strong, sentimental, mystical, and irrational current toward the Communist International."[138] At Paris the partisans of adherence had buried their opponents beneath a landslide of over 13,000 votes; and even the conservative Federation of the Nord had passed the Souvarine-Frossard motion by a margin of almost two to one. Within the leadership the final alignments had taken place. Heine's Ultra-Left, Loriot's Left, and the Frossard-Cachin Center would go to Moscow; Blum's Right already spoke of a new organization; Longuet's group would opt for independence, even if the cost were schism. Renaudel? Thomas? Varenne? In two years the party had moved so far leftward that they no longer had a voice.

### TOURS

Despite its preordained result, the Congress of Tours (December 25–30, 1920) was an exciting and eventful moment in the history of the French working-class movement. All the elements of high melodrama were there, from the clandestine arrival of the Comintern's representative, Klara Zetkin, to the impassioned plea for the independence of Indochina by a young delegate who was later to be better known as Ho Chi Minh. Another Comintern delegate, Zalewski, who was at this time passing under the name of Alexandre, prowled the halls and cornered members of the congress for hurried talks in which he urged a split with the Center. The speeches were carefully prepared and stirringly delivered, the repartee razor-sharp. But there was an air of unreality about the entire affair. It was almost as if the 285 delegates who crowded into the Salle du Manège were speaking for posterity and not for their immediate audience, perhaps because everyone knew that the various factions had come to Tours not to make up their minds, but to register their verdict before history.[139] Only the setting lacked stature: a small hall, run-down and dark, hung with red tapestries and crowded with iron folding-chairs hastily borrowed from a cafekeeper. Lying on the speakers' platform were a few garlands and affixed to the walls no fewer than three portraits of Jaurès, as if the memory of the dead tribune could somehow guide the party through this difficult moment. Behind the speakers' stand there were two large calico banners which proclaimed in bold characters: "The emancipation of the workers will be the work of the workers themselves," and "Workingmen of all countries, unite!"

The congress began in an atmosphere of high excitement and taut nerves. Each side suspected the other of wanting a split—and it was true that such preparations were afoot. The first conflict came when the Left attempted, successfully, to set aside the order of the day established by the CAP and pass directly to the question of the Third International. The Right immediately accused Frossard of a "coup de force."[140] Another debate was occasioned by Frossard's suggestion that each of the federations briefly outline its position before the main discussion was opened. This procedure was not customary; but from Frossard's point of view it had the great advantage of showing the mood in which the party was going to Moscow.

These preliminary reports, delivered by militants of the second and third rank—who seldom had the opportunity to voice their opinion before the entire party—showed two things, the combination of which could hardly be encouraging for either the Left or the Right. First, the rank and file of the party wanted the SFIO to adhere to the Third International—not because they were fascinated by Bolshevik ideology, but because they felt that this would mean a policy of action and a repudiation of War Socialism. As Gomichon, a delegate from the Loire-Inférieure, put it:

Yes, comrades, we see that the policies that we have followed are disastrous policies, and we don't want to fall back into the same errors. We say this precisely because our comrades have collaborated in the government. We have voted for adherence to the Third International and have accepted the Twenty-One Conditions because we think that these Twenty-One Conditions will prevent the Third International from foundering in shame and dishonor like the Second.[141]

Second, alongside the drive to repudiate War Socialism and make the party revolutionary—that is, oppositionist—there was also a general desire to preserve the party's unity, or at any rate not to purge Longuet and the Center. Most of those who voted for the motion of the Left had voted for it in the sense Frossard had given it; they did not mean to endorse Souvarine's policy of expulsions." Thus, the federations wanted action, they wanted greater control over the parliamentary Group, and they very definitely wanted to demonstrate their solidarity with the Russian Revolution; but they also wanted to preserve

---

" The case of the Isère was typical. After approving the Cachin-Frossard motion, the Federation of the Isère unanimously passed a motion by Mistral, which stated that the congress accepted the resolution with the guarantees given by Frossard at the Congress of the Seine. *Le Populaire*, 14.xii.20.

A letter from a provincial Communist in the Federation of the Cher to Rappoport makes the same point: "There are only two or three of us here who are clearly won over to the Third International. But I am the only one who is completely committed. I have sold almost all the Socialists in the neighborhood of Verzon on the idea of the Third International, but I have not been able to bring even the most convinced to see the necessity of a break between us and the *majoritaires* of every shade." (Auguste Gavin to Rappoport, 27.vii.20. Rappoport Archives.) On December 23, 1920, the Kienthalian Pierre Brizon summed up in *La Vague* what was probably the attitude of the majority of delegates: "Let's all join the Third International, without unnecessary conditions or divisions on the left."

the unity of the party, and, more particularly, they wanted a unity of the Left that would include Longuet and, in some cases, even Blum. As for Moscow's conditions, they had no wish to quibble; twenty-one or 21,000, they would approve any conditions that would restore the party's ideological innocence and combativeness.[142]

The leaders of the Right and the Center did their best to point out the follies of adherence during the general debate; but they had little to add to what they had said and written before the congress except a note of pathos and a plea for unity. Marcel Sembat, in a brilliant speech, showed the conflict between Jauressianism, with its synthesis of reform and revolution, and the Bolshevik tradition. Bolshevism, he urged, was a product of Russian conditions that did not exist in France.[143] Léon Blum, in a weak voice that had to surmount heckling from the Left, presented once more, with almost professorial dignity, his demonstration that Bolshevism was not traditional Socialism, but something new in all its essentials, a kind of Blanquism à la tartare, which saw in the conquest of public power the end rather than a means. "We are convinced to the depths of our being," he said in conclusion, "that while you go seek adventure, someone must stay to watch over the old house."[144]

The leaders of the Center did not have much to add to the remarks of the Right, for all their supposed desire to go to Moscow. Jean Longuet argued that the Third International was a product of special historical circumstances, and that Russian methods and Russian discipline could not be applied to other countries.[145] Paul Faure had the good grace to illustrate his attitude toward the Third International and its conditions with a humorous anecdote that made the Center's point as well as any historical demonstration:

One day, Rappoport decided to leave Russia to come to Paris, to shores that at the time no doubt seemed more hospitable to him, where he became one of our wittiest citizens. When he left Moscow, either out of principle or out of poverty, he rejected the "conditions" of the Russian railways, and he traveled without a ticket. At the first station, a brutal conductor made him get off with a kick you know where. (*Laughter.*) Rappoport did not get discouraged; he waited for the next train; a second conductor subjected him to the same treatment. Thus, from station to station, from conductor to conductor, he managed to leave the country of his birth and get to France! Now it is proposed that we make the trip in the opposite direction, but with more or less the same humiliating conditions.[146]

Cachin and Frossard bore the brunt of the defense; and the major part of their argument was devoted to de-emphasizing the importance of adherence. Cachin invoked the stability of the Russian Republic and denied that there was anything in Bolshevik methods that ran counter to the French tradition. Bolshevism, in his interpretation, was merely Guesdism warmed over.[147] Frossard insisted once more that he and Cachin had never agreed to the exclusion of Longuet and the Center. When they had gone to Moscow, he pointed out, Reconstruction had already failed. The only solution had been adherence to the Third International. Their main consideration had been to render this adherence as painless as possible.[148]

The way was thus cleared for a last-minute reconciliation between the Left and the Center in the name of the party's revolutionary unity. Such maneuvers had succeeded before. The Bolsheviks, however, had taken steps to forestall this possibility. On the fourth day of the congress, Zinoviev, still flushed from his oratorical feats at Halle, sent a telegram to the congress in the name of the Executive Committee. In it Zinoviev made clear that the Third International did not want Longuet and his friends as members. "The Communist International," his message read, "can have nothing in common with the authors of such resolutions. In the present circumstances, the worst disservice one can do the French proletariat is to think up some mixed-up compromise that will later be a veritable ball and chain for your party."[149] Later on the same day, Klara Zetkin, the wrinkled old German Socialist, arrived unexpectedly, after eluding the French police, to make the same point: "For this congress to fulfill its great historical mission, you must divide in order to achieve union."[150]

The Zinoviev telegram had its desired effect: it destroyed what chances there might have been for a compromise between the Center and the Left. It did no good for Frossard to define adherence as a simple matter of preparing minds and making hearts "firmer and better placed"; nor for him to scoff at the threat of dictatorship within the party; nor even for him to guarantee once more that no one would be expelled.[151] The Center was now resolved to force the issue; and the Right prodded it on. On the fifth day, after the party had voted to join the Third International by a solid majority (3,208–1,022), Paul Mistral submitted a motion repudiating the Zinoviev telegram, and declaring that the congress refused to shatter the unity of the party by embarking on systematic exclusions.[152] Manier, speaking for the members of the Center, made it clear that if this motion were accepted, they would stay in the party; if not, they would leave.[o] Renoult, speaking for the Left, pointed out that the Cachin-Frossard motion did not call for the expelling of anyone. But at the same time, he emphasized that it would be ridiculous to vote for adherence to the Third International one minute, and the very next repudiate the

---

[o] SFIO, *18e Congrès,* p. 481. There is some controversy on this question. Verfeuil, who belonged to the Center, claimed that if the Left had given in on this question, the Center was planning to wage the same sort of battle on the issues of minority rights within the party and attendance at the Congress of Vienna. (*L'Humanité,* 7.i.21.) Frossard, too, later maintained that Faure and Pressemane had decided upon a split even before the congress had begun. (*Le Journal du Peuple,* 1.ix.21.) It is difficult to discover the truth under the charges and counter-charges. The fact is that positions had hardened to the point where a split was almost unavoidable.

authority of the Executive Committee.[153] Renoult then presented a motion which stated that no one would be expelled for his actions in the past, and that no party member who accepted the decisions of the present congress would be barred. Renoult insisted that this gave the Center all the guarantees it needed to stay in the party.

But Longuet was adamant. The dialogue between Longuet and Renoult illustrates the obstacles which the issue of the Third International had managed to erect even between the best of friends:

*Renoult*: My dear Longuet...
*Longuet*: No! No! I'm an agent of the bourgeoisie, I can no longer be dear to you.
*Renoult*: I told you, my dear Longuet...(*noise in the Center*)...you know it, we told you during our discussion this afternoon, we completely reject the interpretation you have given this phrase of Zinoviev's....
*Longuet*: It's not an interpretation; those are the words.
*Renoult*: Like you, I've read them, and I tell you we are absolutely certain (*noise in the Center*)...I am certain, I tell you, that this phrase does not have the insulting connotation which, in view of your past, Longuet, you obviously would have the right to object to indignantly. It simply means that the man who used the phrase feels that certain policies...
*Several delegates*: Say whose.
*Renoult*:...that certain policies, which are in his eyes too timid and too hesitant, are likely to contribute, indirectly and against the wishes of the defenders of these policies, to the prolongation of the capitalist regime. (*Protests in the Center.*)[154]

Frossard also emphasized that he did not agree with Zinoviev that Longuet was a servant of bourgeois interests. Nevertheless, the Center stuck to its resolution and the Left refused to give way. Cachin and Frossard had gone too far to desert the Third International now. Longuet, on the other hand, refused to break with his entourage; and his friends had now resolved that a split was necessary and inevitable. The Renoult motion carried by a vote of 3,247 to 1,398, and the Right and Center stalked out of the hall after reading their respective statements. The time was about 2 A.M. on the morning of December 30. The majority met on the following day to organize the new party, while the rump claimed the succession of the SFIO. As the Communists made ready to disband and leave Tours, Frossard dismissed the congress with a concluding remark that can only seem ironic in view of what was to follow. "We have finished," he said, "with internal dissension, with discord, with debates on matters of secondary importance. All together, with a single heart, with a single will, we are going to work for the universal Revolution in this great Socialist Party, which carries on the traditions of its founders and which intends to remain true to its glorious past and to all its revolutionary traditions."[155] Seldom has prophecy been less prophetic: Frossard himself would be among the first to go.

Though the old Socialist Party—the party of Jaurès, Guesde, and Vaillant—died at Tours, the political organization that we now call Communist had yet to make its appearance. It would therefore be premature to discuss its origins. However, a few preliminary observations both can and must be made in order to make the later argument more meaningful. What is offered here, then, is not a conclusion but a report, a quick look backward before hurrying on to the second and equally important installment of our story. Let us begin by posing a few questions, to which we must, for the moment at least, content ourselves with partial answers: Why were the French Socialists so drawn to Bolshevism, a doctrine that could not contrast more sharply with their own Jauressian Socialism? Why did the Russian Revolution become the object of a cult rather than study and critical evaluation? Why were the leaders of the Center either swept aside by the revolutionary enthusiasms of 1919–20, like Longuet and Faure, or driven to Moscow, like Frossard and Cachin? And why did the Bolsheviks opt in favor of the kind of party they did?

The first two questions are really one, for in 1920 it was still impossible to know what the doctrine of Bolshevism was. The Congress of Tours came before the main outlines of Bolshevik ideology had clearly emerged in the West—or in Russia itself, for that matter. It is easy enough for us to read back into the Russian revolutionary tradition the excesses of Stalinism; but in 1920 Bolshevism contained the tantalizing attraction of an unopened book. Few French working-class leaders had taken the time to study Bolshevism. Those who had, had merely seen in it a more effective version of the prewar ideologies of the Left Wing. For Loriot, Bolshevism was "Marxism in action"; for Monatte and Rosmer, it was an updated version of revolutionary syndicalism; for Péricat and Chauvelon, it was anarchy—godless, federal, and anti-parliamentary. For Lefebvre, Vaillant-Couturier, and Barbusse, it was revolutionary pacifism, enlightened internationalism, and direct democracy—in short, the avant-garde. Moderate Socialists, like Faure and Blum, agreed with this analysis; and in condemning Bolshevism, the terms that they employed most readily were "Hervéist," "Blanquist," and "anarchist." What they meant to express by such historical references was that Leninism represented a new flowering of the left-wing heresies that the Socialist movement had rejected twenty years before.

Most French Socialists and syndicalists, however, did not bother with such fine doctrinal distinctions: for them, Bolshevism simply meant "the Revolution." If they followed Lenin, it was not because they knew what Leninism was, but because Lenin was the leader of the Socialist Revolution and they were revolutionaries.[156] This equation was not so obvious in 1920 as it may seem today. The first Russian Revolution, that of 1905–6, had inspired interest, enthusiasm, and sympathy—but no tendencies toward emulation. Its sequel, once captured by the Bolsheviks, had been met with reservations. Even the Russian Revolution's most ardent French defenders had at first viewed the methods of the Bolsheviks with distaste. Of imitation there had been no question, except among a handful of extremists. French Socialists, like the Bolsheviks themselves, had assumed that the great revolutionary drama would be played out on the central stage of European history, and not in its backward and half-barbaric wings.

By 1920 all that had changed. Events in Russia appeared in a new perspective. The Bolshevik Revolution was no longer just a democratic revolution that Socialists defended out of a Wilsonian concern for self-determination. The Soviet regime had begun to stand for *the* Revolution, and by fighting for the existence of Soviet Russia, Socialists had come to feel that they were fighting for revolution in France. Bolshevik Russia, in the words of Daniel Renoult quoted earlier, had become "the common homeland of all Socialists" and not just "any country." And the press of circumstances was such that the most moderate of Socialists felt compelled to reaffirm their dedication to the Russian Revolution, even while condemning the doctrine of Bolshevism.

How had a portion of the French working-class movement come to identify its own hopes for liberation with the fate of the Soviet State? For the answer to this question we must turn to the experience of 1917–20. The mystique of the Russian Revolution took root in a historical situation determined, on the one hand, by the unexpected success of the Bolsheviks in Russia and, on the other, by the unexpected failure of reformism in France. Only the sad showing of the second made possible the great prestige of the first. Reformism had given everything and gotten nothing in return. It had not succeeded in moderating French war aims; it had not won the working class a voice in national affairs; it had even proved unable to prevent the French government from engaging in a reactionary Russian intervention. In short, the French working-class movement had failed in its historic task. Yet the opportunities had been great; and even so dark a pessimist as Merrheim had to acknowledge that the situation had been pregnant with revolutionary possibilities.

Whose was the fault? What had gone wrong? From the impression of revolutionary opportunity and the evidence of reformist failure it was no great step to the decision that Lenin had been right: that patriotism was wicked; that bourgeois democracy was a sham; that peace was impossible within the conditions of capitalism; that violence was necessary; and that the Revolution could only be made by the dictatorial use of State power. Hence the worship of the Russian Revolution; for had not the War and its aftermath shown that the only true patriotism was class patriotism? Hence the commitment to the Third International; for only in this manner could the sins of the Sacred Union be expiated and Socialist innocence regained. Hence also the incredible durability of the Communist appeal; for what French workers and intellectuals admired in Moscow was not the Russian reality but their own revolution, the one that they had failed to make in 1919–20.

Amidst this ideological turmoil and social strife, the leaders of the Socialist Center tried to steer a middle course. Their first instinct was to pretend that nothing had changed. The great majority undoubtedly wished nothing better than to return to the Jauressian formulas of the prewar years. Blum's electoral program had been such an attempt. But Jauressianism required class peace and a progressive bourgeoisie that would cooperate in its own destruction or transformation; and both of these factors were notably absent in postwar France. With the breakdown of the Second International and the desertion of its most revolutionary parties to the newly created Third, the French Centrists found themselves isolated not only at home but abroad as well. Reconstruction was a last effort on the part of the moderates to save themselves from the grip of the Bolsheviks. Caught between the desire of the masses for a revolutionary gesture and their own democratic habits, the Center searched for a third way, which would bring the Russians to Europe rather than the French to Moscow.

Two years earlier or two years later Reconstruction would certainly have succeeded. But 1920 was a bad year for the middle way. The issues raised by the Russian Revolution did not permit equivocation. Socialists abroad were busy choosing sides. Within the party the drift was toward the Left. A new generation of Socialist leaders had arisen from the cinders of the War, a generation that had no time for compromise or tradition, only for the Revolution. The eternal conflict of generations developed. The new men were not affected by the subtle distinctions of Léon Blum, the scrupulous orthodoxy of Longuet, or the tears of Sembat.[p] They spoke in the language of extremism that the mass of new recruits understood. The shift in mood was shown by the changing position of Jean Longuet. In 1916 Longuet had been considered a dangerous radical and defeatist; by 1918 he had become a moderate; two years later he was branded as a counterrevolutionary. He had not changed so much as the circumstances had. Between him and his audiences lay the Russian Revolution and the shattered hopes of 1917–20.

---

[p] A number of Socialist leaders noted this conflict of generations. Vaillant-Couturier wrote: "A good deal more than an internal party struggle was involved. It was a conflict between two civilizations. As convalescents from a period of murderous decadence, of abdication and disorder, we had an absolute need for order and health." (*Clarté*, 15.xi.22, p. 27. See also Longuet's article in *L'Humanité*, 11.ii.20, and Frossard, *De Jaurès à Lénine*, pp. 28–29.) Paul Faure reports that at Tours certain delegates on the Left sneered during Sembat's speech. According to Faure, Mistral, "outraged and furious," shouted at them, "Salauds! Salauds!" Faure, *La Scission socialiste en France et dans l'Internationale* (1921), p. 7.

To the War generation Bolshevism seemed to offer everything that Jauressianism lacked. The Bolsheviks had never indulged in class collaboration; they
had never been deceived by the allures of liberalism; Lenin had never wavered
in his stand against both the War and the tyranny of the bourgeoisie. Moreover, there was the impressive fact that the Bolsheviks had made a revolution
rather than merely talked about one. To a generation that admired action, this
was an inducement. The abortive general strikes of July 21, 1919, and May
1920 drove home the impotence of traditional Socialist tactics. The platitudes
of Cachin and Longuet had done nothing to mitigate the bite of French steel.
Many Socialists, particularly those whose participation in the working-class
movement was new, had drawn from these events the same lesson as Raymond
Lefebvre, when he wrote, shortly before leaving for Moscow, that what the
party needed was "a faith that has never been dirtied in the mud of class collaboration," and "method, dedication, and systematic and carefully considered
violence, which must be farsighted, calculated, and precise."

Confronted with this situation, the Centrist leader could take one of two
stances: he could brave the leftist wave, sacrifice his popularity, and reaffirm
his dedication to the old, discredited ways; or he could follow the masses. For
all but the most conservative, the most detached, or the most maligned by
Bolshevik propaganda, the first course was forbidding. In any case, a lifetime
of devotion to the masses and revolutionary phrasemongering had not prepared the Centrist leaders to check this movement toward the Left. In their
hearts they felt guilty for War Socialism, for their reckless honeymoon with
nationalism and liberalism, and for their failure in the revolutionary eddies
of 1919 and 1920. They, too, as Frossard said, were "in search of a mystique."
Was it opportunism, careerism, or idealism that drove men like Frossard and
Cachin to Moscow? The very question is naive. It was the essence of French
Socialism that all these motivations were inextricably mixed with one another.
One should not by any means discount the role of ideology. Life may blunt
ideology; but ideology can also shade the way life is experienced. The revolutionary side of Jaurès came back to haunt the Center; for, after all, these men
were revolutionaries; and now that the revolution was in Moscow, the logical
thing to do seemed to be to follow it.

The Bolsheviks were well aware of the attraction exercised by the Russian
Revolution and played it for everything it was worth. They had decided in
early 1920 that they wanted a mass party in France, and not a sect. The first
wave of revolution had not destroyed the old order. The lesson of 1919 seemed
to be that spontaneous mass movements would not end in revolution unless
led by disciplined Communist parties. The Left Wing in France was devoted
but weak. To base a Communist Party on this group alone might mean to
lose the masses and jeopardize the future of the revolution. Moreover, there
were now signs that the Center was in the process of differentiation. Thus, pre-

cisely at the moment that the French Socialist Party moved toward the Left, the Bolsheviks took a step to the Right to meet it. To the great consternation of the French Left Wing, Lenin's International set out to woo the Centrist majority.

In the course of the negotiations that followed, the Bolsheviks showed a wiliness and a flexibility that contrasted sharply with the image of revolutionary purity and intransigence that they had conveyed the year before. Adherence to the Third International was made as painless as possible for Frossard, Cachin, and those who followed them. The Bolsheviks treated the two Frenchmen roughly in Moscow; but it was made clear that this was a penance for their sins during the War, and they were given to understand that total redemption was possible for those who wanted it. Frossard and Cachin were told repeatedly that no one expected them to make a revolution; they were merely required to prepare for it. Lenin presented the Russian Revolution as a universal event, and even more important, as a direct continuation of the French Revolution. Thus, the trip to Moscow had the great advantage of being both conservative and radical: conservative because the Russians were faithful to French traditions "as the river is faithful to its source in flowing toward the sea"; radical because to adhere to the Third International meant to repudiate, once and for all, the dishonor and disgrace of War Socialism.

The Bolsheviks, then, made concessions to the French in order to attract them to the Third International, concessions which, as Serrati complained, the Italians were denied.[157] But there was one favor the French were not granted. Longuet was was not permitted to join. Much against their will, Frossard, Cachin, and Renoult were forced to separate from Longuet and Mistral. Why Cachin and Frossard, two recognized opportunists, and not Longuet? Because, consciously or unconsciously, Bolsheviks were seeking that unquestioned dedication to the Russian Revolution that would later degenerate into subservience under Zinoviev and corruption under Stalin. Cachin was no more revolutionary than Longuet, and probably less. But he was willing to accept the scolding and reproaches of Moscow; and the Bolsheviks were confident that he would either unlearn his opportunism or be swept aside by events. Longuet, on the other hand, was considered dangerous precisely because he was a man of principle, who would not knuckle under.

If the aim of the Bolsheviks had been to restore the orthodoxy of prewar Socialism, as they claimed and perhaps even thought, then this choice would have been indefensible. For men setting out to create a new kind of political movement, however, the decision to bar the door to Longuet and his friends made excellent sense. Sentimentalists like Cachin could be remolded. One day they might even make Leninists. Opportunists like Frossard could be used and if necessary discarded. Socialist leaders of Longuet's type would simply be a hindrance. Too reflective to overlook the implications of Bolshevik methods, too honest to let themselves be used, too committed to the old ways to be won over to totalitarianism in the afternoon of their careers, they had no place in a party whose objective was political power rather than social justice.

What then can be said about the split of 1920? Those who blame the division of the Socialists on the irresponsibility of the Left Wing, the opportunism of the Center, or the malevolence of the Bolsheviks fail to appreciate the narrow limits within which these men acted and the ambiguous outcome of their deeds. Events had pushed the groups competing for the allegiance of the French working class into strange and unforeseen paths. This was as true for the Russians as it was for the French. For all their emphasis on will and the ability of men to shape history, the Bolsheviks could not take credit for the split of 1920; they had merely exploited the favorable situation created by the success of their Revolution and the climate of political and social reaction in France. Moreover, if Tours was a great triumph from the point of view of Bolshevik ingenuity, it was a great defeat from the point of view of Bolshevik ideology. The mass of the SFIO had been won only by compromising the principles proclaimed in 1919. These compromises would perhaps not have been important if the Revolution had been at hand. But it was not. Already doctrine had been sacrificed to personal loyalty, and the line between Bolshevism and Machiavellianism had begun to fade.

## Chapter six

# The Great Friendship

Notre unité révolutionnaire est complète.... Le
parti devient peu à peu ce que nous voulions qu'il
fût: une grande amitié en même temps qu'une
formation de bataille.
—*L.-O. Frossard, March 1921*

The founding of the French Communist Party coincided with the passing of
the atmosphere that had produced it. This circumstance explains the unreal, almost surrealistic story of the party's first years, a tale of sound and fury, in
which debates were endless because without purpose, the clash of personal ambitions replaced the confrontation of ideologies, and social forces seemed to
vanish from the stage, leaving the working-class leaders declaiming like has-
been actors before half-empty halls. We should not be deceived: the social
forces were there. But they were not the forces that had created the revolutionary situation of the immediate postwar period. Before going on to study the development of the party in detail, we must stop for a general picture of the context, both national and international, within which its leaders had to operate
during the years between 1921 and 1924.

### THE NEW PERIOD

By 1921 the revolutionary onslaught had been stopped. The last acts of this
reversal were the defeat of the Red Army before the gates of Warsaw and the
failure of insurrection in Italy in September 1920. Its epilogue came in Germany, where left-wing impatience, Comintern interference, and government
provocation combined to produce the fiasco of the March Action. The responsibilities for this senseless putsch have been disputed up to this day.[1] The results were clear. Even the Bolsheviks were forced to acknowledge that the
European proletariat had been temporarily thrown on the defensive.

In France the prospects for a revolutionary party were not good. Trotsky,
that eternal optimist of world upheaval, might continue to assert (to Frenchmen) that "in Europe it is still France that will be the first to follow us."[2] He

could point to certain facts. The French State was bankrupt. Its quest for security and reparations would inevitably cause it to fall out with its former allies. Such problems, however, could unite the nation as well as divide it. Most important of all, the French working-class movement was not what it had been in 1919–20. For one thing, the balloon of mass syndicalism had burst. By the spring of 1921, the CGT had been reduced to its prewar strength of 600,000 members. For another, the combativeness of the working class had diminished. Strikes were markedly fewer and further between; and when there were large strikes, as at Roubaix in August 1921, at Lille in May 1922, and at Le Havre in the summer of 1922, they were invariably defensive in origin, economic in objective, and unsuccessful in result.[3] It was not that the workers had given up their hostility to power and the State. They still felt oppressed and discriminated against. They continued to favor some kind of vague but total social transformation. Revolution, one might say, was in their blood, where working-class parents, propaganda, and experience had put it. But the workers were confused and disgusted by the constant feuding of the postwar years between this faction and that. What they sought above all was peace and quiet and a secure job. With luck they could live almost as well as before the War; with a wife who worked they could live even better. The appeals of agitators might win their sympathy, but they could not get them on the streets.[4]

The frustration of revolutionary hopes in the West must be viewed in conjunction with the internal development of the Bolshevik Revolution. In the spring of 1921, the Bolsheviks faced what Lenin himself termed the greatest internal political crisis in the history of the Soviet regime.[5] By the beginning of that year, the Bolsheviks had passed victoriously through the most critical stage of the civil war. An armistice had been signed with Poland in mid-October 1920; and Baron Wrangel's forces, despite French recognition and some French assistance, were driven into the Crimea and then into the Black Sea a month later. But the people which emerged from that ordeal by fire was hardly in a condition to make the additional leap required to pass from the realm of necessity to the realm of freedom. The cost of victory, in both human and material terms, had been high: Petrograd had lost one-third of its population; factory output was down 85 per cent in comparison with 1913; and over 7,000,000 people had lost their lives since the beginning of the Revolution. As if to underline the tragic destiny of the Russian people, the man-made catastrophes of war and revolution were followed in the fall and winter of 1921–22 by the natural disaster of famine, which according to official estimates took some 5,000,000 additional lives.[6]

Physical suffering could be borne and transcended; the loss of support for the regime was something else. In the spring of 1921, the Bolsheviks were confronted with the brutal fact that they could no longer count on the sympathies of the majority of the peasantry and the proletariat in their advance toward

Communism. Uprisings in the South and East announced the growing dissatisfaction of the peasantry with the rigors and confiscations of War Communism. Of even more threatening implication for the future of the regime was the Kronstadt rebellion, which broke out on March 2, 1921, while the Tenth Congress of the Bolshevik Party was in session. The sailors of the Kronstadt naval base revolted in the name of the October Revolution; their rallying cry was "Soviets without Bolsheviks"; and they defended the concepts of Soviet democracy and the Workers' State against the encroachment of bureaucratic centralism.[7]

Threatened by the prospect of peasant disorders, burdened with a disintegrating economy that had to be rebuilt from the bottom up, and now under fire from that very sector of the working class in whose name they had made their Revolution and with whose help they had overcome their enemies, the Bolshevik leaders realized that they had to either execute a retreat or face the possibility that their regime would be overthrown. Admitting that "we have gone too far on the road of nationalizing trade and industry," Lenin appeared at the Tenth Party Congress to propose the New Economic Policy. "We know," Lenin stated, "that only an agreement with the peasantry can save the Socialist Revolution in Russia, until the Revolution breaks out in other countries."[8] NEP meant the Bolsheviks would end the policy of forcible requisitions from the peasantry, replace these by a fixed tax in kind, re-introduce a certain measure of free enterprise, and retire to the commanding heights of industry and transport. In the phrase of Ryazanov, NEP was the "peasant Brest."

NEP was more than an economic policy; it announced the opening of a new era in the history of the Soviet regime. In the realm of foreign affairs, the Bolsheviks now sought more diligently to establish normal relations with the outside world. Less than a week after the adoption of NEP, the Soviets signed a trade agreement with Great Britain and a treaty of friendship with Turkey.[9] By the end of 1921, the Bolsheviks had established trade delegations in Finland, Estonia, Latvia, Lithuania, Poland, Sweden, Norway, Germany, Czechoslovakia, Austria, Italy, Great Britain, Turkey, and Persia. In April 1922 the Bolsheviks were admitted, at least temporarily, into the community of nations when they were invited to attend the conference of Genoa; and the treaty of alliance between Russia and Germany during that conference only further demonstrated that the Bolshevik regime could no longer be dismissed as a revolutionary and outlaw regime. The road to recognition, though still uncertain, was opened; by the end of 1924, the Soviet regime was recognized by Great Britain, Germany, Italy, Austria, Greece, Norway, Sweden, and even France. After March 1921, the Bolsheviks were permanently torn between their role as leaders of a worldwide revolutionary movement and their respon-

1. The Socialist leadership on the eve of the War at the Mur des Fédérés. Center to right: Jean Jaurès, Edouard Vaillant, Pierre Renaudel (wearing armband). Second figure on Jaurès's right (behind coat), Pierre Brizon.

2. Léon Jouhaux

3. Charles Rappoport, the Guesdist conscience of the SFIO

4. Georges Anquetil's "Communist" weekly, originally *Le Bolchéviste*; May 1919

5. Striking railroad workers, February 1920

6. A gathering of French Bolsheviks: Paris, 1920

7. The SFIO's delegation in Russia, June 1920. Cachin, between Frossard and Zinoviev, being greeted by Russian official.

8. Alfred Rosmer at the Second Comintern Congress, 1920. *Drawing by Isaak Brodsky.*

9. Raymond Lefebvre at the Second Comintern Congress. *Brodsky drawing.*

10. Marcel Cachin addressing a workers' meeting

11. The great friendship: Paul Vaillant-Couturier (left) and L.-O. Frossard (right) at the Congress of Tours, December 1920

12. The "Trial of the Plot," March 1921. In the dock, front row, from left to right: Pierre Monatte, Boris Souvarine, Fernand Loriot, Gaston Monmousseau. At table, second from right, Henry Torrès.

13. L.-O. Frossard.
*Sketch by DuKercy.*

14. Renaud Jean.
*Sketch by H.-P. Gassier.*

15. Amédée Dunois.
*Gassier sketch.*

16. Fernand Loriot.
*Gassier sketch.*

17. Pierre Monatte

18. A. Lozovsky

19. Dmitrii Manuilsky, Boris Souvarine, and Alfred Rosmer in Moscow, 1922

Maurice Thorez (center, facing camera), at the Congress of Lyon, January 1924

21. Jacques Doriot

22. André Marty

23. Jaurès's catafalque being carried to the Panthéon by six miners from Carmaux, November 1924

24. The heirs of Jaurès. From left to right: Jules Racamond, Pierre Sémard, Florimond Bonte, Benoît Frachon, Gaston Monmousseau, Marcel Cachin, Paul Vaillant-Couturier, Maurice Thorez, Jacques Duclos, Marcel Gitton, Raymond Guyot, and Lucien Sampaix.

sibilities as the masters of a huge State, with the latter gaining in importance at the expense of the former as the prospects for world revolution faded.

The inauguration of NEP had certain unanticipated consequences for the nature of the regime and the internal constitution of the party. If the majority of the peasantry and the proletariat were now opposed to the regime, it was no longer possible to pretend that the Communist dictatorship was a "dictatorship of the proletariat." The answer might have been to recognize the divergence of social interests and to permit the re-emergence of opposing parties. Instead, NEP was accompanied by a hardening of the dictatorship. Lenin and the Bolsheviks, however, could not admit the fact that the party no longer represented the proletariat—Lenin had always identified the interests of the proletariat with the interests of the party—and the result was a growing gap between ideology and reality, between what the regime represented itself to be and what it was.[10] Thus the interests and destinies of the party and the proletariat, which had perhaps coincided for one brief moment during the years 1917–20, while the European Revolution had hung in the balance, diverged increasingly after 1921. Of the dictatorship of the party and the dictatorship of the proletariat, one became a reality, the other a myth, as Soviet democracy, that will-of-a-wisp of 1917–20, withered away and the party consolidated its power.

As the Bolshevik leaders fastened their dictatorship ever more tightly on the proletariat, so did they consolidate their dictatorship of the party. As Isaac Deutscher has pointed out, "In suppressing all parties, the Bolsheviks wrought so radical a change in their political environment that they themselves could not remain unaffected."[11] If the party no longer represented the proletariat and if the party were engaged in a life-and-death struggle for the future of Socialism against the peasantry within Russia and imperialist powers without, it was necessary to tighten ranks and ensure party unity. Controversy within the party could not be allowed once the leadership had decided to make concessions both to the peasantry and to the outside world. If an army is to be capable of maneuver, it must possess an iron discipline. And, therefore, at the Tenth Party Congress, the same party congress at which NEP was announced and approved, it was decided to ban factions within the party. This process did not originate with NEP. Centralization was a legacy of War Communism and the Civil War. Nevertheless, the Tenth Party Congress was an important turning point. The irreversible steps had been taken in the process that would lead to Stalin's dictatorship. Democracy within the party was equated with factionalism: factionalism was condemned; and bureaucratic assignment increasingly took the place of local party elections.[12]

These events in Russia had their repercussions in France. Beginning in 1921 the workers no longer followed the Bolshevik Revolution with anywhere near the same unanimity or devotion. True, Communist leaders like Souvarine, Vaillant-Couturier, and Cachin praised the Soviet regime to the skies and scoffed at its critics in the pages of *L'Humanité*. They were widely read; they were widely believed. No self-respecting worker could hesitate between the bourgeois complacency of his own government and the aspirations of the Bolsheviks.

But for the militant who thought for himself, there were reasons for doubt. The anarchists revealed the persecution and imprisonment of their comrades in Russia, and announced that the Soviet regime was a dictatorship of the Bolshevik Party over the workers and not a Workers' State. For them, by the spring of 1921 Bolshevism was dead, and the Soviet dictatorship of the proletariat was just another regime "of oppression and lies."[13] The alienation of the Bolsheviks from the Ultra-Left was paralleled by their reconciliation with the bourgeois Left. Recently returned from a trip to Russia, where he was feted royally by the Communists, Edouard Herriot announced in November 1922 that the Soviets had given up their plans for world revolution. NEP was more than an expedient: it marked a real turning point in the development of the Revolution. Henceforth, Communism was "only a fiction."[14] The Soviets themselves in their foreign policy and their overtures to the outside world seemed to lend credence to this interpretation. Chicherin flirted with Lloyd George, Rathenau, Briand, and even Poincaré.[15]

Communists themselves had divided feelings about the course the Russian Revolution had taken. Less involved party leaders, like André Morizet, while praising certain aspects of the Soviet regime, criticized its Jacobinism, its militarism, and its de-emphasis of unions and cooperatives. And when schism followed schism and the working-class movement found itself incapable of response to capitalist provocation, militants complained of Russian interference in French affairs and grumbled that the mess the party and the unions were in was all "Moscow's fault."[16] Did these developments destroy the mystique of the Russian Revolution? Not in the least. The faithful remained, more convinced than ever of the perfection of their cult and the infallibility of its priests. But for every militant who believed, there was probably another who was skeptical and a third who was hostile.

### LEADERS AND FOLLOWERS

Before disbanding and leaving Tours, the delegates who had accepted the verdict of the party met once more on the day after the congress to settle certain administrative questions. Not all the members of Longuet's faction had followed him to union with the Right. Raoul Verfeuil and Charles Lussy had returned to the congress hall in protest against the tactics of the Right, to whom they ascribed the immediate responsibility for the schism.[17] Frossard instructed the delegates to return to their federations and to attempt to win them to the decision of the congress. If the federation proved recalcitrant, he warned, it might be necessary to organize a new one. The congress then approved the new leadership, which had been presented to it *en bloc* after the prior agreement of the Left Center and the Left. Frossard became General Secretary of the new party; Cachin, Director of *L'Humanité*; Loriot, International Secretary; Souvarine, representative to the ECCI; Eugène Dondicol, Treasurer; and Verfeuil, André Julien, Lucie Colliard, and Veyren were named as *délégués à la propagande* or propagandists.[a] Veyren could not accept his post and was replaced by Albert Treint.

The Souvarine-Frossard motion had called for a Comité Directeur (CD) of 24 members, which was to be the sovereign body of the party. Elected to the CD at Tours, once more by prior agreement of the two factions, were: Alexandre Blanc, Boyet, R. Bureau, Cachin, Joseph Cartier, Antônio Coën, Dondicol, Dunois, A. Fournier, Frossard, Henri Gourdeaux, Antoine Ker, Lucie Leiciague, Georges Lévy, Loriot, Paul Louis, Méric, Rappoport, Renoult, Louis Sellier, Servantier, Souvarine, Albert Treint, and Vaillant-Couturier. The editorial board of *L'Humanité,* a Control Commission, and a Conflict Commission were chosen in similar fashion, and contained many of the same men.[18] The real work of organization, however, was left for an Administrative Congress that was to meet in three months' time. A special commission of 12 members was chosen to draw up the new party's statutes.

Let us look more closely at these Communist leaders. We have already made acquaintance with several of them: Frossard, bald despite his youth, invested with both French intelligence and French guile, a persuasive orator, a meticulous administrator, respected, admired, liked, a man with a future who seemed destined for a ministerial portfolio; Cachin, stocky, mustached, a lover of words, especially his own, whether printed or spoken, a man of the people who was never happier than when among the people; Loriot, tall, gaunt, burned-out eyes, bearded like a prophet, his nervousness showing in every gesture, his speeches and articles painstakingly prepared and arduously delivered, a pedagogue of the Revolution rather than a tribune; and Souvarine, small, his eyes crowned by thick brows, quick to criticize, quick to learn, sarcastic, liable to enthusiasms, more at home in the study than before an audience, where he was embarrassed by a light stutter, reminiscent of Trotsky in the power and venom of his pen but without the range of interests and diabolical humor that were Trotsky's charm.

From the Reconstructors came Amédée Dunois, Daniel Renoult, and Louis Sellier. Dunois was a soft and mild man who had made his way to Socialism

---

[a] Propagandists were paid party officials whose assignment it was to spread the Communist gospel throughout the country. Combining the functions of publicist, campaign manager, and administrative troubleshooter, they were on permanent loan to lower party bodies that requested their services.

by way of anarchism and revolutionary syndicalism. A lawyer by education, he earned his living writing for left-wing journals, among them *L'Humanité*, of which he became an editor in 1918. From the beginning he devoted himself to the problem of relations between the syndicalists and the party, on which he could bring to bear the advantage of his connections with the *Vie Ouvrière* group. Daniel Renoult had been a member of the SFIO since 1906. Like Dunois he wrote for *L'Humanité*, where he covered parliamentary affairs. His Socialism was learned from Jaurès and bore the imprint of the idealism of 1848. A man of sincerity and probity according to those who knew him well, in character he was stormy and extreme.[19] Louis Sellier was another Jauressian. An elegantly upturned mustache gave him a look that could be interpreted as affable or slippery; close associates found him both. Sellier's talents lay in the direction of administration and vote-getting rather than journalism. In 1914 he had taken Cachin's place as a municipal councillor in the Eighteenth Arrondissement.

Charles Rappoport, Paul Vaillant-Couturier, and Albert Treint represented the Committee for the Third International. A polylingual scholar and journalist of Russian Jewish descent, Rappoport had been a Zimmerwaldian of the earliest hour. Enthusiastic as he was about the Russian Revolution, his Marxist convictions, and perhaps his Socialist Revolutionary past, stood between him and any fondness for Lenin, whose dissolution of the Constituent Assembly he disapproved. It was not until after the Conference of Berne that he had come to terms with the Bolshevik Revolution and rejoined Loriot's group to fight for adherence to the Third International. Rappoport's wit and erudition were famed among French Socialists, and his speeches, for all their theoretical sweep, were eagerly listened to by working-class assemblies. Vaillant-Couturier, by contrast, was a typical representative of the generation brought to the party by the War. The offspring of a Parisian family of artists, his development paralleled in almost every respect that of his boyhood friend Raymond Lefebvre. Like him he had served at the front; like him he had been wounded; like him he had aspirations as a writer and a poet. In November 1919 he had been elected a deputy in Paris. An open, sincere, and intense young man who burned with hate for war and the bourgeoisie, Vaillant-Couturier had no patience with those who wanted to temporize or maneuver. Treint had joined the SFIO in 1910, but his Socialism, like Vaillant-Couturier's, bore the imprint of the War. A schoolteacher by profession, he had emerged from the War with the rank of captain and the honorific title of Chevalier de la Légion d'Honneur—which earned for him, in party ranks, the nickname of "Captain Treint." This epithet summed up his character. A man of extremes with a mind that leaped over obstacles rather than working its way through them and a suspicion of others that verged on paranoia, Treint was a storm trooper of the Revolution, a man who applied to Socialist politics the disciplinary methods of an army camp.

Three more men deserve mention, though none belonged to the first CD. Renaud Jean was a farmer who had been elected deputy of the Lot-et-Garonne, in December 1920, after a furious campaign in which he had gained for Socialism an area that had previously been impervious to collectivist ideas. After Tours he followed the majority. A former soldier of forthright and even ostentatiously independent convictions, Jean turned the Lot-et-Garonne into his personal fief. He quickly became the party's specialist on agricultural questions and represented in Communist councils the point of view of those peasants who had returned from the War anti-militarist, anti-government, and more than slightly envious of the workers' position.[20]

Alfred Rosmer and Pierre Monatte require little introduction. In January 1921 Rosmer was still in Moscow, and Monatte had not yet joined the party. Both, however, were to play leading roles in the years to come. A civil servant by occupation, Rosmer was a thin, stooped man, friendly, sincere, self-effacing and absolutely dedicated to the liberation of the working class. Forty years later the brittle fire of his spirit could still be glimpsed through sparkling eyes. Consistent in a way that few men dare to be, he made of his entire life a revolt against the hypocrisy of bourgeois society.[b] Honesty, not power, was his aim. Without personal ambition, Rosmer moved in the shadow of more self-assertive men. His connection with Trotsky had immediately won him an important position in the Comintern, where his scorn for the leaders of French Socialism and his ties with the union movement were much appreciated. Monatte fitted the description of a working-class militant given by Pelloutier.[c] Like his friend Rosmer a déclassé, Monatte had made his way from Blanquism to anarchism to revolutionary syndicalism, the doctrine to which he remained faithful throughout his life. A rarity in a country noted for its opportunists, Monatte dedicated his life to the working-class movement, yet always remained on its wings, preferring the role of conscience to the positions of leadership that could easily have been his. Though he was a journalist rather than an organizer, his prestige in syndicalist circles was immense. To many he seemed to symbolize the coming revolution.[21]

These were some of the most interesting and important men who founded the Parti Communiste Français (PCF) and were called to lead it during its formative years. But there were others, of course, who left their mark on the party even though many of them merely passed through it on their road to

[b] It is thus no accident that Rosmer, whose real name was Griot, took his pseudonym from the protagonist of Ibsen's play *Rosmersholm*. Like Ibsen's Rosmer, he was unable to come to terms with the everyday lies that people call reality.

[c] See pp. 24–25 above.

careers in other political parties or the university: Georges Pioch, the flamboyant Secretary of the Federation of the Seine, who often appeared at meetings in his evening clothes, on his way either from or to a play which he was to review; Antoine Ker, another officer and teacher, who specialized in social and economic questions; Victor Méric, Bohemian son of a Radical Senator, "famed for the harshness of his adjectives and the joviality of his character";[22] the lawyer Ernest Lafont, more syndicalist than the syndicalists themselves; Charles Heine, a doctor of psychiatry and a dabbler in Surrealism; C.-E. Labrousse, an ardent young historian who often wrote about the parallels between the Russian and French Revolutions; Joseph Tommasi, aviation worker by trade, Soviet espionage agent by avocation; Henry Torrès, lawyer and specialist in defending cases of subversion; Marie and François Mayoux, pacifists, syndicalists, champions of lost causes.

Both at the summit and at the base this was a party of young people.[23] Almost all the leaders were under 40: Loriot at 50, Cachin at 51, and Rappoport at 55 lent the weight and experience of age; but Souvarine and Vaillant-Couturier were only 27; Frossard, 31; Jean, 33; Tommasi, 34; Treint, 36; Renoult, 40; and Dunois, 41. The second rank was filled with young men in their twenties and early thirties. From the point of view of social origin and occupation, the Communist leaders were almost solidly bourgeois: for the most part, schoolteachers, like Frossard, Treint, Ker, and Blanc; journalists, like Renoult, Dunois, Souvarine, and Cachin; men of letters, like Vaillant-Couturier and Rappoport; lawyers, like Lafont, Torrès, and Coën; and post office employees, like Sellier, Gourdeaux, and Verfeuil; only a very, very few workers like Tommasi or farmers like Jean.

These men were as heterogeneous in ideological background as they were similar in social origin. In general, the Communist leadership was a mixture of three currents: prewar Socialism (Cachin, Frossard, Rappoport, Renoult, Sellier, Blanc, Gourdeaux, Paul Louis); the traditional Left Wing (Dunois, Rosmer, Méric, Lafont, Morizet, Marie and François Mayoux); and those younger men who had come to Socialism and later Bolshevism as a result of the War (Souvarine, Vaillant-Couturier, Treint, Jean, Ker). But even within these categories there were enormous differences between Guesdists like Rappoport and Jauressians like Frossard; and between revolutionary syndicalists like Rosmer and anarchists like Méric. Oddly enough, the last group was the most homogeneous because it was the least subject to the pull of the old traditions.

What had brought these men to Communism? Certainly a myriad of factors. But in each case, one seems to have predominated. Fidelity to the letter of Socialist doctrine (Loriot, Rappoport); a conviction that the War necessitated a radical renewal of French Socialism (Renoult); an emotional attraction to the first proletarian State (Cachin); hatred of war and those who made it (Vaillant-Couturier, Jean); a fascination with the novelty of Bolshevik ideas and methods (Souvarine, Treint); the belief that Bolshevism carried on the legacy of revolutionary syndicalism (Rosmer, Tommasi) or anarchism (Heine, Méric). For all, the desire not to be separated from the proletariat; for some, the ambition to be leaders of a great party. A tangled web of motives in which only revulsion against War Socialism, conviction that reformism was chimerical, and unwillingness to be left outside the movement of the masses remain constant.

What did these leaders expect from their party? The majority, certainly, a more effective version of the prewar SFIO. A few, the long-awaited realization of that truly revolutionary party of the Left Wing, which would be anti-militaristic, anti-parliamentary, and anti-statist. A handful, like Souvarine, the remaking of the French party in the image of Bolshevism. Revolution? Yes. But a revolution to which each assigned his own meaning and his own date, varying in imminence and in interpretation from Rappoport's organized social democracy and Frossard's Jauressian Republic to Dunois' society of free producers and Méric's anarchist utopia.

These were the leaders: the generals, the captains, and the lieutenants of the Revolution. Who were their troops? We would like to know in detail the social origins, occupations, and state of mind of the 110,000 Socialists who followed the party into the Third International in the first six months of 1921. This information is lacking, and it may never be assembled. What we know we must infer from other data. We know, for instance, that the creation of a professedly revolutionary party at Tours attracted a certain number of recruits from the ranks of the syndicalists and the Ultra-Left. Though not by any means a flood, this current of enrollments helped to conceal the fact that many of the militants who had voted for the Souvarine-Frossard motion before Tours did not follow the party into the Third International.[24] The majority of these recruits were probably new to the working-class movement. Older militants like Monatte, Monmousseau, Péricat, and Chauvelon did not join the party. The centers of Communist strength were much the same as those in the prewar SFIO: the North; the Seine and its environs; the Valley of the Rhone; the area to the northeast and southwest of the Massif Central (the Allier, the Dordogne, the Gironde, the Haute-Vienne); and the bastion of the Moselle and Rhine Valleys, inherited from the German Social Democrats. For lack of information to the contrary, we must assume the same continuity in the party's social composition. The only significant sign of change was the influx of peasants. Despite concentrations of industrial workers, the Socialism which the Third International captured at Tours was for the most part "a Socialism of medium-sized enterprises, a small-town Socialism, a 'provincial' Socialism."[25]

Were these new recruits to Communism bent on revolution? Some were. They were to be found mostly among the middle-class members of the Federation of the Seine, the peasants of a few provincial departments like the Lot-et-Garonne, and the youth movement. But what the great majority sought in joining the Communist Party was the repudiation of War Socialism, resistance to the government, and a vague commitment to solidarity with the Russian Revolution: what might be called the policy of the universal no, what sociologists would term a protest against the insecurities, both economic and psychological, of the postwar world. Young, rural, petty-bourgeois, unschooled in Socialist doctrine, more than a little tainted with syndicalism and anarchism, the French Communist Party as it was constituted in the first six months of 1921 was far from being that union of revolutionary Marxists and revolutionary workers which the Bolshevik leaders had prescribed for the ills of the French working-class movement in 1919 and 1920.

ENEMIES WITHOUT

Both Blum and Frossard had emphasized at Tours that despite the schism, which they accepted as inevitable, they would continue to speak of their fellow Socialists without bitterness. Blum had concluded his speech with a plea for mutual tolerance between the warring factions: "Even if we are to go our separate ways, let us all remain Socialists; no matter what happens, let us remain brothers, brothers divided by a bitter quarrel, but a family quarrel, brothers who may one day find a common home."[d] Schism, though, even between ideological brothers, had its own harsh logic. Within a few days of Tours, the Communists (despite their caution they were not able to escape the title) and the Dissidents (this was the epithet fixed on the Right) found themselves locked in a life-and-death battle for the inheritance of the SFIO. Each side, knowing the attachment of the rank and file to unity, accused the other of having wanted and planned the split.[26] The Bolsheviks, of course, had no time or inclination for the pleasantries of camaraderie between dissident parties. Trotsky and Zinoviev had both advised their French allies to strike hard and discredit their opponents in the eyes of the workers.[27] The younger French Communists were the quicker learners. Already on January 12, Vaillant-Couturier noted that Longuet's group were now the prisoners of the Right; and that whether they wanted to or not, they were becoming the "agents of the bourgeoisie." "Should we take no interest in their maneuvers?" asked Vaillant-Couturier. "Certainly not. Between them and us, it's war to the death."[28]

In the short run, the Communists swept their Dissident opponents from the field. Out of the 96 federations, 89 followed the new Communist Party. Only 13 of the 68 deputies of the Socialist parliamentary Group declared themselves Communists; but this fact in itself seemed to indicate that the party had chosen the truly revolutionary path. In terms of total membership, out of 179,800 mem-

d SFIO, *18ᵉ Congrès national* [1920], p. 275. Frossard made a similar vow: "For my part, tomorrow I will speak of you without bitterness. Tomorrow I will not utter a single wounding word about you. I consider you Socialists and I will say so." *Ibid.,* p. 384.

bers of the SFIO in December 1920, 110,000 went over to the Communist Party, while the Dissidents were scarcely able to rally 30,000.[e] Also at issue were *L'Humanité* and the party's financial resources. The Dissidents wanted the Communists to abandon the title *"L'Humanité,"* not to claim Jaurès as its founder, and to give them three-fifths of the party treasury. Their argument was that the distribution of deputies, as well as the vote at Tours, should be taken into account.[29] A stockholders' meeting was held, at which Louis Camélinat, the principal stockholder, divided his voting power according to the numerical breakdown at Tours. Philippe Landrieu, who held the stock emanating from the German SPD, gave all his votes to the Communists. These two blocs of votes allowed them to prevail and to claim the succession of Jaurès, which they have done up to the present day. The Communists, however, were not satisfied with their victory, and they accused the Dissidents of having seized the party's treasury and leaving it with only 1,500 francs, a charge they would repeat periodically whenever new brooms with which to beat the Dissidents were scarce.[30] In this manner, any hope of "brotherly" relations between the two parties disappeared, as they fell not to quarreling over ideological issues, but to dickering like greedy relatives over a fat inheritance.

The Communists had other reasons for optimism. Though the revolutionary threat was over, they were the last to know it. Government persecution gave them the sensation that they were a threat to social peace. At the end of January, Ker was arrested. The offices of the party were searched by the police. A few days later, Dunois followed Ker to prison for his role in the so-called "Affair of the Checks." The "Affair of the Checks" revolved around the person of a Comintern agent named Zalewski, whose clandestine activities at the Congress of Tours were noted earlier. Unable to show himself because of close police surveillance, Zalewsky had passed Dunois 50,000 francs worth of checks, drawn on American Express. Dunois, in turn, had had the checks cashed by Ker, Griffuelhes, and an industrialist friend, and had then remitted the cash to Zalewski's contact, whom Dunois later described as a young, pretty blonde of the Russian student type. The money was destined for a French edition of the *Communist International*—according to *L'Humanité*. More likely, it was intended as subsidies to the Left (Souvarine's faction) and the Jeunesses Com-

---

[e] The party gave two sets of figures for its membership in October 1921: 131,476 and 109,391. The second figure is no doubt closer to the truth than the first. (Kriegel, II, 846–47.) It is likely, however, that at least 10,000 members were lost between April 1 and October 1, 1921. Frossard claimed on May 10, 1921, in *Le Journal du Peuple* that the party had distributed 122,308 cards by the end of March. See also *De Jaurès à Lénine* (1930), p. 187, where he gives the figure of 130,000, as opposed to 30,000 for the SFIO. It is useless to look for precise membership figures. More often than not, the party itself did not know how many *permanent* members it had. Moreover, a distinction has to be made between those who took out a card and those who kept up their membership. The point is that the party attracted a great many members at the beginning of the year who later let their membership lapse.

munistes.[31] Dunois and Ker were released at the end of March; Zalewski sat in prison until May, at which time he vanished into Eastern Europe, rumor has it at the request of the French party, which preferred to do without his aid.

The "Affair of the Checks" was followed by the "Trial of the Plot." No incident better illustrates the confusion in which the PCF was born. The ten defendants, a fantastic mixture of anarchists, revolutionary syndicalists, and Communists, ranging from Loriot and Souvarine to Monmousseau and Sigrand, were the working-class leaders who had been arrested the previous May during the general strike. Loriot and Souvarine had already made plans to escape from Clairvaux, where they assumed they would be sent after their conviction.[32] To their great surprise they were unanimously acquitted on March 17 by the Jury of the Seine, after a noisy and often ludicrous trial. The prosecution could not make up its mind whether it was prosecuting the Third International or the Strike Committee, and it had no way of connecting the two.[33] A long chain of witnesses for the defense appeared, which included such stellar figures as Barbusse, Victor Basch, Victor Dalbiez, Robert de Jouvenel, and Marc Sangnier. The persecution of the Communists had become unpopular. Besides, from the Communists' point of view, it had served its purpose. *L'Humanité*'s circulation had risen to 200,000. A subscription drive initiated by Frossard had succeeded in raising 440,000 francs in three months. Finally, a by-election in the second sector of Paris, in which Souvarine and Loriot routed their Dissident opponents, showed that the party had benefited from its new revolutionary stance. True, Loriot and Souvarine had run as victims of reaction and not as Communists. True, the candidates of the Bloc National had won the run-off. But as Cachin pointed out, that merely indicated that the French masses were still susceptible to the evocation of the Bolshevik peril, especially when it was coupled with the hint of hidden German influences and gold.[34]

### TROUBLEMAKERS WITHIN

What illusions of power the Communists might have nurtured were shattered during the brief war crisis of April and May 1921. The French government had been struggling throughout 1920 for what it considered its due share of reparations. At Paris, in January 1921, the French had at last succeeded in getting the English to agree to a sum of 148 billion francs, of which the French would receive 52 per cent. The German government dickered over this sum; and on March 8, after an ultimatum, the French retaliated by occupying the towns of Dusseldorf, Ruhrort, and Duisburg on the right bank of the Rhine. Declaring that France would not retreat until the Germans had paid, Briand authorized Barthou to draft the class of 1919 in the event it became necessary to occupy the Rhineland. The English, however, were not nearly so enthusiastic about these gestures of force as the French. The Reparations Committee developed a new plan calling for reparations of 132 billion francs from the Germans. The

German government balked at this figure when it was presented as an ultimatum on May 5; but a new Cabinet accepted it on May 11, and the French forces were withdrawn from the Rhine.[35]

The Communists had mentioned the possibility of military action on the Rhine as early as February 21. Renoult had reminded *L'Humanité*'s readers what the policy of the party would be. The ambiguities of prewar Socialism on militarism and national defense, he wrote, had ended. No army, no matter how democratic, could be anything but the bulwark of the bourgeoisie's dictatorship. The policy of the Communists, he concluded, was "violent anti-militarism." On March 8, in response to the occupation of the Rhineland cities, the CD established a Vigilance Committee linking the party, the minoritaire United Trade Unions of the Seine, and the Association Républicaine des Anciens Combattants. Between March 9 and April 25, the attention of the Communists shifted to other matters. But at the end of April, the party launched a huge press campaign against "the threat of a new war" and the drafting of the class of 1919. Frossard wrote that the nation was being led straight to war, and that the party must do everything in its power to prevent its outbreak.[36] The Jeunesses Communistes (JC), who had no training in the intricacies of traditional Socialist tactics, set out to apply the program of Renoult and Frossard to the letter. Placards were posted reading: "Class of '19, don't go." Treint was indicted. A number of JC's were arrested for their anti-militarist propaganda among the troops.

This was the situation that had led to insurrection in Germany the month before—with the difference that the excitement of the party and the JC was not shared by the workers; and Frossard was no Brandler. May 1 passed with hardly a disturbance. The campaign against war, no matter how violently pursued by the journalists of *L'Humanité* and the agents of the JC, was met with indifference by the public.[37] The Parisian sections of the party sent representatives to the meetings of the CD to plead for a forward policy. Did the party intend to let the JC fight the mobilization alone, asked the JC paper, *L'Avant-Garde,* at the beginning of May.[38] The answer, it seemed, was yes. Neither Frossard nor the Left was anxious to repeat the experience of the KPD. On May 5 Frossard issued an appeal for "sangfroid and discipline." The Parisian sections were at fever pitch, wrote Frossard. The bourgeoisie, on the other hand, hoped to lead the party to adventure. Some members of the class of 1919 had come to ask him what they should do, and he had been compelled to say that he could not advise them to ignore their orders. "It is easy to issue appeals, but if they fall amidst general indifference, if they cover their authors with ridicule, and if they are only followed by the same handful of militants who are always ready for every sacrifice, they end by destroying what it has cost so much effort to build."[39] To emphasize that this was not a personal opinion, a notice appeared in the name of the CD calling for the "necessary discipline," and stating that the Committee would not receive anyone during its meetings except authorized persons.

This announcement spelled the rejection of a policy of adventure. It was interpreted as such. But the "left danger" reappeared in a slightly different form at the Administrative Congress (May 15–16, 1921) and the Congress of the Federation of the Seine which preceded it (May 8 and 14). Both assemblies met at the height of agitation and excitement over the threat of a new war with Germany. Frossard's theme, both before and during the congress, was that all was for the best in this best of all possible parties. Recruitment was up. The loan had been a great success. The Dissidents' party was disintegrating. Within the leadership itself, the differences between Reconstructors and the partisans of the Third International had vanished, and the CD functioned in complete unanimity. As for relations with the Comintern, here, too, agreement prevailed. Moscow had not tried to order the party to do anything. No one had been expelled. The party was well on its way to becoming "what we wanted it to be: a great friendship as well as a battle formation."[40] The representatives of the Left did nothing to trouble this impression of harmony.

The Parisian Ultra-Left was not so obliging. Both congresses witnessed a grassroots rebellion that the leadership could limit but not entirely quash. The special committee appointed by the CD had prepared a list of statutes, which were an attempt to dress up the traditional organization of the SFIO in the leftist language of 1919–20. The National Congress was to be the sovereign body of the party. The principle of proportional representation was maintained. During the interim between congresses, a CD composed of 24 members directed the party. The CD would be controlled by a National Council (CN), comprised of the CD and the representatives of the federations. The parliamentary Group was reminded that its chief function was propaganda; the CD was to control it by means of a permanent liaison between the two bodies. The party press was placed under the political control of the party's majority; but the party and the federations could create organs in which discussion would be completely free. The only real changes were in the direction of greater federalism. The federations were encouraged to form regional unions; and though they had to enforce discipline, they were free to devise their own statutes so long as they did not conflict with the statutes of the party. The name of the party would be changed to "Communist" on January 1, 1922.[41]

The Congress of the Seine, instead of ratifying these statutes, went on to amend them.[42] Most of the amendments tended toward control of the Center by the rank and file, a manifestation of the traditional suspicion of parliamentarians and journalists which was a product of the French past and which had helped take the party to Moscow. It was decided that the party would present no candidates at the senatorial elections; that although the CD could eliminate names from the electoral lists, only the federations could replace them; that

although certain civil servants might be delegates to the congress, they would
have consultative votes only; that there could be a maximum of four deputies
on the CD; that the CD would have to include one member of the JC, some
women, and at least ten union members; that no more than a third of its members could be in the liberal professions; that one-third of its members would
have to be replaced each year; that the Congress, not the CD, would appoint
the editors of party journals; and that no more than a quarter of the Communist deputies could ever be present at the Chamber. Some of the sections
had gone so far as to suggest that party members should not be allowed to wear
decorations or go to church; and to top things off, the JC had submitted a
motion criticizing the leadership for its refusal to recommend desertion during
the war crisis. These last resolutions were mercifully rejected. But the amendments of the Seine, if accepted by the Administrative Congress, would have
reshaped the party in the image of Péricat's Parti Communiste.

The mood of Paris, however, was not the mood of France. At the Administrative Congress, Frossard could bring to bear both the support of the provincial federations and the support of Loriot. His performance was that of a
master fencer, lunging now to the Right, now to the Left, always sure of his
ground, never using force where dexterity sufficed. When Verfeuil complained
that the congress did not have on its agenda a discussion of the resolutions of
the Second World Congress (which he, for his part, was unwilling to accept), Frossard replied that at the party's first congress there were other things
to do than to quibble over details when everyone was agreed on essential
points.[43] On the second day, the Parisian Ultra-Left began their onslaught of
amendments. They wanted the statutes to include the rejection of national defense under a capitalist regime; the salaries of deputies and party journalists
to be reduced; the deputies to devote themselves entirely to propaganda; and
the party to abstain from participation in senatorial elections. French Socialism
had a traditional way of dealing with such deviations: they were buried in the
Resolutions Commission. When the seven delegates of the Seine declared before the congress that they were withdrawing because their amendments had
not been put to a vote, Frossard stepped in with his usual adroitness and
shamed them into staying. A whispering campaign, he claimed, was under
way against the leadership of the party. "Only three months after our party has
again become a revolutionary organization, is it permissible, is it thinkable,
that at our first congress seven delegates should stage a demonstration that
amounts to an attempt to sabotage the congress?"[44]

After Frossard's plea for unity, the congress rolled on smoothly toward its
preordained destination. The statutes devised by the Commission were accepted, and the amendments of the Federation of the Seine ignored, except for
the one limiting the number of deputies on the CD to four. The JC and the
Ultra-Leftists, however, were still not satisfied. An anonymous motion was

circulated in the Seine in June, which divided the party into three factions: a Right, which included many of the old Reconstructors and which was characterized by stagnation and inertia; a Center, emanating from the old Committee for the Third International, which was tainted by its compromises with the Right; and a Left, which drew its support from the progressive elements of the masses and which had no means of self-expression. The critique was a masterpiece of confusion: in the same breath it complained about the centralization of the party and demanded the full application of the Twenty-One Conditions.[45] This motion and the debates at the Administrative Congress reveal that on the eve of the Third World Congress, many French "Communists" were in great confusion about what they had chosen in following the SFIO into the Comintern. In the spring of 1921 it was still possible to call for decentralization in the name of the Third International. Before such incoherence and Hervéism, the Left had every reason to unite with the Center.

### THE THIRD CONGRESS

In March, Zinoviev announced the convocation of the Third World Congress of the Comintern, two months ahead of schedule. The reason for the change in date, explained Zinoviev, was that a Right had developed in the ranks of the International, which was all the more dangerous because it had appeared at a moment when one could detect "a certain slackening" in the international proletarian movement. As examples of this opportunistic deviation, he gave the Italian Giacinto Serrati, the German Paul Levi, and the Czech Bohumir Šmeral.[46]

The Third Congress introduced a new era in the history of the Comintern. Zinoviev, who was afflicted with a passion for generalizations, explained the change by pointing out that whereas the Second Congress had laid the bases for a Communist strategy, the Third Congress would give the International its definitive structure.[47] This was so; but its significance only emerges against the backdrop of the changing evaluation of the prospects for European revolution. The Third Congress assembled in the aftermath of failure. The main subjects of debate were the March Action and the hesitations of the Italian Communists in breaking with the Center. Both Lenin and Trotsky admitted that their original estimates of the time required for the expansion of the Revolution were mistaken: what had seemed a matter of months in 1919 might now be a matter of years.[48] In such circumstances—with the Revolution neither imminent nor postponed to the indefinite future (Trotsky emphasized that European capital would not be able to recover from the blow of the War)— the obvious tactic was to lay the bases for an organization that would be able to take advantage of the next revolutionary upsurge. How was this objective to be attained? The Bolshevik answer paralleled very closely the decisions taken on domestic policy at the Tenth Party Congress: opportunism without, unity within. The masses must be won; concurrently, the party must be centralized and subjected to a rigid discipline. The trouble was that one precluded the other.[49] If European Communist parties were to transform themselves from sects into mass organizations, they needed more autonomy and more flexibility, not more centralization or direction by the Executive. Yet all the resolutions of the Congress, particularly the monster resolution on organization, emphasized the need for tighter bonds between the various sections and the Executive. And if the attitude of the Bolshevik leaders toward the March Action indicated a rejection of revolutionary putschism, their rude treatment of the Italians was a sign that they intended to make no allowances for national differences.

The Third Congress marked, for the French, the beginning of their international life as a Communist Party. The period from Tours to the Third Congress had been a time of preparation, of incubation, of feeling the way. No one was quite sure what a Communist Party was or what it should be. The leaders of the Left were imprisoned until late March, and then prepared, almost immediately, to leave for Moscow. They had only six weeks to find their bearings. Frossard, who had reason to know what the Bolsheviks expected, was trying hard to forget. The French delegation was chosen by the CD. It included (among others) Loriot, Souvarine, Vaillant-Couturier, Tommasi, the schoolteachers Lucie Colliard and Lucie Leiciague, André Morizet (mayor of Boulogne-sur-Seine), the young scholar André Julien, and Delagrange, a railroad man and syndicalist militant from the Dordogne. Maurice Laporte represented the Young Communists. Cachin and Frossard, it will be noted, were diplomatically absent.

The CD gave its delegates the mandate of "neither subordination nor absolute independence." They were left free to decide the German and Italian cases on their merits. But they were instructed to emphasize the danger of sporadic revolutionary movements, and to indicate that attempts of this nature in France would lead to certain failure. The attention of the ECCI was to be drawn to the peculiar situation of the French syndicalist movement and the necessity of respecting its autonomy.[50] Perhaps the chief characteristic of the French contingent was its lack of briefing on the burning questions of the day. Dependent on interpreters (the language of the congress was German) and constantly at a loss for information, the French complained periodically of being asked to vote on resolutions whose implications they did not understand. Yet after minor qualifications, they voted with the majority.[51]

At any rate, the main action for the French took place not during the congress debates, but at the gathering of the Executive Committee that preceded the congress. The delegation was first brought before the Presidium, where Loriot and Souvarine gave a short review of the events that led up to the Congress of Tours and followed it. After this introduction, the Executive Com-

mittee devoted three sessions to the French party. There is no doubt that the
Bolshevik leadership had been pleased with the outcome of Tours. In March,
during his report to the Tenth Party Congress on the activity of the Comintern, Zinoviev had gone so far as to refer to Tours as a "brilliant operation,"
which "has given us a purged party."[52] Along with Halle, he considered it his
own personal triumph. The Executive Committee, however, was of the school
that believed that to spare the rod was to spoil the child; and the discussions
often became violent. The French retaliated by refusing to approve Zinoviev's
report, an unheard-of act of revolt, and at one point, when Radek flung at
them the epithet "opportunist," they got up and left the room in protest.[53]

As International Secretary and ranking member of the Left, Loriot reported
on the activity of the party since Tours. Those who criticized the French party,
argued Loriot, did not always take into account the special circumstances in
which it was born. The French masses were deceived by the illusion of democracy; this explained the enthusiasm with which the French had fought the
War of 1914. The reaction against the War was long and difficult. The Leninist point of view was unknown until the very end of the War. "By instinct we
went toward the most revolutionary solutions," said Loriot, "but we went
toward them in the dark."[54] The party formed at Tours, despite the evident
sincerity of many of the Reconstructors, was a union of the Center and the
Left, and could not be fully Communist. As for the unions, they were now
"the essential problem," but the party had to deal with the traditional hostility
of the revolutionary syndicalists toward political parties.

After Loriot's report, the delegates belonging to the Left of the Congress cut
loose in criticism. Laporte, speaking for the Young Communists, repeated his
accusation that the leadership of the party had been too passive in their opposition to the mobilization of the class of 1919. The delegate from Luxemburg,
Rheiland, noting that Frossard was not a Communist and never would be,
demanded that the ECCI require the French party to expel him. The Hungarian Lekai called for the censure of the French section. Finally, Béla Kun,
one of the artisans of the March Action, concluded what the stenographic account termed "an indictment of the French party" by demanding that a commission be formed to rule on the admission of the PCF to the Third International.

Loriot, looking tired and weak, replied to these criticisms as best he could,
rejecting out of hand the demand for Frossard's exclusion as an act that would
have "disastrous consequences." But it was the Bolshevik leadership itself—
Trotsky, Lenin, and Zinoviev—who dealt most tellingly with the Left. Their
remarks were harsh but paternal. Trotsky scoffed at the criticisms made by
Laporte, Rheiland, and Lekai. "To be a revolutionary," he said, "it's not
enough to have revolutionary feeling and the will to act; it's also necessary to

have a clear vision of things, without which you may set into motion a lot of movements, but you won't emerge victorious." Trotsky admitted that he had been pessimistically inclined toward Cachin and Frossard when they had come to Moscow the year before because he knew the parliamentary climate of Paris. But he was satisfied with their conduct since, particularly the exclusion of the Center and the creation of a Communist Party. What criticisms he did make were aimed not at Frossard's handling of the mobilization crisis, but at *L'Humanité* and the inactivity of the Communists in the unions. Lenin intervened briefly in order to cut down Béla Kun, "who thinks...that to defend Communism is to systematically defend the Left. But if the Left succeeded in making Béla Kun's views prevail, that would destroy Communism."[55] Lenin, too, approved Frossard's appeal to sangfroid and discipline, and even praised the efforts made by the PCF in the unions. Zinoviev outlined the attitude of the Executive toward the French. The French section, he admitted, had been given preferential treatment before Tours and even after. The Executive, said Zinoviev, had been fully aware that the party formed at Tours was not fully Communist, and that even now there were Centrist and half-Centrist elements who kept the old traditions alive in the party, the press, and the Chamber. Nonetheless, the Executive had concluded a silent agreement with the Communist group in the party (that is, the Left), to leave them a few months' breathing time in which to reorganize the party and group their forces. The President of the Comintern emphasized that in France the danger came not from the "left folly," but from the opportunistic elements. He took to task *L'Humanité,* and pointed out that contrary to what Lenin had said, the French did not have the right line on the trade-union question. Like Trotsky, he brushed aside the demands for Frossard's expulsion. Concluding on a note of optimism, Zinoviev observed that a new spirit was dominant in the party, and that for its part, the Executive felt it necessary to put its confidence in the French leadership. Lest the French grow complacent, however, he added ominously that the PCF might yet have to go through a great crisis and perhaps a split.

Laporte, Radek, and Lozovsky spoke on specific points, particularly *L'Humanité* and the unions, but the demand for Frossard's expulsion was dropped after such prestigious opposition. Loriot, concluding for the PCF, emphasized that he had supported Frossard during the mobilization crisis, and insisted that the trouble with the party was a crisis of growth and organization, not opportunism. "If the French party isn't yet what it should be," he summed up, "it isn't because Cachin and Frossard don't always act like Communists, but simply because circumstances have not permitted the immediate creation of a real Communist Party in our country."[56] The discussion ended, it was decided to name a commission on the French question, which would draft an appeal to the party. This commission was dissolved before the appeal was written, and the Executive finally limited itself to passing a short resolution on the PCF which "advised" the CD to reinforce its control of the press.[57]

Both the Bolsheviks and the French were reasonably satisfied with this first encounter. Zinoviev and Trotsky were sometimes annoyed by the manner of the French. After the French contingent left the hall of the Executive in protest, Zinoviev turned to Rosmer and said: "Your friends think they're in parliament.... They're really tiresome with all their points of order."[58] The French, on the other hand, complained of their housing accommodations, their food, the irregular hours they were compelled to keep, and the brusqueness with which decisions were taken at the congress.*[f] In France what attention was devoted to the Third Congress and its decisions—and there was not much— dwelt on the salutary aspects of the discussions between the Russians and the French. For Renoult, the consensus of the congress was that "the French Communist Party has already done well. It would have liked to do better. It will do better."[59] Dunois, discussing the resolution of the congress on tactics, interpreted the slogan "To the masses" as meaning that the party should sweep aside the Socialist and syndicalist bureaucrats who were an obstacle to the unity of the proletarian front.[60] Nothing could better illustrate the unpreparedness of the French for the slogan of the united front. Only Rappoport had the bad grace (and the perspective) to point out that in the congress's most important debates, the French delegation had "shone by their absence." The Third World Congress marked a turning point in the history of the Comintern. But in France it passed "almost unnoticed."[61]

---

*f* André Morizet, *Chez Lénine et Trotski* (1922), p. 13. In the Trotsky Archives at Harvard there is a copy of a memorandum that Trotsky sent Lenin, reporting that Rosmer was "trembling with indignation" at the crowded living quarters the French delegates had been assigned. T679*.

## Chapter seven

# The Battle in the Night

En vérité, la faute de tout cela n'est pas aux
hommes. Il y a plus grave, il y a pis que cela,
il y a que l'atmosphère communiste, elle-même,
manque en France.
—*Raymond Lefebvre, in a letter written
from Moscow, September 1920*

In the spring of 1921 an unusual constellation of circumstances had given the
party an aspect of fighting spirit and unity that was more illusion than reality.
The events of May dispelled the impression of combativeness. The alliance of
the Left and Center, however, lingered on, never stronger than at the Third
Congress, where Loriot identified his own group with the policies of the CD.
This coalition, fragile as old china, was made possible by four factors: the "left
danger"; the élan and growth of the party's cadres; the nonintervention of
Moscow; and the forbearance of the Left itself. The Ultra-Left was dealt a
crippling blow at the Third Congress by the Bolshevik leadership. Besides, it
had no real following in the party outside Paris. The other three conditions of
party unity disappeared in the fall of 1921. The result was a crisis that lasted
more than a year and a half, until it was finally resolved as a result of the direct
intervention of the International. It was in the process of this struggle that the
PCF lost its independence.

### THE MAKING OF THE CRISIS

The crisis began curiously. On September 5, 1921, Frossard published an un-
usually frank article, in which he admitted that the party was passing through
a "difficult hour."[1] A malaise affected the party, and Frossard did not hesitate
to see it as indicating the beginning of a new crisis. After the spectacular debut
of January, February, and March, recruitment had fallen off. Only a few hundred cards had been bought since April. The intellectual level of the party was
low, and its meetings were either ignored or poorly attended. Frossard saw in
this malaise a reflection of the fact that the party had no policies, only a mystique. "On est inquiet, on manque de securité d'esprit, on cherche sa voie, on

a l'impression d'une marche tâtonnante dans la nuit, on hésite, on s'interroge." This was a strange admission for the party's General Secretary to make; one might have seen in it an implicit critique of the leadership. Frossard's solution for the party's difficulties was even stranger. Too much, he said, had been expected of the 24 men who made up the CD. The leadership was only as good as its troops. Frossard concluded by calling for the opening of a great debate within the federations on the problems of the day.

This was federalism in action. Unfortunately, the leaders of the new International had a different concept of the relationship between the Center and the rank and file. After the Third Congress, the Executive improved its organization and attempted to establish closer relations with the national sections. In this sense, too, the Third Congress initiated a new era in international Communism—that of the struggle for direct control over the life of the Western Communist parties. The main part of the Executive's work was handled by the Presidium, a policy-making group composed of seven members: Zinoviev, Bukharin, Radek, Béla Kun, Egido Gennari, Fritz Heckert, and Souvarine. The Comintern secretaries—Humbert-Droz, Kuusinen, Rákosi, Souvarine, Safarov, and Minkin—took care of the day-to-day administrative tasks. Lenin and Trotsky intervened in Comintern affairs only from time to time, when some important issue arose or some question of special interest caught their eye.

Beginning with the Third Congress, the affairs of the PCF became a matter of central concern for the Executive. It was as if the fiasco of the March Action had freed the Bolshevik leaders from their obsession with the German revolution and turned their eyes farther West. Resolutions were passed; directives were issued; manifestos and appeals were published; a high-ranking Comintern delegate was sent to Paris. Immediately following the Third Congress, Trotsky himself dispatched a series of letters to France: one to Monatte on July 13, a second to Cachin and Frossard the following day, two more to the CD on July 23 and 26. After the silence of the spring, the effect was that of a bombshell.

It would be unnecessarily tedious to reproduce in detail the contents of these documents.[2] Four themes recur in all of them: the need to gain control of the unions, to centralize the party apparatus, to establish closer relations with Moscow, and to popularize and control the party press. All four of these directives played their part in the making of the crisis, but it was the last that triggered the conflict. The Bolshevik leaders attached a great deal of importance to the press; it was through the press that the party leadership transmitted its orders to the rank and file. Moreover, in a country like France, the party paper could be a magnificent instrument for winning over the masses. To be effective, the central party organ had to speak with one voice and to use language that workers could understand. In the view of the Bolsheviks, *L'Hu-*

*manité* satisfied neither of these requirements. It lacked a central line; it devoted too much space to parliamentary debates; it appealed to the cultured bourgeois rather than to the proletarian. "Stop a hundred workers in the street as they leave their factory and read them *L'Humanité*'s account of parliament," wrote Trotsky. "I'm sure that 99 won't understand or learn anything, and as for the hundredth, perhaps he'll understand something, but he won't learn anything."[3] Even more disturbing to the Bolsheviks was the fact that the party journalists wrote what they liked and where they liked, sometimes contributing articles to the bourgeois press. The proposed answer of the Executive was to lower *L'Humanité* to the level of the masses (*Pravda* was the suggested model), and bring the party journalists under the control of the CD. No member of the party was to own, direct, or contribute to any publication that was not under party discipline, under pain of expulsion.[4]

These instructions not only violated the spirit of Jauressian Socialism, they flew in the face of every tradition of left-wing journalism. *L'Humanité* was not the paper it had been in the days of Jaurès and Herr; but neither was it the vulgar and boring sheet it is today. Understandably, neither the intellectuals of the Center nor the intellectuals of the Left showed any desire to transform the paper of Jaurès into a repository for proletarian poetry and letters from factories, as the Executive had suggested they should do. But the question of control was another thing; it involved Communist orthodoxy. And, by the fall of 1921, Communist orthodoxy was very much at issue in the PCF.

The centers of Communist dissidence were Henri Fabre's *Journal du Peuple* and Pierre Brizon's *La Vague*. A number of prominent Socialists, while joining the PCF, had never accepted the verdict of Tours as final. Fabre, Brizon, and Raoul Verfeuil were the spokesmen for this right-wing opposition. They cried over the split with the Dissidents, called for a policy of rapprochement with Longuet's group, and observed that neither Zinoviev, nor Loriot, nor Souvarine, nor even the Executive had the right to give French Communists orders. "The Communist Party," wrote Fabre, echoing the old Jauressian formula, "is a party of free discussion, which gathers men who share an ideal but who may differ over secondary questions of propaganda or tactics."[5] Fabre, Brizon, and Verfeuil were joined by other men of rebellious temperament who refused to worship uncritically at the shrine of the Bolshevik Revolution. At a time when the Soviets had just succeeded in driving their enemies from Russian soil, Georges Pioch wrote odes to pacifism, and offered the opinion that any proletariat which extended the life of its dictatorship past what was absolutely necessary would have failed in its historic task.[6] Communism, he was to say later, in a phrase that would arouse Trotsky's anger, was "the organized form of love." Charles Rappoport, wittingly or unwittingly, did his bit to fan these flames. Writing in his own *Revue Communiste,* he reaffirmed his affection for Serrati, even after his expulsion, and argued for a relationship between the Executive and the various sections that would avoid the overcentralization of the First International and the exaggerated national autonomy of the Second.[7]

The Left watched the emergence of this Right with mounting indignation. The leaders of the Committee for the Third International had given up their hopes for a small and select Communist Party only grudgingly. But once they had concluded their bargain with the leaders of the Center, they had stuck to it faithfully. Nonetheless, they had not disarmed completely. Instead of disbanding the Committee, they had reorganized it, announcing that the members of the faction would serve as a sort of elite corps or shock troop within the party until the old SFIO had become truly Communist.[8] For a variety of reasons, this detachment had never seen action; and after the Third Congress, the Executive had passed a resolution officially dissolving the Committee. Souvarine, writing from Moscow in early October, announced this decision, remarking that the former categories of Right, Left, and Center no longer had any meaning. "The Committee for the Third International is dying," said Souvarine. "It dies a natural death, having accomplished its mission."[9]

Souvarine affected an optimism in public that he did not feel in private. The CD had made no move to carry out the Executive's directives. Trotsky had received no answer to his letters. It was not that the CD rejected the International's suggestions; it merely ignored them and buried itself in secondary matters.[10] Frossard jousted amicably with Fabre and his collaborators on *Le Journal du Peuple* (he himself was one of Fabre's most consistent contributors), and chided them for their desire to reunite with the Dissidents. Though disapproving their ideas, he made no attempt to discipline them. In July the CD had voted to bring Brizon before the Conflict Commission; somehow the hearing never took place. It was almost as if Frossard considered the Right a necessary constituent of the party's balance.

The inactivity of the Center annoyed the Left and aroused the concern of the Executive. Loriot's answer to Frossard's announcement of a crisis had been to rebuke him for his pessimism, and to remind him that as General Secretary of the party, he had better things to do than engage in idle polemics with Fabre.[11] In October, Humbert-Droz, the Comintern's roving ambassador and troubleshooter, appeared in Paris to investigate the state of the party and to try to obtain the enforcement of the Executive's resolutions.[12] He met little resistance. The Comintern's delegate left with the impression that the leadership had agreed to reinforce the party's discipline, organize the control of the press, streamline the apparatus by creating a Presidium, and develop the proletarian character of the party. Nevertheless, after Humbert-Droz's departure, the same resistance to change arose, and the promises made to him remained a dead letter.

To complicate the situation, the question of relations with the International became entangled with the personality of Souvarine, the French delegate to the Executive. Caught up in the intoxicating atmosphere of Moscow, increasingly influenced by the Bolshevik leaders with whom his knowledge of Russian enabled him to establish close relations, Souvarine grew exasperated with the slow response of the French leadership to the directives and suggestions of the ECCI. Discussing this episode many years later, Souvarine argued that he was trapped between two fires: on the one hand, the lackadaisical French, who wanted to be left alone and accused him of egging on the Russians; on the other, the Bolsheviks, who blamed him for the petty-bourgeois ways of his French comrades.[18] There is no doubt, however, with which fire Souvarine's sympathies lay in 1921.[a] During July, August, and September of that year he wrote ten letters to the CD, each more critical and more abusive than the one preceding, in which he described the impatience of the Russians and complained of the slowness of the French in putting the directives of the International into practice. In reply he received nothing except a personal letter from Loriot. At the end of September, Souvarine wrote again, pointing out that the Comintern had been more than lenient in its dealings with the French. The ECCI had taken care not to publish the resolutions on the PCF it had passed after the Third Congress, because it had not wanted to hamper the activity of the party. "It is impossible," wrote Souvarine, "to imagine a more generous approach and, besides, this 'special treatment' with regard to the French party has been very noticeable to all the delegates." Three months after the adoption of these resolutions, there was still no sign of their application. Moscow had asked the PCF to send representatives regularly to the ECCI. Three months

---

[a] It should nonetheless be pointed out that even in 1921 Souvarine was not the uncritical admirer of the Bolshevik regime that he appeared in print and in his relations with other French Communists. Soon after arriving in Moscow for the Third Congress, he had insisted on visiting the prisons in which anarchists were being detained; and Taratuta, the combination guardian angel, guide, and watchdog of the French delegation in Moscow, had charged him with consorting with the Workers' Opposition and indulging in brutal criticism of the Soviet regime. A revolutionary tribunal, consisting of Lunacharsky and Uritsky for the Russian party, and Loriot and Vaillant-Couturier for the French, had been established to hear these charges, and Souvarine had been cleared. Taratuta was removed from his post at the demand of the French. The incident had an aftermath. When Souvarine was appointed a member of the Presidium in Rosmer's place and a secretary of the Executive, Béla Kun had objected, pointing to Souvarine's contacts with the anarchists and the Workers' Opposition. It was Lenin who insisted on keeping Souvarine on, saying: "That is the only way the French will lose their prejudices against us—by working with us." (Interviews with Souvarine, 20.ii.61 and 26.vi.61.) According to Henri Guilbeaux, the French delegates to the Third Congress did not hesitate to criticize the Bolsheviks in private. "Among themselves, most of the French did not scruple to sneer, sometimes crudely, at Russia and at the Russians they extolled so much in the press and in their speeches." *Du Kremlin au Cherche-Midi* (1933), p. 246.

later, there had been no delegates, no reports, no response to the messages of
the International. The Executive had suggested that the price of *L'Humanité*
be decreased in order to raise its circulation; it had recommended a reorganization of the CD to give the party a real leadership. "To all these reasonable
and flexible proposals, *we have received no answer.*" Souvarine warned that
"if the Comité Directeur does not abandon the silence in which it has taken
refuge, it will bear the responsibility for opening a conflict with the International. And I am convinced that the great mass of our party would disavow it
in this event."[14]

Such letters could not help but have their echo in the factional war that was
developing in the fall of 1921; and the Right picked as their target the young
French Bolshevik who found it so difficult to distinguish between a criticism
and a personal attack. Fabre and Verfeuil began to suggest, with a minimum
of proof and a maximum of innuendo, that it was Souvarine who was pushing
the Bolsheviks to make demands on the French, and that he had dictatorial
ambitions within the party. "I am not in on the secrets of the gods," wrote
Fabre, "but I have heard it said that some instructions signed 'Souvarine' have
arrived from Moscow. Souvarine intends, it seems, to run the Comité Directeur and the Communist Party. *Il y a fort, notre cher Boris.* Aren't we old
enough to handle our own affairs?"[15] In October, Méric turned his pen against
Souvarine, making fun of him in article after article in *Le Journal du Peuple,*
ridiculing his views on electoral tactics and discipline, and reminding him that
as representative of the PCF in Moscow, he was its servant and not its master.[16]
As for discipline, Méric agreed; but it must be a discipline assented to freely
by the party itself "en pleine discussion, en pleine lumière." Above all, there
had to be "liberty to laugh when the leaders are ridiculous—leaders, moreover,
who are temporary and weak, who are hoisted to the top by events and who
can fall back tomorrow into the nothingness from which chance caused them
to emerge."[17]

The meetings of the CD, which should have been devoted to the discussion
of policy, now became the stage for personal vendettas. On October 25 the CD
received a long letter from Souvarine reporting on the activity of the Executive. Instead of discussing the essence of the letter, the CD concentrated on
certain epithets Souvarine had used.[18] On November 8 the Left brought before
the CD an article Méric had written in *Le Journal du Peuple,* discrediting
Souvarine and submitting the International to ridicule. The Left wished to
censor Méric; instead, the session turned into an attack on Souvarine. Finally,
a motion was passed condemning personal polemics between Communists.
Méric agreed to publish an article making clear that he had not intended to
make light of the International. November and December passed; no dis-
avowal of the earlier article appeared. Meanwhile, under pressure from the
Left, on November 11 Renoult drew up a motion on control of the press, but

the Left considered it unsatisfactory and directed against Souvarine rather than motivated by a wish to carry out the resolution of the Executive. Frossard hesitated to commit himself one way or the other; his contribution at the meetings of the CD was to suggest that both Méric and Souvarine were in the wrong.[19] Nevertheless, under pressure from the Left, he agreed to resign as a contributor to *Le Journal du Peuple,* while making clear that his decision was taken regretfully and under discipline.[20] Fabre retorted angrily by accusing Souvarine of undermining Frossard's position by depriving him of his sounding board, and he vowed that he and his friends would attempt to prevent Souvarine's re-election to the CD at the Congress of Marseille.[21]

Souvarine was not a man to take these attacks lying down. On December 15 he brought the struggle out into the open and denounced the formation of a Right in the party, which he identified specifically with the persons of Méric, Rappoport, Verfeuil, and Fabre. The characteristics of this Right, wrote Souvarine, were its nationalism, its desire for unity, its attempt to apply NEP to France, its opportunism, its demand for abstention in the unions, and its opposition to discipline under the guise of opposition to sectarianism. There was no crisis in the party, argued Souvarine. The drop in recruitment was to be expected and not to be regretted. What crisis there was consisted of "a sort of physical and moral laziness on the part of the leadership." Through inactivity the CD had compromised its authority. The authority of the CD must be reinforced, the inactive elements must be eliminated from the leadership (a clear threat against the Right and Center), and whatever disagreements there were must be taken out of the corridors and brought into the open.[22]

In his private correspondence Souvarine was even more threatening.[23] Rappoport, he claimed, had schemed against him and tried to undermine his position within the party and with Humbert-Droz. For six months *Le Journal du Peuple* had attacked him with impunity. This was no mere question of personalities. Fabre, Méric, Verfeuil, and Rappoport were all united by their dislike of the resolution giving the party control of the press. He would say nothing until after Marseille, Souvarine promised. But then he intended to clear the air. "Besides, what is deferred is not lost. On my return there will be one of those reckonings that will have a serious impact on the movement in France."

The stage was set, then, for the Congress of Marseille. The Right (Verfeuil, Méric, Pioch, Rappoport) hoped to teach Souvarine a lesson and in the process reassert the independence of the French party. The Left (Loriot, Vaillant-Couturier, Dunois, Souvarine), though avoiding an open struggle, was determined to force the leadership to declare either for or against Moscow. Frossard and the Center had every reason to fear this confrontation, for the very essence of their position was the avoidance of choice. The rank and file? What could they know or care about these quarrels among Parisian journalists and politicians? They merely followed Frossard and put their faith in the Russian Revolution. But before turning to the Congress of Marseille and its preliminaries, we must consider the problem of the party and the unions.

### A FAMILY DISAGREEMENT

This problem was a legacy of history. Guesde's POF had been pushed bodily from the unions. The cornerstone of French unionism, the Charter of Amiens, had as its central tenet independence from all political parties. The SFIO had never overcome this handicap, nor had it really tried. Faced with a hostile union movement, the Jauressian solution had been cooperation without interference—not so much a policy as the recognition of a necessity. For the Bolsheviks, the Jauressian formula of "libre coopération" and "libre entente" was an abdication. They believed that the economic and political struggles were inextricably bound together, and that the unions' role with relation to the party should be that of the circumference to the center. In this metaphor, the idea of subordination was clear, if not explicit.[24] For them the very idea of a Communist Party with no direct influence on the working masses was a mockery. They could never understand the concern of French syndicalists for the autonomy of the union movement. The union, in their view, was merely another weapon to be used in the revolutionary struggle; and a Communist must act as a Communist not only in the party, but also in his union, his cooperative, his sporting club, or wherever he might find himself. Besides, the only truly independent working-class organizations were those "permeated with the idea of Socialism." All others were subject to the influence of the bourgeoisie.[25] The most urgent task of the PCF was thus to conquer the union movement for Communism.

The attitude of the Bolsheviks toward this question of the party and the unions must be understood on several levels. First, history. Because of the backward state of the Russian political system, the trade unions "from their beginning led their existence in the shadow of the political movement."[26] The Bolsheviks had thus never had to deal with a fully developed union movement. Second, theory. It was basic to Lenin's whole approach that without the aid of a revolutionary party (of intellectuals), workers could not progress beyond "trade-union consciousness," that is, reformism. Third, personal experience in France. Lenin, Trotsky, and Lozovsky had all been disgusted by the neutrality of the SFIO during great strikes. They blamed the very existence of anarcho-syndicalism on the excessively parliamentary and reformist nature of the Socialist Party.[b] Fourth, the development of the Russian Revolution itself.

---

[b] Krupskaya recounts how both she and Lenin were disgusted by the SFIO's aloofness from the great postal strike of 1909, on the pretext that it was an affair of the unions and not of the party. (*Lénine et la France*, 1925, p. 36.) Trotsky and Lozovsky had much the same reaction to the French labor movement.

It is not without interest that the Bolsheviks turned their attention to this question in France immediately after having dealt with it in Russia. In 1920 and 1921, a Workers' Opposition had arisen within the Russian Communist Party, which called for the domination of the State and the administration of the national economy by the trade unions, as the Party Program of 1919 had promised. A great debate over the role of the trade unions was opened, in which Lenin and Trotsky played active roles. The policy adopted at the Tenth Party Congress was a Leninist compromise between the syndicalist solution and the militarization of labor, which Trotsky had supported—a compromise, however, in words only. For Lenin and Trotsky agreed on the essential: the need for the unions to accept the leadership of the party. Henceforth, the unions were to be a "school for Communism," which is to say that they were to be subordinated to the State.[27]

It was with these ideas and experiences that the Bolsheviks approached the problems of the French labor movement. If the CGT was a revolutionary party called forth by the failure of French Socialism to fulfill its historical role —as Trotsky, for one, thought it was—then it was logical to assume that once a Communist Party had been formed, the division between the political movement and the unions would lose its raison d'être.[28] Trotsky had excellent reasons for this hope. The War and the Russian Revolution had changed many things. There had been the Committee for Resumption, the Committee for the Third International, the *Vie Ouvrière* group. It could be argued that the party was now more revolutionary than the CGT. Both reformist and revolutionary syndicalists had given up their objection to cooperation with political parties as such. The minoritaires agitated in favor of joining the Third International. They accepted the dictatorship of the proletariat. Why then did history come back to haunt the Communists? Why did the syndicalists invoke traditions that events had made obsolete? Three new factors caused this turn in the year that followed the Second World Congress: the refinement of the Comintern's doctrine and organization; the formation of a French Communist Party based on an alliance between the Left and opportunist elements; and, in the background, the changing image of the Russian Revolution.

The first shadow of conflict was cast by the organization of the Profintern. Up to July 1920, syndicalists had assumed that the Comintern would include not only political parties, but also revolutionary unions. During the Second World Congress, as the outlines of the Comintern's statutes and tactic became clear, the Bolsheviks realized that it would be necessary to create a separate Trade Union International, in order to retain the allegiance of the revolutionary syndicalists who would never accept the Leninist concept of the party.[29] It soon appeared, however, that Profintern and Comintern would be as close in spirit, tactics, and personnel as their names indicated. The circular announcing the creation of the new organization made no secret of the fact that there would be a link between the Trade Union International and the Comintern. A member of the Profintern leadership was to sit on the Executive Committee of the Third International; and conversely, a member of the Executive Committee was to participate in the work of the Profintern's Executive Bureau.[30] To the Bolsheviks, this "organic liaison," as it was called, was merely the reflection of the union between the economic and the political aspects of the revolutionary struggle. For a French revolutionary syndicalist, such a relationship suggested the subordination of the unions to the party.

The Twenty-One Conditions raised the same question. The Comintern's conditions did not explicitly demand the subordination of the unions to the party, but they did call upon the Communists to win the trade unions for the Communist cause, and to create cells that "must be completely subordinated to the party as a whole." Aware that such phrases might awaken resistance within France, and only too conscious of their own lack of influence within the trade-union movement, the leaders of the Committee for the Third International had specifically modified the Twenty-One Conditions, in their motion for adherence to the Third International, to read that although the unions and the party would "coordinate their action, neither organization would be subject to the other." The syndicalist section of the motion, written by Dunois and Paul Louis, spoke of "penetrating" the unions and winning the syndicalists to their ideas; but they were careful to speak of the relationship between the party and the unions as an alliance between equals.[31] Many syndicalists would consider even that claim excessive. The trouble caused by this question is suggested by the fact that in his private correspondence, Loriot felt compelled to assure the syndicalists that the party did not intend to force its views on them or subordinate the unions to the party. The exact form of the relationship between the two movements, he promised, would be left open to further discussion.[32]

The issues of "burrowing from within" and subordination of the union movement to the party had immediate repercussions on the struggle in the CGT between majoritaires and minoritaires. The uncertainty of the partisans of the CSR was revealed at the Congress of Orléans in September 1920. The resolution of the minoritaires called for adherence to the Moscow International, and stated that the CGT would be ready to cooperate with a political organism that was revolutionary in deeds and not only in words, but would at the same time maintain its complete autonomy.[33] Frossard made a dramatic appearance at the congress to assure the syndicalists that he considered the autonomy of the union movement a "French necessity," and to repeat that he did not accept the Russian thesis of subordination. However, with the kind of verbal pirouette that was his stock-in-trade, he added that the party had the right to expect that its members who belonged to unions would not forget they were Socialists.[34] This formula pleased no one: it was either meaningless or an attempt to hedge on his earlier guarantee of autonomy. Moreover, the very presence of Frossard, Renoult, and Rappoport in the congress hall made a bad impression.[35]

The minoritaires' doubts worked to the advantage of the majoritaires, who were able to accuse the Communist International of being the enemy of syndicalist autonomy. The final vote gave the majority 1,515 to 552 for the minority, with 44 votes going to a peripheral motion by Georges Verdier and 83 abstentions.[36] This vote decided nothing. The CSR continued to exist, despite the threats of the majority, and the CGT drew closer to a split. At the same time, the minoritaires began to fall out with one another over the development of the Russian Revolution. Future problems were anticipated in an article written by an anarchist in the aftermath of the congress. This commentator pointed to the subordination of the Russian unions to the State, and concluded: "It's a type of organization that has absolutely nothing in common with the one that the French syndicalists sketch in their outlines of the future. Let them study the Russian experience more closely."[37]

The revolutionary syndicalists followed the events leading up to the Congress of Tours with a sympathetic but skeptical eye. Suspicion of Socialists, even revolutionary Socialists, had never died out entirely. Cooperation had proved difficult within the Committee for Resumption; Loriot and Monatte had quarreled in the Committee for the Third International.[38] One can imagine, then, the disappointment that the Comintern policy of rapprochement with the Reconstructors produced in France. The presence of such well-known opportunists and politicians as Cachin and Frossard at the head of the Communist faction could hardly arouse the enthusiasm of syndicalists for whom the essence of Bolshevism was anti-parliamentarism, Soviet democracy, and the general strike. The majority of unionists decided to reserve judgment until the party had proved its mettle and broken with the past. The syndicalists, wrote Pierre Monatte, would not prevent the creation of a truly revolutionary party. But even given its existence, they would continue to prefer their own class organization, the union. And Monatte allowed himself to wonder whether a hundred years of petty-bourgeois democracy might not have made the formation of such a party unlikely, if not impossible.[39]

Preference for the union did not necessarily mean rejection of the party. After Tours the existence of the PCF became confused with the struggle within the CGT. It is hard to see how it could have been otherwise. The leadership of the CGT immediately declared war on the Communists, charging that their aim was to subordinate the CGT to a political party. Despite this maneuver—or perhaps because of it, in view of the psychology of the French working-class movement—many syndicalists joined the PCF during the first months of 1921. One would suppose that revolutionary syndicalists joined the party; that majoritaires opposed it; and that pure syndicalists—that is, those who rejected altogether any role for the State and political parties—boycotted it. This was not the case. Monatte and Monmousseau did not take out party cards, though their close collaborator Pierre Sémard did. On the other hand, it was not uncommon for a Communist to vote with the reformists in his union. All the leaders of the pure syndicalists—Verdier, Quinton, Griffuelhes, Mayoux—were members of the party.[40]

One can understand the hesitation and inertia of the Communist leadership faced with this muddle. What is less comprehensible was their abdication of ideological leadership. Instead of pointing out the need for new directions, they rivaled the syndicalists themselves in praising the tradition of confederal independence. Instead of advertising the necessity of a revolutionary party, they agreed that any revolution in France would have to be realized through the unions and not by the PCF alone. At their most daring, they suggested what had become a commonplace during the War: temporary cooperation between the party and the unions for specific aims. Most of all, they assured the syndicalists that they had no intention of subordinating the unions to the party.[41]

This assurance was not necessary: the Communists had no foothold in the unions and no hope of getting one without the help of the syndicalists themselves. Moreover, it did no good. New snatches of Leninist theory, Frossard's moderate leadership, and revelations of Red terror against anarcho-syndicalists in Russia had made the syndicalists more suspicious than ever of the organic liaison. The Constituent Congress of the Profintern, held concurrently with the Third World Congress (July 3–19, 1921), completed the process of alienation that had begun the previous year. The French minoritaires sent a large delegation to Moscow to defend their concept of syndicalist independence. What they heard confirmed their fears. Lozovsky, General Secretary of the Trade Union International, made it clear that Communism and syndicalism would have to go "hand in hand"; otherwise they would go against one another. This was "the only alternative."[42] Tommasi pled the special circumstances of the French labor movement and asked for a compromise between the French and Russian points of view. A hard core of French delegates, led by the pure syndicalist Henri Sirolle, merely fell back on the Charter of Amiens. Among the French, only Rosmer accepted the Bolshevik position, and he was not a union leader.

In the end, the French delegation split, half presenting a resolution defending the complete independence of the Profintern, the remainder, including Rosmer, Godonnèche, and Tommasi, voting for the majority motion, which called for an organic liaison between the two Internationals and close relations between the various Communist parties and Red unions. The Bolshevik text triumphed by a vote of 282 to 35. Some semblance of harmony was maintained by a last-minute statement, signed by Sirolle and other members of the French minority, which explained that the meaning of the vote was not subordination but unity in action. Still, the theses voted by the congress were there for all who cared to read them. They stated in black and white that the party, "the vanguard of the proletariat," was to control the trade unions through its cells.[43]

The reaction of the minoritaires in France was amazement and anger that two of their delegates had approved such a document. The CSR immediately responded with a declaration, signed by Monatte, Monmousseau, Sémard, Quinton, Verdier, and others, which disavowed Tommasi and Godonnèche and stated that a syndicalist international based on these concepts would be unable to gather the forces of revolutionary syndicalism. The CSR demanded another congress to discuss the question of the organic liaison, and announced that the minoritaires would limit themselves at the Congress of the CGT at Lille to asking for the withdrawal of the CGT from the Amsterdam International, leaving the question of adherence to the Profintern for a later congress.[44] "Full stop?" asked Monatte. "No!" he replied. "Simply a momentary halt." The Russians, he said, refused to understand that in France the unions were not reformist, but revolutionary. In France a party would never lead the revolutionary syndicalists into action. It might be at their side, and Monatte hoped it would be, but it would never precede them.[45]

The conflict caused by the statutes of the Profintern could not have come at a worse time. The minority was at that very moment engaged in a life-and-death struggle for the leadership of the CGT. In November 1920 the National Confederal Committee had voted to give the departmental unions and federations the authority to expel members of the CSR from their midst; and in February 1921 the CCN had gone one step further, condemning the CSR's as "divisive bodies that dry up syndicalist recruitment, make unified action difficult, and lead to general discouragement," and declaring that individual or collective membership in the CSR was an act of hostility to the CGT.[46]

The showdown between the two factions came at the Congress of Lille (July 25–30, 1921). The minority arrived at the congress divided into revolutionary syndicalists, Communists, and pure syndicalists. Of the three groups, the Communists were the weakest. To complicate matters, the other two groupings were led by members of the Communist Party. The minoritaires disagreed on almost everything except their opposition to the majority. Monatte and his friends had no desire for a split. They were merely determined that the congress condemn the majority's policy of reformism and class collaboration and that the leadership readmit the unions that had been expelled. A group of pure syndicalists, led by Pierre Besnard, had already resolved on a schism and were eager to create a new Central.[47] The majoritaires stood fast. They did not want a split, but neither had they any desire to deliver the CGT to the Communists. The majority was able to evoke the specter of the Communist subordination of the unions, as they had done the year before at Orléans; and the debates showed that many minoritaires had lost their enthusiasm for Moscow.[48] An appeal from the Profintern assuring the French syndicalists that Moscow had no intention of subordinating the syndicalist International to the Comintern had little effect.[49] After five days of deadly heat, bitter recriminations, and physical combat, the majority managed to carry the day by a vote of 1,556 to 1,348, with 46 abstentions. The victory, however, was pyrrhic and the majoritaires knew it. In less than a year the minority had captured 700 unions and doubled its forces.[50] The two factions had reached a stalemate; important segments of both groups now wanted a split. Frossard came back from Lille convinced that it was a "congrès d'avant-scission."[51]

Meanwhile, the leaders of the party attempted to play the role of moderator between the minority and Moscow. Frossard dismissed the dispute as a "family disagreement," and promised that the party would continue to respect the independence of the syndicalist movement in the future as in the past. Dunois and Treint echoed this restraint. "The party, as a party," the latter wrote on July 21, "has no business intervening in the debate."[52] At Lille the Communists had no policy except to avoid upsetting the shaky coalition among the minoritaires. Only Loriot, Tommasi, Godonnèche, and Rosmer chose to defend the Profintern. Loriot pointed out the absurdity of the position of those Communists who contested the right of the party to interfere in the union movement.[53] Rosmer, on the other hand, had remained true to the position of *La Vie Ouvrière* in 1919 and 1920. For him, as for Tommasi and Godonnèche, Bolshevism carried on the spirit of syndicalism. What was the "daring, forceful, and farsighted minority" of prewar syndicalism, they asked, except the party? Was this not the lesson of the Russian Revolution?[54]

Perhaps. But few French Communists felt the force of Loriot's and Rosmer's logic. They saw no reason to tamper with the tested methods of the past. In the meantime, while the French leaders fiddled, the Bolsheviks chafed, annoyed by the passive position the PCF had taken with respect to the unions. Trotsky, in his letters to the CD, insisted that the party must set out to "conquer the unions from within."[55] At the Third Congress the French Communists had promised to increase their efforts to penetrate the unions; but, like their other promises, this had remained a dead letter. The Bolsheviks were not impressed by the insistence of the French that the situation in France was different from the situation in Russia. What looked like a "French necessity" in Paris only seemed to be a surrender in Moscow.[56] When Humbert-Droz came to Paris in October 1921, one of his chief objectives was to persuade the revolutionary syndicalists to join the party and prod the CD to more decisive action. What he found was a complex situation.[57] Though many syndicalists belonged to the party, they did not consider it their own. They felt more at home in their union, and they left the leadership of the party to politicians and journalists. Monatte and Monmousseau had made a theory of this peculiarly French situation. They envisaged a situation in which there would be a division of labor between the syndicalists and the Communists. The former would prepare the proletariat for the Revolution; the latter would take charge of the peasantry and the intellectuals.

Humbert-Droz pointed out the dangers in these ideas. If the PCF followed the course set for it by Monatte and Monmousseau, it would eventually become a petty-bourgeois group without influence on the working class. But he also warned against trying to subordinate the unions to the party. Loriot and Tommasi, he wrote, were wrong in their interpretation of the decisions of the Executive Committee; in agitating for the subordination of the unions to the party they had only reinforced the strength of the anarchists and pure syndicalists while causing disputes among Communist union leaders. At Marseille, concluded Humbert-Droz, the party must make it clear that reformists and pure syndicalists had no place in its ranks. But it must also reject the subordination of the unions and the faction that supported this view. Humbert-Droz's attitude coincided with a more moderate tone on the part of the Russians. A declaration issued by the two Moscow Internationals in October 1921 denied any attempt at subordination, and suggested that a mixed action committee, consisting of Communists and syndicalists, would satisfy its demand for coordination between the unions and the party.[58]

The thesis on the unions which Dunois drafted for the Marseille Congress was close to Humbert-Droz's suggestions. It affirmed that the unions and the party were equally necessary to both the revolutionary struggle and the dictatorship of the proletariat. The image chosen was military: the unions provided the revolutionary army while the party formed its vanguard. Subordination and burrowing from within were rejected; at the same time, Communists were said to have the right and duty to penetrate the unions "not as a party . . . but as an idea, with rights and freedoms equal to those of all the other ideas that meet there."[59] From its first word to its last, Dunois' text was an attempt to find a compromise between the Russian and French traditions, perhaps the best example of his ingenuity being the formula that while the unions were administratively self-sufficient, they were not self-sufficient in everything.

It is hard to see how Communists could have been more moderate. The party was merely asking for the same rights as anarchists, reformists, and Dissidents. Revolutionary syndicalists nonetheless found these claims excessive. When Dunois presented his thesis to a meeting of *Communist* unionists on November 2 and 3, Verdier rejected it altogether, and Mayoux, Quinton, Sémard, and Bert offered a counter-motion, which denied that Communism was superior to syndicalism as a doctrine and came out against the formation of cells in the factories. Mayoux pointed out that it was impossible for the party to dictate a line to its members in the unions without violating syndicalist autonomy; for what would the party do if the decision of the union as a whole differed from the policy the party recommended?[60] Even to Communists, this reasoning seemed unassailable. The party rejoiced when Monmousseau declared in a speech before the United Trade Unions of the Seine on November 27, 1921, that "le syndicalisme ne suffit pas à tout." It was grateful for small favors; for Monmousseau added that he was not in agreement with the CD's thesis and objected to the party's pretensions to being the vanguard of the proletariat. The proletariat, he countered, would find its vanguard in the unions; and the alliance between the party and the syndicalists would be concluded in the heat of revolutionary action.[61] It was on this note of frustration that the party went to Marseille to discuss its policy on the unions—and other, no less exciting issues.

### BEFORE MARSEILLE

Dunois' performance (the image of a tightrope is almost inescapable) was one attempt to fill the void in party policy that Frossard had pointed to in September. Meanwhile, Rappoport, Renoult, and Jean had drafted theses on national defense, electoral tactics, and the agrarian problem for submission to the National Congress at Marseille. Rappoport's motion on national defense repeated the shibboleths of prewar Socialism: it promised to oppose the voting of all war credits; affirmed the support of the PCF for the independence of all peoples; and declared that in case of war, the Communists would respond with a general strike and the slogan "Au système capitaliste pas un homme, pas un sou." Electoral tactics presented a more complex problem. What elections the party had contested during 1921 had been conducted on the basis of opposition to the Bloc National, with very little talk of Communism or Marxism. The election in the second sector of Paris had been the outstanding example. Renoult's motion, like Dunois', was a compromise between the Communist ideal and the French reality. It stated that for the Communists electoral action had only a secondary value, and that they would not consider alliances with other parties. The first round of elections would always be used to proclaim Communist doctrine and for a "revolutionary affirmation." Where there was a possibility of victory, the struggle would be continued on the second ballot with a "redoubled energy." However, where the Communist candidate had no chance of success and where maintaining him during the second round might anger the Leftist electorate, the party would simply withdraw its man, leaving its voters free to choose whom they wished. In the last analysis, it was left to the individual federations to choose the tactic on the second ballot that was best suited to their situation. Renaud Jean's draft on agrarian questions acknowledged the resistance of the French peasant to the idea of collectivization, and pronounced in favor of an intermediary system that would end sharecropping, renting, and hired farm labor, and give the peasants the perpetual use of the land.[62] Little need be said about these texts here; unlike Dunois' effort, they merely restated the policies of the prewar SFIO, with perhaps a dash of Communist language here and there and abundant references to the lessons of the War.

As the Congress of Marseille neared, relations within the CD worsened. The scandal of the press was a running sore. Fabre, Méric, and Verfeuil struck daily at Souvarine and the International from the columns of *Le Journal du Peuple*. In Paris rumors circulated that Souvarine and Loriot were plotting a dictatorship over the party, and that Souvarine no longer had the confidence of the Russians. Rappoport submitted a motion calling for the control of the delegate to the International. On December 15, Fabre was finally brought before the Conflict Commission for an article attacking the Comintern he had published two months before. To the shock and indignation of the Left, instead of being expelled, he was gently scolded and reminded to observe discipline.[63]

The problem of organization became another source of dissension. Like the questions of the press and the unions, this issue had its origins in decisions of the Third Congress. The theses adopted at the Third Congress had called for the reorganization of the foreign Communist parties according to the Bolshevik model. At the Fourth World Congress, Lenin remarked that although excellent in its content, this resolution was too long, too Russian, and unintelligible to foreigners.[64] Lenin's comment was wise, if a little late. The majority of French Communists did not bother to read the resolutions of the Congress; of the few who did, the majority did not understand them; and of the handful who understood them, the majority tried to ignore them.

The Bolsheviks, though, were nothing if not insistent. Trotsky took up the issue in his letters to the CD. Humbert-Droz raised it again in October. Before he left he was promised that the leadership would present a reorganization project at Marseille; specifically, he was told that a presidium would be formed to give the party stronger leadership. November passed; nothing was done about reorganization. The Left, determined not to let the matter die, presented its own project on November 29. Loriot's draft called for the enlargement of the CD to 36 (of whom 12 would reside in the provinces), and the formation of a Bureau of five members to handle current business. In an unfortunate phrase, the draft stated that the CD would meet *at least* once a month. This was immediately interpreted as an attempt to impose a dictatorship on the party; the other members of the CD rejected Loriot's project without discussion. Nothing was said for ten days. Then, on December 10, 1921, Frossard presented his own reorganization plan, which had been drawn up without the knowledge or cooperation of the Left. Frossard's project did not differ markedly from Loriot's draft—except that it retained the CD of 24 members and emphasized that the Bureau would keep the CD informed of its decisions. Frossard's plan was discussed by the CD and adopted.[65]

I have recounted this episode in detail because it indicates the prevailing atmosphere of mistrust and the degree to which leadership had broken down by the end of 1921. What was involved in this dispute was not so much the precise mechanisms of the two projects as the will to put into practice the decisions of the International. Neither group wanted to destroy freedom of discussion within the party. For that matter, the Frossard project could have been used as a basis for reorganizing the party along the lines laid down by the Third World Congress. But the Left no longer trusted Frossard's good faith, and it felt that he wished to keep the levers of leadership weak so that he could continue to manipulate the CD against the Left and postpone indefinitely the application of the International's decisions.

The hidden tensions and undercurrents working in the party exploded into the open for the first time at the Congress of the Seine, which met on the successive Sundays of December 4, 11, and 18, 1921. The Ultra-Left had been nurturing its resentment ever since the events of the spring. These meetings gave it a forum. Refusing to distinguish between Loriot, Frossard, and Méric (they were all leaders, hence all opportunists), Heine, Soutif, and Cartier led the attack on the CD in the name of federalism, international discipline, and the Twenty-One Conditions. A greater muddle could not have been imagined. Heine set the tone. His program was to combine "federalism with democratic centralism in an attempt to achieve revolutionary unity."[66] These sallies would have been mere pinpricks and nothing more, had it not been for the fact that the Ultra-Left controlled the majority of the votes. Over Loriot's objection, the congress decided on the first day to establish its own list of candidates for the CD, and voted by a huge majority to bind its delegates to the National Assembly to the positions it would adopt.[67]

While Loriot flailed against this incoherence, the Right delighted in it. All other issues were forgotten except "oligarchy," for and against. To Méric, what the Left offered was not even "oligarchic centralism" but "sectarian centralism"; and it was the party's delegate in Moscow who was the "instigator of this cabal against the party." Loriot tried to shift the discussion to another ground. His project, he said, implied no dictatorship. "Two states of mind? Yes. Those who accept the resolutions of the International and those who oppose them with the force of their inertia so that nothing gets done." Frossard sidestepped this issue nicely and brought the debate back to the question of dictatorship. "For some weeks," he said, "a battle has been fought in the night." This conflict revolved around personalities, not ideas. It was not true that the majority was against the application of the International's resolutions. The trouble was that Loriot's project created a political presidium rather than an administrative bureau. The minimum of one meeting per month for the CD would soon become a maximum. In the end, Loriot's presidium would replace the CD and deprive it of its political power. Frossard complained of Souvarine's brutality and sympathized with the indignation of Méric and Rappoport. A party, he concluded, could not be led with a cudgel. Those below had as much right to express themselves as those above. "In a great party like ours, a party that is a great friendship, I don't intend to settle questions with a punch in the nose."[68]

The last day of the congress was devoted to the selection of delegates to the National Congress and the passage of a motion on general policy. The text of the Executive Committee of the Seine defeated easily both the motion of the majority of the CD (Ker) and the counter-motion of the Left (Loriot-Treint). Heine explained that what had prevented the leadership of the Federation of the Seine from voting for Ker's version was that it contained the sentence, "Le Comité Directeur dirige le parti." The words "directeur" and "dirige" were incompatible with their interpretation of Communism.[69] Frossard need not have been perturbed by this small defeat. The Congress of the Seine had been one of his finest hours. He had succeeded in using one enemy (the Ultra-Left) to rout the other (the Left). He had posed as the champion of democracy against oligarchy, of freedom of opinion against dictatorship, of comradeship against brutality. Most remarkable of all, he had managed all this while representing himself as the true and devoted servant of Moscow.

### MARSEILLE

Such virtuosity grew more difficult as the demands of the International became better known. The Executive took advantage of the opening of the Congress of Marseille (December 25–30, 1921) to address a message to the PCF.[70] Trotsky himself wrote it. The importance of the communication was not so much in what it said (the members of the CD already knew what the Executive wanted) as in the fact that the International had chosen to speak to the party directly. All of the directives of the past few months were summarized and repeated. The effort of the party, it was announced, had been great; it had not been sufficient. The party lacked firm leadership. What was needed was a bureau of five members, which would direct the activity and ideas of Communists day by day. A greater sense of discipline must be established. The Executive demanded that party members act like Communists in the unions. The party must take a clear position on the control of the unofficial Communist press, in particular *Le Journal du Peuple* and *La Vague*. At the Third Congress the French delegation had agreed to settle this matter; thus far nothing had been done. The congress must deal with the groups that were calling for a rapprochement with the Dissidents and revival of the Left Bloc. Closer relations should be established with the factory workers by bringing them into the CD. Finally, the French should take a greater interest in the work of the International and the life of the other parties. The message, though firm, was phrased in warm and comradely terms; Trotsky allowed the Executive's impatience to show through only when mentioning Fabre and *Le Journal du Peuple*.

This was work for two congresses. The greatest efforts of the delegates at Marseille, however, were devoted to a question that Trotsky's message had not even mentioned: the absent figure of Boris Souvarine. The onslaught began before the congress could even get to its agenda. Rappoport claimed that Souvarine had distorted the meaning of his article on Serrati. Méric brandished two letters from the Executive and suggested slyly that Souvarine had been disavowed by Moscow. Verfeuil celebrated the opportunism of the Third World Congress (which, in his interpretation, had rejected the sectarian principles and tactics laid down the year before), and declared that Loriot had tried to steal the leadership of the party from Frossard at Moscow. Loriot denied this accusation angrily. Amidst the uproar of the congress, he defended Souvarine and his letters, and insisted that what was at issue was a political conflict.

It was at this point that Frossard entered the debate, the very incarnation of reason and compromise. The General Secretary pointed out that the CD had worked together unanimously until December. If the leadership had made mistakes, if it had shown a lack of initiative, it was not himself or Cachin who was responsible, but rather the Committee as a whole. He denied that Méric, Rappoport, and Verfeuil were Rightists. They held no ideas in common (this was only a half-truth; they despised Souvarine and objected to the ordering about of the PCF by the Executive). The cause of the present malaise, he found, was not a conflict of factions, but a clash of personalities. He concluded with an appeal to unity. "We must be united. I have said what I think. I am ready to turn the page, but I repeat, the party must become a great friendship. (*Applause.*) We must make a party where personalities do not count and where ideas come first."[71]

After these early confrontations, the congress appeared to have settled down and the debates proceeded in greater calm. The third, fourth, and fifth days were devoted to the discussion of the theses submitted by the CD. Considering the importance of the issues, they aroused surprisingly little serious debate.[e] This was in part because no one had anything new to say, in even greater

---

[e] In the perspective of history, the debate over Rappoport's thesis on national defense takes on a certain interest. There were two points of view: the Tolstoyan pacifism of Pioch and Méric, and the revolutionary anti-militarism of Vaillant-Couturier. Pioch objected to Rappoport's confusion of "the pacifism of the drawing room and the government and the pacifism of Tolstoy." Tolstoy's pacifism, Pioch admitted, might have failed; nevertheless, it expressed "the best that man has dreamed of." Méric agreed, adding that "Our party will be anti-militarist or it will not be." For Vaillant-Couturier, Tolstoyan pacifism was

part because the party's leaders now had their minds on other matters. On the second day of the congress, the subcommittee on general policy had met, as was customary, to draw up a unanimous motion laying down the party's future course of action. A text drafted by Frossard had been accepted; it approved the idea of an administrative bureau, rejected the united front with the Dissidents, and rebuked Souvarine for his polemics. Frossard's motion said nothing of *Le Journal du Peuple* or *La Vague*, and went out of its way to condemn the principle of "oligarchic centralism."

Horrified by this revolt against international discipline, the delegates of the International, Bordiga and Walecki, immediately demanded a closed conference with the representatives of the subcommittee. Agreement was not easily reached. Bordiga and Walecki pleaded with the delegates of the subcommittee, Renoult, Rappoport, Brodel, Soutif, and Treint, not to condemn the united front and the concept of centralized political leadership. Had not the French delegates to the Third Congress approved the theses on organization and tactics? The French disputed this interpretation of the Third Congress. Besides, they countered, they were merely the instruments of the party's will; and this was the way their comrades wanted it. Walecki demanded a "coup à droite" against Fabre and Brizon. Rappoport replied that "no one takes Fabre seriously." Renoult added that Souvarine had poisoned the atmosphere of the congress with his personal polemics. Everyone, he said, agreed on *Le Journal du Peuple* and *La Vague*. Renoult assured Walecki that Fabre's attacks would cease and that "this time there will be not words but acts from our side." Rappoport then interjected: "If only you had acted through letters instead of firing Moscow's big cannon." To which Walecki replied: "We've written more than ten times."[72]

Finally, after three days of debate, a motion was composed by Renoult that everyone except Treint agreed to sign. An incredible mixture of double entendre and innuendo, it was a document that could hardly cheer the Left or the International.[73] What was given with one hand was taken away with the other. It was promised to control *Le Journal du Peuple* and *La Vague*; at the same time, personal polemics among Communists were forbidden, a slap at Souvarine as well as Méric. The idea of a presidium or bureau was accepted;

---

not enough. War was hell. Everyone agreed on this. But before we can end war we must win the Army and, if necessary, adapt to circumstances. (*L'Humanité*, 30.xii.21.) What we have here is basically a conflict of generations. The men of the traditional Left Wing could not bring themselves to use militaristic and unprincipled methods in fighting militarism. The younger men had no such scruples. They felt that pacifism had been discredited in 1914 and that Tolstoy's noble idealism had to be replaced by Bolshevik toughness. The full implications of the debate and the meaning of "adapting to circumstances" would not become clear until the late 1930's. In 1921 it required an extraordinary imagination to conceive of a militaristic Communist Party in France.

but to drive home the point that its role would be administrative rather than political, it was stressed that the concentration of power in a few hands was necessary only in time of civil war. Souvarine was praised for his work as delegate to the International; but the same clause stated that there were no political disagreements between him and the CD, thus implicitly approving Frossard's leadership and making Souvarine's criticisms appear personal outbursts. The intervention of the International's delegates had been vigorous; it could not by any means be called successful. Despite Walecki's warning that to reject the Executive's tactic of the united front would be to put the party into opposition "against almost the entire International," the French had gone ahead to write into their motion a clause that specifically ruled out the possibility of any alliance with the Dissidents.

The last night of the congress arrived. In a series of quick votes, the delegates approved the theses of the CD by huge majorities. Even Mayoux's counter-motion on the unions received only a sprinkling of votes. After a minor change in the wording demanded by Loriot, Renoult's text on general policy was approved unanimously. It seemed that Frossard had repeated his success at the Federation of the Seine. The opposition of the Left had been neutralized by the Right. The General Secretary arose to announce the vote on the selection of the CD. Souvarine's name did not appear on the list. A murmur ran through the hall, which ended only when Loriot took the speaker's stand. The leader of the Left thanked the congress for his own election, but declared that he could not accept the post. "The non-election of Souvarine," he said, "poses a problem of conscience for me." Treint, Dunois, and Vaillant-Couturier made the same declaration of solidarity, as the Left of the congress shouted bravos.[74]

A frantic effort was made to heal the breach caused by the resignation of the four. Bestel, a member of the Left, asked the four to change their minds. Ker also intervened, and said that he would remain on the CD if Souvarine's mandate as delegate to the International was renewed. Frossard took the floor and made another appeal for unity. What had happened, he said, was the result of the absurd method of voting. The congress had reached agreement on all essential questions. It did not have the right to split over such an issue. "Think it over, comrades," he concluded. "We cannot separate in this way. We must look for a solution bringing immediate unity. . . . I would not want to remain at the head of the party if we cannot make this effort at unity." Loriot replied that Frossard's attempt at unity had come too late. "The trouble was not born today. It was born at the Congress of the Seine, and Frossard said nothing. Whether one likes it or not, there are disagreements over doctrine between us." He and his friends would return to the ranks. Loriot refused Bestel's offer of a compromise. Souvarine would be too proud to accept a lesser post. Ker then demanded that the congress re-elect Souvarine as delegate to the International. Renoult, Méric, and Jean all took the speaker's platform to insist that Loriot and his friends withdraw their resignations. Jean pointed out that the party had already voted on the questions of policy and had accepted the texts submitted by the CD unanimously. "S'il y a conflit de tendances, on se trompe ou on nous trompe." He demanded that Loriot accept Ker's proposition. The session was suspended for half an hour while Frossard tried to make a deal with the Left.

Finally, at 2:30 in the morning, Frossard appeared on the speaker's platform. We accept Ker's proposition, he began. We are ready to say, with Bestel, Ker, and Tommasi (all members of the Left), that there are no political differences between Souvarine and us, and we will vote to renew his mandate. "To Loriot, Treint, and Vaillant-Couturier I say, 'You place us at the head of the party; we accept.'" The congress passed Ker's proposition with near-unanimity. Ironically, as a consequence of the resignation of the four, Souvarine automatically became a member of the CD. All these negotiations and accusations had taken place in an atmosphere of turmoil and confusion. Most delegates were stunned by the sudden conflict between the Center and the Left. Many of those present must have sympathized with Lafont, who asked: "Why has no political question been raised during the course of these five days, and why, when someone fails to be elected, is it discovered that there is a political difference? ... I don't understand anything."

### THE FIRST YEAR OF COMMUNISM

Thus the first year of the party, the first year of that "grande amitié" of which Frossard spoke so often, ended amidst personal squabbles, recriminations, threats, and above all, confusion. Enemies of the party did not hesitate to profit from its embarrassment. Comparing the practice of the PCF with the statutes of the Third International, Paul Faure concluded that Bolshevism in France was a "farce" and an "imposture."[d] Léon Blum had already detected the irony inherent in the French opposition to the united front. Noting that Souvarine had objected to the Executive's new tactic, Blum wrote: "The French Communists are bringing us one surprise after another. While Moscow gives Paris lessons in orthodoxy via Souvarine's pen, Paris is giving Moscow lessons in intransigence via Souvarine's mouth."[75] The bitterness of Faure and Blum showed how wide the gap between former comrades had grown in only a year. Le Temps' evaluation may have lacked subtlety; its general conclusion can hardly be disputed:

[d] Faure, Le Bolchevisme en France: Farce et imposture (1921). Faure certainly did not lack for cases. One of the most humorous (p. 57) concerned a Communist named Devienne, head of the textile strike committee in Lannoy, who was leading a demonstration when he was suddenly approached by the brigadier of the local gendarmerie and told that he had been appointed a member of his unit. Without hesitation, Devienne quit the procession. As of Faure's writing, this Communist militant was a dedicated gendarme.

In less than two years Communist propaganda has ruined the working-class organizations; it has driven out of them all the sound elements that Socialist formulas
had temporarily succeeded in leading astray. Today all that remains are agitators, in
violent conflict with one another, who quarrel over the means of bringing about a
revolution that they all hope for with equal fervor, but that is now scarcely within
their power to organize.[76]

Not that the year had been a total disaster. Frossard could boast of the 131,476
cards that the party had succeeded in distributing by October 15, 1921; the
580,000-franc loan that had been raised in a few weeks to restore the party's
finances and acquire a new home for it; and the electoral campaigns of the
second sector of Paris, where Loriot and Souvarine had outrun the Dissidents,
and Charonne, where André Marty had become a municipal councillor.[77]
During this first year, the party had made some progress in the use of the
front organization. At the threat of an occupation of the Ruhr, the CD had
set up an Action Committee against War along with the CSR, the United
Trade Unions of the Seine, ARAC, the Fédération Ouvrière et Paysanne des
Mutilés, and the JC. This, in turn, had been transformed into a Comité de
Résistance aux Lois Superscélerates (July); and when this campaign was won,
into a Committee of Aid to the Russian People (September), to combat the
famine that struck Russia in 1921. In three months this committee raised more
than a million francs.[78]

These achievements looked impressive on paper. They were less so when
placed in their proper perspective. The early influx into the party after the Congress of Tours was more a gesture of sympathy for the Russian Revolution
than an espousal of the principles of Bolshevism or the Third International.
Frossard was the first to admit that recruitment had fallen off sharply after
April.[79] In those elections which the party had contested, it had presented
itself not as the incarnation of Bolshevism, but as the champion of opposition
to the Bloc National and war. The campaign against the occupation of the
Ruhr had found no echo among the masses. As for the unions, the Communists
were more isolated than ever from the real sources of working-class power.
They had promised to penetrate the unions "as idea"; but as yet the PCF's
leaders could not even make an appearance at a syndicalist congress without
arousing a protest, more likely than not led by members of their own party.
Le Temps notwithstanding, the Communists could not take on themselves the responsibility for the approaching schism of the CGT. For if the
anarchists and revolutionary syndicalists were anxious to free themselves from
Jouhaux and Dumoulin, they were in no hurry to throw themselves into the
arms of Moscow. All in all, an unprejudiced observer might conclude from
the record of this first year that the Communists had been least effective when
they acted most like Communists (as they did during the occupation of the

Ruhr), and most effective when they presented themselves as the vanguard of the progressive Left (as they did in the election of the second sector of Paris). Frossard was too shrewd a politician not to have noticed this; one wonders what his thoughts were as 1921 drew to a close.

Within the party the year had seen the progressive deterioration of relations among the members of the CD. It was still too early to speak of factions, but four tendencies had emerged, which sometimes represented four different positions but which just as frequently merged into two. On the extreme Left there were the federalists of the Seine (Heine, Latouche, Soutif, Cartier), who carried on the legacy of the "Parti Communiste" and "Fédération des Soviets." Calling themselves the "Left" were the remnants of the old Committee for the Third International (Souvarine, Loriot, Vaillant-Couturier, Treint) and a few reinforcements from the Reconstructors (Dunois, Tommasi). Despite their name, the members of the Left were not so much itching for revolutionary action (Loriot was even something of a pessimist) as anxious that the decisions of the International be applied to the letter. Frossard and Cachin had no policy except procrastination and the maintenance of freedom of opinion within the party. The Right, an invention of Souvarine's prolific pen, was a motley assembly of former members of the Committee for the Third International (Rappoport, Méric, Pioch), Reconstructors (Verfeuil), and independent left-wing journalists (Fabre, Brizon) who had little in common except a dislike of Souvarine and an unwillingness to take orders from Moscow. Was this conflict one of personalities, as Frossard insisted, or one of ideas, as Loriot claimed? For the moment, it was a little bit of both. Older militants like Rappoport and Méric resented Souvarine's manner and were jealous of his meteoric rise to power in the International.[80] Souvarine, for his part, made no distinction between personal disagreement and ideological deviation. Behind the personal vendettas, however, there loomed a larger question: that of the relationship between the Comintern and the French.

Thus far, relations with the International, if not ideal, had been amiable. Trotsky had reined in his natural sarcasm and impatience when dealing with the French. When one remembers the scorn and even brutality with which the leader of the Red Army treated Cachin and Frossard in 1920, the *politesse* of his letters in 1921 seems truly amazing. Lenin and Zinoviev had had words of praise for Frossard and Cachin at the Third Congress; and the personal mission of Humbert-Droz to Paris had gone off without conflict. The Bolsheviks had been particularly careful not to mix in the internal quarrels of the PCF. To demonstrate their good faith, they had encouraged the Left to disband the Committee for the Third International. In its own relations with the CD the Executive had "suggested" and not "commanded." At no time had it wielded that absolute power over the French party which the decisions of the Second and Third Congresses gave it.[e] Why this un-Bolshevik restraint? Zinoviev explained that it was because the PCF was a young party. A more plausible answer is that the Bolsheviks were trying to avoid a repetition of Livorno, where the impatience of the Comintern had lost it the majority of the Italian Socialist Party. A French Livorno would be even more disastrous.[f] Walecki's threats at Marseille suggested that this period of grace might be coming to an end.

The most significant development of 1921, however, was not to be found in relations with the Comintern, but rather in the crystallization of an attitude of inferiority toward and imitation of the Bolsheviks. This was not the doing of secret messengers, disapproving letters, or congress resolutions. It was inherent in the logic of the historical situation. Ever since 1917 the Russian Revolution had been a trump card that the Left Wing of the working-class movement could play against its more moderate foes. Longuet had used it in October 1918 to rout Renaudel. Not that he identified himself with the Bolshevik regime; but he defended the right to revolution, anywhere, any time. Frossard had gone one step further. Answering Merrheim's anti-Bolshevik speech at Orléans in 1920, he had argued that a working-class militant did not have the right to criticize the Russian Revolution, even if he disagreed with it. For if the Bolsheviks were defeated, he concluded, reaction would triumph and the chances for the liberation of the working class would be compromised.[81]

One might think that this manipulation of the Russian Revolution would have ceased to have any meaning among Communists. But such was not the

[e] The French, however, had no reason for illusions on the nature of relations between the Executive and the member sections. The invitation to the Third Congress, reported in the *Bulletin Communiste,* 9.vi.21, read, with regard to the Executive's authority: "It is possible to appeal one of its decisions, but during the intervals between congresses the Executive has full authority. Its decisions must be carried out. Otherwise the very existence of the Communist International as a centralized and disciplined international organization would be impossible." And the Forty-Sixth Thesis on organization passed at the Third World Congress read: "The party as a whole is under the leadership of the Communist International" and "Directives and decisions of the International are binding on the party and of course on every individual party member." Quoted in Jane Degras, *The Communist International, 1919–1943, Documents* (London, 1956), I, 267.

[f] As a result of Livorno, the Comintern was forced to build its Italian section upon the foundations of Gramsci's group at Turin and Bordiga's group at Naples. Since neither of these factions had any real following among the workers, the creation of a mass Communist Party in Italy was substantially retarded. The leaders of the International blamed this defeat on Serrati, who henceforth became a symbol of rebellion against the Comintern. Soon thereafter, Paul Levi, the Chairman of the German Communist Party, was excluded for his criticism of Béla Kun's and Rákosi's policy of the offensive in Germany. There is a brief but good account of these events in Franz Borkenau, *World Communism* (Ann Arbor, Mich., 1962), pp. 208–20. The best analysis of the events leading up to Livorno is to be found in Donald W. Urquidi, "The Origins of the Italian Communist Party, 1918–1921" (unpublished doctoral dissertation, Columbia University, 1962).

case. The Left, in combating the opportunism of the old Reconstructors and the new Right, appealed to the superior wisdom and eventually the infallibility of the Bolsheviks and the International. Still obsessed by the memory of August 1914, the young Communists put their faith in internationalism, and chose as their chief foe the nationalist deviation. Souvarine admitted that the Bolshevik Party played a predominant role in the International. Its influence, however, was legitimate in his view. "What Socialist Party has as much claim to the gratitude of the proletariat as the Bolshevik Party? What party has made so many sacrifices for the Revolution? What party can produce militants comparable to the leaders of the Russian revolutionary movement? What party has the learning, the experience, the practice, of the Russian Communist Party?"[82]

Since the Bolsheviks had this superior insight into the mechanics of revolution, it was only natural to emulate their organization, their discipline, their theory, and even their language. Souvarine, Vaillant-Couturier, and Treint became more Bolshevik than the Bolsheviks themselves. We have already seen the lengths to which this compulsion for imitation could lead. Souvarine's letters from Moscow, in addition to being the product of a natural enthusiasm and a talented pen, were also an attempt to introduce into the PCF the Leninist habit of violent political polemics without regard to personal sensibilities. Frossard himself had been forced to flail the Dissidents as counterrevolutionaries. It was Vaillant-Couturier's restatement of Bolshevik dogma ("Between them and us, it's war to the death") which had triumphed.

In 1921 the full implications of these Bolshevik patterns were not yet clear. In May, Souvarine considered the question raised by Levi's expulsion from the German party. How, he asked, did one draw the line between criticism and hostility? What rules governed the right of minorities within the party to express their ideas? Admitting the difficulty of drawing such a line, Souvarine answered that "it is the job of the party, or of its chosen representatives, to use their political sense in judging what contributes to or decreases its effectiveness."[83] Implicit in that formula was Souvarine's own downfall.

Chapter eight

# The Cold Wind from Moscow

Nos adversaires de mauvaise foi nous accusent
d'avoir ajouté à ces "21 conditions" une 22ᵉ
disant: "Les 21 conditions ne comptent pas."
—*Charles Rappoport, February 1922*

Human affairs have their own crazy logic: what was meant by all parties to be
an end was only a beginning. The Congress of Marseille exacerbated rather
than dissipated the malaise that gnawed at the party. Or perhaps it would
be more accurate to say that the malaise found itself at Marseille and became
a crisis. The "battle in the night" of which Frossard had spoken so regretfully
now burst out into the light of day. What had been tendencies became factions.
The clash of personalities merged almost imperceptibly into a conflict of ideas.
If 1921 was a year of grace during which the French were able to avoid the
logical implications of their adherence to the Comintern, 1922 was a year of
reckoning. Positions were taken; harsh words were exchanged. Moscow
sniffed treachery; Paris cried "ukase." The great misunderstanding upon
which the party had been founded could no longer be kept from view. The
"French question" became a permanent fixture on the agenda of the Executive. And all the while the French Bolsheviks dug themselves deeper into that
moral grave of Leninism from which only two exits were possible: expulsion
by the very instruments that they had forged; or corruption and subjection to
Moscow.

## THE UNITED FRONT

The great majority of delegates returned from Marseille convinced that justice
had been done. The Right, of course, exulted; for after all, Verfeuil had been
elected to the new CD and Souvarine defeated.[a] The Center also interpreted

[a] The new CD was composed of Barabant, Marthe Bigot, Jules Blanc, Louise Bodin, Paul
Bouthonnier, Cachin, Cartier, Eugène Dondicol, Ferdinand Faure, Frossard, Jean Gachéry, Henri Gourdeaux, Jean, Ker, Leiciague, Georges Lévy, Paul Louis, Méric, Marius

the results of the Congress as a reaffirmation of the party's unity and freedom of opinion. Writing in *L'Humanité*, Cachin observed with an obvious personal reference that "Our meeting in Marseille has served notice with éclat that the party will not permit anyone to lay a hand on its unity of organization and action. An enormous majority has served notice, just as emphatically, that it will not allow either personal attacks or threats against militants, all of whom have given themselves to the party without reservations."[1] Realizing the confusion in which the congress had ended, Loriot and Dunois tried to give political substance to their gesture of resignation. Both attempted to show that the refusal to elect Souvarine to the CD represented an act of revolt against Moscow. This was possible only by anticipation. Dunois discovered the existence of a Centrist danger, which had crystallized at Marseille around the issue of Souvarine. The struggle for the Third International, he wrote, was not yet won. It had resumed in the form of an offensive against internal Centrism. Dunois spoke ominously of finishing "the work begun at Tours."[2] The new leadership, however, had no intention of delivering itself into the hands of the Left. It replied to the threats of Dunois and Loriot by passing a resolution in which it denied the existence of a Right tendency and affirmed "its absolute solidarity with the Moscow International."[3]

The reaction of the Bolsheviks to the fiasco of Marseille was hardly encouraging for the Left. The papers describing the final session at Marseille did not arrive in Moscow until January 9, 1922. Souvarine immediately resigned as a member of the CD and the delegate to the Executive. That day the Presidium of the ECCI met and passed a resolution stating that it considered the resignation of Loriot and his friends a "mistake." It refused to accept Souvarine's resignation, and wired the PCF to send a delegation to Moscow, including two members of the CD and two members of the minority. After hearing the report of Ker, who had left for Moscow almost immediately after Marseille, the Presidium decided to postpone the previously scheduled meeting of the Enlarged Executive until the arrival of the French delegation.[4] Meanwhile, in two private letters to the CD, Zinoviev left no doubt where the Executive stood in the Souvarine affair. The French delegate, wrote Zinoviev, was right in his opposition to Verfeuil and other "quasi-reformists." But the Bolsheviks were well aware that Souvarine's personal polemics could be vexing, and Zinoviev emphasized that "in these matters you must never identify Souvarine with the Executive." The choice of their representative to the International was for the French to make. "Every representative of the PCF," Zinoviev concluded, "will be received fraternally by us."[5]

Paquereaux, Rappoport, Renoult, Soutif, Tommasi, and Verfeuil; with Emile Auclair, Emile Bestel, Colliard, Pierre Dormoy, Victor Hattenberger, R.-P. Philippe, Pioch, and Servantier as alternates. For Fabre's and Verfeuil's reaction to Marseille, see *Le Journal du Peuple,* 4.i.21.

The Executive had no desire to encourage a personal struggle within the French party, if only because it had more important things to think about. In December 1921, Zinoviev had announced the adoption of a new tactic, the united front. The idea of the united front, like so many other Comintern policies, had its origins in the experience of the KPD. As early as January 1921, Karl Radek and Paul Levi had published an open letter in which they proposed the united action of workers' parties to shift the burden of reparations "from the shoulders of the proletariat to the shoulders of the bourgeoisie."[6] Because of the March Action and Levi's conflict with Moscow, the tactic had been dropped temporarily in the spring of 1921. But after the Third Congress, it was revived by Ernst Meyer, the new Chairman of the German party. With Radek's encouragement, Meyer argued that NEP marked the end of an era, that the German revolution had reached a stalemate, and that a new policy of joint action with other labor and middle-class groups hinging upon the question of reparations must be initiated.[7] Lenin and Trotsky approved of Meyer's line; it coincided with their own conviction that the period of the revolutionary offensive was over, and that a new period had opened in which the emphasis must be upon the organization and training of Communist parties for future combats.[b] The slogan "To the masses," announced at the Third Congress, thus took on an unexpected interpretation: "to the masses" by way of their reformist leaders. The tactic received its first concrete application in Thuringia in October 1921, when a Social Democratic "workers' government" was constituted with Communist support.

It was Zinoviev who took it upon himself to define the theory and practice of the united front, first in a speech before the ECCI in December 1921, then in a series of theses and articles rained upon the European Communist movement in January 1922.[8] The revolutionary spirit of the world proletariat was rising, wrote Zinoviev. The characteristics of this "new wave" were (sic!) the offensive of international capital against the economic positions of the working class, and the constantly growing threat of a new imperialist war. The response of the workers to these attacks was an irresistible surge toward unity. Considerable portions of the old Social Democratic parties had become dissatisfied with the policies of their leaders. They desired unity with the Communists. Nevertheless, they still had confidence in their reformist leaders and hesitated to leave their old organizations and join the Communist Party. The Communists, concluded Zinoviev, must lead this aspiration to unity.

[b] In August 1921, Lenin observed that though the Communists had a worldwide army, it was still badly trained and organized: "This army . . . must be trained, organized properly, and put through all sorts of maneuvers, in widely differing clashes and in both offensives and retreats. Without long and painful experience, it is impossible to win." *L'Internationale Communiste,* December 1921, col. 4795.

True, the new tactic raised certain problems. The situation in France, for example, was very different from the situation in Germany and Italy. In the latter countries the united front was a means by which the Communists could gain access to the working class; in France the Communists had the majority, while the Dissidents were a general staff without troops. Did this mean that the united front could not be applied to France? Just the contrary. By proposing united action to the reformists, the Communists would unmask "Jouhaux, Merrheim, and Co." before their own followers.[9] Of course there was the danger that some French Communists might interpret the tactic in an opportunistic fashion. Zinoviev mentioned by name Fabre, Verfeuil, Rappoport, and Renoult. But what seemed at first glance a disadvantage was in fact a blessing. For the application of the united front would speed the ideological consolidation of the weaker Communist parties by exposing the reformists, isolating them from the truly Communist Centrists who sought contact with the masses, and educating "the impatient and sectarian elements through experience."[10]

Zinoviev scoffed at those French Communists who feared the unsettling effects the united front might have on a party that had just recently been taught to regard the Dissidents as counterrevolutionaries. The stronger a Communist Party, said Zinoviev, the clearer its ideology and the greater its capacity for maneuver. Even the weakest Communist Party must learn how to gain access to and win over the unorganized masses. Or as the President of the Comintern put it in one of his least successful metaphors, "In learning to swim, one may drown, but this is nevertheless no reason for not learning how to swim."[11]

For all the prose that flowed from Zinoviev's pen, he raised more questions than he answered. Was the united front a means of reaching the masses, a method of discrediting reformist leaders, or a strategic device aimed at the consolidation of the Communist parties themselves? Did it signify the abandoning of the Revolution, or was it merely a temporary maneuver? How far might the surge toward union go? Here Zinoviev had been extremely vague. Despite the fact that the Communists were (and always had been) the most fervent partisans of unity, he said, they could not give up their independence or their right to criticism. Organic unity with the reformist Internationals was out of the question.[12] Still, there was the German precedent of the Open Letter and the "workers' government." Did this mean that Communists should enter Socialist governments? Understandably, Communists of the best intentions took away very different impressions of what the International had in mind, and Communists of the worst intentions had a field day. Nowhere was the confusion greater than in France.

From the very beginning, the reaction of the French Communists to the concept of the united front was hostile. The question had first been raised at a meeting of the ECCI in September 1921. The majority of the Executive Committee had voted to set up Committees of Aid throughout the world for the purpose of collecting famine relief for Russia. These committees would appeal to all working-class organizations, whether Communist or reformist. Souvarine had opposed this decision, and it was in deference to his opposition that the Executive had made the Committees of Aid a suggestion rather than a directive, a suggestion which the French had then gone on to ignore.[c] This seems to have been one of the few points on which Souvarine and the majority of the CD agreed.

The relevant documents on the united front were not yet available at the time of the Congress of Marseille. Hence no debate on this question had been scheduled. But Ker had just returned from a trip to Germany, where he had undoubtedly been briefed on the uses of the new tactic, and the way the meeting between the subcommittee on general policy and the delegates of the International unfolded shows that the party's leaders had already made up their minds. Bordiga and Walecki pleaded with the French to at least leave the question open. Renoult was adamant in his opposition. "Mass movements? Yes. United front? No."[13] Rappoport was simply amused. "Now that the Russians are in power, they find themselves in a moderate zone, while we are in a tropical zone. The cold air seems to be coming from Russia." Only Treint favored the new policy. Walecki insisted that the resolution of the committee was unacceptable and ended with a threat: "Whatever text you vote, this will not be the conclusion but the opening of the debate."[14] The most the delegates of the International could do was see that the united front was not explicitly condemned. The motion finally passed by the congress, with one negative vote,[d] proclaimed that "there is no possibility for the Communists of this country of rapprochement with the Dissident leaders, allies of the bourgeoisie and of the government, or with the syndicalist leaders who have abandoned the class struggle."[15]

The French Communists went directly from the factional struggle at Marseille to the consideration of the united front. Inevitably, this question of tactics became involved with the intra-party struggle between the majority and the Left. The new CD met on January 17, 1922, to determine the attitude of its representatives to the Enlarged Executive, which had been convoked to consider the problem of the united front. The unanimously passed motion not only reiterated the impossibility of any alliance between the PCF and its re-

---

[c] Souvarine to the CD of the PCF, Moscow, 28.ix.21. (Rappoport Papers.) Souvarine did not oppose the united front as such, but he thought that it must be made over the heads of the opportunist leaders by appealing to the masses. Most of the famine aid for Russia was gathered in Germany, Holland, and Switzerland. E. H. Carr, *The Bolshevik Revolution, 1917–1923* (New York, 1953), III, 404.

[d] That of Treint.

formist foes in the SFIO and CGT, but affirmed that the CD considered this tactic to pose certain dangers for the International, "against which guarantees will have to be secured."[16] The French delegates (Cachin, Renoult, Sellier, Métayer) were instructed to defend this point of view in Moscow, and to insist that the question of the united front be placed on the agenda of the Fourth World Congress. To buttress the authority of the delegation, Frossard hastily summoned a conference of federal secretaries, which met on January 23–24 and approved the position of the CD by a vote of 46–12, after being assured that the united front would inevitably lead to parliamentary collaboration and eventually to organizational unity with the Dissidents.[17]

Meanwhile, the formulation of the united front by Zinoviev called forth a deluge of articles in the French left-wing press. The members of Souvarine's Right went their separate ways, according to their background. Their only common denominator was confusion. Rappoport approved the united front, arguing that it was merely traditional Marxist method.[18] Brizon in *La Vague* and Fabre in *Le Journal du Peuple* rejoiced in the new line; but they interpreted it (as Zinoviev had predicted they would) in the sense of the "Bloc des Rouges" and reunion with the Dissidents.[19] Méric and Verfeuil were opposed because, of all reasons, the united front would lead to opportunism. According to Méric, the new tactic would lead straight to the "outmoded, repudiated, and stigmatized ministerialism, of which the Dissidents themselves no longer want to hear."[20] Verfeuil accused the Executive of basing its tactics on the policies of the Soviet government.[21] Renaud Jean, on the other hand, objected to the International's practice of universalizing a tactic which had emerged quite naturally out of the situation in Russia, Germany, and Italy, but which had no relevance in France.[22]

Not even the Left could muster much enthusiasm for the turn. Dunois accepted it in principle, but he admitted that its application posed great difficulties in France.[23] Loriot's only contribution was his advice that the French should not reject today what they would have to accept tomorrow.[24] Not surprisingly, it was Frossard who dealt most tellingly with Moscow's tactical innovation. His arguments were motivated not by opposition to the International, not by personal animosity, but by a sense of political realities. He realized that it was impossible to lead a party which had just been taught to hate the Dissidents into union with the Dissidents' leaders. He knew, furthermore, the desire that many more vacillating Communists felt for reunion with Longuet, Pressemane, and Faure. Alliances with the SFIO might destroy the Communist organizations locally. Most of all, he understood the compulsion of his countrymen for intellectual clarity. This was the land of Descartes, not of Hegel. As the meeting of the Enlarged Executive neared its end, Frossard published a criticism of the united front that struck at the very nature of Leninism as it was in the process of being redefined. "Whatever one may say," he wrote, "a party is not an army. In any case, the discipline it imposes on its troops cannot be a mechanical discipline buttressed by military penalties.... We need clear slogans that seem to be inspired by a constant political direction."[25]

### THE ENLARGED EXECUTIVE

Trotsky had complained in his message to the Marseille Congress that the French did not take a sufficient interest in the affairs of the International. The debates of the Enlarged Executive, which convened in Moscow from February 21 to March 4, 1922, should have satisfied the Bolsheviks that the French intended to break their isolation and bring to bear what influence they could upon the policies of the Comintern. The Enlarged Executive had been staged carefully to approve the tactic of the united front.[e] The Bolsheviks, with their sense of historical unity, made no attempt to conceal the fact that the new tactic was the reflection in Comintern policy of NEP in Russia. Zinoviev went forward bravely to meet what objections this connection between Russian domestic policy and world revolutionary tactics might arouse by arguing that the situation in Russia and the struggle for world revolution were intimately connected. It was impossible, he insisted, for the interests of the only proletarian government not to correspond to the interests of the world proletariat as a whole.[26] The French delegation to the conference consisted of Cachin, Sellier, Renoult, and René Métayer for the CD, with Treint as a non-voting representative of the minority. The Left was further strengthened by the presence of Ker and Souvarine. The Bolsheviks indicated their confidence in Souvarine by re-electing him to the new Presidium, along with Zinoviev, Bukharin, Radek, Heinrich Brandler, Louis Sellier, Umberto Terracini, Karl Kreibich, and Carr.

After two brief reports by Klara Zetkin and Cachin on the use of the united front in Germany and the situation in the PCF, Zinoviev took the floor to inform the delegates about the work of the Executive and comment on the tactic of the united front. It was obvious that the President of the Comintern was annoyed by the recent behavior of the French majority. From the beginning, he said, we knew that "a party that only yesterday was not Communist and that today moves toward us would be in a difficult position and develop slowly." Now the Executive would be forced to take a closer look at the French situation, and it was likely that in the "very near future" it would be France that would "attract most particularly our attention."[27] Coming to the French objection to the united front, Zinoviev agreed that if the CD ac-

---

[e] Daniel Renoult later charged (*L'Humanité*, 23.iv.22) that the decisions had been made before the Executive began, so that the delegates had been presented with a fait accompli. Radek, he claimed, had already initiated negotiations with Adler in Berlin before the principle of agreements with heads of the other Socialist parties had been approved. This was a revelation in 1922, but it merely reflected the reality of Bolshevik predominance in the Comintern. Two years later no one would think it unusual or out of order.

tually believed that the International was proposing fraternization with the leaders of the Second International, then it was their right to sound the alarm and demand a congress to discuss the question. But what they did not have the right to do, he went on, was to falsify the tactic of the International in *L'Humanité* before the eyes of the French working class. It would take a month to repair the harm done by the distortion of the united front. And a few minutes later, replying to the objection of the French that the united front was not applicable in their country because they had the majority, Zinoviev returned to his central theme. "It's not possible," he said, "for the national interests of a party to be contrary to the international interests of the working class."[28]

The delegates of the CD refused to be intimidated. Renoult presented Frossard's objections to the united front, and went on to argue, as he had been instructed, that the tactic of alliances with reformist leaders was dangerous for the International as a whole.[29] He registered the protest of the PCF against the proposed Conference of the Three Internationals. Renoult was supported by Roberto and Terracini of the Italian delegation. The French had to bear the onslaught of both the Bolsheviks and their own comrades of the Left. Radek remarked sardonically that "the Italian comrades are hostile to the united front because they are the minority; the French because they are the majority."[30] Ker, Souvarine, and Treint presented a statement claiming that Renoult's speech did not represent the point of view of either the entire delegation or the PCF.

Zinoviev's method was to bully, to threaten, and to scoff, Radek's to ridicule. Trotsky's way was historical analysis; and it was he who made the most sustained and closely reasoned attempt to demolish the French position. It was not a question, he said, of uniting with Longuet and the Dissidents, but of exposing them before the masses. We are for the Revolution; the Dissidents are against it. At the present time the proletariat does not understand this difference, and we must show it to them.[31] Trotsky warned the French that the party which mechanically opposed the demands of the working class for unity would inevitably find itself condemned in the eyes of the masses. The French Communists must take the lead in the struggle to preserve the unity of the CGT. Trotsky pointed out that the revolutionary syndicalists in France had accepted and applied the tactic of the united front naturally, without outside guidance.[f] The Communists must offer as an alternative to the Left Bloc the

---

[f] As usual, Trotsky identified the French revolutionary syndicalists with Monatte, who was enthusiastic about the new strategy. Monmousseau, on the other hand, whose effective influence on the French union movement was much greater, rejected the idea of agreements with the reformists out of hand. (*La Vie Ouvrière*, 3.ii.22.) Cadeau, another revolutionary syndicalist, was of Monmousseau's mind. "They are not going to drag us to Amsterdam via Moscow." (*Le Journal du Peuple*, 15.iv.22.) Here, then, was a new source of conflict between the French syndicalists and Moscow.

bloc of the working class against the bourgeoisie. All those within the party who favored the Left Bloc must be driven out. This would convince the best workers that the united front was not a policy of compromise or reconciliation with the reformists.[32] Trotsky denied that contact with the reformists was dangerous, but his argument was sounder than Zinoviev's aquatic fantasies. If we lose those elements that joined accidentally, argued Trotsky, we will gain important working-class support. He concluded on his favorite theme: the party must win *decisive influence* within the unions.[33] The next day Treint reduced this complicated reasoning to a simple formula that showed how difficult it was for foreign Communists to follow the subtleties of Bolshevik thought: "Nous nous rapprochons et nous nous éloignons alternativement des réformistes comme la main se rapproche et s'éloigne de la volaille à plumer."[34]

Internal questions went more smoothly than the debate on the united front. On the first day of the conference, a committee composed of Klara Zetkin, Zinoviev, Trotsky, Humbert-Droz, Walecki, Ambrogi, and Vasilii Kolarov was named to meet with the French delegation for the purpose of studying the French question. In his preliminary report to the committee, Renoult argued that the causes of the crisis were personal rather than political. At the end of the second session, Zinoviev submitted a series of questions to the majority: (1) What did it plan to do to end the progress of the Right, as represented by *Le Journal du Peuple* and Fabre? (2) What did it plan to do with regard to the four who had resigned? (3) What would be its attitude toward the unions? (4) What was its attitude toward the existence of factions in the party? During the next meeting Renoult read the response of the majority, which promised that the French delegation would ask the CD (1) to bring Fabre before the Conflict Committee and expel him; (2) to reintegrate the four into the leadership; (3) to apply the Marseille resolution on the unions; and (4) to put an end to the existence of factions.[35] The committee found this answer satisfactory; on March 2, 1922, Trotsky presented the committee's resolution, which found the majority and the Left equally at fault, observed that the present organizational crisis was a stage in the growth of the party, and registered with approval the pledges made by the French delegation to eliminate the causes of the crisis.[36]

The Russians had hoped to end the conference on a note of unanimity, and a committee had been named to work out an agreement between the partisans of the united front and its opponents (the French, the Italians, the Spanish, and the Australians). But this effort at compromise proved a failure. The resolutions of the Executive approving the continuation of the united front tactic and accepting the invitation of the Vienna International to a conference in Berlin were approved by 46 votes, with the French, Italians, and Spanish casting their 10 votes against. The three Latin delegations combined on a minority resolution reaffirming the appeal to the masses, but rejecting any rapprochement with political parties and declining the invitation to the Berlin conference. After the vote, Cachin read a declaration in the name of all three delegations, stating that the minority would remain "disciplined and faithful to the resolutions of the Third International," but observing that the Executive had committed itself to applying the new tactic with the greatest possible allowances for the peculiar national situation of the country involved.[37]

After adopting resolutions on a whole series of questions touching the world revolutionary movement, which ran from the syndicalist problem (the French abstained) to the Near East, the conference disbanded. Neither of the factions within the party could view the results with much satisfaction. The Left had been rebuked for its gesture at Marseille; the objections of the majority to the united front had been thrust aside. From the Russian point of view the conference represented a great step forward, for the French majority had promised to deal with Fabre and had signified its willingness to observe international discipline in the application of the united front. The only question was whether the French would fulfill their pledges; and on this point Cachin's closing remarks seemed to promise trouble.

### THE BERLIN CONFERENCE AND ITS AFTERMATH

The French delegation returned to Paris on March 14, 1922. That night *L'Internationale,* the newly founded Communist evening daily, published an interview with its editor, Daniel Renoult, in which he discussed the significance of the Enlarged Executive in the most ambiguous terms. Asked if the Executive's point of view had triumphed, Renoult answered affirmatively. But he added that the debates, though very thorough and very interesting, had not succeeded in reconciling the French conception of the united front—an appeal to the masses—with the Russian interpretation, which required agreements with reformist leaders. Renoult concluded: "Now the question is clarified, and in the international discipline to which the French Communists naturally cannot help but submit, the action of each party will manifest itself in accordance with the conditions of its context."[38]

The most determined reader could not have wrenched a clear direction from this tortured sentence; but its meaning became clearer at the end of the month, when the CD published three resolutions it had passed in response to the pledges made to the Executive by its delegation in Moscow. The CD agreed to bring Fabre before the Conflict Committee, "which will judge in complete sovereignty and in complete independence"; decided to propose to the next CN the readmission to the CD of the four men who had resigned; and resolved to maintain its prior opposition to the united front, observing that it (the CD) "is more than ever persuaded of the impossibility of putting this tactic into practice, and, in any case, of its dangers for the Russian Revolution and international Communism." The CD agreed, however, "for reasons of discipline," to allow Frossard to participate in the Berlin conference, and added, in a concluding phrase that now appeared to be either a non sequitur or a provocation, that the PCF yielded to the decisions of the Executive.[39]

The party's journalists, meanwhile, continued to play havoc with the interpretation of the united front. Every possible variation on the theme was offered—except the one the Executive wanted. Méric, writing before the decisions of the Executive were known in France, suggested that the united front was merely a means of helping the Soviet government overcome its difficulties. He concluded that the present moment might be propitious for re-examining the relationship between the Soviet government and the International. If the Executive persisted in its tactic, "The French Communist Party will be required either to reverse its position nationally, by submitting to the International, or to reverse its position internationally, by resisting it."[40] Fabre demonstrated daily his total incomprehension of Bolshevism by protesting that the united front would make no sense if he were expelled from the party. Was he not the most fervent propagandist of unity with the Dissidents?[41] He accused "Boris" (Souvarine) of having misinformed the Russians, and compared unfavorably the Socialist culture of Souvarine, Treint, and Vaillant-Couturier to that of Longuet and Faure.[42] Renaud Jean intervened in the debate with a more concrete objection to the Executive's strategy. He insisted that the demands on which the united front was to be based (resistance to the offensive of capital, the eight-hour day) would fail to interest the French peasants. Jean suggested that the Communists emphasize instead the campaign against militarism and rearmament.[43] This proposal caused Trotsky to write in exasperation that in any other Communist Party the kind of articles, statements, and speeches that one found in the French party press, attacking revolutionary violence and written "in a spirit of insipid and sentimental humanitarianism," would be "unthinkable."[44]

In one of its most controversial resolutions, the Enlarged Executive had voted to send a delegation to Berlin to meet with the representatives of the Second and Second-and-a-Half Internationals. This was the united front at its most daring, an attempt to capture the leaders of the reformist Internationals and use them for revolutionary (that is, Communist) ends. Despite French opposition to the project, the Executive chose Frossard to complete the Communist delegation of Radek, Bukharin, Bordiga, and Zetkin. The conference took place in Berlin on April 2–5, 1922. From the beginning the negotiations went badly. For some reason, the reformists were reluctant to let themselves be used. At one point, the meeting came close to shipwreck when Vandervelde would not admit to the agenda a discussion of the reparations or the Treaty of Versailles. Radek, though, was determined to show that the united front could work; and the conference was saved.[45]

From the Communist point of view, the results of the meeting were meager indeed. A committee of nine members was formed for the purpose of organizing future conferences of the three Internationals. The committee could not make decisions by majority vote; thus there were few possibilities for manipulating it and playing the Center off against the Right. Workers of all countries were invited to organize common demonstrations against the capitalist offensive, and in favor of aid to Russia during the famine and the resumption of political and economic relations with the Soviet government. In exchange Radek agreed to allow the representatives of the reformist Internationals to attend the trial of the Socialist Revolutionaries in Moscow; promised that no matter what the verdict, the death penalty would not be applied; and authorized the Committee of Nine to investigate the situation in Soviet Georgia and report on it at a later date.[46]

Lenin was convinced that the Communists had "paid too dearly" for the results they had attained. "The bourgeoisie in the person of its diplomats," he wrote, "had once more proved cleverer than the representatives of the Communist International."[47] Lenin's evaluation turned out to be correct. The Socialist Revolutionaries, though convicted, were spared. On the other hand, nothing came of the projected cooperation of the three Internationals, and when the Committee of Nine met in Berlin on May 23, Radek accused the Second International of having sabotaged the united front and announced the secession of the Communists. In the spring of 1923, the Second and Vienna Internationals were merged.

Frossard observed discipline at Berlin. But he did so in such a way that the leaders of the Comintern were further enraged. Though a disciplined Communist in public, he had abstained when Radek's deal with Vandervelde was put to a vote within the delegation itself. He came back from Berlin more convinced than ever that the united front, as it was interpreted by the ECCI, was a dangerous and mistaken tactic.[48] After his report, the CD passed a resolution in which it (1) pointed to the dangers of the Committee of Nine, which seemed "to give an unacceptable character of permanence to a rapprochement that even in the International's view was supposed to be accidental, temporary, and provisional"; (2) fixed the date of its demonstration for May 1, in order to coordinate its activity with that of the newly formed CGTU (Confédération Générale du Travail Unitaire); and (3) rejected an offer from the Dissidents of joint action on May 1.[49] The rejection of the SFIO's offer of a united front was commented upon with amusement by Longuet, who noted: "It is curious that we 'agents of the bourgeoisie' can at present act in agreement with Moscow, while our purer-than-thou's scoff at its advice and its resolutions."[50] At any rate, the question remained academic, for neither the PCF, the CGTU, the CGT, nor the SFIO was able to organize a working-class demonstration of any size. May 1, 1922, passed with hardly a disturbance, except for the strikes of the taxi and bus drivers' unions, neither of which, as the Dissidents maliciously pointed out, belonged to the CGTU.[51]

The CD had once more defied Moscow; but Frossard and his friends seem to have been convinced that if they could persuade the Russians that the party was behind them the Comintern's hands would be tied, and they would be free to yield to "French necessities." In line with this strategy, a National Council was convoked for April 22–23. Frossard and Renoult led the attack on the united front before provincial delegates who still had little idea of what the new strategy was.[g] Both emphasized the difficulties the united front would cause with the CGTU; both interpreted the Committee of Nine as the prelude to reunification with the Dissidents. Neither of these arguments was wholly sincere. That, however, did not prevent them from being effective. With the mood of the National Council overwhelmingly against the united front, the central issue became the interpretation of the relationship with the Executive. Treint claimed that the CN had no jurisdiction to discuss a policy that had been approved by a meeting of the Enlarged Executive. The majority of delegates, reasoning along the lines of the PCF's organization, thought that such an important departure in strategy could be decided on only by the Fourth World Congress.[52] Frossard, who knew better, tried to reconcile the necessity of international discipline with the right of the party to express its own opinion. Unfortunately, this middle way was becoming more and more slippery. The resolution, voted by a majority of 3,337 to 627 for Treint's text, with 235 abstentions, approved the CD's decision to reject alliance with the Dissidents on May 1; deplored attempts at parliamentary cooperation between Communists and Social Democrats in other countries; and stated that only the Fourth World Congress could rule on the question of the united front. Souvarine, Loriot, Dunois, and Vaillant-Couturier were re-elected to the CD, but only after a vote (2,497 to 1,068, with 600 abstentions) which showed that the antagonisms of Marseille still subsisted.[53]

The doors had scarcely closed on the National Council before the polemic over the united front was resumed in the Communist press. For the first time in five years, Loriot did not lead the Left's attack. Waning health and concern for his family's future had persuaded the former schoolmaster that he must give up his career as a Communist leader for the more sedate existence of a Left Bank bookseller. However, despite Loriot's withdrawal, critics of the party's leadership were not lacking. Among these Souvarine was, as usual, the most direct. He saw in the decision of the CN and the articles in the Communist press a renascence of the atmosphere that had existed before Tours. Moreover, the party's representative in Moscow no longer hesitated to use the word

***

[g] The reports of the party's delegates to the conference of the Enlarged Executive in Moscow had still not been published. See Méric in *L'Humanité*, 21.iv.22.

"enemy" for the group writing in *Le Journal du Peuple*.[54] The leaders of the CD did not shy away from the confrontation over the Executive's tactic or its implications. "Ne nous en plaignons pas," wrote Daniel Renoult. "Il faut que l'abcès crève; l'affaire doit être liquidée à fond."[55]

### THE VIEW FROM MOSCOW

The resolutions of the April National Council opened a period of acute conflict with the International. An abundance of documents, unusual in Comintern history, makes it possible to follow the unfolding of this crisis on three levels: the debates and decisions of the Executive, Trotsky's articles and private correspondence, and the reports of the International's delegate in Paris. The result is a fascinating case study of the way in which the Comintern brought to heel a rebellious national party.

The French suspected the indignation their attitude would arouse in Moscow and took steps to assuage it. Lucie Leiciague, who had been delegated by the CD to replace Sellier as representative to the Executive, arrived in Moscow around May 1. She reported on the French situation and read to the Executive the motion on the united front that the CN had passed on April 23. Leiciague explained the nature of the Conflict Committee and argued that opposition to the purging of Fabre should not be interpreted as agreement with his political position. She ended on a note of optimism, pointing out that things had now taken a turn for the better, and that the united front was under serious study. After listening to Leiciague's report, the Executive devoted three sessions (May 8, 9, and 19) to a discussion of the French question in the presence of Leiciague, Sellier, and Souvarine.

Souvarine took issue with Leiciague; in his judgment the opposition to the International had gained in strength since the meeting of the Enlarged Executive. Nevertheless, he opposed expelling the editor of *Le Journal du Peuple*. For if Fabre were expelled and Méric and Verfeuil, who defended the same policies, remained, the masses would be confused. "What the French party needs," he concluded, "is a political program that will determine once and for all who can remain in the party and who cannot."[56] Souvarine proposed that the Executive send an open letter to the PCF, informing it of how relations between the CD and the International had developed.

The Bolsheviks were furious. Trotsky made a special appearance at the Executive to speak on the French question. During the Third Congress, he said, he had been optimistic about the development of the PCF. After the Enlarged Executive he had been less optimistic. Now Leiciague's report had made him pessimistic. He demanded that the French party become disciplined in deeds as well as words; that *L'Humanité* publish an authentic interpretation of the resolutions of the International and the pledges made by the party; and that Fabre and whoever else attacked the principles of the International be expelled.[57] Zinoviev was even more peremptory. The PCF, he claimed, had sabotaged the demonstration of April 20 against the Entente. The French had even gone so far as to demand Frossard's recall from the Committee of Nine. Never, he said, since the creation of the Third International, had such indiscipline been seen. Zinoviev proposed that Article 9 of the statutes of the Comintern be invoked to expel Fabre, and that the PCF be informed by telegram.[58]

On the next day (May 9), Sellier spoke in defense of the party and tried to make light of certain tendencies which, he felt, the Executive exaggerated. Sellier dismissed Fabre's expulsion as ill-timed, and warned that this could make a martyr of him. The Executive should inform the party before taking any "premature steps."[59] Souvarine agreed. The Russians and Germans, however, were convinced that the time had come for a showdown, and that day a committee was formed, composed of Trotsky, Bukharin, Jordanov, Ambrogi, Brandler, Leiciague, Sellier, Souvarine, and Doriot (for the Jeunesses Communistes), for the purpose of expelling Fabre and drafting a letter to the CD.

The work of the Committee was presented and commented on by Trotsky on May 19. Fabre was to be expelled on the basis of Article 9 of the Comintern's statutes. The Executive's decision was explained in a message to the PCF (to be published in L'Humanité), which emphasized that the right to think or write against the party could exist only *outside* the party's limits.[60] A letter to the CD was to be sent along with the resolution, reviewing the history of relations between the International and the PCF in the previous year and airing the grievances of the Executive. Further steps would be taken if the past pattern was not replaced by one of "frank and friendly revolutionary sincerity." Trotsky explained the reasoning behind these decisions in his report to the Executive. There were two possible coalitions: the coalition of the Center with the Left and the coalition of the Center with the Right. Of these two possibilities the International preferred the former, but it would not hesitate to break with the Center if Cachin and Frossard continued to flirt with the Right. Trotsky went on to criticize the Center for its position on the united front, its tolerance of pacifist deviations, and its failure to capture the unions.

At this point Sellier interrupted. The Center, he said, had borne the reproaches and criticisms of the International because it had the responsibility for leading the party. If the Left had controlled the CD, he insisted, things would have been no different. Besides, continued Sellier, the Russians were very badly informed on the life of the French party; they knew only what they read in the papers. Leiciague supported Sellier's position, attacking Trotsky's division of the PCF into Center, Left, and Right as "too mathematical."

To these objections, Trotsky replied that they expressed a kind of fatalism. They assumed that the present CD was conducting the best Communist policy possible. But this was not the case. It was precisely the fatalism and passivity of the CD, said Trotsky, that the Executive deplored. Three or four members of the Central Committee might play a decisive role at a critical moment in the history of the party. Such a moment, he suggested, is before us now. As for the accusation that the Russians knew nothing of the inner life of the party, Trotsky replied that what was involved was not the inner life but the policy of the CD. The French, he said, voted for the resolutions of the International at congresses. Then they rebelled against those resolutions and declared that the Russians were badly informed. "Let the abscess burst!" he concluded. "Let the misunderstanding disappear! ... A new stage is before us, after the preparatory stages we have passed through. Now more energetic and more decisive methods are necessary, and that is what we propose."[61]

Trotsky further developed his view of the crisis in the French party and its solution in a series of articles and personal letters written in May and June 1922. Trotsky, of course, was not the Executive. But he still exercised tremendous influence—one is tempted to call it magic—over its members. And contrary to what one might think, the evidence suggests that his ideas were shared by Zinoviev, Lozovsky, and Bukharin, the other Comintern figures most directly concerned with French affairs. *Faute de mieux,* namely the International's files, the available information gives an important insight into the thinking of the Bolshevik leader chiefly responsible for the formulation of Comintern policy in France.

The picture of Trotsky that emerges is of a man who was at once an informed and talented historian, a shrewd and cautious negotiator, and, in the end, a believer. Trotsky found the causes of the French crisis in the weight of the past and the passivity of the CD. Commenting on Marcel Martinet's play *Le Drame du prolétariat français,* Trotsky observed that no other proletariat had such rich historical memories as the French proletariat, for no other proletariat had had such a dramatic fate. Now, however, this glorious tradition weighed down the French working class and acted as a threat to its future liberation. "The dead tenaciously hold back the living. Each stage bequeathed not only its experience, but its prejudices, its formulas devoid of all content, its sects that were unwilling to die."[62] The "terrible poison of the French working-class movement," "the danger," "the threat," "the most malignant rust," were those orators, "leaders," journalists, bureaucrats, individualists, syndicalists, and poets (he was thinking of men like Lafont, Fabre, Mayoux, and Pioch) whose passivity before events lay concealed beneath radical phrases.[63] The CD, burdened by this past, did nothing to throw it off. Instead, it used the prejudices of syndicalists, the extremism of bureaucrats, and the individualism of journalists as an excuse for a policy of inactivity and waiting. Trotsky saw the laziness and indifference of the French CD reflected in the conduct of Rappoport. In Moscow on private business during the meetings of the Executive in May, Rappoport had been invited by Zinoviev and Trotsky to the Kremlin to explain his position on the French crisis. When the hour of the session arrived,

Rappoport was nowhere to be found. Repeated searches failed to turn him up. Thus, concluded Trotsky, a member of the CD of the PCF shines by his absence from a meeting of the Executive at which the most important questions relating to French Communism are under study.[h]

What was the solution to the crisis? Writing to Rosmer on May 22, Trotsky confessed that "from here, the general situation in the party appears extremely alarming."[64] It was "absolutely obvious" that the PCF had reached a critical point in its development. If the Center, in agreement with the Left, struck at the Right, then the party "so to speak, would be promoted to the next class." But if the Center remained in its present state of lethargy and continued to make light of the united front, "then the renascence, the consolidation, and the development of the Left faction are absolutely inevitable, and the fate of the party will be in its hands." It was Trotsky's opinion that the prudent and to some extent passive policy the Comintern had followed in dealing with its French section had now outlived its usefulness, and had to give way to a more forceful policy. The Executive had not yet given up hope of a merger of the Left and the Center against the Right. But it had come to the conclusion that the only means to force the Center to act against the Right was to pose openly and energetically all the pending questions before the party and the International. If the French CD did not respond satisfactorily to the letter from the Executive, then the International would publish it and appeal to the party as a whole. A week or so later Trotsky received a letter from Ker, in which the party's International Secretary accused Rosmer of pessimism and failure to understand the need for caution in handling the French situation. Trotsky replied on June 6, countering that it was not he and Rosmer who were pessimistic, but Ker.[65] "It would seem that in your opinion the French party must be treated like an invalid: speak in a soft voice, walk on tiptoes." The Executive

[h] Trotsky to Rosmer, 22.v.22. "Lettres du camarade Léon Trotsky à quelques camarades français, 1921–1922, à propos des problèmes du mouvement ouvrier français et du développement du parti" (collection in the Bibliothèque Nationale), p. 19. Rappoport's version is in his "Mémoires" (ms. in the Bibliothèque Nationale), p. 283. On May 23 Rappoport published an article in *Izvestiya* warning the Bolsheviks that they had to proceed cautiously in dealing with the French movement. It was necessary, he said, to grant the PCF "the right to some independence in its application of the major principles of the Third International—which are, of course, obligatory for all sections." Trotsky replied on May 25 with a slashing attack in which he asked: Just what does Rappoport mean by "caution" and "independence"? The incident is significant because it suggests Trotsky's infinite capacity for treading on people's feelings and making enemies. Though he later (1927) rose to Trotsky's defense, Rappoport could not bring himself to like the Russian Carnot. Writing to Radek in his exile at Tomsk on June 5, 1929, the old philosopher confessed that he had never been able to share Radek's illusions about Trotsky's opposition. "I have studied him since the beginning of the century, and I have always seen in him a lonely meteor, in love with his own character and incapable of carrying behind him anything or anybody." Rappoport Papers.

did not agree. "We think that in its essential proletarian core the French party is profoundly healthy and revolutionary, and eagerly looks forward to a more definite situation and a more decisive leadership."

Trotsky's evaluation of the French crisis was based on his belief that even in "the least favorable case" of a split between the Center and the Left, the party would end "by finding the right road." "The subsequent inevitable displacements in the proletariat," he wrote to Ker, "will orient themselves toward the Left, and not the Right. The politicians who act under the impetus of passing difficulties and retreats ... will be swept aside by events." The Executive's delegate in Paris was not so optimistic. On May 17 Zinoviev had telegraphed Humbert-Droz in Madrid, where he was assigned to the Spanish Communist Party, directing him to proceed to Paris. His mission, Rákosi informed him on May 27, was to report to the Executive on the state of affairs in the PCF, and to interpret for the French the documents of the International, in particular the confidential letter sent to the CD after the discussion in the Executive.[66] The historian has reason to be grateful for Humbert-Droz's prudence and his feeling for important documents. Throughout his stay in Paris, he managed to preserve duplicates of his reports to Moscow. A mediator of finesse, with wide-ranging contacts throughout the party and among the revolutionary syndicalists, the former Swiss pastor was a correspondent of determined objectivity. His letters are an invaluable source for both the situation in the PCF and relations between the Executive and the CD.

The picture presented by Humbert-Droz's first report to the Presidium was somber indeed.[67] "An extraordinary confusion reigns on all questions, and the general situation of the party is far from hopeful," he wrote. The recent elections of municipal councillors had shown that in a great number of *départements,* and even in certain industrial regions, the Communist movement was still superficial and far from having the influence among the masses that the Executive had thought. For all their rhetorical intransigence, many federations had formed alliances with the Dissidents and Radicals. The greatest confusion of all existed over the question of the united front. The united front was accepted not only by the Left, but also by the entire Right, which interpreted it as a return to unity with the Dissidents and the Left Bloc. Humbert-Droz gave as an example the editor of the Communist paper in Dijon, who in one breath had agreed with Treint about the advantages of the united front and in the next had gone on to support its application in the Left Bloc. It was dangerous to label people on this question, Humbert-Droz warned, because the Right current favoring the Executive's policy was stronger than the Left. The delegate of the International pointed out that the confusion over the united front was based on the realities of the political situation. Unless the party could get the proletariat to break with the left wing of the bourgeoisie during the coming elections, the Communist organizations would be swept into the Bloc des

Gauches. Thus, the arguments of the opponents of the united front were not groundless. "In the party's present state of confusion," he concluded, "the application of the united front is a real danger."

Humbert-Droz arrived in Paris in time to attend the meeting of the CD on May 30, when the Executive's directive expelling Fabre was discussed. At this session the CD unanimously approved the motion of the Executive. Humbert-Droz reported to Moscow that Fabre's expulsion had touched off "a movement of very bad feeling" against the Executive. Even so, the debate in the CD was less violent than he had expected. Daniel Renoult's proposal that the CD protest the procedure of the Executive was rejected by the other members of the committee. At Humbert-Droz's insistence, Frossard agreed to go to Moscow in June to attend the meetings of the Enlarged Executive. In turn, Humbert-Droz promised to hold off the publication of the Executive's open letter to the party. The CD had confined itself to publishing the Executive's motion expelling Fabre, along with an embarrassed commentary that said the CD had done everything possible, within the limits of the party's statutes, to carry out the pledges to the International made in February.[68]

Humbert-Droz found "an attitude of distinct hostility toward the Executive." It was still difficult to speak of tendencies within the party. Indeed, if such tendencies had existed, the situation would have been less confused. Humbert-Droz divided the party into a Right (Fabre, Verfeuil, Barabant), which was favorable to the united front and hostile to the International; a Center, which oscillated from left to right and followed Frossard; a Left, which wanted to be in agreement with the International in every respect; and an extreme Left, which varied from the phrasemaking of Méric and Renoult to the syndicalism of Heine and Métayer. Only the Left was organized into a real faction. But even the Left was far from homogeneous. Dunois and Vaillant-Couturier were ready to cooperate with Frossard, while Treint and his friends were eager for a split. Rumors were afoot of a French Livorno. Humbert-Droz warned against such a policy. The Left was very weak, and the International could not hope to carry away from a split the forces it had retained in Italy after Livorno. As for Frossard, he was a "strong political intelligence and a clever tactician, but he lacked direction." He maneuvered for the sake of maneuvering. After talking to him, however, Humbert-Droz came away convinced that he was anxious to resolve the crisis and form the "stabilizing nucleus" that would give the party real leadership. "Il faut arriver à le 'fixer,' et lui donner une direction politique claire et ferme." Humbert-Droz was hopeful that Frossard's visit to Moscow might permit the necessary rapprochement and end the scandalous polemics that racked the PCF. The great obstacle, however, to such a rapprochement was the united front. On this issue, counseled the delegate of the International, it was necessary to strive for some kind of minimum understanding with the present leadership.

FROSSARD IN MOSCOW

If Frossard's first trip to Moscow had been a "Chemin des Dames," his second was a Verdun. The Enlarged Executive of June 1922 assembled the delegates of 27 countries. Representing France, besides Frossard, were Souvarine, Sellier, Leiciague, Cartier, and Rappoport. As in February, the major question on the Executive's agenda was the united front and the crisis in the French party. Zinoviev launched the proceedings by observing that despite the collapse of the Committee of Nine, the united front remained a sound tactic. The struggle for the united front had been initiated from above and had not obtained much in the way of results. Now it must be pursued even more energetically from below. However, the united front was not possible unless the French and Italian parties did their part and carried out their orders. They must apply the united front in deeds as well as words. To consolidate these parties was the great task of this conference of the Enlarged Executive.[69] The French, said Zinoviev, claimed that they had nothing to gain from the united front because they had a majority of the working class.

I hope and wish that we obtain this majority, but this is at present only a wish and not a reality. Never count your chickens before they are hatched. And so we will wait until Comrade Frossard's syndicalist chickens are really with us. Comrades, there is yet another point against our French comrades. It appears that in France the reformist party of Renaudel obtained more votes than we did in the North at the last departmental elections. And then they come and say, "We have a majority." It is an optical illusion on the part of our French comrades. The united front aims to obtain a true majority of the working masses.[70]

On June 8 Frossard presented his report on the crisis in the PCF.[71] In general, despite occasional expressions of optimism and confidence, the picture he painted was one of dark decline. The party's strength, he said, had been undermined by the prevailing atmosphere of distrust and factionalism. Between January and March 1922, membership had fallen from 120,000 to 60,000. The Communists had been disappointed in the recent local elections. Their influence in the cities was diminishing. It was the opinion of the party that the Executive had set a dangerous precedent by invoking Article 9 to expel Fabre. The party, he said, recognized the importance of the united front; but it must be allowed to apply this tactic in a way that reflected the situation in France. The question of principle had to be distinguished from the question of opportunity. The PCF, for example, could not cooperate with both the CGTU and the reformists: it must choose one or the other. The Executive could rely on the French to carry out its decisions; the Center was ready to cooperate with the Left. But the prerequisite for a healthy PCF was the ending of the factional struggle. It was a clever and tactful speech, designed to appease the International and isolate the Left, while at the same time leaving the French party sufficient room to maneuver within the limits of "French necessities."

Souvarine followed Frossard with the report of the Left, in which he submitted the party and particularly the leadership to thoroughgoing criticism. The party, he said, was undergoing a great crisis because it had not fulfilled the obligations it had taken on at Tours. The party had broken with the bourgeoisie, but it had not broken with bourgeois ideology. The PCF had remained a propaganda organization; it had no discipline; it did not lead the unions, but was led by them; its press was not Communist. In brief, the mentality of the party had remained unchanged. The PCF must now do what it should have done after Tours. It was the duty of the International to intervene in order to resolve the crisis; otherwise the French party would be lost.[72]

Trotsky spoke next. His words struck home like the blows of a fancy boxer—now playful, now indignant, jabbing their way toward a brutal climax. Both the clever report by Frossard and the entirely contradictory speech by Souvarine, he began, proved that the party had reached a critical point in its evolution. Trotsky dealt severely and sarcastically with the deviations of Renoult, Rappoport, Jean, and Méric. Méric, he said, wrote in the party press that the International was badly informed on the situation in France and made its decisions on the basis of rumors. This was not true. We have the party's newspapers, he said. We have the reports of the CD. We have the reports of the French delegates. We have the reports of the members of the Executive. We have the reports of Humbert-Droz, Bordiga, and Walecki. We have the reports of the Jeunesses Communistes. And if, despite all this, you insist that we understand nothing of the situation in France, what are we to do, what course of action are we to take, dear Comrades, he cried in a voice filled with exasperation.[73]

The International might make mistakes, but its errors could not be compared with those of the French leadership. In arguing against the united front, you claimed that the Dissidents were insignificant in strength. The last elections have shown that you were mistaken. The Federation of the Seine was a study in chaos and confusion. It was false to compare the organization of a Communist Party with the Federation of Soviet Republics in Russia. The party is not a federation, but a highly centralized organization. The leaders of the Federation of the Seine were wrong to try to emulate the Soviets. France was not in a situation like that of 1917, but rather in the preparatory period that Russia had gone through between 1905 and 1917.[74] Frossard had invoked the tradition of Jaurès in defending the inactivity of the Communist leadership in the unions. Trotsky replied that Jaurès's tactics had been the product of necessity; he was not able to apply our tactics. Now the situation had changed. The party must direct the activity of the Communist syndicalists in the unions.[75] Frossard had said that the time of democratic illusions had passed for the working class. Trotsky denied this. If you offer the French workers nothing but revolution, he said, they will choose the Left Bloc. The French worker was skeptical. He had been deceived many times throughout history. But if you offer him a bloc of proletarian forces against the bourgeoisie he will respond.[76] Trotsky concluded with a threat. If the International was forced to choose between a resolute Right and a Left in the process of formation (the Center would inevitably disintegrate), then the International would have no choice but to give its authority to the Left. This was "inescapable."[77]

The floor was then thrown open to discussion. Bordiga, Kreibich, and Zetkin all criticized the French leaders for their lack of discipline, though Klara Zetkin noted in passing that "the so-called Left has up to now often behaved clumsily."[78] Brandler opposed drastic measures at this point on the grounds that the French working class would not understand the position of the International. He advised waiting until after the Fourth Congress.[79] Trotsky replied that Brandler was too pessimistic. There was no need to speak to the French working class in a whisper and take measures of extraordinary caution. The working-class movement and the revolutionary elements were completely sound. The French, he said, complain of a lack of men. The men were there, but they were in the syndicalist movement. It was up to the CD to bring them into the party.[80]

Frossard came back to answer the various criticisms that had been made of the French leadership. The situation, he said, was not as gloomy as Souvarine had indicated. The party had made many advances. Frossard was not too optimistic about the possibilities of doing anything in the union movement before the Congress of St.-Etienne. But at least the Communists in the unions could be organized. He admitted that the party had yet to win the masses; the Left, however, had to bear its responsibility for this state of things along with the Center. The essential prerequisite for the development and flourishing of the party, he concluded, was an end to factional struggle.[81] Frossard assumed personal responsibility for the pledges the French delegation might make.

Zinoviev followed Frossard on June 10 and summed up the debate. No one, he said, could ever accuse the International of having acted overhastily. We have done everything to avoid the growth of factions, and we have not favored the minority.[82] The real source of the crisis, Zinoviev asserted, lay in the motley social composition of the party, and in the fact that it did not feel that it represented the working class. Hence its mistaken position on the syndicalist question. The party must support Rosmer's group in the unions, since for the Communists, the unions were the crucial battlefield. The Left (with which, Zinoviev added, the Executive was far from being in agreement) had to be absorbed into the party. Zinoviev stated that he was not satisfied with Frossard's speeches; he found in them no real program, no indication of how he planned to resolve the crisis or of what kind of Central Committee he planned to form.[83]

It was once more Trotsky who wrote and presented the resolution of the Executive on the French question. This time the Executive pulled no punches. Its motion called for setting up a homogeneous CD, of which at least half the members had to be workers; the assumption by the CD of the right to expel members when necessary; the creation of a Bureau Politique residing in Paris; the alteration of the federalistic statutes of the Federation of the Seine and the creation of a liaison between the CD and the Committee of the Federation of the Seine; the elimination of the pure syndicalists; the application in practice of the united front; control of the press; and the unifying of the majority of the party against the Right. The Left was told not to create a faction and to cooperate actively with the Center in practical work. The resolution censured Renoult and *L'Internationale* for not having carried out the pledges made by him in February, and stated that the Executive regarded his campaign in *L'Internationale* as the principal reason for the disrepute of the united front in France.[84]

The Executive's resolution, for all its sternness, was obviously drawn up in the hope of saving Frossard and the great majority of the party. The Left was gently scolded and told to cooperate with Frossard. In this sense Souvarine had been rebuked, for the situation before Tours was re-created. At the same time, Renoult was made to bear the responsibility for the disrepute of the united front in France—which diplomatically ignored the fact that at every level of the party the vote against the tactic had been overwhelming. Perhaps the most novel thing about the resolution was its insistence that the CD include workers in its midst. Trotsky and Zinoviev had now decided that the party would only become truly Communist if it were a workers' party, run by workers. That conclusion was not as obvious as it might seem.

Trotsky's resolution was adopted by the Enlarged Executive unanimously, with the French abstaining. Before the vote Frossard made a statement declaring that, "on the whole and from a general point of view," the motion appeared to the majority "to assure the party of important points of support for its formation and subsequent development."[85] The majority, he said, could accept without reservation all sections of the resolution except those bearing on the unions, the past activity of the party, the united front, and the personal responsibility of Daniel Renoult. If there were any rebuke to be administered, Frossard remarked, the entire CD should receive it, and not just Renoult. However, Frossard had no illusions about the result of the vote. He promised that the majority would faithfully report these resolutions, explain them, and defend them before the party. "And I hope, if you will permit me to end on this note, that at the Fourth Congress of the Communist International, it will not be the French question that will absorb the attention of the International."[86]

## Chapter nine

# The Bursting of the Abscess

We have learned to grasp the reins
Of spirited rearing steeds
To break their stubborn backs
To subdue the will of refractory beasts . . .
    —*Alexander Blok, "The Scythians," 1918*

Frossard came home from Moscow bearing the resolutions of the International and determined to do his best to put them into practice. Always a realist, Frossard now recognized that the ECCI would not brook further indiscipline. As he told the Executive's delegate, the decisions of the International were "the indisputable basis on which we must work and which it is no longer our place to discuss."[1] One may speculate on Frossard's private thoughts at this point; he may, with good reason, have been pessimistic about the possibilities for a lasting alliance between the Center and the Left. But it seems clear that he wished to give the way of the International its chance, and he undoubtedly was sincere when he told Trotsky in Moscow that he had no intention of playing the role of a French Serrati. Obedience, though, was more easily promised than delivered. The situation Frossard encountered upon returning to France was enough to test the wits and the good faith of the most determined Communist leader. Never had the gap between Russian demands and French realities seemed wider. Never had the creation of a French "Communist" Party seemed less imminent.

### ST.-ETIENNE

The immediate problem facing Frossard when he arrived home in late June 1922 was the approaching Congress of the CGTU in St.-Etienne. Both Zinoviev and Trotsky were convinced that the major source of the weakness of French Communism was to be found in its failure to infiltrate and win control of the union movement. "As long as our French comrades do not have their groups in the unions," Zinoviev had said at one point during the meeting of the Enlarged Executive, "they will not have a real party. Let us proclaim this loudly!" There were two reasons for the importance the Executive ascribed to this question of the unions. First, it was through its groups in the unions that the PCF would reach the workers and become capable of launching mass movements. Second—and this was a point that both Trotsky and Zinoviev hammered home during the meetings of the Executive in June—the introduction of workers and union leaders into the CD would counterbalance the journalists, lawyers, and intellectuals who blocked application of the International's decisions by insisting on autonomy, freedom of thought, and elaborate legal procedures, and thus would help the PCF overcome its crisis and become a disciplined Communist Party. It would not be an exaggeration to say that in the second half of 1922 the second motivation was more important than the first. At any rate, Trotsky's instructions to Frossard had been specific and incapable of misinterpretation. "At the Congress of St.-Etienne," he said, "there must be a Communist faction, led by representatives of the Comité Directeur, that has a well-defined program of action and is truly disciplined."[2] Frossard had protested the special circumstances of the French labor movement, and had expressed pessimism about the chances for any real accomplishments before the congress, which was due to meet in less than three weeks. But he had promised to do what he could.

Frossard had sound reasons for his pessimism. The split in the CGT, foreshadowed at the Congress of Lille, became a reality in December 1921. A new confederation, the Confédération Générale du Travail Unitaire, was formed by the leaders of the CSR during the first six months of 1922. By July the CGTU claimed 350,000 members, with 250,000 remaining to the CGT. One might assume that the villains of the plot were the Bolsheviks, and that Lozovsky had gained in 1921 at Paris what Zinoviev had accomplished the year before at Tours. In the sense of ultimate causation, this may be partly true: the Russian Revolution did help to exacerbate differences within the French labor movement. From the point of view of deliberate policy, however, this was not so at all. Uncompromising splitters in the Socialist movement, the Bolsheviks had been uncompromising champions of unity in the labor unions.[3]

It made little difference, though, that the official Communist position on the trade unions was unity; for the Comintern had no direct control over what happened in the French trade-union movement in 1921. Up to the Congress of Lille, the struggle against the CGT majority had been led by a disparate coalition of anarchists, anarcho-syndicalists, and revolutionary syndicalists in the name of the Russian Revolution and the traditional principles of French syndicalism. As the split neared, differences within the minority coalition appeared. One of these differences was the attitude of the various factions toward a split. Pierre Monatte, the father of the CSR, wanted to make further concessions to the CGT leadership. The anarchists, however, led by Pierre Besnard, had made a pact in February 1921, and wished to push onward to a break. When Monmousseau and the other revolutionary syndicalists of *La Vie Ouvrière* refused to support Monatte on the issue of unity, he resigned his post on the paper.[4] Thus, not only was the split in the CGT not the work of the Communists, it was carried out by anarchists and anarcho-syndicalists against the will of those who, like Monatte, stood closest to the Bolsheviks.

Once the split within the CGT was consummated, the anarchists went on to take over the leadership of the new confederation and turn it against the Communists. The temporary alienation of the Monatte-Monmousseau group from the Profintern after July 1921 left the field open to anarchist infiltration and control. By 1921 the anarchists had ceased all pretense of solidarity with the Russian Revolution. Fully as hostile to Communism as the reformists in the CGT, they had pledged themselves to fight "against those 'minoritaires' who seek to make the unions the fiefs of political parties, and ... tend to make the workers not the masters of their destiny and the free artisans of their happiness, but the slaves of a so-called proletarian State."[5] When Lozovsky addressed a letter to the CGTU in March 1922, asking it to send delegates to Moscow to help prepare the next international congress, the Administrative Council (CA) replied with a refusal, adding that it had agreed to participate in a congress of anarcho-syndicalists to be held in Berlin on June 16–18.[6] Nor did the anarchists controlling the CGTU stop there. On March 15, with particular reference to the trial of the Socialist Revolutionaries in Moscow, the CA passed a resolution declaring that French revolutionary syndicalism was the "rigorous adversary of all forms of government, *whatever they might be,*" and emphasizing, furthermore, that the CA did not confuse any government or party with the revolutionary conquests of the proletariat.[7] The threat was clear. Not only had the Bolsheviks lost the CGT; they now faced the terrifying prospect of being driven out of the union movement altogether.

Fortunately, from the Russian point of view, the policies of the anarchists had not gone unchallenged. By June 1922, three groups had emerged within the CGTU that opposed in greater or lesser measure the anti-Communism of the leadership: the pure syndicalists; the Communist faction; and the syndicalists of *La Vie Ouvrière*.[8] It is no easy matter to distinguish these shades of syndicalist opinion. It would not be worth the trouble were it not for the fact that the syndicalists themselves felt the differences so deeply. The pure syndicalists were torn between their commitment to the principles of traditional syndicalism and their sympathy for the Russian Revolution. The Communists had the most clear-cut position of all. They stood for the direction of the unions by the party. Zinoviev had said at the Enlarged Executive that the future of the PCF lay with "Rosmer's group" of Communist syndicalists. He was wrong on two counts. Rosmer did not have a group but a journal, *La Lutte de Classe,* which he published with Russian subsidies. His collaborator, Tommasi, led the Communist faction, which still had little influence. It was the *Vie Ouvrière* group that represented the future of French Communism. Monmousseau and his friends still wavered between Communism and syndicalism. They accepted the dictatorship of the proletariat and were ready to cooperate with a truly revolutionary party. Yet they could not accept the superiority of the party or the organic liaison. Three-fourths of this group were members of the party.[9]

The Congress of St.-Etienne, which met from June 25 to July 1, 1922, was a test of force between the *Vie Ouvrière* group and the anarchists, with both factions bidding for the support of the pure syndicalists. Monmousseau's motion opted for adherence to the Profintern on the condition that the autonomy of French syndicalism be respected. Besnard's counter-motion rejected membership in an International that would have any connection with a political organization, and empowered the CGTU to send delegates both to Moscow and to the Berlin International Syndicalist Conference. The Communist motion urging unconditional adherence to the Profintern was never seriously in the running. Frossard kept his pledge to the International. On the second night of the congress he convoked a meeting of 130 Communist delegates, and informed them that the party was satisfied with neither the Besnard nor the Monmousseau motion, but that on the question of the statutes the Communists should vote with *La Vie Ouvrière*.[10] This meeting was mostly for show, since the great majority of Communists present went on to vote for Monmousseau's motion anyway. But Frossard had made his gesture and the delegate of the International was overjoyed. St.-Etienne, he wrote Zinoviev, had been a "great victory" for the party.[11]

The issue underlying all the debates was the Russian Revolution, its meaning, and its relevance to French revolutionary syndicalism. The anarchists claimed that the Russian Revolution had degenerated and had no lessons for French syndicalism; the Communists and the *Vie Ouvrière* group insisted that the French must accept the lessons of the Russian Revolution and declare their solidarity with the Soviets. Many of the most impassioned speeches against the party were given by Communists. Mayoux referred to Monmousseau as a "dupe" and a "politician" of the party, and defended the Besnard motion. For him it was not "natural" that the "leaders" of the PCF should mix in the business of the CGTU.[12] Ernest Lafont, angry because one of his articles had been refused by *L'Humanité,* circulated a statement attacking Treint and Lozovsky and defending the CGTU's right to independence.[13]

Despite such incongruities, the Monmousseau motions on the statutes and on the international orientation of the CGTU managed to carry by votes of almost two-to-one (779–391 and 743–406). The new bureau was composed of Monmousseau, Marie Guillot, Léopold Cazals, and Claudius Richetta, all *Vie Ouvrière* stalwarts. As Monatte pointed out in his commentary, the crucial element in the victory of the Communist syndicalists had almost certainly been the impression given by the anarchists that they wanted to condemn and repudiate the Russian Revolution.[14] The victory at St.-Etienne did not mean that the Communists had won the unions. But it did represent a transitional step from the revolutionary syndicalism of pre-1914 France to that of a Communist dominated and controlled CGTU. The congress overwhelmingly accepted the postulate of syndicalist autonomy, both national and international. The real question had been, with Moscow or against it? On those grounds the anarchists had been routed.

The Bolsheviks could congratulate themselves on this victory in more than one respect. They had helped earn it with their propaganda, their tactical flexibility, and their personal pressure. St.-Etienne was to Lozovsky what Halle had been to Zinoviev. Perhaps an even greater success; for the head of the Profintern had to deal with prejudices that did not exist in the German Independent Party, and unlike Zinoviev he could not point to a revolutionary upturn. Throughout the first six months of 1922, Lozovsky had carried on a personal correspondence with the revolutionary syndicalists of *La Vie Ouvrière,* in which he prodded them, in amiable but frank language, to take action against the anarchists.[a] His polemics against the anarchists were published regularly in the French Communist press. These campaigns had their effect; in the spring of 1922, both Monatte and Monmousseau moved closer to Communism.[b] The great danger at St.-Etienne had been that the anarchists would

---

[a] For example, Lozovsky wrote Monatte (15.v.22) to warn him that under the leadership of the anarchists, the CGTU was becoming a sect. "The ineffectiveness of the CGTU is now obvious. Just look at what your friends are doing in Genoa, where a conference is convening at a time when the entire bourgeois world has declared war on Soviet Russia. These great strategists and diplomats haven't been able to find anything better to do than lodge a protest against the Soviet government. They pay no attention to their own government. Neither Poincaré nor Barthou interests them. They don't see that the Soviet government is struggling against great difficulties, and that these difficulties are the logical consequence of the impotence of the working-class movement in all countries and especially in France. If instead of babbling to their hearts' content they had put pressure on their government, if they had given first place to the struggle against reaction, if they had expended their energy in struggling against their bourgeoisie, would Poincaré and Barthou have dared to adopt such a cynical attitude? The arrogance of Poincaré and Barthou is in direct proportion to the stupidity of these blunderers. I think that you will forgive me for expressing myself so brutally, but it pains me to see the French working-class movement fail to learn from the experience of the War and the Revolution. These men haven't learned a thing; like parrots they repeat old slogans, while holding on for dear life to the Charter of Amiens as if it had been devised for all times, for all peoples, and for every problem of life and death." Monatte Archives.

[b] Trotsky remarked to Rosmer in March that he had been told by one of Monatte's best friends, Fritz Brupbacher, that Monatte was impressed by the fact that the younger generation was going into the party and not into the syndicalist movement. ("Lettres du camarade Léon Trotsky à quelques camarades français, 1921–1922, à propos des problèmes du mouvement ouvrier français et du développement du parti," collection in the Bibliothèque Nationale, p. 17.) In the spring of 1922, Monatte began to write a column on the unions for *L'Humanité.*

rouse the anger of the delegates by accusing the Communists of trying to deprive the CGTU of its independence. Lozovsky staved off this threat in his message to the congress, by emphasizing that the organic liaison was desirable but not obligatory. The Profintern, he wrote, left the task of defining its relationship with the party to each national organization.[15] Nor was Lozovsky content to watch the fate of the French labor movement being decided from afar. Crossing into France illegally, he appeared at the congress on the fourth day to reiterate the reasonableness of the Profintern. It is difficult on the basis of the stenographic record to know what impression this flamboyance made on the delegates. Part of the assembly broke out into cries of "Long live the Russian Revolution!" and sang the *Internationale*. The anarchists replied by yelling "Long live Kronstadt!" and intoned *La Révolution*. We may assume from the vote, however, that the delegates felt assured by Lozovsky's gesture that in choosing Moscow they were opting for alliance with men who made revolutions and did not just sing about them. After his speech, Lozovsky slipped away as mysteriously as he came, evading the police despite elaborate attempts to apprehend him.[16]

THE ALLIANCE OF THE CENTER AND THE LEFT

By assembling the Communist delegates at St.-Etienne, Frossard had made the first step toward realization of the Executive's program. The remaining obstacles to agreement with the International were acceptance of the united front and alliance with the Left. As Moscow's man in Paris, Humbert-Droz had the responsibility of overseeing the application of the Comintern's line. His task was difficult; and although he was entirely faithful to the Executive's policy, his interpretation of what that policy was often differed from that of his superiors.

Through Humbert-Droz the Executive had at last established in practice that liaison between Paris and Moscow that the Third World Congress had decreed in theory. The delegate of the International reported weekly, and sometimes even daily, to the Presidium on the situation within the party. He attended the meetings of the CD and presented the point of view of the Executive. He interpreted the documents sent by the International to the PCF. He published articles in the Communist press (under the pseudonym Jean-Christophe) on the proper interpretation of the united front.[c] In dealing with the leaders of the Center and the Left, Humbert-Droz attempted to favor neither; inevitably, he antagonized both. Alliance between the Center and the Left

---

[c] For example, *L'Humanité*, 17.vi.22. "Jean-Christophe" was the pseudonym given to Humbert-Droz by Rosmer, Monatte, and the poet Martinet. Romain Rolland, it seems, failed to see the connection between his famous protagonist and the Comintern's emissary, and when he protested, Humbert-Droz became simply "Christophe." *L'Oeil de Moscou à Paris* (1964), p. 92.

was, of course, the official policy of the Executive. In Humbert-Droz's case, this middle way corresponded to his personal observations, and perhaps to his temperament. Though critical of the Center's indecisiveness and "politique du silence," he was no admirer of Souvarine and Treint. He noted that they spent their time in idle polemics rather than constructive action; and, agreeing with Trotsky and Zinoviev that the party's only hope was to attract the revolutionary syndicalists, he could not help but be struck by the fact that Monatte and Monmousseau were even more hostile to Souvarine, Treint, and Vaillant-Couturier, who "have little contact with the working class and know little of its life," than they were to Frossard.[17]

The Left was not unaware of the feelings of Humbert-Droz. They noticed that he worked through the CD rather than consulting beforehand with the Left. In late June, Souvarine retaliated by addressing a memorandum to the Presidium in which he accused the Executive's delegate of having contact only with the Center, and further, of encouraging the Center in its resistance to the Left. By his actions, wrote Souvarine, Humbert-Droz had made the alliance of the Left and the Center an impossibility.[18] Humbert-Droz immediately wrote to Dunois and Rosmer asking them to confirm or deny Souvarine's accusations by return mail. Both denied Souvarine's charges indignantly, though Dunois admitted that certain comrades of the Left resented the neutrality of the Executive's representative.[19] Humbert-Droz retorted by reminding the leaders of the Left that he had never been invited to their meetings.

The Executive knew Souvarine well enough to ignore his accusations. But in its interpretation of the alliance between the Center and the Left, the Executive stood closer to the Left than to Humbert-Droz. This was brought out in an incident that took place at the end of June. On June 23 the Executive had demanded the exclusion of Verfeuil on the grounds that he had continued to publish in *Le Journal du Peuple* after Fabre's exclusion.[20] The Executive reminded the French party that its resolution on Fabre had declared that all those who continued to support him or contributed to his paper "will be automatically expelled from the International." The Left wanted to proceed with Verfeuil's exclusion. The Center, on the other hand, thought it would be more politic to let Verfeuil exclude himself, which in their view was only a matter of time. They advised limiting the action of the CD to a rebuke, and appealed to the Executive not to carry out its threat, using as the basis for their request certain pledges made by Verfeuil. Humbert-Droz (along with Thalheimer, Lozovsky, and Walecki, who were in Paris at the time) agreed with the Center, and wrote as much to the Executive.

Zinoviev replied in a furious letter, in which he wrote that it was necessary to operate as soon as possible on "the appendix of Centrism" from which the French party was suffering.[21] The French question, Zinoviev announced, was now the most important in the international Communist movement. The

Executive no longer intended to temporize; it must know in the very near future whether the majority of the party intended to struggle against the Right. The Executive, he revealed, had unanimously passed a resolution which ruled that if the Verfeuils were not excluded from the party by July 15, the Executive would have recourse to Article 9, which gave it the authority to expel not only individuals but groups and whole parties. Let no one say, Zinoviev went on, that it would weaken the party to eliminate the Verfeuils. Who, he asked, would seriously argue that the expelling of Levi, Geyer, and Friesland had weakened the German party? As for the factional struggle, the ECCI agreed with Humbert-Droz; it, too, wanted the union of the Center and the Left. "But if this bloc were to be a reality and not just a wish, the Frossard-Cachin-Ker group would have to break once and for all with the Right, expel a dozen scoundrels from the party, and *make L'Humanité* a militant organ against *the Right*." The International, Zinoviev wrote, was aware of the errors of Treint and Souvarine. But it supported the principles of the International in the struggle against the Center, and it was Humbert-Droz's duty to support the *ideas* of the Left. The President of the Comintern ended his letter with a typically Zinovievan flourish. Referring to a meeting that Humbert-Droz had reported between himself and Verfeuil, Zinoviev concluded in a postscript: "You were too polite to this gentleman. The only way 'to converse' with such persons is with a whip in hand."

Zinoviev was as good as his word. On July 14, the ECCI appointed a committee composed of Trotsky, Zinoviev, Zetkin, Jordiana, Souvarine, Leiciague, and Rappoport to take action on the French question. The committee produced a resolution explaining the nature of Article 9; censuring the PCF for its hesitation in expelling Verfeuil, Lafont, and Mayoux; demanding that the statutes of the Federation of the Seine be replaced with a more centralized organization; insisting that the International's point of view be represented in the party press; announcing the intention of the International to send representatives to the Paris Congress of the PCF on October 8; and ruling that henceforth the national congresses of the various Communist parties would be held *after* the congresses of the Comintern.[22] The brusqueness of the International offended the majority of the CD; but after a lull of several weeks, the CD responded with a series of resolutions on the organization of the party, the Federation of the Seine, the expelling of Verfeuil, Lafont, and Mayoux, and the control of the press, in which it promised to defer to the wishes of the International.[23]

The Executive's procedure was brutal; it was not unpremeditated. For want of a better term, the policy which Moscow now pursued might be called the instant cure. The PCF was infected with the bacilli of Centrism, pacifism, journalistic individualism, and anarcho-syndicalism; only a stiff purgative could save it; the more drastic the remedy, the less painful and the less prolonged the recovery. And in the event the patient died, a new one would be born to take its place.

For a brief interlude in August it appeared that the medicine had been effective: the alliance between the Center and the Left was taking shape. Souvarine returned to Paris in early August, and Humbert-Droz noted a change for the better. "I can scarcely recognize the abrupt, haughty, and intransigent Souvarine I knew in Moscow," he wrote to Zinoviev.[24] Frossard in turn had abandoned Renoult, and had come out in favor of the united front, though he opposed its application on the electoral and parliamentary level. On August 20, Frossard joined with the Left to ensure that the extremely federalistic statutes of the Federation of the Seine would be replaced by a more centralized organization.[25] Souvarine was so pleased with Frossard's speech that he termed it "a first step toward the union desired by the International and by the Left. One can say now that the formation of a real Communist Party is well under way."[26]

Meanwhile, Frossard, Ker, Rosmer, and Souvarine met under the chairmanship of Humbert-Droz and agreed to draw up joint motions on general policy, the united front, and the syndicalist question for the coming Congress of Paris.[27] The Center, at Frossard's urging, accepted the drafts on general policy and the united front written by Souvarine, while the Left agreed to accept Frossard's modification of Rosmer's resolution on the unions. Both the motion on general policy and the motion on the united front implicitly criticized the party's leadership and justified the position of the Left. The text on the unions provided for "workers' committees" that would penetrate the unions and propagate Communist ideas.[28] Humbert-Droz gave credit for the compromise to Frossard. Souvarine, he claimed, hoped that the Center would refuse the terms of the Left, and that the International would intervene.[29] Not all the leaders of the majority were willing to follow Frossard in this retreat from the intransigence of the spring. Renoult accused the party's General Secretary of having abandoned his position on the united front.[30] The Parisian Ultra-Left charged that he had become a partisan of "oligarchic centralism." The hero of 1921 threatened to become the villain of 1922. "Frossard," wrote Humbert-Droz to Zinoviev on September 17, "sticks it out with an energy which I sometimes admire and of which I didn't think him capable."[31]

Despite Frossard's efforts, the alliance of the Center and the Left was fragile. Even Humbert-Droz, who had negotiated the compromise that led to the joint motions, remained pessimistic. Undermining all relations between the two factions was a lack of trust that made any lasting cooperation impossible. Souvarine distinguished between those in the Center with whom it was possible to deal (Ker, Frossard, Jean, Soutif), and those whom it was necessary to reject at all cost (Cachin, Renoult).[32] Frossard came upon a letter by Treint advocating cooperation with the Center as a temporary expedient.[33] At the

Congress of the Federation of the Seine, the Left had succeeded in getting the majority of the places on the Executive Committee. This inspired it to ask for two-thirds of the positions on the new CD. When asked by Humbert-Droz to collaborate with the Center on the basis of parity, Souvarine replied, "There is nothing in common between them and us; we are Communists, they are not!"[34] Faced with such obstinacy, Humbert-Droz threw up his hands in despair. Frossard, disgusted by this constant factionalism, announced his intention to resign his post as General Secretary. Finally, on September 24, the leaders of the Center (Frossard, Cachin, Ker, Louis, Faure, Lévy, Julien) issued their final word: they were willing to join the Left in wiping out the remnants of the reformist past, but they refused to read the partisans of other motions out of the Communist family. Only those who called into question the Tours Charter were clearly outside the party.[35] After two years of Communism, the French had yet to define what they meant by party discipline.

The cost of this bitter factional struggle was the party's decline as a fighting organization. Throughout June, July, and August 1922, Humbert-Droz complained to Moscow of the PCF's inertia and apathy. This, he insisted, was not a question of factions; the Left was just as guilty as the Center. Unlike Trotsky and Souvarine, Humbert-Droz believed that the party was sick not only at the level of the CD, but also at the level of the federation and section. What was needed was a persevering and thoroughgoing educational effort.[36]

Humbert-Droz's reflections were inspired by the example of the Le Havre general strike. The metallurgists and shipyard workers of Le Havre had been on strike ever since June 19, when the management announced that their wages would be cut by 10 per cent.[37] During July and August, tension between the employers and the strikers mounted. In mid-August the port workers and sailors joined the movement, bringing the number of strikers to 40,000. On August 25, after the arrest of some workers, the local unions called a one-day general strike. The next day there were bloody encounters between the police and the strikers. Three workers were killed, fifteen more were wounded. The CGTU replied by calling a general strike for the 29th. The night the general strike was declared, there was no one at either *L'Humanité* or party headquarters. The leaders of the Left were all on vacation. The next day's edition of *L'Humanité* did not even carry the strike order. *L'Internationale* and the Federation of the Seine came out in favor of the strike, but with little effect.[38] The correspondent of *The Times* reported that the strike was only partial, and that "a casual observer might not notice its effects." The essential services of transport, lighting, and food distribution, he wrote, had scarcely been affected.[39] The Bolsheviks were disgusted, and the delegates of the International to the Paris Congress of the PCF were instructed to say both at the meetings and in private conversation that the Comintern considered "such an attitude toward the mass movements of the proletariat a veritable crime."[40]

### A FRENCH LIVORNO

These orders were only a small example of the care the ECCI took in preparing for the Paris Congress. The Bolsheviks were determined that the fiasco of Marseille would not be repeated. In mid-September, Manuilsky arrived in Paris to lend the International's delegation added prestige—and perhaps a push to the Left.[d] Trotsky and Zinoviev personally worked out the instructions that Humbert-Droz and Manuilsky were to follow. In these instructions the alliance between the Center and the Left received its clearest formulation up to that time. Humbert-Droz and Manuilsky, Zinoviev wrote on September 20, must explain to the Left in the most friendly manner that the two-thirds requirement was not possible, for to insist on it "is, in our opinion, to risk failure on every count."[41] However, in the new CD the Left would in fact have the preponderance, for "it has had and will continue to have behind it the Executive Committee of the Communist International." Among the representatives of the Center on the new CD, Zinoviev continued, there must be a group of workers who can be won to the policy of the Left. To accomplish this, these future members of the CD should be specially invited to Moscow. Because of the police, it might be more sensible for Manuilsky not to speak at the congress. But this, wrote Zinoviev, would not prevent him from being present throughout the duration of the session or from participating in private conversations, "which will be decisive." From one end to the other, the congress was to be controlled by the delegates of the Executive. A set of supplementary instructions sent the same day, perhaps as an afterthought, called for the Left and the Center to form a small committee under the chairmanship of Humbert-Droz and Manuilsky to work out a position on all questions to come before the congress. Agreement on all projects, Zinoviev emphasized, should be reached in the committee, and the projects sent to Moscow for approval before being submitted to the delegates. The decisive posts in the party would be allocated in Moscow, during the Fourth World Congress.[e]

These instructions aimed at a control which the Comintern did not yet have the power to exercise. In the last two weeks before the opening of the congress (October 15), relations between the Center and the Left broke down altogether. Humbert-Droz came back to Paris on October 5 after ten days in

[d] Manuilsky was both close to Zinoviev and a good friend of Souvarine's.
[e] Humbert-Droz Archives. Further instructions were sent on October 7, 1922. According to these more detailed directives, the Right (Verfeuil and Lafont) had to be expelled, Renoult's resolution on the united front condemned, and Renoult himself denounced as a confirmed "enemy of the Communist International's tactic." *L'Humanité* must be reorganized. The united front had to be put into practice, the "regime of factions" to end. Loriot must enter the CD. All projects submitted to the congress should be sent to Moscow, so that the Executive Committee could approve them first. Close relations between the German and French parties had to be established.

Switzerland to find the situation greatly deteriorated. Frossard continued to support loyally the policy the International had dictated after the June Executive. But Cachin had published an article in the *Bulletin de la Presse Communiste* which spoke of the motions on general policy and the united front as rough drafts that could be reworked at the congress; and Paul Louis had publicly criticized Rosmer's resolution on the unions, and then inspired the Federation of the Somme to accept the Souvarine texts with reservations.[42] The Left cried sabotage and treachery, and announced that it would boycott the CD if it were not given the means to carry out the International's policy.[43] Souvarine was determined to oust Cachin not only from the editorship of *L'Humanité* but also from the CD. Never had this policy been less feasible. Many federations had passed the Souvarine motions with reservations, particularly with respect to the electoral united front. The Renoult minority had shown itself to be quite strong and composed in large part of workers, while the Left, on the contrary, had overestimated its strength within the party.[44]

It was under these delicate circumstances that the International's delegation stepped in to negotiate the crisis and impose the solution of the Executive. A mixed committee consisting of representatives from the Center and the Left was set up. Negotiations began a few days before the opening of the congress and lasted right up to the climax. Both factions agreed, after a certain amount of discussion, to the International's solution of parity on the CD. Then the question of personalities was raised. Souvarine and Treint insisted that Paul Louis and Cachin be removed from the CD. They wanted *L'Humanité* to be directed by the Left. Souvarine intervened to state his position with his usual brutality. "Je n'accepterai une minute ... de subir le contact de Cachin. S'il n'est pas éliminé, je me retire."[45] The Center refused. At the next meeting of the committee, Humbert-Droz and Manuilsky offered a new proposition: parity on the CD and direction of *L'Humanité* by the Bureau Politique, which would consist of four members of the Left and three members of the Center. The Left agreed to this proposal. The Center refused, saying it could not accept the elimination of two of its members, and announced its intention to take the question before the congress.

Finally, on October 15, the day on which the congress opened, Manuilsky and Humbert-Droz announced their final offer of arbitration: parity on the CD (12–12); parity (3–3) on the Bureau Politique, with deadlocks to be decided by the delegate of the International; double editorship of *L'Humanité* (Cachin-Rosmer); and Frossard as General Secretary, with a member of the Left as his assistant. The delegates of the International emphasized in their letter that this decision was "final," and that the faction that rejected it would be "responsible before the party and the International for the rupture and its consequences." The Center replied the next day that it could not accept this offer of arbitration. It proposed instead: parity on the CD and BP; Cachin and

Frossard as co-editors of *L'Humanité*; and the General Secretaryship to the Left. The congress would have to decide on all these questions, the letter concluded.[46] It was over Cachin that negotiations had broken down. The Left refused to leave him the editorship of *L'Humanité*; the Center refused, on principle, to abandon him. In view of later developments, these negotiations have a certain irony.

The stage was thus set for the congress; and a tawdry stage it was. The meetings took place at the Maison de la Grange-aux-Belles in Paris. The hall was bare. There were no decorations on the walls except for a dilapidated portrait of Marx. Nothing had been prepared, no program had been arranged, no direction was given the debates.[47] The first two days of the congress went smoothly enough. The real debate, as we have seen, was taking place in the corridors and in the negotiations between factions. On the third day the discussion of the motion on general policy began. Ker took the speaker's stand to defend the Frossard-Souvarine project; instead, his speech turned into an attack on the Left and a defense of Cachin. The Left, he said, wanted to scuttle Cachin because he had formulated reservations on the motions. But Frossard himself had emphasized that these motions would be open to modification. Ker described the discussions between the Left and the Center leading up to the congress. The Center, he remarked, had felt that the congress must decide the merits of the case. He concluded by throwing down a challenge whose implications everyone in the hall recognized: "It is a matter of knowing whether the French party will be free to choose for itself the men who are to lead it."

The Left booed Ker as he descended from the platform. Souvarine rose to speak next, and there was applause mingled with shouts of "dictator." Souvarine answered Ker by saying there was a difference between formulating reservations and openly opposing a resolution: how could the Left have confidence in Cachin when he had written in favor of Renoult's motion? The Left, he said, would take no part in the leadership as the Center conceived it. Souvarine consented to the closed session suggested by Pioch, and the negotiations with the delegation of the International were described to the delegates. This was the morning of the third day. In the afternoon Manuilsky appeared mysteriously (this was de rigueur for emissaries from Moscow), and delivered a two-hour speech in which he attacked both Cachin and Renoult. Renoult, he said, represented "confusionism." "I am convinced, Renoult, that you will remain in the Third International. But your present activity is disastrous to the party." Manuilsky stressed that the Left had carried out the policy of the International, and that the Center had been responsible for the breakdown of negotiations.[48]

The next day, Frossard took the floor to urge a last attempt at reconciliation. He suggested that some delegates from the provinces gather and devise a homogeneous CD. Souvarine replied in the name of the Left. He placed the responsibility for the crisis squarely on the shoulders of Frossard. "Do you think," he asked, "that it is possible to form a homogeneous Comité Directeur that includes men who have made degrading accusations against us? Perhaps this is politics the way professionals play it. We fail to understand. We'd rather be little boys and not understand."[49] Souvarine concluded by demanding that the Center take all responsibility for the leadership of the party.

Frossard followed Souvarine to the platform. Up to this last day, he had presented a picture of apathy and lack of interest in the proceedings. He had made only a few appearances on the rostrum. One could see him, wrote one participant, reclining on his bench as if it were a chaise longue. When he rose to speak, however, he was a man transformed: his voice became warm and gripping; his sentences were clear and well-balanced; his gift for the right image and his ready wit held the audience in an attitude of passionate attention.[50] According to Louise Bodin, who could not withhold her admiration for the man despite her personal antipathy for his policies, this was one of the finest speeches Frossard ever made.

"Let me tell you," he began, "I've had enough." What were the reasons for the crisis, he asked. For two years, Frossard confessed, he had been torn between his fidelity to the International and the best interests of his party. "Inside me there is a permanent crisis, a crisis of duty. Are there different attitudes in me? It's because I'm not sure of myself." We could not go any faster in our work with the unions, he insisted, without creating resistance. "I admit that, faced with certain inapplicable decisions of the International, I played for time. I preferred that to destroying my party." Frossard explained why he had changed his mind about the united front. He believed after the June Executive that the time had come to re-establish confidence between the party and the International. Moreover, the situation had been propitious. The CGTU itself had taken the initiative for the united front. Now the negotiations between Left and Center had broken down over a question of personalities. The Left wanted to eliminate Cachin and Paul Louis; the Center refused this sacrifice. "And now, what will the congress do? Will the Left maintain its announced positions? If the Left persists in leaving the leadership to us alone, I declare, in the name of all my comrades of the Center, we will take it. (*Applause.*) We will take it in order to carry out the International's policy with energy, sincerity, and perseverance."[51]

The most exciting moment of the congress was yet to come. Late in the morning of October 20, Mazé, the young rapporteur of the Conflict Committee, which was controlled by the Left, appeared to read his report expelling Brizon, François Mayoux, Marie Mayoux, Henri Sellier, Verfeuil, and all those who had signed Verfeuil's motion. In explaining the expelling of Sellier, Mazé used the phrase "S'autorisant de la tradition de Jaurès ... Henri Sellier voudrait faire du Parti Communiste un grand parti démocratique." The outburst was immediate. From the depths of the hall Charles Lussy cried: "You have just expelled Jaurès." Some delegates shouted "Long live Jaurès!" Frossard leaped from his bench, ran to the platform overturning benches as he went, and announced: "You have just insulted Jaurès. I will not remain here a minute more; I refuse to work with people who insult Jaurès." With those words Frossard picked up his papers and his hat, and tried to leave. His friends restrained him and tried to quiet him down. To the demand of the Left that the exact phrase be read, Cachin replied: "The report has been destroyed. A shameful text that so dishonors its authors cannot be preserved even for an instant." Mazé, "pale as a dead man," was booed. Henri Sellier took the platform and, after accusing the Jeunesses Communistes of venality, demanded that the congress exclude him. Cachin had to drag him from the speaker's stand in order to get him to shut up. Vaillant-Couturier finally restored order by announcing that the Left had no intention of calling the Jauressian tradition into question, since Jaurès stood above all factions.[52]

It was in this mood, after nearly thirty hours of continuous session, that the delegates got around to voting on the motions and selecting the leadership. The motions of the CD passed easily. Vaillant-Couturier then came to the platform to ask the congress to accept the arbitration of the Executive, that is, parity in the important posts. Cachin replied for the Center, demanding that the congress designate a CD formed of members of the Center, to direct the party until the Fourth World Congress. The motion of the Center carried by a close vote of 1,698 to 1,516, but there was a large bloc of 814 abstentions. Directly after the vote, Vaillant-Couturier read a declaration by Manuilsky saying: "Faced with a French Livorno, the International asks the Left to enter the CD on the basis of parity, as well as to take the posts that the congress will assign it both in the Bureau Politique and in the other organs of the party."[53] The Left, said Manuilsky, would have the right to protest at the Fourth Congress.

Cachin asked the congress to recess for a moment so that the Center could discuss Manuilsky's proposal. Ker, Paquereaux, and Bestel went to the Left and proposed parity on the CD; a majority for the Center on the Bureau Politique; the General Secretaryship and the editorship of L'Humanité to the Center. The Left accepted. Then, according to Bodin, who is the only source for this incident, Cachin arrived, and said in "a strangled voice" that the Center would take the leadership alone.[54] Cachin asked the congress to ratify the Center's decision, which meant, for all practical purposes, turning down the International's offer. This may have been the result of calculation, of personal antagonism, or of fatigue; most likely, it was the product of all three. Tommasi read a statement by the Left saying that it would abstain on all future votes and appeal to the Fourth Congress. The delegates sang the Internationale. The congress ended in a disorderly fashion with the expelling of Verfeuil (which he himself requested) and François and Marie Mayoux. The other cases were sent back to the CD. It was 1 P.M. of the second day of continuous session when the delegates dragged themselves, exhausted, from the congress hall.

### THE FOURTH WORLD CONGRESS

The Congress of Paris ripped the last veil from the antipathies and suspicions that had been poisoning the party's atmosphere for over a year. The "meddling" of the International; the "opportunist" Cachin; the "dictator" Souvarine; the "politician" Frossard; the sanctity of "syndicalist autonomy"; the "tradition of Jaurès"—no appeal to emotion was spared. The impression made on those in attendance was uniformly bad. It was one of the most painful congresses that had ever yet been seen, said one delegate.[55] "You would have thought you were at a congress of lunatics," commented another. "Nothing but screeching, whistling, booing, yelling, fits of rage, disorder, confusion, incoherence."[56]

Neither faction wanted to take responsibility for such chaos; each swung into action to pin the blame on the other. The Left was more convincing because more convinced of its own righteousness. Declaring that "the decisions of the congress bear witness to the desire of the faction now leading the party to break with the Communist International," the leaders of the Left and their followers resigned their posts in the party apparatus and on *L'Humanité.!* Rosmer and Monatte's group of revolutionary syndicalists (Maurice Chambelland, Robert Louzon) accepted this interpretation of the congress, and came out in favor of the Left.[57] The Center responded to these accusations by choosing its Bureau Politique (Cachin, Frossard, Dormoy, Ker, Georges Marrane, Soutif, Paquereaux), and issuing a statement affirming its "undying fidelity" to the International and its intention to carry out the International's policy "in its spirit and its letter."[58] The chief point of disagreement at Paris, claimed the leadership, had been whether "the congress could be deprived of its right to choose the men in whom it invests its confidence." To prove that the Center did not dispute the policies of the International but simply its methods, Frossard initiated a noisy campaign for the united front with the Dissidents.

The distinction between the policies of the International and its methods was impossible to sustain; Frossard must soon have realized it. Cachin and Soutif attacked the motion on the syndicalist question, and accused the Left (read the International) of not taking into account the national conditions in which the decisions of the International had to be applied.[59] The Left accused the Center of trying to take the party out of the Third International, and called

---

*f L'Humanité,* 20.x.22. The next day Bigot, Colliard, Bernard Lecache, Paul Bouthonnier, Vernochet, Labrousse, and Fernand Desprès announced their resignation from the staff of *L'Humanité.*

for the union of the Center and the Left at the party's base, that is, without its leaders.[g] Manuilsky supported the Left, and stated in the name of the International's delegation that the Center was completely responsible for the failure of the congress.[h] This left the Center in the embarrassing position of protesting its fidelity to an organization whose representatives had condemned its policies. Under these circumstances, the only course left was for both factions to present their case before the tribunal of the World Congress, which was scheduled to meet in Moscow on November 4, 1922.

The Left, of course, accepted this solution gladly. The leaders of the Center, for reasons just as obvious, did their best to avoid the trip to Moscow. It was first decided that Dormoy would lead the Center's delegation to Russia. He had just departed when Frossard and Cachin received "imperious telegrams" insisting that they attend the congress.[60] Frossard refused to leave. Cachin weakened, taking with him Renoult and Ker, who had wanted to avoid the trip because of the poor state of his health.[61] All in all, 24 French delegates made their way to Moscow, including Souvarine and Rosmer for the Left; Cachin, Dormoy, Ker, and Faure for the Left Center; Renoult and Jean Duret for the Right Center; and Renaud Jean representing his own peculiar viewpoint. Only the Right (Verfeuil) and the Ultra-Left (Heine) were absent, which represented the final recognition that these opinions no longer had any place in the Third International.

The Fourth World Congress marked the demise of the Comintern that was founded in 1919, but few delegates sensed it at the time. The last congress of the Third International at which Lenin appeared, it was also the last congress which approximated that free and frank colloquy of international revolutionaries which the Comintern had been meant to be. This coincidence caused many Communists to take away the impression that Lenin had stood for freedom of discussion, and that while he lived, debates had been unmanaged and decisions multilateral. No new tactics were adopted. The Fourth Congress merely ratified the united front and reinforced the emphasis that had appeared in 1921 on the organization, training, and discipline of the revolutionary forces. The most startling event of the congress was the report made by Bukharin on the Program, in which he analyzed the consequences of the present situation for the attitude of the various parties toward national defense. Now that a proletarian State existed, said Bukharin, the problem of national defense could no longer be posed in the same way. The proletarian State can and must

---

[g] *Cahiers Communistes*, 9.ix.22, p. 4. *Cahiers Communistes* was founded by the leaders of the Left after the Congress of Paris. Only six numbers were published.
[h] *L'Humanité*, 23.x.22. Humbert-Droz wrote from Berlin to announce his agreement with Manuilsky. *Ibid.*, 1.xi.22.

be defended not only by its own proletariat, but also by the proletariat of all other countries. Could a proletarian State form an alliance with a bourgeois State? In principle, explained Bukharin, there was no difference between an alliance and a loan. The Bolsheviks, Bukharin concluded, were now big enough to conclude a military alliance with one bourgeois government in order to overthrow another. The duty of the Communists of all countries in such a case would be to contribute to the victory of the two allies. If victory was attained, Bukharin remarked maliciously, "another problem arises (*laughter*), which I don't have to sketch for you here, but which you will understand readily."[62]

The French delegation contributed little more to these debates than they had the year before. The French had no talent for the kind of soaring historical analyses of the world situation in which the Bolsheviks delighted. Abstract theses on this or that question bored them. Besides, from the minute they arrived, the eyes of the French were riveted on the work of the French Commission, whose 23 members would decide the fate of the PCF. The Bolsheviks themselves were no less absorbed by this question. The importance which they ascribed to the PCF is suggested by the fact that the Russian members of the French Commission were Lenin, Trotsky, and Zinoviev. How was the crisis to be resolved? Here the Bolsheviks faced a dilemma. Both Trotsky and Zinoviev emphasized that the International approved of the conduct of the Left and considered it the truly Communist branch of the party.[63] They were convinced that there had to be a purge. But at the same time, to abandon the Center and base the PCF on the Left would mean to weaken French Communism immeasurably, and perhaps to reduce the party to a small sect without influence. The problem was thus to keep the bulk of the Center, while "assisting Centrism out through the door," as Zinoviev picturesquely put it.[64]

We know from a secret memorandum, sent by Trotsky to Zinoviev, Lenin, Radek, and Bukharin, that the Bolsheviks devoted careful thought to this matter of how to neutralize the leaders of the Center without losing their followers.[65] The trick was to select a reliable CD at the congress without making it appear to be handpicked by Moscow. It was Trotsky who suggested the answer: the CD would be named at the congress after negotiation with the three factions.[i] All the delegates would sign the agreement. Cachin would tell the congress that the French delegation had unanimously recognized the need to organize the CD in this way. The French delegates would then pledge themselves to get this list approved by an extraordinary congress or National Council, whose date the Executive would set. This procedure, Trotsky noted, had the advantage of compromising the members of the Center and forcing them to carry out the policy of the International with the support of the Left. If in

---

[i] The three factions referred to are the Left, the Center, and Renoult's group.

two months' time the Centrist CD had done nothing, then it would have discredited itself completely.

For all its ingenuity, Trotsky's tactic assumed that the men could be found in the PCF's majority to agree to the International's solution. Cachin and Ker were expected to swallow in Moscow what they had turned down in Paris. The Bolsheviks pursued this end in several ways. Trotsky talked to Cachin. The charitable interpretation would be that the Centrist leader was convinced that his duty lay with the International and not with those French conditions he had lately been defending so ardently; the less charitable that a stern lecture and the promise of the editorship of *L'Humanité* brought him around. We can be sure only of the result. When Trotsky proposed to draw up a list for the CD during a meeting of the subcommittee on the French question, Cachin disoriented his comrades by interjecting quickly: "Agreed.... Tomorrow our faction will bring you its names."[66] In Renoult's case, conversations with the Bolshevik leaders and a deep moral commitment to the Third International seem to have persuaded him that his opposition was mistaken. Chosen by Zinoviev and Trotsky to be the Serrati of French Communism, he deceived his accusers and like a disciplined soldier yielded to the decision of the ECCI. Still, what of men like Frossard and Ker? Would they accept what Cachin had agreed to out of weakness and Renoult out of respect for discipline? What was needed was a weapon to use against the more troublesome leaders of the Center that would disgrace them in the eyes of the workers and give the International an excuse for demoting them.

Trotsky found this bombshell in the question of Communist membership in masonic lodges. Trotsky was well aware that many French working-class leaders belonged to these lodges and to the Ligue des Droits de l'Homme et du Citoyen. He had even written a study of Freemasonry in France before the war.[67] It must, however, have come as something of a shock to him when it was brought to his attention that a number of Communist leaders were masons, including at least two members of the Bureau Politique. In any case, such an incongruity confirmed Trotsky's belief that the great sickness of the PCF derived from the leading role played by bourgeois elements. Here was one more way in which the bourgeoisie subjected the proletariat to its influence and blunted class antagonisms. Perhaps even more important at the time, Trotsky understood the hostility of French workers to politicians and intellectuals, and he knew that this issue could be used to discredit the Center.

The example Trotsky chose was the sickly Ker. One evening, as Trotsky was addressing the French Commission, he said: "I am informed that some of the leading comrades are members of Freemasons' lodges." Was it true, he asked, that the Secretary of the party and leading members of the parliamentary Group were Freemasons? Radek has left a dramatic description of the scene that followed:

Those words took effect like the lash of a whip. Trotsky stood erect amidst the French comrades. Ker turned pale and let his head sink. For a moment an oppressive silence reigned. Then a quiet voice was heard: "With regard to me, Comrade Trotsky, you are correctly informed." Trotsky turned brusquely to the worker from Frossard's faction seated at his left. He laid his hand on his shoulder and addressed him in sharp and cutting sentences: "Do you know what the Freemasons are? Do you know that they are an organization of bourgeois career hunters, who govern the economic and political life of France, and deceive the workers with the aid of democratic phrases, in the interests of plutocracy? And a proletarian like you permits the Secretary of the party to belong to a Freemasons' lodge?" Ker rose to his feet: "Up to now there has been no resolution forbidding membership in a Freemasons' lodge. I have continued my membership out of laziness, but I shall give it up if the party demands it." The session was closed.[68]

Depending upon how one reads Trotsky's character, one can interpret this attack as the result of conviction, of calculation, or of desire for revenge.[j] There is no doubt that it had the desired effect. A subcommittee, headed by Trotsky and consisting of Zetkin, Bordiga, Vasilii Kolarov, Humbert-Droz, Sen Katayama, and Manuilsky, was chosen to draw up a resolution on the French question and a program of action for the coming year. The cause of the crisis within the PCF was said to lie "in the indecisive and hestitant waiting policy of the Centrist leaders, who, before the urgent requirements of party organization, tried to play for time, thus disguising a policy of out-and-out sabotage on the questions of the unions, the united front, the organization of the party, and others."[69] It was recognized that despite specific errors of the Left, "on the major problems of the revolutionary movement ... it has occupied the right position in the face of the Center and the Renoult group."[70] By January 1, 1923, the CD must liquidate all connections between the party and both Freemasonry and the Ligue des Droits de l'Homme. All members of the party who were Freemasons had to publicly announce their resignation from their lodges before January 1. They would be barred from holding any responsible posts in the party for a period of two years.[71] Before January 1, all those contributing to bourgeois newspapers who held responsible posts in the party had to choose between bourgeois and party publications. They could not write for both. Henceforth, nine-tenths of the candidates presented by the party at elections would have to be Communist workers and peasants.[72] The PCF and CD were instructed to devote more attention to the colonial question.

The new CD was to consist of ten members of the Center (including Cachin, Frossard, Henri Gourdeaux, and Louis Sellier); nine members of the Left (among them Dunois, Rosmer, Souvarine, Tommasi, Treint, and Vail-

---

[j] Revenge for Ker's defense of the party's autonomy at the Congress of Paris. Ker, it will be remembered, had originally been a member of the Left. During the course of 1922 he moved toward Frossard.

lant-Couturier); four members of Renoult's group but not Renoult himself; and Renaud Jean. Two members of the JC would sit on the CD with a consultative vote. The BP would be composed of three members of the Center, three of the Left, and one from Renoult's group. Cachin was allowed to remain Director of *L'Humanité*, but Dunois was added as General Secretary, and it was emphasized that the BP would control the press. The secretariat would be shared by Left and Center. Frossard and Souvarine would represent the party and their factions in Moscow for at least three months.[73]

Trotsky reported the findings of the committee to the congress on December 1, 1922. His speech turned into a violent attack on those intellectuals, journalists, and politicians who spent nine-tenths of their time in a bourgeois milieu, worked at an occupation that separated them from the working class, then came to the party meetings on Sunday to criticize, throw doubts on the principles of Communism, and demand freedom of thought. After creating confusion in the minds of the workers, they returned to their bourgeois milieu. "The party," he said, "must be freed of those elements who see nothing in it besides an open door to a job or an office." The workers must be shown that they had been misled, and that these people had "used them as a springboard for their careers."[74] Trotsky's hardest blows were reserved for Frossard. Every time he read Frossard's statement at the Congress of Paris in which he said that he had tried to gain time, Trotsky remarked, he had the same shock. "What! A person belongs to the International for two years, and now he says that a certain resolution passed by the International threatened to destroy his party! Then why does he belong to the International?"[75]

Before the vote on the French resolution, each faction made a short statement in which it promised to apply the decisions of the International loyally. Cachin, speaking for the Center, admitted the mistakes of his group, but insisted that Trotsky had not sufficiently indicated the responsibilities of the Left for the crisis. Renoult stated that his opposition to the united front had been based on fears which the explanations of the congress had now banished. Souvarine noted that Trotsky's report had justified the attitude of his group. The Left, he said, would always obey the resolutions of the International, "which it places above everything."[76] Only Renaud Jean, speaking in his own name, sounded a discordant note in this chorus of abnegation. He saw a dangerous precedent in the designation of the CD by the congress. This, the reorganization of *L'Humanité,* and the measures against the masonic lodges and the Ligue des Droits de l'Homme were, in his view, a breaking of the contract between the International and the party. Though "morally against" the resolution, however, he promised to submit to discipline and work for its application.[77] The Brazilian delegate asked for a discussion of these issues, but a proposal not to open the French question for debate was quickly passed. Trotsky then replied briefly to the points raised by the French statements. He objected strenuously to Jean's statement that the congress had designated the CD. On the contrary, he said, acting on the appeal of the party, the congress had attempted to formulate a proposition that would be submitted to the National Council for ratification.[78] The stenographic account records no opposition to Trotsky's description of the International's procedure.

### A RABBIT IS BAPTIZED CARP

The strategy behind Trotsky's harshness toward the leadership of the PCF was his conviction that the humiliation and elimination of bourgeois elements would show the workers that the party was not just another parliamentary, careerist organization, and would attract them into its ranks. For every journalist lost, the PCF would gain a proletarian.[79] Still, the party could never become a truly revolutionary organization until it had captured the leadership of the CGTU. As Rosmer pointed out during the congress, despite all the talk of the subordination of the unions, it was the CGTU that led the party and not the other way around.[80] The leaders of the CGTU wanted partnership with Moscow; they were even willing to cooperate with a revolutionary Communist Party in France. But first they insisted upon the modification of the statutes of the Profintern, and the removal of Article 11, which called for an organic liaison between Profintern and Comintern. Without this concession, they said, the CGTU would be split, and its effectiveness would be nullified. Thus, the corollary of the Comintern's resolution on the French question was the decision of the Profintern to conciliate the French syndicalists. For perhaps the first time in the history of the Communist International, the central authority yielded on a crucial question.[81]

It would be interesting to be able to follow the making of this concession in confidential Comintern documents. Lacking such records, we are forced to rely on the official pronouncements of the French and the Russians. All the same, the main outlines of the process seem clear. The motion of the majority at St.-Etienne, it will be recalled, had instructed the new leadership to send a delegation to the Second Congress of the Profintern, for the purpose of obtaining the modification of its statutes. If the offending paragraphs were removed and the autonomy of French syndicalism respected, the CGTU's delegation was empowered to apply for membership. During the five intervening months before the opening of the Profintern's congress (it met simultaneously with the Fourth World Congress), Lozovsky had been careful not to do anything to jeopardize his success at St.-Etienne. When 31 members of the anti-Communist minority of the CGTU wrote him in September 1922, asking him to notify them by return mail whether he would remove Article 11 and thus "put an end to the terrible threat hanging over the head of the world proletariat," Lozovsky replied in polite terms that as the French knew very well, the Bureau could not change the decisions of a congress. This would be an of-fense against the "elementary rights" of the union movement. Nevertheless, the Bureau could state with the greatest clarity that it would do everything in its power to come to an agreement with the syndicalists. To demonstrate its desire for an understanding, the Profintern had even invited the anarchist Federation of Building Trades to send delegates to the congress. "For us," Lozovsky wrote, "proletarian revolutionary unity comes before any formula or paragraph."[82]

The Bolsheviks had good reason for treading gingerly in their relations with the leadership of the CGTU. When Frossard convoked the meeting of Communist delegates during the Congress of St.-Etienne, Monmousseau had flown into a rage. Shortly afterward, when informed that the party intended to create syndicalist commissions with which to infiltrate the unions, Monmousseau had cried: "If you do that, it's war between the CGTU and the Communist Party!"[83] The leadership elected at St.-Etienne, he said, intended to practice "syndicalism pure and simple, the syndicalism that has been practiced for a good many years despite all this talk." They had no intention of "playing the game of a party of any sort whatsoever." During the crisis within the party that followed the Congress of Paris, Monmousseau had taken refuge in ambiguity: he refused to sanction either the Center or the Left, declaring that the crisis itself was a justification of the CGTU's policy of autonomy, for otherwise the CGTU might have been divided into fractions.[84] However, for all its neutrality, *La Vie Ouvrière* did not hesitate to take advantage of the crisis to publish an attack on the Left's policy of infiltrating the unions.[85] And Monatte, who had come out strongly in favor of the Left, considered Monmousseau's avowed neutrality the cover for a flirtation with Frossard.

Since Monmousseau and his friend Sémard were to play roles of decisive importance in the history of French Communism, it might be appropriate to digress briefly at this point to say something about them and their backgrounds. Gaston Monmousseau and Pierre Sémard were both railroad workers of lower-class origin.[86] Both were autodidacts, neither having passed beyond the stage of elementary education. Both had aspirations to rise above the drudgery of manual labor. Both had learned to write and speak with some effect. Both viewed middle-class Socialists with scorn and suspicion. In all these ways, the two leaders of the CGTU corresponded to the prototype of the prewar syndicalist militant. Yet Monmousseau and Sémard differed from a Merrheim or a Monatte in one essential respect. Where Merrheim and Monatte had learned their syndicalism during the decade of the Dreyfus case, Monmousseau and Sémard had risen to leadership in the working-class movement during the last stages of the War. This meant three things. First, internationalism. For dedication to the Russian Revolution and pacifism were the touchstones of the *minoritaire*. Second, a "political" approach to syndicalism. For men like Monmousseau and Sémard, the union was not an end in itself, but a means for struggle against the bourgeoisie and a battlefield on which to defeat reformists. Finally, it implied an uncertainty about the validity of the traditional techniques of syndicalism. Both Monmousseau and Sémard had experienced directly the failure of the syndicalist movement in 1919–20. That failure had not made them any less dedicated to the revolutionary goal; it had, however, made them more open to new approaches. Thus, though still firm believers in syndicalist ideology, Monmousseau and Sémard were willing to accept the need for a strong and repressive revolutionary State.

It was these two men—roughhewn, ambitious, lacking in culture and finesse —who led the CGTU's delegation to Moscow in November 1922. Shortly before the congress opened, the two French syndicalists were granted the honor of a brief interview with Lenin. Lenin asked, with some astonishment, how the two heads of the CGTU could work together in such perfect agreement when one was a member of the party and the other was not. Sémard and Monmousseau answered that a party card was no gauge of Communism in France. Lenin then asked: granted that it were true that the PCF would only be a truly Communist party when it was proletarian from the top down; and granted that this would only happen when the best elements of the CGTU joined it and entered its ruling bodies; what had to be done so that the CGTU leaders who still did not trust the PCF would join it? The two Frenchmen immediately responded that the Comintern should order the PCF to adapt its syndicalist tactic to the peculiarities of the French movement, and, most important of all, that organizational ties between the party and the unions had to be discontinued. Did they suppose that this would lead to the results desired by the Comintern, Lenin asked with a smile. Monmousseau and Sémard answered that they were convinced of it. Excellent, Lenin responded, they had a bargain. But it went without saying that this concession, which might be fraught with serious consequences for the international Revolution, would be an exception to the rule, and should not in any case be interpreted as a breach driven in the Communist International.[87]

This was the account of the meeting published by Monmousseau a year and a half after the event. Though probably accurate in its main outlines, we may be sure that certain aspects of the conversation were left unrecorded. For example, it is extremely likely that the two French delegates agreed to meet the Russian concession halfway by working for a closer relationship between the CGTU and the party.[88] At any rate, Monmousseau was a different man when he stepped before the congress a few days later. For him, he emphasized, the modification of Article 11 was not a matter of sentiment or ideology, but simply a question of technique.[89] The French syndicalists did not want a rupture with the Communist Party or the Comintern; on the contrary, they would welcome their intervention in the revolutionary struggle. The Russian, German, Italian, Spanish, Bulgarian, and Polish delegations then presented a resolution, adopted unanimously, stating that even though they continued to believe in the necessity of giving the leading role to the Communist Party in each country and to the Communist International on the international level, they were ready to accept the CGTU's resolution. Sémard responded in the name of the French delegates by announcing their joy and gratitude at this concession; and Monmousseau declared that the CGTU now belonged to the Profintern.

The Bolsheviks left no doubt about the spirit in which they had made this concession. Zinoviev explained the reasoning of the Russians in one of his speeches before the Fourth World Congress.

The French movement as a whole is extremely important for the International. To speak in arithmetic terms, one can say that the French labor movement counts for 50 per cent of the International. Why? Because Paris and the policy of the French bourgeoisie are the home of world imperialism and the heart of world reaction. The present task lies in overcoming the prejudices of the French labor movement and in creating a party in France which brings the masses together. This is the International's most important task. In these conditions we must be ready to make the necessary concession.

Monmousseau was wrong; he would soon recognize his error. Besides, added Zinoviev slyly, with the confidence of a man who is in the know, the tie between the two organizations would not be weakened.[90] As Frossard was to put it a few weeks later, the "rabbit organic liaison" had been baptized "carp." This, however, does not mean that the Bolsheviks were pleased. Addressing the French Commission a few minutes after this speech, Zinoviev reminded them that "this concession was nonetheless a humiliation, which we owe the French party and which it should have spared us."[91] The irritation of the Bolsheviks was unwarranted. Their step backward was indeed the prelude to later advances. Writing a year and a half later, Monmousseau observed that it was "from this date that the leaders of the CGTU drew close to the Communist Party."[92]

#### "I CAN OR I CANNOT"

For all their faith in the leftward leanings of the proletariat, the Bolsheviks were fully aware that it was one thing to pass a resolution in Moscow, another to carry it out in Paris. Optimism and threats in public often gave way to prudence and deals in private. Cachin is an excellent example of the way principles and even personal antagonisms could be forgotten before the dictates of power. The situation left behind by the delegates who went to Moscow was full of uncertainties. Even the Left urged caution. "The moment is grave,"

Rosmer's wife wrote Humbert-Droz on November 2, 1922, "and a blunder or the use of brute force could ruin everything."[93] The leaders of the Left repeated these warnings on arriving at the congress. To name the CD in Moscow, they advised Trotsky, might offend the sensibilities of the French workers and play into Frossard's hands.[94] This was the Bolsheviks' main concern. Both Trotsky and Zinoviev suspected Frossard of secretly plotting to take the French party out of the Third International. Their game was to provoke him without provoking the mass of the party. Thus, despite the brutality with which they treated the French during the debates, they took care to emphasize that the International rejected the idea of a split.[95] After the congress, the situation was still extremely delicate. The negotiations with the Center had gone well enough in Moscow (here the buckling under of Cachin had been crucial), but Jean, Ker, and Renoult were still unknown factors. Furthermore, it was feared that Cachin's loyalty to the International might weaken under Frossard's influence. Just before leaving Moscow to return to France, Humbert-Droz was summoned for a last interview by Zinoviev, who invested him with full powers for the handling of the crisis. Zinoviev confessed that the International expected to lose *L'Humanité* and a good section of the party to Frossard. "Save what can be saved," said Zinoviev.[96]

The Left had greeted the decisions of the Fourth Congress with mixed reactions. Souvarine, Treint, and Reynaud felt that the International's solution was bad. They were in favor of leaving the responsibilities of leadership to the Center and remaining in the opposition. Souvarine, moreover, was personally disappointed because he had not been given the editorship of *L'Humanité*. He turned down the post of General Secretary in exchange for the *Bulletin Communiste*.[97] Dunois, Rosmer, Vaillant-Couturier, and the great majority of the Left, on the other hand, considered the International's solution a good one, because it would force the Left to take an active role in the life of the party.[98] On December 14, 1922, the Left published an unconditional acceptance of the decisions of the Fourth Congress.[99] As Vaillant-Couturier had foreseen earlier, it was now necessary for each member of the party to say "I can" or "I cannot."[100]

The reaction of the Center was elusive. On December 7, Frossard published and commented on the decisions on the French question made at the Fourth Congress. So far, he wrote, the information was fragmentary. Only the composition of the CD and the distribution of posts was known. The Center, he said, would have to consult with its delegates before it made any final decisions. "We are at a turning point in the history of our party," remarked Frossard. "The hour of choice has come. Vaillant-Couturier has posed the terms of our dilemma: 'Work or disappear!' "[101] Privately, Frossard was furious at Cachin for having deserted him under fire. In a violent encounter between the two men after Cachin's return from Moscow, Frossard said that he could not ac-

THE BURSTING OF THE ABSCESS

cept the resolutions. Cachin replied that they had been passed by the congress, and added that he was "l'homme de l'Internationale."[102]

The CD heard the reports of its delegates from December 12 to 16. Cachin was *"introuvable,"* and had to be sought out.[103] Ferdinand Faure was the only returning delegate to take a clear position of hostility. On the 16th, the CD passed a motion, submitted by Louis Sellier, accepting the decisions of the International in their entirety and promising to apply them loyally and immediately.[104] The vote was 15-4 with André Morizet, Cardon, Ledoux, and Soutif voting against, Frossard voting for. Both the Center and Renoult's group broke down into those who were ready to follow the line of the International (Ker, Cachin, Leiciague, Sellier, Marrane, Paquereaux, Werth) and those who resisted (Morizet, Cardon, Ledoux, Soutif, Jules Nadi, Antônio Coën, Ripert). On December 21 Soutif and Nadi were expelled. The delegates returning from Moscow who remained faithful to the International were dispatched to the federations to explain the decisions.

As Trotsky had foreseen, the difficulty and risk of purging the party of Freemasons and careerists bound the Center and the Left together. On December 17, Ker announced his resignation from the CD, from his post on *L'Humanité,* and from the Freemasons.[105] Four days later, a delegation headed by Coën and Ripert asked the CD to postpone the execution of the decisions on the masonic lodges and the Ligue des Droits de l'Homme until the Fifth Congress. This was the same procedure that had been used with the united front. This time, however, no one, least of all Frossard, had any illusions that procrastination could work. On December 24, the CD published a statement ratifying the decisions of the Fourth Congress. A committee consisting of Humbert-Droz, Rosmer, and Cachin was set up to purge the staff of *L'Humanité* and reinstate the journalists of the Left who had resigned after the Congress of Paris.[k] The situation was confused because during the period between the Congress of Paris and the return of the party's delegates from Moscow, Frossard had taken charge of *L'Humanité* and won over to his views three-fourths of the staff, including several persons who had formerly been associated with the Left, such as Noël Garnier, Henry Torrès, Bernard Lecache, and Tourly.[106] These young intellectuals were purged along with the holdouts of the Center. With the former factions crumbling, a new one was in the making, the faction of the International. The Left, however, refused to die. Souvarine and

---

[k] Humbert-Droz arrived in Paris on December 27, after crossing the border illegally. When he had first tried to pass into France legally from Switzerland on the 17th, he had been arrested and detained for five days. On releasing him, the Swiss authorities informed him that the French Minister of the Interior had issued an order for his expulsion from France the previous September 8. These exciting and mysterious activities are described in Humbert-Droz to Zinoviev, 25.xii.22. Humbert-Droz Archives. See also *L'Oeil de Moscou,* pp. 166–67.

306 THE BURSTING OF THE ABSCESS

Treint, having once more taken over the *Bulletin Communiste,* used it to threaten further measures against the Center.[1]

Battle lines had formed: Morizet, Pioch, Méric, Lussy, Torrès, Garnier, Lecache, Tourly, and Gassier would leave the party; Cachin, Ker, Sellier, Renoult, and Leiciague would stay. The only uncertainty was the course of action Frossard would choose. A legend has grown up to the effect that Frossard had prepared a plot to take the PCF out of the Comintern.[107] This is to misunderstand the man's character. As Humbert-Droz had pointed out so often, Frossard's essential characteristic was indecisiveness, the lack of a firm political line, the absence of a plan. Humbert-Droz himself later admitted (in a report to the Comintern) that had Frossard resigned right after the return of the delegation from Moscow, the delegates undoubtedly would have been disavowed and Frossard would have taken with him *L'Humanité* and the great majority of the CD and the party.[108] Who knows what schemes might have crossed Frossard's mind in those last weeks of December? He was young; his political career was just beginning; he had cut himself off from his Socialist friends by his campaign to discredit the Dissidents as counterrevolutionaries. Everything tied him and his future to the party—financial considerations as well as political ones. Yet to remain with Moscow after what had been said at the Fourth Congress, after what had been thought, if not expressed, in Paris during the last weeks, seemed impossible. Then there was the fact that Frossard was a mason.[109]

For two weeks, Frossard said nothing. It seems that he had decided to go to Moscow to take up his post as representative to the Executive. On the night of December 31, he invited Humbert-Droz to dinner. The most recent issue of the *Bulletin Communiste* had depressed him. He did not believe a serious and lasting collaboration with the Left was possible. Souvarine and Treint, he thought, would only be satisfied when they had thrown Frossard and his friends out of the party. He asked Humbert-Droz to reinstate Garnier and Tourly on *L'Humanité.* Humbert-Droz refused. That night Frossard read and reread Trotsky's speech at the Fourth World Congress. He was convinced that it was designed to provoke his resignation.[110] His companions, Aimé Méric and Gassier, encouraged him in this interpretation and pressed him to act. After painful self-debate, Frossard drew up a letter of resignation. "The incidents of the last few days," he wrote, "have profoundly upset me. I have made the greatest of efforts to accept their consequences, out of Communist discipline. I have not succeeded. Consequently, I cannot associate myself with a policy one of whose aspects they express with singular clarity."

[1] The brunt of Treint's and Souvarine's attack was directed against Ker and Frossard. Treint in particular suspected Frossard of having circulated rumors to the effect that he had volunteered for military service against the Bolsheviks in Poland and had only resigned after failing to be promoted. See the strange letter distributed to the members of the Left by Treint after the Paris congress. Monatte Archives.

A delegation of Renoult, Cachin, Sellier, Marrane, and Paquereaux was sent by the Bureau Politique to dissuade him; but to no avail. His mind was now made up. He expanded on the reasons for his resignation in a second letter, dated January 2, 1923. As soon as he had heard the decisions of the Fourth Congress, he wrote, he had wanted to resign. They constituted a revision of the Charter of Tours imposed on the party from without:

I considered them, moreover, impossible or dangerous to carry out. Finally, I saw in them the affirmation of a policy of extreme centralism which, throughout the international Communist Party, tends to reduce, in a way I believe fatal for great working-class movements, the decision-making power of the national sections and their ability to adapt themselves to the special conditions of their struggle.

Pressed by his friends to accept, he had been on the verge of leaving for Moscow. But the events of the last few days had convinced him that his effort at discipline was pointless. "The so-called faction of the Left treats the party like a conquered country." We were told, said Frossard, that we must finally choose. We "must say 'I can' or 'I cannot.' Well then, I choose: I cannot. All that remains for me then is to go, simply, honestly."[111]

### THE FROSSARD YEARS IN RETROSPECT

The history of these two years, 1921–22, was the history of a misunderstanding. In some cases, an honest misunderstanding, a bargain concluded in good faith without full knowledge or comprehension of the engagements undertaken; in other cases, a less honest misunderstanding, where one and sometimes both of the parties to the transaction hoped to improve the terms to their advantage after the agreement was signed. Frossard and his friends had gone to Moscow because they thought it was possible "to associate in a harmonious synthesis the audacity of Lenin's revolutionary achievement with the vast humanity of Jaurès."[112] That is a rather grand way of saying that they hoped to drape traditional French Socialism, which was now in disgrace because of its participation in the Sacred Union, with the prestige of the Russian Revolution and the Bolshevik regime. The conception was broad enough to attract both Left Wingers and Jauressians. It is true that leading syndicalists and Socialists pointed out that their ideologies were incompatible with Leninism; but the great majority of the party put their confidence in Frossard when he said that the new party would be neither a "church" nor a "barracks," and went forward to make a gesture of support for the Russian Revolution.

Frossard assumed, or rather hoped, that the Bolsheviks would accept the adherence of the French for what it was, then leave them alone to apply the strategy of the International as they could. The first six months of the party's existence were, if anything, encouraging. Loriot's group was silent, while the Bolsheviks themselves seemed the very soul of moderation and consideration. This, however, was the calm before the storm. For the Bolsheviks were in the process of effecting the shift from revolutionary audacity to tactical flexibility. The slogan "To the masses," which was the tactical contribution of the Third World Congress, was soon thereafter given the specific content of the "united front." Tactical flexibility, in turn, demanded iron discipline and ideological homogeneity. The tactic of the united front and the increased centralization of the International were two sides of the same coin. Leninism, which for a brief historical moment had been interpreted in terms of spontaneity, returned to its earlier emphasis on consciousness. The revolutionary elite corps, that is the party, had to be tightly organized, rigidly centralized, and capable of the most complex maneuvers.

The great conflicts of 1921 and 1922 in France were all fought over this question of centralism and federalism. The issue of the Presidium, control of the press, selection of the CD, the statutes of the Federation of the Seine, the statutes of the CGTU, the relationship of the party to the unions, the running sore of the organic liaison, the debate over Fabre and the Conflict Committee, the question of whether national congresses of the party were to follow or precede the congresses of the Comintern—all these conflicts led back to the basic question of the relationship of the center to the periphery. The disagreement was "irreducible." As Frossard himself later observed, it was a conflict between the Jauressian concept of the party as a "grande amitié" in which men of different tendencies could meet and discuss, and the Leninist view of the party as a disciplined army in which it was necessary to submit to the leadership or be expelled. Even more fundamentally, it was a struggle between the French and Russian styles of authority. For whereas the French tradition tolerated dissidence, so long as it was separated from responsibility, the Russian tradition stressed obedience.

The French heroically resisted the recognition of this conflict. Their delegation voted for the measures of increased centralization passed at the Third Congress, then came home to ignore them. The conflict between centralization and federalism was implicit in the disagreements preceding the Congress of Marseille; but it was so overlaid by the clash of personalities that the opponents of the International's conception could in good faith deny the existence of the problem, and assert that they stood foursquare for the policy of the Executive. It was the united front and the problem of the unions which forced the conflict into the open. The French stubbornly refused to accept the united front; the Bolsheviks stubbornly insisted that it had universal validity. Moreover, the Russians grew angry at the chaos of the French Communist press and made an example of Fabre, which, to minds long schooled in the importance of legality, raised the question of jurisdiction.

By June 1922, it was no longer possible to escape the implications of the conflict. The Jauressian Verfeuil, the anarchist Méric, and the syndicalist Lafont had moved into positions of outright hostility to the International. Frossard, however, made one last stab at cooperation with the Executive. He accepted both the necessity of the united front and the infiltration of the unions. He did so not out of conviction, but out of the belief that the party had to reach an agreement with the Executive at any cost. His gamble might have worked, he might even have managed the transition from Jauressian Socialism to a French version of Leninism, if it had not been for the wolves of the Left, who pushed him to the wall and tried to force him to abandon his closest associates. The case of Cachin was a dramatic example of where Leninism might lead. Frossard balked at the experience. And thus he entered into conflict with the International once more, a conflict from which the only exit was departure or submission. It should not be thought that Frossard did not consider submission; its advantages were considerable. But once more the violence and insatiability of the Left decided him. It would be impossible to work with men like Treint and Souvarine. And so he left.

The Bolsheviks, too, played something of a double game during these two formative years. Both Zinoviev and Trotsky believed that the French party would very probably have to suffer the same schism as the Italian party. Both were convinced that in the long run, the Bolshevik cause could not help but triumph. Both maintained private relations with the leaders of the Left. Nevertheless, in their practical, day-to-day dealings with the Centrist leadership, Zinoviev and Trotsky showed great caution and even cunning, as is shown by the behind-the-scenes negotiations at the Fourth Congress and the frequent reprimands handed out to the Left. The reasons for this un-Bolshevik restraint were discussed quite frankly by Trotsky in a short preface to a Russian collection of his writings on French Communism, published in the spring of 1923.[118] The weakness of the Left, he explained, had prevented any action against the Frossard group in 1921 and 1922, even though Frossard and his friends had given plenty of reason for their expulsion. Had the International taken action it would not have been understood by the masses. Moreover, a split would have left the International with only a motley group, itself in need of a purge. The Left had to gather around itself the significant part of the proletariat and become conscious of its tasks before a split was possible. In Italy the split with the Center had been forced by events; in France it had been the International which had chosen the moment for the break. All this, of course, was only half true. It had not been the International which had chosen the moment for the split at all; it had merely reacted to the movements of the Left and the Center. But Trotsky's article does point to one important fact: the International dared not act sooner because it had no confidence in the forces of the Left.

Why was the International so anxious to split the French party and purge it of its reformist remnant? On this point students will necessarily differ, depending on their approach to politics and men. Some will say that it was

ideology, others the drive of the Bolsheviks for power. Whatever one's prefer-
ences on this point, it is of interest to know what the Bolsheviks themselves
thought they were about. Trotsky's speech at the Fourth Congress on "The
Russian Revolution and the Prospects for World Revolution" addressed itself
precisely to this issue. Trotsky felt the Revolution would be incomparably
harder to come by in the West than it had been in Russia, but, once it was accomplished, the hardships would be fewer because the Western countries were
more advanced. The Western bourgeoisie, Trotsky pointed out, had learned
from the Russian case, and had armed itself to the teeth. During this period of
calm in the world Revolution, it would try to lull the proletariat with pacifist
and reformist illusions. And it would succeed, for these illusions were still
strong in the West. But when the Left Bloc came to power in France, as
Trotsky was sure it would, a strong wave of disillusionment would seize the
French working class. When this moment arrived, the workers must be able
to turn to the Communist Party and find in it a party of "the rude and brutal
truth." It was for this reason that the party had to free its ranks of elements
who might serve as purveyors of pacifist and reformist illusions. Frossard,
Trotsky added, had once described the party to him as "a great friendship."
This is all well and good, but only a thoroughgoing selection can give rise to
this great friendship. "In other words, there must be a great selection before
the party can become a great friendship."[114]

The members of the Left meanwhile continued to support the policies of the
International with all their force; and one can study in their thoughts the
progress of Leninist attitudes and concepts. Treint, whose mind seemed made
for the vulgarization of complex ideas, defended the united front and the need
for centralization in the crudest of terms. For him, the united front meant that
the reformists were fowl "to be plucked," while federalism was "shameful."[115]
In attempting to justify the International's position, Treint argued that centralization of the party's organization was necessary both in times of revolution and in quieter periods. In a period of revolutionary struggle, it was obvious that decisions must be made directly by the Center. But even in calm
periods, the great number of decisions to be made did not permit the consultation of the sections and federations. This would require an enormous bureaucracy. Besides, in a calm period the party must learn how to react quickly to
events. Still, Treint assured his readers, even though decisions were not made
by the sections, all authority derived from them. The leadership of the party,
even if limited to a few men, was accountable to the congresses, the national
councils, and the CD, and could be recalled.[116] The merits of the system, as
Treint himself pointed out, depended on the closeness of the tie between the
leadership and the masses of the party. But what would happen if this tie
broke down? And how could it be kept alive when the sections no longer had

any role in the formulation of policy? To these crucial questions, Treint had no answer; nor, it must be said, did he feel it necessary to raise them.

Another problem, closely related to the first, was the question of discipline and freedom of speech within a Communist Party. Once more the leaders of the Left decided in favor of the authority of the International. Commenting on the Fabre affair, Humbert-Droz attempted to define the line between liberty and discipline within the party. His conclusion was that, "He who joins the party, who becomes an *active member* of it, accepts a *limitation on his individual liberty*." Before a decision is made, the minority has the right to discuss it; afterward, however, it must submit out of discipline. The penalty for nonsubmission was exclusion. "For the worker's conscience there is no doubt: he who does not accept discipline is a traitor." The limitation of individual liberty was the essential condition of all collective struggle.[117] Treint went Humbert-Droz one better. No one within the party, he wrote, had the right to think like an anti-Communist. He did not attempt to define, however, what was Communist and what was anti-Communist.[118] It was obvious that the epithet anti-Communist was a weapon that could be used with terrible ambiguity. For who was to decide who was an anti-Communist and what was anti-Communist? The International? And what if the International fell into evil hands?

Souvarine added the final touch to this debate on the right of criticism within a Communist Party. In discussing the deviation of the Ultra-Left (Heine, Soutif), Souvarine, showing himself a good pupil of Lenin, was led to identify it with the deviation of the Right. Even the terminology was unmistakably Leninist. "Scratch the surface of the Ultra-Left," wrote Souvarine, "and you will immediately find the core of the Ultra-Right." Then Souvarine went on to ask, "What is opportunism?" Opportunism, he replied, "is error, abundant and various, fluctuating and diverse." The Opportunists are now on the Right, now on the Left. *"But at the decisive hour, they oppose the Communist idea in unison; they combine forces against the Revolution."*[119] The formulas of Treint, Humbert-Droz, and Souvarine were extremely vague when it came to defining what was permissible in the way of criticism and what was counterrevolutionary. Only one thing seemed clear: it was the leadership of the party that would decide what was Communist or anti-Communist in the sections and the federations; and it was the Executive that would decide what was Communist or anti-Communist in the leadership of the party.

No one, whether of the Right, the Left, or the Center, could argue that 1922 had been a successful year for the party in terms of influence among the masses. The decrease in membership that was already marked in the summer of 1921 became a mass exodus in 1922. Frossard claimed 78,828 members for the party as of the end of July 1922. Sixty thousand is probably closer to the true figure.[120]

Membership had dropped by over 5,000 in the all-important Federation of the Seine; in all, the party had probably lost some 30,000 adherents in the course of the year. Membership figures, as the Bolsheviks like to say, were not everything. But every indication pointed to the impotence of the Communist Party. The cantonal elections of May 1922 showed that the Communists had lost ground in the cities; that in the key working-class centers of the Nord, the Pas-de-Calais, the Bouches-du-Rhône, and the Gironde, the PCF was weaker than the SFIO; and finally, that in many federations, Communists had disregarded the electoral motion passed at Marseille and had joined alliances with the Bloc des Gauches in order to defeat reactionaries.[121] The fiasco of the Le Havre general strike was a convincing demonstration that the organic liaison between the CGTU and the party was yet to be established. On the parliamentary front, the small band of Communist deputies had done nothing to draw to the party the attentions of the nation. With the exception of Vaillant-Couturier and Renaud Jean, there was little to distinguish the Communist Group from the Socialists. Thus far, the party had no colonial program. Moreover, its North African sections refused to accept the notion of alliances with the native bourgeoisie. Only the Communist press maintained the link with the masses, and this fact was in itself proof of the party's inability to break with its Jauressian past. With a record of this complexion, it was clear that any change must be for the better. The "Communist" party envisaged by Lenin and Trotsky seemed, if anything, further from realization than it had two years before. It was with the hope of forming such a party that the new leadership looked forward to 1923.

## Chapter ten

# The Left Takes Charge

*Le mouvement ouvrier français entre enfin dans
sa voie véritable.*
*—Zinoviev to Cachin, February 11, 1923*

By January 1923, the Left had attained the goal for which it had fought so
stubbornly during the previous year and a half. The Verfeuils, the Piochs, the
Mérics, the Lafonts, the Fabres, the Verdiers, the Mayoux, were gone, either
expelled or resigned. Cachin, Marrane, Rosmer, Sellier, Souvarine, Treint, and
Werth comprised the Bureau Politique; Sellier and Treint divided the chores
of the Secretariat.[a] In theory, this was the working alliance of the Center and
Left, symbolized by the dual secretaryship. In practice, it was the alliance of
the Center and the Left according to the interpretation of the Executive, which
meant (and had always meant in the minds of Trotsky and Zinoviev) that
those men of the Center who were trusted by the working class would be
forced to carry out the policies of the men of the Left, who were not. Only
Souvarine could continue to sulk over what was in every sense a victory for
the ideas and personnel of the Left. Cachin might remain as Director of
*L'Humanité*; Sellier might take Frossard's post as party Secretary. But it was
Dunois and Rosmer who in fact controlled the policy of the party's daily, Souvarine who tended to the orthodoxy of French Communism, and Treint who
dominated the new apparatus. The two additions to the leadership, Georges
Marrane and Gérard Werth, were both open to the ideas of the Left. Of the
troublemakers of 1922, only Renaud Jean retained his influence: Renoult, Ker,
and Rappoport were all relegated to the limbo of unimportant party work.

[a] The new CD consisted of Sellier, Cachin, Louis Jacob, Gachéry, Leiciague, Marrane,
Gourdeaux, Laguesse, Paquereaux, Henriot, Rosmer, Treint, Vaillant-Couturier, Sou-
varine, Marcel Cordier, Bouchez, Tommasi, Demusois, Dunois, Vital Gaymann, Froment,
Dubuc, Werth, and Renaud Jean. *L'Humanité*, 22.i.23.

Despite the rout of Centrism, the International's solution had its unexpected sides. The principle of Trotsky's "great selection" had been such that Frossard had gone and Cachin had remained. Yet it had been over Cachin that the Congress of Paris had split. Even Souvarine had been willing to work with Frossard, whom all considered, despite his faults, "une force et une intelligence politique." Why Frossard and not Cachin, Sellier, or Renoult? This was a question which French Communists did not feel it necessary to ask in January 1923. At this date, it was still taken for granted that revolutionary fiber was equated with fidelity to the International. However, in 1922 and 1923 the Bolsheviks themselves did not shrink from such dilemmas. Writing in *Inprecorr* in June 1922, Radek had already indicated the attitude of the Bolsheviks toward the situation in the French party with a frankness whose consequences perhaps even he himself did not recognize fully. The clarity of thought with which the members of the party understood Communist theory, wrote Radek, was quite unimportant when compared to their willingness to reject this or that group of leaders.[1] Radek did not go on to explore the implications of his statement further; he did not have to. What he meant was clear enough: discipline and loyalty to the International mattered more than any understanding of doctrine. By January 1923, Radek's principle was accepted by both the International and the leadership of the PCF. It led in a quite different direction from Trotsky's "great selection" of revolutionaries.

Having eliminated the enemy within, it was now the task of the Left to transform the party, to make it revolutionary. The theses on tactics adopted at the Third Congress had said that Communist parties could develop "only in struggle."[2] The occupation of the Ruhr and the promise of great events in Germany gave the PCF a chance for action that it had never had before. Great strides were made in the application of the International's decisions. It might be said that this was the year in which the party won its spurs. But the experience of 1923 was to show that Communist orthodoxy did not necessarily lead to mass influence; nor did it put an end to intra-party dissension.

POINCARÉ SAVES THE PCF

Frossard had expressed the desire to leave the party "simply, honestly." But this was no more possible for him than it had been possible for the Communists and Dissidents to treat each other as comrades. The Communists, aware of their vulnerability, feared the creation of a rival party. Soon after the return of the French delegation from Moscow, a Comité de Défense Communiste had been established in the Department of the Seine to protest against the decisions of the Fourth World Congress. The declaration of the Committee, signed by Méric, Pioch, Lafont, Torrès, and 84 others, warned the International that its policies would lead to "an automatic obedience, which is the very negation of revolutionary action," and asserted the confidence of the Resistants (they had thus been christened to distinguish them from the Dissidents, whom they had temporarily replaced as the villains of the French working-class movement) that, no matter what the response of the International, "the proletariat remains with us."[3] In the federations of the Drôme and the Loire the party faced rebellions that were traceable to the expelled deputies Nadi, Lafont, and Faure, whose fiefs these were. The CGTU had its minority, too, grouped around Pierre Besnard's Comité de Défense Syndicaliste. With Frossard at their head, these elements might be welded into a party of revolutionaries that could mine the PCF, the CGTU, and perhaps even the SFIO. Humbert-Droz warned the ECCI that at best, the party could count on a loss of from 50 to 60 per cent of its membership. At this juncture, he wrote on January 9, "any hesitation . . . would be fatal for the party."[4]

To head off this danger (the Bolsheviks thought in terms of a party that would stretch from Longuet to Verdier), the delegate of the International intervened, and demanded forceful action: namely, the expelling of those Resistants who had not resigned, and the launching of a campaign to discredit Frossard in the eyes of the working class. Sellier dispatched Roger Rieu to the Drôme and the Loire to save these federations for the party and explain the decisions of the Fourth Congress. The political execution of Frossard was prompt and merciless. Frossard was made the scapegoat for the entire crisis of 1922. Dunois accused him of preparing a plot to carry the party out of the International, with the fantastic dream of returning to Moscow on his own terms.[5] Manuilsky devoted a six-page article in the *Bulletin Communiste* to "the suicide of L.-O. Frossard," and concluded that he had played a double game with the French and the International throughout the two years that he had led the party.[6] Manuilsky could refer to Frossard's own speech at the Congress of Paris for evidence of his duplicity; Souvarine did not bother with such subtleties. "Treason," he wrote, "had been permanently installed at the party's summit. Any enemy of the International could safely enter into contact with Frossard for any purpose harmful to the party."[7]

One suspects that Humbert-Droz and Zinoviev were overpessimistic in their forecasts of doom. The Committee of Communist Defense was composed of Parisian intellectuals without contacts with the masses. Besnard and his followers had already been routed at St.-Etienne. There is no evidence that Longuet desired to join his erstwhile foes. All this, however, must remain conjecture and nothing more. For providence, in the unlikely form of Poincaré, intervened to save the Communists. On January 11, 1923, the French Premier, exasperated by the failure of the Germans to pay and the unwillingness of the English to make them do so, ordered the Republic's troops to occupy the Ruhr. That day Monmousseau, Treint, Marrane, Gourdeaux, Joseph Lartigue,

Charles Piétri, Léopold Cazals, and Jules Massot were arrested and accused of plotting against the internal and external security of the State. Two days later, Ker and Charles Hueber were arrested. On January 19, the Chamber of Deputies voted after a stormy session to lift Cachin's parliamentary immunity and authorize legal proceedings against him; the next day he was arrested.

From one day to the next, the outlook for the Communists changed. Frossard's resignation, which could have been a political act of great significance, calling attention to the incompatibility between traditional French Socialism and Bolshevism, now appeared an act of desertion. The Communists lost no time in exploiting the government's repression against their Resistant enemies. "At such a time," Manuilsky wrote, "let us admit it, the party's abandonment by its General Secretary is desertion before the enemy, and as such, according to martial law, merits the punishment of political death."[8] (How these Bolsheviks were drawn to military analogies!) Scarcely a week after reporting on the grave crisis facing the party, Humbert-Droz was able to send Moscow an optimistic view of the PCF's situation and prospects. The government had cut the ground out from under the Resistants just when they seemed most dangerous, and had allowed the party to regain its equilibrium. At the same time, the energy of the Centrist CD had inspired confidence in the Left, and there were signs of the disappearance of factionalism. "The ideological unity of the party," concluded Humbert-Droz, "is in the making and is becoming a reality."[9]

### THE PARTY WINS ITS SPURS

Ever since the spring of 1919, the Left of the working-class movement had stood in unbending opposition to the Versailles Peace Treaty. That opposition, however, seldom took the form of action outside the offices of *L'Humanité* or the Palais Bourbon. This was as true of the Communists as it had been of their Socialist predecessors. The reason for their timidity is easily understood. Communist leaders knew full well that the great majority of Frenchmen were hostile to Germany and favored making the "Boches" pay. The struggle against the occupation of the Rhenish towns in April and May of 1921 had been conducted on the grounds of anti-militarism, and even so had met with general indifference, except among the Communist youth. Official Comintern policy, on the other hand, called for solidarity with the German working class. The theses on tactics adopted at the Third Congress called it the duty of the French Communists "to do everything they can to make the French soldiers in the occupied zone understand the part they are playing as policemen for French capital and reject the shameful task assigned them."[10] Solidarity with the German proletariat was meant to take the form of cooperation with the KPD. According to the resolution on the organization of the Executive Committee passed at the same congress, neighboring Communist parties were supposed to "maintain the closest contact with each other with respect to information and organization."[11] This meant reciprocal attendance at important conferences and congresses, and the exchange of representatives.

These resolutions, like so many others, had remained a dead letter. Méric had been delegated to the German party during its action of March 1921; Ker had visited Germany in December 1921; Treint had gone to the congress of the KPD in 1922. That same year the French and Germans had met in Cologne, and had reached agreement on joint strategy. But in general the liaison between the French and Germans had been weak and uneven.[12] This was partly because of the French political environment; partly because the French Communists had been too preoccupied with their own crisis to undertake any concrete steps against the Versailles Peace Treaty; partly, however, because the Russians themselves had not emphasized this issue. Up to the end of 1922, the hostility of the Bolsheviks to the Versailles settlement had merely been one of the elements in their theory of the contradictions of the capitalist world. At the Fourth World Congress it became, in the words of E. H. Carr, "the pivot of a whole analysis of the international situation."[13] Significantly, it was Cachin, a former admirer of Poincaré and a Frenchman, who was chosen to make the report on the Versailles Treaty. The resolution proposed by him (and, we may be sure, written by the Russians) declared that the treaty had turned the states of Central Europe into "colonies of English and French capital," and Germany into "a plaything in the hands of England and France." The French party was instructed to "fight with all its strength against the imperialist aspirations of the French bourgeoisie," to demand the withdrawal of French troops from the left bank of the Rhine, and to struggle against the projected occupation of the Ruhr. Anti-patriotism, the resolution emphasized, was no longer sufficient in France; "today it is necessary to fight the Versailles peace at every step."[14]

The Versailles Peace Treaty took on importance in Bolshevik eyes for two reasons. At the most, the clash between France and Germany over reparations could weaken the German bourgeoisie, sharpen class antagonisms, and provoke the outbreak of a revolution. At the least, it could separate Germany from the West and thus offer a wedge for the action of Soviet diplomacy, which had already proved itself brilliantly at Rapallo. Both policies were pursued simultaneously in 1923, though the emphasis was now on one, now on the other. These prospects for Soviet diplomacy and Comintern agitation thrust the French Communist Party into a new and important role that had little, if anything, to do with making a revolution in France itself. A powerful PCF could aid Bolshevik policy on both levels, by immobilizing the French government in the case of a German revolution and by swaying public opinion toward rapprochement with the Soviet Union. This explains Zinoviev's almost frantic concern with the fate of the PCF and his repeated assertion at the end of 1922 and beginning of 1923 that the French party was "the most important section" in the International.[15]

The French delegations came home from the congress determined to put its resolutions into action. They seem to have been informed in advance of the steps that were coming, whether from the French or Russian side it is difficult to know. On the initiative of Monmousseau, a Comité d'Action contre l'Impérialisme et la Guerre was formed on December 21, 1922, by the party and the CGTU. The Anarchist Federation was invited to take part, but refused. The CD delegated as its representatives Cachin, Marrane, Gourdeaux, Paquereaux, and Treint; the CGTU, Marie Guillot, Cazals, Monmousseau, Lartigue, and Piétri.[16] This Committee organized a meeting at the Grange-aux-Belles for January 3, to protest against the threat of an occupation of the Ruhr. Cachin and Treint spoke for the PCF, Monmousseau and Sémard for the CGTU. Rosi Wolfstein, a disciple of Rosa Luxemburg, represented the KPD. Treint emphasized that the Red Army would not stand by and watch the German revolution be suppressed. "And if the Soviet troops reached the banks of the Rhine," he boasted, "it would be we, comrades, who would go open the gates of our towns and greet them in the name of the French proletariat." According to L'Humanité's account, Treint's words were met by a "salvo of applause."[17]

Three days later, on January 6, 1923, the Communist parties of France, Germany, England, Belgium, Italy, Holland, and Czechoslovakia met in conference at Essen to plan their strategy against the occupation of the Ruhr. Representing France were Cachin, Ker, Treint, Béron (from the Moselle), Hueber (from the Bas-Rhin) for the party; Pierre Provost for the JC; and Monmousseau, Sémard, Jacob, and Massot for the CGTU.[18] The French delegates cut a rare figure of revolutionary determination. Monmousseau delivered 11,000 francs sent by the CGTU for the strikers of Ludwigshafen (the money may very possibly have been provided by the Profintern) and declared that everything must be done "to prevent and sabotage" the occupation of the Ruhr. Cachin attacked the policy of the French government in violent terms. Ker pointed out the risks which the French delegates ran, but emphasized that this did not worry them "because we will never again find such a favorable occasion for winning influence over the masses." The conference pronounced in favor of sabotaging the military undertakings of the French bourgeoisie and preparing for a general strike in France in case of war or a lasting occupation of the Ruhr. A resolution was passed calling upon the French workers to "raise their voice together and with might against the occupation of the Ruhr basin."[19] An international Action Committee was formed, as well as three Franco-German committees, one each of railroad workers, miners, and metallurgical workers. Steps were taken to distribute Communist propaganda and undermine the morale of French troops.[20] Before returning to France, the

French delegates separated and delivered inflammatory speeches throughout western Germany. An example of their language was Hueber's statement at Stuttgart that "if arms are placed in the hands of the workers, they must turn them against those whom it is necessary to eliminate first of all."[21] Not since Hervé's time had such phrases been heard from responsible party and union leaders; and this time they were backed up by organization, money, and coordination on an international level.

After the close of the Conference of Essen, the Action Committee continued agitating in France. Public meetings were held in Le Havre, Strasbourg, Saverne, Bourges, Cherbourg, Laon, St.-Etienne, Nantes, and Lyon.[22] Tracts were distributed. *L'Humanité* denounced Poincaré's policy in huge headlines ("Poincaré prépare l'aggression," "L'impérialisme français se prépare à frapper l'Allemagne désarmée"), and announced that "La Résistance ouvrière s'organise."[23] When the government arrested the first Action Committee (January 11), new ones were formed, on both the national and the departmental level.[24] The reorganized Committee of Action called a huge meeting for January 15, and declared in a manifesto that "Le Comité des Forges veut la Ruhr."[25] On January 18, 19, and 20, thirty meetings were held in different quarters of Paris protesting the occupation of the Ruhr. *L'Humanité* published an appeal from the Comintern and Profintern to the French workers (January 19) declaring that "Your enemy is at home." It was the duty of all French workers and soldiers to do everything to oppose the Poincaré government and prevent a new war. On January 26, the Central Action Committee announced to the proletariat that "the official mobilization order, calling up several classes and thus marking the beginning of a real danger of war, will be for you the signal for the general strike."[26]

Such appeals were bluffs, but they were shrewd bluffs, based on the awareness of the Communist leaders that Poincaré dared risk no more than a limited action. With the occupation of the Ruhr a fact, the Communists went forward with plans to organize another international conference, this time a meeting of both Communist and Social Democratic parties and revolutionary and reformist unions, which would make the united front a reality and demonstrate the solidarity of the European proletariat. Officially organized by the factory councils of the Rhine and Westphalia, the conference met in Frankfurt on March 19, the anniversary of the Paris Commune. As a manifestation of the solidarity of the European proletariat, the conference was unconvincing: 200 of the 250 delegates were German; of these, only 10 were Social Democrats and 17 Independents. The rest of the assembly belonged to the group of the Comintern and the Profintern.[27] For the French delegation, however, the conference was something of a success. Those French Communists who succeeded in sneaking past border guards were congratulated on their "brilliantly sustained" campaign, and told that they should continue to apply the united front. Their immediate tasks, they were told, were to prepare "congresses of factory, shop, and mine delegates, regional at first, national afterward, which will deliberate upon syndicalist unity and the danger of war," and to organize a week of protest against the occupation of the Ruhr, which was to take place on an international scale during April 15–22.[28]

The French party did what it could to carry out these directives. On March 17, the Action Committee had organized a mass meeting of solidarity with the German proletariat and the Frankfurt Conference, at which the German Communist Emil Höllein spoke. In April and May, the party intensified its propaganda effort in the form of press campaigns, public meetings, and candidacies for local elections. If government repression is any gauge of revolutionary ardor, the French did their duty. *L'Humanité* was submitted to the indignity (or honor) of a search, for the first time since its foundation. By the end of April, the Santé was bursting with Communists (Cachin, Marrane, Gourdeaux, Paquereaux, Treint, Hueber, Béron, Höllein), syndicalists (Monmousseau, Piétri, Lartigue, Cazals, Jacob, Massot, Sémard, Keim, Guillot), and Jeunesses Communistes (Gabriel Péri, Maurice Laporte, and others) who were charged with an impressive array of offenses running from "provocation to crimes against the external and internal security of the state" to "provocation of soldiers with the intention of diverting them from their duties, in the cause of anarchist propaganda."[29]

The attempt of Poincaré to bring these culprits to justice gave the Communists the opportunity for a minor victory over the government. On May 5, 1923, the parliamentary committee set up to investigate the charges against Cachin pronounced in favor of freeing him. Millerand reacted to this defiance of the government's wishes by issuing a decree (May 7) bringing all of the above-mentioned defendants before the Senate High Court. The first hearing was scheduled for May 24. To make the charges more plausible, they were changed to "Communist plotting." In the interim, Péri and Höllein embarked on a highly publicized hunger strike to secure their liberation from the Santé; and André Marty, the still imprisoned "hero of the Black Sea mutiny," was victorious in ten different local elections.[30] When the Senate met, it declared the matter outside its competence by a vote of 145 to 104. The Premier immediately offered his resignation, but Millerand refused it and Poincaré stayed on to liquidate the affair of the Ruhr, the costs and unpopularity of which were mounting by the day. This second "Trial of the Plot" had its epilogue when, after winning 42 different elections, André Marty was released and amnestied on July 21, 1923.

As in 1921, the French political establishment was unwilling to condone forceful measures against the Communists for their agitation.[b] But this should

[b] See above, p. 220.

not be interpreted to mean that the PCF had succeeded in rousing the indignation of the working class against the occupation of the Ruhr. On the contrary, we know from the reports of Humbert-Droz that during the spring of 1923, the Communists' campaign foundered on the indifference of the masses. The first successes of January and February could not be repeated in March and April. The meetings organized at the time of the Frankfurt Conference were "a great failure." The party had to postpone its observance of International Propaganda Week until the last week of April, so that it would end with the traditional celebration of May 1. During this brief period of agitation, the circulation of *L'Humanité* actually dropped.[c] Despite the exchange of representatives with the KPD, the liaison between the German and French parties was still not good. The French were often in the dark about the KPD's situation and political prospects; Radek and Brandler complained of the inactivity of the PCF.[31] These feelings inspired Radek to write in the June issue of the Comintern journal that thus far the International's policy in France had attained only "feeble results."[32] Humbert-Droz defended the PCF against Radek's and Brandler's criticisms. French opinion, he noted on June 14, was dominated by the coming elections, and was indifferent toward questions of foreign policy. "Those comrades who have undertaken the job of propaganda," he wrote, "are unanimous in saying that the part of their speeches aimed at the Ruhr policy was greeted with indifference by their audience."[33] Still, Humbert-Droz could not deny Radek's statement that the French proletariat was so weakened by the Sacred Union that it lacked the strength to turn economic strikes into a political struggle against Poincaré and his "expedition of plunder."[34]

### THE JEUNESSES COMMUNISTES AND THE SUBVERSION OF THE ARMY

The greatest Communist successes were attained not in France, but in the occupation army itself, and these were the work of the tiny Fédération des Jeunesses Communistes.[d] This is a glorious but dark chapter in the history of the French

[c] Humbert-Droz to Zinoviev and Trotsky, 21.iv.23; Humbert-Droz Archives (HDA). Circulation figures for *L'Humanité* are hard to come by. According to the Communists themselves, the circulation of *L'Humanité* rose from 160,000 in November 1922—the low point to which it had plunged during the crisis of that year—to 218,000 by January 15, 1923. It remained high (210,000) throughout February, but leveled off at 180,000 on February 28. If these figures are correct, and they probably are approximately so, then we may conclude that circulation had settled at about 170,000 or 175,000 in the spring of 1923.

[d] The Federation of Communist Youth played a much more important role in the formation of the PCF than is generally recognized. In July 1923 its National Committee claimed "close to six thousand members," as opposed to 30,000 for the German Communist Youth organization and 15,000 for the Swedes. This figure must indeed have been approximate, for a later commentator, heartened by the rapid growth of Jeunesses Communistes in the

Communist Party. Without the records of French Army Intelligence and the reports of the Comintern agents in Germany, it is difficult to know in detail how profound the infiltration of the occupation army was. We must be satisfied with snatches of information here and there, along with the impressions of some of the men who were in a position to judge the scope and effectiveness of Communist propaganda, for a picture of "the first Leninist anti-militarist experiment attempted in the Western countries."[35]

Ever since the spring of 1921, the Fédération des Jeunesses Communistes had viewed the party with ambivalent feelings. The two organizations had coexisted without cooperating. The Jeunesses Communistes accused the CD of neglecting them and even of sabotaging their operations; the leaders of the party, on the other hand, devoted no more attention to the JC than the Socialists had to the Jeunesses Socialistes before 1914. As a result, the relations of the Jeunesses Communistes to Moscow were much closer than their relations with their own party. Their activities were financed and directed by the Communist Youth International (CYI)—and ultimately, of course, by the Comintern. This was particularly true in the case of their work in the army. Anti-militarism was the very raison d'être of the Jeunesses Communistes; it was to the perfection of their anti-militaristic techniques that they devoted their greatest efforts in 1921 and 1922. One can imagine that for this reason, they were highly valued by Moscow. At any rate, the leaders of the JC—Maurice Laporte, Jacques Doriot, Gabriel Péri—had already attained an independent position in the Comintern by the end of 1922.

The leaders of the JC were first briefed that important events were coming in the Ruhr at the end of 1922. Around that time (probably in December), Voja Vujović, the delegate of the CYI, had passed through Paris to organize the agitation of the Young Communists in the Ruhr and to discuss the possibility of financial aid.[36] Further arrangements were made through Pierre Provost in Essen. When French troops marched into the Ruhr on the night of January 10–11, they were met by an appeal signed by the Fédération des Jeunesses Communistes informing them that they unwittingly were acting against "the interests of the proletariat of France, Germany, and the entire

---

fall of 1924, recalled that the federation had had only 4,000 members in May 1923 at the time of its Congress of Lyon. (*L'Avant-Garde,* July 1–15, 1923, and November 1, 1924.) For the origins of the JC, see Annie Kriegel, *Aux origines du Communisme français* (1964), II, 718–24. The primary source for the development of the JC is its journal, *L'Avant-Garde Ouvrière et Communiste,* which commenced publication on September 25, 1920, and appeared bimonthly throughout 1921–24. Maurice Laporte's books *Les Mystères du Kremlin* (1928) and *Espions rouges* (1929) shed little light on the activities of the organization of which he was Secretary, but Henri Barbé's "Souvenirs" (ms. at the Hoover Institution) is of first-rate importance, both for the federation as a whole and for the local branch in St.-Denis.

world," and calling upon them to revolt against their rulers.[37] From this date on, the Jeunesses Communistes took an active role in the Action Committee and the struggle against the Ruhr. Their main effort took the form of written propaganda. Over two million tracts, leaflets, and manifestos were distributed to the Army of Occupation, often right in their barracks.[38] These tracts were published in German, French, and Arabic, the last designed to reach the 20,000 Algerian and Tunisian troops who had been sent to the Ruhr. The JC's paper, *La Caserne,* was issued to new recruits, at first monthly, later bimonthly; a series of pamphlets with such titles as "Why Jacques Bonhomme is here" was published. Unlike the party, the JC did not confine themselves to manifestos and appeals. Cells were created in Army units; contacts were established with local Communist organizations: JC leaders like Doriot moved in and out of the area of occupation. These activities were conducted under the direct control of a group of Comintern officials, headed by two Red Army generals who went under the names of Anton and Pierre.[39]

How successful was the operation? This depends on one's point of view. Judged in the perspective of what had been done in the past and what could be done, there is no doubt that the activities of the JC marked a new departure in the tactics of the French Communist Party. By May 1923, there were nearly 200 cells in French military units. More than sixty-five Communists or Communist sympathizers held important posts as noncommissioned officers.[40] French soldiers fraternized with German workers, gave them food, sometimes refused to fire on them when ordered—and, perhaps most important of all, eased their lives by simply disregarding orders whenever possible. Because of the presence of Communist noncommissioned officers, like Henri Barbé, it was possible for notorious Communists to operate under the very eyes of the French military authorities.[41] For all this, however, a good part of the French troops, probably the majority, remained resistant to Communist propaganda. This was especially true of the Belgian contingent and French soldiers from regions that had been occupied or invaded by Germans during the war. Barbé, for example, could not guarantee the friendly attitude of his troops in the case of an order to fire on a German demonstration.[42] Communist agitators often ran into an attitude of hostility and incomprehension on the part of their listeners and readers. As one former Communist propagandist put it, "The great majority of occupation troops entered the Ruhr with the fierce will to take care once and for all of these 'Boches' who did not want to pay. Take care of them once and for all . . . even . . . by a scrap . . . ; this was the eventuality to which the soldiers were resigned, and the most rebellious among them were far from fraternizing with those they held responsible for their troubles."[43] That quotation does not do justice to the real accomplishments of the JC; but it does indicate the limits within which they had to work. Taking those limits into account, their operation in the Ruhr was a brilliant success.

Declarations of official optimism abounded in the Communist press in the first months of 1923.[44] They were inspired by the conviction of the PCF's leaders that the party had at last become truly Communist. The metaphor chosen to illustrate the party's recovery was invariably medical. Writing in April, for example, Souvarine described the PCF's transformation in terms worthy of the most dashing TV doctor. "Its rotten limbs amputated, our party, formerly the victim of a whole series of working-class sicknesses, has rapidly begun to convalesce. In less than three months after beneficial surgery, its recovery is an accomplished fact."[45] Souvarine's diagnosis was premature. The PCF's con-valescence from the operation performed at the Fourth Congress was long, uneven, and marked by frequent relapses. The first of these relapses came in March 1923 and lasted through December. It took the form of dissension among the leaders, listlessness, and overcentralization.

January and February had passed in harmony and goodwill. With Poin-caré's aid, the Communists had kept the inroads of the Resistants to a mini-mum.[46] Under the stimulus of government repression, factionalism within the leadership had virtually disappeared. The Left had been impressed with Sel-lier's energy, and Humbert-Droz had asked him to stay on in the Secretariat.[47] The National Council of January 21, which met to ratify the decisions of the Fourth Congress, took place in an atmosphere of calm that contrasted sharply with the tumultuous assemblies of 1921 and 1922. Paquereaux delivered the report of the delegation to the congress in the name of both Left and Center in order to signify the end of "the regime of factions." The lists for the CD, the BP, and the Conflict Committee were accepted unanimously. When two delegates protested against the expulsion of Heine, their statement was met with "bursts of laughter."[48]

It seemed that the party had at last attained its ideological unity. But, despite the disintegration of the factions of 1922, the departure of Frossard did not end the tendency toward petty quarrels that had plagued the party during the first two years of its existence. Notwithstanding the repeated warnings of Hum-bert-Droz, Souvarine was sent home in mid-January to bolster the depleted ranks of the leadership. Six weeks had scarcely passed before the *Bulletin Communiste*'s irascible editor came into conflict with the imprisoned Treint. The immediate cause of their disagreement was Bukharin's statement at the Fourth Congress that it might be necessary for a proletarian State to conclude a military alliance with a bourgeois State against another bourgeois country. It was typical of Treint that while all other French Communist leaders treated Bukharin's remarks with extreme caution and did their best to avoid the issues they raised, Treint rushed on blindly to embrace his conclusions. In his en-thusiasm, Treint went beyond Bukharin to formulate the concept of "workers' imperialism." The Russian army, said Treint, was not a national army, but rather the army of the Communist International. There was no question of Russian imperialism here, as the opponents of the International had charged. But there was a different kind of imperialism—a class imperialism, a workers' imperialism, a Red imperialism. "And what is Communism," Treint asked, "the old Marxist Communism, identical with the young Bolshevik Communism, if not workers' imperialism conquering from parasites the riches, all the riches, of the world?"[49]

The leadership wisely considered this slogan both meaningless and dangerous, and Sellier said as much in print. When Treint wrote a long-winded reply in which he tried to define his concept of "workers' imperialism" further, it was not published.[50] The question was further confused because Cachin, too, complained that his articles had been cut, rewritten, and buried on the second page of the paper, of which he was theoretically the Director. In protest against this maltreatment, the two men resigned their posts as Secretary and Editor of L'Humanité. Humbert-Droz intervened on behalf of the prisoners to end the dispute. He insisted that all important decisions be made at the Santé, after consultation with the leaders of the CGTU, and he availed himself of the occasion to request once more that Souvarine be recalled to Moscow. "His presence here and his personal methods of work," Humbert-Droz wrote, "are a continual danger in the period of the party's convalescence."[51] It was Souvarine, however, who seemed to emerge victorious. When Treint's article was finally published, it was accompanied by a condescending reply by Souvarine, in which he pointed out that the party Secretary's understanding of Lenin's concept of imperialism was completely erroneous.[52] These skirmishes at the summit of the party would not require telling were it not for the fact that they marked the beginning of a falling-out between Souvarine and Treint that had a significant sequel the next year.

While the leadership quarreled, the party and its federations sank into the apathy and inertia already described in connection with the campaign against the occupation of the Ruhr. By March 13, only 40,000 cards had been sold, marking a drop of 6,000 in comparison with the figure of the previous year.[e] The decline of certain key federations was even more striking. Under the leadership of the Left, the membership of the Federation of the Seine sank from 8,000 to 4,000 in less than a year. There was a scarcity of speakers and propagandists. The few public meetings held were badly organized. Instead of trying to recruit, the federations isolated themselves in uncompromising sectarianism, which cut them off from any hope of rallying the masses behind their slogans for the approaching election year.[53]

[e] Humbert-Droz to Zinoviev, 13.iii.23. On April 3, 1923, Humbert-Droz wrote Zinoviev and Trotsky that the party's membership had risen to 50,000! HDA.

It is hard to know whether the decline of the party as a mass organization was the effect or the cause of its overcentralization. In early May, Treint emerged from the Santé to take up his post as Secretary alongside Sellier. Treint soon succeeded in dominating the former Centrist. Under his authoritarian leadership, both the CD and the BP lost influence to the Secretariat. Major political questions were not even submitted to the BP.[54] The members of the CD began to complain that they were not being consulted on the important questions affecting the party. The Secretariat and the BP often made decisions in the absence of Cachin, with the result that there were "painful incidents."[55] In June a conflict arose between Treint and Dunois. Through some mishap, a declaration of the Action Committee was lost in the offices of *L'Humanité*. Treint insisted that Dunois and his assistant, Labrousse, be held responsible and given an official rebuke. To obtain this sanction, the party Secretary threatened to resign. The conflict was finally settled by the arbitration of Humbert-Droz and Tommasi, after Dunois and Treint had exchanged a number of threatening letters.

The delegate of the International took away from this encounter the conviction that Treint's methods were a menace to the party, and that Rosmer must be called back to Paris because he and Souvarine were the only two members of the BP who would stand up to Treint. As early as June 14, he had written Zinoviev that Treint had "a completely mechanical concept of discipline" and insisted on drawing up all theses "without consulting the party organs that could give him the information he lacked."[56] On June 23, he accused Treint of exercising a kind of permanent blackmail on the other members of the BP by continually threatening to resign. "A crisis," he concluded prophetically, "is brewing. The forming of a party of the elect within the party could one day have serious consequences. Moreover, despite the quite friendly and private warning I gave him [Treint] about his authoritarian and brutal methods, he continues to lead the party as if it were a regiment."[57]

Treint replied to such criticism by drawing up a plan for the reorganization of the party, which was adopted by the CD and published in July 1923.[58] This report is worth summarizing in detail, for it gives an overall view of the party's organization in the summer of 1923. Little seems to have changed since the Fourth World Congress and the departure of the Resistants. The chief organs of the party, according to Treint, were (a) its press (*L'Humanité*, *La Voix Paysanne*, the *Bulletin Communiste*, and the *Bulletin de la Presse Communiste*); (b) the Administrative Council of *L'Humanité* and the Communist press; (c) the parliamentary Group; (d) the group of propaganda delegates; (e) the Council of Economic Studies, which also functioned as a center for documentation; (f) the Council of Colonial Studies; (g) the publications service; (h) the Syndicalist and Cooperative Committees; (i) the Women's Secretariat and its journal, *L'Ouvrière*; and (j) the Fédération des Jeunesses Communistes and its principal organ, *L'Avant-Garde.* The party was directed by (1) the CD, "whose essential role is to make decisions of great importance and sweeping consequence ['haute portée'] on major issues"; (2) the Secretariat and the BP, which reported to the CD and were responsible for determining the day-to-day policy of the party; and (3) the different committees of the CD, charged with special tasks and responsible to the CD and the BP.

The two chief defects from which the party suffered, argued Treint, were (1) that the execution of decisions was too haphazard because there was no control apparatus; and (2) that the party's center was submerged with paper work in its relations with the almost one hundred federations. Treint suggested as a remedy the creation of regions and regional delegates. Instead of being in direct contact with the federations, the center would work through regions. Each region would have its own political leadership, its own propaganda center, and its own weekly paper. The permanent delegates for propaganda would act as regional delegates and would maintain the liaison between the center and the mass of the party's members. According to this plan, the directors of the central organs of the party would meet in conference at least once a month. The center would then distribute directives, while the various party officials would raise issues, make suggestions, etc.

These measures of reorganization were designed, in Treint's phrase, to eliminate "the bureaucratic vice from which the party suffers."[59] The idea was not new: a similar plan had been proposed at the SFIO's Congress of Amiens in 1914.[60] Neutral in themselves, Treint's recommendations might have been used for purposes of centralization or decentralization, depending on the spirit in which they were applied. Here was the rub. The party leadership was trying to reshape a basically Jauressian party in the image of Lenin's highly centralized organization of revolutionaries. To appeal to spontaneity would have meant to return to the federalist traditions of pre-1914: freedom of the press, ideological heterogeneity, and the Left Bloc. The outcome of Treint's establishment of regions and regional delegates was thus predetermined: it reinforced his own hold on the party and deprived the federations of what sense of initiative remained to them. By the end of September, the regional delegates had become "veritable prefects of the BP, with very great authority over the federations, directing them politically, receiving their letters, and answering them in the name of the party leadership without the leadership's having any knowledge of it except through the reports of the delegates."[f]

---

[f] Humbert-Droz to Zinoviev, 29.ix.23. (HDA.) It is interesting to note that the same process occurred in the Soviet Union, where the agencies designed by Lenin to limit bureaucracy actually helped in consolidating Stalin's hold over the party. See pp. 356–61 below.

The issue of Treint's dictatorship and the stagnation of the party at its lower
and intermediate levels arose simultaneously with the problem of applying the
united front, and soon became confused with it. One might have assumed that
the operation performed by the Bolsheviks at the end of 1922 would have resolved once and for all the question of the united front. Such was not the case.
The trouble did not stem from indiscipline or lack of opportunity. By January
1923, the leaders of both the PCF and the CGTU were unanimous in their
acceptance of the Executive's tactic. The occupation of the Ruhr, the violence
of the Right, the struggle for the amnesty, and the prospect of revolution in
Germany all offered excellent occasions for cooperation with other working-
class organizations. But the experience of 1923 showed that what was accepted
in principle might be extremely difficult to realize in practice. Part of the problem derived from the ambiguity of the strategy itself, part of it from the peculiarities of the French situation. For example, did the united front mean that
the Communists sincerely hoped for joint action with the Socialists? Or did
they merely seek to embarrass the Socialists and the reformist syndicalists in
the eyes of the working class? The most careful reading of the tons of Communist pronouncements on the united front will not resolve this question. Nor
could the Bolsheviks themselves. For what they wanted was both; and since
the reformists refused to act as the Comintern wished them to do, the outcome
was that first one approach was adopted, then the other.

The other problems were specifically French. How far should the united
front reach? Should it extend to the Resistants, who had formed their own
Parti Communiste Unitaire? Should it include the anarchists, who attacked
the Soviet regime? Should the united front be restricted to strikes and demonstrations against the danger of war and for the amnesty? Or should it also apply
to the coming national elections? If so, how could the united front be distinguished from the traditional Bloc des Gauches, which threatened to absorb the
Communist Party in the general surge of revulsion against the Bloc National?
Finally, what if the Socialists or Resistants took the initiative and proposed a
united front to the Communists in order to support them "like the rope supports the hanged man" and deprive them of their working-class support? The
Communists discovered to their discomfort that the united front could be a
double-edged sword.

The Action Committee against the occupation of the Ruhr and the danger
of war was formed on December 21, 1922. On January 31, the Central Committee of the CGTU submitted to the congress of the CGT a proposal for a
reunification of the two unions' centrals, and also a concrete offer of a united
front against the occupation of the Ruhr. These offers were refused. On February 4, Sellier and Tommasi, the two acting party Secretaries, proposed joint

action against Poincaré's Ruhr policy to the SFIO's Congress in Lille. The Socialists refused for the same reasons they had given Frossard in November; they feared they were being manipulated, and they did not want to be the dupes of the Communists.[61] These offers of a united front were repeated at the time of the Frankfurt Conference. The French Socialists and the CGT, however, did not participate; and it is difficult to see how they could in good conscience have done so after the campaign of vilification that Souvarine conducted in *L'Humanité*, in which he referred to the Socialists as *"capons traditionnels"* and "scabs," and accused them of "permanent betrayal" of the working class.[62]

Souvarine's articles set off a debate within the leadership over the application of the united front. Treint and (according to his testimony) the other prisoners at the Santé felt that Souvarine had given the Socialists a pretext for turning down the Communist offer of united action and protested to the CD.[63] The CD agreed with Treint, and Souvarine was forced to interrupt his campaign. In an article published in the *Bulletin Communiste* in late March, Souvarine admitted that there were situations in which the reformists could loyally and efficaciously participate in joint action with the Communists, thus augmenting their authority with the working class.[64] The editor of the *Bulletin Communiste,* however, was not a man who liked to eat crow, especially when administered by Treint, and the conflict dragged on into the next month. On April 18, the party once more proposed the united front to the SFIO on the basis of the program drawn up by the Frankfurt Conference.[g] This proposal was no more successful than the preceding ones, nor was the CGTU able to organize a joint demonstration with the CGT for May Day. Souvarine considered these overtures to the SFIO and CGT too conciliatory, and the BP felt it necessary to submit this question of the interpretation of the united front to the Executive for a final decision. As Humbert-Droz put it, it comes down to whether we are really trying to constitute a united front, or whether we only make these proposals in order to have them rejected.[65]

Meanwhile, the Communists had encountered an embarrassing situation within the Action Committee. The National Confederal Committee of the CGTU met in March 1923, and demanded the enlargement of the Action Committee to include "all regularly constituted groups giving revolutionary guarantees and taking their inspiration from the principle of class struggle." The CGTU's position was seconded by the Executive Committee of the Railroad Workers, which threatened to withdraw its recognition of the Action Committee unless it was opened to the Anarchists, Dissidents, and ARAC.[66]

[g] The offer consisted of a week of agitation against the occupation of the Ruhr, a joint demonstration for May 1, and attendance by the SFIO at the World Workers' Conference, which it had been decided to call at the Frankfurt Conference. *L'Humanité*, 18.iv.23.

These demands put the Communists in a dilemma: just ten days before, Humbert-Droz had emphasized to Zinoviev in his report that the Resistants were still a threat, and that a mistake by the party might give them control of the CGTU.[67] To admit Frossard and his friends to the Action Committee would be to give them access to influence over the working class. Humbert-Droz advised Cachin to admit the Anarchists and ARAC, but not the Resistants. The party, he emphasized, must threaten to resign if the Parti Communiste Unitaire is admitted.[68] The PCF's position was rendered more awkward by the fact that Frossard, having learned his lesson well, had become the great champion of the united front. The solution finally found, in cooperation with the *Vie Ouvrière* group, was to dissolve the Action Committee and to establish new committees for more specific purposes, such as the Committee against Fascism and the Committee for the Defense of the German Revolution. These committees at first included the Anarchists, the Resistants, and the ARAC; but they were later reconstituted to include only the party, the CGTU, and the ARAC.[69] Thus the Communists failed both in their attempt to bring the Socialists and reformist syndicalists in and in their attempt to keep the Resistants and Anarchists out of the Action Committee. They were finally left with those groups they controlled themselves—and no united front.

The ineptitude of the Communists was further shown in June, during the uproar created by the violence of the Action Française. On the evening of May 31, Marius Moutet, Marc Sangnier, and Maurice Violette were attacked by royalists and beaten while on their way to address a leftist meeting protesting Poincaré's policy in the Ruhr. The indignity was compounded when Fernand Bouisson, a venerable republican politician, received a threatening letter accompanied by a packet of dung.[70] Public opinion reacted violently against this emulation of Mussolini's strong-arm tactics. For the first time since the election of the Bloc National, the Radicals came out in clear opposition to the government. Here, with the alliance of Right Center and Left Center in disintegration, was the situation for which united front tactics had been designed. Theoretically the Communists should have taken the leadership of the Left's forces and mounted a huge campaign against the danger of fascism in France. Instead, the PCF's leaders tried to escape the contagion of a true united front.

During the great debate of June 1, the Communist parliamentary Group played an insignificant role, leaving the leadership of the republican forces to Herriot and the Socialists. When the Ligue des Droits de l'Homme invited the Communists to participate in a huge demonstration against the Action Française, the BP refused. Humbert-Droz intervened to insist that the Communists take part, marching separately in order to distinguish themselves from the Radicals and Socialists.[71] The BP, however, feared that such an action might compromise the party by bringing it into contact with the Bloc des

Gauches; it countered by calling for a demonstration of the CGTU, the CGT, the SFIO, the ARAC, and the Union Anarchiste in another part of Paris for the same hour. The Socialists and the CGT of course rejected this offer, and made ready to participate in the protest of the Ligue des Droits de l'Homme, which had been postponed for a week.

The party took advantage of this postponement to try to steal a march on its republican competitors by organizing the entire manifestation. In its appeal to the working class, it attempted to explain that only the proletariat could combat fascism, since fascism was itself a product of capitalist society.[72] But this reasoning was undoubtedly a bit subtle for the Parisian worker, who interpreted the demonstration in terms of the traditional mechanics of republican defense. When the march was prohibited by the authorities, the party submitted almost gratefully.[73] Finally, the Communist-controlled departmental Action Committee against War and Fascism called the people of Paris to a demonstration against the Action Française on June 23. Cachin claimed that "the success obtained far exceeded what one could expect"; but he himself admitted that the Communists had been accused of sabotaging the demonstration of the Ligue des Droits de l'Homme and calling off their own.[74] Humbert-Droz commented with typical understatement: "Je crois que le parti ne sort pas grandi de cette manœuvre."[75]

### THE WORKERS' AND PEASANTS' BLOC

Electoral strategy presented an even more sticky dilemma than the application of the united front for specific purposes. The incidents of June 1923 opened the electoral campaign in earnest. Defending the policy of his government before the Chamber on June 15, Poincaré refused to repudiate the "extremists" of the Right with the determination the Radicals would have liked. The enthusiasm of the Action Française for Poincaré and the new moderation of the SFIO did the rest: the alliance of Radicals and Socialists, which would sweep into power the next year, was conceived. What would be the attitude of the Communists toward this Left Bloc? Tradition offered two varieties of Socialist electoral tactics. One provided for the party to submit its own candidates on the first ballot, and then to vote against reaction on the second wherever Socialist candidates had no chance of winning.[h] This was substantially the solution chosen by Renoult in his electoral thesis for the Congress of Marseille. The other alternative called for the party to maintain its candidates on the second ballot, as in the ill-starred elections of 1919. It was a variation on this second tactic that Trotsky had proposed to the Communists at the Enlarged Executive of February 1922. The PCF, he said, must form a Workers' and Peasants'

---

[h] This was the course decided upon at the Congress of Amiens in 1914.

Bloc. When forced to choose between union with the proletariat and a bloc with the bourgeoisie (the Left Bloc), the Dissidents would opt for the latter and would be unmasked.[76]

Trotsky did not say it, but this reduced the elections to an exercise in the use of the united front. Nevertheless, when the question of the elections arose in 1923, it was to Trotsky's Workers' and Peasants' Bloc that the Communists turned. In the midst of the debate between Poincaré and the Radicals on June 15, Cachin announced that the Communists would not take sides in the coming struggle between "two clans of the bourgeoisie," but instead would fight against both.[77] That same day Renaud Jean developed the PCF's position in more detail and with greater éclat. His theme was that there was no real difference between the Bloc National and the Bloc des Gauches. They had been elected on the same program; they were only separated by minor differences; and on the essential questions Right and Left (that is, the Radicals) had almost always voted together against the proletariat. "Entre la droite et la gauche, nous n'avons pas à choisir." The Communists, Jean concluded, would form a Workers' and Peasants' Bloc, which they would oppose to the Bloc des Gauches. The Socialists, he warned, would be committing the worst of mistakes by concluding a pact with the left wing of the bourgeoisie instead of with the proletariat.[78]

Despite the bravado with which Jean announced the Communists' new slogan, it soon turned out that the leaders of the party had little idea of what they meant by the Workers' and Peasants' Bloc. When Humbert-Droz asked the BP to discuss this question, he was presented with three different interpretations of what the Workers' and Peasants' Bloc should be. Treint saw it as the electoral form of the united front, with joint electoral lists that would include Communists, Socialists, and Dissidents. Cachin and Sellier understood it as meaning separate lists for the party, which would be open to syndicalists and Left Socialists who condemned the Bloc des Gauches. The remnants of the old Renoult group thought that the party had to present its own list, and did not think the united front could be extended to elections. Humbert-Droz warned that the party's concept of the Bloc Ouvrier et Paysan was extremely vague, and that some federations had already interpreted it as meaning that the party would be ready to renounce its own list and vote for the Socialist candidate—in other words, traditional republican discipline. He requested the ECCI to issue the party some directive on this subject.[79]

The Executive responded with a message on the elections written by Trotsky. The bourgeoisie, read the message, hoped to have the proletariat and the peasantry pay the cost of the War. Only the Radicals and Socialists could carry out this policy for the bourgeoisie; they would do so by trying to revive the democratic and pacifist illusions of the population. The Bloc des Gauches thus became the Kerensky period of the French revolution, during which the bourgeoisie had to turn to Leftists to carry out its program. The Communist Party must pose as the defender of the workers and peasants and unmask the Radicals and Socialists. It must reject all signs of reformism or careerism; otherwise it would not hold the respect of the masses. The party must present as its candidates principally men "taken from the bench and plough." Candidates without party affiliation ("sans-parti") could be included if they had proved their attachment to the working class. Any attempt to throw a bridge between the party and the Left Bloc must be met with immediate expulsion in full view of the working class. Only such a policy could win the confidence of the proletariat. The message ended with a typically Trotskyist paean to the coming revolution. The electoral campaign, he wrote, must be conducted in such a way that its revolutionary and class character would be obvious to all. "For the Communist Party, participation in the elections will be a preparation, and circumstances permitting, a direct introduction to the revolutionary seizure of power."[80]

This message was probably the least inspired that Trotsky had ever addressed to the French Communist Party. His talk of the seizure of power and revolution was either official optimism, and thus hypocrisy, or else the reflection of an abysmal ignorance of French conditions. A casual reading of the reports of Humbert-Droz would have dispelled any illusions he might have had about the fighting capacities of the PCF or the chances of a successful campaign based on appeals to revolution. Since Trotsky was an intelligent man, if a fanatic one, and since we know that he followed the French press closely, we must assume that the ECCI's major concern was to protect the PCF from the temptations of the Left Bloc. Even so, its message raised more questions than it answered. Agreed that the campaign would be revolutionary, agreed that the PCF's candidates would be workers and peasants, what attitude would the Communists take toward the Socialists and Dissidents? How would they act on the second ballot? Should they admit members of other parties to their lists? What should be their platform? Again we must suppose that the ECCI's silence was deliberate.

All these ambiguities were much in evidence during the two sessions that the CD devoted to the Executive's resolution. The problem was not indiscipline, as in 1922, but simply confusion about what the International meant. After the leadership had accepted the project unanimously, there were three quite different opinions on the question of how to put the Executive's tactics into practice. The former Renoult group thought the party should address the masses directly. Cachin, supported by Doriot, proposed that the Communists draw up an offer of a united front, but in such terms that the other proletarian parties would feel compelled to reject it. Humbert-Droz and Rosmer agreed with this general idea, but argued that the proposal for joint action should be worded in such a way that it would provoke a discussion among the

Socialist and Resistant rank and file. In their view, this object could be attained if the only condition required for the united front was the rejection of the Bloc des Gauches by the Socialist leaders. Unable to reach a decision, the CD shelved the problem for later consideration.[81]

## THE DOLDRUMS

These barren discussions indicate the sorry state to which the party had sunk by September 1923. Scarcely a week passed that Souvarine and Treint did not feud over the united front. Both agreed on the end, but one thought the Socialists should be unmasked before, the other after, joint action.[82] Their medieval hair-splitting hid the fact that the party was incapable of any kind of positive action because of its overcentralization, declining membership, and lack of faith in its own revolutionary determination. Treint's reorganization had choked the last life out of the federations. A federal congress no longer dared take the smallest initiative without the approval of the BP. Treint, in turn, bullied the BP and did as he pleased.[83] Recruitment continued to drop: in less than a year, the party lost 25,000 members.[i] Instead of exploiting its Socialist and Dissident competitors through the united front, the PCF was exploited by them.

The campaign for the amnesty at the end of September may serve as an example. The party belonged to a General Committee for the Amnesty, which included the various working-class organizations and the usual non-Socialist Leftists. André Marty had been the Committee's electoral candidate throughout 1923, and this had redounded to the glory of the party. In July, Marty was released from prison. Neither the BP nor the Bureau of the Federation of the Seine acted, and the Resistants rushed in to propose the name of Jean Goldsky, a left-wing journalist imprisoned for subversive activity by Clemenceau. Once more the party was confronted with the united front in reverse. The BP wanted to withdraw from the Committee for the Amnesty because it feared the implications of Goldsky's candidature. From Goldsky it was only a small step to Caillaux, and the party would be involved in a kind of embryonic Bloc des Gauches. To abandon the Committee, however, would be to risk discrediting the party. Finally, the PCF took the risk and went ahead to run its own candidate, the fugitive railroad worker Lucien Midol, in the by-elections being held in the Santé and Charonne quarters. Things went well enough in the Santé quarter, where Midol defeated Goldsky handily. However, in Charonne, Goldsky ran ahead of Midol, and the party chose to withdraw its candidate on the second ballot rather than infuriate left-wing opinion. Midol was with-

---

[i] Humbert-Droz is comparing the party's membership to that *claimed* in October 1922. A likely estimate would be that the PCF's real membership was somewhere between 45,000 and 50,000 in the fall of 1923.

drawn in the name of the Workers' and Peasants' Bloc, but not without losing a great deal of face for the party and embarrassing it before the working class.[84] It was no easier to convince the Parisian proletariat that they should vote for Marty or Midol, but not for Goldsky, than it was to explain why the party had not joined with the other leftist organizations to protest against the outburst of fascist violence in June. The PCF seemed locked in a dilemma: it could be either Communist and pure, or opportunist and effective. Ten years would pass before it would learn how to be both.

The delegate of the international did what he could to guide the PCF through this difficult period. His role had been extended and had changed in character. In 1922 he had been an observer and an adviser; in 1923 he added to these tasks the responsibilities and power of a regular party leader. In addition to reporting to the Executive on the state of the French party and writing articles for the Communist press to clarify troublesome aspects of the International's strategy,[85] he asked for minor party work "compatible with the discretion I must maintain," attended all meetings of the BP and L'Humanité's editorial board that dealt with political questions, and intervened when necessary to secure action from the leadership or to arbitrate a conflict. French security precautions made life exciting; they did not, however, prevent the Comintern's emissary from discharging his mission, nor, for that matter, from enjoying life. Humbert-Droz could rent a comfortable apartment in Neuilly; he could send for his wife and two children; he could house visiting Communist dignitaries like Rákosi and Vujović; when circumstances dictated, as they did in March, he could even manage to be present for the meetings of the BP held in the Santé. On April 3, 1923, Humbert-Droz was able to inform Zinoviev, "I am playing an ever greater role in the party's life."[86]

Owing to his energy, his tact, and his assiduity in reporting to Moscow, we know a lot more about the inner life of the party and its leading organs than we would otherwise be able to learn from official documents. The reports of Humbert-Droz also allow us to judge the state of relations between the Executive and its French section. The first conclusion must be that the Bolsheviks were well informed about the state of the PCF. What illusions they might have had about the militance and capabilities of their French section had their origin in Moscow, not in Paris. The Comintern's agent made no attempt to tell his superiors what they wanted to hear. While critical of the party's inadequacies, he was careful to emphasize the limitations imposed by the national context within which the PCF had to operate. He never ceased to stress, for example, that in its present condition a true united front represented a danger for the party.[87]

For all his awareness of the difficulties the PCF had to face, however, Humbert-Droz saw the great weakness of the party in the pernicious role of personalities and the lack of competent and well-intentioned leaders capable of working with one another in a spirit of cooperation. The experience of 1923 only reconfirmed his earlier impressions of the leaders of the Left. Throughout January, February, and March, he repeatedly urged the recall to Moscow of Souvarine, whose presence he considered "a sword of Damocles" poised over the party.[88] Knowing the PCF's need for experienced journalists and propagandists, he recommended that Renoult, Ker, and Rappoport be used, instead of being forced to serve out their punishment in unimportant tasks. Rappoport's great crime, he noted, was to have been Souvarine's enemy during the past few years.[89] Beginning in May, Humbert-Droz became increasingly disturbed by Treint's methods, and by late September he had come to the conclusion that the former captain must be removed from the Secretariat, if the party were to be brought back to life. He proposed to Zinoviev a major reorganization in which Rosmer would be given Treint's position, Monatte given control of *L'Humanité*, and Treint recalled to Moscow to represent the PCF to the Executive. While in Russia, he urged, Treint should be "warned against the personal line he's following."[90]

The reports of Humbert-Droz do not seem to have received the attention they deserved. The PCF was sick, extremely sick. But the Bolsheviks, those dedicated physicians of 1922, evidently saw no cause for alarm. Souvarine was not forced to curb his pen. Renoult, Ker, and Rappoport were not given positions of responsibility. Treint was rebuked lightly by Zinoviev at the Enlarged Executive of June 12–23 for his use of the term "workers' imperialism" and for his interpretation of the united front.[91] His more important faults, however, went uncriticized. "The party," Zinoviev said in that now outworn cliché of 1923, "has passed into healthy convalescence. It was obliged to undergo a severe operation, but it has been proved that the health of the party was sound."[92] Having listened to these trivialities, Treint came home to reinforce his dictatorship through the creation of regional delegates. During the next few months, Humbert-Droz came close to losing contact with Moscow altogether. Time and again he complained that the ECCI was not answering his letters or issuing the directives he needed to guide the PCF.[93] In September it appears that he himself ceased to write because of the Executive's failure to respond. All this suggests that despite the presence of a representative who for all practical purposes was an integral member of the party leadership, who played an active role in the determination of party policies, and who mediated party conflicts, the PCF still had a great deal of independence in 1923.

Perhaps too much. For ironic as it may seem, what the French party needed above all was guidance. Owing to the operation performed at the end of 1922, the PCF lacked men, vigor, and imagination. The Left had never stood for policies, only for the International. Its absence of political sense showed through clearly once it had assumed power. The journalistic skills of Souvarine, the brutality of Treint, even the real qualities of Rosmer, were no substitute for the cadres that had been lost through the clumsy policies of 1919–22. This was unfortunate from the point of view of French Communism. For the first time since the formation of the Third International, the Bolsheviks were in no position to offer the guidance the French party required. They had their own problems. One was the struggle for power within their own party. Another was the German revolution. Both were to affect the development of the PCF profoundly.

### ACROSS THE RHINE

After two months of relative silence concerning the Ruhr, *L'Humanité* announced on August 1 that "Germany is on the eve of great struggles." "Will there be fighting tomorrow in the streets of Berlin?" the Communist daily asked. "Will there be civil war? Will there be a fascist putsch? Or will a workers' and peasants' government be proclaimed at last?" In anticipation of such reports, the CD issued a manifesto calling upon the workers of France "to give their exclusive attention to events in Germany." The French proletariat must understand, the manifesto read, that the defeat of the German revolution would mean the reinforcement of capitalist exploitation in France. And to its own members the CD declared that "The federations, the sections, the regional propaganda delegates, the papers, the party's speakers, must from this day forth, until new orders are received, devote all their concern, all their work, to the German situation."[94] The CGTU immediately constituted a Committee for the Defense of the German Revolution, which the party, the CGT, the SFIO, the Resistants, the ARAC, and the Anarchist Union were invited to join.

With these appeals and directives, the policy of the PCF toward events in Germany entered a new and basically different stage. The campaign against the occupation of the Ruhr mounted by the French in January and February, and continued with renewed vigor (if not renewed success) in March, April, and May, had been essentially negative. It had emphasized the danger of war, and had played on the traditional anti-militarism of the French lower and middle classes. The line adopted in August, September, October, and November 1923 emphasized the coming of the German revolution and the need for the French proletariat to prepare itself for the coming struggle, in which it would be expected to prevent its own bourgeoisie from choking off the German revolution in its early stages. The party, Souvarine explained on August 22, should gird itself for the counterrevolutionary offensive of the French government, ranging from the imposition of censorship to the abrogation of parliamentary rights.[95]

This shift in the rhythm and emphasis of French Communist policy had its source in the radicalization of the German situation and a sudden change in the attitude of the Bolsheviks toward the KPD's prospects for seizing power.[96] The origins of this change went back to May and June, when the Soviet Union suffered a collapse in its relations with Great Britain, culminating in the presentation by the British Foreign Office of the Curzon ultimatum. The impression of imminent crisis was further reinforced by Marshal Foch's state visit to Poland and the assassination of the Soviet delegate to the Lausanne Conference, Vatslav Vorovsky. "What the most irreconcilable sections of international imperialism are now planning," wrote Zinoviev on May 16, "is nothing less than a new campaign against the Russian Revolution."[97] The effect of these events was to increase the emphasis of the Bolsheviks on the possibilities of revolution in Germany.[98] How was this revolution to be accomplished? Where were its partisans to be found? Karl Radek suggested an answer at the Enlarged Executive of June 12–23, when he pointed out the revolutionary potential of German nationalism. Not content to limit himself to the drab style of his fellow delegates, the flamboyant Bolshevik leader went on to dramatize his point in terms that would later cause a great commotion throughout the Communist world. Commenting on Klara Zetkin's report on fascism, Radek referred to Albert Schlageter, a German nationalist shot by the French for sabotage, as "the brave soldier of the counterrevolution" and "the wanderer into nothingness." It was now up to Schlageter's comrades, said Radek, to decide whether they wished to join the capitalists of the Entente, who were trying to enslave the German and Russian peoples, or the Communists, who were fighting for their liberation.[99]

The objective of the so-called Schlageter line was not an alliance between German fascism and Communism, but rather the conversion to Communism of those middle-class elements—officers, government officials, intellectuals, and freebooters—who had thus far been attracted by the nationalist program. In their propaganda the Communists emphasized that they alone could save Germany from Entente imperialism and the greed of German capitalists who gambled with the Fatherland's existence.[100] That the KPD had no intention of yielding to right-wing extremism was shown on July 19, when the Zentrale of the German party announced plans for demonstrations against fascism on July 29. This proclamation marked the initiation of a new activist policy on the part of the KPD leadership. During the first ten days of August, it seemed as if the German party might benefit from the rising tide of indignation against the failure of the government to check inflation. Attempts were made to turn the strike of August 10 against the Cuno government into a general strike that might lead to the formation of a "workers' and peasants' government." What hopes the Communists might have had for revolution, however, were dashed when Cuno fell and was replaced, on August 13, by Gustav Stresemann, whose policy was union between the Center and the Social Democrats and accommodation with the Entente.

The German revolution was over, "stillborn," as a recent author has called it. But the Bolshevik leaders, who gathered in Moscow on August 23 to discuss the meaning of recent events in Germany, drew a very different conclusion. They were convinced that the long-awaited crisis was approaching, and after consultations with Radek and Brandler, they decided to support the revolution with all the resources at their command.[101] The next five weeks were devoted to preparations. A special conference of the Russian, German, French, Czech, Polish, and Bulgarian parties was called in Moscow by the Executive, and met during September and the first week of October. Cachin, Treint, Sellier, and Souvarine represented the PCF. No stenographic account of this meeting was ever published—and with good reason. For the first time in the history of the Comintern, the Communists plotted revolution instead of analyzing past mistakes or issuing propaganda slogans.[102] The main subject of discussion seems to have been the date. Trotsky suggested that the insurrection be set for November 9; Brandler, whose common sense had been shaken but not destroyed altogether by the optimism of the Bolshevik leaders, demurred. Finally, it was decided that the insurrection would take place in the next four, five, or six weeks, with the responsibility for the ultimate decision being left in the hands of the German leadership.[103] The Communists would begin their move by entering the Social Democratic governments of Saxony and Thuringia. These workers' and peasants' governments would serve as the basis for revolutionary operations throughout Germany. News of the failure of insurrection in Bulgaria on September 23 sobered Brandler and Radek, but did nothing to cool the enthusiasm of Zinoviev or Trotsky.[104] Armed with his instructions and the best wishes of Trotsky, Brandler left Moscow at the beginning of October to take up his new ministerial post in Zeigner's Saxon government.

Meanwhile, the campaign for the German revolution was not going well in France. The PCF's opening manifestos in August had been met with a "conspiracy of silence."[105] Moreover, the KPD's appeal to national sentiment had sown confusion and doubt in the ranks of the party and the CGTU. To those who had followed the evolution of the Comintern since 1922, it was obvious that the Schlageter policy was the concrete application of Bukharin's declarations at the Fourth World Congress; the International was now "big enough" to conclude an alliance with a nationalist bourgeoisie, just as the Soviet regime was "big enough" to sign a pact with one bourgeois State against another. From here it was but one short step to the fear that the German revolution might be carried out to the rallying cry of a patriotic war of liberation against France as the symbol of the Treaty of Versailles. The French Communist press did nothing to put these suspicions to rest. Treint's contribution would have done justice to Zinoviev. There was a great danger, he admitted, that the KPD might be contaminated by nationalism. All doctors who fight a disease run the risk of catching it. But was that any reason for the doctor to shut himself away in his office while the epidemic raged outside?[106] Manuilsky scoffed at the "primitive a-nationalism" of the PCF, and suggested that the struggle of the German people against the occupation of the Ruhr might turn into a just national war, which the entire international working class would be obliged to support.[107] Rosmer denied that the German Communists were cooperating with the nationalists, but added significantly that for the Communists, in any case, "the proletarian State, the Republic of workers and peasants" was the *patrie*.[108] Here was material and more for any malicious opponent. Both the Socialists and the Dissidents leaped to the bait, launching press campaigns in which they accused Radek of calling for a nationalist-Communist war against the Versailles Peace Treaty.[109] As Paul Faure explained it on September 28, there were at the present time two threats to world peace: Radek and Poincaré.[110]

Humbert-Droz saw the harmful effects of the Socialist campaign on the morale of the party, and did what he could to refute the assertions being made by Grumbach, Faure, and Frossard. On September 17, he began a campaign in L'Humanité under the title "The Revolution is Peace," in which he argued that Poincaré was using the Socialists in order to weaken the support for the German revolution in France and thus prepare the way for a policy of aggression. A German revolutionary government, he insisted, would accept the Treaty of Versailles, just as the Soviets had done in the case of the Treaty of Brest-Litovsk.[111] The working class, however, was not convinced. Nor, for that matter, was the leadership of the PCF itself. The party leaders, Humbert-Droz wrote to Zinoviev on September 6, could understand the necessity of defending the *patrie révolutionnaire*; but they could not see why the *patrie* had to be defended when it was still governed by the bourgeoisie and had not yet become *révolutionnaire*.[112] On September 29, the Comintern agent again emphasized the hesitations of the French. The BP, he reported, had recently had to postpone its scheduled day of agitation for the German proletariat and a projected loan because it feared a weak response. "You will understand the extent of the danger that the KPD's strategy has provoked when you learn, for example, that Monatte was convinced that the German party was treading the same path as the Socialists in 1914!"[113]

The return of Cachin, Treint, and Sellier from Moscow dispelled any doubts the leadership might have had about an alliance between German nationalism and the KPD.[114] Rosmer, who as Secretary of L'Humanité was in a position to know, claims that the reports the delegates brought back were so contradictory and divergent "that it was impossible to know exactly what had happened in Moscow and what had been decided."[115] If so, uncertainty did not prevent enthusiasm. Cachin, the first to arrive, informed an assembly of the Federation of the Seine that the German revolution was now inevitable. "Every Communist must from this day on consider himself MOBILIZED in the service of the German revolution, and hold himself ready to act by any means, whatever it might be."[116] These orders were repeated in greater detail to some 200 provincial delegates during a closed session of the National Council on October 14. Both the National Committee of the Jeunesses Communistes and the Bureau of the CGTU threatened to unleash a general strike if Poincaré moved to crush the German revolution.[117] No one gave the impression of greater determination than the leaders of the CGTU. Reporting from Germany on October 26, Monmousseau declared that the CGTU had concluded a "pact of alliance" with the German revolution. "The French proletariat," he said, "will intervene when necessary."[118]

All this was magnificent, but hollow. In the unlikely case that Poincaré had acted to smother a nascent German revolution, the French Communists could have done nothing to stop him. In contrast with 1914 and 1921, certain concrete measures had been taken. Moscow had provided an emergency fund with which to purchase a radio transmitter and launch the PCF's evening daily, *L'Internationale,* which had been forced to close up shop in 1922 for want of readers.[119] After talks with Vujović, who had passed through Paris in late September, Vaillant-Couturier, Tommasi, and Doriot had taken steps to intensify the demoralization and subversion of the Army of Occupation.[120] If the reaction of the government and the army is any gauge, this activity was not without effect.[j] But it was one thing to annoy the government, another to paralyze it. Vaillant-Couturier himself admitted on October 26 that despite the agitation of the PCF, it would be false to say that the great majority of troops in the Ruhr were favorable to Communism.[121] That was the Communist way of admitting that the struggle for the Army of Occupation had been lost. Moreover, for all the thought given to organization, the party was less able than ever to withstand a serious attack by the government. In the event of a crisis, reported Humbert-Droz on October 5, all the authorities need do is arrest a hundred leading militants and the party and the CGTU would be paralyzed.[122] The situation was even worse than Humbert-Droz indicated.

---

[j] On November 17, 1923, General Degoutte issued an order calling on his staff to "follow the movements of the Communist Party very closely, and as soon as possible put it in a position where it can do no harm. You will take advantage of every opportunity to arrest the ringleaders." (Quoted in André Marty, *Le Procès de Mayence,* 1924, p. 12.) The orders were rapidly put into effect. Within the month there were 135 arrests, including that of Robert Lozeray, the delegate of the Federation of Young Communists. The defendants were tried the next June at Mayence. Lozeray was convicted and sentenced to ten years in prison. Two of his comrades, Mahmoud Ben Lekhol and Albert Lemire, received five and two years, respectively. They were released, however, soon afterward. See André Ferrat, *Histoire du Parti Communiste Français* (1931), pp. 137–38; Gérard Walter, *Histoire du Parti Communiste Français* (1948), I, 100–101; *La Révolution Prolétarienne,* July 1925, pp. 19–26; and Marty, *Le Procès de Mayence,* pp. 14–15.

The CGTU was already paralyzed: the Besnard minority did not consider the situation revolutionary, and the anarchists opposed any revolution that would be connected with the Soviet regime. Small wonder that despite Monmousseau's threats, nothing concrete had been done to prepare for a general strike.[123]

As it turned out, it was of purely academic interest whether the leaders of the PCF and CGTU were capable of effective action against the government. They had no masses to follow them. The French workers, even those normally sympathetic to Communist appeals, watched the PCF's campaign in favor of the German revolution with bored indifference. *L'Humanité*'s circulation fell because of constant emphasis on events in Germany, and meetings featuring the party's best speakers were sparsely attended.[124] "Public opinion and working-class opinion," confessed Humbert-Droz to Zinoviev on October 5, "is far from realizing the seriousness of the situation in Germany, and the responsibilities that weigh on the proletarians of France."[125] Three weeks later, on the supposed eve of great struggles in Germany, the picture had not improved. "Comrades returning from the provinces make pessimistic reports: sparse and unsympathetic audiences! Attention is still concentrated on questions of domestic politics."[126]

The Communist campaign did not convince the French working class of the imminence or importance of the German revolution; one wonders whether it convinced the Communist leaders themselves. The militants of the CGTU were the most committed to the revolution; they seem to have been the most shaken by its failure. Among the Communist leadership there was more than one skeptic. Rosmer has left an interesting account of the difficulties of making up *L'Humanité* during this hectic month of October:

If, acting on a precise bit of information, we maintained a reserved tone about the preparation of the movement, irritated protests assailed us: Germany was on the eve of revolution; the French Communists must be kept in a state of alert! Articles in the *Bulletin Communiste* were entitled: "On the threshold of the German revolution," "The proletarian revolution is in sight." But we couldn't write that every day when we had no other fact, no other sign announcing the revolution, than the entry of three Communists into the cabinet of the left-wing Socialist Zeigner. Finally, after having announced the revolution, it was necessary to record the terribly laconic dispatch saying that the "workers' government" had collapsed without struggle and that the Reichswehr had entered Dresden, brass bands playing.[127]

Zeigner's government fell on October 21, after a conference of workers' organizations meeting at Chemnitz had refused to agree to Brandler's request that they declare a general strike and oppose General Müller's entry into Dresden.[128] It was weeks, however, before the French Communists realized that the German revolution had ended without ever having really begun. Their incomprehension was understandable. The Germans and Russians themselves were not sure whether the insurrection had been stopped or only halted temporarily.[129] Monmousseau and Richetta, who had witnessed the events in Chemnitz, came back from Germany convinced that the revolution was already under way. "The first attack of the Reichswehr against the [proletarian] hundreds," Monmousseau wrote on October 24, "will be the signal for civil war. Perhaps it has broken out at this very moment, so unstable is the situation."[130] The next day the CD appealed to Socialist workers to form joint Action Committees with the Communists over the heads of their leaders. "Civil war," the CD cried, "is imminent, the proletarian revolution inevitable!"[131] L'Internationale reappeared on November 7 (in time for the anniversary of the October Revolution and in anticipation of the scheduled German insurrection), and immediately devoted itself to events in Germany and life in the army. Vaillant-Couturier, its editor, had little to write about, for the newspaper's purpose had vanished two weeks before in the dust of General Müller's advancing army. Finally, the bitter task could no longer be postponed. On November 12, the CD issued an official statement on the civil war in Germany, in which it blamed the temporary setback on the betrayal of the Left Social Democrats and approved fully the KPD's strategy of retreating rather than provoking an insurrection. The German party, the text read, "has had the courage to decide on a retreat, thus saving all revolutionary hopes."[132]

No further official interpretation of the failure of the German revolution was ever given, because the party's leaders did not know what to say. The KPD's retreat had left behind confusion and disappointment. "Many comrades don't understand anything that is going on," Humbert-Droz reported to Zinoviev on November 23. To the French the situation seemed to be revolutionary; they did not understand the reasons for the German retreat.[133] On December 8, the Comintern's agent added that the campaign on behalf of the German revolution had been stopped because of the lack of precise information. Everyone here, he said, understood the reasons for the retreat; but no one comprehended "the casualness with which this action had been planned." The French militants, he continued, had lost their confidence in the KPD because of what they considered a policy of bluff. It was obvious that it would be difficult to restore that confidence. Moreover, the policy followed by the German party in the Saxon government had called forth a new offensive against the united front. The adversaries of the united front had taken up their own cry: "With the mass, but not with the leaders!" Humbert-Droz concluded with a plea for some kind of directive from the International.[134] That was precisely what he could not get. For the Russian leaders themselves were undecided; and it was not until 1924 that the full implications of the German defeat would be drawn.

### THE RUSSIFICATION OF MONMOUSSEAU

Despite the inglorious finale of the campaign for the German revolution, the year 1923 marked a giant step forward in the development of the French Communist Party. Not only had its militants proved their mettle and their dedication to the proletariat by their struggle against the occupation of the Ruhr; not only had it proceeded with the centralization of its apparatus; but, most important of all for the future of the Communist movement in France, the party had at last succeeded in bringing into its ruling group the revolutionary syndicalists of *La Vie Ouvrière*. The mere recitation of events may conceal the fact that the battles of 1923 were fought jointly by the party and the CGTU. Both syndicalists and Communists had gone to Essen. Both syndicalists and Communists had been struck by the government's repression.[k] In October it had been difficult to tell who was leading whom in the preparations for the defense of the German revolution. The symbol of this rapprochement between the Communists and syndicalists was Monatte's long-awaited decision to lend the party the prestige of his name and his reputation. For Trotsky, Monatte's act of joining was the justification of the policy the Bolsheviks had followed at the Fourth Congress.[135] More significant, however, from the point of view of future events was the development of the Monmousseau-Sémard group. In committing themselves to Communism, they gave the party control of the CGTU.

Monmousseau, Sémard, Dudilieux, and Berrar had gone to Moscow in November 1922 as the defenders of the traditional ideas of French syndicalism.[l] They came back Leninists. The change was not immediately detectable. On returning to Paris, Monmousseau defined the terms of the CGTU's membership in the Profintern in a formula that any French syndicalist could accept: "No organic liaison either below or above, but below as above, the possibility of mutual agreements between revolutionary forces, agreements dictated by circumstances and given concrete form by Action Committees, which will be constituted every time circumstances necessitate it, every time the defense of proletarian interests requires it."[136] Such committees were not new; they had been formed with greater or lesser frequency ever since 1914. But what began as a temporary cooperation within an Action Committee formed for a specific purpose soon turned into permanent collaboration between the CGTU leadership and the BP of the Communist Party.[m] Whether this development was the result of Lenin's persuasiveness, the atmosphere of crisis created by the occupation of the Ruhr and the later prospect of a German revolution, or sheer Machiavellianism is a question that cannot be answered here. What matters, in any case, is the result, and not the motivation. Close associates of Mon-

---

[k] Among those arrested during 1923 were Cachin, Treint, Marrane, Gourdeaux, Hueber, Ker, and Vandeputte for the party; Monmousseau, Lartigue, Piétri, Cazals, and Massot for the CGTU; and Doriot, Péri, and Féguy for the Jeunesses Communistes.
[l] See p. 301 above.
[m] As early as April, Humbert-Droz suggested to Cachin that all important decisions be taken in conjunction with the leadership of the CGTU. Humbert-Droz to Cachin, 2.iv.23. (HDA.)

mousseau observed that he and his friends had returned to France convinced of the superiority of the Communist Party over the syndicalist movement. As Benoît Broutchoux put it bitterly, the French delegates "had got themselves naturalized as Muscovites and were more Russian than the Russians."[137]

Coalitions seem made to be broken. The coalition of revolutionary syndicalists assembled at Orléans in 1920 had split over the question of the development of the Russian Revolution. The coalition formed at St.-Etienne now splintered over the attempt of Monmousseau and Sémard to tie the CGTU to the coattails of the party. Disagreements had arisen at the Santé during the spring of 1923 between Cazals and Monmousseau over the make-up of the Action Committee against the occupation of the Ruhr. Cazals wanted the committee open to all revolutionary forces. Monmousseau and Sémard, following the Comintern's orders, insisted on keeping the Anarchists and Resistants out.[138] The struggle was carried on simultaneously on another ground. On March 23, Broutchoux presented a motion to the Executive Committee of the CGTU that condemned the syndicalist commissions of the party as an attempt to subordinate the union movement. Louis Clavel replied with a resolution observing that the Executive Committee had no business interfering in the affairs of the PCF. Clavel's text was accepted by a vote of 12–6. At this point a minority, led by Cazals, Marie Guillot, and Broutchoux, crystallized within the CGTU on the question of the party's syndicalist policy.[139]

The minority was right in sensing a danger, but they had picked the wrong target. The syndicalist commissions existed only on paper.* The real problem was that the syndicalists of *La Vie Ouvrière* had subordinated themselves to the Comintern. The question of the syndicalist commissions came before the CGTU once again in July, during the meeting of the National Confederal Committee (CCN). In a manifesto published on June 30, the party had demanded the right, along with the anarchists and anarcho-syndicalists, to organize a faction within the unions for the purpose of spreading Communist ideas.[140] The *Vie Ouvrière* group supported this demand in a statement reaffirming loyalty to the Russian Revolution and refusing to deny an outside group the right to influence the unions. "It is not up to the editorial committee of the *VO*," the declaration read, "to judge the means by which a political or syndicalist group spreads or wants to spread its ideas in the syndicalist movement."[141] This supposed attitude of neutrality toward political organizations bent on capturing the unions concealed a radical new departure in the attitude of the CGTU majority. Sémard confessed as much in August, when he asked "Is syndicalism above parties?" and answered negatively by pointing out that the Russian Revolution had rendered the Charter of Amiens obsolete. The French revolutionary syndicalists, he said, could not hold themselves aloof

* See p. 381 below.

from an international movement which had carried out a proletarian revolution in Russia and which constituted the revolutionary opposition in Germany, Poland, Czechoslovakia, Finland, and Bulgaria.[142] The Guillot-Cazals group, however, was not convinced. It was satisfied with the CGTU's membership in the Profintern, but opposed the party's penetration of the unions through its syndicalist commissions. When its motion condemning these commissions was once more rejected by the CCN on July 27, the minority resigned from both the Executive Committee and the Bureau and demanded the calling of a congress. Under the threat of schism, the majority agreed.[143]

The Congress of Bourges, which met from November 12 to 17, 1923, marked an overwhelming victory for the Monmousseau group and thus, indirectly, for the party. Three factions clashed: the anarchists, concentrated in the building trades, who wanted a pure and simple retreat from the Profintern and the affirmation of the Charter of Amiens; the Guillot-Cazals-Lartigue group, who while accepting membership in the Profintern condemned the syndicalist commissions of the party and the Action Committees; and finally the majority, assembled around *La Vie Ouvrière,* who under the guise of neutrality defended the right of the Communists to win the unions to their views, arguing that the experience of the Ruhr had demonstrated that the PCF had changed and was no longer a group of politicians. Inevitably, the two branches of the minority tended to merge: their speakers accused the majority of having subjugated the union movement to the party, and furthermore of having pursued a policy of bluff with respect to the German revolution.

Both charges were correct, and had the mass of CGTU members been given their choice, it is possible that they would have opted for the proposal of the Lartigue faction for membership in the Profintern without subordination to the party. The issue, however, never presented itself in these terms, for Lartigue's group was discredited by the support of the anarchists, who went so far as to assert that should the Communists try to monopolize the German revolution, they would find the anarchists on the other side of the barricades. This left Monmousseau and his friends to play the card of loyalty to the Russian and German revolutions. Lozovsky's message, read by Monmousseau amidst murmurs and exclamations, put it bluntly but effectively. Instead of aiding the German proletariat effectively, he wrote, the CGTU had "demoralized and discouraged the French working masses by interminable discussions and quibbling about the Charter of Amiens, with respect to Paragraph 11 of the statutes of the RILU [Profintern], by articles and speeches on the danger of the Communist Party's syndicalist commissions, and by repeating ad infinitum the words 'autonomy and independence.' "[144] This stern language attained its objective. Despite the ritual references to the demagoguery and reformism of the Communist Party, Sémard's resolution, rejecting that interpretation of the Charter of Amiens that the syndicalist movement was closed to other political and philosophical groups, was voted by a huge majority.[145] "You have consciously voted for subordinating syndicalism to the party," the partisans of the Guillot-Lartigue motion replied.[146] The new Bureau was composed of Monmousseau, Edouard Dudilieux, Jules Racamond, and Berrar, all Muscovites.

The conversion of the CGTU's leadership was not the only Communist victory of 1923. In July both the Association Républicaine des Anciens Combattants and the Fédération Sportive du Travail were captured by the party.[o] Earlier Henri Barbusse had taken out a card in the PCF to great fanfare: his adherence presaged later Communist successes in attracting intellectuals. For the moment, however, these triumphs were of minor significance compared to the change in the attitude of the Monmousseau-Sémard group. After the Congress of Bourges, the leadership of the CGTU drew ever closer to Moscow.[p] In 1924 Monmousseau and Sémard entered the party's Bureau Politique. By January 1925, Sémard was willing to call the CGTU's doctrine "syndical Leninism." Lenin, he wrote, had not only taught the French syndicalists the role of the unions, he had also shown them "the indispensable necessity of a doctrinal group with iron discipline, the vanguard of the proletariat—the Communist Party."[147] The ties between the party and the CGTU were made public in 1926; and three years later Marcel Cachin would represent the PCF at a congress of the CGTU and hear his party officially recognized as the "avant-garde dirigeante du mouvement ouvrier."[148]

The conversion of the CGTU's leadership to Communism had an unexpected result. Instead of conquering the CGTU, as the Bolsheviks demanded, the party was itself conquered.[q] Beginning in the spring of 1923, Monmousseau and Sémard began to take a more and more active role in the affairs of the

---

[o] For the ARAC, see *L'Humanité*, 6.viii.23. At the ARAC's Congress of Clermont-Ferrand in July, André Marty, Barbusse, Guy Jerram, Georges Lévy, Treint, and Vaillant-Couturier became members of the new Central Committee. For the FST, see *Le Populaire*, 24.vii.23.

[p] The revolutionary implications of the new policy, however, were by no means clear to all revolutionary syndicalists, including those who were highly placed. Adolphe Herclet, the CGTU's first permanent delegate to Moscow, defended syndicalist autonomy with traditional fervor at the meetings of the Profintern's Central Council in June 1923. *Otchet o rabotakh III sessii Tsentralnogo Soveta K.I.P. 25 iyunia–2 iyulia 1923 g.* (Moscow, 1923), pp. 11, 19. In his report to the CGTU of October 8, 1923, Herclet insisted that the statutes and decisions of the Profintern were being respected in both their letter and their spirit. There were no other ties between the Comintern and the Profintern, he wrote, except for the international Action Committee, where delegates of the two organizations met in equal numbers and on equal terms. But Herclet himself noted, a few lines later, that the Comintern and Profintern followed the same policies, and that this obviously proceeded from the fact that the great majority of the members of the Executive Bureau of the Profintern were Communists and also members of the Comintern. Later Herclet himself became a full-fledged Leninist. There is a copy of his report in the Monatte Archives.

[q] Humbert-Droz had warned Zinoviev against this possibility as early as March 13, 1923. (HDA.)

party. Their influence, understandably enough, was exerted in the direction of rendering the party more proletarian and less intellectual or parliamentarian. The first fruits of this pressure came at the National Council of October 14–15, when Treint submitted an amendment barring any party official or journalist who was not already a deputy from running for office in the coming elections. After a long discussion, Treint's proposition passed with only three votes short of unanimity.[149] Treint later explained that "some dramatic gesture was necessary to do away with the feeling among the masses that the leaders of the party were interested only in getting elected."[150] More specifically, it was necessary to placate Monmousseau, who wanted concrete evidence for his argument that the party had changed.[151]

The ironic logic of these changes should not be allowed to slip by unnoticed. In October 1922, Monmousseau had argued that the revolutionary syndicalists should not take sides in the internal disagreements of the Communist Party. In July 1923, he and Sémard had defended the right of the party to penetrate the unions with its ideas, arguing that the syndicalist movement was open to all factions. By January 1924, Monmousseau was willing to draw the implications of his argument. Writing in *La Vie Ouvrière,* he defended the CGTU leadership against those who criticized it for interfering in the internal affairs of the Communist Party. The confederal leadership, he urged, had an obligation to search out the reformists in the party since those same tendencies reflected themselves in the syndicalist movement.[152] In other words, if the Communists were free to influence the syndicalist movement, then the syndicalists themselves must watch over the ideological purity of the party. It was on the basis of these arguments that the leadership of the CGTU was to play an active role in the party struggle of 1924.

### THE FRENCH NEW COURSE

Meanwhile, the situation within the party had deteriorated. The crisis of overcentralization and bureaucratization, exposed and condemned by Humbert-Droz in his letters of the summer, received no solution at the September-October meeting of the Executive. During the month of October, in an attempt to curb Treint's dictatorship, the delegate of the Comintern had suggested that the Secretariat of the party be divided into two bureaus, with Treint in charge of political affairs and Sellier responsible for organization. By December it was clear that this division of labor had not helped: Treint was everywhere and insisted on having a hand in everything. Though Sellier was supposedly responsible for relations between the Center and the federations, Treint was able to control them through his manipulation of the regional delegates, who exercised their own dictatorship over the federal secretaries. The Federation of the Seine continued to turn in upon itself and refuse new members, even though the moment was propitious for recruitment. When criticized by the BP and Humbert-Droz, its secretary, Suzanne Girault, could call on Treint for support. The party tended more and more to become a sect and lose all influence on the masses. Confronted with this fact, Treint transformed it into a theory. The party, he claimed, must choose between winning the organized proletarian elite of the CGTU and appealing to the broad working masses. Treint's sectarian position was sustained by Monmousseau. A Treint-Monmousseau-Girault bloc seemed in the making. On November 23, 1923, Humbert-Droz wrote Moscow that a new secretary must be found: anyone, he urged, would be better than Treint.[153]

The stormy atmosphere in the party's leadership was further charged by Souvarine's return in November. While they were both in Moscow in September, relations between Souvarine and Treint had degenerated to the point where they no longer spoke to each other. In October, Humbert-Droz had communicated to the Executive Rosmer's fears about the turn affairs would take when the two men returned to France. "I believe I know them well enough," he wrote, "to agree with Rosmer that neither one will abandon his feuding in the interest of the party and its activities."[154] These fears proved justified. At the first meeting of the BP that he attended, Souvarine lashed out at Cachin and Rosmer for their direction of L'Humanité, then at Treint for the strategy and policy of the party as a whole. When the BP refused to give him Dunois' position as director of the party's publications and insisted that he take Vaillant-Couturier's place as Editor of L'Internationale, he stalked out of the meeting, slamming the door behind him. Despite the efforts of Humbert-Droz to intervene (the delegate of the International scolded him for acting like "a young intellectual who only wants to do what he pleases"), Souvarine maintained his opposition and threatened to take his differences with Treint before the party at the approaching congress, which, it had been decided, would be held in January at Lyon.[155]

Souvarine's opposition might have done more to consolidate Treint's position than to weaken him, if it were not for the fact that it coincided with general resentment of Treint's methods felt on all levels of the party. Humbert-Droz warned the Executive in a report written on December 8, 1923, that a Souvarine-Renoult-Jean bloc might coalesce during the congress, based on a common hostility to Treint's policy of overcentralization, the sectarianism of the Federation of the Seine, and Treint's concept of the united front. In an effort to forestall a possible conflict, Humbert-Droz appealed to Moscow to intervene, and recommended that the International (1) come out against the methods of organization being used by the Federation of the Seine; (2) request the party to revoke Treint's electoral amendment; (3) give an interpretation of the Workers' and Peasants' Bloc; (4) change the leadership of the Federation of the Seine; (5) eliminate the dual secretaryship and find a new Secretary; and (6) call Treint to Moscow after the congress.[156]

Treint was not unaware of the attitude of Humbert-Droz; he must have imagined the tenor of the reports that were being sent to the Executive, even if he did not see them. Nor did Treint intend to give up the Secretariat without a struggle. In mid-December he wrote to the Executive, complaining of the policy of the delegates of the International (Rákosi had recently joined his Swiss colleague) and arguing that it was not he alone who was responsible for the malfunctioning of the party's apparatus, but the BP as a whole. Treint's defense was that he and a few other comrades had heroically taken upon themselves the work the BP had no time to accomplish.[157] For the moment, however, the Executive turned a deaf ear to Treint's protests, and he was left alone to meet the mounting wave of criticism his leadership had inspired.

The last week of December showed that Treint's prospects were not good. Rákosi and Humbert-Droz complained of the haphazard way in which the congress was being organized, and demanded that Treint clarify the issues confronting the party; Souvarine stood ready to mount a full-fledged offensive; and the debates at the Federation of the Seine brought home to Treint that the French delegate to the Executive was no isolated malcontent.[158] Obviously, some sort of reckoning could not be avoided. Should he attack or retreat? The former army captain found his solution in the precedent of the Russian party's self-examination, which had been initiated by Zinoviev two months earlier.[r] On January 3, Treint opened a discussion of the PCF's problems in the pages of *L'Humanité*. His call to debate was the epitome of hypocrisy. "Formerly in the party, there was a lot of talk and little work. Today, there is a lot of work, but not enough discussion. True, this ill is less serious than the first. But it is an ill nevertheless."[159]

It was a strange discussion. With the exception of Souvarine, the party leaders kept silent and allowed militants of the second rank to have their say. Their articles showed that Humbert-Droz's reports had not been unfair or overpessimistic. The party was overcentralized. The BP had usurped the functions of the CD. On the pretext of maintaining discipline, all discussion at the lower levels had been eliminated. The sections, barred from participating in the resolution of political questions, had become absorbed with purely administrative matters.[160] The party was in disarray. Deluged with administrative lectures during the year, it had suddenly been presented with a flood of reports and circulars on the Congress of Lyon, which it was supposed to digest and approve or disapprove in the course of two or three meetings.[161] Despite the victory at Bourges, the party's prestige among the proletariat as a whole was still slight.[162]

In anticipation of such criticisms, Treint included in his political report for the Congress of Lyon a section pointing to the dangers of overcentralization,

[r] See p. 362 below.

passivity, and sectarianism.[163] He still, however, refused to accept personal responsibility for the development of "military centralism"; and, while admitting the inadequacies of the party during the previous year, he took advantage of the opportunity to flay the editors of *L'Humanité* for their lack of political perspective and their failure to anticipate the development of the German situation. This *autocritique* took some of the edge off Souvarine's assault, printed in the same issue of the *Bulletin Communiste,* in which he held Treint personally responsible for the ills of the party. But it did nothing to satisfy Humbert-Droz, who was more than ever convinced that Treint must be replaced by a new Secretary. Humbert-Droz was disgusted by Treint's political dishonesty, and he accused him of trying to keep his position at any cost. "If this *autocritique* was sincere," wrote Humbert-Droz, "and if Treint was really convinced of the bad influence of his methods, everything would be fine, but this only creates new confusion. *On se bat actuellement dans la nuit.* Treint, who has made a political retreat with the purpose of maintaining himself in the leadership, continually feels on the defensive, and the tone of discussions about trivial matters takes on an aggressive and hostile note that is very dangerous. Treint sees every member of the BP who does not agree with him as a personal enemy."[164]

### THE CONGRESS OF LYON

The party congress met at Lyon on January 20–23, 1924. A storm cloud hung over the assembly; and its origin was not Moscow, but Paris, where a clash between Communists and anarchists had taken place at the Grange-aux-Belles on January 11. Two workers had been killed and several others wounded.[165] For weeks it was feared that the incident might lead to the split of the CGTU and the creation of a rival anarchist organization. The situation was grave enough to occasion an unscheduled trip to France by Lozovsky, who attended the congress discreetly and without the fanfare of his earlier performance at St.-Etienne.[166]

The Congress of Lyon marked the point of transition between the tumultuous congresses of the 1914–22 period and the more boring and perfunctory assemblies of the late 1920's and the 1930's. Despite the fears of Humbert-Droz, the basic issues dividing the leadership were settled successfully in the meetings of the CD that preceded the congress and were never brought before the rank and file. A political commission of 40 members was chosen to judge the party's past performance and chart its future course. The first day was devoted to greetings from foreign parties. On the second day a message was read from Zinoviev, in the name of the ECCI. Zinoviev's communication concentrated heavily on the coming elections and the proper interpretation of the Workers' and Peasants' Bloc. For the Communist Party, Zinoviev explained, the Bloc des Gauches was on the same level as the Bloc National. Thus, the policy of the party would be "resolute and unrelenting war against the Bloc des Gauches and the Bloc National; no concessions, no compromises."[167] Every worker must understand this basic truth, that "whoever is with the Bloc des Gauches is against the working class." Zinoviev followed the advice given by Humbert-Droz and ruled that all agreements with other parties must be dependent on two conditions: their rupture with the bourgeois Left and their willingness to make such agreements national rather than local. Whatever the response of the Socialists, the party must go ahead to organize the Workers' and Peasants' Bloc, and the elections must be used to conquer the masses.[168] Despite this last injunction, however, and despite the repeated pleas of Humbert-Droz, the ECCI did not order the party to reject Treint's amendment forbidding the candidacies of officials and journalists who did not already hold office. This policy, Zinoviev emphasized, was "certainly correct." A CD composed of non-deputies would be more capable of controlling the parliamentary Group.[169] Thus, the party was given the impossible task of winning the masses with a sectarian tactic.

After remarking that the party must intensify its anti-militarist propaganda and anti-colonialist agitation, Zinoviev went on to the subject of the party's internal organization. The sections, he noted, were not nearly active enough. The source of this stagnation, however, lay neither in Treint's methods nor in the overcentralization of the party, but in the party's structure. According to Zinoviev, the party could not be effective until factory cells were created. "The revitalizing of the party," concluded the message, "more intense activity in the sections, the gradual creation of factory cells as the Communist Party grows—these are the organizational tasks that confront the PCF."[170]

The congress itself was more a manifestation of party unity than an assembly at which policy was debated and resolved. Treint and Souvarine joined forces to defend the resolution on candidacies. The motion, passed with only one negative vote, said that the party would present proletarian candidates whenever possible, that the present deputies who belonged to the CD would run again, and that in all doubtful cases the CD would decide. On the third day (January 22), the reports on the state of the party and its policies were discussed. Renoult attacked the sectarianism of the leadership. "We understand," he said, "that it has been necessary to confine ourselves to the work of internal organization, but today we think that we must open the window and look at what is happening outside."[171] Paul Marion, an up-and-coming militant who had taken an active part in the discussion before the congress, complained of the lack of liaison between the Center and the sections. He agreed with Zinoviev that the only way to establish a link between the party and the masses was by the creation of factory cells. At six o'clock a hush fell over the assembly when Souvarine interrupted the debate to announce that Lenin had died the day before.

Souvarine spoke on the last day. By comparison with his earlier articles and statements, he was the soul of moderation. Evidently he felt that he had obtained full satisfaction from the CD and that there was no need to drag Treint's corpse before the congress. In an unusual conciliatory gesture, he even went so far as to remind the federations that if the party suffered from overcentralization, it was partly their own fault for putting up with it. Treint defended the Secretariat against the charges of bureaucratization, and argued that the failure of the united front strategy had been the fault of *L'Humanité*. Sellier, in turn, came to the tribune to accept his share of the responsibility for the mistakes of the past year.[172]

The resolutions unanimously passed by the congress seemed to signify the triumph of Treint's critics, and especially of Souvarine. The resolution on tactics and organization blamed the leadership for the overcentralization and bureaucratization of the party; announced that the CD would henceforth exercise leadership and not the BP; and accused the leadership of sectarianism and of having misunderstood the decisions of the Third Congress, which called for mass Communist parties. The new leadership was instructed to maintain close contact with the federations, to speed the creation of factory cells, to fight for the re-establishment of syndicalist unity,[173] to convince the working class of the need for a united front (and to do this sincerely, not just by open letters but also by preparing a program of immediate reforms), and finally to steer between the two perils of electoralism and anti-parliamentary demagoguery. The resolution on *L'Humanité* admitted the mistakes of its editors, but blamed them on the lack of a clear political line from the Center. In addition, the congress passed a number of detailed resolutions, stating the tasks and goals of the party in the cooperatives, in the unions, among the peasants, in the Fédération Sportive du Travail, in the colonies, and among the children and women of France.[174] All this represented a quite impressive plan of attack for the future. Perhaps most significant was the resolution on the colonies, which affirmed the intention of the Communists to devote their efforts to the support of indigenous native nationalist movements. Up to this point, the PCF's accomplishments in this area had been practically nil.[8]

The new CD was composed of Marcel Brout, Cachin, Cordier, Jean Crémet, Dallet, Doriot, Dunois, Dupillet, Gaymann, Girault, Gourdeaux, Jacob, Jean, Marrane, Midol, Monatte, Rosmer, Sellier, Sémard, Souvarine, Tommasi, Treint, Vaillant-Couturier, and Werth from Paris; and Bazin, Maurice Boin, Cadeau, Guy Jerram, and Gabriel Péri from the provinces. On the list of alternate members from the provinces could be found the name of Maurice Thorez, a young militant from the Pas-de-Calais. This Comité Directeur went on to choose a BP consisting of Cachin, Crémet, Marrane, Rosmer, Sellier,

---

[8] See pp. 407–8 below.

Souvarine, and Tommasi. The name of Treint was absent. The Secretariat was given to Sellier, with Crémet and Marrane as his assistants. Cachin and Rosmer were kept on as Directors of *L'Humanité*. Gourdeaux was made head of the Central Syndicalist Committee. Finally, Souvarine and Treint were appointed co-delegates to the Executive.[175]

The Congress of Lyon, therefore, seemed to represent a victory for the ideas of Humbert-Droz. Both Treint and Souvarine were to be shipped off to Russia, where in the snows of Moscow they might continue their feud without damage to the party. Sellier was to be given undivided sway over the Secretariat. The Workers' and Peasants' Bloc had been defined much as Humbert-Droz had suggested that it should be. The methods, if not the personnel, of the Federation of the Seine were condemned. And the leadership had been instructed to pursue a true and not a specious united front, by drafting a program of concrete reforms. The unanimous verdict of the congress seemed to be that the party was overcentralized and that what was needed was an injection of free discussion and greater activity on the level of the sections and federations. This, it was agreed, was to be obtained through the gradual creation of factory cells. A detailed program of party policy had been worked out, which ran from agitation among the women of France to the penetration of the unions. On February 15, 1924, Souvarine commented on the results of the congress with a sense of satisfaction that suggests he considered himself the victor. "The Congress of Lyon has been unlike anything our party, either the old or the new, has ever seen. Instead of the everlasting haggling of the old days, instead of platform effects and incidents cleverly contrived by parliamentary strategists, instead of factional struggles and coalitions devised in the corridors, we have had a congress with a record of effective work and real unity."[176]

## Chapter eleven

# The Way Traced by Lenin

Merci au parti bolshevik, qui a fait de nous de
véritables révolutionnaires, qui nous a délivrés
des préjugés démocratiques, des illusions humani-
taires, des erreurs réformistes, qui a suscité par son
exemple d'autres partis à son image dans tous les
pays du monde. Nous nous efforcerons de marcher
sur ses traces, de profiter de ses enseignements,
de servir comme lui la Révolution. Nous sommes
fiers d'appartenir au même parti mondial. Nous
n'avons d'autre orgeuil que celui d'avoir sa confiance, d'autre ambition que celle de nous en
montrer dignes.
—*Boris Souvarine, March 1923*

The struggle for power within the Russian Communist Party burst forth from
the bounds of the Politburo and was dragged before the International in the
first few months of 1924. Out of fear that their critics might find allies in
other Communist parties, perhaps in part out of a sense of ideological com-
pleteness, the Bolshevik majority insisted that the International join in the
condemnation of the Opposition. Foreign Communists, no matter how much
they might have wished to abstain from commitment, were not allowed to remain neutral. Ambassadors of the Russian majority were sent throughout the
world to obtain condemnations of Trotsky and his fellow oppositionists. Those
Communist leaders who resisted, either through considerations of integrity
or for reasons of personal loyalty, were purged and replaced by men subservient to the Russian majority. As in 1922, qualities of leadership were prized
less than reliability in the factional struggle.[a] Frequently, those elements who
resisted this process the most stubbornly were the very men who had done the
most to create the Communist parties in the immediate postwar period.

In France the eruption of the Russian conflict entangled international and
Russian issues with what had been purely local conflicts. The "Russian question" was superimposed on and confused with the "French question." Personal antagonisms were disguised under ideological differences that often had
only the most fragile basis in reality. By the fall of 1924, Treint had managed to
re-install himself as leader of the party; Souvarine had been expelled from the
International; Rosmer and Monatte had been identified as leaders of the "in-

---

[a] See p. 314 above.

ternational Right"; and the PCF had embarked on the process of corruption, self-deception, and subjection known as "bolshevization."

The method used by the Russians to obtain this result, as Boris Souvarine has written from experience, was "to dupe the naïve, neutralize the hesitant, fanaticize the mediocre, corrupt the politicians, and isolate the men who were most honest and aware."[1] But such techniques would not have sufficed had it not been for the transformation the PCF had undergone in the first three years of its existence. By February 1924, the French Communist Party was more proletarian, more centralized, and more internationalist: more proletarian from the point of view of social composition, values, and behavioral patterns; more centralized because the federations and the sections had been deprived of all sense of responsibility and initiative; more internationalist in the sense that its leaders had shown themselves willing to sacrifice the effectiveness and influence of their organization to the higher necessity of a general line dictated in Moscow, which might or might not be applicable in France. These changes made the PCF more Communist. They also made it less able to withstand the crisis that spread through the International like a cancer in the wake of Lenin's death. Precisely because the French Communist Party had already been "Leninized" in 1922 and 1923, it proved itself unable to resist "bolshevization" in 1924.

But before recounting this story of intimidation, corruption, and confusion, we must shift the focus of our study to Moscow and return to the year 1922, to sketch briefly the development of the Russian Revolution after the adoption of NEP. To proceed otherwise would be to describe the results of bolshevization without revealing its mainsprings. For better or for worse, the success of the Bolsheviks in subordinating and Russifying the European Communist parties meant that their fate was joined to the fate of the Russian party. The relationship between the PCF and the development of its mother party was not one of simple cause and effect. At more than one point, the French situation seemed to reproduce in a miniature and somewhat distorted scale what had happened in Russia. France had her "New Course," her Zinoviev, her Trotsky, her Radek, and even her "Workers' Opposition." Lurking in the background were several young candidates for the role of the French Stalin. Moreover, the reasons for the failure of the French Opposition closely paralleled the reasons for the failure of the Opposition in Russia. Thus both the dictates of historical analysis and the spur of curiosity require some attention to the situation in Russia.

### THE RUSSIAN THERMIDOR

It was the peculiarity of the Russian Revolution, as well as a testimony to the genius of Lenin, that the Bolsheviks succeeded in avoiding the fate of Thermidor by executing their own retreat before it was too late.[2] However, implicit in this tactical maneuver, made possible only by the iron discipline of the party, was a dilemma: the Bolsheviks saved the proletarian Revolution only by halting their advance toward Communism and by making concessions to the peasantry, that class which Marx identified with reaction and "rural idiocy." Concrete manifestations of this dilemma did not fail to appear in 1922 and 1923. The peasantry appeared to have emerged as the chief beneficiary of the Revolution, while the proletariat both declined in numbers and lost its distinctive character.[3] There was the danger, as Maxim Gorki confided to André Morizet during the summer of 1921, that "the immense peasant tide will end by engulfing everything."[4] The recovery of heavy industry lagged. By 1923 many members of the old intelligentsia had made their peace with the regime, and had returned to reclaim their former positions in the administration and society. Despite the repeated denials of its leaders, the Bolshevik Revolution seemed to have entered upon what Crane Brinton has called the period of "convalescence from the fever of revolution."[5]

The Bolsheviks themselves recognized that the difficulties of their position derived from the fact that they had seized power in a backward country that did not fit the Marxist model. Lenin and Trotsky each put it in their own characteristic language, one matter-of-fact and direct, the other cosmic and flamboyant. The Bolsheviks, said the former, had achieved only the political half of Socialism; the economic basis was still to be created.[6] "History," wrote the latter, "as always, moved along the line of least resistance. The revolutionary epoch burst upon us through the least barricaded door."[7] The policy of the Bolsheviks in such unfavorable circumstances could only be that of a beleaguered fortress, behind whose battered ramparts the Russian proletariat would seek to hold out until the European working class could come to its rescue.[8] But by the end of 1922, the date of that relief, seemingly so close in 1919 and 1920, had to be postponed into the indefinite future. Radek, annoyingly realistic as ever, was left to articulate what the other Bolshevik leaders preferred to leave unsaid. It was a "historical fact," he pointed out during the Fourth Congress, that the seizure of power by the proletariat did not stand as an imminent task upon the order of the day. The masses of the proletariat no longer believed in the possibility of taking power. "They have been forced on the defensive."[9]

It would be a mistake to think that the Bolsheviks gave up their hopes for European revolution. On the contrary, these hopes were revived in the fall of 1923 and burned with heightened brilliance, all the more intense for their desperation. But at the same time, there was an increasing emphasis on the possibility of creating the base for Socialism by the use of State power. The crucial year in this development was undoubtedly 1921; for it was in February 1921, as Lenin himself admitted, that the Bolsheviks realized that they had against their regime not only the great mass of the peasantry, but also a good part of the working class.[10] The answer was NEP: the Bolsheviks would abandon their front-line positions, retire to the commanding heights of industry, and attempt to create the economic and cultural basis for Socialism while waiting for revolution in the West. Orthodox Marxists like Karl Kautsky and Otto Bauer interpreted this decision as the death knell of the Soviet regime. Admitting capitalist forces into the economy, they argued, would inevitably bring about a transformation of the political superstructure. Trotsky replied that this was true enough—if NEP were to last forever. But the Bolsheviks, he stressed, were determined that it should not. They would win the struggle against capitalism and conquer the peasant market just as they had earlier won the civil war against the Whites. "Wir standen in Kampfe," Trotsky cried before the Fourth World Congress;[11] and it was precisely this spirit of activism which Western Communists admired and sought to emulate during this first stage in the life of the Third International.

If this was Thermidor, then, it was Thermidor with a twist; for the revolutionary forces had retired in good order to a new redoubt, from which they intended to carry on the struggle. However, such a sustained campaign against both the peasantry within the country and the imperialist powers without demanded a strongly disciplined and ideologically homogeneous party whose unity was assured;[12] and by 1923, this unity was subject to serious strain. In May 1922, Lenin suffered his first stroke. He recovered sufficiently in the fall and winter of 1922 to reclaim his position of leadership within the Bolshevik hierarchy. But a second stroke in December forced him to withdraw altogether from active participation in party and government affairs, though he continued to write and follow political problems from afar.

Lenin's illness opened a contest for predominance in the party and the State between the *troika* of Zinoviev, Kamenev, and Stalin on the one hand, and Trotsky on the other. It would be a mistake, as E. H. Carr has commented, to view the struggle for the succession simply as a personal struggle for power in which issues were unimportant.[13] But it would be just as misleading to assume that it was a struggle over ideological alternatives alone. Personal rivalries and policy differences were hopelessly intertwined. The conflict over planning and industrialization is an example of this confusion. Who could maintain that the Bolshevik leaders did not honestly differ over the pace and manner of industrialization? Who, though, could deny that economic differences were often subordinated to and colored by personal antagonisms? Zinoviev certainly resented Trotsky's brilliance and the fact that he had stolen the position he, Zinoviev, had coveted, that of tribune of the Revolution.[14] And Stalin very likely nurtured an antagonism against them both for their oratorical skill, their flamboyance, and their Westernism.

Still, for the moment Stalin had every reason to make common cause with Zinoviev and Kamenev: Trotsky represented the immediate danger. At the beginning of 1923 a whispering campaign was launched against the Father of the Red Army, in which he was described as a threat to the future of the Revolution. The memory of Bonaparte and Danton was evoked. It was recalled that Trotsky was not an "Old Bolshevik."[15] In the meantime, Stalin profited from the increasing bureaucratization of the revolutionary regime to carve out a position of power as General Secretary and Commissar of Nationalities. By the Twelfth Party Congress, in April 1922, he had already become the "decisive" figure within the party.[16] His meteoric and unnoticed rise had been made possible by his control of the apparatus. The pattern of dictatorship within the party organization set down by the Tenth Party Congress had developed to the point where, as the Platform of the 46 put it,[b] "beneath the external form of official unity" there was "the ever increasing, and now scarcely concealed, division of the party between a secretarial hierarchy and 'quiet folk,' between professional party officials recruited from above and the general mass of the party, which does not participate in the common life."[17]

Writing soon after Lenin's death, Trotsky defined Leninism as "above all realism, the superior qualitative and quantitative appreciation of reality from the point of view of revolutionary action." Leninism, he insisted, was incompatible with "the flight from reality."[18] Lenin's last speeches, notes, articles, and testament, written in the six months preceding his third stroke, do indeed indicate awareness of the critical stage reached by the Russian Revolution. In his brief and somewhat confused speech before the Fourth World Congress, Lenin attacked the resolution on organization passed the year before as "too Russian" and incomprehensible to a foreigner. "My impression," he said, "is that we have made a great mistake with this resolution, that we have blocked our own way to further progress."[19] In a series of notes and articles that he dictated in December 1922 and January 1923, Lenin called for a reform of the government machinery, the expansion of the Central Committee, and the replacement of the Workers' and Peasants' Inspectorate (formerly administered by Stalin) by a new control body, staffed by workers and peasants and designed to sweep away bureaucratism by subjecting the party administration to surveillance by the rank and file.[20] At the same time, Lenin entered into conflict with Stalin over his handling of the Georgian question. The proletariat, Lenin wrote in his notes on the nationalities question on December 31, 1922, must win the confidence of the nationalities either by its "behavior" or by "concessions in regard to the minorities."[21] On Christmas Day, Lenin composed his testament. Ten days later he added a postscript, in which he described Stalin as "too rude" and proposed that he be replaced as General Secretary. Lenin's distrust and dislike of Stalin turned him increasingly toward Trotsky. On March 5, 1923, he wrote urgently to Trotsky to ask him to de-

[b] See p. 362 below.

fend the Georgian case in the Central Committee against Stalin and Felix Dzerzhinsky. Trotsky was told by Lenin's secretary that he was preparing a "bombshell" against Stalin.[22]

But for all his realism and honesty, Lenin was not successful in leaving his party a testament that might have allowed it to avoid the pitfalls of Russification of the International, of bureaucratization, of Great Russian chauvinism, or even of personal dictatorship. The cause of Lenin's failure must be sought not in self-deception, but in a fundamental limitation of intellect, a narrowness of vision that was the basis of his political genius.[23] To see this one has only to return to the final documents in which he sought to deal with the problems of the Bolshevik Revolution. Lenin criticized the resolution on organization of the Third Congress not for its principles, but rather for the incomprehensible way in which these principles were stated.[24] He saw the origin of bureaucratic abuses primarily in the fact that the administration had been infiltrated by hundreds of thousands of old Tsarist functionaries, and secondarily in the economic and cultural backwardness of the country.[25] Finally, Lenin blamed Great Russian chauvinism and abuses against the nationalities either upon this same "alien" and "bourgeois" bureaucracy taken over from the old regime, or upon individual faults of character (in the case of the Georgian affair, "the hastiness and administrative passions of Stalin" and Grigorii Ordzhonikidze's lack of self-control).[26]

Never for a moment did Lenin stop to think that it might be the system itself which was at fault. Never for a moment did he stop to re-examine his basic concept of organization, that principle to which he always remained true: the idea that it was the party which had to give revolutionary consciousness to the masses, and further, that within the party, all members must be bound by the decisions of the Center. Implicit in these organizational formulas were the worst excesses of bureaucratization, for the citizen and the party member were left without institutional safeguards. Implicit, too, was the cancer of Great Russian chauvinism, for who was to distinguish between proletarian zealousness and Russian oppression of subject nationalities? Implicit in this theory of centralization was also the degeneration and Russification of the Comintern, for who could draw the line between internationalism and Russian domination once the European revolution had failed? Lenin could not explain satisfactorily the degeneration of the Revolution into bureaucratization because it was his own organizational formula which had led to it. His last-minute thrust at Stalin was without success because it was Stalin who was his legitimate heir.[27]

### THE TRIUMVIRATE VERSUS TROTSKY

The "bombshell" against Stalin reportedly being prepared by Lenin was never detonated. On March 9, 1923, Lenin suffered a third stroke; thereafter he was unable to do more than wave weakly in response to the greetings of visiting delegations of workers and peasants.[28] Despite Lenin's request for aid against Stalin in the Georgian question, Trotsky abstained when this issue came up for debate at the Twelfth Party Congress (April 17–25). Mindful as ever of the need for a unified leadership, Trotsky confined himself to delivering Lenin's notes on the nationalities question to the Politburo, which, not surprisingly, decided to suppress them.[29] At the congress itself, Trotsky was hailed as a hero of the Revolution, and his theses on the necessity of a central plan and rapid industrialization were accepted as the official policy of the party. But the victory was only a superficial one, for the theses were not applied, and Trotsky's very popularity was used as an argument by those who sought to portray him as a potential Bonaparte. This, if ever, was the moment when Trotsky should have made his move against Stalin. He had working for him both his own immense prestige and the support of Lenin's authority. Unassailed by Trotsky, the Triumvirate of Zinoviev, Kamenev, and Stalin emerged from the congress with its authority intact. The Central Control Commission and the Central Committee were enlarged, as Lenin wanted them to be. However, these bodies only fell further under the influence of Stalin, who was able to staff them with his own appointees. Lenin's remedy for bureaucratism thus ironically, though not accidentally, contributed to the consolidation of Stalin's power.[30] How could the rank and file control the apparatus when it was inherent in the organizational theory of Bolshevism that the Center controlled the party? The party could be only as high-minded and selfless as the men who directed it, and these men were now locked in a struggle for power.

The Twelfth Congress did not alter the leadership of the party, at least not officially. Lenin, Trotsky, Zinoviev, Stalin, Kamenev, Alexei Rykov, and Mikhail Tomsky still constituted the Politburo. But Trotsky was increasingly excluded from the actual process of decision-making.[c] Throughout the spring and summer the usually vociferous Soviet leader said nothing that could have been interpreted as criticism of the ruling Triumvirate. Then, in the fall of 1923, at the very moment when hopes for revolution in Germany were reaching their height, the smoldering crisis within the party burst into flame. The precipitating factor was the sudden downturn in the economic situation and the resurgence of the opposition groups. Toward midsummer the problem of diverging industrial and agricultural prices—what Trotsky called the "scissors" —reappeared to haunt the party leadership and underline the uneven recovery

[c] Alfred Rosmer relates how once, in May 1923, he was summoned to Zinoviev's apartment to report on the progress of the French Communist Party, and fortuitously found himself in the midst of a secret conclave of the Politburo from which Trotsky was excluded. After Bukharin, Kamenev, Stalin, Tomsky, and Rykov had all been assembled, he was shuffled out by Olga Ravich, who told him: "Ça ne va pas être amusant pour vous à présent: ils vont tous se mettre à parler russe." *Moscou sous Lénine* (1953), pp. 283–84.

of the Soviet economy. In August and September, unemployment rose. There was an outburst of wildcat strikes. The Workers' Truth and the Workers' Group rose once more to champion the cause of the proletariat. A subcommittee set up by the Central Committee in September to study the crisis recommended a more thorough repression of opposition groups. All party members would be required to denounce to the secret police anyone associated with the underground opposition. Simultaneously, an attempt was made to undermine Trotsky's position within the government by expanding the Revolutionary Military Council, of which he was chairman.[31]

These developments roused Trotsky to act. On October 8 he addressed a letter to the Central Committee, in which he denounced the trend of events within the party after the Twelfth Congress and put the blame for the resurgence of underground opposition on the lack of discussion. "The bureaucratization of the party apparatus," he wrote, "has developed to unheard-of proportions by means of the method of secretarial selection."[32] The Politburo replied by dismissing Trotsky's letter as a bid for personal power. This interpretation of Trotsky's act, however, was called into question when the Politburo received on October 15 the so-called Platform of the 46, in which 46 well-known party militants repeated Trotsky's criticisms in even stronger form.[33] In late October, the Plenum of the Central Committee supported the Politburo by condemning the Platform of the 46 as factional, and by accusing Trotsky of threatening to injure the unity of the party. Then, on November 7, 1923, Zinoviev suddenly gave a new turn to the crisis by opening a general debate among the party's rank and file. With consummate hypocrisy Zinoviev wrote: "It is necessary that intra-party workers' democracy, of which we have spoken so much, begin to a greater degree to take on flesh and blood....Our chief trouble consists often in the fact that almost all very important questions go predecided from above downward."[34]

The debate at first proceeded on comradely enough lines. As yet the rank and file could not have grasped the depth or the real implications of the disagreement. A provincial correspondent reported in *Pravda* that "the discussion of internal party questions has taken the provinces unawares," and that the majority of party members did not know what to think.[35] The Triumvirate meanwhile did its best to salvage the appearance of party unity by coming to a compromise with Trotsky, whose popularity they still feared. After a number of meetings held around Trotsky's sickbed in his private apartment, the Politburo reached a unanimous resolution on party democracy, which it published on December 7, 1923, in *Pravda*. This resolution seemed to grant the majority of the demands of Trotsky and the 46. It denounced bureaucratization, pointed to its origins in the contradictions of NEP, and called for freedom of controversy and election within the party—while reaffirming that it was impossible to tolerate factional groupings. But suspicion had now crept into the relations among those in the ruling group. Trotsky was determined that the Politburo's resolution be applied and not remain a mere scrap of paper. And thus, on December 8, he addressed an open letter to a party assembly in which he presented his interpretation of the New Course.[36]

Trotsky began by emphasizing that it was up to the party to realize this new regime, and not to the bureaucrats who stood by ready to pay lip service to the New Course and then bury it in practice.[37] "In short: *the party must subordinate its own apparatus,* without ceasing to be a centralized organization."[38] The party apparatus, Trotsky insisted, must be renovated by the introduction of new elements. All bureaucrats who had sought to use terror and sanctions to curb freedom of criticism within the party must be purged. Moreover, Trotsky threw out the suggestion, threatening if only in its ambiguity, that, *"It is only by a constant and active collaboration with the new generation, within the framework of democracy, that the Old Guard will conserve its character as a revolutionary factor."*[39] To prove his point, Trotsky gave the example of the degeneration of the Old Guard of the Second International, who had been direct disciples of Marx and Engels and who had nonetheless turned to opportunism. Trotsky's postscript, written two days later, in which he reminded his readers that the "revolutionary character" of the epoch did not in itself constitute a guarantee against the degeneration of the Old Guard, could hardly have reassured his fellow members of the Politburo or the bureaucrats of the party.[40]

If this was to be the opening shot of a determined attack against the Triumvirate, the terrain and the moment could not have been more badly chosen. Trotsky's letter on the New Course threatened the most sweeping changes in the State and the party without explaining clearly how he differed from the majority. Such reticence from a man noted for his steely logic might easily be mistaken for personal ambition.[d] The *troika* did not immediately react. Then, on December 15, the armistice of late November and early December was broken by Stalin and Zinoviev, who set out to impugn Trotsky's credentials as a Bolshevik. This was not the light skirmishing of the preceding months, but a massive campaign designed to destroy Trotsky's prestige in the party and the International. Writing in *Pravda,* Stalin pointed out that Trotsky was in no position to concern himself with the fate of the Old Bolsheviks, for he had never been one. And he concluded: "Comrade Trotsky is in a bloc with the democratic centralists and a part of the 'Left' Communists: that is the political meaning of Comrade Trotsky's action."[41] That same evening Zinoviev leaped

---

[d] As Boris Souvarine has remarked, the letter on the New Course said either too much or too little: "Too much for a leader who shared responsibility for the regime's policies and who had just voted for an official resolution; not enough for an opponent who had decided to re-establish forgotten truths and bring a dead movement to life. Too much to disarm the masters; not enough to arm the slaves." *Staline* (1935), p. 322.

into the fray, with a speech delivered to the Petrograd party organization. He developed the concept of Trotskyism, defining it as a view of the party as a "conglomerate of individual factions and tendencies."[42] In response to Zinoviev's persuasive oratory, the Petrograd party workers passed a motion condemning Trotsky and accusing him of having broken the discipline of the Politburo. Similar motions were passed in other party organizations throughout the country, a testimony to Stalin's command of the apparatus.[43]

With the intra-party struggle out in the open, both the Triumvirate and the Opposition rallied their forces for the test of the Thirteenth Party Conference. Though resistance manifested itself on the lower levels of the party, the machine developed by Stalin in 1922 and 1923 worked with deadly precision to sort out potential supporters of the minority. The actual conference, which met from January 16 to 18, 1924, included only a few isolated members of the Opposition. Trotsky himself was absent: just a few days before the conference was to convene, he left for the Caucasus, where he hoped to recover from the nagging illness that had undermined his health throughout the last months of 1923. Organization, however, was not the only explanation for the ease with which the majority routed its opponents. The Opposition was surprisingly unsuccessful in rallying the support of the workers.[44] To ears long accustomed to bitter denunciations of the "bourgeois" liberalism of the West, the appeal to democracy rang false. Appropriately enough, it was Stalin who was assigned the task of discrediting Trotsky and the Opposition. After accusing Trotsky of trying to form a faction, Stalin revealed the ban on inner party groupings passed by the Tenth Party Congress in 1921. The resolution on the party crisis adopted by the conference identified Trotsky as the leader of the Opposition, and condemned it as "not only an attempt at the revision of Bolshevism, not only a direct departure from Leninism, but also a clearly expressed *petty-bourgeois deviation*."[45]

The Thirteenth Party Conference promised "a systematic and energetic struggle of our whole party" against Trotskyism.[46] That this was no empty threat was shown by the events of the spring of 1924. Lenin's death, on January 21, was used as an opportunity to transform the doctrines of the great revolutionary leader into a cult and a dogma—a cult and a dogma that could in turn be used against Trotsky as weapons in the intra-party struggle. A new journal, *Bolshevik,* was created for the express purpose of "the defense and consolidation of *historical* Bolshevism, the struggle against any attempts at distorting or perverting its foundations."[47] In the name of a "Lenin levy," 200,000 new members were admitted to the party. These recruits, most of them workers and unschooled in the traditions of Socialism, only further undermined the Opposition. In April 1924, Stalin delivered a series of lectures at Sverdlov University on the "Foundations of Leninism," which presented Lenin's teachings as a canon and Stalin as its humble, but first, interpreter. The Thirteenth Party

Congress, which convened in May 1924, only confirmed the rout of the Opposition. The note sounded throughout was the necessity of unity within the party. Trotsky was present, but ineffectual. "The allegation that I am in favor of permitting groupings is incorrect," he said at one point.[48] The Central Committee was charged by the congress "to guard, as determinedly and firmly as before, the unity of the party and the established line of Bolshevism from any deviations whatsoever."[49]

### THE RUSSIAN CRISIS STRIKES THE INTERNATIONAL

It is forgotten today that the Third International was meant to be a forum for the discussion of the problems of the Russian Revolution as well as a fighting organization for the subversion and overthrow of bourgeois governments. Neither the Bolsheviks nor the Western Socialists had ever considered the Soviet regime a purely Russian affair. It was taken for granted by the founders of the Comintern that one day the leaders of the foreign Communist parties, having made their own revolutions, would repay the aid given them by the Russians by saving the Soviet State from its dilemma of economic and cultural backwardness. In anticipation of this moment, the Bolsheviks were scrupulous to report periodically to the world Communist movement on the progress of their revolution.

By the end of 1923 the Third International had failed in both the purposes for which it had been designed. There had been no European revolution; and Communist internationalism had become a monologue, in which advice and orders were given but not received. Trotsky talked often and with pride of Bolshevik internationalism. The Russians, he said, unlike the French, did not consider it demeaning to take their conflicts before the International.[50] It was true that in 1922 the Workers' Opposition had appealed to the Enlarged Executive, and that there had been hearings, presided over by Cachin, at which Trotsky and Zinoviev had testified for the Russian majority. But the very unanimity and indifference with which the committee formed for this purpose brought forth its verdict suggest that European Communists were satisfied to put their faith in the leaders of the October Revolution. After all, how could a Cachin judge a Trotsky? Further participation by foreign Communists in Russian affairs was not encouraged by the Bolsheviks, who presented a solid front whenever discussing the problems of the Soviet State—or, for that matter, those of other Communist parties. One might have expected, then, that the struggle within the Russian leadership would not be brought before the International. There were two reasons, however, why foreign Communist parties were likely to become involved. First, both Trotsky and his ally, Radek, had special positions of prestige and influence in the French and German Communist parties. Second, Zinoviev, Trotsky, and Radek were all deeply involved in the preparation of the abortive German revolution.

It would be convenient to avoid the German tangle altogether. Unfortunately, this is no more possible for the student of bolshevization than it was for the Bolsheviks themselves. The German events were entangled with the Russian crisis, and both were in turn brought before the International in the spring of 1924. All the Soviet leaders had approved the projected insurrection in Germany, though with varying degrees of enthusiasm.[51] The dispute thus hinged upon "the lessons of the German events." There were three issues: the interpretation of the overthrow of the Zeigner government; its implications for subsequent applications of united front tactics; and the changes in the KPD's leadership called for by the defeat. The German Zentrale itself had met on November 3, 1923, to discuss the abortive uprising. Brandler, supported by Radek and Georgii Pyatakov, had submitted theses describing the dissolution of the Saxon government as "the victory of fascism over the November Republic." Brandler's theses attributed major responsibility for the defeat to the Social Democrats, and maintained that henceforth the united front would have to be pursued from below. Armed insurrection remained "on the agenda," but the struggle for the proletarian dictatorship would have to begin with a program of concrete (and not particularly radical) reforms. Despite the opposition of the German Left, led by Ruth Fischer, the *enfant terrible* of the KPD, Brandler's theses were accepted by the German Zentrale. A new development, however, was the emergence of a Center (Hermann Remmele, Hugo Eberlein, August Kleine) which asserted that the retreat, though necessary, should not have become a "timid and passive surrender."[52]

It was at this point that the German question became confused with the Russian struggle. Zinoviev at first endorsed the point of view of the Radek-Brandler group. Then, as the enormity of the disaster became clear, the vulnerability of his own position must have come upon him. The intra-party struggle was under way. As President of the Comintern, he could be held responsible for the KPD's defeat. At the same time, Radek, Pyatakov, and Brandler were all close to Trotsky; a blow against them would become a blow against Trotsky. In response to these considerations, Zinoviev pirouetted about in late November, and blamed the defeat on the leadership of the German party for having turned participation in the Saxon cabinet "into a banal parliamentary coalition with the Social Democrats."[53] The fall of Zeigner's government was not the victory of fascism over the Republic, but the victory of Social Democracy *and* fascism over the Communist workers. The implication of these rather vague statements was clear to the Communist initiate. The German leadership had misinterpreted the united front. Instead of using Zeigner's government as the springboard for military action against the Republic, it had played into the hands of the Social Democrats.

Zinoviev himself does not seem to have been sure how far this issue should be taken. His most urgent concern at the end of November was to extricate himself from any responsibility for the defeat of the KPD.[54] What hesitations he and his fellow Triumvirs might have had, however, disappeared in mid-December, when the Russian delegation returned from Germany. Speaking before a party meeting in Moscow, Radek claimed that even if the majority of the Russian Central Committee turned against Trotsky, he would find defenders in the French and German Communist parties.[55] The relevance of his remark was brought home about the same time by a letter to the Russian Central Committee from the leadership of the Polish party. The letter expressed "the gravest anxieties" about the language being used in the Russian debate, and stressed that "we cannot admit the possibility that comrade Trotsky could find himself outside the ranks of the leaders of the [Russian Communist Party] and of the International."[56]

Here was a threat the Triumvirs could not ignore. The specter of a coalition of Old Guard Bolsheviks, students, military officers, intellectuals, and foreign Communists, all led by Trotsky, had appeared. Zinoviev moved to meet the danger. On December 27, 1923, the Politburo adopted a resolution condemning Radek's policy in Germany, particularly his support of Brandler against the Left. The Politburo of the Russian party, it was stated, based its policy on the alliance of the Center and the Left, while criticizing "the gross errors of the Right."[57] Radek replied, with what must be considered either a very naïve or a very foolhardy gesture, that he was responsible for his actions in Germany to the world congress of the International, and not to the Central Committee of the Russian party.[58] Ten days later, on January 6, 1924, Zinoviev denounced Trotsky before the Executive Committee. Trotsky, he said, was "an outspoken individualist" and had "no feeling for real economic relations in Russia."[59] Zinoviev's speech ended with an attack on Radek and the Central Committee of the Polish party for having intervened "in favor of the Trotsky faction."[60]

By this time the campaign against Trotsky was under way in earnest. Each day in *Pravda* some new flaw was discovered in his economic views, his associations, or his revolutionary past. As has already been narrated, these attacks bore their fruit at the Thirteenth Party Conference, where the 46 and Trotsky were equated and condemned. The equivalent in the International was the simultaneous debate on the German question, which began on January 11, with the representatives of the various factions of the KPD in attendance. After ten days of discussion and recriminations, during which Radek proved unrepentant, a resolution was passed unanimously that listed the errors of the Right.[61] Though not the victory that Stalin had obtained at the Thirteenth Party Conference, the Executive's resolution cleared the way for the changing of the KPD's leadership. When the Zentrale of the German party met to reorganize itself on February 19, the Brandler group was dropped and a new

Committee, consisting of five members of the Center and two of the Left, was formed. Within two months, the Center had disintegrated, and Ruth Fischer's faction had taken over the leadership of the party.[62]

The German Left had thus ridden to power in the wake of the German defeat and the campaign against Trotsky. For the first time in the history of the Communist International, a foreign Communist group had been sacrificed to the requirements of a purely Russian conflict. The strategy of the united front and the meaning of the October defeat had been reinterpreted in order to bolster Zinoviev's position. These events had not gone unchallenged from abroad: the Polish party had raised its voice in protest, first in December, and again at the January meetings of the Executive.[63] Would other parties follow the Polish party's example? This disquieting question turned the attention of the Russian leadership toward that other section of the International on which Radek had claimed that Trotsky could count: the PCF.

### THE FIRST FRENCH REACTIONS

Radek's boast showed a curious misunderstanding of the relationship between the French and the Russian Communist parties. It suggests that the Bolsheviks themselves may not have realized the degree to which their roughshod leadership had deprived the Western parties of all sense of initiative. Up to December 1924, the French Communists knew little of what went on in Russia and the Russian party. Those journalists like André Morizet who brought to the analysis of Russian affairs anything but an attitude of hagiography had been replaced or expelled during the crisis of 1922. The Workers' Opposition found defenders neither in the PCF nor among the syndicalists of *La Vie Ouvrière*, who might have seen the Russian Opposition as their counterpart. After January 1923, a French Communist was a man who obeyed automatically when Moscow commanded. This meant that the French were not prepared for the issues that were thrust upon them at the beginning of 1924. They required a crash course in the history of the Russian Revolution.

Souvarine, Rosmer, and Treint were exceptions to these generalizations. They visited Moscow often, knew and corresponded with Bolshevik leaders, and followed developments in the Russian party. The same was true of Monatte, though for one reason or another, he had never been to Russia. Even these men, however, were unaware of the depth of the conflict in the Russian party until the end of 1923. The sense of discipline among Bolsheviks was such that they did not discuss their internal problems with foreigners, not even with foreign Communists.[e] Personal loyalties had never been a factor in the

---

[e] Interview with Rosmer, 13.ii.61. "The International knew nothing about what was happening in Russia, and Trotsky felt neither justified in enlightening it nor capable of doing so." Souvarine, *Staline,* p. 342.

crises of the PCF. Rosmer, for example, had managed to be on good terms with Zinoviev, Trotsky, and Lozovsky. Souvarine called both Trotsky and Manuilsky friends.*' What might seem strange in the perspective of history was perfectly normal in 1922 and 1923. These men were regarded not as past or potential enemies, but as members of an iron phalanx of Bolshevik leaders whose personal antagonisms would always be subordinated to the higher interests of the Revolution.

There was thus no Trotskyite faction in France at the beginning of 1924. But there was a Trotskyite cult. Its roots went back to the War. Lenin and Trotsky—from 1917 on these two names had always been mentioned in one breath. Moreover, whereas Lenin had remained distant, Russian, admirable but incomprehensible, Trotsky had caught the imagination of the French working-class movement. He had become theirs, and his involvement in the affairs of the PCF had made him the best-known Bolshevik leader in France. A few militants had known the future organizer of the Red Army during his stay in Paris. If they had not, they had read about him in *La Vie Ouvrière* or seen the striking portrait of him in *La Vague*. Those Communists who followed the party press at all consistently had read dozens of Trotsky's articles, theses, and speeches during the 1920–23 period. They had been astounded to see the assurance with which the Soviet leader prescribed remedies for the ills of the French working-class movement. What doubts they might have had were quashed by the comments invariably accompanying these texts, which observed that Trotsky had a phenomenal theoretical and firsthand knowledge of French conditions.

Loriot, Rosmer, and Monatte had initiated this cult back in 1919. None of these men, however, was suited by temperament to adulation. They admired Trotsky as one revolutionary admires another. It was Souvarine who turned him into a legend. Souvarine worshiped Trotsky with the intensity that one intellectual reserves for another who has combined a commitment to great ideals with the manipulation of great power. Trotsky's works, wrote the Editor of the *Bulletin Communiste* in April 1923, were among the classics of revolutionary literature. "Marvelously endowed as a thinker, writer, and orator, with great historical and economic knowledge and the temperament of an indefatigable man of action, he is incontestably one of the greatest forces of the Russian and world Revolution."[64] In September 1923, Souvarine dashed into print to acclaim Trotsky's solution to the reparations question (the United States of Europe), and to contrast it with Treint's mechanical echo of the German slogan ("expropriate the national expropriators of 51 per cent of their capital"), which was "obviously an erroneous, inopportune, and anachronistic

*' When Manuilsky was in Paris he stayed with Souvarine, and when Souvarine was in Moscow he stayed with Manuilsky.

tactic, which failed to take into consideration the concrete conditions of post-war Europe and the relative strength of the different States and of the classes in each State."[65] Trotsky, Souvarine wrote at various times during 1923 and 1924, was a "superman"; a continuator of Marx and not merely a commentator; and, with Lenin, the only contemporary figure whose contribution to the Revolution was so great that "one can say that anything which harms him also harms the Revolution."[66]

It was thus appropriate and significant that it should be Souvarine who brought the Russian crisis to the attention of the French Communists in December 1923. Souvarine had always admired the brutality with which the Russians argued with one another, and he considered this courageous self-criticism a sign of health within the party.[67] Before coming home to Paris in late November, he had witnessed the beginning of the dispute in the Russian party. It is not likely that he had bothered to conceal his own sympathy with Trotsky's ideas. It is even possible that he had hinted to Zinoviev and others that the French party as a whole would stand by its mentor and spiritual father. These suggestions must remain speculations; for if Souvarine talked of these matters, he did so in private to a narrow circle of his own friends. In public he gave no sign of his concern. Writing in the *Bulletin Communiste* on December 6, Souvarine took note of Zinoviev's article in the November 7 *Pravda* opening the discussion of the tasks of the party, and approved it thoroughly. "All that," he observed, "is full of interest, and having raised the question, we will have to study it. For the French Communists, like those of Russia and elsewhere, must profit from this revolutionary experience, since the affairs of the Russian Communists are also our affairs."[68]

It was the traditional appeal to Communist internationalism, and it seems to have been received as such. Throughout the month of December, Souvarine continued to supply his readers with translations from the discussion in the Russian press, including, on December 27, Trotsky's letter on the New Course. His own interest, however, does not seem to have been reciprocated by his subscribers. Despite successive appeals, only five readers bothered to write in to ask him to report the debate in greater detail.[69] It is easy to understand the indifference of the French Communists. They knew nothing of the personal antagonisms between Trotsky and the Triumvirate. Both camps were saying things that they had always taken for granted. For that matter, they had trouble discovering what the issues were and who stood for what. They assumed that this debate would end as others had ended.

During the first few weeks Souvarine might have agreed; but after receiving *Pravda* for the last two weeks of December, he must have realized that the dispute had taken a new and alarming turn. Beginning with the first of the year, there was a note of concern to be detected in the commentaries he appended to each article. On January 4, 1924, Souvarine protested that there were

no factions in the Russian party: those who accused the Opposition of forming a faction were momentarily blinded by the heat of the polemic. He
criticized Evgenii Preobrazhensky, Timofei Sapronov, and Mikhail Rafail
(members of the 46) for their "maladresse" in continuing to make criticisms
after the publication of the resolution of the Central Committee passed on
December 5. But his sharpest barbs were reserved for Stalin, whom he accused
of giving a personal turn to the dispute. "We know how much is owed to
Stalin, what his merits are, and what part he has played in the history of the
party. But precisely because we know all that, and know Stalin as frankness
itself, even to the point of brutality, we say to him straight out: anyone who
thinks that he can separate the names of Lenin and Trotsky in the eyes of the
world proletariat is deceiving himself."[70] Souvarine supplemented these remarks with a personal letter to Zinoviev, protesting against the attacks being
made on Trotsky's reputation.[71]

After these opening salvos, the Russian question was temporarily eclipsed by
the interest of the French in their own Congress of Lyon. Souvarine devoted
himself to obtaining Treint's demotion; when Treint opened the French
discussion in January, Souvarine turned the *Bulletin Communiste* over to
letters from the rank and file. The Russian conflict was not an issue at the
Congress of Lyon. Knowing Trotsky's popularity in France, Zinoviev apparently hesitated to throw such a bombshell into a party congress without
careful preparation. For somewhat different reasons, the German revolution
had not become a subject of debate. In September and October, the French
leadership had been unanimous in supporting the KPD's projected insurrection. In November it had been unanimous in condemning the German party's
parliamentary combinations with the Left Social Democrats and its insufficient
agitation among the masses.[g] Treint dared not raise either issue: the first
because he could not yet be sure of what the outcome of the Russian struggle
would be, the second because he had been a warm supporter of Brandler's use
of the united front. Though quick to shift his ground in November, the embattled party Secretary could hardly make capital of the German revolution

---

[g] In November 1923, Treint was delegated by the party as its representative at the meetings of the KPD. Before Treint left for Germany, the BP approved a letter of criticism
proposed by him which censured the leadership of the KPD for (1) misevaluating the
balance of social forces in Germany, (2) misevaluating the degree to which Social Democracy had decayed, (3) trusting the Left Social Democrats in Saxony and Thuringia, and
(4) participating in parliamentary combinations with the leaders of the Left Social Democrats and failing to agitate sufficiently among the masses. Treint's fifth criticism—that the
German majority had not called for a proletarian dictatorship and the formation of soviets
as soon as the revolution was considered imminent—was rejected unanimously by the BP.
It would also seem that, on Treint's initiative, the BP dispatched a letter to the German
Left sometime in November—probably in mild support of its position. *Bulletin Communiste*, 4.iv.24.

against opponents who had all along criticized him for his desire to sacrifice party principles to the formation of a true united front. It was thus that the Congress of Lyon, though meeting in the aftermath of the campaign against Trotsky and Radek, came to be almost totally devoted to internal problems.

### TREINT STRIKES BACK

The next events are shrouded in mystery and controversy. Accusations and counteraccusations make it difficult to know what happened in the ensuing weeks. According to the Treint-Girault group, the Congress of Lyon had merely postponed a conflict that had been brewing ever since November 1923; according to their opponents, the Russian question was thrust upon a happy and unsuspecting party. These seemingly contradictory interpretations are not really contradictory at all; they simply represent two different perspectives on the same events. What happened was that new issues were found by Treint and Girault to reopen the discussion that had been closed at Lyon. These issues were discovered in Trotskyism and the new Labour government in England, then were joined neatly to the earlier disagreements about Treint's dictatorship and the Federation of the Seine's sectarianism, and finally, with the aid of the Executive's directive on factory cells and Zinoviev's diagnosis of the German situation, were turned into a theory of bolshevization. Though scarcely credible in the pure form in which Treint presented it, this theory provided a reason for taking away the leadership of the PCF from those men who refused to condemn Trotsky, and thus had its usefulness for Zinoviev in the spring of 1924.

The results of the Congress of Lyon have already been described. At the first meeting of the new CD, Henri Gourdeaux proposed that Treint be reappointed as Secretary. This motion was defeated, and Treint requested that he be named delegate to the Executive.[72] With Treint out of the way, Souvarine went after the leadership of the Federation of the Seine. At the Federal Congress, which met on February 18, he attacked Girault's Federal Bureau, demanding that half its members be replaced and accusing it of not applying the Lyon resolutions. By a very narrow margin, Girault's faction succeeded in retaining control of the Federal Bureau.[73] This skirmish between Girault and Souvarine, tactfully hidden on a back page of L'Humanité, revealed that the bitter pill of Lyon had not been swallowed whole by the Treint-Girault forces.

About the same time as the meeting of the Federal Congress of the Seine, delegates from the Executive and the KPD arrived in Paris and confronted the French CD with the most recent decisions of the Executive on the crisis in the Russian and German parties. Precise information on this episode is lacking, but it appears that the French leadership was asked to take a position on both the Russian and the German questions—that is, they were called upon to join in the general condemnation of the Brandler tendency in Germany and

Trotsky in Russia. Souvarine, meanwhile, had grown alarmed at the lengths to which the discussion in the Russian party had gone during the month of January. Whereas during December he had tried to interest the French in the Russian question and complained of the general indifference, he now tried to shield his fellow Communists from the worst excesses of the dispute. What possible good could come from publishing articles which the French could not understand and which would require whole volumes to explain to them, he said in reply to a complaint by his old enemy Rappoport that he had suppressed an article in which Stalin had attacked Trotsky. "The role of the French Communists," he wrote, "is to study the Russian debates in order to profit from them, and not to get involved in a dispute when they have so much to do at home."[74]

For the moment, the French CD was convinced by Souvarine's argument in favor of nonintervention. After listening to the reports of the delegates of the KPD and the Executive, the CD adopted a resolution proposed by Souvarine, which affirmed the neutrality of the French party in the Russian crisis and refused to distinguish between the majority and the Opposition in the Russian party, saying they were "equally animated by a desire to work for the glory of the party and the triumph of the worldwide Russian Revolution," and instructed the delegate of the Executive to convey to the Russian party the concern of the French at the form the dispute had taken.[75] Only Treint and Suzanne Girault voted against this text. The same policy of abstention was adopted with respect to the crisis in the KPD. On February 19, after a heated discussion during which both Souvarine and Sellier presented drafts, the CD agreed on a compromise motion declaring that the CD had never supported one faction of the German party against the other, and calling on the federations and the sections not to proceed to a vote until the necessary documents for a serious discussion had been placed at their disposal.[76] Souvarine, from the pages of the *Bulletin Communiste,* appealed to the PCF to remain above the struggle; but the language in which his remarks were phrased left no doubt about his own sympathies. "If it is understandable that the Bolsheviks should be carried away by a certain internal logic of conflict, and give themselves over to unjust attacks, it would be intolerable for these attacks to be renewed in the French party by comrades who do not have the excuse of being inflamed by blows given or received. The French Communist who allows himself to defame Trotsky in France is either irresponsible or a scoundrel."[77]

Meanwhile, a new source of conflict had arisen. On January 23, 1924, a Labour government headed by Ramsay MacDonald came to power in England. J. T. Walton Newbold, one of the leaders of the British Communist Party, asked the French CD to react by sending an open letter to the Labour Party. Rosmer was assigned by the CD to draft the letter; after revision by a special subcommittee of the CD, Rosmer's draft was adopted on February 5 over the negative votes of Treint and Girault, who objected on the ground that it lacked vigor and a definite program of action and agitation. The gist of the letter was very simply that the Labour Party had been entrusted with a great responsibility by the workers of England; that it could only fulfill this responsibility by attacking the capitalist regime without delay and without mercy; and, finally, that its task would be facilitated if it joined forces with the British Communist Party and concluded an alliance between England and the Soviet Union.[78] The letter was phrased in polite language, it is true; but as Souvarine later pointed out at the Thirteenth Congress of the Russian party, the French Communists were trying to lay the foundation for a united front between the British Communists and the Labour Party, and they saw no point in sending a sharply critical letter to people they were trying to interest in a policy of cooperation. Apparently the representative of the Executive made no protest at the time. At any rate, the question was academic, for the letter was never sent.[79]

Involved, of course, was the perennial dilemma of the united front. Six months before the Executive would have been only too happy to see that the French had abandoned their intransigence and their sectarianism. But since the defeat of the German revolution and the intra-party struggle in Russia, the official view of the united front had changed. The united front from above now suggested Chemnitz; and Chemnitz in turn had become a battle cry in the controversy between the Russian majority and the Opposition. On February 2, 1924, Lozovsky had published an article entitled "No Illusions!" in *L'Humanité,* in which he had emphasized that the coming to power of the Labour government did not constitute a victory for Socialism, but rather "a victory of the bourgeoisie over Socialism."[80] This was not the nonsense it seemed: Lozovsky was stretching Zinoviev's interpretation of the German defeat to fit England. Rosmer either did not get the point or thought it stupid. A week later he replied mildly and with a note of surprise that Lozovsky had put the question badly: it was not the French Communists but the British workers who had illusions about the Labour government, and verbal intransigence would only have the effect of alienating the workers and isolating the British Communists from the masses. It was not by denouncing the Labour Party, but by fighting in its midst, that the British Communist Party would win influence over the workers and disabuse them of their illusions. This, of course, added Rosmer, did not mean that the British Communists should not recall the past of the Labourite leaders (that is, expose them as reformists) when it was of use in illuminating the present.[81]

The issue might have died at this point. Rosmer had added nothing new or startling to the interpretation of the united front; what he had said was merely a reformulation of the orthodoxy of 1922 and 1923. That was the problem. The orthodoxy of 1923 had become the heresy of 1924. Moreover, Rosmer was a personal friend of Trotsky, an enemy of Treint, and a member of the coalition that had refused to condemn the Russian Opposition.[h] All this is necessary for understanding what happened. Rosmer found himself at the center of a debate that concerned not only Lozovsky and himself but also those two paladins of party orthodoxy, Treint and Souvarine. The whole discussion proceeded in an atmosphere of absurdity that is only comprehensible if we remember that the participants were more interested in discrediting one another than in saying something for its own sake.

Rosmer was accused from within his own party of having recommended "la manière douce" with respect to the Labour Party. He replied that it was not "la manière douce" that he favored, but "an intelligent, comprehensible, and fruitful manner." Returning to Lozovsky's assertion that the coming to power of the Labour government represented a victory of the bourgeoisie over Socialism, Rosmer remarked that this opinion was "debatable" (he might have said "absurd"). "If this were the case, the bourgeoisie would win at every turn: when it loses as well as when it triumphs."[82] Writing from Moscow, Lozovsky repeated his original point that Communists did not understand clearly enough what the Labour experience in Great Britain represented. Was the British working class in power? Definitely not. The British Communists must expose the Labourites constantly as the reformists they were. Then, in conclusion, came the key point: the Communists should not be afraid of being denounced as sectarians.[83] At this point, Souvarine leaped into the debate to attack the "agitators" in the party "who demand that we approach the Labour Party with a thick rope in our hand and gallows on our shoulder." He could not refrain from recalling Treint's phrase of 1922, when he described the Socialists as a "fowl to pluck" by means of the united front. The Communists in Great Britain, he concluded, "must present themselves to the Labourite workers not as wily enemies, but as auxiliaries resolved to aid them in their task, to sustain them *in their struggle*."[84]

Thus far there had been no hint that the balance of forces within the party had changed. But on March 14, the *Bulletin Communiste* published an article by Treint in which he listed the errors of the "majority" in its evaluation of the Labour Party. Treint's article was a clumsy mixture of outright lies, fabrications, and exaggerations, amazingly reminiscent of the polemical style of Stalin in its repetitiousness and use of innuendo. Its theme, repeated *ad nauseam*, was that the new leadership had allowed *L'Humanité* to publish a statement that "we would support the Labourite government with all our might, no matter what policies it followed."[85] Accompanying the article was a short note by Souvarine, in which he referred to Treint's interpretation of the united front as "anti-Communist" and protested that the Secretariat of the party had forbidden him to comment on Treint's assertions. One week later, another note appeared in the *Bulletin Communiste,* announcing that Souvarine

[h] See p. 377 below.

had been removed as Editor by the decision of the CD and that he was being sent to Moscow as a delegate to the ECCI. The reason given for Souvarine's transfer was that he had disregarded the decision of the CD, and had inserted his comment on Treint's article just before the issue went to press. "Communist criticism is one thing," said the notice; "personal and unfriendly polemic is something else."[86]

The full implications of Souvarine's removal only became clear the following week, in the March 28 issue of the *Bulletin Communiste*. Writing under the title of "The Way Traced by Lenin," Treint reviewed the history of the party over the past year and presented the CD's new theses on the tactics of the PCF and the problems facing the International. A whole series of disagreements among the party's leaders had arisen during the past months, he asserted: over the Ruhr, the evaluation of the Labour Party at the time of its victory, the evaluation of the Russian Opposition, the conditions of the party's development and relations with other working-class organizations, relations between the party and *L'Humanité,* the implementation of the principle of centralism. Why had these questions not been resolved at Lyon, Treint asked. Because the party had not been informed; these events had been too recent. Definite factions had not yet formed. After Lyon, the situation had evolved rapidly: a Right, a Left, and a Center had emerged. The Right, Treint maintained, consisted of Souvarine, Rosmer, and Monatte. It attenuated criticism of the Labour government and favored the Russian Opposition under the guise of neutrality. It denied the beginning of a crisis in the French party, and refused to recognize the existence of factions in the International. "In all circumstances it manifested a dangerous pessimism, which is a reflection of the momentary withdrawal of the world revolution required after the October retreat in Germany." The Left, on the other hand, Treint explained, had approved from the beginning the line that was later adopted by the International: preparation for great struggles in France; criticism of the Labour government; support of the leadership of the German party and the Central Committee of the Russian party. The Center had wavered, sometimes voting with the Right (as in February), but it had finally rallied to vote for a common set of theses with the Left. Treint concluded his announcement of the overturn in the party's leadership by stating for the first time what was to be the party's slogan in 1924: "No debolshevization of the Russian party; on the contrary, bolshevization of all Communist parties."[87]

### ZINOVIEV INTERVENES

One would like to know when and how Treint came to understand the gravity of the Russian conflict and its potentialities for his own use. Unfortunately, Humbert-Droz's reports leave off in January 1924, when he was transferred to Italy. Since we lack the necessary documents, proof must give way to hypothesis. In November 1923, Treint was delegated by the CD to represent the PCF at the meetings of the German party. While in Germany, the irascible Secretary must have become sensitive to the conflict between Brandler and the German Left.[i] However, no more than any other French Communist leader did he foresee the explosive uses to which these differences would be put. After Lyon what Treint needed was an issue, a wedge with which to force his way back into the party leadership. The opportunity presented itself almost immediately. Before returning to Moscow, Lozovsky outlined "the Bolshevik point of view on the Russian question" at a meeting of the CD. Rosmer rose to Trotsky's defense; Girault, Sémard, and Calzan declared their agreement with the Russian majority.[88] No decisions were made. Then, in mid-February, the delegates of the Executive and the KPD arrived in Paris. Treint undoubtedly talked with these envoys; he may even have made a deal with them. At any rate, he and Girault voted to support the Russian and German majorities; and immediately after the adoption of the resolutions proclaiming the neutrality of the French CD, Treint and Girault began to organize meetings of sections and federations to denounce Souvarine's presentation of the Russian question and accuse him of partisanship. The Federal Bureau of the Seine voted such a censure in early March.[89]

This grass-roots movement, proclaimed with great fanfare later, would not have gotten beyond the limits of the Federation of the Seine had it not been for the direct intervention of Zinoviev. In mid-March, Manuilsky arrived in Paris. He was accompanied by delegates of the German majority. A joint meeting of the CD and the leadership of the CGTU was organized for March 18.[j] Manuilsky and the Germans reported on the situation in the International and demanded that the French take a stand. This time the foundation had been carefully laid. Treint produced a set of theses, signed by fourteen members of the CD, which condemned the Russian Opposition and its French supporters in extremely harsh language, using the words "bolshevization," "debolshevization," "revisionism," "liquidationism," "Menshevism," and "confusionism."[90] Sellier and François Chasseigne, the Secretary of the Fédération des Jeunesses Communistes, countered with another text, less extreme but also designed to commit the CD. After a first subcommittee had failed, a second succeeded in combining the two projects.[91]

The compromise theses, entitled "On the Tactics of the French Communist Party and on the Problems Facing the Communist International," stated that the party had to conduct its electoral campaign on the basis of the Workers' and Peasants' Bloc while fighting against the Rightist deviation within. It

[i] See p. 371n.
[j] A dramatic illustration, by the way, of how close the link had become between the party and the leadership of the CGTU.

was announced that the primary organizational task was the transformation of the party on the basis of factory cells. Concerning the British Labour government, it was admitted that the PCF had not been harsh enough in its criticism, and that it had not been sufficiently prompt in exposing its inability to carry out a truly proletarian policy. The German Right was condemned; and the French party signified its agreement with the decisions of the Thirteenth Party Conference. Trotsky's name was not explicitly mentioned, but the resolution read that "The Bolshevist Old Guard ... presents, as a group, the best guarantees of experience, firmness, and Communist clear-sightedness."[92]

Souvarine, Monatte, and Rosmer were caught unawares. Unlike Treint and his friends, they had not gotten together in advance to work out a common strategy.[93] Souvarine voted against the theses of the second subcommittee and presented his own, which stated that the role of the International was not to make the differences in the Russian party deeper, but to find a basis on which the Bolsheviks might re-establish their unity. The decisions made at Lyon, he charged, had remained a dead letter, and the party had become mired in "a mechanical, bureaucratic, and irresponsible centralism."[94] According to the *Bulletin Communiste,* Souvarine's theses were opposed by "almost the whole of the CD." Rosmer abstained from the vote and resigned from his positions on the BP and *L'Humanité.* Monatte joined Souvarine in voting against the subcommittee's theses, and made a statement to the CD in which he insisted that the basic cause of the present malaise in the party was not the German defeat, the Russian question, or the coming to power of the Labour government, but the mechanical centralism that existed long before October 1923. Monatte refused to accept the assertion of the new majority that the Russian Opposition was tainted by Menshevism. The French party, he argued, had no business interfering in the Russian question—especially when it did not have access to the necessary information for an intelligent judgment. "Bien heureux ou bien présomptueux, ceux d'ici qui peuvent distribuer le blâme ou la palme à ceux qui les dépassent de cent coudées," concluded Monatte, with characteristic disdain for the personalities of French Communism.[95]

The events of February and March 1924 should now appear in sharper focus. Lozovsky had leaped on Rosmer not for his views on the British Labour Party, but in retribution for his defense of Trotsky at the meeting of the CD after Lyon. Souvarine's removal from the editorship of the *Bulletin Communiste* had been merely a superficial reflection of the overturn within the party leadership that Manuilsky had obtained. Treint's article on "The Way Traced by Lenin" had marked his victory over the coalition that had ejected him from the Secretariat at Lyon. Though he had written with the seeming authority of the CD, Treint had in fact used the very language that the CD had refused to accept. Now, however, Treint dared all, for he knew that he had behind him the authority of the International, and he was playing this card for all that it

was worth. In the course of his article, Treint even managed to let fly a
threatening shaft at his fallen rival. Souvarine, he wrote, "is moving in a
dangerous direction."[96]

Souvarine, though, had no intention of yielding to Treint, or, for that matter, to Zinoviev. The President of the Comintern had replied to Souvarine's
letter of January 6, and accused him of waging a "factional struggle" and lend-
ing his support to "an opposition which represents no more than one per cent."
Souvarine struck back on March 20, with a long letter that showed anything
but a spirit of contrition. Denying indignantly that he was a "factionalist" or
a "Trotskyite," Souvarine asserted that the Russian majority's campaign had
injured the party, the Revolution, and the International rather than Trotsky
himself.[97] About the same time, the deposed Editor of the *Bulletin Communiste* sent his former subscribers a letter, in which he declared that the real
motives for his demotion had not been "personal disagreements" as the new
majority claimed, but his point of view on the Russian question.[98] Souvarine,
Rosmer, and Monatte followed this act of revolt by the publication of Trotsky's
articles on the New Course, financed out of their own funds. The articles were
accompanied by a highly inflammatory introduction by Souvarine, which
pointed out that these texts would show "the absence of intellectual and moral
scruples that characterizes the way in which certain people have presented
things in France, and perhaps also elsewhere."[99] The CD responded to Souvarine's letter to the subscribers of the *Bulletin Communiste* by accusing him
of having violated party discipline. The rank and file was reminded that it
had been Souvarine who had single-handedly written the resolution placing
the party press under the absolute control of the leadership. "The worker members of our organization, who scrupulously respect party discipline themselves,"
the announcement cunningly observed, "would not understand it if the most
highly placed militants enjoyed special treatment."[100]

### THE REACTION OF THE PARTY

The new majority, meanwhile, prepared to explain the recent events to the
lower echelons of the party. A conference of federation secretaries was summoned for April 6–7, and a federal assembly of the Seine heard both the
majority and the opposition explain their positions on April 2, 4, and 11.
Only the results of the conference of federation secretaries were made public:
of the 75 federations represented, 59 voted confidence in the CD, two voted
against, and 14 abstained.[101] The account of the meetings of the Federation of the Seine was fragmentary; for the first time since the foundation of
the PCF, *L'Humanité* resembled *Pravda*. Souvarine was reported to have
brandished Trotsky's *New Course* and exclaimed, "Something is being hidden
from the French party!" He was then supposed to have added: "There's something rotten in the party and the International: it will have to be burned out."

The BP merely quoted these incriminating statements out of context, and then replied blandly that it had no intention of slandering Trotsky, and that it had asked Souvarine to publish the *New Course,* along with the responses made in *Pravda,* as soon as possible.[102]

Successive meetings of the assembly of the Seine were more fully reported. Treint spoke on April 4, and, in highly tendentious fashion, accused the "opportunist Right" (that is, Trotsky and Radek and their foreign friends) of having sabotaged the German revolution.[k] Souvarine, Rosmer, and Monatte were allowed to defend themselves on the 11th. They denied Treint's allegations and repeated the statements they had made to the CD on March 18. Girault concluded the meeting by remarking with shocked innocence that any Communist Party worthy of the name must be capable of coming to a conclusion on such an important issue as the Russian question.[103] This lecture on Communist ethics was provoked by the unreceptive mood of the audience. Monatte was applauded when he said that the French were not in a position to judge the Russian question, and the audience protested when the assembly's chairman tried to limit his speaking time. No vote was taken, but a contemporary unpublished account concluded that the majority of the hall remained uncommitted. According to this spectator, two-thirds listened, one-third expressed an opinion; and of this one-third, the majority seemed to favor Monatte and Rosmer.[104]

The unrepentant attitude of the Opposition and the unenthusiastic tenor of these first party debates only spurred Treint on to greater heights of fantasy. His theme, repeated with the subtlety of a pile driver, was that Souvarine, Rosmer, and Monatte were the French representatives of a Right whose partisans could be found everywhere in the International, most notably in England, Germany, Poland, and Russia. This charge was not easily substantiated, and Treint had to stretch his memory and his readers' sense of reality to make the accusation possible, not to say plausible. Groping for possible deviations in the past, Treint recalled that Monatte had proposed the establishment of a web of syndicalist commissions independent of the party—the old anarcho-syndicalist error. Rosmer, on the other hand, had made the mistake of telling the BP before the Congress of Bourges that he was skeptical of the value of the syndicalist commissions. The fundamental charge, however, was pessimism: "All that Monatte, Rosmer, and Souvarine do is discourage the party and spread in its ranks the demoralizing doubt that they have within themselves." And again with even greater imagination: "Our Opposition is truly an opposition of the Right, of liquidationism, of pessimism, and of revolutionary defeatism."[105]

---

[k] *L'Humanité,* 5.iv.24. A short correction by Rosmer was run in *L'Humanité* the next day, claiming that none of the quotations read by Treint and attributed to him were actually from his pen.

The real charge—that Souvarine, Rosmer, and Monatte had refused to condemn Trotsky—was carefully dodged. Trotsky himself was approached gingerly—like a stricken giant whose strength, though reduced, could not be discounted altogether. "What is the meaning of this sad, sentimental defense of Trotsky, which our Opposition tried to substitute for a discussion of the great problems of the Russian Revolution at the conference of federation secretaries?" Treint asked on April 11, in the *Bulletin Communiste*. "Nothing is more dangerous for a revolutionary movement than to place a man, no matter how great he might be, above all political criticism. . . . For our part, we remain firmly attached to the Old Guard of the Bolshevik Party." And lest the Opposition take advantage of the opportunity to point out that it represented the Old Guard in France, Treint hastily added: "There is no Old Guard in France. An Old Guard is formed through severer struggles than those we have seen."[106]

These wild accusations were bitter fruit for men who associated the revolutionary movement in general, and the Communist Party in particular, with what Trotsky had called "the rude and brutal truth." Monatte had never spoken in favor of creating a web of syndicalist commissions independent of the party. He had merely repeated before the CD and the assembly of the Seine what every informed person had known already: namely, that the syndicalist commissions created in 1923 existed thus far only on paper.[107] It was true that Monatte wished "to syndicalize the party," but in a more profound sense than Treint could ever understand. In Monatte's own phrase, he wanted "to communize" both the party and the unions, which meant that he hoped to make both the party and the unions revolutionary and proletarian organizations—but "revolutionary" and "proletarian" in Pelloutier's sense and not in Lenin's.[1] In protest against Treint's accusations, Monatte resigned his post on *L'Humanité* on April 22; his friends, Rosmer, Godonnèche, Chambelland, Antonini, and Ferdinand Charbit, followed him the next day. All the resignees denied that they had formed a faction with Souvarine.[108]

By the date of the national elections in May the smoke had cleared somewhat, and the alignment within the party leadership could be summarized. Treint's return to power had been made possible by the support of Girault (and thus of the Federation of the Seine) and Sémard (representing the CGTU), and by the weight brought to bear on the more hesitant members of the leadership by Manuilsky. The Russian envoy had presented the question in such a way that to vote against the new theses was to enter into conflict with the majority of the Russian party and the International. What was easy

---

[1] See Monatte's speech before the Federation of the Seine, in *L'Humanité*, 13.iv.24. Monatte thought of the syndicalist commissions as designed not only to win the unions to Communism, but also to teach the party's wartime recruits the importance of union activity. See his pamphlet *Les Commissions syndicales* (1923), p. 9.

in December 1921 was inconceivable in April 1924. Faced with this choice, it is clear, many voted against their inclinations and their consciences in order to break the stalemate and preserve the unity of the party.[109]

Few members of the CD, however, wished to follow Treint in his aping of the Russian dispute and his talk of "bolshevization," "Menshevism," and "liquidationism." Sellier, for example, while he continued to support the theses passed at the meeting of March 18, refused to group Rosmer and Monatte with Souvarine. Nor was he willing to attack Trotsky. His line was that Souvarine had tried to cloak his own indiscipline with the thought and personality of Trotsky, who had nothing to do with these minor squabbles.[110] Renaud Jean was unenthusiastic about the new majority; and Vaillant-Couturier, alarmed at the conduct of Treint, wanted to draw up a new set of theses and restore the party's unity.[111] Dunois, the party's delegate to the Executive, had been willing to sign the theses of the CD when he first received them to show that he was not bound by personal friendship. But when he saw Treint's article "The Way Traced by Lenin," he not only decided not to sign them, but resolved to vote with Monatte and Souvarine against them.[112] The Fédération des Jeunesses Communistes, though ready to condemn the Russian and French Oppositions, was critical of Treint for having attempted to transpose mechanically the Russian and German crises to the French scene. It pointed out that the party faced a danger not only from the Right, but also from the Left.[113] For their part, Monatte and Rosmer insisted that they formed no faction, and that they had nothing in common with Souvarine except the desire to protect Trotsky's name from slander.[114] Souvarine himself, intrepid if not always wise, had left for Moscow, where he attended the Thirteenth Party Congress and spoke in defense of Trotsky and himself.

If the leaders of the party hesitated to follow Treint in his more extreme accusations and wished to go slowly in condemning the Russian Opposition, the militants of the provinces were simply confused and bewildered by the sudden outburst of the crisis. Florimond Bonte, a revolutionary of long standing, wrote Monatte on May 28 (the date of Treint's article) to ask: "What does all this mean? What is this bomb that has exploded in the midst of the battle?"[115] The young Maurice Thorez, not yet admitted to the inner councils of the party, hastened to assure Souvarine that he agreed with him that the French crisis was artificial. Souvarine, he said, could count on his support for his theses.[116] Three weeks later Thorez wrote again to Souvarine, describing the impact of the crisis on his Federation of the Pas-de-Calais. "All our sections" are still "unaware not only of the problem, but also of the positions certain people have taken on the problem. A very small number of militants are trying to figure it all out. Of these, the majority agree that Trotsky is not a Menshevik, and that the real Rightists are not those that are now being designated as the party's Right."[117]

Ignorance, apathy, and skepticism toward the intrigues of Parisian "leaders" were the decisive weapons of Treint's faction in the battle to win control of the provincial federations. The secretary of the Federation of the Seine-Inférieure, Bruyère, wrote Souvarine to ask if it were true that Trotsky wanted "to social-democratize" the Russian Revolution. While passing by the Secretariat, Bruyère had been stopped by Treint and Jean Crémet, who asked him what his federation thought about the crisis. They had told him that everyone in the party had to judge the questions at issue, and that these questions were in fact very simple. Trotsky, they maintained, wanted to extend NEP, open the Russian market to foreign competition, transfer Russian industry to the centers of raw materials, and give the Planning Commission (which was run by non-Communists) full powers.[118]

It is easy to see how a provincial Communist leader could waver when confronted with accusations that he himself had no way to check and told by men he had been accustomed to trust that it was necessary to make a choice. He might decide to put his faith in the Bolshevik majority, as he had done before in 1920 and 1923; he might decide to wait and see; or he might, like the schoolteacher Louis Bouët, suspect that this was another personal conflict similar to those the PCF had seen in 1921 and 1922. Writing to refuse his old comrade Monatte space in the *Ecole Emancipée* in which to attack the party leadership, Bouët expressed what was probably the dominant mood of the provincial Communist:

We do not yet see clearly in the new party conflict. Why, in particular, was Treint removed from the leadership of the party at Lyon? How is it that today Souvarine is with Rosmer and you, when authoritarian methods formerly had no warmer partisan? ... I could pose several other questions that would give you cause to believe that, in this new internal affair, I accord more importance to personal quarrels than to the battle of ideas; but really, for someone who lives far away from Paris and has only the *Correspondance Internationale* and the *Bulletin Communiste*—and perhaps some snatches of conversation while passing through the capital—to inform him, it is difficult to form a firm opinion.[119]

### THE ELECTIONS AND THEIR AFTERMATH

It was the misfortune of the French Communists that their crisis coincided with the national elections held on May 11, 1924. Inevitably, the question of electoral tactics became an issue in the intra-party struggle. In the wake of the occupation of the Ruhr, a great wave of opposition to the Bloc National had gathered. The mechanism of this resurgence of the Left was the Cartel des Gauches, the alliance of all those progressive forces—Radicals and Socialists—who wished to see the Bloc National driven from power. The question was: how far would this cartel reach? Would it include the SFIO? Would it include the Communists? Or would the PCF remain alone and isolated?

The Communists had their answer ready. The Workers' and Peasants' Bloc was first proposed to the Socialists and Resistants on December 17, 1923, and then again during the Congress of Lyon. It was specifically stated in the first offer that the Socialists would have to break off all cooperation with the Radicals, that they had to renounce all previously established electoral cartels, and that they had to abandon their practice of collaborating with the bourgeois press and stop appearing at meetings of the Bloc des Gauches. Two alternatives were presented to the Socialists: "With the Communist Party in constituting the fighting unity of the working class against the Right and Left bourgeoisie; or with the Radical Party against the Communist Party, which refuses absolutely to practice class collaboration."[120] We know, of course, that these prerequisites for joint action were designed to make the offer unacceptable. The Congress of Lyon decided, at Lozovsky's urging, to add another condition: the Socialists and Resistants had to join in the struggle for syndicalist unity.[121]

There is no doubt that some Socialists felt tempted by the idea of a Workers' and Peasants' Bloc. Such Left Socialists as Longuet and Verfeuil would have liked to make common cause with the Communists. But even Longuet despaired when the ECCI outlined in detail its concept of the Workers' and Peasants' Bloc. For Longuet the most important thing was to defeat the Bloc National, even if it meant running the risk of coalitions with the Radicals in the provinces, as it inevitably did.[122] For the majority of Socialist leaders, the choice was easier: they were no more anxious than the Communists to attempt the hazardous experiment of electoral alliances. At their Congress of Marseille, which immediately followed the Communist Congress of Lyon, the Socialists accepted the idea of the cartel to defeat the Bloc National. The Socialist federations were instructed to appeal to the Communist organizations wherever their cooperation might be necessary to defeat the Right. But the offer of a general and exclusive alliance was specifically rejected; and the Socialist statement denounced "the insolent injunction" that would oblige the party to work for the destruction of the CGT and the Amsterdam International under the guise of the struggle for syndicalist unity. It pointed out, moreover, that the Workers' and Peasants' Bloc would mean the victory of the Bloc National in many departments.[123]

This, of course, was a potent weapon to use against the Communists in the eyes of the working class. The Communists replied by appealing to the Socialist workers over the heads of their leaders. "Reject this contradictory and incoherent policy affirmed by your opportunistic leaders at Marseille, which consists, by means of clever balancing, in allying here with revolutionary Communists and there with conservative Radicals, and whose only objectives are inconsequential electoral successes achieved at the expense of principle.... Rally to the flag of the Workers' and Peasants' Bloc!"[124] The Communists, this circular stated, would no longer appeal to the Socialist leaders, but they would be glad to discuss the united front with federations or sections of the Socialist Party. This encounter ended the negotiations between Socialist and Communist leaders. The Communists were hardly anxious to become involved in cooperation with the Socialists at a time when the united front was under attack and the disaster at Chemnitz was fresh in mind. Nevertheless, both the Communists and the Socialists took a bad conscience away from these discussions. Working-class disunity was always difficult to explain to the rank and file. And *Le Populaire* and *L'Humanité* clashed daily during the spring of 1924, each trying to blame the leaders of the other party for making impossible a collaboration that both sets of leaders feared.[125]

The Communists conducted their electoral campaign in a mood of extremism. The resolutions of the Fourth World Congress prescribing that nine-tenths of the party's candidates must be workers and peasants and the Treint amendment barring party officials from running for office were observed.[126] Carried away by the success of his own theses, Treint instructed the party's militants to evoke the specter of revolution, the soviets, and the dictatorship of the proletariat during the electoral campaign. The Workers' and Peasants' Bloc, he maintained, made sense only if it led to power; and this in turn meant a Workers' and Peasants' government.[127]

The nation, however, could not have cared less about soviets or a government of workers and peasants. Its attentions were focused on the struggle between the Bloc National and the Cartel des Gauches. Bolshevism and foreign conspiracy were not central issues. For *Le Temps,* that stronghold of French values, the terms of the electoral contest were clear: "On one side, the France of order, peace, work, thrift, property, the family, and inheritance. On the other, the France of disorder, pacifism, sloth, and Socialism, which abolishes property, breaks up the family, and eliminates inheritance."[128]

The Cartel des Gauches, led by Herriot, Painlevé, and Blum, swept to a decisive victory. The Socialists, who formed an important part of the coalition, shared in the triumph, electing a hundred deputies. The Communists, with their Workers' and Peasants' Bloc and a good deal of Russian money, managed to elect only 26 of their candidates. Of these 26, 19 were in the Seine and the Seine-et-Oise, and only seven in the provinces. Three of the seven provincial deputies were elected in the heavily industrialized Nord. All the former provincial deputies, with the exception of Renaud Jean, were defeated. Cachin and Vaillant-Couturier succeeded in being re-elected; André Marty and Jacques Doriot entered the Chamber for the first time.[m]

It was hard to know whether the Socialists exulted more in their own suc-

---

[m] The Communists received 900,000 votes, 309,000 of which were in the Seine.

cess or the Communists' failure. Analyzing the results of the election, *Le Populaire* concluded that "Communism is just about nonexistent in the provinces. Communism is a Parisian movement."[129] This was perhaps somewhat overstated. What one can say is that in the provinces, the Communist tactics had clearly proved disastrous. The progressive-minded electorate outside Paris had voted for the Cartel des Gauches against the Bloc National, for the Left against the Right. In this clash between the forces of movement and the forces of reaction, Communism had seemed irrelevant. The new leaders of the PCF, however, drew another conclusion from the election. Treint and Girault pointed to the disparity between the Communists' electoral successes in Paris and their failure in the provinces, and claimed that this proved that the Federation of the Seine had followed the right political line.[130] Speculating on the future of the party, Treint went on to predict "a wave of inflation and great labor struggles." "The petty-bourgeois and peasant masses are also threatened. Their disillusionment in the face of the failure of the Left Bloc can lead them toward Communism as well as toward fascism." The party's task, he concluded, was to begin an immediate struggle "against the birth of fascism and against the growth of the anarcho-fascism observed during these last months."[n]

Having conducted a truly Communist electoral campaign and having detected a fascist danger on the horizon, the new majority of the PCF returned to its major preoccupation: the intra-party struggle. The Comintern's Fifth World Congress had been convoked for July 1924. Its purposes were to celebrate the triumph of Bolshevism over the Trotskyite Right, and to bring the International's strategy up to date in the light of the German defeat. What was intended was a wake, not a discussion. Thus it was essential, from Zinoviev's point of view, that each party come to the congress bearing a condemnation of Trotsky and the international Right.

For a brief moment in early May it appeared that the PCF might not do its duty. Bruyère's Federation of the Seine-Inférieure passed a resolution proposing that the French party go to the Fifth Congress uncommitted.[131] There is

[n] *Bulletin Communiste*, 13.vi.24. The French Communists had first become preoccupied with fascism and its causes during the struggle in the Ruhr. On March 13, 1924, Vaillant-Couturier observed that, "The coming of a fascist era now seems to be a threat in France. The point is to figure out if it will come immediately, without elections, or if it will arise from the democratic failure of the Bloc des Gauches, after the elections. It is only a question of time." *L'Internationale Communiste*, February–April 1924, p. 118.

Treint quickly seized on the term and made it part of his political vocabulary, frequently coupling it with the prefix "anarcho." Other French Communists were more cautious in their approach to the phenomenon. Borel, writing soon after the elections, pointed out that fascism would not arise from a struggle between the Bloc des Gauches and the reactionary bourgeoisie, but rather in reaction to the working-class movement. "Either French fascism will be a movement arising in reaction to the upsurge of the revolutionary proletariat or it will not be at all!" *Bulletin Communiste*, 13.vi.24.

no question that this approach appealed to many of the provincial federations, whose members were perplexed by the rapid way in which the crisis had un- folded. A small grass-roots rebellion might even have developed had it not been for the vigorous intervention of the delegates of the Executive, Kirsch and August Kleine, who flayed the motion of the Seine-Inférieure for its "political passivity."[o] Would the PCF go to the congress as "one of the greatest parties of the Third International," Kirsch asked—"that is, well-informed, well pre- pared for participation in the debates, capable of expressing its own opinion, of contributing to the discussion of the events of the past year of international life?" Or would the French party, "following the disastrous traditions and prejudices of its heavy Social Democratic past," come to the World Congress to seek information, to study, to engage in verbal duels "without bringing its firm, conscientious, and clear opinion to bear on all the great problems on the agenda of the Fifth Congress?"[132] Despite the clumsy language in which this question was phrased, no French Communist could ignore the appeal to avoid the pitfalls and habits of the Social Democratic past. To make sure that the right positions were espoused, Kleine himself appeared at meetings of pro- vincial federations, where he was able to participate in the deliberations and influence the outcome. His theme was that Trotsky was trying to "social- democratize" the Russian Revolution and the Bolshevik Party.[133]

The pressure of the delegates of the Executive was decisive; the federations fell smartly into step. At the Thirteenth Party Congress in Moscow, Manuilsky was able to brandish a telegram from the CD of the PCF which proclaimed its support for the Russian majority, and which announced that several feder- ations had declared against the Opposition on the Russian question.[134] On May 18, the Congress of the Seine approved the theses of the CD by an overwhelm- ing majority of 134 to 15.[135] The National Council that met on June 1 and 2 at St.-Denis put the finishing touches to the rout of the Opposition. The new leadership was invested with the full prestige of the International. Zinoviev's message noted that the PCF had become "a great Communist Party," con- gratulated it on its "great electoral success," and singled out the Federation of the Seine for special praise.[136] After accusing the Right of panic and pessimism, Kleine complimented Treint on his unerring instinct for deviations. Treint, he said, "voit loin et juste." After its great electoral victory, Kleine explained, the next task of the party was to become "un véritable parti bolchevik, net, propre, et clair dans ses mouvements."[137] The implication of these vague words was clear to all. It was Sellier who put it most bluntly: even if the French could not grasp all the nuances of the Russian discussion, he said, they had a "devoir de conscience et de responsabilité" to take a position on the crucial questions.

[o] Kleine had also been an active participant in the German party crisis. See p. 366 above.

The delegates had evidently been selected carefully. Only Monatte raised his voice in protest,[138] and he was made the scapegoat of the council. Speaker after speaker marched to the platform to denounce him and the "international Right" he supposedly represented. The discussion was not drawn-out; a vote was taken on the CD theses on the first evening. The result was overwhelmingly in favor of the new majority, 2,353 to 3, with ten abstentions. A telegram was immediately sent to the Comintern announcing the results and affirming the solidarity of the PCF with the Central Committee of the Russian party on all points of the discussion.[139] To anyone who had followed the events of the past two months, it was clear that this nearly unanimous verdict was not the result of reasoned deliberation, but rather a blank check that the French had signed to signify their confidence in the superior wisdom of the Bolshevik majority.

THE FIFTH WORLD CONGRESS

The docility of the federations assured, the scene of battle shifted to Moscow, where the Fifth World Congress convened from June 17 to July 8, 1924. The French were represented by a large delegation of some forty persons which included Treint, Girault, Sellier, Cachin, Marrane, Tommasi, Guy Jerram, Parreye, and Leiciague for the party, Monmousseau, Sémard, and Jules Racamond for the CGTU, and Doriot, François Chasseigne, Roger Gaillard, François Billoux, and Henri Barbé for the JC.[p] Amédée Dunois was present by virtue of his position as delegate to the International, as was Souvarine, who still retained his position as a member of the Executive. Rosmer also attended, though without a mandate from the party. Despite personal entreaties by Lozovsky and Herclet and an urgent invitation by telegram from Zinoviev himself, Monatte chose not to make the trip.[q] Rosmer, who arrived in Moscow in early June, was at first not unduly alarmed by the situation. Writing to Monatte shortly before the congress was to begin, he remarked that he had seen Lozovsky and had attacked "vigorously." Lozovsky scarcely reacted, but just muttered "Diable! Diable!" "He is surely not happy with the fancy business that's been going on, and it disturbs him when he is faced with the facts." As for the crisis in the French party, Rosmer reported that he had heard from diverse sources that Souvarine and Treint would be kept in Moscow, and that

[p] Some attempt evidently was made to select a delegation that would toe the majority's line. On June 19, Monmousseau told Lucie Colliard: "The CGTU's delegation must be made up of comrades with enough guts to smash any rightist faction in the party when they return." Monatte Archives.
[q] See Monatte's letter to Zinoviev, dated June 16, 1924. Lozovsky wrote to Monatte on May 7, 1924, asking him to come and spend some time in Russia; and Zinoviev telegraphed him, on June 6, inviting him to attend the meeting of the Presidium that was scheduled to take place before the opening of the congress. Monatte declined on the grounds that after the National Council he would represent no one but himself. Monatte Archives.

he and Monatte would be asked to resume their posts. "On the whole," he summed up, the situation "remains the same as we have always seen it, aggravated by an unrelenting and hypocritical persecution of the Opposition."[140]

The Fifth World Congress reflected the sorry state to which the world Communist movement had fallen since its last congress in November 1922. No more were there the eager comradeship and the fervent hopes of the Second Congress; no more were there even the firm determination and unyielding optimism that had characterized the Third and Fourth Congresses, when Lenin and Trotsky had led the Russian delegation. Lenin was now dead, and Trotsky, in the shadow of his recent disgrace, was notable chiefly for his absence from the debates. Appropriately, it was during the Fifth Congress that Stalin became known to the delegates of the International for the first time.[141]

The opening of the congress was marked by great pomp and circumstance: there were effusive tributes to Lenin, in the course of which he was compared to Marx; the Russian party was recognized as the repository of Lenin's wisdom; a delegation of pioneers dressed in red scarves came to salute the congress and parade before the Presidium to the beat of drums; the workers of the "Comintern" textile mill presented Zinoviev with a set of overalls and named him an honorary worker in their factory; two funeral marches were played to start the congress, one for Lenin and one for the Bulgarian Dmitri Blagoev; there were cheers for Trotsky and the Red Army; and finally, the workers of the "Red Proletarian" factory brought to the congress an iron hammer, symbol of the struggle against the bourgeoisie.[142] The ceremony was so grand and the language so familiar that few delegates noticed that conspiracy had been replaced by showmanship, or that the debates, far from being a discussion of the possibilities for overthrowing the European social order, had been turned into a kind of elaborately staged ritual in which the triumph of one Russian faction over another was celebrated.

As had always been the case, the treatment accorded visiting Communists was highly selective. Now, however, what counted most was one's stand on the Russian question. Those leaders, like Treint and Girault, who had sniffed out the new line and led the attack on the Right, were praised and taken into the secret councils of the Russian majority or at least given the impression that they were. Those new elements, like Monmousseau and Sémard, who might prove decisive later on, were fêted, pampered, and carefully talked to.[143] Those Communists of the first hour, like Rosmer and Souvarine, who had refused to participate in the condemnation of the Opposition, were ostracized by men whom they had formerly counted their friends and their comrades.[144] There was little pretense at discussion: decisions were merely made behind locked doors, then announced. And in the corridors, the members of the Politburo were already sounding out potential supporters for the next round of intraparty conflict.[145]

The Fifth Congress was Zinoviev's congress in a way the earlier ones never had been: he staged it, directed it, and played the major role in it. The prolific President of the Executive had sounded what was to be the major note of the congress in an open letter sent to all the sections of the International in late April. The Comintern, he wrote, "is between two waves of the proletarian Revolution. One wave has passed, the other is not yet rising."[146] It was this vague text which Zinoviev developed in his four-hour report to the congress. With the Revolution stalemated, he explained, it was inevitable that a Right deviation should tend to emerge. The residual force of Social Democracy in the Communist parties was much greater than had ever been imagined. It was now the task of the International to root out these remnants of Social Democracy, but this could only be done if at the same time the International repressed the extreme Leftist deviation before it began to take on importance. It was true that this extreme Left was small, but "small brooks make big rivers."[147] To those Communists who accused the International of acting without principles in its continual changes of line, Zinoviev replied disdainfully with his favorite rhetorical device, the analogy: "Imagine that we have to steer a warship through a minefield. We have no chart; the mines are located now to the Right, now to the Left. Would you call the captain who swerves to avoid them 'unprincipled'?"[148] This description of the internal dangers facing the International was only matched by Zinoviev's unembarrassed forecast of the prospects for revolution in his closing comments. There were two possibilities, he said: either the crisis of capitalism would develop rapidly, leading to revolution in three, four, or five years; or there would be a temporary stabilization of the capitalist system, in which case revolution would come more slowly. The two prospects were equally likely.[r] The slogan of the new period was to be "Go to the masses by means of the bolshevization of the party."[149]

These ambiguous statements took on meaning only when Zinoviev got down to describing the problems and tasks of each national section. The Executive, he said, had had to fight against the resurgence of a new Right in the PCF. One of the principal errors of this Right was its exaggeration of the importance of the Labour government in England. "The Executive will do everything in its power," Zinoviev pledged, "to prevent the further development of the Right represented by Souvarine, who refutes himself with every word he

[r] "We were somewhat taken aback by this ambivalent and contradictory conclusion," recalled Barbé. When Doriot and other members of the French delegation spoke to Heinz Neumann about it, he responded with an anecdote. To prepare his report, Zinoviev needed statistics on world production, unemployment, and price fluctuations. For these data he turned to the Hungarian economist Eugen Varga, who shot back at Zinoviev: "How do you want your statistics? Indicating a capitalist crisis or proving, rather, the stabilization of capitalism?" Varga had statistics proving both. Henri Barbé, "Souvenirs de militant et de dirigeant communiste" (ms. at the Hoover Institution), pp. 58–59.

speaks, and who in general has no worse enemy than himself, and by Rosmer and Monatte, from whom we expected better. The French party has justly and resolutely fought this tendency."[150] It was now the task of the former Left (Treint) and Center (Sellier) to form a compact Left without factions. The PCF must break out of its isolation and win the great working-class centers. The united front must be applied in such a way that the Communists could appeal to the Socialist workers over the heads of their leaders, and call on them to join the struggle against the Cartel des Gauches on the basis of economic demands. In this way, the Socialists would be torn between their intrigues with the bourgeoisie and their following in the proletariat. In the field of organization, the French party must develop its apparatus and extend the system of factory cells. It must go to the peasants and win the support of the lower strata of the peasantry. The slogan of the Workers' and Peasants' government was more applicable in France than any other country. "A good Communist press, a solid apparatus, better economic liaisons," concluded Zinoviev, "these are the objectives."[151]

As had been the case at previous congresses, the French delegation cut an unimpressive figure. Treint rushed into the debates like hot air into a vacuum, to praise Zinoviev and declare his "unbroken and unbreakable loyalty to 'Leninist principles.' "[152] But his performance was too clumsy to be admired either by the Russians or by his own delegation. Few of the French delegates understood the aims the Bolshevik leaders were pursuing. The great majority, says Barbé, let themselves "be duped by the debates and the pomp of the congress."[153] The apparent unanimity of the French delegation in its condemnation of the Russian Opposition hid serious differences. Monmousseau and Sémard were "arch-hostile" to the Treint group and considered it "too sectarian" and "too 'political.' " A number of the Communist leaders from the Federation of the Seine and the provinces were both critical of Treint's leadership and suspicious of the syndicalists, whose rapprochement with the party they considered too recent to be relied upon. The Sellier-Cachin group tried to avoid the internal disputes of the delegation, but it was opposed to Treint's methods and favored a return to the traditional parliamentary methods of the old Socialist Party. The JC, on the other hand, led by Doriot, wanted the PCF to devote itself to social activities amidst the working class and to anti-militarist agitation.[154]

The congress had its interesting sidelights for the French. Souvarine arranged a confrontation with Trotsky. Despite the protests of Treint and Girault, the delegates insisted on going to see the embattled Bolshevik leader in his quarters at the Commissariat of War. Though defeated and under attack from all sides, Trotsky was still able to impress and intimidate the French. "His lion's mane, his sparkling eyes, his energetic and scoffing expression, his biting irony, his brilliant oratory delivered in remarkable French, his impetuous fits of anger, and above all his knowledge of the working-class movement bowled me over," recalls Henri Barbé. After Souvarine had said a few words, Trotsky "took off in a storm" to explain his views on the development of revolutionary action in France. Having finished, he threw the floor open to questions. Monmousseau asked if it were true that there were differences of opinion between him and the other Bolshevik leaders. Here is Barbé's recollection of the answer.

"It is perfectly possible that disagreement exists among us. I know that I am being called a counterrevolutionary, a Menshevik, and many other things. But," he said, addressing Monmousseau, "while it may be true that I am an international Menshevik, in any case I would have preferred to have my hand cut off rather than sign the disgraceful compromise that you, Monmousseau, signed in Paris with the anarchists after the meeting of January 11, 1924, when the anarchists fired on our men." Taken aback by the violent tone of Trotsky's remarks, Monmousseau did not know how to reply, and the delegates filed out.[155]

Some ten days later, Suzanne Girault took the French delegation to see Stalin at the offices of the Central Committee. Though the interview was very short, Stalin impressed the French by his "contained violence" and his air of inscrutability as deeply as Trotsky had by his vehemence and his brilliance. "I can say without exaggeration," writes Barbé, "that the pose he struck—that of a sphinx smoking a pipe—transfixed the delegation."[156]

Meanwhile, the French delegation was busy arguing over the fate of Souvarine. On June 12, during the meetings of the Executive Committee preliminary to the opening of the congress, Marrane presented a motion in the name of the French delegation condemning Souvarine for his failure to observe discipline and asking that he be deprived of his vote on the ECCI. "Souvarine," the text read, "does not by any means represent the opinion of the French party." Radek, Zinoviev, and Bukharin all spoke against the proposition on the grounds that it violated the statutes of the International. Their argument was that Souvarine did not represent his party on the Executive Committee, but had an independent status as an elected member of the Comintern's ruling body.

Souvarine, taken unawares by Marrane's motion, demanded half an hour to prepare a refutation of the accusations against him. He returned with a bitter statement, in which he warned against the "atmosphère de pogrom" that reigned in the International and complained that it was impossible to express an opinion without becoming suspect. Unanimity, he said, had become "à la mode" in the International. Zinoviev had evidently wished for nothing better than a pretext to chastise Souvarine for his repeated refusals to bend to the Russian majority. He answered Souvarine's charges: "Souvarine, who has always been his own greatest enemy, has taken advantage of the opportunity he was given to make a political statement. We do not hold against him a few violent words, but several of his words have an anti-Communist ring. People who have uttered similar ones have turned out badly from the political point of view. Is it such a bad thing that unanimity should reign in a party?"[157]

A committee was then formed to discuss the "Souvarine case," with Stewart of the British party as chairman, and Mikhail Frunze, Walecki, Vujović, and Marrane as members. Evidently, however, the entire French delegation took part in its deliberations. Treint demanded Souvarine's "pure and simple" expulsion. Guy Jerram made a counterproposition. He suggested that Souvarine be divested of his membership in the CD and of all party posts for one year. A debate followed, during which Monmousseau and Sémard were particularly implacable in their opposition to Souvarine. According to Rosmer's account, "Kleine was active in the corridors and wanted to avenge himself for the scornful fashion in which S. [Souvarine] had treated him publicly." Finally a vote was taken. Jerram's motion got 11 votes (including those of Dunois, Tommasi, Rosmer, Leiciague, and Parreye), which was not enough for passage. Treint then made another harsh proposition, and the Russians replied with yet another more moderate motion, which stated that Souvarine's expulsion was only temporary. Everyone except the Italians accepted the Russian motion.[158]

Shortly after the congress ended, the Souvarine case was taken before the Enlarged Executive. Jerram, Palmiro Togliatti, and Amadeo Bordiga pled extenuating circumstances and spoke against the decision of the committee. Stewart replied for the majority: "Either we are disciplined parties or we are not. The adoption of the resolution will convince the entire Comintern, and, what is still more important, the enemies of the Comintern, that infractions of discipline are not tolerated in our ranks."[159] After Stewart's report, the proposition of the committee was adopted against the five votes of the Italian delegation. Souvarine was expelled from the International and from the PCF on the condition that the French party could propose his admission to the Sixth Congress if he demonstrated his loyalty toward the party and the International in the interim. It was also decided to send an open letter to the French party reminding its members of the "real meaning of discipline," and urging them "to see that it was strictly respected by energetically opposing all deviations and all personal policies, from whatever quarter they might come."[160]

Souvarine's expulsion opened the way for the reworking of the French BP. At the Fourth Congress, the Executive had chosen the new leadership of the PCF, but only after an effort had been made to give the impression that the French themselves had solicited the intervention of the International. The degree to which the PCF had evolved since December 1922 may be measured by the fact that eighteen months later, the designation of the leadership by Moscow no longer seemed a strange procedure. Though we possess no confidential documents describing the exact role the Bolsheviks played in the realignment of the French BP, the principle of selection is easily discovered. Those who had stood most firmly for the Russian majority during the crisis of the spring (Treint, Girault, Sémard) were raised to the leadership; those who had either opposed the condemnation of Trotsky (Rosmer, Souvarine) or consented to it with insufficient enthusiasm (Tommasi) were dropped. The services rendered by the *Vie Ouvrière* group and the party's proletarian aspirations were simultaneously recognized by Sémard's promotion to the position of General Secretary. The new BP (Sémard, Sellier, Treint, Girault, Cachin, Marrane, and Crémet) represented a coalition of three currents: the Treint-Girault Left, the survivors of the old Center, and new blood from the CGTU. Monmousseau's fears that the expulsion of Souvarine and the sudden elevation of Sémard might cause trouble in the party and the CGTU were swept aside by Treint, who reproached him for his timidity.[161]

### A PROFILE OF THE PCF

While at the Fifth Congress, the leaders of the PCF filled out a questionnaire for the files of the Comintern in which they described the structure and evaluated the forces of their party as of the summer of 1924. This document, a copy of which has been preserved in the archives of Pierre Monatte, provides a handy profile of the party on the eve of bolshevization.[162] According to this questionnaire, the PCF was divided into 14 regions and 92 federations. It was governed by a Comité Directeur of 24 members with five additional members chosen from the provincial federations. It counted 50,000 dues-paying members, including 2,000 women and 5,000 candidates who had not yet completed their period of probation. There were 1,500 sections and 250 factory cells. Three-fourths of the party's members lived in cities, and one-fourth in the countryside. Of the urban three-quarters, one-half were workers and the other half civil servants. The party maintained five daily newspapers, 18 weeklies, and three foreign-language newspapers, for a combined circulation of 270,000. Of this total, the Parisian and southern editions of *L'Humanité* accounted for 200,000. In the elections of 1924, the PCF had obtained close to 900,000 votes. The Fédération des Jeunesses Communistes numbered about 7,000 members, the ARAC (whose central council was dominated by Communists) some 20,000, and the CGTU 400,000. These forces were to be compared to the SFIO's 49,000 members, the Union Socialiste Communiste's few hundred adherents, and the CGT's 260,000. This was out of a population of 40,000,000, which included 9,000,000 industrial workers and 3,300,000 agricultural laborers.

These figures speak for themselves, but there are certain points that require emphasis. The Socialist Party had gone to the Congress of Tours almost 200,-000 strong; the newly formed Communist Party had emerged with a still sizable following of 133,000. By June of 1924, the party could claim only 50,000 members. Together with the 50,000 of the SFIO, this amounted to the 100,000 of the Unified Socialist Party in 1914. Ten years of war, revolutionary disturbance, and class conflict had not added one whit to the strength of the Marxist forces in France. The same might be said of the union movement. The 400,000 of the CGTU and the 260,000 of the CGT, discounting for exaggeration and leaving aside the question of the accuracy of the proportion, merely add up to the 600,000 members that the CGT claimed on the eve of the War. There is a similar continuity in social composition. Of the 9,000,000 industrial workers in France, only 18,750 were members of the Communist Party, or fewer than one in 40; and these workers were counterbalanced by an equal number of civil servants. On the other hand, though not proletarian, the party was overwhelmingly urban: 8,000 of its members, 50,000 of the readers of its papers, and 300,000 of its voters lived in Paris; only 12,500 of its militants could be found outside city walls.

The organization of the PCF represented a mixture of the old and the new. The old federal relationships were replaced by a centralized apparatus. The ad-hoc leadership of deputies and journalists gave way to the disciplined and unanimous direction of a Bureau Politique. For all this, the grass-roots structure of the party remained unchanged. Only half the 250 factory cells claimed actually existed; of these, the majority functioned badly if at all.[163] Contact with the masses still took place almost exclusively through the press, the campaign meeting, and the section. Consequently, the tie with the masses was subject to the vagaries of public opinion and political enthusiasm, strong during election campaigns, potentially weak in times of international or internal crisis.[8]

These observations are necessary for understanding the historical significance of the period that followed the Fifth World Congress. The superstructure of the PCF had been transformed by the summer of 1924, but the basis remained unchanged. Though subordinated to Moscow, centralized, and tied to the union movement by bonds that had never existed before the War, the PCF had not yet become an organization capable of manipulating masses. The prime obstacles in its way were the party's structure and its strategy, which was directed toward the elite that the SFIO and the CGT had appealed to before 1914. A mass party in France would have to appeal to unskilled workers, discontented peasants, unassimilated foreigners, and rebellious colonial peoples, as well as to skilled workers and petty-bourgeois elements. The question, which only history could answer, was whether such a party was compatible with the revolutionary ideology in whose name the PCF had been formed.

[8] See pp. 341–42 above.

## Chapter twelve

# Bolshevization

Il n'y a rien de plus à gauche que la ligne léniniste
de l'Internationale et...tout ce qui s'en écarte,
malgré le verbalisme radical dont on le recouvre,
*se classe fatalement à droite,* c'est-à-dire aux con-
fins de l'opportunisme et de la confusion.
> —*Theses of the Comité Directeur, issued
> after the Fifth World Congress, August
> 1924*

Nothing is more difficult in the study of the Third International than to discover what lies hidden beneath a word. The history of international Communism is studded with words—"the united front," "to the masses," "the workers' and peasants' government," "class against class"—that almost always turn
out to mean something very different from what they seemed to mean at first
glance. It is not just that the Communist leaders tried to deceive their followers. More often than not they had only the slightest idea what they meant
themselves. The future was dim; only the present seemed important. The
emphasis in Bolshevism on activism for History's sake encouraged its prac-
titioners to opt for today. Yet because the Bolshevik leaders had a passion for
generalizations, their retreats, sidesteps, and deviations from Marxist ideology
had always to be disguised with resounding slogans. Though misleading, these
slogans were not necessarily empty. They usually announced a major change
in the organization, tactics, or leadership of the Communist parties. Bolshevization was such a word.

The French Communists had first encountered the term "bolshevization"
in the pages of the *Bulletin Communiste* in late March 1924, when Treint
called on the party to oppose the "debolshevization" of the Russian party and
support the "bolshevization" of all other Communist parties. Treint's newly
found and reluctant allies on the CD had not followed him immediately in
the use of these extremely vague and unwieldy words. But the former captain's political acumen (and perhaps his direct connection with the Russian
majority) was borne out when Zinoviev announced to the Fifth World Con-

gress that the great slogan of the coming period was to be the bolshevization of the Communist parties.[1]

The theses on tactics adopted by the Fifth Congress defined bolshevization as "the transfer to our sections of everything in Bolshevism that has been and still is of international import." It was emphasized, however, that bolshevization did not mean the mechanical application of the experience of the Bolshevik Party to the other Communist parties. Five essential characteristics of a Bolshevik party were listed:

1. The party must be a real mass organization. That is, whether it is legal or illegal, it must maintain a close and indispensable contact with the workers and express their needs and hopes.

2. It must be able to maneuver. That is, it must not have a dogmatic and sectarian tactic, but must use against the enemy any strategic maneuver it can without ceasing to remain itself. Their frequent failure to understand this is the chief mistake of our parties.

3. It must be an essentially revolutionary and Marxist party.

4. It must be a centralized party, permitting neither factions, nor tendencies, nor groupings—a monolithic party cast in a single block.

5. It must devote itself systematically to the task of propaganda and organization in the bourgeois army.[2]

During the next ten months, Zinoviev returned continually to the theme of bolshevization in an attempt to give it greater meaning. In January 1925, at a meeting of the Presidium of the Executive, he stated that, "To bolshevize a party means to understand in the given moment how to concentrate attention in a given country upon those concrete main tasks which will provide the party concerned with the possibility: (1) of becoming a mass party; (2) of becoming a party of fighting Leninism."[3] Then, in April 1925, after assuring the Fifth Enlarged Executive that despite the retardation of the world revolution the slogan of bolshevization had more validity than ever, Zinoviev offered two analogies as aids to understanding the International's program. Bolshevization, he said, was both "knowing how to avoid the Scylla of sectarianism and the Charybdis of amorphism and opportunism," and "the art of seizing the most important 'link,' which makes it possible to pull the entire chain." "This 'link,'" he hastened to add, "cannot be identical in all countries because of the diversity of their social and political conditions."[4]

Quite obviously, no good Communist could find fault with the basic concept of bolshevization as it was phrased so cautiously by Zinoviev. In its broadest and most meaningful sense, bolshevization had been under way in France ever since the Congress of Tours. What, after all, were the Twenty-One Conditions, if not an attempt to isolate "everything in Bolshevism that has been and still is of international import." The same might be said of the theses on organization produced by the Third Congress. From the point of view of a wholehearted acceptance of the principles of Leninism, 1923 had been the crucial year in the history of the PCF. For it was in 1923 that the Communists had broken definitively with the traditions of French Socialism: namely, they had defied the government and acted "illegally" to subvert the army; they had embarked on the development of a centralized apparatus; and they had captured such organizations as the CGTU and the ARAC.

Bolshevization, then, cannot be understood simply in the sense of the transformation of the French Communist Party along Leninist lines. Nevertheless, Stalin was quite right when he wrote, in October 1924, that the last six months had brought a "radical change in the life of the Communist parties of the West," though his own efforts to describe in what that change consisted—"a decisive liquidation of the Social Democratic remnants," "the bolshevizing of the party cadres," "shedding the opportunist elements"[5]—may be dismissed as a clumsy and willful attempt at mystification. Zinoviev and Stalin were unable to define bolshevization because out of conviction, calculation, or the inertia of a lifetime's commitment, they were bound to the terminology of revolutionary Marxism. We need not share their limitations. Bolshevization was the last stage in the process, begun in the spring of 1920, by which the Western Communist parties were transformed from left-wing, elitist, and revolutionary organizations into mass movements[a] subordinated to the requirements of Soviet foreign policy. As such, bolshevization was the reflection of a similar change in Russia, which witnessed the transformation of the Soviet Revolution of 1917–19 into a conservative and nationalist regime, more intent on preserving and extending Communist power than in extending the limits of man's freedom.

Though neither of these developments can be considered a radical departure, they did represent a new, significant, and unexpected extension of patterns that had been set earlier in a quite different spirit. This explains why men like Trotsky in Russia and Rosmer in France, who had been the most enthusiastic supporters of earlier "bolshevization," now entered into opposition. They sensed, dimly it is true, the dangerous direction in which Bolshevik practices were heading. More important for the moment, they could not bear to see them applied by men they considered mediocre, incompetent, or unprincipled.

[a] I am using the term in the sense given it by William Kornhauser, to refer to movements that appeal to "large numbers of people who are not integrated into any broad social groupings, including classes." (*The Politics of Mass Society,* Glencoe, Ill., 1959, p. 14.) Hannah Arendt makes a similar point. "The totalitarian movements," she writes, "aim at and succeed in organizing masses—not classes, like the old interest parties of the Continental nation-states; not citizens with opinions about, and interests in, the handling of public affairs, like the parties of Anglo-Saxon countries." *The Origins of Totalitarianism* (New York, 1958), p. 308.

It is here that personal and ideological issues intersect, to produce an Opposition that did not itself yet realize the extent of its alienation from the new Bolshevism and the men who embodied it.

These preliminary remarks are necessary so that the reader will avoid the twin dangers of regarding this period either from the point of view of the victory of the ideas and organization of revolutionary Marxism, in which case the struggle against Trotsky and his supporters becomes secondary and even incomprehensible; or exclusively from the point of view of the persecution of the "Right," in which case the transformation of the party is overlooked. Bolshevization in France had three aspects: the recasting of the party's organization and strategy for the purpose of winning greater influence over the masses; the expulsion or hounding from the party of those men who refused to accept the changes begun in the spring of 1924; and their replacement by new men who were subservient to the majority of the Russian Central Committee. Each of these developments will be considered in turn.

### THE TRANSFORMATION OF THE PARTY

If the Communists had learned any lesson in the four years since 1920, it was that internal crises were more easily surmounted when they were overshadowed by other concerns. This was the experience of 1921; it was also the wisdom of 1923. Thus the first act of the CD[b] after its leading members returned from Moscow in August 1924 was to adopt theses directing the party's attention toward the concrete tasks which the Fifth Congress had assigned the PCF.[6] Chief among these tasks, proclaimed with the fanfare merited by the opening of a new era, were the reorganization of the party on the basis of factory cells; agitation among the peasants; a campaign for the independence of the colonies; the reunification of the syndicalist movement; and the subversion of the bourgeois army. These were, in fact, the areas in which the party exerted its greatest efforts. But theses, no matter how detailed, always left unsaid the most essential points. What was implicit in the theses of August 1924 was that every change announced would be doubled by another, which would bind the party more tightly to Moscow and reduce the PCF's independence and spontaneity to the point at which quantity turns into quality. These innovations may best be discussed under the headings of organization, finances, and tactics.

[b] With the exception of Souvarine, the CD remained the one that had been elected at the Congress of Lyon. (See pp. 353–54 above.) The result was that it lost its decision-making function, and was replaced by the BP. After the Fifth Congress the CD met irregularly, and when it did, the members of the "Right" were sometimes not informed. In other words, the official leadership was superseded by a semi-official group that had Moscow's confidence.

*Organization*

There is no doubt that the most spectacular change in the party after the Fifth Congress lay in the transition from the traditional Socialist organization of sections to the new base unit of factory cells. Where before party members had been grouped according to the area in which they happened to live (the commune in the provinces, the quarter in Paris and other large cities), they would now be organized according to their place of work. The Communist would thus be approached not as citizen or voter, but as producer and potential conspirator, and as rebel against the capitalist system that enslaved him. The idea was that the party would penetrate to the center of the working class, express its needs, defend its interests, identify its aspirations with Communist goals, and in so doing establish an unbreakable liaison between the proletariat and the party.[7] It should be noted that this project paralleled closely the prewar revolutionary syndicalists' dream of constructing a proletarian citadel within the capitalist world, with the difference that the Communists, as good Leninists, approached the working class as masses to be manipulated rather than as elites to be educated.

The history of this development in organization shows how unevenly the Russians moved toward the reshaping of Western Communism in the image of their own party. Factory cells had been used by the Bolsheviks in their struggle against the Tsarist autocracy. During the Revolution, the Red Guards had been organized according to place of work. Yet the Bolshevik leaders were slow to apply this form of organization to the West. Both the Twenty-One Conditions and the theses on organization adopted at the Third Congress spoke of factory cells. But in France these references were interpreted as applying mainly to Communist groups or factions within unions and other organizations, such as the ARAC; and the Bolshevik leaders did nothing to discourage this reading of its directives. Up to January 1924, only the JC had made any sustained effort to create factory cells in France.[c]

---

[c] The Second Congress of the Communist Youth International (July 1921) had passed a resolution requiring Communist Youth organizations to make "a transition from the current exclusively territorial organization of Communist Youth to the formation of Communist League cells." (Quoted in E. H. Carr, *Socialism in One Country, 1924–1926*, 3 vols., London, 1958–64, III, 917.) No attempt to put this directive into practice was made during 1921 or 1922; but it was reapproved and reiterated with greater urgency at the CYI's Third Congress, in December 1922. (*The Minutes of the Third Congress of the Y.C.I.*, Berlin, 1923, pp. 49–52.) At the Congress of Lyon in May 1923, the JC accepted the idea of transforming its organization on the basis of factory cells, and declared it the federation's number one objective. (*L'Avant-Garde*, 6–15.vi.23.) Such a program was difficult because of the JC's overwhelmingly bourgeois composition, but it was pursued with dogged persistence. At the PCF's Congress of Lyon in January 1924, the report on the function of factory cells was given by one of the JC leaders, Roger Gaillard; and it was a

It was the German events of October 1923 that caused the Bolsheviks to focus their attention on the importance of factory cells.[8] The German revolution had failed because the KPD's link with the masses had been too weak. The logical conclusion was that some more effective form of organization was required. On January 21, 1924, after the meeting of the Executive that analyzed the failure of the German revolution, a directive went out ordering all Communist parties to transfer the center of gravity of their organizational work to the cell.[9] The French Communists, it will be remembered, were informed of the Executive's new policy in Zinoviev's letter to the Congress of Lyon. The JC responded enthusiastically, but the debates revealed that the great majority of delegates to the congress had no clear idea of what factory-cell organization would entail.[10] Plans were made to proceed slowly with the creation of factory cells as complements to territorial organization.[d] At this turn, the question of reorganization became entangled with the Russian struggle and the conflict between Treint and the so-called Right. Treint and Girault saw an issue to their liking in the unwillingness of the leadership elected at Lyon to proceed immediately with a total reorganization of the party's cadres. The Federation of the Seine rushed hastily to create—on paper—as many cells as possible; Treint followed his article "The Way Traced by Lenin" with another the next week, in which he linked bolshevization with the new organization. "To bolshevize the party," he announced, "is above all, at this time, to root it in the factories."[11] Treint's feeling for the winds blowing in the Comintern was shown at the Fifth Congress, when Zinoviev informed the French delegation that its most pressing task was to complete the entire reorganization of the party by December 31, 1924. Thus factory cells were not meant to complement the sections, as had originally been thought, but to supplant them.

The party's new organization has been described in detail elsewhere, and there is no point in repeating here the work done by others.[12] As always, the Comintern eschewed half measures. The entire structure of the party was reworked from base to summit. Socialist organization had been modeled on the administrative subdivisions of the Third Republic. The Communists now broke with these bourgeois conventions. All members of the party who worked in factories or businesses were required to form cells. The unemployed, the self-employed, and those working in isolated occupations (domestics, *concierges*) were permitted to organize street cells. Street and factory cells met by quarters. Several quarters formed a *rayon*. The rayons of a city elected a *comité de ville*. City and provincial rayons formed a departmental committee.

---

recognition of the JC's pre-eminence in this field when Gaillard was charged to prepare a pamphlet on this subject for the federations' use. *L'Avant-Garde* was justifiably proud of the role the JC had played at Lyon, and January 1924 may be taken as the date for the final acceptance of the JC by the party. *L'Avant-Garde*, February 9–23, 1924.

[d] See pp. 352, 354 above.

The federations themselves, traditionally the backbone of the party, were compressed into 27 regions, for the purpose of greater control.[13]

The problems involved in the reorganization were immense.[14] French factories were small; consequently, cells were so limited in membership that they were lifeless. Workers feared reprisals from their employers. Many workers commuted long distances to their place of employment. In the Nord the old traditions were deeply entrenched. In general, both bourgeois and workers preferred the old system to the new. The leadership resisted these objections, despite the loss of thousands of members.[e] Obstacles were surmounted. When they could not be surmounted, they were ignored. By April 1, 1925, the party could announce that its reorganization was complete. Later modifications in the party's structure were required. Many cells never functioned; others existed only in the pages of the Secretary's report.[15] Eventually, the preference for the street cell had to be acknowledged. Nonetheless, the PCF has retained to this day, with minor modifications, the organization imposed on it in 1924–25.[16]

The transition from sections to factory cells was supposed to make the party more proletarian. It did. By the end of 1924, the proportion of workers in the PCF was undoubtedly much higher than it had been at the beginning of the year.[17] After the first prejudices had been discarded, the worker, particularly the unskilled worker, found that the cell offered him advantages that the section could not provide. In addition to being a political and revolutionary organization, the cell was a school and a community in which the worker could find friends and roots. Inside, with his fellow Communists, he belonged; outside, he was a stranger in a bourgeois world that refused him admittance to its temples and hierarchies.[18] But if the first effect of the reorganization was to bring the party closer to the working class, its secondary result, no less important, was to make the party itself less democratic. Cells were smaller, less bourgeois in the good sense of the word, less concerned with theoretical and political questions, more easily controlled by the Center. While offering a splendid link with the masses and a potential basis for illegal and clandestine activity, they protected the leadership from potential rank-and-file rebellion. In short, the creation of factory cells institutionalized the malady of overcentralization that had afflicted the PCF in 1923, and made it both the party's weakness and its strength: weakness in time of social peace, strength in time of social crisis.

[e] Ferrat, who played an active role in the reorganization, writes that there was a turnover of some 70 per cent of the party's membership in the course of 18 months of reorganization. Though precise figures are lacking, it would seem that membership rose to 60,000 in the fall of 1924 and remained there throughout 1925. This would indicate that 42,000 Communists abandoned the party between July 1924 and December 1925. (Ferrat, *Histoire du Parti Communiste Français*, 1931, p. 144.) There is an analysis of the PCF's membership in *BEIPI*, March 1–15, 1955, p. 24.

Concurrently with these measures of reorganization, less publicized steps were taken to strengthen the apparatus and tie the PCF more closely to Moscow. After four years of drift, the parliamentary Group was finally incorporated into the party and put under the control of the BP.[19] If this could be achieved with so little friction, it was because the members of the parliamentary Group owed their power to the party and not the other way around, as had been true in the prewar SFIO. With the exception of Cachin, Jean, and Doriot, the Communist deputies were nonentities raised to their high estate by the play of chance and the whim of the party's sectarian tactics. Realizing this, they obeyed. *L'Humanité* was reorganized, its staff cut, and the salaries paid its employees reduced. The reorganization resulted in a tightening of control; it also produced a lowering of journalistic standards. It was at this date that *L'Humanité* acquired the drab and vulgar format it has retained to the present day. Russian patterns were imitated both in form and in content. An organizational bureau was established (Thorez was later its director); the practice of transferring personnel from one part of the country to another was initiated; even the name of the Comité Directeur was changed to Comité Central.[20] The number of paid bureaucrats was increased sharply, though no figures were ever released on this aspect of the party's reorganization.

One of the greatest problems was to find trained organizers to aid provincial federations in making the transition to the new type of party structure. This gap was partly filled through the establishment of a Leninist school in Bobigny, which put 65 party members through a two-month course in organization during the fall of 1924. Other similar schools were set up in the Paris region and in the provinces.[21] Comintern agents oversaw the teaching of these schools, as well as the work of reorganization. Kleine, Zinoviev's *homme de confiance,* returned to France after the Fifth Congress to complete the work he had begun so successfully in the spring; and it would seem that thereafter the assignment of a representative of the Executive to the PCF was standard practice. This in itself constituted no innovation: Comintern agents had visited France ever since 1920, and a permanent delegate had been assigned to the PCF as early as May 1922. Yet there was a difference in the emissaries who came after the Fifth Congress. What distinguished men like Kleine from earlier agents like Humbert-Droz was that they represented a Russian leader as well as a policy, and possessed a prestige that no French leader dared challenge. "They had the power to demand everything," recalls Henri Barbé, "including changes and transfers of leading personnel.... Every word that issued from their mouth was considered sacred and irrefutable."[22]

*Finances*

Money, says tradition, is the root of all evil. More than one former Communist has seen in the corrupting effects of Russian subsidies the source of the degeneration of the Comintern.[23] The financial aspect of bolshevization may be summed up in a sentence. The reorganization of the party, the expansion of its apparatus, and the development of new cadres required money; and the leadership's need for money, which it had no means of raising, made it more dependent than ever upon Moscow.

Not much has been said in this study about finances, and for good reason. The prewar SFIO operated on a shoestring. As late as 1914, it employed only five paid bureaucrats: a secretary, two assistants, a treasurer, and an archivist. Deputies doubled as propagandists; and though the results were not good, expenses were kept at a minimum. In 1913, for example, the party spent only 5,500 francs.[24] The CGT managed on the same slim budget. After the War everything went up—hair, skirts, and the expenses of running a working-class party. Even the organization of a small opposition group cost more money than it would have before the War. Politics was expensive, and beginning in the spring of 1920 the Bolsheviks sent subsidies to the French Communists. These sums, smuggled across the French border by visiting agents, were intended for specific purposes, such as the publishing of the *Bulletin Communiste,* the diffusion of Comintern propaganda, delegations to Russia, and the support of the journals and anti-militaristic activities of the JC.[25]

After Tours this aid was continued and indeed increased, but the party itself lived on its own income.[1] This was possible in part because of the relatively high membership of the PCF during the first two years and the enthusiastic response it met from the working class, in part because the apparatus was kept small. From 1921 to 1923, the party employed only four permanent propagandists, and the JC only one. Their salaries were low: 1,000 francs a month and 25 to 30 francs *per diem* traveling expenses. The General Secretary himself received only 1,200 francs a month. *L'Humanité* supported the party newspapers and journals that operated at a loss, such as Renaud Jean's *La Voix Paysanne, L'Ouvrière,* and *L'Humanité de Nîmes.* When Renoult's *Internationale* proved to be a financial failure at the end of 1921, its publication was discontinued. According to the financial report published by the party at the end of 1922, its expenses had been 676,856 francs and its income 260,561 francs (of which 218,421 had been obtained by the sale of party cards), with the deficit financed by public subscriptions advertised in *L'Humanité.*[26] This may be taken in its broad outlines as a true picture of the party's finances during the first two years of its existence. Only the Fédération des Jeunesses Communistes received large subsidies.[27]

---

[1] Frossard, *De Jaurès à Lénine* (1930), pp. 189–90: "As long as I stayed in the party, not one ruble went into the treasuries of the organization or the paper. Cachin, Renoult, Dunois, and I were absolutely uncompromising on this issue. We felt that subsidies from Moscow would not only deprive us of our independence, they would lead the party to forget the importance of individual effort by its members."

Even so, there was grumbling at the pernicious role played by Moscow's gold. The most dramatic incident came at the Fourth World Congress, during a meeting of the French Commission. The Left and Center, it will be remembered, were engaged in a bitter conflict. Renaud Jean and other members of the Center had threatened to raise the question of subsidies to the Leftist JC. One day, at the end of a long and tiring session, when the last item on the agenda had been dealt with, the delegate of the JC rose to ask a qualified representative of the Comintern to remind those comrades who were attacking the Jeunesses that the subsidies of the Executive were a completely natural demonstration of international solidarity. Renaud Jean immediately went up to the platform where Trotsky was seated and engaged in a violent exchange with the Bolshevik leader, which ended when the latter reminded Jean that "the International has nothing in common with a fair at which wily peasants give themselves over to bargaining."[28]

Another slightly different but equally significant episode took place the following February, after the delegates had returned from Moscow. Ilbert, a member of the Treint-Girault group, had been accused of stealing money from a workers' solidarity fund some years before. A Conflict Commission, set up by the Federation of the Seine, ruled that although he need not be expelled, Ilbert must resign from all official party positions. Suzanne Girault ignored the decision and arranged for Ilbert to retain his posts. When these events were discussed at a meeting of the Left, Treint defended Ilbert, saying that the morality which condemned theft was bourgeois and thus inapplicable to a Communist. Monatte, who witnessed this meeting, was so disgusted that he decided to put off joining the party.[29]

As in so many other matters, the great change in the party's finances came between March and October 1924. Treint's reorganization in the summer of 1923 had required expanding the apparatus to include 24 regional delegates. Though it is not known how much they were paid, it can be assumed that the party's expenses expanded proportionally. In October 1923, the PCF was provided with a special emergency fund to be used in the event the German revolution broke out. Part of this money was used to buy a radio transmitter and to relaunch the defunct *Internationale*. Most of the fund was not used, and when the crisis provoked by the Russian question broke out in the spring of 1924, the new majority turned to this money to create an apparatus.[30] The elections followed. Whatever their results from the point of view of agitation and propaganda, they were a disaster financially. Of the 300,000 francs that Sellier claimed to have raised in the party's subscription drive, only 30,000 had actually been collected.[31] By the Fifth Congress the CD admitted to a deficit of 700,000 francs, and the true figure seems to have been closer to 2,000,000.[32] Only massive subsidies from Moscow could have saved the party during this period. Though temporary cutbacks were made in the number of party papers and regional delegates during the summer and fall,[g] new sums were necessary to finance the operations of the Organizational Bureau and the Leninist school. The subscriptions and loans so loudly proclaimed in the press were mostly designed to conceal the influx of Russian money.[33]

It is difficult to know how much money was funneled into France during the next years through the services of the Comintern's secret transportation and financial branch, the OMS (Otdel Mezhdunarodnoi Svyazi). At the end of 1927, Souvarine mentioned the figure of 25 million francs for the preceding four years.[34] Even allowing for exaggeration, the sums must have been very large indeed to allow the PCF to weather the storm of the reorganization and its own ineptitude. Perhaps the greatest damage done by these subsidies was to the moral caliber of the party. Money was dispensed loosely; consciences were often bought; the Ilberts tended to predominate rather than the Monattes. Rappoport's remark sums up the change: "On a remplacé des valeurs par des voleurs."[35]

### Tactics

Up to 1924 the greatest efforts of the party had been devoted to winning the revolutionary elite of the working class and the progressive bourgeoisie, organized in the CGTU and the ARAC. These objectives had been successfully attained in 1923, but only at the cost of losing the unorganized masses who had been drawn to the SFIO in 1919–20.[h] After the Fifth Congress, the Communists widened their net and extended their agitation to include other groups hitherto unexploited: specifically, the reformist workers in the CGT, the oppressed peoples in the colonies, and the discontented sector of the peasantry. The implications of this change in tactics were not immediately clear because it was carried out in a spirit of sectarianism that contrasted sharply with the party's avowed aim of winning the masses. But, though the new tactics were not destined to bear fruit until a later era, the foundations of Communist action were laid in 1924–25.

Little need be said about the Communist campaign to reunify the CGT and the CGTU. Throughout 1922 and 1923, the strategy of the CGTU leadership had been to win as many workers as possible for their own revolutionary unions. Comintern and Profintern directives to the contrary had been either rejected or ignored. Though united front tactics were accepted after the Fourth Congress, they were interpreted exclusively in the sense of unity from below. Few Communist union leaders believed in the possibility or even the

[g] The regional apparatus was reduced from 24 to six during the Fifth Congress. *Bulletin Communiste*, 18.vii.24.
[h] By January 1924 the PCF numbered only one-fourth the total enrolled in the SFIO at the end of 1920.

desirability of cooperating with the reformist leaders.[i] At the Congress of Lyon, Lozovsky had persuaded the Communists (and thus the leaders of the CGTU) to campaign for syndicalist unity. This tactic had patent disadvantages, for in France the Communists had the majority of the organized workers. Nevertheless, the Communists buckled down and urged on the reluctant reformists their heartfelt desire for a reconciliation. Proposals for a unity conference were made in January 1925 and again in August, during the CGT's annual congress. The development of a Left among the reformists permitted the hope that these advances might be reciprocated, but the Communist campaign foundered in September, when the leaders of the CGT boycotted the CGTU's congress of unity. Hopes for unity faded on both the national and the international levels in 1926. Two gains were registered, however, which stood as portents for the future. First, the Communist leaders themselves had been won over to the slogan of trade-union unity, and henceforth the PCF began to establish factions in the CGT. The struggle over principle had been won.[36] Second, the events of September 1925 showed that a sizable number of CGT delegates responded to the plea for unity. A crisis would cause them to break discipline and force their leaders into the arms of the Communists. The reunification of the CGT and the CGTU thus awaited the right atmosphere and the right shock.

The most dramatic change in Communist tactics in 1924–25 was the PCF's increased attention to the colonial question. The prewar SFIO had opposed colonialism, but its efforts in this area had been devoted almost exclusively to unmasking the relationship between war and imperialism.[37] The party had no specific colonial policy. Socialist federations did exist in Algiers and Constantine, and there were also isolated Socialist groups in Tonkin and Senegal, but together they counted less than 500 members in 1914. On the eve of the War, the Algerian federation was in decline.[38] After Tours the majority of the Algerian federation joined the PCF. The emphasis of the Bolsheviks on colonial questions inspired a short-lived interest in overseas matters among the French Communists. A forum on the colonial question was opened in *L'Humanité* in 1921, and a propagandist, André Julien, was assigned to North Africa. These first steps toward a colonial policy were submerged in a sea of indifference, at least in France. Moreover, the articles that appeared under the colonial rubric showed that few Communists agreed with the Twenty-One Conditions, which required Communist parties "to support every colonial liberation movement not merely with words but with deeds."[39] Julien pointed out, for example, that the Algerian Communists had "come out clearly against nationalist movements and nationalist revolts, unanimously and without a single

[i] See p. 263n.

voice being raised to sustain a contrary point of view, without a single native comrade having made the slightest comment."[40]

Julien seems to have reflected accurately the sentiments of the North African Communists. When the Comintern drafted an appeal for the liberation of Algeria and Tunisia in May 1922, the Algerian section of Sidi Bel Abbès replied with a memorandum requesting that its publication in Algeria be countermanded.[41] Despite their long tradition of Leftism, the memorandum read, the Communists of the Sidi Bel Abbès section could not accept the International's colonial policy. The liberation of Algeria would be reactionary, not progressive, if it came before a victorious revolution on the mainland. The native population of North Africa was composed in major part of elements hostile to the economic, social, and intellectual development necessary to enable an autonomous State to build Communism. The job of the PCF in North Africa was therefore to establish a favorable attitude toward Communism. These propositions were accepted unanimously by the Second Communist Interfederal Congress of North Africa, on December 7, 1922.[42] The attitude of the North African Communists was that appeals to revolt and Communist propaganda among the native population would be not only premature, but dangerous. Meanwhile, the memorandum of the section of Sidi Bel Abbès had earned the French a dressing down by Trotsky at the Fourth World Congress. Communists, he said, who sustained such opinions could not be tolerated in the party for an instant.[43] The resolution on the French question passed at the congress instructed the CD "to devote infinitely more attention, force, and means than it heretofore has to the colonial question and to propaganda in the colonies, and, among other things, to create a permanent Bureau of Colonial Action closely related to the CD."[44]

A Comité des Etudes Coloniales was created, but it does not seem to have functioned during the following year. As late as June 1924, an Arab Communist could write that since the Fourth Congress the party had done "almost nothing" for the masses in the colonies.[45] The leadership was aware of this gap. At the Lyon Congress an impressive and detailed report was presented by the Comité des Etudes Coloniales.[46] It promised a program of agitation among the natives in both metropolitan France and the colonies. Two types of nationalist movements were distinguished: one reformist, which collaborated with colonial governments; the other proletarian and anti-bourgeois. The party was to oppose the first and sustain the second. It was emphasized, however, that the PCF would not hesitate to support any nationalist group during the early stages of its struggle for independence. More specifically, it was recommended that the post of colonial delegate be re-established, that the colonial forum in L'Humanité be reopened, and that the Comité des Etudes Coloniales be represented on the CD.

Whatever might have been done to implement these recommendations in the spring of 1924 was forgotten in the furor over the party crisis. At the Fifth Congress the French, along with the British Communists, were castigated by Manuilsky for their sluggishness in supporting colonial liberation movements.[47] The party leadership was either too uninterested or too absorbed by other matters to pay much attention to such peripheral matters as the colonies. But the JC took Manuilsky's reproach to heart. Doriot and Chasseigne came back from Moscow determined to embark on the kind of anti-colonialist campaign that the JC had conducted in the Army of the Ruhr during 1923. An opportunity for concrete action now presented itself. In July 1924, war had broken out between the Spanish and the followers of the Moroccan chieftain Abd-el-Krim. On August 19, Chasseigne announced to a meeting of the Federation of the Seine that "the most immediate task of the PCF is work in Morocco." The party, he said, must infiltrate the French army. Soon afterward Sémard and Doriot sent Abd-el-Krim a telegram in the name of the CD, the parliamentary Group, and the Fédération des Jeunesses Communistes, congratulating him on his successes against the Spanish army. "For the first time," wrote Sémard and Doriot, "the French party is taking a clear position."[48]

No clearer demonstration was ever given of the difference between the JC and the party, between the generation of Doriot and the generation of Cachin. For Cachin a verbal defiance of government authority was enough— and perhaps, on such a delicate issue as the colonies, too much. Doriot insisted on translating the party's threats into action.[49] The French JC made contact with their Spanish counterparts. Arrangements were made for joint action. An appeal was issued calling on French and Spanish soldiers to fraternize with the hordes of Abd-el-Krim. Doriot scandalized the Chamber of Deputies by reading the party's telegram from the tribune.[50] The opening of hostilities between the French and Abd-el-Krim in May 1924 offered Doriot an opportunity to intensify and extend the party's campaign. Though opposed by Cachin and Girault, he had the support of the CGTU's leadership, whose activism was always easily brought to the surface. An Action Committee was organized. Congresses of workers and peasants were staged throughout the country, the largest held in Paris on July 4–5, 1925, drawing almost 2,500 delegates. For the first time since Tours, militants of the SFIO and the CGT were persuaded to participate in a true united front with the Communists.[51] In the summer of 1925, Doriot led a JC delegation to Morocco itself, in an attempt to make contact with Abd-el-Krim and establish a liaison with local nationalist movements.[52] The party's campaign was halted by a strong counterattack by the government in the fall of 1925. Abd-el-Krim and his followers were defeated and pacified. The first beginnings of united action between Communists and reformists had no aftermath. But it was indisputable that in the space of a year, the party had uncovered a whole new area of operation and untapped reserves of discontent, as well as a new and popular leader: Doriot.

The third group which the PCF reached out to embrace for the first time in this period was the peasantry. Like the colonial question, the problem of the peasantry was inherited from the prewar SFIO. Despite the fact that the party of Jaurès and Guesde had several strongholds in the provinces, it had never succeeded in attracting large numbers of peasants before the War. There were two reasons for this. Aside from the personal efforts of Compère-Morel, the party had no agrarian program. Its propaganda was overwhelmingly political and ideological, and thus it tended to find converts in the provincial bourgeoisie—among lawyers, notaries, and schoolteachers. Where the party did draw peasants, it was not as Socialists or potential revolutionaries, but as good republicans determined to rout the reactionary opposition, or as anti-militarists determined to avoid their military service. The second and most important reason was that before 1914, peasants were conservative, and when they were not conservative, they were politically apathetic.[53]

A cluster of peasant recruits in 1919 and 1920 and their surge toward the most leftward positions at Tours seemed to indicate that the War had revolutionized the peasantry. Renaud Jean's agrarian theses, drawn up for the Marseille Congress, were designed to attract these angry farmers to Communism.[j] Immediate collectivization was dismissed in favor of a transitional regime, in which the profit motive would prevail and working peasants would be guaranteed hereditary use of their land. Strong emphasis was placed on the relationship between capitalism and war and the need to create a milieu in which proletarian and peasant could make their way toward Communism in harmony rather than in conflict. Analyzing these theses, Lenin concluded that Jean's basic point—"namely, that the immediate application of integral Communism to the conditions of *small peasant farming* would be profoundly erroneous"—was "correct and important from the practical and theoretical point of view."[54] These early hopes for peasant support, however, were not fulfilled in the years that followed. The peasants seemed to retreat into their prewar apathy. And when in 1922 Jean suggested that the party formulate its slogans so that they appealed to the peasantry, Trotsky replied with a blistering article in which he reminded the French peasant leader and war veteran that the proletariat was the only really revolutionary class.[55]

The turn came in 1924 after the national elections, when only four non-industrial provincial federations elected Communist deputies.[56] Zinoviev instructed the French at the Fifth Congress to begin serious work among the peasants, and Jean's theses returned to favor. As Gordon Wright observes:

By the end of 1925, the Communists had built up a whole new apparatus of national and regional agrarian committees; they had added courses in peasant action to the curriculum of the Central Leninist School; and they had founded, alongside

[j] See pp. 244–45 above.

their union for farm laborers, a new union (the Confederation of Toiling Peasants) designed to recruit smallowners, tenants, and shopkeepers. In the municipal elections of 1925 the Communists registered their only notable gains in the rural villages; and in 1926 the party reported to the Comintern that 70 per cent of its most recent converts were peasants.[57]

None of these tactical innovations was successful in the 1924–25 period. The campaign for syndicalist unity was dashed by the opposition of the reformist leaders. The agitation against the Riff War lost the party more supporters than it won.[58] Work among the peasants ground to a halt in 1926. These programs were unsuccessful in 1924 and 1925 partly because they were clumsily applied, partly because they were identified with an irresponsible policy of adventure and class war, but most importantly because the economic and political situation was not propitious. The Dawes Plan had brought stabilization to the European economy, and between 1924 and 1929 the French, like other Europeans, enjoyed a period of relative prosperity. Moreover, a Leftist government made Communist cries of fascism and imperialism appear ridiculous to the great majority of Frenchmen, and even to Communists themselves.[59] In the perspective of history what is important about this period is that the Communists themselves were converted to the Leninist tactics they would use later, in a period of social upheaval and political instability. It was Renaud Jean who summed up the new attitude toward tactics that crystallized in 1924: "When doctrine is in conflict with the Revolution, it is the Revolution which is right."[60] This phrase expressed succinctly the real import of the transformation that the party underwent in 1924–25. The traditional doctrines and methods of the Left Wing had been sacrificed to the goal of Revolution. But what if the goal itself was sacrificed to a higher necessity—the preservation and strengthening of the proletarian State? That happened only in the 1930's, under Stalin, when Communism at last was able to effect a reconciliation with nationalism, under the guiding hand of Soviet foreign policy.

### THE FATE OF THE OPPOSITION

For those with a sense of what is personal in history, there is something tragic about the fate of the Opposition. Those men who had been the earliest and most enthusiastic converts to Bolshevism became its victims, defeated by the very instruments they had helped to forge. The experience of rupture with the party was a shock of such proportions that the majority of former Communists never recovered from it. For two, three, and in some cases even four decades, they lived in the shadow of these five years between 1919 and 1924, lonely and superfluous figures out of the past, carefully rehearsed and dedicated players whose historic roles had been canceled on the eve of great events. There is a further irony to be noted. Though the leaders of the Opposition promised eternal loyalty to the principles of Communism upon their departure or expulsion, they were eventually led to become the most violent and irreconcilable enemies of the party which embodied those principles. This was no accident. Once the Comintern had resolved to break with the traditional precepts and methods of the Left Wing, it was inevitable that it would break with its representatives. The Opposition, on the other hand, could not remain faithful to an organization that negated in spirit and in practice their conception of a proletarian party. Some of these men later abandoned the ideas they had held in 1919–24; others did not, believing that the principles remained valid but the men who applied them were corrupt. Whether of one persuasion or the other, they were all termed "enemies of Communism." This was a fate they did not deserve. Without them the Communist parties would never have been born. The story of the Opposition is a story of successive disillusionments. For the sake of brevity it will be told here in three stages: the expulsion of the "Gauche Ouvrière"; the rout of the Opposition carried out in the name of the International's slogan of "normalization"; and the development of the Opposition after the Congress of Clichy in January 1925.

## The Expulsion of the Gauche Ouvrière

There is no doubt that even after the upheaval of the spring and that drab ritual of conformism and political liquidation which was the Fifth World Congress, the French "Right" retained every intention of remaining within the party, where it conceived of itself as playing the role of a vociferous but loyal opposition. For those who despaired, of course, there was always the example of the War, during which the minorities in both the SFIO and the CGT had organized themselves and succeeded either in wresting control of their organization from the hands of the patriotic majority, as in the case of the party, or at least in pushing the leadership leftward, as in the case of the CGT. In late May of 1924, during the height of the campaign against Trotsky and his French defenders, Monatte had written to Parreye, a member of the CD of the Federation of the Nord, to stiffen his resolve and dissuade him from resigning from the party. "I shall stay in the party as a rank-and-file militant, and I shall defend my point of view in the hope and the conviction that future events will prove us right." As for those militants who supported the International in the crisis, Monatte was inclined to be tolerant. The majority had yielded because the International had spoken; they thought they were thus being more faithful to the International than we; they were mistaken, and in the long run they would realize that they were wrong and understand that it was the Opposition who remained faithful to the spirit of the International. "The future," Monatte assured Parreye, "will prove us right. Let us be patient and steadfast."[61]

It was taken for granted by the Opposition that it would be allowed the weapon of criticism, if nothing more. As Rosmer explained to Monatte in mid-August, after informing him that he had attacked Sellier "brutally" during the August 6 session of the CD, it was their strategy "to throw themselves on the 'Leftists' as well as the politicos like him [Sellier], who denounce our 'Menshevism,' and who are forced, because of their supremely intelligent policies, to eliminate with pell-mell brutality both what is useless and what is indispensable to the party."[62] Monatte made a first step in this direction at the conference of federation secretaries, which met in Paris on September 22–23 to hear the reports of the French delegation on the proceedings of the Fifth Congress. Much to the consternation of Sémard and Girault, who had planned an orderly and uneventful demonstration of approval for the resolutions of the congress, Monatte insisted on the question period customary at former assemblies of the Communist Party. When his own turn came to speak, the veteran militant defended Souvarine and pointed to inconsistencies in the statements of certain party leaders. His dissatisfaction was echoed by Edmond Guillou, Secretary of the Federation of the Vendée, who raised the question of Lenin's testament, and asked why the French delegation had demanded Souvarine's expulsion in Moscow when the issue had not been discussed at the National Council of June; by Delagarde, who expressed amazement that Trotsky's name had not been mentioned during the reports; and by Roger Rieu, who criticized the financial policy of the leadership.[63]

But 1924 was not 1914, and the new majority had no intention of tolerating an awkward and dangerous opposition within its ranks, especially at a moment when it was so patently open to criticism. Moreover, it now had at its disposal both the authority of the International (personified by Kleine) and the sanction of discipline. Since Rosmer, Monatte, and Delagarde still held their places on the CD, the first response of the leadership was to circumvent this body and make all important decisions within the BP, which was a clear violation of party statutes. Second, it was made clear to the minority that by their opposition they were treading a path that led inevitably to expulsion from the party. At the conference of federation secretaries, Cadeau had pointed his finger threateningly at Monatte and Rosmer and said: "You who are almost outside the party...."[64] The motion passed by the conference unanimously (with "some abstentions") warned that the federation secretaries would view any attempt to reopen the Russian discussion, "now theoretically and practically closed, as a desire to harm and break up the party by obstructing its political work and its work of reorganization on the basis of factory cells." And to ram home the point, a special resolution was passed at Kleine's suggestion, which instructed the leadership to obtain either the support of the Opposition or their resignation.[65]

After the conference of federation secretaries, the leadership set out to assemble a dossier that could be used to justify Monatte's and Rosmer's expulsion. Proofs of anti-Communism were taken wherever they could be found. Both the Secretariat in Paris and Treint in Moscow wrote Monatte asking him to write an article condemning the Swedish Communist Zeth Höglund, whose major crime had been his refusal to cooperate in his own political liquidation.[66] Monatte demurred. Immediately after the conference of federation secretaries ended, the BP addressed letters to Monatte, Rosmer, Delagarde, and Rieu demanding that they state: (1) whether they accepted the decisions of the Fifth Congress and the conference of federation secretaries; (2) whether they were ready to work in the party for the accomplishment of its political and organizational tasks; and (3) how they stood on the crisis in the Swedish party.[67] In short, the Opposition was asked to condemn itself. Rieu answered the first two questions affirmatively, and the third by saying that he supported the ECCI against Höglund; at the same time he protested against the accusation that he was anti-Communist, and insisted that his opposition had been totally distinct from that of Rosmer and Monatte, which indeed it had been.[68] Rosmer, Monatte, and Delagarde gave the sought-after replies on October 5, 1924, but did so in an aggressively worded letter that left no doubt of the contempt in which they held the party's leadership.[69] Their letter reminded those Leftists of the moment who tried to class them with the Right that in 1914 they had been among the small handful of those who had saved the cause of internationalism in France, that in 1915 they had defended Zimmerwald, that in 1919 they had been among the first to join the Third International, and that in 1922 they had defended the tactic of the united front. The three Oppositionists gave no promise of silence. On the contrary: their letter implied future confrontations. "No one will succeed in passing us off as saboteurs of the party and of the efforts to prepare the proletariat for revolution," they warned.

Such reminiscences were hardly designed to heal the breach between the Opposition and the majority. More than one member of the new leadership had a record of resistance to the decisions of the International. Both sides girded for the battle. The leadership reserved its first blows for the entourage of Monatte and Rosmer. On October 7, Maurice Chambelland was expelled after he accused Werth, a member of the new majority, of having stolen 14,500 francs from the party treasury.[70] The following week (October 13) a representative of the CD was sent to the Federation of the Vendée to secure the expulsion of Guillou, at least in part for his intervention at the conference of federation secretaries.[71] On November 5, Rosmer wrote Sémard to complain of the way in which he and his friends were being slandered by the members of the BP, and to demand that their letter of October 5 be published. "We are constantly insulted and spoken of in the most contemptuous way by the members of the BP—particularly by the General Secretary of the party—who pursue us with a personal hatred and attribute to us ideas that we have never had and plots we have never dreamed of. At the same time, we are given no chance to present our point of view in the party organs."[72]

At this point international factors intruded to force the conflict between the

Opposition and the leadership to a climax. During the months of August, September, and October, the majority had sought to avoid all mention of the Russian question. Its policy, dictated by Sellier's natural cautiousness and Monmousseau's fears, was to pretend that the Russian discussion was now closed, that Trotsky, good Communist that he was, had resumed his posts, and that the Bolshevik leader had nothing in common with his undisciplined French followers.[73] During the latter half of November, however, the Russian question once more came to the fore, this time in a much more violent and direct form than the previous spring. In early November, Trotsky published the preface to the third volume of his collected writings, entitled *The Lessons of October*. The core of the article was a historical demonstration that the Bolshevik Revolution had been made in spite of Zinoviev and Kamenev, who, Trotsky reminded his readers, had opposed Lenin on all crucial points of the insurrection.[74] These historical footnotes were no more welcome to the Triumvirate than the Monatte-Rosmer letter of October 5 had been to the French leadership. They were a devastating and unanswerable reply to the Triumvirate's argument that Trotsky had never really been a Bolshevik. Unanswerable, that is, so long as Bolshevism was equated with revolutionary activism. But the emphasis in Bolshevism had now been shifted to party discipline and organization. Exploiting this subtle but decisive transfer, the Russian majority's counterattack asserted that Trotsky had elevated himself above Lenin, the Central Committee, and the Petrograd organization.[75] A massive campaign against Trotsky was mounted in the Russian press; and the dispute was carried into the International by Zinoviev's henchmen, Kuusinen, Kun, and Kolarov, who pointed to Trotsky's mistakes in the interpretation of the international situation. These errors, as Zinoviev succinctly summarized them in December, were "overestimation of the democratic-pacifist era, overestimation of the miraculous peacemaking quality of American super-imperialism, underestimation of the counterrevolutionary nature of Social Democracy, underestimation of fascism."[76]

This time the foreign parties fell quickly into line. On November 10 the KPD declared its solidarity with the Central Committee of the Russian party. Its gesture was repeated by the Polish, Czech, Balkan, and American parties —and even by Brandler and Thalheimer in Moscow, who joined in asking for the speedy liquidation of the Opposition.[77] No foreign Communist showed greater enthusiasm for the new round of conflict than Treint, just recently returned from Moscow by way of Czechoslovakia, where he had represented the Executive at the congress of the Czech party.[k] On Treint's motion, the French CD passed a resolution on November 28 condemning the attempt of

---

[k] While in Czechoslovakia, Treint distinguished himself by the violence of his attacks against Karl Kreibich and A. Zapotocky, the Czech equivalents of the "international Right." Carr, *Socialism in One Country*, III, 182–83.

Trotsky and the Opposition to reopen the struggle against the Leninist Central Committee of the Russian party, and a campaign was begun to obtain similar resolutions from the party's cells, rayons, and federations.[78] Reckless as always and eager to anticipate his mentor Zinoviev, Treint sought to create a philosophy out of the struggle against Trotskyism. The essence of Trotsky's position, he explained in a set of theses he presented on November 28, was a belief in the fading of the prospects for revolution and the prediction of a long period of bourgeois democracy.[79] Treint drew opposite conclusions from the present situation. The period of pacifist democracy was now over. It was giving way to a period of "decisive struggles and of victorious revolutions in the East as in the West." In order to defend itself, the bourgeoisie would have to resort to "extremely complicated methods," including the use of fascism, Social Democracy, and anarchism. There was a "fundamental identity" among these three movements, Treint announced excitedly, basing himself on the German events of the previous year and throwing in the troubles of the French Communists with the anarchists for good measure. "The nuances are secondary."

The Triumvirate was making similar statements; but it combined them with a foreign policy of accommodation with the capitalist world.[80] Soviet reasonableness and Realpolitik bore fruit on October 28, when France, the most stubborn and anti-Communist of European Powers, at last conceded de jure recognition to the Bolshevik regime.[81] Treint misread the purpose of the anti-Trotskyite campaign. Unlike Zinoviev, he believed his own ideological inventions. What was worse, not content to make revolutionary assertions on the theoretical level, he rushed to put them into practice. An opportunity came with the atmosphere of crisis that followed the depositing of the ashes of Jaurès in the Pantheon on November 23.[82] A successful demonstration on that day convinced Treint that France was on the eve of great proletarian battles.[1] The party's new slogan—"Fascism is here!"—might have succeeded in winning the PCF influence among the workers and the democratically inclined middle class had it not been combined with an appeal to revolutionary violence. Forgetting that the demonstration had been carried out in the name of Jaurès and not of Lenin, Treint, followed by his allies in the CGTU and JC, lumped Socialism, Radicalism, and fascism together in the anti-proletarian camp, and called for the dictatorship of the proletariat, the revolutionary tribunal for Rightists such as Millerand, workers' control of industry, and the turning over of all land to the peasants without compensation.[83] The predictable result was a wave of popular hostility against the Communist Party and the undermining of the leftist government that had come to power in

---

[1] Fifty thousand Communists marched behind the formations of the democratic Left. It was the most successful demonstration to that date in the history of the party.

May 1924. Paradoxically, Treint's predictions were self-fulfilling, at least in part. Fascists, Royalists, Conservatives, and Radicals alike called for action against the PCF, and Herriot was forced to prove the government's determination by raiding the party school at Bobigny.[84]

It was in the light of Treint's new crusade against Trotskyism that Rosmer and Monatte decided that they could not remain in the party. As Monatte later explained in a commentary that was never published, the BP had tried to muzzle them and they were not people to be muzzled.[85] They could have had no illusions about the trend of events in the party. Ever since the Fifth Congress, the leadership had emphasized that no opposition to its policies would be tolerated. In the first issue of the new *Cahiers du Bolchévisme,* which was launched on November 21 to replace Souvarine's old *Bulletin Communiste* as the party's theoretical journal, Treint made it clear that the Right was to be eliminated from all responsible posts in the party: "Homogeneous ideology, homogeneous policies, homogeneous structure, homogeneous leadership, we will build our party of a block of steel that nothing can split." In the last days of November, Monatte, Rosmer, and Delagarde addressed what was intended to be the first in a series of open letters to the members of the party for the coming congress in January.[86] As a precedent, they could not have helped but have in mind the letters Rosmer had issued during the War in the name of the Committee for the Resumption of International Relations.

After the last conference of federation secretaries, read the letter, where we were classified as anti-Communist elements, we replied by stating our position in a declaration addressed to the CD. This statement was not communicated to the CD, nor did it appear in the party press. "It will be understood if after a long wait, we make it known to the members of the party by the sole and feeble means that we have left." We have been accused of belonging to the Right. This we know is untrue. If we must be classified, we would belong to the "Gauche Ouvrière." We have been accused of supporting the Russian Opposition. Unfortunately, we are not acquainted with Trotsky's speech given in July at the assembly of Moscow veterinarians or with his preface to *1917.*[87] For Trotskyists we lack vigilance. However, "certainly we have been heard from, and moreover we will be heard from, every time that Trotsky is insulted, because his name and his efforts, alongside the name and efforts of Lenin, are identified with the Russian Revolution. We will say more: we think that at the present time, it is Trotsky who is really thinking and acting in the spirit of Lenin, and not those who are persecuting him with their attacks while draping themselves in the cloak of Leninism." If Trotsky captured the majority in the Russian Central Committee tomorrow, those same French Communists who are insulting him would be the first to adulate him, and to find us insufficiently Trotskyist.

The remainder of the letter was devoted to a criticism of the policies of the Treint-Girault leadership and an analysis of the way it had come to power. At the beginning of 1924, the three explained, the PCF had been confronted with two crises: one international and the other national. The latter was provoked by Sellier and Doriot, who declared that they could no longer work with Treint in the central apparatus. Moreover, they were not the only ones to think that Treint must go. Humbert-Droz, the delegate of the International, had said that as long as Treint and Souvarine remained at the head of the party, it would be impossible to have a Communist Party in France. Not long ago, Doriot had deplored the fact that Rosmer and Monatte had not been more aggressive in attacking the so-called Left; tomorrow, perhaps, he will demand their expulsion from the party. The Left had now had control of the party for ten months. What had they accomplished? They had bypassed the CD to such an extent that its members had learned of the coming party congress in the party press. They had ruined *L'Humanité*. And they had put the party in a state of continual financial crisis. The leaders of the party cry out so loudly against the Right because they fear the results of their own leadership: "From top to bottom of the party, we are confronted with a cascade of instructions that we must obey without understanding and above all without muttering anything except the sacramental, 'Captain, you are right!' A barracks-room mentality is in the process of being formed, and the morals of noncommissioned officers become the norm." Yesterday it was the Center that one wanted to torpedo, in the person of Sellier, for its financial policies. Today it is the "Gauche Ouvrière." Whose turn will it be tomorrow? "The French party," the letter concluded, "threatens to resemble the South American Republics in which there is a coup d'état every three months."

The Opposition's attack could not have come at a worse time. The party was in the midst of its reorganization and its campaign against fascism. As in 1923, an appeal to principle could be dismissed as an anti-Communist stab in the back. On December 2, 1924, the BP declared Monatte, Delagarde, and Rosmer "enemies of the party and the International," and called an extraordinary conference of the party to expel them.[88] The conference, composed of the members of the CD, one representative per federation, and one representative per regularly functioning rayon, met on December 6. The great majority of the delegates had probably not even read the brochure for which the three members of the CD were being excluded; nor were they supposed to.[89] Doriot and Treint led the attack. Doriot accused Rosmer, Monatte, and Delagarde of having betrayed the party at a moment of grave danger. Treint demanded their expulsion. The motion excluding the three was passed unanimously, with three abstentions. Rosmer could only state, in the name of himself and his friends, "We will work from outside to hasten the day when the party becomes a real Communist Party."[90]

*Normalization*

It is easy to see why the leadership did not feel it could tolerate an Opposition. Bolshevization was not going well, and failure forbade discussion. Though the rate of recruitment was high, membership losses were even higher. The methods of the new leadership drove many veteran militants from the party in disgust. A year later the party would admit that 70 per cent of its cadres had been replaced in 18 months of bolshevization.[91] Thus far the reorganization had hardly gone beyond Paris, the Nord, and the Lyon region; the target date for its completion had had to be quietly extended to April 1, 1925.[92] Financially the party led a precarious existence, with rumors of embezzlement and bankruptcy too widespread to be without foundation. Internal chaos might have been more lightly borne had it not been coupled with political fiasco. Treint's anti-fascist campaign had failed to move the working class. Instead, its only immediate result, aside from covering its author with ridicule, had been to isolate the party, create an atmosphere of reaction, and stimulate the formation of anti-Communist defense committees and proto-fascist groups like Pierre Taittinger's Jeunesses Patriotes.[93]

Moscow was not pleased by Treint's sudden show of zeal. According to Souvarine, who was in Moscow at the time, the expulsion of Rosmer and Monatte caught the Presidium by surprise.[94] Bukharin demanded an explanation, and when Marrane, the PCF's delegate, proved incapable of accounting satisfactorily for the leadership's action, Paris was ordered by telegram to send the materials "immediately." The source of the Bolsheviks' annoyance is not far to seek. The expulsion of the Gauche Ouvrière would hamper the party's recruiting in working-class circles. Even more important, Treint's anti-fascist campaign endangered the Soviet Union's rapprochement with France. What the Soviets wanted was a mass party capable of tipping the French political balance, not a small band of embattled revolutionaries.

Evidently the materials sent by the French leadership were not deemed sufficient; for in late December, Treint himself was summoned to Moscow, where he was told bluntly by Zinoviev that his theses were best consigned to the nearest wastebasket. The expulsions, added the Comintern's President, were a fact, but they must be the last.[95] These reproaches were given suitable ideological dress in a major speech by Zinoviev on the French situation given before the Presidium on January 10, 1925.[96] The PCF, he said, "must carry on the main fight against against social fascism." But it must conduct the struggle "as a defensive struggle." This was not opportunism, but "an adaptation of Bolshevism to the concrete conditions of France." The party's chief task was "the creation of a *tradition of a revolutionary mass workers' party*." This meant 50,000 members in Paris and winning the provinces, "chiefly the industrial districts of the Nord." Within the party, the new slogan was to be "normalization." "The party must be told: the period of crisis is at an end, the purging process has been carried out; steady work, feverish organizational activity, steady continuation of agitation and propaganda work are necessary."

Chastened, but still invested with the authority of the International, Treint rushed home to attend the Congress of Clichy. Why had the Executive not removed a man whose leadership threatened to ruin the French section and whose zeal ill accorded with the objectives of Soviet foreign policy? The situation was not so simple when viewed from the perspective of the Comintern's President. To demote the French party Secretary at such a crucial moment would have been to call the entire policy of bolshevization into question, with resulting damage to Zinoviev's own prestige and standing in the Russian party. Forced to choose between subservience and new political directions, the already vulnerable Triumvir could not hesitate. Treint and Girault were to be used and even defended so long as they were necessary.[m] Meanwhile the first items in their own dossiers of exclusion had been entered.

That Zinoviev had taken the only course open to him was shown by events in Paris. A new Opposition had arisen, led this time by Dunois, Berthelin, and Loriot, who had come out of a three-year retirement to protest against the distortions of bolshevization. Loriot and Berthelin had drawn up theses on the international situation, which were opposed in every particular to those of Treint.[97] The Loriot-Berthelin theses rejected as "simplistic" the idea that revolution was imminent; pointed out the unsuitability of factory cells for education and discussion; condemned the dictatorial system prevailing in the party; observed that the present PCF was the result of a specifically Russian conflict; disagreed with Treint's theory that fascism, Social Democracy, and anarchism were identical; and concluded that the Communists had every reason to seek a united front against fascism. Loriot and his friends expounded these ideas to receptive audiences throughout the Paris region in the weeks preceding the Congress of Clichy.[98] Recalling that "we accepted the political and tactical principles of Bolshevism under special conditions, at a time when we could count on the world Revolution," Loriot observed that "today all that must be called into question."[99] When the Opposition defended this point of view before the General Assembly of the Paris region, Berthelin was expelled and

---

[m] About this time, Zinoviev wrote Humbert-Droz to suggest that he deny "Rosmer & Co.'s" allegation that he, Humbert-Droz, had favored Treint's demotion. (HDA.) Humbert-Droz responded with an article published in the *Cahiers du Bolchévisme* on January 23, 1925; but though he criticized Monatte and Rosmer and pointed out the dangerous implications of their opposition, he made no attempt to conceal his differences with Treint during the course of 1923. Treint riposted angrily: "It would take at least a pamphlet to re-establish the truth behind every error made by Humbert-Droz." (*Cahiers du Bolchévisme*, 6.ii.25, p. 738.) Humbert-Droz continued to consider Treint a danger to the party, and had more than a little to do with his fall in 1927.

Loriot's case was turned over to the BP for further study. Loriot would undoubtedly have gone the way of Rosmer, Monatte, and Berthelin if Treint had not been directed to halt the purges. Instead, the former schoolteacher's theses were printed in the *Cahiers du Bolchévisme,* and he was given permission to address the Congress of Clichy, which met on January 17, 1925, in the industrial suburbs of Paris.

In its leading figures, its methods, and its results, the Congress of Clichy marked a fitting conclusion to the period that had begun at Tours. Doriot, Thorez, and Sémard sat on the Presidium alongside Treint, Sellier, and Cachin, thus symbolizing the union of the new and the old. Sémard's opening report struck all the predictable notes. The period of the purge was now over, and the conflict of personalities ended. If the CD had shown no life up to the present, that did not mean that this situation would continue after the congress. These dreary formalities completed, the Opposition launched its attack. Dunois began by defending Souvarine, Rosmer, and Monatte. The present leadership, he noted, had committed more mistakes than its predecessor; in continuing its policies, the BP risked destroying Communism in France. As soon as Dunois had left the speaker's platform, Thorez, the temporary chairman, read a motion stating that "Amédée Dunois' speech has caused the congress to waste its time, and [the congress] has decided not to have any discussion of this speech." And so it went. Loriot's charge that the party had been subjected to the dictatorship of a bureaucracy was answered by Suzanne Girault, who countercharged that Rosmer and Monatte had deserted the party in its hour of peril. No one, except the Oppositionists themselves, seemed to mind that the issue had never been fairly joined.

The case for an "international Right" was capped by Treint on the afternoon of the first day. The people that Rosmer defended, he said, desired a split in the party and a crisis that would endanger the Soviet Union. To prove his point, Treint read excerpts from a letter written by Souvarine to Rosmer on November 26, 1924, in which Souvarine had observed that "salvation would lie in a great crisis which put the Revolution in danger. Then the whole party would turn toward Trotsky." In another passage, Souvarine had suggested the need for an "intellectual center, which would serve as a rallying point for all those who cannot find their way in the present situation." These statements, concluded Treint, were evidence that a counterrevolutionary group was organizing both in Russia and elsewhere. Taken aback, Dunois could only mutter that he could not join those who wished the Revolution ill. According to *L'Humanité*'s highly selective account of the proceedings, "The reading of this document caused a tremendous stir. And it was amidst a clamor provoked by uncontained and uncontainable indignation that the session was brought to an end."[100]

The next morning, Rappoport spoke. He was disturbed by the weakness of

the party in the provinces. The Paris region outweighed the provincial organization by a factor of eight to three. The party "as a whole" did not understand the expulsions.[101] Suzanne Girault quickly slapped him down, recalling
that he had sometimes supported the Mensheviks against Lenin. Rappoport,
irrepressible as ever, sprang back. The effect of the purge had been to stifle all
discussion. "I regret the absence from the congress of certain workers and intellectuals who have withdrawn in order to escape suspicion." This was the
last flicker of opposition. One after another, the new leaders took the floor
to refute the criticisms of Dunois, Loriot, and Rappoport, and to assert that
the party had never had greater influence among the working class. The fashion was to welcome the passing of "the intellectuals." Dunois had bewailed
L'Humanité's new look. Lenain scoffed at these criticisms. "Our working-
class comrades sometimes make mistakes in syntax, but they don't commit the
political mistakes that the international Right has committed." The session
ended with the unanimous adoption of Sellier's report on the state of the party
and the ratification of the expelling of Monatte, Rosmer, and Delagarde, with
only one negative vote.

On the third day, Treint reported on the international situation. The menace,
he announced, was Trotskyism. As for the French party, its task was "to
normalize." Lest the new slogan be interpreted as a reproach to the leadership, the delegate of the International elaborated on the meaning of normalization. He denied that the Comintern had ordered the leadership to change its
tactics and halt the purge. Since the Fifth Congress, there had been no differences between the French and the ECCI. "We are in absolute agreement on
all points concerning the reorganization of the French party." The remainder
of the delegate's speech was devoted to a rebuttal of Rosmer's and Monatte's
open letter. The crisis of 1924, he insisted, was French, specifically French, and
had not been imported from Russia. The Paris federation had wanted to reorganize the party; the "Rosmer-Monatte-Souvarine leadership" had refused.
This struggle was now over. Normalization of the party meant winning the
masses.[102] Treint summed up in the afternoon. "The double meaning of this
congress is the liquidation of Trotskyism within the party and preparation
for the conquest of the masses." Mahouy's attempt to answer Treint was
shouted down, and on this note the congress ended. It was clear that the Opposition had been routed. But the optimistic took heart from the new slogan, and
the malicious noted that Treint's theses had never been put to a vote.[103]

*After Clichy*

Up to January 1925, the members of the Opposition had been lonely and
dispersed; this was one reason for their ineffectiveness. To find a core of shared
ideas and evidence of organizational links in the motley crew of those expelled from the party in the second half of 1924 was a task that even Treint
found difficult. The second Opposition was no more coordinated than the

first. Dunois, Loriot, and Rappoport had spoken at Clichy as isolated individuals. And the uncertainty and hasty composition of this last group may be gathered from the fact that Berthelin was excluded a month after he himself had voted for the exclusion of Monatte and Rosmer.

After Clichy the Opposition took steps to count its numbers and gird itself for long and painful battles. The first necessity was a journal. In January 1925, Monatte, Rosmer, Louzon, and Chambelland launched a review, *La Révolution Prolétarienne,* in which disaffected Communists could find a forum and a haven. Its position, as Rosmer defined it in February, was not Trotskyist, "since there is no Trotskyism," but "Communist syndicalist."[104] A chain was formed that extended from *La Révolution Prolétarienne,* on the outside, to Communists like Loriot, Dunois, and the lawyer Maurice Paz, who remained inside the party. Souvarine, Herclet, and Pierre Pascal ensured a steady flow of news from Moscow.[105] With party publications at a new low, Monatte's journal quickly won an audience among the Communist elite. The things that no one dared say in *L'Humanité* and the *Cahiers du Bolchévisme* appeared with impunity in *La Révolution Prolétarienne.* And when Souvarine returned from Moscow later in the year, he revived the *Bulletin Communiste,* thus adding a more specifically Marxist review to the Opposition's arsenal.

From what sections of the party did the Opposition draw its support? What were its dimensions? No sure statements about the sociology of the Opposition can be made until more detailed studies are done on the local level. But its leading elements seem to have come from three groups: the old revolutionary syndicalists; middle-class intellectuals, many of them with roots in the prewar Left Wing; and provincial civil servants, who objected to the destruction of their organizations. In 1925 this coalition appears to have rallied considerable grass-roots support, if the frenzied reaction of the leadership and the concern of the Comintern are any indication. By December 1925, 250 militants were in overt rebellion against the leadership of the party, and their complaints were no doubt shared by hundreds of others who dared not carry their opposition to the point of risking expulsion.

Certainly grounds for criticism were easily found. Membership fluctuated so much that the Comintern itself was not sure how many members its French section had.[n] Reorganization had reduced the party to a skeleton in the provinces.[106] Leadership had been replaced by demagoguery and bluff. Relations

---

[n] In December 1926 Kuusinen observed: "Some comrades maintain that the party has recently lost members during the reorganization, others deny it—nobody knows for certain. The membership of the party is therefore somewhat indefinite, which is also a sign of its lack of development. The fluctuation in membership seems to be rather large." (*Inprecorr,* December 1926, p. 1517.) The Opposition put it more bluntly: "The party," Roger Hairius wrote in July 1926, "has become a roadside inn for political travelers, with more people checking out than checking in. It is unable to keep its members or leave its mark on them. It is the ideal strainer." *La Révolution Prolétarienne,* July 1926, p. 10.

were not good between the Treint-Girault group and the leaders of the CGTU. And the municipal elections of May 1925 showed that the party had lost 50,000 voters in Paris. A democratic party would not have tolerated the methods of Treint and Girault. During the War the majority of the SFIO had been overthrown with less provocation. But the opportunities for protest were not what they had been in 1917. Critics from the camp of the expelled were dismissed as saboteurs and agents of the bourgeoisie. Within the party, discussion was not permitted. The leaders of the Opposition were placed where they could not influence the rank and file; access to the party press was denied them; and on those infrequent occasions when they were given an opportunity to speak or write, their words were misinterpreted and distorted to the point where true debate was impossible.[107]

Unable to overcome the leaders' dictatorship from within, the Opposition addressed itself directly to the Executive in a series of letters and theses, beginning in February 1925 with the "Letter of the 80."[108] The central theme of these communications was the need to return to the tactical and organizational principles of the Third and Fourth Congresses: specifically, the Opposition demanded the re-establishment of freedom of discussion; the revival of the section as the base unit of the party, to function alongside the factory cell; and the sincere application of the united front, not just from below, but also with the Socialist leaders. Most of all, the Opposition deplored the suppression of all criticism and the inauguration of the vote of confidence. "The party," complained the Letter of the 80, "no longer has the right to think or express its opinion, but it must nevertheless declare itself; it is called on to vote." The criticism of the Opposition was not just negative, Loriot assured Zinoviev in an accompanying letter.[109] For the oligarchic centralism now practiced by the leadership, he and his friends wanted to substitute the democratic centralism provided for in the statutes of the International.

The leaders of the Opposition assumed that the Executive would remove Treint and Girault once it understood the extent of their incompetence and the disastrous direction in which their policies were heading. They were sadly mistaken. The last thing that either Zinoviev or his allies wanted was the restoration of democracy in the Communist parties of the West. This was demonstrated at the Fifth Enlarged Executive, which met during March and April 1925. Treint and Sémard went to Moscow determined to obtain a condemnation of the Opposition and *La Révolution Prolétarienne*. For the first time in the history of the PCF, there was no representative of the minority present to defend its point of view. The Opposition's letter was duplicated and distributed, but there was no official discussion of it.[110] Nor could there be. For whatever Treint's tactical inadequacies, his brand of anti-Trotskyism (and hence Zinovievism) was very much in favor. Left to himself, the eccentric captain launched a massive attack on the French Right, all the longer and more repetitious because there was so little encouraging news to report about the progress of the PCF. Though a masterpiece of logical incoherence and a study in redundancy, Treint's speech left no doubt about the prospects for democracy within the party. "Normalization," he said at one point, "yes." But normalization in the sense that "the party is normal, that is, that there is no abnormal situation in which the enemies of the International can exert an influence."[111] There was no rejoinder from Zinoviev, nor for that matter from any other qualified member of the Executive.

From every point of view, the Fifth Enlarged Executive represented a major setback for the prospects of the Opposition. Souvarine, Rosmer, and Monatte were inscribed among the enemies of the International, their names henceforth to be identified with such symbols of anti-Communism as Levi, Balabanova, and Höglund.[112] Not satisfied with this achievement, the French leadership demanded that Trotsky declare his attitude toward *La Révolution Prolétarienne*. As Treint put it, we know that Trotsky does not condone the acts of our Right. But "objectively, what we have here is a chain that goes from Comrade Trotsky to the bourgeoisie by way of the Right."[113] This proposal was adopted. Pascal had already noted in mid-April that Trotsky was avoiding the Frenchmen, whose company he formerly had sought. "I am convinced," he wrote Rosmer, "that sooner or later, under one form or another, he will damned well drop you."[114] Pascal's prediction was premature, but correct. In October, Trotsky condemned *La Révolution Prolétarienne* as counterrevolutionary and repudiated its defense of himself.[115] His advice to Rosmer and Monatte, whom he praised as "tempered old revolutionaries," was to discontinue the review immediately; to act like soldiers of the party even while remaining outside the party; and to apply to the ECCI for readmission to the Comintern. "There is no other way," Trotsky concluded.

It would be both dreary and long to narrate the history of the Opposition in detail. Its leaders continued to urge on the International their own fidelity and the incompetence of the men who were ruling the party. Their arguments, circulated in letters and by word of mouth, gained new converts with every month. In May the 80 became 130; in December their numbers swelled to 250. The party leadership, threatened by this constantly growing rumble of discontent, demanded that the Opposition be silent or be purged. No weapon was spared to throttle the spokesmen of the rebellion. "The battle in the party is depressing," Loriot wrote Monatte in asking him for the latest number of *La Révolution Prolétarienne*. "Never in the worst days of the War did I feel so sick at heart."[116] The International opposed the leadership's policy of purges. It was only too aware of Treint's shortcomings. The Comintern's delegate, Kleine, was no less critical of the leadership than Loriot himself. His articles in the months after the Fifth Executive supplement rather than contradict the letters of the Opposition.[117] But in the last analysis, the Executive always came down in favor of obedience, as indeed it had to. For whereas the Opposition yearned for the democracy—let us be more specific, the libertarianism—of the prewar French working-class movement, the Comintern leadership looked forward to the authoritarian discipline of twentieth-century political movements. Between these two points of view, there could be no reconciliation.

Condemnation of the Opposition did not mean approval of the leadership, whose inefficiency the Comintern deplored. In 1926 Treint and Girault were removed from the BP; and in 1927 the two Zinovievites were expelled. But the Opposition did not benefit from their demotion. By the Congress of Lille in July 1926, the great majority of Oppositionists had been either hounded from the party or reduced to silence. When Treint and Girault went, they yielded their places not to Loriot and Dunois, but to Thorez, Doriot, and Marty. A new Communist Party, the Communist Party of Stalin, had been born.

### The Logic of Expulsion

The events of 1925–26 presented the Opposition with a set of dilemmas. Was Communist activity possible outside the Communist Party? Or was it true, as Herclet wrote Rosmer in January 1925, that at the present time it was impossible for revolutionaries to work outside the Comintern and Profintern?[118] Second, what attitude should a revolutionary take toward the Soviet Union? This last dilemma was put most squarely by Pierre Pascal in a letter to Rosmer dated April 12, 1925.[119] The Soviet regime, Pascal explained,

tends to draw its support from a peasant aristocracy, a labor aristocracy, and a class of government officials, to the detriment of the mass of the people, who made the Revolution. In this sense, then, it is counterrevolutionary. It would seem necessary, therefore, to attack it by every means. But things are not so simple because it is so closely connected with the Revolution itself; it is so well blended with the Revolution that it poisons and kills, that every blow struck against it also strikes the Revolution. If it falls, the Revolution would not be set free in such a way that it could simply continue its uninterrupted march: everything would remain to be done again.

The Opposition reacted to these dilemmas in various ways. After a brief period of silence during which he applied repeatedly for readmission to the Comintern,[o] Souvarine broke violently with Communism. By 1933 the former

---

[o] Souvarine obviously entertained real hopes of being readmitted to the Comintern. On December 10, 1925, he applied for readmission. This request was turned down in January by the Presidium. *Bulletin Communiste*, 29.i.26; *Inprecorr*, 11.ii.26, p. 181.

leader of the PCF had proclaimed the death of the Comintern, and had declared war against the Soviets, the "usurpers, exploiters, and parasites" of the Russian Revolution.[120] Souvarine's own views tended toward the reconciliation of Marxism and democracy. Like Trotsky a historian at heart, he published a brilliant and carefully documented biography of Stalin in 1935, which exploded for the first time the myths in which the Soviet leader had so painstakingly cloaked his past.[121] Today he is a relentless and informed critic of Communism and the Soviet Union, his pen no less active, its lash no less biting, than in the apocalyptic days of 1920. Monatte, by contrast, never an enthusiastic convert to Leninism, returned to revolutionary syndicalism after 1925. His *Révolution Prolétarienne* became the organ of all those who called for the independence of the unions. He died in 1958, as respected and dedicated a militant at the end as he had been a half-century before. His memory lives on, as does his journal. Rosmer's course was different from either Monatte's or Souvarine's. Always an admirer of Trotsky, he broke with *La Révolution Prolétarienne* in the late twenties, in order to devote himself to the organization of a Trotskyite opposition in Europe.[122] Later he fell out with Trotsky's associates and returned to devote his efforts to the revival of the CGT. In 1936 he published the first volume of an immense work on the French working-class movement during the War, which fairly breathes his commitment to the ideals of the prewar Left Wing: internationalism, anti-parliamentarism, and truth.[123] He died in 1964. To the end he never gave up his belief in the Leninism of 1917–22, which in his view was corrupted but not called into question as a doctrine.

Of the others, Dunois remained in the party until 1927. After a brief fling in Sellier's and Louis' Parti de l'Unité Prolétarienne (PUP),[p] he rejoined the SFIO, where he was never completely at home. He died in 1944 in a German concentration camp after being apprehended for publishing a clandestine edition of *Le Populaire*. It was a fitting and noble end for this artisan of the printed word. From the intellectual point of view, Loriot represents the most interesting case of all. Disgusted by the development of the party, the former schoolteacher failed to renew his membership in 1926. His cooperation with Paz's and Colliard's group on *Contre le Courant* convinced him of the futility of "Communist opposition."[124] He died in 1932, but only after subjecting the Russian experience to a searching examination. His conclusion, published in *La Révolution Prolétarienne* and presented with his usual dogged honesty,

[p] The PUP was formed from the merger of Louis' Parti Socialiste Communiste (which had existed since 1924) and the Parti Ouvrier et Paysan, the creation of six municipal councillors who had broken away from the PCF in 1929. The PUP aspired to provide a necessary middle ground between the "sectarianism of the Communists" and the "opportunism of the Socialists."

was that the Leninist concept of the party had to be rejected in favor of the syndicalist theory of a class represented by a union organization open to all proletarians, without regard to their political opinions.[125]

Rappoport, unlike the other founders of the party, remained in the PCF throughout the twenties and thirties. After the Congress of Paris in 1922, however, he increasingly withdrew from political activity, confining himself to journalistic tasks. From that date, he says, he was convinced that the PCF was "totally 'domesticated' by Moscow."[126] To the end he refused to curb either his critical spirit or his wit. In 1934 he was talked into running as a Communist candidate in the Fourth Arrondissement of Paris. When asked by a reporter what his situation in the party was, he replied: "Mes rapports avec le parti communiste sont les mêmes que ceux de Voltaire avec Dieu. On se salue de temps en temps, mais on ne cause pas."[127] In 1938 he resigned from the PCF, the Comintern, and *Izvestiya,* of which he had been the Paris correspondent, in protest against the purge trials; and in 1940, when Stalin invaded Finland, he telegraphed Paul Faure his adherence to the SFIO. He died in 1941, still faithful to the Marxism for which he had abandoned Jaurès forty years before.

Expulsion carried its own logic. Despite the determination of these men to act like disciplined soldiers of the party while remaining outside it, they were almost all led to become opponents of the Comintern and critics of the Soviet Union. This was no accident. Once ideology had been superseded by a theory of organization, to be a Communist outside the party made no sense. What Communists shared after 1924 was less an ideal than an allegiance, an operating code, and a subculture. Nor was it a coincidence that the founders of the party almost to a man returned to the ideologies of prewar France. Even the obedient Treint rejoined the SFIO in 1934, after a brief flirtation with the Trotskyist Opposition. Only Girault, this "second-rate Catherine the Great, brutal, vulgar, ferociously ambitious,"[128] escaped the logic of expulsion. She was taken back into the party in 1933; and in 1948, a decade and a half of faithful service to Thorez was rewarded when she was elected a Communist senator. Her case only proves the rule. Of all the Communist leaders she was the least attached to any ideology. A political manipulator rather than a working-class militant, she was almost certainly an agent of the GPU.[129]

### THE NEW MEN

The transformation of the party and the defeat of the Opposition were accompanied by a development of equal if not greater importance in the history of the PCF: the emergence in the leadership of new men, who represented a different approach to the problems of the working-class movement. Between the Congress of Lyon and the Congress of Clichy, the composition of the party leadership changed. The CD named at Lyon rested on a coalition of the former Center and the former Left, with certain additions from the syndicalists, the JC, and the provincial federations. The balance of power, however, clearly remained with the second group, the men who had taken power after the Fourth World Congress. Clichy saw the crystallization of a new grouping. What was left of the original leadership (Cachin, Sellier, Marrane, Gourdeaux, Treint, Vaillant-Couturier, Renaud Jean) now shared power with the syndicalists (Sémard, Monmousseau, Jacob) and the new elements (Doriot, Thorez, Marty, Chasseigne, Girault, Crémet) brought into the ruling circle during the course of the struggle against the Opposition. With key additions and subtractions, these groups constituted the leadership of the PCF throughout the next fifteen years of its history.[130]

Little need be said about the remnant of the original CD. Those who survived to 1925 had done so by subordinating their critical spirit to their allegiance to the Soviet Union. Petty-bourgeois by origin, journalists, deputies, and civil servants by profession, they differed in no marked respect from the leaders of the prewar SFIO. Not surprisingly, the majority leaned toward the use of traditional parliamentary methods. But whatever tactics they favored, they had learned to roll with the changing Comintern line. With the exception of Treint and Sellier, they all survived the vicissitudes of the twenties and thirties. Their survival, however, was earned at the cost of a partial withdrawal from intra-party politics. None of them except Marrane ever played a leading role in the party apparatus. Cachin and Vaillant-Couturier concentrated on journalistic and parliamentary chores; Renaud Jean made his specialization in agricultural matters a form of inner emigration. For those who learned to play their roles, there were honors to ease the pains of age and conscience. When Cachin died in 1958, he was *doyen* of the Fourth Republic's Senate. Marrane lived to be a minister, a councillor of the Republic, and the party's presidential candidate against De Gaulle in 1958. Even Daniel Renoult, the leading Oppositionist of 1922, came back to be elected the mayor of Montreuil in 1935.

The syndicalists represent a different case. Proletarians by origin and profession, they stood for *ouvriérisme,* activism in the anti-militarist field, and attention to the workers' interests. Their leading characteristic was their rejection of theory for the lessons of the everyday struggle. The most ignorant worker, Sémard explained at Clichy, was worth more than the intellectual, for he suffered from exploitation and thus could express the aspirations of his class. As for revolutionary theory, the party Secretary admitted that a brief encounter with Marx's *Das Kapital* (which he referred to as "Capital and Labor") had "bored him to death."[131] In 1926, Monmousseau, Benoît Frachon, and two other members of the CGTU leadership were brought into the BP en masse, thus completing the process that had begun at St.-Etienne in 1922. Sémard and Monmousseau both stayed in the party until their death. Sémard was shot by the Germans in 1942; Monmousseau died in 1960. The two syndicalists are buried in Père Lachaise cemetery, the final resting place of Communist heroes.

The third group, the new men, stood closer to the syndicalists than to the old leadership, both in terms of social origin and in their approach to the problems of the working-class movement. The majority were metallurgical workers (Doriot, Barbé), miners (Thorez), clerks (Billoux), or déclassés (Marty). Like Sémard and Monmousseau, they favored anti-militarism, anti-colonialism, and agitation among the workers. The new elements followed different roads to power. Some, like Thorez, came from the provincial party organization. Twenty-five years of age in 1925, a blond and ruddy-complexioned young man of some personal charm, Thorez was the son of a miner from the Pas-de-Calais.[132] As we have seen in a previous chapter, he wavered briefly during the spring of 1924, indicating his support for Souvarine and Trotsky in a series of letters that survived to haunt him. The events of the summer of 1924 cleared up these first misconceptions. Whether through ambition or through an overweening sense of commitment to the Russian Revolution, Thorez was to be found on the opposite side of the barricade by the fall of 1924. His well-timed conversion was rewarded handsomely when in October he was appointed Secretary of the Nord region. From this point on, the climb of Thorez was rapid, the two main channels of his advance being the reorganization of the party and the struggle against the Riff War, in which he played a spectacular but secondary role.[133] He was above all the man of the apparatus. Theory bored him, and it was not until the late twenties that he made any attempt to acquire a Marxist education.[134] His combination of physical dynamism, opportunism, ruthlessness, and obedience to Soviet directives turned out to be the perfect set of qualities needed for success in Stalin's Comintern.

André Marty, on the other hand, entered the party from the outside without any previous experience in the French working-class movement. Marty's credentials derived from his role in the Black Sea rebellion in April 1919. After spending four years in the prisons of the Republic, he was released in July 1923. In the interim the publicists of the party had inflated him into a revolutionary hero of nationwide reputation. Lacking any better alternative, he entered the party, where his rise was contemporaneous with bolshevization. Older than most of the new men (he was 39 in 1925), a figure of chilling grayness from whose flesh the prison pallor never disappeared, Marty quickly became known as an *homme à tout faire*. Neither principles nor popularity impeded his advancement. He will probably always be branded by Hemingway's description in *For Whom the Bell Tolls,* where he appeared as a bloodthirsty and vain Commissar of the Loyalist forces.

The majority of the new men received their training in the Jeunesses Communistes. Doriot was both their leader and their idol. "A tall, strong, dark-complexioned boy with a manly face and solemn eyes,"[135] Doriot made his way to prominence within the party as a leader in the anti-militarist and anti-colonialist struggle. In the early twenties his chief characteristics were his dynamism, his daring, and his almost ascetic dedication to the revolutionary cause.[136] These qualities, unusual in the PCF of the period, attracted to him a considerable personal following, including, among others, Henri Barbé, François Billoux, François Chasseigne, André Ferrat, Roger Gaillard, Raymond Guyot, and Henri Lozeray. Only twenty-seven in 1925, Doriot was already a deputy and a veteran of Comintern politics. No Communist leader seemed to have a more brilliant future before him than "le grand Jacques."

Though as different from one another in personality and manner as men can be, this second generation of Communist leaders had a great deal in common. To begin with, the great majority were in their twenties. The essential, however, was not age, but a shared experience. None of them had been involved in the prewar working-class movement. For all of them, the years of war and social conflict from 1914 to 1923 had been the formative period in their lives.[q] Barbusse's *Le Feu*, Lenin's *"Left-Wing" Communism,* and Trotsky's *Terror and Communism* were the books on which they had been weaned. One might say that they were open to the novelties of Bolshevism in a way that men like Rosmer, Monatte, Loriot, and Dunois never were and never could have been.[137] Second, their Socialism was non-theoretical in character. None of them had any training in Socialist or syndicalist theory as it was understood before 1914. The world of Jaurès and Pelloutier was as far removed from them as the world of Charlemagne. For all these men, Communism meant action for action's sake. Third, unlike the previous generation of Socialist leaders, they were oriented toward social questions rather than toward politics. In that sense, they had absorbed the anti-parliamentarism of the syndicalists. It was no accident that Doriot's Jeunesses Communistes had led in the creation of factory cells and the reworking of the party's strategy.

---

[q] The JC were highly aware of themselves as a generation who differed from their elders. Take, for example, Jean Duret, who wrote in 1920: "Consciousness, in general, is determined by the conditions of the historical period in which it is formed. The product of a democratic and law-abiding period, the consciousness of our older leaders cannot be the same as that of our young Communists, whose revolutionary consciousness was formed, in most cases, under the impact of the World War, in a period of social revolution. The result is that the two groups give a different meaning to essential Socialist concepts such as 'revolutionary tactic,' 'political struggle,' 'dictatorship of the proletariat,' 'social revolution,' etc. ...The group that will push the West's working-class movement back to the Left will emerge from the Jeunesses [Communistes]; their job is to get ready for the struggle." (*L'Avant-Garde,* 27.xi.20.) This point is so strongly emphasized by Barbé that it sometimes appears to be the theme of his memoirs. See his "Souvenirs de militant et de dirigeant communiste" (ms. at the Hoover Institution), p. 12.

Finally, these new elements were alienated from the society in which they lived to a degree the Socialists never had been. The War and its revolutionary aftermath had left them with an impression of destroyed consensus. Their social backgrounds and occupations as workers and clerks reinforced their feeling that they lived in a grim age of masses and machines. What they sought in Communism was not only an ideology, but also sport, entertainment, good fellowship, and the feeling of belonging.[188] Their anti-patriotism and their commitment to the Soviet Union was the result and not the cause of this alienation. It is again highly significant that the JC took the lead in anti-militarist and anti-colonialist activities.

During the decade from 1925 to 1935, a homogeneous Communist leadership was hammered out of these three groups, a leadership of revolutionary opportunists, whose hallmark was their allegiance to the Soviet Union, their lack of scruples, and their indifference to ideology. Few emerged from the atmosphere of the Comintern with their faith intact. Cynicism was the usual byproduct of success in Communist ranks.[139] During the 1930's the temper of the party turned toward opportunism and nationalism, a reflection of similar changes within the Soviet Union. Those like Thorez, Marty, Guyot, and Duclos who reacted most nimbly to these changes became the party's leaders;[r] those like Sellier, Barbé, and Doriot who made false steps were left by the wayside. Of the second group some, like Sellier and Ferrat, returned to Socialism; others, like Doriot and Barbé, turned to fascism; still others, like Chasseigne, Gaillard, and Marion, became involved in Vichy. Their story is for others to tell. But it should be remembered that the contenders for power were the men who came to the fore with bolshevization, the generation born around the turn of the century, the products of the revolutionary crisis of 1917–23.

[r] Duclos came to the party from the leadership of the ARAC. It was only in 1928–29 that he began to play an active role in the party's ranks. Barbé, "Souvenirs," p. 240.

# Conclusion

Il y avait là bien plus qu'une lutte intérieure du
parti. C'était le conflit entre deux civilisations.
Nous avions, en convalescents d'une époque de dé-
cadence meurtrière, d'abdication et de désordre,
un besoin absolu d'ordre et de santé.
    —*Vaillant-Couturier, on the schism of French
    Socialism*

With the events of 1924–26 this study reaches its conclusion. The PCF, let us
hasten to add, had not yet completed its agonizing period of adolescence. Nor
had it mastered thoroughly its arsenal of weapons. The uneasy affair with
the intellectuals had hardly passed the point of covert glances.[a] The Palais
Bourbon still seemed to most Communists a seat of iniquity rather than a
springboard for further operations. Patriotism had yet to be reconciled with
devotion to the Communist cause. Such changes would require time, struggle,
and upon occasion the heavy hand of Muscovite discipline. Yet growth, when
it occurred, would come within the patterns set by bolshevization. Having
accepted the Machiavellianism of one State, it was no great step to accept the
Machiavellianism of another. The break with prewar precedent had been
made—that was the essential. A new party had been born.

How can we account for the appearance of this new political formation in
a terrain already staked out and occupied by earlier arrivals? What shall we

[a] To be sure, there had been intellectuals sympathetic to Communism ever since 1919.
Barbusse flirted with the party and then joined it in 1923. Anatole France contributed
money and the prestige of his name. The *Clarté* group wrote approvingly of the Bolshevik
Revolution and the Soviet State, and certain of its members played an active role during
the Communist Party's formative years. Nevertheless, the PCF's relationship with the intellectuals during this era was not what it later became. The party had not learned how
to use them; nor had they accepted the necessity of being used. After the Fifth World
Congress many Communist intellectuals abandoned the party as a protest against bolshevization. (See David Caute, *Communism and the French Intellectuals, 1914–1960*, New
York, 1964, pp. 59–92.) Like Caute, I have used the term "intellectual" to refer to those
workers of the mind—philosophers, writers, artists, scientists, lawyers, doctors—whose
field of activity was not primarily politics.

choose as our theme? Have we to do with the rise of a truly revolutionary party, as Leninists assumed; with its decline, as left-wingers always insisted; or with the remnant of a shattered working-class movement transformed along totalitarian lines, as Social Democrats were inclined to think?[1] The answer is, of course, that the PCF was all these things. It began as the embryo of that left-wing party which was so long talked about but never realized. Its decline began even before its founding. And it was transformed through the action of external forces. We have to do, then, with the rise, fall, and transformation of a left-wing party. But these developments take on their full significance only when viewed within a larger context: the crisis of the working-class movement as a whole. Communism would not have arisen unless the prewar organizations had failed. And their failure would not have been such a traumatic experience if their opportunity had not been so great. Thus, our first theme takes its place within a second: the opportunity, failure, and metamorphosis of the French working-class movement.

A labor movement is not an isolated system that behaves according to predetermined laws. It seeks contact with a working class that is itself undergoing constant change. It is led by men of flesh and blood, who are brilliant or not so brilliant, dedicated or not so dedicated, farsighted or not so farsighted—men, in short, who bend their wills against the winds of history with greater or lesser luck. Most of all, a working-class movement partakes of a national culture, and inherits a past that limits the directions it may take and the pace at which it may develop. When working-class leaders think, they think in categories which they have inherited from their fathers and which they have tested against the facts of life. When they organize, they choose the forms of organization that historical experience lays before them. This legacy, which dogs the footsteps of working-class leaders as relentlessly as shadows trail men, determines the way a labor movement reacts to crises. In particular, it determined the way Western labor movements reacted to the storms of 1914–24. It could either propel them toward Social Democracy or channel major portions of them toward Communism—and the unyielding opposition such a stance implied. This push in the direction of extremism was History's legacy in France. The French working-class movement underwent a number of radical changes between 1914 and 1924; but from the standpoint of democracy these innovations led backward, toward the past.

Before we discuss these events, however, one more comment of a general nature is required. We have widened our perspective to include the syndicalists and the anarchists and deepened it to uncover the legacy of the past; we must also, if we want a meaningful picture, lengthen it in time. For to understand why the prewar movements failed, we must first know what aims they cherished and what means they recommended. The aftermath of the First World War has ordinarily been interpreted as the beginning of an era; it would be equally correct to see it as an end. The personalities, the ideas, and the methods that filled the stage during these years were, with very few exceptions, those of the period before 1914. Their failure, moreover, was as much the failure of a system as the failure of its individual parts. Nor should the analysis of this collapse be confined to France alone. The failure of democracy in Russia and the schism of the Socialist movement in France were not unrelated events; connecting them was a crisis of liberal values which announced itself before the War.

Like so many other twentieth-century movements, French Communism had its roots in the decade that preceded the War. By 1905 three ideological alternatives had been articulated to fill the void left by the decline of the older working-class doctrines of Proudhonism and Blanquism, both of which had been discredited by the failure of the Commune. They were Guesdism, Jauressianism, and revolutionary syndicalism. Guesdism was a vulgarization of Marxism; after an early period of militance, it came to be at once passive and inflexible, by opposing class collaboration and progress within capitalist society. Jauressianism held out the dream of class reconciliation in a new, postbourgeois society. Revolutionary syndicalism stood for class isolation and irreconcilable class struggle. The touchstone of all these movements was their attitude toward the State. Where Jauressians wished to use the State and Guesdists were sure of inheriting it, revolutionary syndicalists rejected it altogether in favor of the union. Though the SFIO was unified on Guesde's terms, it soon fell under the influence of Jaurès. This was possible, however, only because Jaurès accepted Guesde's language and came to terms with his attitude toward the bourgeois State.

In European terms, Guesde represented a distorted French reflection of Kautsky's Marxist orthodoxy. Because his Marxism was innocent of both economic training and philosophical interest, it was eventually reduced to dogmatism; at its best it displayed a kind of sterile positivism and faith in science typical of the period. The embryo of a Left Wing existed in the area between the SFIO, the CGT, and the anarchist groups. The characteristics of this Left Wing were its heterogeneity and its isolation from the masses. Three strands, one Socialist, one syndicalist, and one anarchist, may be detected. Still, despite its organizational division, it shared the European Left's emphasis on activism, anti-parliamentarism, anti-militarism, and spontaneity—doctrines that in France were most closely identified with the CGT. There could be no true revisionism in France because there was no true Marxism.[2] Instead, there were isolated individuals like Albert Thomas and Alexandre Varenne who wanted the SFIO to abandon its revolutionary language, that is, to accept its role as a party of reform. Jauressianism must be counted an original French form of Socialism, which combined flexibility in means with a commitment to the goal of revolution. Activist without being opportunist, pointed toward the liberation of the future while at the same time appreciative of the progress of the past, it deserved more truly than any other working-class ideology in Europe the label of Social Democracy. What distinguished the French movement from other European labor movements was the division of the party from the unions, the continual and institutionalized contact between working-class leaders and the bourgeoisie, and the tendency of both Right and Left to be swallowed up in the Jauressian version of the European Center.

The tactics of both Jaurès's SFIO and Griffuelhes's CGT were based on their reading of the direction of change in France during the period 1880–1905. The SFIO's basic assumption was the growth of the proletariat and the steady progress of its organization and influence. Jaurès believed, moreover, in the existence of a liberal bourgeoisie that would cooperate in its own transcendence. The CGT, for all its activism, its anti-intellectualism, and its rejection of bourgeois values, was just as linked to the liberal world as the SFIO.[a] Implicit in its methods was a vision of society in which employers were small, feudal, and unorganized, the State was limited and capable of being overthrown, and the worker was revolutionary. The élan of both the SFIO and the CGT in 1905–10 was inspired by the conviction of their leaders that history was developing in their favor, and by their faith that even if victory eluded them today, it would be theirs tomorrow.

Around 1910 signs appeared that the working-class organizations had lost their momentum. The setback was relative rather than absolute, but for a movement that prided itself on its thrust forward, to stand still was to decline. For the Socialists the most pressing problem was organization: the SFIO was growing, but it was growing slowly, and it was far from winning the majority of the population which Marxism promised. Why was the SFIO's growth not commensurate with the march of industrialization? And how, given the SFIO's minority status, could Socialists be effective without ceasing to be Socialists? Such questions raised the issue of the scope of Socialist activity, the kind of tactics Socialists should follow in their relations with the State, and the nature of the SFIO's ties to the International. In the CGT the crisis took the form of concern about the waning of revolutionary ardor and the possible implications of mass industrial unionism. Did industrial unions, for example, mean reformism? Many syndicalists feared they did.[b] And yet how else were strikes to be won and capitalism to be overthrown when employers were forming associations for the purpose of resisting syndicalist demands and influencing the State? One innovation seemed to call for another, and a further

[b] Some syndicalist leaders did not hesitate to link this danger to the introduction of assembly-line methods, thus exposing the ambivalent attitude of syndicalism toward industrialization. As Emile Pouget put it, "With the automation of the worker, with his degradation to the position of servant and subject of a machine, all initiative, all dignity, even all intelligence...and consequently all spirit of revolt are killed in him." Quoted in Michel Collinet, *Esprit du syndicalisme* (1952), p. 44.

impulse to change came from the example of foreign lands. In Germany, Sweden, Belgium, and England, the improvement of the workers' lot was being attained through the State rather than over its cadaver. Might not the same methods be applicable in France?

These new preoccupations caused dissension in both the SFIO and the CGT. A Right reappeared within the SFIO which called for collaboration with the bourgeoisie. The orthodox Marxists stood firm. Jaurès, on the other hand, though still faithful to his commitment of 1905, recommended new directions and greater flexibility. The problem was still pending on the eve of the War because of the unwillingness of the Radicals to commit themselves to a program of social reform. Within the CGT, differences appeared between the traditionalists, who clung to the storming tactics of Griffuelhes, and the innovators, who tended in the direction of what might best be called "revolutionary reformism." The farsighted might have seen the possibility here for an alliance between a reformist CGT and a Jauressian SFIO, and in fact there was increasing cooperation between Socialists and syndicalists on the eve of the War. At the same time, the time now seemed ripe for the development of a left-wing party. But all attempts to form such a party failed because of the reach of the Jauressian synthesis and the attachment of the CGT to its original doctrines. Precisely because the SFIO and the CGT were federalist organizations based on a noninterventionist style of authority, conflict was delayed and contradictory approaches to the burning questions of the day were able to coexist. Yet the cost of coexistence was stagnation, and obeisance to the formulas and methods of the past.

The War and its revolutionary aftermath broke this stalemate. On the one hand, the transformation of French society proceeded with astonishing rapidity. The masses, whose presence had never been more than a shadow before 1914, now burst upon the scene. On the other hand, the effect of the War was to lay bare the choice that working-class leaders had earlier avoided: collaboration with the bourgeoisie or violent revolution. The former was certainly the more attractive, and it was toward Sacred Union that the leaders of Socialism and syndicalism instinctively moved in August 1914. But, as soon became clear, class collaboration came tied to a nationalist foreign policy; one could not be had without the other. And this was a price that the majority of Socialists and syndicalists, pacifists out of ideology and deep conviction, could not bring themselves to pay. When the leaders of the SFIO and the CGT hesitated to abandon their new practices, minorities arose that called for a return to the syntheses of the past. For one brief moment in 1916–17, it seemed that Wilsonianism might offer the pillar of consensus around which the French working-class movement could repair its fractured unity. These hopes were quickly dashed, however, by the coming of the Bolshevik Revolution and the opening of a period of Europe-wide revolutionary crisis in 1917. One can argue about what might have happened had there been no Russian Revolution; what did happen is clear. The Bolshevik success gave the left-wing position a prestige it had never had. At the same time, the growing conservatism of the ruling groups and the mounting violence of workers and soldiers made the Bolshevik vision of the world seem true. Thus, just as the beginning of the War had thrust the working-class movement's center of gravity toward the Right, the continuation of the War thrust it toward the Left.

Because of the uncertainty of the War's outcome and France's exposed position, the SFIO did not feel the full impact of the revolutionary wave until the spring of 1919. The Socialist leadership had risked its honor and its innocence in the name of future victories. The masses, home from the War and out of the factories, demanded the changes the War had deferred. At no time since 1848 had the level of expectations been so high—or so vague. Faced with the demands of working-class leaders for sweeping structural changes, the government adopted an attitude of evasion and finally of utter refusal. The failure of Wilsonianism only further underlined the point: class collaboration was a chimera that Socialists and syndicalists of goodwill must now reject. The leaders of the Center responded to the crisis by retreating angrily into opposition, and by trying to dress the old formulas in Leninist language. Their grip on their organizations, however, was quickly undermined by a great influx of members whose imaginations had been fired by the Russian Revolution and the new Soviet regime. A new coalition was formed out of many diverse elements: former Socialists ashamed of the humiliation of War Socialism; anarchists and syndicalists who had never before taken an active role in the affairs of the SFIO; new men brought to Socialism by the War; and a great mass of new recruits who were responsive to left-wing language. At one only in their rejection of class collaboration and their enthusiasm for the Russian Revolution, the rank and file swept their moderate leaders aside and pushed the SFIO toward Moscow.

It seemed as if events were leading toward the creation of a left-wing party that would join the new Communist International. This was certainly what revolutionaries like Souvarine, Lefebvre, and Monatte wanted. They saw in Bolshevism all that was best in the past, as well as all that was most promising in the future. But as enthusiasm for Moscow mounted, the prospects for revolution declined. Whatever chances there were for successful insurrection slipped by in the spring of 1919. The elections of November 1919 and the general strike of May 1920 showed that the bourgeoisie had begun its counterattack. Seeing that the left-wing element in France was small, divided, and ideologically heterogeneous, and fearing that its hold over the masses was insecure, the Bolsheviks rejected the idea of a left-wing party and opted instead for a mass organization that would rest on a coalition of left-wing and centrist groups. It was this unwieldy and hybrid political formation that joined the Third International at Tours: an unstable compound of conflicting elements whose unifying principle—the revolutionary crisis—was about to disappear.

The dominant characteristic of the period that followed was its ambiguity. To be sure, everyone agreed that the Revolution had come to a halt; but no one knew how long the wait might be. Anything but passive, the Bolsheviks resolved that when the next revolutionary wave arrived, they would not be caught unprepared. Thus they set about transforming the PCF into a disciplined and battle-ready organization. The Left Wing was at first the beneficiary of this process. By 1923 it occupied the party's ruling heights. But the defeat in Germany revealed that what all had thought to be a third and final act was actually an anticlimax. The tendency everywhere was not toward revolution but toward stabilization of the capitalist regime. The ebbing of the revolutionary tide coincided with the succession struggle in Russia. This was no accident; for the Bolsheviks, too, like revolutionaries elsewhere, were forced to weigh the lessons of the Revolution's failure. Were they to stake all on one last revolutionary fling? Or was it the time to retrench and consolidate what had been won? This question had every bit as much relevance in France as it had in Russia, though the leaders of the Left Wing refused to admit it. It was resolved, as we have seen, with Trotsky's defeat and the decision to turn NEP into a long-term policy rather than a short-term expedient. Bolshevization in France was the natural corollary of Stalin's Socialism in One Country. In both France and Russia, energies formerly held alert for a resumption of revolution were now to be devoted to more constructive tasks. Bound by their loyalty to Trotsky—bound even more by the leftist principles for which he stood—the Souvarines, Rosmers, Monattes, and Loriots were soon driven out of the party.

The leaders of the Opposition thought that Communism had entered upon the way of Social Democracy, and that the policies of the PCF were merely Jauressian policies brought up to date.[4] They could not have been more wrong. Communism offered an answer to the dilemmas that had paralyzed the SFIO on the eve of the War. For one thing, the scope of the party's potential influence had been enlarged. Where Jaurès's SFIO had approached its clientele as prospective converts to Socialism, asking them for their votes, their money, and their presence at meetings and demonstrations, the PCF had a much more variegated appeal at its disposal. To the militant, it offered a life of dedication, unceasing activity,[c] and perhaps eventually paid

[c] Georg Lukács noted the importance of this side of the Communist appeal in September 1922. It was only in becoming "a world of activity for each of its members," he wrote, that the Communist Party could transcend the passivity of bourgeois democracy. Lukács thus saw active participation as subversive of liberal democracy. (*Histoire et conscience de classe*, 1960, p. 379.) A recent study by two American political scientists supports Lukács's contention: see Gabriel A. Almond and Sidney Verba, *The Civic Culture: Political Attitudes and Democracy in Five Nations* (Princeton, N.J., 1963), pp. 473-76.

employment. To the member it extended the possibility of community and political protest. And, finally, through its factory cells and its front organizations, the PCF provided a means of reaching the workers who were not ready or willing to commit themselves fully to the party.[d]

Second, there was the matter of the State. The SFIO, for all its congress debates, had never been able to decide whether it wished to overthrow the bourgeois State or reform it. The PCF resolved this problem, in part with its new structure of authority, which silenced or eliminated those members who deviated from the party line, but above all by a shift in its social structure. Where the SFIO had appealed to skilled workers, the petty bourgeoisie, and the liberal professions, classes that were democratic but inconsistently revolutionary, the PCF pitched its propaganda to industrial workers, clerks, peasants, colonials, foreigners, and in general all the sectors of French society rendered irrelevant or discontented by the march of industrialization. Consequently, just as the SFIO was always drawn toward class collaboration, the PCF was bound to be a party of irreconcilable opposition so long as its social base rested in these groups. The clearest example of discontinuity, of course, was on the question of the International. The SFIO had tried to be both nationalist and internationalist, and had succeeded in being neither. The PCF did away with the problem altogether by identifying the interests of the French proletariat and the Soviet State. Henceforth, it could claim to be both the nationalist and internationalist party par excellence.[e]

Communism, then, might be said to have begun where the prewar movements faltered. Its task was to carry on an old struggle with new and more potent weapons. Socialists, syndicalists, and left wingers had all in their own way aspired to educate the masses; Communists were satisfied to manipulate them. Therein lay the importance of the change. Why had such a movement arisen? Because of the ambiguous outcome of the postwar crisis. The times had been revolutionary; hence the traditional forecast had proved right. But the various working-class organizations had failed to take advantage of the opportunity; hence the traditional methods had proved mistaken. Jaurès's bourgeois allies, Guesde's proletarian army, and Griffuelhes's revolutionary workers had all neglected to show up for their rendezvous with destiny. In-

[d] Almond and Verba ascribe the success of the Communist Party in countries like France and Italy to its technique of creating its own infrastructure and channeling negative feelings of discontented people "*against* the legitimate structures of the polity rather than *into* them." (*Ibid.*, p. 144.) See also Charles A. Micaud, *Communism and the French Left* (New York, 1962), pp. 77–100, and the brilliant discussion by Hannah Arendt, *The Origins of Totalitarianism* (New York, 1958), pp. 306–88.

[e] Which is not to say that this problem has not come back to haunt the Communists. In fact, it has only been in those periods during which French national interest and Soviet foreign policy seemed to converge, as in 1933–39 and 1941–47, that the Communist Party has come close to wielding political power.

stead, there had been a reactionary bourgeoisie, masses whose mood was as shifting as sand, and helpless working-class elites. Out of this failure of history to either realize or discredit the libertarian vision arose the PCF, a left-wing organization revamped, retooled, restructured, and remanned in the backwash of an unsuccessful revolution.

As interpretations go, the thesis of "the prewar movements that failed" is a good one. It tells us, for example, why the leaders of the PCF so admired the Bolsheviks. Having failed themselves to make a revolution, they could not help but find extraordinary qualities in a group of men who had succeeded. It suggests a reason for their pessimism about the revolutionary potential of the masses. The uncontrolled movement of the masses had failed them once; there was no reason to suppose that it would not fail them again. It also explains their fierce attachment to centralized organization. For had not the *révolution manquée* of 1919–20 lacked only a reliable organizational link with the masses? Yet alone and unsupplemented, this interpretation does not suffice. It accounts for the atmosphere within which the party developed; it does not account for the party itself. Having discovered that the prewar movements failed, one wants to know *how* and *through whom* Communism succeeded in establishing a stronghold in the French labor movement. The search for the answer to these questions takes us both into the day-to-day acts of individual working-class leaders and into the structural characteristics of French society.

The role of the Bolsheviks, of course, should not be overlooked. They could bring to bear the financial powers of a great State, the services of secret envoys, and the prestige of a successful proletarian revolution. It is possible, though difficult to prove, that it was these resources alone that permitted them in 1924–25 to keep afloat and overhaul a party which might otherwise have floundered. Equally effective was the dynamism and the flair with which the Bolsheviks pursued their policies in France. Not content to watch the unfolding of events from afar, they constantly intervened in French affairs. But for the decisiveness with which Zinoviev and Trotsky moved in the second half of 1922, the Comintern might have lost the French party altogether; similarly, it was largely owing to the unflagging energies of Lozovsky that the CGTU was brought under Communist control. Nor, for all their sense of righteous indignation, were the Bolsheviks unwilling to forget the dictates of revolutionary morality when political realities required. Though appropriately *pur* and *dur* in public declarations, they were careful to guarantee the success of their operations by careful behind-the-scenes preparation. The survival of Cachin through repeated crises is sufficient evidence of their sense of Realpolitik.

Still, without French allies the Bolsheviks would have been powerless to carry into practice that force of will and keenness of historical vision on which they so prided themselves. These agents they found among the Socialists, the Left Wing, and the younger generation. About the Socialists little need be added to what already has been said. They had the defects of their virtues. Taught to believe in the workers as medieval men believed in God, they had no choice but to follow them when they veered to the left in 1919. If and when they reneged on their commitment, it was with a heavy heart. Frossard remains the best example. Too much the populist to withstand the movement of the masses, too wedded to the purposes of a proletarian party to take up happily the role of a Millerand, he whiled away his life in futile intrigues, an early martyr to the Socialist split. As he himself observed with brutal candor (and perhaps with an undercurrent of surprise), he had never, not even at his most enthusiastic, been a Communist. Yet in a real sense he was a founding father of French Communism. Without his political talents, the PCF would not have received the rousing send-off it did; and to this party, which first slandered him and then blotted him from the pages of its history, he taught an early lesson in the technique of cloaking Bolshevik innovations in the language of Jaurès.

The Left Wing represents an altogether different case. The most enthusiastic partisans of Bolshevism in 1919, they were also its most tragic victims in 1924. This outcome was to a large extent their own doing. In centralizing the party, in bringing proletarian leaders into its midst, and in tying it to Moscow, they laid the basis for its transformation. Looking back over the record of these years, one is struck by the degree to which these men were the servants rather than the masters of their fate. They did not so much act as react: even their innovations were against. If they were centralists, it was because federalism had led to the debacle of class collaboration. If they favored united front tactics, it was because their enemies opposed them. They did not stop to think that a heedless internationalism might have its dangers: it was enough that Social Democrats clung to some measure of national autonomy. The logic of reaction had a strange result. When the leaders of the Communist Left came to power in 1923, it was in the name of Moscow's policies, not their own. The tactics and methods later identified with Stalinism were put into practice either by them or with their consent in 1923. By the time they understood the dangerous direction of these policies, it was already too late. Loriot and Rosmer were no more able than Trotsky had been to reverse the processes that they themselves had set in motion.

Their places were taken by new men, for the most part members of the younger generation. Only with the arrival of this third group of leaders did the party fully lose its independence. Loriot and Rosmer had favored Russian methods out of a deep conviction that the day of reckoning was close at hand, and that only thus rearmed could the proletariat overwhelm its foe; Thorez and Monmousseau fell into line with the Soviet directives like disciplined soldiers, aware that theirs was not to reason why. The difference between the two sets of leaders is so striking that one is tempted to agree with Rappoport that high-minded men had been replaced by thieves.[f] Nonetheless, it would be a mistake to ascribe this change to defects of character alone. Ever since the 1890's the working-class movement had been plagued by leaders of doubtful dedication. Moreover, if men like Thorez and Monmousseau were opportunists, they were opportunists of a very special sort. Sincere in their hatred of the capitalist regime, they were at the same time too close to the events of 1917–23 to be confident of overthrowing it. Their idealism, therefore, could easily turn to cynicism, and no doubt often did. What remained of their original commitment, however, once hope of revolution had faded, was activism and unyielding opposition to the bourgeois State.[g] This made them ideal agents of Soviet foreign policy. Oppressed by the decadence of the society that surrounded them, eager to escape from the passivity of their predecessors, yet without their faith in the benevolence of history, they were dependent on the party both for their livelihood and for their sense of purpose. Through them Moscow ruled those layers of the French working class that the Socialists and Left Wing had won over between 1917 and 1924.

Agents there were, then, in abundance. But, as this book has shown, they were not always receptive to Bolshevik demands. Frossard, Rosmer, and Doriot all eventually broke with Moscow. And yet they failed when they attempted to undermine the party. Loyalty to Moscow proved a one-way street: once granted, support could not be taken back. In this connection it is interesting to speculate on the role of chance in the making of French Communism. If the nature of the Soviet State had been revealed in 1920 rather than 1921, perhaps the verdict at Tours would have been different. If Poincaré had not struck against the party in January 1923, perhaps the Resistants would have carried off the main body of the Communists' support. And if the Opposition had acted with more resolution and harmony of purpose in 1924–25, perhaps bolshevization could have been halted before it had gotten under way.

Yet the very enumeration of these instances leads one to believe that other forces were at work. Otherwise it is hard to understand why events invariably turned to the Bolsheviks' advantage. Certainly the failure of the successive oppositions cannot be laid to lack of talent or qualities of leadership. For if it is true that Frossard's unfortunate penchant for vacillation and intrigue cast doubts on his abilities, the same cannot be said of Rosmer, Monatte, and

---

[f] See p. 406.

[g] Contrast a Thorez or a Doriot, for example, with the Socialist opportunists of Jaurès's generation that Romain Rolland described in *Jean-Christophe* (1931): "These men gave the impression of believing in a new society. Perhaps they had believed in it once; but in reality their only thought was to live off the remains of a society that was in the process of dying. Theirs was a near-sighted opportunism in the service of a pleasure-loving nihilism." II, 209–10.

Loriot, all men of courage and determination, all veterans of the struggle against the War. By contrast, the Communist leaders who came to the fore in 1925 were, with the exception of Thorez, a shady and unattractive lot. Nor is it enough to say that the Bolsheviks tipped the balance with their shrewd appraisal of the French situation: the Russians, as we have seen, consistently misread the meaning of French events. One need only remember Zinoviev's writings in 1919–20 or Trotsky's letters in 1922–23 to realize that when Bolshevik policy succeeded, it was often for the wrong reasons. More than once Russian brusqueness endangered the future of the party. In every case, however, the influence of the Bolsheviks survived these crises, whereas apostates from Communism, no matter how stouthearted, were reduced to sterile opposition. The persistence of this pattern suggests that if the Bolsheviks were able to win over to their banner a substantial segment of the French working-class movement, it was not just because their historical vision was sharper, their opponents more incompetent, or fortune more favorable to their cause. The Russians held a trump card which, if properly played, would always bring them victory. It is not on the player but on the hand that we should focus our attention.

The Bolsheviks' advantage lay in the mentality of the French worker. What I mean by "mentality" is not so much an ideology as the stuff of which ideologies are made: a cluster of attitudes that inclined French workers to respond in certain ways to certain stimuli. The elements in this mentality were all a legacy of the past. They had arisen in reaction to the bourgeois style of life, but like all social reactions they bore the stamp of the attitudes they negated. The bourgeois universalized his values of stability; therefore, the worker did the same with his values of revolution. The bourgeois was a radical nationalist; the worker was a radical internationalist. The bourgeois had rejected the possibility of proletarian participation in his society. The worker responded by excluding the bourgeois from participation in his world. The essence of this mentality was not its activism (as Trotsky thought), but its sense of alienation. At the end of the nineteenth century, it had given rise to revolutionary syndicalism. From 1917 to 1920, it predisposed French workers to embrace the Russian Revolution. In 1924–26 it strengthened the hand of the Communist leadership against the Opposition. For nothing was more difficult than to argue before working-class assemblies that revolution was no longer possible, that trade-union leaders were insufficiently aware of what was going on, that it was necessary to break with the only proletarian State. These were illusions that made life possible in a society that was not so much cruel as indifferent.

The Bolsheviks were further aided by a second factor, not unrelated to the first: the structure of French working-class organizations. To begin with, the combination of centralization and decentralization typical of French groups made them susceptible to sudden overturns of leadership. Like the German party and union organizations, the SFIO and the CGT were oligarchical in the sense that their policies were set by a relatively small group of men who tended to remain the same; but, unlike their German counterparts, the bureaucracies of the SFIO and the CGT exercised little control over the intermediate and lower levels of party and union life. The local fief, not the exercise of a party function, was what gave the Socialist leader his power. The result was that dissidence, once it had begun, was hard to check; for minorities could always retire to the shelter of provincial strongholds. Moreover, the subversive effect of federalism was reinforced by dislike of Paris. Movements of revolt against party and union majorities could always exploit the feelings of hostility and suspicion harbored by provincial militants against the dictatorship of the capital. Both these factors are important in understanding the changes in party and union leadership that took place between 1914 and 1924.

Despite these similarities, however, the organizational situation was not identical in the SFIO and the CGT. In the former, both policies and leaders were determined through elections so democratic that oligarchy may be said to have rested on consensus. Because congress delegates were bound by their federations' mandates, established party leaders had little chance of influencing important votes by eloquence alone.[h] Thus at Tours a temporary movement toward the Left delivered the entire party organization into the hands of the Communists. The case of the CGT was more complex. There voting was not by head, but by union. This prevented the CGT from falling to the Communists in 1920–21. But once the Left Wing had founded their own organization, these same characteristics worked to the advantage of the party. The syndicalists of *La Vie Ouvrière* were able to win control of the CGTU as easily as the anarchists had the year before. A few months later, the conversion of a few key personalities like Monmousseau and Sémard was all that was required to bring the organization securely into Moscow's fold. In this way, working-class attitudes were transformed into organizational successes. Needless to say, these processes were not easily reversible. Once captured, the organizations were restructured and the new leadership was made immune to the danger of the kind of dissident movement that had earlier brought it to power.

Thus while France offered few real opportunities for proletarian revolution, it offered a first-rate terrain for the creation of a Communist Party. In

---

[h] According to Joseph Paul-Boncour, "The Socialist Party's structure was extremely democratic, too much so perhaps.... It could be taken for granted that each delegate represented an existing organization and accurately interpreted the decisions that it had made. Under these conditions, congress decisions reflected *a priori* opinions rather than the sort of opinions that emerge in a gathering at which everyone is free to cast his own vote." *Entre deux guerres* (1945), II, 21–22.

Russia the combination of Westernization and civic backwardness had revolutionized the whole society. In England prosperity and the willingness of the ruling groups to compromise had oriented the working class toward reform. France fell somewhere between these two extremes. Long-term economic advance and political democracy had undercut the bases for a proletarian revolution. Yet the narrow class nature of the republican regime and revolutionary memories kept radical sentiments alive. The worker was an outcast in his own society: a leper who could neither surmount nor destroy the walls that hemmed him in. Hence his susceptibility to Communist appeals. Distrusting bourgeois freedoms, he could accept the party's authoritarian structure. Knowing the limitations of bourgeois truth, he could believe Communist propaganda even when it was patently absurd. This explains what must otherwise remain a mystifying paradox: why the effect of Communism on French national life has been so unfailingly reactionary. Instead of breaking through the walls of non-communication that separated Frenchmen, Communism deliberately set out to reinforce them. It is thus no mere *jeu d'esprit* to call the PCF the greatest bulwark of the bourgeois status quo.[5]

It might be said that we have reached a crisis of interpretation. We have asked why the French Communist Party emerged in the midst of a fully developed labor movement; and we discovered that it was the gap between working-class achievements and working-class expectations that made possible this surprising historical development. We next asked how the Bolsheviks were able to win control of this party; and we saw that the secret of Bolshevik success lay less in the Russians' prowess than in the alienation of the French proletariat, the structure of French organizations, and the existence of French working-class leaders who for one reason or another were willing to do the Bolsheviks' will. The puzzle thus begins to fit together. Certain trends in the French past rendered permanent what circumstances had rendered possible. Yet to complete the puzzle, we still lack one important piece. Lurking behind and determining the emergence of French Communism lay two decisive events: the revolution in Russia and the defeat of the working-class movement in France. If the Bolsheviks had not seized and held power in Russia, there would have been less pressure toward a schism; whereas if the French working-class movement had not met with such stubborn resistance from the representatives of the liberal bourgeoisie, it would have been able to withstand the ideological attraction of Bolshevism. The timing of this coincidence is suggestive, but its significance is by no means clear. Therefore, before we can be satisfied that we understand the reasons for the PCF's appearance, we must first know how the defeat of the French working-class movement was related to the march of the Russian Revolution.

What were the historical connections between Russian Communism and the

Communist parties of the West? No question has been more hotly debated within the European Socialist movement. Since 1917 polemics have raged over the European significance of the Russian Revolution. The Bolsheviks insisted, with almost desperate Marxist fervor, that their revolution had universal validity. The Social Democrats replied with equal passion that it did not. At stake was a whole series of practical issues, such as the attitude that Socialists should take toward the War, the dictatorship of the proletariat, and the Third International, as well as the more basic question of what the Russian Revolution was about. The debate burst out again in 1924, this time within the Communist camp itself. The controversies going on in Russia, said the Opposition, had no relevance to the problems of the working-class movement in the West. Self-respecting Communists, the majority retorted, must take sides. Again a major issue was at stake. The Communist leadership was trying to introduce the Russian system of organization. Their opponents argued that such methods had no place in countries which had yet to have a proletarian revolution. In the course of the discussion, which lasted at least a decade, many left-wingers concluded, like Loriot, that the Russian Revolution had nothing of value to teach the workers of the West. The debate has shown no tendency to die out with the passage of time, at least not in France. Communists still recite their scriptures about Lenin's insights into the disintegration of capitalist society; while Socialists, wittier if not more wise, are content to observe that the PCF is not left but east.

Unlike so many other matters over which working-class leaders squabble, this debate has serious implications. If the Russian and French experiences are related, they must derive from some common antecedent, some general crisis, that will help to explain them both. If, on the other hand, the Russian and French experiences are essentially unrelated, French Communism becomes the product of a misunderstanding, the fruit of certain men's malevolence or ambition, at best the creation of a cruel and capricious fate. In the first case, we have what might be called the thesis of crisis; in the second case, we are left with the thesis of circumstance.

Marxist theories of social evolution being in disrepute, the thesis of circumstance currently holds the field. Its best-known formulation is in the writings of Franz Borkenau.[6] Though Borkenau's interest was not primarily France, an interpretation of French Communism may be drawn from his books. Bolshevism, argued Borkenau, was a movement molded by the Russian conditions within which it developed. Where the Western labor movement was "thoroughly 'bourgeois' in mind and sentiment," the Russian revolutionary movement was profoundly anti-bourgeois. Where the Western labor movement was based on the proletariat, the Russian revolutionary movement was a creation of the intelligentsia. Finally, where the Western labor movement was "unaggressive in spite of a revolutionary creed," the Russian revolutionary movement was oriented exclusively toward the bloody goal of revolution. The former produced the labor movements and reformist Socialism of the West; the latter issued in the Russian organization of professional revolutionaries, "with its peculiar methods of selection and work, its peculiar religious enthusiasm, and its equally peculiar indifference to ordinary moral standards." The history of the Communist International was the history of Lenin's attempt to transfer these peculiarly Russian patterns to the West. Thus while Bolshevism and Western Socialism shared a common ideology, they were in reality quite different, the products of two different cultures.[7]

We owe many insights to Borkenau, but it seems clear that he exaggerated both the Russian nature of Bolshevism and the homogeneity of the Western labor movement. What was the Left Wing of the Socialist movement in the West if not revolutionary, anti-bourgeois, led by members of the intelligentsia, and religious in its enthusiasm? As for the authoritarian element in Bolshevism, one must not forget that it coexisted with a strong libertarian vision of the Socialist future. The most serious defect of Borkenau's interpretation, however, is that it confuses the national circumstances that produced Bolshevism with the international circumstances that made possible its exportation. It explains why Stalin followed Lenin; it does not tell us why Jaurès was followed by Thorez. Why, if Bolshevism was peculiarly Russian, did it strike such deep roots in the West? Borkenau's answer—that Western Socialists were deceived by their own theory—is not convincing. Men sometimes make mistakes in the heat of action; the anarchists of 1919 are an example. But a political movement that has lasted half a century must have some deeper basis.

That basis, it seems to me—that common antecedent of the Russian and French Communist parties—was the crisis of liberal values that affected all of Europe in the years preceding the World War.[8] By "liberal" I refer not merely to a political ideology, but to a view of the world that was held throughout Europe by the end of the nineteenth century. Even where liberal values were not dominant in 1900, as in Russia and Spain, everyone (including Socialists and conservatives) agreed that their triumph was imminent. Liberalism, in other words, was the world view against which all other movements and subcultures measured their methods and defined their aspirations. What were the primary tenets of this system of values? An attachment to some form of representative government; a conviction that social distinctions were both useful and necessary; a commitment to national self-determination; a faith in the basic rationality of man; an unshakable belief in the superiority of Europeans over all other peoples; and most of all, perhaps, a tendency to see the world in terms of individual needs and accomplishments, a facile bent for abstractions, and an optimistic assumption that the advance of technology and the development of the human personality went hand in hand. It was these last habits of thought that united the great majority of the educated inhabitants of prewar

Europe. A good liberal never doubted that virtue could be combined with the exercise of power, nor did he hesitate to universalize his own individual values and apply them to mankind.

Around the mid-1890's, this liberal synthesis entered a period of crisis. The problem was the transition from an elitist society to a society of mass participation. The precipitating factors were political, social, and economic change, speeded by the heady advance of European technology. The suffrage was everywhere extended, thereby endangering the continued political dominance of men of property. Industrialization lured the peasant from his hamlet and the artisan from his workshop, subjected them to an anonymous employer and a new and harsher discipline, threw them into contact with new social groups, and robbed them of their sense of identity. The middle classes, too, felt the winds of change. Small businessmen came up against the competition of large industry; and State taxes and regulations affected more and more people in more and more occupations. The liberal dictum that politics was a branch of economics was secretly but nonetheless surely being replaced by a reality of statist domination. Movements like Socialism arose to oversee the transition from liberalism to democracy. What made their task so difficult and moderate change so rare was that the entrenched groups felt threatened, not only in their interests but also in their way of life (thus they could condemn as evil what was merely dangerous); while the new masses had only the slightest idea of what they wanted. They floundered, they spat in sullen fury, and all the while their numbers mounted. These processes lay behind the troubles of the decade 1895–1905 in Italy, France, and Russia. By 1906 the first crises had been successfully passed. But the new elites who came to power were incapable of dealing with the forces of social disintegration. Hence the violence and ambiguity of the decade that preceded the War.

For those who cared to look, the signs of collapse were clear enough in the years before '14. The great protagonists of prewar French fiction—Rolland's Jean-Christophe, Proust's Swann, Martin du Gard's Jean Barois—all felt the crumbling of the world around them. Moral codes no longer seemed to correspond to feelings. Youth sought outlets in religious commitments or the revival of strange cults. Irrationalism was exalted. Imperialistic ventures attracted Europeans who found their native countries effete and boring. And new movements arose on both the Right and the Left that paraded their disdain for liberal values. In the air there was a feeling of approaching apocalypse. As Hesse's Demian put it to his friend Sinclair, "I sense the coming of conflicts. They will come, believe me, they will come and soon.... The world, as it is now, wants to die, it wants to perish, and it will."[9]

Obviously this crisis affected different countries in different ways. In Russia the autocratic nature of the State, the weakness of the bourgeoisie, and the precarious hold of liberal values made conspiracy and assassination the only effective forms of political opposition. In France the strength of the bourgeoisie and the freedoms which it cherished meant that unrest could be expressed in the form of articles, demonstrations, and protest votes. In Russia the State was practically without allies; in France the peasantry and bourgeoisie stood allied behind the State. In France there was too much stability; in Russia there was not enough. Despite these differences, however, what both countries essentially faced was a crisis of legitimacy. New classes had arisen for which no roles had been assigned. Others were fighting their way to political consciousness. Confronted by the vanguard of the mass society, the elites in Russia and France asked themselves whether those trail-blazing processes loosely termed improvement were not undermining the civilization that lay beneath.

Social Democracy occupied an ambiguous position in the working out of the European crisis. It was both the gravedigger and the standard-bearer of liberalism. On the one hand, Social Democrats rejected the egoism and elitism of the liberals. Convinced that the day of conservatism was over, they reserved their harshest blows for the liberal elite, and from this militancy came much of their success. On the other hand, Social Democrats were deeply involved in the fate of the bourgeois society that they aspired to supplant. Reduced to its essentials, Social Democracy was little more than an attempt to extend to other classes those values that the bourgeoisie had hoarded for itself. Hence the aversion of the Social Democrats to violence and their enthusiasm for parliamentary procedures. This made them doubly vulnerable: vulnerable from the Left because they dared not alienate their class support; vulnerable from the Right because they dared not undermine the values they esteemed and the groups with whom they planned to build a new society. Their most sensitive area, however, was on the question of nationalism. As Socialists, they were internationalists. As democrats, they aspired after national unity. Small wonder that Social Democrats wavered hopelessly on the question of the War.

The first three years of war brought all these dilemmas to the fore. In France the outbreak of the War offered the working-class movement its great opportunity: never before had the working class been so closely identified with the nation. Unhappily, however, it soon became clear that national unity could be achieved only by giving up internationalism. The Socialists could triumph only by ceasing to be Socialists. In Russia the War provided the forces of Social Democracy with an even greater opportunity, arising from the collapse of state authority. But the opportunity meant a choice, the same choice as in France. Just as the French Social Democrats had learned that they could only be democrats by ceasing to be Socialists, the Russian Social Democrats discovered that they could only be Socialists by ceasing to be democrats. For the French, as for the Russians, 1917 was the crucial year. Clemenceau's arrival in power and the Bolshevik coup d'état were two aspects of a similar process: the failure of Social Democracy to achieve its ends.

It would be comforting to think that this outcome was inevitable; it was certainly anything but accidental. In France the break between the Socialists and the liberal bourgeoisie had long been pending. It was called for by an irreconcilability of social interest. A bourgeoisie trained to think of itself in absolutes could not accept a program that aimed at its transcendence, no matter how nobly conceived. Proletarians, on the other hand, could not be expected to act like the reformists they were not. What was needed was a shock of such proportions as to make the potential benefits of renovation outweigh the bitter pleasures of class hatred. Contrary to what might be expected, the threat of war did not produce this psychological reorientation; nor did the prewar economic advance. On the contrary, their effect was to turn the bourgeoisie toward reaction. For if the uncertain international situation convinced the average bourgeois that France was surrounded by foreign enemies who conspired against her, the creeping evidence of modernization made him worry over the decline of traditional values. Both experiences pushed him toward the Right.[10] Meanwhile the working class, too, was in the process of being transformed. The artisan was being replaced by the unskilled worker, who was both more apathetic and less responsive to democratic slogans. Such proletarians did not constitute a majority of the population, nor would they later. Yet they were the raw material with which a Socialist party had to work. This helps to explain the confusion of Socialists on the eve of the War. It also sheds light on Jaurès's new insurgency: in 1914 it was harder to be both a revolutionary and a liberal than it had been in 1905.

In Russia the prognosis for democracy was even more uncertain. Forces working for democracy existed, but the obstacles to their success were great. Chief among these was Russia's responsibilities as a great power.[11] To strike roots and develop, Russian liberalism needed peace. "Give us ten years and we will be safe," the Russian liberal Shidlovsky said in 1914. These hopes were shattered when Russia was drawn into a conflict which she did not want and for which she was desperately unprepared. For three years Russia's rulers were torn between their commitment to make war and their desire to maintain the status quo. When the autocracy fell in 1917, the liberals of the Provisional Government and the more moderate Socialists of the Petrograd Soviet discovered to their surprise that they had inherited the autocracy's dilemma. The prerequisite for the survival of Russian democracy, once established, was peace. Yet circumstances did not permit a general peace in 1917.[12] France, it should be noted, played a greater role than most European powers in the unfolding of the Russian drama. Uncompromising opponents of a negotiated peace in 1917, the French were also the driving force behind the intervention of 1918–20. Both policies worked to the Bolsheviks' advantage. The first made possible the Bolshevik coup d'état; the second helped the Bolsheviks to consolidate their authority. The fates of French and Russian Social Democracy thus turned out to be curiously related: the policies pursued by France helped undermine the position of the Social Democrats in Russia, while the failure of Social Democracy in Russia contributed to the split of the working-class movement in France.

If the hopes of Social Democracy were dashed by the War, the Left Wing fared no better in the stormy years that followed. The Left Wing, it will be remembered, had developed as an alternative to Social Democracy. Left Wing-ers rejected certain liberal values that Social Democrats shared, such as a belief in parliamentary methods, an abhorrence of violence, and a commitment to the tenets of bourgeois morality. Seen in this perspective, the development of the European Left Wing was one of the manifestations of the liberal crisis. Yet the paradox at the center of the left-wing movement was the fact that its concept of revolution was rooted in the liberal world—a world in which men were free to pursue the cultivation of the self unfettered by discipline or the responsibilities of power; a world in which the State was less important than the society that lay behind it; a world, too, in which moral standards were so taken for granted that their outward manifestations could be assaulted and abandoned without endangering their content. The left-wing view of revolu-tion was a negative projection of this world: a liberation from all authority and restraint that was conceived in esthetic and moral rather than political terms. Though European revolutionaries differed in their means of struggle, all of them—Socialists, syndicalists, and anarchists alike—shared this vision of the future, a vision inspired, it is hardly necessary to say, by a profound dis-content with the realities of the European present.

It is this fact—what might be called the reactionary ethos of the Left Wing—which gives the events of 1917-20 their irony. With every year the advance of industrialization lessened the chances for a revolution of the left-wing type. The direction in which European and even French society was heading in the years before 1914 was toward more discipline, more power, more national unity, not less. Only the War and the outbreak of the revolutionary crisis obscured this trend. The Bolsheviks and the French Left were suddenly given opportunities to wield power that they never had before 1914, and that they had reason to believe they would never get. The Left Wing's sudden change of fortune came because the liberal elites could not cope with forces they them-selves had unleashed. War speeded the process of industrialization, created new masses, and destroyed the prestige of the European ruling classes. A tawdry peace completed what a bloody war had begun. The result was a fur-ther disintegration of liberal values, values in which, as we have seen, the Social Democrats themselves believed. Bolshevism, therefore, was indeed what Charles Rappoport had called it in 1919: "the punishment for this great crime: the War!"[13] Without the political and social strains induced by three years of murderous conflict, neither the Bolsheviks nor their Western allies would have attained the importance they did.

The Left Wing's moment was short-lived. In France the Rosmer-Souvarine group had demonstrated their failure by 1923. It was not merely that the men of the Left had been unable to carry out a revolution; they had also shown little talent for the creation of a mass political party. This outcome was implicit in their prewar premises: prophets of self-cultivation, they had nothing to offer the masses, whose objective was not finer minds but fatter paychecks, not the inauguration of a new society but a fuller enjoyment of the one that already existed. The Bolsheviks were no more successful in carrying out the left-wing revolution. The difference was that they were Russians. This meant not that they were more Marxist, more anti-bourgeois, more revolutionary, or more fanatic, but that they were more alive to the problem of power, more conscious of the irrationality of masses, more ambivalent in their attitude toward Western values. Unlike the Left Wing in the West, Lenin had always distrusted spontaneity. This placed him in a more advantageous position to meet the crisis of 1920–21. To save the Revolution's future, Lenin sacrificed its left-wing present, and broke irrevocably with libertarian aims. Lenin saw this retreat as temporary, an expedient required by the postponement of the European Revolution. He assumed, like many other Europeans of his age, that libertarian ends could be achieved by illiberal means. He was wrong, and before he died a rift had opened between the party's practice and its aspirations. Power was wielded without regard to its revolutionary results. The goal of personal transcendence faded increasingly from sight. In its stead appeared a worship of technology for technology's own sake.

All this should not blind us to the brilliance of Lenin's innovation: finding the members of his party stunned and disoriented by the failure of their revolution, he revived them, regrouped them, and headed them down a more promising path. Dazzled as his followers were by the success of the maneuver, few noticed that in the process of changing direction, the end had become nothing, the movement all. The inspiration for Lenin's innovation was undoubtedly Russian, an unexpected legacy of Russia's historic need for authority and power; it was nonetheless applicable to the West, where the coming of the mass society and the breakdown of liberal values had cut the ground from beneath the Left Wing's hope for a revolution of the libertarian kind. Hence the importance of the younger generation in the making of the French Communist Party. It was a post-liberal generation that was best suited to lead a movement that denied the liberal virtues of individualism, stability, and absolute morality. That generation was a product of the War, of the revolutionary crisis, and of the disillusionment which their outcome engendered. The Rosmers were replaced by the Doriots, the anarchists by realists for whom ideology was something to be manipulated rather than believed. We are accustomed to thinking of Communism as a creation of the early twentieth century, a twin to such movements as integral nationalism and corporatism. The reality is more complex. The radical movements of prewar Europe, no less than the bourgeois movements they arose to combat, were victims of the liberal collapse. Their successors inherited everything but the dream of liberation that made these movements tick. That dream died in the disappointments of 1919–23. Communism, both in France and in Russia, was a product of the Revolution's failure, not of its success.

# Notes

# Notes

Unless otherwise indicated, all books mentioned are published in Paris. In addition to the abbreviations used in the text, the following abbreviations are used in the notes:

BC          *Bulletin Communiste*
BEIPI       *Bulletin d'Etudes et d'Informations Politiques Internationales*
HDA         Humbert-Droz Archives
IC          *L'Internationale Communiste*
JP          *Le Journal du Peuple*
Kriegel     Annie Kriegel, *Aux origines du communisme français, 1914–1920: Contribution à l'histoire du mouvement ouvrier français.* 2 vols., 1964.
OJJ         *Oeuvres de Jean Jaurès.* 9 vols., 1931–39.
Rosmer      Alfred Rosmer, *Le Mouvement ouvrier pendant la guerre.* 2 vols., 1936–59.
VO          *La Vie Ouvrière*

Official proceedings of Socialist national congresses are cited in the form "SFIO, $9^e$ Congrès," followed in most cases by the city and date of the congress in brackets.

## Chapter one

Epigraph: SFIO, $9^e$ *Congrès* [Lyon, 1912], p. 223.

1. SFIO, $1^{er}$ *Congrès* [Paris, 1905], pp. 13–14.

2. Guesde still awaits his biographer, who should be able to make an important contribution to our understanding of the development of French Socialism before the War. The best introduction to his thought and life is to be found in Claude Willard's introduction to Jules Guesde, *Textes choisis* (1959); Samuel Bernstein, "Jules Guesde, Pioneer of Marxism in France," *Science and Society*, IV (1940), 29–56; and I. Belkin, *Zhiul Ged i borba za rabochuyu partiiu vo Frantsii* (Moscow, 1952). Alexandre Zévaès, *Jules Guesde, 1845–1922* (1929), and Adrien Compère-Morel, *Jules Guesde, le socialisme fait homme, 1845–1922* (1937), may also be consulted.

3. Some of Guesde's articles from this period are collected in Jules Guesde, *Ça et là* (1914). See in particular pp. 151–52.

4. The Russian revolutionary Georgii Plekhanov was converted to Marxism in 1880–81 while an exile in Paris. See Samuel H. Baron, "Plekhanov and the Origins of Russian Marxism," *Russian Review*, XIII (1954), 38–51.

5. D. W. Brogan, *The Development of Modern France, 1870–1939* (London, 1953), p. 294.

6. Marcel Cachin, "Le Centenaire de Guesde," *Pensée*, No. 5 (Oct.–Dec. 1945), p. 23.

7. Jules Guesde, *Le Socialisme au jour le jour* (1899), p. ii. See also Jules Guesde and Paul Lafargue, *Le Programme du parti ouvrier*, 6th ed. (1902), p. 21.

8. Jules Guesde, *Le Socialisme, Double réponse à MM. de Mun et Paul Deschanel* (1945), pp. 13–14.

9. *Programme du parti ouvrier*, pp. 7–8.

10. There is an excellent summary of Guesde's ideas in Bernstein, "Jules Guesde," pp. 48–50. See also Milorad M. Drachkovitch, *Les Socialismes français et allemand et le problème de la guerre, 1870–1914* (Geneva, 1953), pp. 8–12, and, of course, Guesde's own works, in particular *Ça et là* and *Le Socialisme au jour le jour*.

11. The articles, originally published in *Le Cri du Peuple*, are reproduced in *Le Socialisme au jour le jour*, pp. 433–37.

12. For Zinoviev, see Georges Zinoviev, *Les Socialistes français et la guerre: Jaurès, Sembat, Guesde* (Petrograd, 1920), pp. 46–48; for Cachin, see SFIO, *18ᵉ Congrès* [Tours, 1920], pp. 189–91.

13. For the issues at stake in this split, see Aaron Noland, *The Founding of the French Socialist Party*, pp. 21–23, and Brogan, pp. 295–96.

14. According to Jean Maitron, *Histoire du mouvement anarchiste en France, 1880–1914*, 2d rev. ed. (1955), p. 275, the Allemanists were sometimes called the "allemarchistes," and Fernand Pelloutier referred to their party as "la pépinière de l'anarchie."

15. Drachkovitch, *Les Socialismes*, pp. 15–17; Marcel Prélot, *L'Evolution politique du socialisme français, 1789–1934* (1939), pp. 105–6; Brogan, pp. 296–97.

16. Brogan, p. 297.

17. Charles Rappoport later wrote of Guesde: "His mind seemed to have been created to grasp and point out the social antagonisms that tear our world apart." *IC*, No. 22 (Aug.–Sept. 1922), p. 70.

18. Joseph Caillaux, *Mes mémoires* (1947), III, 96; Georges Sorel, *Réflexions sur la violence*, 10th ed. (1946), pp. 81–82. Clemenceau complained that when Jaurès wrote, his verbs were always in the future tense. (J. Hampden Jackson, *Clemenceau and the Third Republic*, New York, 1948, p. 139.) There are now at least three good biographies of Jaurès: Harvey Goldberg, *The Life of Jean Jaurès* (Madison, Wis., 1962); Marcelle Auclair, *La Vie de Jean Jaurès* (1954); and J. Hampden Jackson, *Jean Jaurès* (London, 1943). Goldberg's massive study is more than a biography; it is a history of the Third Republic during the years 1884–1914 from the point of view of the Left. Auclair is very good on Jaurès's personal life and the atmosphere of the period. Read together, these books make Jaurès appear one of the most attractive political figures of modern times, and perhaps one of the greatest.

19. In his famous lecture on "Idealism and Materialism," Jaurès observed that "the thrust of man's thought in the four centuries since the Renaissance has been toward reconciliation, toward the synthesis of opposites and even of contradictions: this is the hallmark of modern philosophical and intellectual development." *OJJ*, VI, 8.

20. Max Bonnefous, in his introduction to Vol. III of *OJJ* (no pagination).

21. See his *Etudes socialistes*, in *OJJ*, Vols. III and VI.

22. *OJJ*, III, 160.
23. *Ibid.*, VI, 262–63.
24. *Ibid.*, p. 301.
25. *Ibid.*, p. 272.
26. *Ibid.*, p. 133.
27. SFIO, 2ᵉ *Congrès* [Chalon-sur-Saône, 1905], p. 101.
28. SFIO, 4ᵉ *Congrès* [Nancy, 1907], p. 277.
29. See his speech on "Idealism and Materialism," *OJJ*, VI, 6–19.
30. *OJJ*, III, 160–61; VI, 18. Also Kurt Vorländer, *Kant und Marx* (Tübingen, 1926), p. 105.
31. *OJJ*, VI, 96.
32. *Ibid.*, p. 83.
33. *Ibid.*, III, 162–63.
34. *Ibid.*, VI, 152–53.
35. *Ibid.*, III, 348.
36. *Ibid.*, p. 399.
37. For the evolution of Guesde and Jaurès and their *rapprochement*, see Goldberg, *Life of Jaurès*, p. 185; on Vaillant, consult Drachkovitch, *Les Socialismes*, p. 15; for the development of Marxism as a whole during this period, the best work is George Lichtheim, *Marxism: An Historical and Critical Study* (New York, 1961), pp. 203–58.
38. Quoted in Goldberg, p. 185.
39. See the debate between Jaurès and Guesde on "Les Deux méthodes," *OJJ*, VI, 187–218.
40. Emile Vandervelde, *Souvenirs d'un militant socialiste* (1939), p. 157, remarks that after 1905 Jaurès drew closer to Vaillant, and that Vaillant became "the overseer of his Socialist conscience."
41. See H. Stuart Hughes, *Consciousness and Society*, Vintage ed. (New York, 1961), pp. 67–104, for the details of this critique.
42. Roger Martin du Gard, *Jean Barois* (New York, 1949), p. 317.
43. For the Action Française, see Eugen Weber, *Action Française: Royalism and Reaction in Twentieth-Century France* (Stanford, Calif., 1962); for revolutionary syndicalism, see below, n. 72.
44. Romain Rolland, *Jean-Christophe* (1931), III, 168–69.
45. SFIO, 5ᵉ *Congrès* [Toulouse, 1908]. For J.-L. Breton, see p. 225; Jobert, pp. 407, 434–35; Lagardelle, p. 264; Lafargue, pp. 135–36; Vaillant, p. 159.
46. Prélot, *L'Evolution politique du socialisme français*, p. 175. Victor Serge recalled in his *Mémoires d'un révolutionnaire* (1951), p. 51, that "in those days, the world had such a cohesive structure, such a look of permanence, that it did not seem possible really to change it." This is an interesting testimony, coming from a Russian anarchist who knew Western revolutionary circles well.
47. SFIO, 5ᵉ *Congrès* [1908], pp. 144–45.
48. For the text of this document, see *ibid.*, pp. 484–85.
49. SFIO, 4ᵉ *Congrès* [1907], pp. 487–88.
50. See Noland, *Founding of the French Socialist Party*, pp. 51–56, for an excellent discussion of the evolution of Guesdism. Vaillant recognized that the party was moving toward reformism, and he considered this development an inevitable result of French political and social development. But he was confident that when circumstances changed and class conflict again became acute, the party would respond in corresponding fashion and rediscover its revolutionary spirit. SFIO, 4ᵉ *Congrès* [1907], p. 505.
51. Noland, p. 56.
52. Goldberg, *Life of Jaurès*, p. 258. See also Leslie Derfler, "Le 'Cas Millerand': une nouvelle interprétation," *Revue d'Histoire Moderne et Contemporaine*, X (Apr.–June, 1963), pp. 81–104. Derfler emphasizes Guesde's jealousy of Jaurès and the ascendancy he was gaining over the working-class movement. Perhaps. But in the case of a man like Guesde it is extremely difficult to distinguish concern for his own position from concern

for the movement as a whole; and on the basis of Guesde's previous career I would be inclined to put more weight on the latter than the former.

53. Goldberg, p. 223 and p. 518, n. 149. Brogan writes that after the Dreyfus case "it was almost necessary for self-respect for a young man who graduated from the Ecole Normale to be 'Socialist.' The Alsatian librarian, Lucien Herr, made it his business and duty to indoctrinate the young Normaliens. And when he failed, as with Edouard Herriot, it was a kind of scandal." *The French Nation from Napoleon to Pétain, 1814–1940* (New York, 1957), p. 216.

54. L.-O. Frossard, *De Jaurès à Léon Blum* (1943), p. 24.

55. My approach to these questions owes a great deal to Maurice Duverger's classic work, *Political Parties* (New York, 1963 ed.).

56. Bernstein, "Jules Guesde," p. 47. See also Robert Michels, *Political Parties* (Glencoe, Ill., 1958 ed.), pp. 48–49, which points out this tendency in the European Socialist movement as a whole. Edouard Berth, *Les Nouveaux Aspects du socialisme* (1908), called Guesdism "une sorte de *napoléonisme* ouvrier" (p. 3) and described it in the following way (p. 10): "A strong organization; iron discipline; concentration and centralization of power; an all-powerful general staff followed by fanatically loyal and blindly obedient troops: the Guesdist army was supposed to march in close order to the conquest of the State." Claude Willard, however, remarks that "this discipline was only relative. There are numerous examples of groups that failed to respect the general policy of the party, and of officeholders, local leaders, and just plain militants who were guilty of insubordination against their own groups or federations." "Contribution au portrait du militant guesdiste dans les dix dernières années du XIX siècle," *Le Mouvement Social*, No. 33-34 (Oct. 1960– Mar. 1961), p. 63.

57. *OJJ*, II, 292.

58. Goldberg, pp. 308–11.

59. For these statutes, see SFIO, *1er Congrès* [1905], pp. 23–32. In the department of the Seine and at Lyon, the groups of the same arrondissement in the suburbs were to form a section.

60. *OJJ*, II, 438.

61. These figures are taken from Louis Dubreuilh's report at the Congress of Lyon in 1912. (SFIO, *9e Congrès*, p. 93.) The total circulation of *L'Humanité* was 87,844 at the end of 1913, as opposed to 55,719 at the beginning of the year. SFIO, *10e Congrès* [Brest, 1913], p. 140.

62. Unfortunately, the kinds of data that one would like on the Socialist vote are not yet available. Before any trustworthy generalizations can be made we must have detailed regional studies on the development of the Socialist electorate. Georges Dupeux has made a first step in this direction with his *Aspects de l'histoire sociale et politique du département de Loire-et-Cher de 1881 à 1914* (The Hague, 1962).

63. *L'Echo de Paris* remarked on May 14, 1914: "There is a considerable and worrying phenomenon—the progress of revolutionary Socialism among the rural population. In certain regions the peasant has become revolutionary and votes for the SFIO." Quoted in Eugen Weber, *The Nationalist Revival in France, 1905–1914* (Berkeley, Calif., 1959), p. 137.

64. François Goguel, *Géographie des élections françaises de 1870 à 1951* (1951), pp. 55–64.

65. The source for this statement is Hubert-Rouger's *La France socialiste*, 2 vols. (1912–14), in which there are numerous biographies of leading Socialists. If one can judge from the composition of the parliamentary Group, the SFIO was becoming more bourgeois, not less, on the eve of the War. Georges Lefranc, *Le Mouvement socialiste sous la Troisième République* (1963), p. 189.

66. Drachkovitch, *Les Socialismes,* p. 84; Michels, *Political Parties,* p. 271.

67. Albert Thibaudet, *Les Idées politiques de la France* (1932), p. 197.

68. See the interesting discussion of bourgeois in the Socialist movement in Michels, pp. 247–81. Guesde's Parti Ouvrier followed the same pattern. Even though its rank and file were largely of working-class origin, its leaders had come from the petty bourgeoisie. Willard, "Contribution au portrait du militant guesdiste," p. 60.

69. SFIO, *3ᵉ Congrès* [Limoges, 1906], pp. 173–74, and SFIO, *4ᵉ Congrès* [1907], pp. 466–67.

70. J. H. Clapham, *The Economic Development of France and Germany, 1815–1914* (Cambridge, Eng., 1936), p. 240; Gordon Wright, *France in Modern Times* (Chicago, 1960), p. 360.

71. Jacques Chastenet, *Jours inquiets et jours sanglants, 1906–1918* (1957), p. 151.

72. There is a considerable literature on the origins and doctrines of revolutionary syndicalism. Some useful books are Jean Montreuil, *Histoire du mouvement ouvrier en France* (1946); Edouard Dolléans, *Histoire du mouvement ouvrier,* 2 vols. (1946); Val R. Lorwin, *The French Labor Movement* (Cambridge, Mass., 1954); Louis Levine, *Syndicalism in France,* rev. ed. (New York, 1914); and R. Goetz-Girey, *La Pensée syndicale française* (1948). But perhaps the two best books for an understanding of the historical situation in which revolutionary syndicalism arose are Jean Maitron's *Histoire du mouvement anarchiste en France,* and the same author's *Le Syndicalisme révolutionnaire: Paul Delesalle* (1952).

73. According to J. H. Clapham, "France remained to the end [of the nineteenth century] a home of artistic trades, of *ateliers,* of small workshops, many of which made no use of power. In 1896 a census of industries and professions showed that the 575,000 'industrial establishments' in the country averaged 5.5 workpeople each day. Only 151 establishments had 1,000 or more workpeople. More than 400,000 of the establishments had only one or two workpeople, and another 80,000 had only three or four. Of the 575,000 establishments, 534,500 had less than ten." *Economic Development of France and Germany,* p. 258.

74. Dolléans, *Histoire du mouvement ouvrier,* II, 34.

75. "Direct or indirect, simple or complex, government of the people will always be a swindle of the people." P.-J. Proudhon, *Idée générale de la révolution au XIXᵉ siècle* (1851), p. 140.

76. Clapham, p. 272. See also David Thomson, *Democracy in France,* 2d ed. (London, 1954), pp. 175–76.

77. Wright, *France in Modern Times,* p. 364. See also Jean Fréville, *Né du feu* (1960), pp. 31–32.

78. Maitron, *Mouvement anarchiste,* pp. 249–62.

79. Quoted in *ibid.,* p. 251, from a police report of Nov. 6, 1892.

80. *Ibid.,* p. 279.

81. Maitron, p. 310; Drachkovitch, *Les Socialismes,* p. 18; Pierre Monatte, *Trois scissions syndicales* (1958), pp. 115–16.

82. There is a short biographical sketch of Pelloutier's life by Victor Dave in Pelloutier's *Histoire des Bourses du Travail* (1902), pp. i–xx.

83. *Ibid.,* p. 160.

84. *Ibid.,* p. 26.

85. Mermeix (Gabriel Terrail), *Le Syndicalisme contre le socialisme,* 6th ed. (1907), pp. 192–203.

86. Roger Picard, *Le Mouvement syndical pendant la guerre* (1929), p. 19.

87. *Ibid.,* pp. 21–22.

88. Weber, *The Nationalist Revival,* p. 40.

89. Quoted in *ibid.,* p. 41.

90. Quoted in Dolléans, *Histoire du mouvement ouvrier*, II, 126.

91. Joseph A. Schumpeter, *Capitalism, Socialism and Democracy*, 3d ed. (New York, 1962), p. 340.

92. Edouard Berth, *Les Nouveaux Aspects du socialisme*, p. 4. Berth's works, of course, say more about himself and his friends than about syndicalism.

93. John Bowditch, "The Concept of Elan Vital: A Rationalization of Weakness," in Edward Mead Earle, ed., *Modern France* (Princeton, N.J., 1951), pp. 32–43.

94. For this bizarre episode, see Weber, *Action Française*, pp. 68–85.

95. Schumpeter, p. 340. For the argument that "revolutionary syndicalism is historically an important root of the antidemocratic philosophy of communism as well as fascism," see Carl Landauer, *European Socialism*, 2 vols. (Berkeley, Calif., 1959), I, 345.

96. Quoted in Maitron, *Mouvement anarchiste*, p. 298.

97. *Le Mouvement Socialiste*, Jan. 1905, pp. 14, 17.

98. Quoted in Maitron, p. 286.

99. G. D. H. Cole, *The Second International, 1889–1914* (London, 1956), Part I, p. 362.

100. According to Emile Pouget. Quoted in Mermeix, *Le Syndicalisme contre le socialisme*, p. 201.

101. Once again according to Pouget. Maitron, p. 474.

102. Quoted in Landauer, I, 345.  103. Mermeix, pp. 199–201.

104. SFIO, *4ᵉ Congrès* [1907], p. 367.  105. Mermeix, p. 2.

106. Choloz memoir on the French working-class movement, probably written in 1922. Monatte Archives.

107. Quoted in Mermeix, pp. 210–11.  108. Goldberg, *Life of Jaurès*, p. 391.

109. Quoted in Maitron, p. 301.  110. Quoted in *ibid.*, p. 306.

111. The phrase is Goetz-Girey's (*La Pensée syndicale française*, p. 37). See also Léon Jouhaux, *Le Syndicalisme et la C.G.T.* (1920), pp. 147–48.

112. Quoted in Dolléans, *Histoire du mouvement ouvrier*, II, 198.

113. SFIO, *3ᵉ Congrès* [1906], p. 103. Socialists were required by the party statutes to belong to a union if they were eligible for union membership.

114. See Hubert Lagardelle's speech in Jules Guesde, Hubert Lagardelle, and Edouard Vaillant, *Le Parti socialiste et la Confédération du Travail* (1908).

115. SFIO, *3ᵉ Congrès*, p. 190.  116. *Ibid.*, p. 187.

117. *Ibid.*, p. 194.  118. *Ibid.*, p. 184.

119. SFIO, *5ᵉ Congrès* [1908], pp. 348–49, and *Journal Officiel de la République française, Débats, Chambre*, 11.v.07.

120. SFIO, *5ᵉ Congrès*, p. 350.

121. Guesde, Lagardelle, and Vaillant, p. 5.

122. Annie Kriegel, "Jaurès, le Parti socialiste, et la C.G.T. à la fin de juillet 1914," *Bulletin de la Société d'Etudes Jaurésiennes*, No. 7 (Oct.–Dec. 1962), pp. 7–9.

123. Duverger, *Political Parties*, pp. 146–51.

124. See, for example, William Kornhauser, *The Politics of Mass Society* (Glencoe, Ill., 1959).

125. See p. 25n, and Jesse R. Pitts, "Continuity and Change in Bourgeois France," in Stanley Hoffmann *et al.*, *In Search of France* (Cambridge, Mass., 1963), pp. 235–62.

126. *La Guerre Sociale*, Mar. 22–29, 1910.

127. On Freemasonry, see Mildred J. Headings, *French Freemasonry under the Third Republic* (Baltimore, Md., 1949); Albert Lantoine, *Histoire de la franc-maçonnerie française* (1925); Henri Coston, *La République du Grand Orient* (1964); and Jean Marques-Rivière, *La Trahison spirituelle de la franc-maçonnerie* (1931). The influence and social role of Freemasonry under the Third Republic merit further research.

128. SFIO, *9<sup>e</sup> Congrès* [1912], pp. 521, 527.

129. Coston, pp. 93–94, and Headings, pp. 74–75.

130. *Ibid.*

131. Membership fees varied from one part of the country to another, but they seem to have averaged 30 francs ($21) a year. SFIO, *9<sup>e</sup> Congrès*, pp. 544–45.

132. *Ibid.*, p. 487.    133. *Ibid.*, p. 462.

134. *Ibid.*, pp. 544–55.    135. *Ibid.*, p. 674.

136. Noland, *Founding of the French Socialist Party*, p. 207.

137. Drachkovitch, *Les Socialismes*, pp. 174, 377.

138. Max Weber, *The Protestant Ethic and the Spirit of Capitalism* (New York, 1958 ed.), p. 27.

139. Eugen Weber, *The Nationalist Revival*, pp. 38, 44. Weber writes of a "progressive Hervéization" of the Socialist Party which caused the Radicals to move toward the Right during this period.

140. B. W. Schaper, *Albert Thomas: Trente années de réformisme social* (1960), p. 63.

141. Goldberg, *Life of Jaurès*, pp. 361–474.

142. Drachkovitch, p. 82.

143. SFIO, *9<sup>e</sup> Congrès*, p. 246.

144. *Ibid.*, p. 253.

145. Jean Jaurès, *L'Armée nouvelle* (1911), pp. 534–35.

146. See, for example, the debate on the party's growth at the Congress of Amiens in 1914, pp. 78–132.

147. The Congress of Lyon in 1912 voted to found a Federation of Young Socialists, but it seems that neither the Center nor the federations showed much interest in its organization. When Young Socialists asked that the question of their Federation be formally discussed at Amiens in 1914, they were turned down and told that the materials were not available. The upshot of the incident was that a committee was charged to study the problem of the Young Socialists in depth. SFIO, *11<sup>e</sup> Congrès* [Amiens, 1914], p. 117.

148. SFIO, *8<sup>e</sup> Congrès* [St.-Quentin, 1911], p. 242. The question of the Second International's power over its national sections is a complex one that deserves careful study. Most Socialist leaders would probably have agreed with Rosa Luxemburg when she said that the International's authority was moral—but immense. (*Sixième Congrès socialiste international tenu à Amsterdam du 14 au 20 août 1904: Compte rendu analytique*, Brussels, 1904, p. 173.) Differences arose when it came to the scope and proper subject of the International's authority. These differences were aired most fully at Amsterdam in 1904. According to Lafargue and Guesde, it was the job of the International to develop a "general international doctrine" and to enforce its application. Jaurès and Vandervelde, on the other hand, thought that it was not the role of the International to expel member sections or enforce a doctrinal orthodoxy. Marcel Sembat said that whatever the International decided, the SFIO would obey; and there is little doubt that the unification of French Socialism on a German program was the International's greatest triumph.

In 1907 at Stuttgart the question of national differences came up again. Heinrich Beer stated the consensus of the delegates: the role of the International was to set down general principles upon which the majority agreed. It was not to write national peculiarities into its decisions, and it was not to intervene in the affairs of the individual sections. The Congress of Copenhagen elaborated on Beer's formulation in a resolution that was approved without discussion. According to this text, the individual sections had the right of choosing the way and the opportune moment to apply the decisions of the International. But the congress insisted "strongly" on the "duty" of the national parties "to do everything in their power" to carry out the decisions of international congresses. And it was decided that the

International Socialist Bureau would submit a report to each congress indicating how well the national parties had carried out the decisions of the International. (*Huitième Congrès socialiste international tenu à Copenhague du 28 août au 3 septembre 1910: Compte rendu analytique,* Ghent, 1911, p. 475.)

Lenin's conclusion, after having attended the Congress of Stuttgart, was that, though its resolutions were not formally binding for the various countries, the International's moral significance and influence were such that non-observance of its decisions would be out of the question, "scarcely more frequent than the non-observance by the separate parties of the decisions of their own congresses." (*Polnoe sobranie sochinenii,* XVI, 80.) In 1914, however, when it appeared that the International might try to force the various Russian Socialist parties to unite, Lenin took a quite different line. Writing to his friend and agent Inessa Armand to assure her that the Bolsheviks stood in no danger from the International, he remarked that the International Socialist Bureau "can only offer us its 'bons offices' for negotiations, for an 'exchange of views' with the other parties, factions, etc. It can only do this. Only this!" (*Polnoe sobranie sochinenii,* XLVIII, 249.)

149. According to Dolléans, the result of Clemenceau's labor policy was 104 years in prison sentences, 667 wounded workers, 20 dead workers, and 392 dismissals. *Histoire du mouvement ouvrier,* II, 145.

150. Landauer, *European Socialism,* I, 347.

151. Michel Collinet, *Esprit du syndicalisme* (1951), p. 35.

152. Quoted in Dolléans, II, 200. Writing in 1917, Monatte spoke of this period as being characterized by "une grande paresse d'esprit ... presque tous, à tous les degrés, nous étions atteints du même mal." Quoted in *ibid.,* p. 203.

153. *Le Mouvement Socialiste,* July–Aug. 1913, p. 128.

154. For a brilliant analysis of these changes and their implications for revolutionary syndicalism, see Collinet, *Esprit du syndicalisme.*

155. Rosmer, I, 36.

## Chapter two

Epigraph: *Compte rendu sténographique non officiel du cinquième Congrès socialiste international tenu à Paris du 23 au 27 septembre 1900* (1901), p. 150.

1. Ilya Ehrenburg, *People and Life, 1891–1921* (New York, 1962), p. 161.

2. Raymond Lefebvre, *Le Sacrifice d'Abraham* (1919), p. 1.

3. Quoted in H. Stuart Hughes, *Consciousness and Society,* Vintage ed. (New York, 1961), p. 338.

4. Romain Rolland, *Jean-Christophe* (Paris, 1931), III, 452.

5. For the details of this switch, see Eugen Weber, *The Nationalist Revival in France, 1905–1914* (Berkeley, Calif., 1959). The transition is portrayed in fictional form in Roger Martin du Gard, *Jean Barois* (1913).

6. Quoted in Hughes, p. 344.

7. L.-O. Frossard, *De Jaurès à Léon Blum* (1943), pp. 155–56, and Weber, *Nationalist Revival,* p. 38.

8. SFIO, *3ᵉ Congrès* [Limoges, 1906], p. 215.

9. *Ibid.,* p. 260.

10. *Ibid.,* p. 232.

11. Quoted in Alexandre Zévaès, *Jules Guesde, 1845–1922* (1929), p. 171. In 1908 Edouard Berth wrote that "Guesde has the soul of a patriot of '92." *Les Nouveaux Aspects du socialisme,* pp. 12–13. For Guesde's early nationalism, see Samuel Bernstein, "Jules Guesde, Pioneer of Marxism in France," *Science and Society,* IV (1940), pp. 31–32, and

Adrien Compère-Morel, *Jules Guesde, le socialisme fait homme, 1845–1922* (1937), pp. 57–58.

12. SFIO, *3ᵉ Congrès*, p. 244.
13. *Ibid.*, p. 256.
14. Jean Jaurès, *L'Armée nouvelle* (1911), p. 534.
15. *Journal officiel*, 11.v.07.  16. Jaurès, *L'Armée nouvelle*, p. 571.
17. SFIO, *3ᵉ Congrès*, pp. 261–62.  18. *OJJ*, II, 294–95.
19. Parti socialiste, SFIO, *4ᵉ Congrès* [Nancy, 1907], pp. 284–85.
20. *La C.G.T. et le mouvement syndical* (1925), p. 99.
21. *Ibid.*, p. 104.
22. *Ibid.*, p. 129.
23. See, for example, Alphonse Merrheim in *Le Mouvement Socialiste*, Nov. 1905, p. 333.
24. *Ibid.*, pp. 328–29.
25. Jean Maitron, *Histoire du mouvement anarchiste en France*, 2d rev. ed. (1955), p. 350.
26. Quoted in R. Goetz-Girey, *La Pensée syndicale française* (1948), pp. 48–49.
27. Quoted in Weber, *Nationalist Revival*, p. 46, from *L'Echo de Paris*, 25.ix.08.
28. *L'Humanité*, 16.vii.14.
29. See William Maehl, "Nationalism in the German Socialist Party," *Journal of Modern History*, XXIV (1952), 15–41; G. D. H. Cole, *The Second International, 1889–1914* (London, 1956), Part I, p. 87; and Milorad M. Drachkovitch, *Les Socialismes français et allemand et le problème de la guerre, 1870–1914* (Geneva, 1953), pp. 245–86. When asked if he would fire at Guesde in case of war, August Bebel had replied: "All right! Yes! I would shoot.... That would be terrible, but I repeat, I would have no choice." Quoted in Drachkovitch, p. 353. This anecdote sums up the position of the SPD on the question of war.
30. Drachkovitch, p. 148.
31. Annie Kriegel, "Jaurès, le Parti socialiste et la C.G.T. à la fin de juillet 1914," *Bulletin de la Société d'Etudes Jaurésiennes*, No. 7 (Oct.–Dec. 1962), pp. 6–7.
32. Ehrenburg, *People and Life*, pp. 162–63.
33. *Le Parti socialiste, la guerre et la paix* (1918), p. 104.
34. *L'Humanité*, 5.viii.14.
35. Kriegel, "Jaurès, le Parti socialiste et la C.G.T.," p. 10.
36. Quoted in Rosmer, I, 152.
37. Barbara Tuchman, *The Guns of August* (New York, 1963), p. 108.
38. Quoted in Rosmer, I, 532–33. Rosmer reproduces on pp. 523–32 the entire text of Dumoulin's pamphlet, *Les Syndicalistes français et la guerre* (1918).
39. *Le Mouvement Socialiste*, Nov. 1905, pp. 166–67.
40. CGT, *XIVᵉ Congrès confédéral tenu à Lyon du 15 au 21 septembre 1919, Compte rendu* (Lyon, 1919), p. 169.
41. *Ibid.*, p. 105.
42. The Stuttgart resolution on war, quoted in James Joll, *The Second International, 1889–1914* (London, 1955), p. 196.
43. *L'Humanité*, 28.viii.14.
44. *Le Mouvement Socialiste*, July–Aug. 1913, p. 129.
45. Quoted in Bernard Georges and Denise Tintant, *Léon Jouhaux, cinqante ans de syndicalisme* (1962), p. 156.
46. Tuchman, *Guns of August*, p. 416.
47. Quoted in Harvey Goldberg, *The Life of Jean Jaurès* (Madison, Wis., 1962), p. 341.
48. According to a joint Franco-Belgian manifesto, adopted on September 6, 1914, the

two parties were convinced that "the French government sincerely wanted peace and was making, as we have been demanding, every effort to preserve it." *Le Parti socialiste, la guerre et la paix,* pp. 113–14.

49. For the atmosphere in working-class circles in August and September 1914, see Rosmer, I; Leon Trotsky, *My Life* (New York, 1930), p. 246; Henri Guilbeaux, *Du Kremlin au Cherche-Midi* (1933); Raymond Lefebvre, *L'Eponge du Vinaigre* (1921); and Roger Martin du Gard, *L'Eté 1914* (1936–40).

50. Tuchman, p. 487.

51. Quoted in N. Lenin and Georges Zinoviev, *Contre le courant* (1927), II, 19.

52. Paul-Marie de la Gorce, *The French Army, A Military-Political History* (New York, 1963), p. 123.

53. Quoted in Joll, *Second International,* p. 172. See also Pierre Renaudel, *L'Internationale à Berne* (1919), which reproduces (p. 42) the minutes of the meeting of the French parliamentary Group with Müller and Huysmans.

54. Joll, pp. 173–75.

55. *L'Humanité,* 29.ix.14.

56. Romain Rolland, *Au-dessus de la mêlée* (1932 ed.), pp. 55–56.

57. Rosmer, I, 214–16.

58. "We remember well those lean and sad meetings of that first winter. They helped all of us ward off despair and disgust." The editors of *La Vie Ouvrière,* 30.iv.19.

59. Lefebvre, *L'Eponge,* pp. 5–6.

60. *VO,* 16.iv.19.

61. Reproduced in Rosmer, I, 180.

62. Quoted in Georges and Tintant, *Léon Jouhaux,* p. 281.

63. Rosmer (I, 288) writes of the opposition: "The Damocles' sword of mobilization was constantly suspended over their head, and generally it came down with a click at a propitious moment—for their enemies."

64. *Union des Métaux,* Aug. 1914–May 1, 1915, p. 1.

65. Max Ferré, *Histoire du mouvement syndicaliste révolutionnaire chez les instituteurs: Des origines à 1922* (1955), pp. 174–77.

66. "From that day on," writes Roger Picard, "syndicalist circles were divided." *Le Mouvement syndical pendant la guerre* (1927), p. 149.

67. Jean Maxe, *De Zimmerwald au bolchévisme* (1919), p. 37.

68. SFIO, *Congrès* [Paris, 1915], *Rapport du Secrétariat,* p. 7.

69. Amédée Dunois in *IC,* May–July 1924, p. 214, and L.-O. Frossard, *De Jaurès à Lénine* (1930), p. 13.

70. Quoted in Daniel Ligou, *Histoire du Socialisme en France, 1871–1961* (1962), p. 13.

71. Rosmer, I, 294.

72. Quoted in Joll, *Second International,* p. 160.

73. Frossard, *De Jaurès à Blum,* pp. 56–57.

74. *Le Parti socialiste, la guerre et la paix,* p. 127.

75. The story of the Zimmerwald movement has yet to be written. The pieces may be gathered from Olga Hess Gankin and H. H. Fisher, *The Bolsheviks and the World War* (Stanford, Calif., 1940); Angelica Balabanova, "Die Zimmerwalder Bewegung, 1914–1919," in *Archiv für die Geschichte des Sozialismus und der Arbeiterbewegung herausgegeben von Dr. Karl Grünberg* (Leipzig, 1926, pp. 320–413; 1928, pp. 232–84); Merle Fainsod, *International Socialism and the World War* (Cambridge, Mass., 1935); Rosmer, Vol. I; Jules Humbert-Droz, *Der Krieg und die Internationale: Die Konferenzen von Zimmerwald und Kienthal* (Vienna, 1964); and Kriegel, I, 97–112. Balabanova's German stenographic record is available at the International Institute for Social History in Amsterdam.

76. Rosmer, I, 371.

77. Quoted in Kriegel, "Sur les rapports de Lénine avec le mouvement zimmerwaldien français," *Cahiers du Monde Russe et Soviétique,* III, No. 2 (Apr.–June 1962), p. 300.

78. So far as I know, no biography of Merrheim exists. This is unfortunate because Merrheim was one of the most interesting and significant revolutionary syndicalists, and both his early career and his role in the War and the immediate postwar period merit close study. This paragraph is based on Pierre Monatte's obituary in *La Révolution Prolétarienne,* No. 11 (Nov. 1925), pp. 11–12; the remarks in Frossard, *De Jaurès à Lénine,* pp. 19–20; Henri Barbé, "Souvenirs de militant et de dirigeant communiste" (ms. at the Hoover Institution), p. 15; Edouard Dolléans, *Histoire du mouvement ouvrier* (1946), II, 167–76 and *passim*; and Georges and Tintant, *Léon Jouhaux,* pp. 274–76.

79. Trotsky, *My Life,* p. 247.

80. Frossard, *De Jaurès à Lénine,* p. 20.

81. *La Révolution Prolétarienne,* No. 11 (Nov. 1925), pp. 11–12.

82. CGT, *XIVᵉ Congrès confédéral,* p. 171.

83. Trotsky, *My Life,* p. 249.

84. Balabanova, "Die Zimmerwalder Bewegung, 1914–1919," p. 320.

85. Angelica Balabanova, *Erinnerungen und Erlebnisse* (Berlin, 1927), p. 114.

86. Quoted from the German *Protokoll* of the Zimmerwald Conference, pp. 138–39, in the Grimm Archives at the Institute for Social History in Amsterdam.

87. Lenin and Zinoviev, *Contre le courant,* II, 14.

88. Rosmer, I, 401–2.

89. *Le Parti socialiste, la guerre et la paix,* p. 129.

90. Hubert Bourgin, *Le Parti contre la patrie* (Paris, 1924), pp. 53–54.

91. Grimm Archives.

92. Rosmer, II, 47.

93. For a partisan but valuable account of this congress, see *Demain,* 15.iv.16, pp. 251–63.

94. There is a copy of Bourderon's motion in the Grimm Archives.

95. In a motion published as a circular by the Socialist section of the Committee for the Resumption of International Relations (January 1916?), Grimm Archives. Lozovsky used almost exactly the same wording in his account of the congress in *Nashe Slovo,* 6.i.16.

96. Alistair Horne, *The Price of Glory, Verdun 1916* (New York, 1963), p. 67.

97. Kriegel, I, 123.

98. Writing seven months after the Committee's formation, Lozovsky described its membership as 70 per cent syndicalist, 20 per cent Socialist, and the remaining 10 per cent anarchist. (*Nashe Slovo,* 18.viii.16.) Kriegel is the best source for the activities of this group. See also the detailed but outdated study by S. Bantke, *Borba za sozdanie kommunisticheskoi partii Frantsii* (Moscow, 1936).

99. Jean Fréville, *La Nuit finit à Tours* (1951), p. 53.

100. Comité pour la Reprise des Relations Internationales, *Les Socialistes et la guerre* and *Conférence socialiste internationale.* Both of these pamphlets date from 1915. They were followed in 1916 and 1917 by a series of pamphlets on different aspects of the War and international Socialism.

101. Merrheim wrote Grimm on July 11, 1916: "Only the majoritaires can get together or take the floor at meetings; that is the present state of freedom in France." (Grimm Archives.) The police received full reports, used by Kriegel in *Aux Origines,* on the meetings of the Committee for Resumption.

102. Letter of 3.iii.16, Grimm Archives.

103. Rosmer, I, 401–3.

104. Frossard, *De Jaurès à Blum,* p. 58.

105. Kriegel, I, 130. Charles Seignobos, Amédée Dunois, Jacques Mesnil, and André Le Troquer joined this group. In the political geography of the period, the Société d'Etudes Documentaires et Critiques sur la Guerre was to the right of the Committee for Resumption and to the left of the Ligue des Droits de l'Homme. See *Les Origines de la guerre: Lettres à la Ligue des Droits de l'Homme* (1921). Morhardt was former General Secretary of the Ligue.

106. *Le Populaire du Centre,* 16.iii.16.

107. Merrheim to Grimm, 27.iii.16, Grimm Archives, and *Le Populaire du Centre,* 2.iv.16.

108. The minority's motion was published in *L'Ecole de la Fédération,* 22.iv.16.

109. For the preparations for this conference, which are reminiscent of World War II spy movies, the best source is the Grimm Archives. Merrheim wrote Grimm on March 24, 1916, that he would do everything possible to have four delegates at the conference; but "this may be difficult, for all our activities and comings and goings are closely watched by the police." Trotsky drafted a manifesto, which was sent to the conference in the name of the *Vie Ouvrière* and *Nashe Slovo* groups; it is reproduced in Rosmer, II, 83–86.

110. Pierre Laval is sometimes said to have been the fourth "pilgrim of Kienthal." I have found no evidence that he was. Henri Guilbeaux, who was living in Switzerland at the time, attended, and also, it seems, Inessa Armand.

111. Even Lenin, that unyielding partisan of leftist positions and admirer of the SPD, was forced to note in 1907, after the Congress of Stuttgart, that it had taken the "sting of French competition" to make the revolutionary position prevail. *Polnoe sobranie sochinenii,* XVI, 80–81.

112. Henri Guilbeaux, *Du Kremlin au Cherche-Midi,* p. 98.

113. Balabanova, *Erinnerungen,* p. 129.

114. Guilbeaux, quoted in Gankin and Fisher, *The Bolsheviks and the World War,* p. 409.

115. Balabanova, *Erinnerungen,* p. 129.

116. *Dix années de lutte pour la révolution mondiale* (1929), p. 266, and the Kienthal *Protokoll,* p. 61, in the Grimm Archives. Brizon "said that it was easy for Lenin, who was living in Switzerland, to preach revolution as the only means of stopping the War, but that he would like to see what position Lenin would take if he were in Russia." Guilbeaux, quoted in Branko Lazitch, *Lénine et la IIIᵉ Internationale* (1951), p. 63.

117. V. I. Lenin, *Sämtliche Werke* (Vienna, 1927–35), XIX, 527.

118. Rosmer, II, 97.

119. *Journal Officiel,* 24.vi.16.

120. *Le Parti socialiste, la guerre et la paix,* p. 146.

121. Rosmer, II, 189–90.

122. Quoted in *ibid.,* II, 189. In an interview with *Le Bonnet Rouge* (17.v.16) Raffin-Dugens claimed to have received "a pile of congratulatory letters" for having gone to Kienthal.

123. According to Kriegel (I, 93), who takes her information from a police report, there were 24,000 Russians living in Paris in 1915.

124. Pierre Monatte, *Trois scissions syndicales* (1958), p. 239. Martov's reply to Hervé was published in *Golos,* 25.ix.14.

125. This paper was founded on September 1, 1914, and was originally called *Golos* ("The Voice"). Around mid-January 1915, it was suppressed, owing to the intervention of Aleksandr Izvolsky. It reappeared again on January 29, 1915, under the name *Nashe Slovo* ("Our Word"). Suppressed again, it was transformed into *Nachalo* ("The Begin-

ning"). After the Revolution of March 1917 it was again banned, only to reappear under the title *Novaya Epokha* ("The New Epoch"). (Henri Guilbeaux, *Le Mouvement socialiste et syndicaliste français pendant la guerre,* Petrograd, 1919, p. 19.) *Nashe Slovo*'s colorful history is recounted in Lozovsky's "Comment nous éditions pendant la guerre des journaux internationalistes," *BC,* 24.x.24, 31.x.24, and Deutscher, *The Prophet Armed,* pp. 217–38.

126. Deutscher, pp. 216, 223.

127. *Ibid.,* p. 223.

128. Ehrenburg, *People and Life,* pp. 170–71.

129. Deutscher, p. 218.

130. *Ibid.,* pp. 236–38.

131. The reports of the Prefecture of Police on Inessa Armand have been examined by Annie Kriegel, whose findings appear in the *Cahiers du Monde Russe et Soviétique,* III, No. 2 (Apr.–June 1962), pp. 299–306. The remainder of this paragraph is based on her research.

132. The letter is included in *Polnoe sobranie sochinenii,* XXVII, 235–39.

133. Comité pour la Reprise des Relations Internationales, *Pourquoi nous sommes allés à Zimmerwald* (1915), p. 4.

134. N. K. Krupskaya, *Pamiati Inessy Armand* (Moscow, 1926), p. 21.

135. Fernand Loriot, *Rapport du Secrétariat, Parti Communiste (S.F.I.C.), 1921.* No pagination. Rosmer writes of Lenin's influence in France before the Revolution (I, 401): "Outside Russian circles he was practically unknown in France, among Socialists and syndicalists alike." A. S. Shapavolov, a Bolshevik living in Paris at this time, substantiates the view that Lenin and the Bolsheviks were almost completely unknown in France before the February Revolution. (*V borbe za sotsializm,* Moscow, 1934, pp. 802–3.) Still, the point should not be exaggerated. French Zimmerwaldians knew that Lenin wanted them to leave their organizations and form a Third International (see, for example, the interview with Louise Saumoneau in *Avantil,* 15.iv.16, in which she rejects Lenin's proposal as "premature, to say the least"); and one of them (probably Charles Rappoport) published and distributed Lenin's *War and Socialism* illegally in Paris. *Polnoe sobranie sochinenii,* XXVI, 310.

136. "Lettres de Lénine à Inès Armand," *Cahiers du Communisme,* Jan. 1950, pp. 1, 41–54. This quotation is from p. 48.

137. I am indebted to Annie Kriegel for much of the following information on the internal evolution of the Committee for Resumption during 1916. Also consult Rosmer, "Trotsky à Paris," *La Révolution Prolétarienne,* Oct. 1950.

138. Trotsky, *Voina i revoliutsiya* (Moscow, 1924), II, 214–15.

139. Quoted from *To the Finland Station* by Edmund Wilson (Garden City, N.Y., 1940), p. 431.

140. Trotsky, *Voina i revoliutsiya,* II, 215–18.

141. *Ibid.,* p. 218.

142. For example, the anarchist Mauricius (his real name was Vandamme) in *Ce Qu'il Faut Dire,* 19.v.17.

143. Loriot wrote the pamphlet in collaboration with Trotsky and Louis Bouët (Rosmer, II, 145). Trotsky's hand in it is obvious.

144. Comité pour la Reprise des Relations Internationales, *Les Socialistes de Zimmerwald et la Guerre* (n.d.), pp. 8–10.

145. *Ibid.,* pp. 14, 28.

146. Trotsky, *Voina i revoliutsiya,* II, 221–22.

147. *Ce Qu'il Faut Dire,* 29.ix.17. The poll was announced in the issue of 1.v.17.

148. Letter of 11.xii.16, in *Vie Ouvrière*, ed., *Vingt lettres de Léon Trotsky* (1919), p. 26.

149. Quoted in Rosmer, II, 210.

150. The mood of the party on the eve of the congress is well described in *ibid.*, pp. 203–7.

151. *Ibid.*, pp. 210–12, and Ligou, *Histoire du socialisme en France*, pp. 289–91.

152. Quoted in Rosmer, II, 211.

153. *Ce Qu'il Faut Dire*, 6.i.17.

154. Rosmer, II, 210.

155. Quoted in Zévaès, *Jules Guesde*, p. 176.

156. Rosmer, II, 204; Ligou, pp. 286–87.

157. Ligou, p. 291.

158. Arno J. Mayer, *Political Origins of the New Diplomacy, 1917–1918* (New Haven, Conn., 1959), pp. 159–60.

159. Quoted in Ligou, p. 292.          160. Quoted in Rosmer, II, 212.

161. Kriegel, p. 154.                          162. Quoted in Mayer, p. 160.

163. Georges and Tintant, *Léon Jouhaux*, pp. 308–9.

164. André Marty, *La Révolte de la Mer Noire*, 4th ed. (1949), p. 123. Marty's Archives show that he was diligent in his research, if not always accurate in his writing. A letter to Raymond Lefebvre (31.v.18) reports that in May 1918 the minoritaire *Le Populaire* was beginning to feel the competition of *La Vague*. Another letter from a sailor who took part in the Black Sea revolt mentions *La Vague* as one of his sources of information about what was going on in France. Gustave Champale to René Bonnefille, 26.v.49, in the Marty Archives.

165. Quoted in Ligou, p. 292.

166. *Vie Ouvrière*, ed., *Vingt lettres de Trotsky*, p. 26.

167. Comité pour la Reprise des Relations Internationales, *Organisation et action de la section socialiste*, 29.iii.17, p. 3.

168. Kriegel, "Sur les rapports de Lénine avec le mouvement zimmerwaldien français," *Cahiers du Monde Russe et Soviétique*, III, No. 2 (Apr.–June 1962), p. 305. Writing in September 1916, Trotsky observed that the influence of the Zimmerwaldians on the party leadership was insignificant, and that it was also weak in the sections. It was incomparably greater, he said, among the syndicalists, the youth, and the women. (*Voina i revoliutsiya*, II, 235.) According to Lozovsky, the Committee for Resumption did not wield a real influence until the beginning of 1917. (*Rabochaya frantsiya*, Moscow, 1923, p. 55.)

169. The letter is printed in Rosmer, II, 228–32.

## Chapter three

Epigraph: Included in Romain Rolland, *Journal des années de guerre* (1952), p. 1209.

1. See Arno J. Mayer, *Political Origins of the New Diplomacy, 1917–1918* (New Haven, Conn., 1959), for the development of this theme.

2. See the concluding chapter of Vladimir Lebedev's *Souvenirs d'un volontaire russe dans l'armée française, 1914–1916* (1917), "L'ami inconnu," for a description of the French view of their Eastern ally.

3. L.-O. Frossard, *De Jaurès à Léon Blum* (1943), p. 67.

4. The resolution passed by the International Socialist Congress of Basel in 1912 stated that "Tsarism is the hope of all the reactionary powers in Europe, and the most formidable enemy of European democracy as it is of the Russian people. The International regards provoking the collapse of tsarism as one of its most essential tasks." Quoted in Alexandre Zévaès, *Histoire du socialisme et du communisme en France* (1947), p. 343.

5. This dispatch is dated February 9, 1905, and is included in "Otrazhenie sobitii 1905 g. za granitsei," *Krasnyi Arkhiv,* II (9), 1925, pp. 39–41. For the French response to the Russian Revolution of 1905, see M. Ya. Domnich, "Nachalo revoliutsii 1905 g. i dvizhenie solidarnosti vo Frantsii," *Voprosy Istorii,* Jan. 1955, pp. 87–94.

6. Marcel Cohen, "Quelques souvenirs politiques jusqu'à 1921," *Pensée,* Jan.–Feb. 1961, pp. 90–94.

7. N. S. Rusanov, *V Emigratsii* (Moscow, 1929), pp. 278–80.

8. *L'Humanité,* 10.vi.05. The second remark is taken from an unpublished essay on the Russian Revolution of 1905, reproduced in *L'Actualité de l'Histoire,* No. 25 (Oct.–Dec. 1958), pp. 38–39.

9. Lucien Herr, *Choix d'écrits* (1932), I, 171.

10. For the reaction of the SPD to the Russian Revolution of 1905, consult Carl E. Schorske, *German Social Democracy, 1905–1917* (Cambridge, Mass., 1955), pp. 28–59.

11. An irate article by a Russian "muzhik" warned Hervé that if he continued to speak of "French liberties" he would no longer be logical and his paper would no longer be proletarian. *La Guerre Sociale,* Mar. 27–Apr. 2, 1907.

12. *Le Parti socialiste, la guerre et la paix,* p. 166.

13. *L'Humanité,* 17.iii.17.

14. *Ibid.*; also Bernard Georges and Denise Tintant, *Léon Jouhaux, cinquante ans de syndicalisme* (1962), p. 302.

15. *L'Humanité,* 23.iii.17.

16. Rolland, *Journal des années de guerre,* p. 1174; Hubert Bourgin, *Le Parti contre la patrie* (1924), p. 211; Ilya Ehrenburg, *People and Life, 1891–1921* (New York, 1962), p. 225; *L'Humanité,* 2.iv.17; *La Victoire,* 2.iv.17; *Le Bonnet Rouge,* 2.iv.17; and *Demain,* May 1917, p. 61.

17. Georges and Tintant, p. 186.

18. Quoted in Edouard Dolléans, *Histoire du mouvement ouvrier,* 2 vols. (1946), II, 263.

19. Paul-Marie de la Gorce, *The French Army, A Military-Political History* (1963), pp. 127–28, and Georges and Tintant, pp. 188–93.

20. Louis-Jean Malvy, *Mon crime* (1921), p. 102.

21. Henri Carré, *Les Grandes Heures du Général Pétain* (1952), p. 33.

22. *Ibid.,* p. 36.

23. Quoted in de la Gorce, p. 126.

24. Carré, p. 49.

25. Raymond Poincaré, *Au Service de la France* (1926–33), IX, 148. For the mutinies and their causes, see Carré, *Les Grandes Heures*; de la Gorce, p. 127; and Alistair Horne, *The Price of Glory, Verdun 1916* (New York, 1963), pp. 322–23.

26. Carré, p. 7.

27. According to Carré (p. 116), 25 of the 224 death sentences handed down by Army courts-martial in May, June, and July were actually carried out. Horne (p. 323), however, is skeptical of the official figures; he quotes the diaries of Haig, who wrote that he had been told in November 1917 that "there were 30,000 'rebels' who had to be dealt with." For Dubail's reaction, see Carré, p. 105, and Malvy, *Mon crime,* p. 76.

28. Carré, pp. 79–92.

29. Malvy, p. 145.

30. *Ibid.,* p. 145, and Georges Clemenceau, *L'Antipatriotisme devant le Sénat* (1917), p. 44.

31. Carré, p. 110.

32. For Stockholm, see Olga Hess Gankin and H. H. Fisher, *The Bolsheviks and the World War* (Stanford, Calif., 1940), pp. 582–703, and Hildamarie Meynell, "The Stock-

holm Conference of 1917," *International Review of Social History*, V (1960), Parts I and II, pp. 1–25 and 202–25.

33. *Le Populaire du Centre*, 22.v.17.

34. Daniel Ligou, *Histoire du socialisme en France, 1871–1961* (1962), p. 293.

35. *Ibid.*, p. 294.

36. *2ᵉ Circulaire de la minorité du Parti socialiste* (1917), p. 31.

37. Albert Thomas, *Discours prononcé par Albert Thomas devant le Comité du Conseil des ouvriers et des soldats, le 12 mai 1917* (1917).

38. According to Merrheim, who had it from Kerensky, CGT, *XVᵉ Congrès confédéral tenu à Orléans du 27 septembre au 2 octobre 1920*, p. 362.

39. See the reprint of the article (which originally appeared in the Menshevik journal *Rabochaya Gazeta*) in *Demain*, Aug. 1917, pp. 242–43, for the "russification" of the French delegation.

40. Maurice Paléologue, *An Ambassador's Memoirs* (New York, 1924–25), III, 300, 354–55.

41. *Avanti!*, 30.v.17.

42. *L'Humanité*, 28.v.17.

43. *Le Temps*, 30.v.17.

44. Charles Rappoport, *La Crise socialiste et sa solution* (1918), p. 26.

45. Albert Thomas, *Le Parti socialiste et la politique nationale* (1917), p. 11.

46. *Ibid.*, pp. 16–20, and Renaudel to Branting, 10.ix.17, in the Branting Archives.

47. Mayer, *Political Origins*, p. 142.

48. De la Gorce, *The French Army*, pp. 129–30.

49. Poincaré, *Au Service de la France*, IX, 149.

50. *Ibid.*

51. Alexandre Ribot, *Lettres à un ami* (1924), p. 261.

52. *Journal Officiel*, 1.vi.17.

53. Georges Bonnefous, *Histoire politique de la IIIᵉ République* (1955), II, 244.

54. Poincaré, *Au Service*, IX, 202–3.

55. *Ibid.*

56. Ligou, *Histoire du socialisme en France*, p. 293. See also Merle Fainsod, *International Socialism and the World War* (Cambridge, Mass., 1935), p. 145.

57. *Le Populaire Socialiste-Internationaliste*, 8.ix.17.

58. Renaudel to Branting, 10.ix.17. Branting Archives.

59. *Le Populaire Socialiste-Internationaliste*, 22.ix.17. Rumor had it that only Thomas's ambition for the Ministry of Foreign Affairs kept the Socialists out of the government. Ribot, *Journal d'Alexandre Ribot* (1936), p. 200, and *Le Populaire Socialiste-Internationaliste*, 15.ix.17.

60. *Ibid.*, 6.x.17.

61. *L'Humanité*, 10.x.17.

62. *Ibid.*, 11.x.17.

63. *Le Populaire Socialiste-Internationaliste*, 13.x.17.

64. Branko Lazitch, *Lénine et la IIIᵉ Internationale* (1950), p. 38.

65. *Dix années de lutte pour la révolution mondiale*, p. 190, and n. 6 above.

66. *Dix années de lutte*, p. 192, and Lenin, *Polnoe sobranie sochinenii*, XIX, 353.

67. *Le Populaire du Centre*, 30.vii.17.

68. *Ibid.*, 6.viii.17.

69. *Le Populaire Socialiste-Internationaliste*, 28.vii.17.

70. *L'Humanité*, 9.xi.17.

71. Marcel Berger and Paul Allard, *Les Secrets de la censure pendant la guerre* (1932), pp. 249, 274.

72. Boris Souvarine, *Eloge des Bolcheviks* (1919), p. 3.
73. *Le Parti socialiste, la guerre et la paix*, p. 201.
74. See Longuet's intervention at the CAP of December 11, 1917, reported in *Le Populaire Socialiste-Internationaliste*, 22.xii.17.
75. *L'Humanité*, 1.i.18.
76. *Journal Officiel*, 11.i.18.
77. See Mistral in *L'Humanité*, 17.ii.18.
78. *L'Humanité*, 1.i.18.
79. *Le Populaire du Centre*, 27.i.18.
80. *L'Humanité*, 15.ii.18.
81. Alexis de Tocqueville, quoted in R. R. Palmer, *The Age of Democratic Revolution* (Princeton, N.J., 1959), p. iii.
82. *L'Ecole de la Fédération*, 24.iii.17, p. 210.
83. *Ibid.*, 7.iv.17, pp. 230–31.
84. Quoted in Rolland, *Journal des années de guerre*, p. 1185.
85. Henri Guilbeaux, *Du Kremlin au Cherche-Midi* (1933), pp. 151–52.
86. The description is Frossard's (*De Jaurès à Blum*, p. 71).
87. *La Nouvelle Internationale*, 1.v.17.
88. By Guilbeaux, *IC*, May 1920, col. 1535.
89. *JP*, 17.iii.18.
90. *La Plèbe*, 27.iv.18. This Zimmerwaldian newspaper managed to publish only four issues before being suppressed.
91. SFIO, *17ᵉ Congrès* [Strasbourg, 1920], p. 439.
92. *La Plèbe*, 27.iv.18.
93. *JP*, 20.xi.17.
94. *La Vérité*, 26.i.18.
95. *Ibid.*, 5.i.18 and 7.iii.18. Merrheim agreed with Trotsky that "official French Socialism is the least qualified of all movements to reproach the Russian Socialists for making a separate armistice and threatening a separate peace." Comité pour la Reprise des Relations Internationales, *Pour l'action: Les Evénements de Russie* (Jan. 1918?), p. 23.
96. Comité pour la Reprise, *Pour l'action*.
97. See his speech at the Thirteenth Confederal Congress in Paris, in 1918, in *XIIIᵉ Congrès confédérale*, pp. 211–14.
98. CGT, *Conférence Extraordinaire, tenue à Clermont-Ferrand les 23, 24, 25 décembre 1917, compte rendu*, pp. 62–63.
99. Quoted in Georges and Tintant, *Léon Jouhaux*, p. 305.
100. Kriegel, I, 206.
101. Quoted from the Péricat papers by Kriegel (I, 213).
102. Georges and Tintant, p. 307.
103. S. Bantke, *Borba za sozdanie kommunisticheskoi partii Frantsii* (Moscow, 1936), pp. 196–206.
104. Kriegel, I, 208–9.
105. Henri Barbé, "Souvenirs de militant et de dirigeant communiste" (ms. at the Hoover Institution), p. 9. Barbé's testimony is valuable since he worked in the Hotchkiss armament factory in St.-Denis. For the motivations of the strikers, see the letter from Berrar, Mayor of Drancy, to André Marty, 5.vii.39, in the Marty Archives. Berrar had his information from the secretary of the union of Parisian metallurgists. According to Louis Marcellin, *Politique et politiciens pendant la guerre*, 4 vols. (n.d.), II, 328–29, the strike was not popular. "In the streets, the strikers were roundly insulted by passersby and by soldiers on leave, who called them slackers."
106. Georges and Tintant, p. 308.
107. Quoted in *ibid.*, p. 203.
108. See de la Gorce, *The French Army*, pp. 132–42.
109. *L'Humanité*, 20.ii.18.

110. *Le Populaire Socialiste-Internationaliste*, 2.ii.18.

111. *L'Humanité*, 6.iii.18.

112. CGT, *Réception de Kerensky par le Comité confédéral, 10 juillet* (1918), p. 8.

113. *Ibid.*, p. 23.

114. *Le Populaire*, 22.vii.18. *Le Populaire* had become a Parisian daily on April 11, 1918.

115. *Ibid.*, 20.vii.18.                          116. *L'Humanité*, 30.vii.18.

117. *Le Populaire*, 20.vii.18.                   118. *L'Humanité*, 20.vii.18.

119. *Le Populaire*, 7.vii.18.                    120. *Ibid.*, 31.vii.18.

121. CGT, *XIVᵉ Congrès confédéral tenu à Lyon du 15 au 21 septembre 1919, compte rendu* (Lyon, 1919), p. 64.

122. CGT, *XIIIᵉ Congrès*, pp. 216–67.

123. *Union des Métaux*, Sept. 1918, pp. 2–6.

124. Quoted in Georges and Tintant, *Léon Jouhaux*, p. 313.

125. *Union des Métaux*, Sept. 1918, p. 6.

126. Dolléans, *Histoire du mouvement ouvrier*, II, 286.

127. *L'Humanité*, 10.x.18.

128. See the speeches of Longuet and Faure, *L'Humanité*, 9.x.18. Also *Demain*, Oct. 1918, p. 320.

129. The letter was published in *La Nouvelle Internationale*, 14.ix.18.

130. Charles Dumas to Branting, 24.x.18. Branting Archives.

131. François Mayoux to Louis Bouët, 16.ii.19. This letter is in the possession of Annie Kriegel.

132. Rosmer, I, 327.

133. Amadeo Bordiga developed a position similar to Lenin's during the War, though independently of his influence. See Donald William Urquidi's very interesting unpublished Columbia doctoral dissertation, "The Origins of the Italian Communist Party, 1918–1921" (1962).

134. Rappoport, *La Crise socialiste*, p. 18.

135. The Russians themselves understood this. See *Golos*, 9.x.14.

136. See the reply of the Zimmerwaldian faction of the SFIO to the Stockholm questionnaire: "In short, the faction calls for the application of international resolutions in their entirety, and a return to the revolutionary traditions of the world proletariat organized in a class party." Comité Organisateur de la Conférence Internationale de Stockholm, *Stockholm* (Uppsala, 1918), p. 343.

137. See *L'Avenir Internationale*, Oct. 1918, pp. 11–12. By 1918 Loriot, Mayoux, Mesnil, Rosmer, and Monatte were all won over to the idea of a new International.

138. Raoul Verfeuil (*JP*, 15.x.18) was typical: "We are inclined to forget the internal quarrels that divide us. We want to forget everything but the struggle against our common enemy. On one condition, however: that the majoritaires are also willing to forget."

139. *JP*, 15.x.18.

## Chapter four

Epigraph: Henri Barbusse, *Le Feu* (1917), p. 368.

1. Jacques Chastenet, *Les Années d'illusions, 1918–1931* (1960), pp. 14–16, and William F. Ogburn and William Jaffe, *The Economic Development of Post-War France, A Survey of Production* (New York, 1924), pp. 51–56.

2. The Dadaist manifesto, quoted in Eugen Weber, *Paths to the Present: Aspects of European Thought from Romanticism to Existentialism* (New York, 1960), p. 253.

3. See Henry Lévi and Gabriel Fargue, *Ancien Combattant, homme nouveau* (n.d.), and Barbusse, *Der Schimmer im Abgrund* (Leipzig, 1920).

4. Lenin, *Polnoe sobranie sochinenii*, XXXVII, 164.

5. E. H. Carr, *The Bolshevik Revolution, 1917–1923*, 3 vols. (New York, 1953), III, 128.

6. Quoted in Francesco Nitti, *Peaceless Europe* (London, 1922), p. 94.

7. Quoted in Carr, *Bolshevik Revolution*, III, 129.

8. *IC*, 1.v.19, col. 46.

9. CGT, *XIVᵉ Congrès confédéral tenu à Lyon du 15 au 21 septembre 1919, compte rendu* (Lyon, 1919), p. 115.

10. Bernard Georges and Denise Tintant, *Léon Jouhaux, cinquante ans de syndicalisme* (1962), p. 291.

11. *Le Populaire*, 13.viii.18.

12. *La Vérité*, 16.viii.18.

13. Quoted in Roger Picard, *Le Mouvement syndical pendant la guerre* (1927), p. 205.

14. B. W. Schaper, *Albert Thomas: Trente ans de réformisme social* (1960), p. 176.

15. *L'Humanité*, 13.i.19.

16. Picard, *Le Mouvement syndical*, p. 88.

17. David Thomson, *Democracy in France*, 2d ed. (London, 1954), p. 45.

18. Gordon Wright, *France in Modern Times* (Chicago, 1960), pp. 402–3.

19. For every 100 women employed in 1914, in July 1918 there were 677 in metallurgy, 461 in transport, and 301 in the building trades. Picard, p. 99.

20. Edouard Bonnefous, *Histoire politique de la IIIᵉ République*, III (1959), 192.

21. Jules Romains, *Cette Grande Lueur à l'Est* (1941).

22. *L'Humanité*, 11.i.19.

23. See Daniel Renoult in *Le Populaire*, 14.x.18.

24. *L'Humanité*, 9.v.17.

25. Parti socialiste, *Circulaire de la Minorité du Parti Socialiste* (1916), p. 15. "What we want is to snatch the International from the ruins of war, and give it new life and strength, and we are ambitious enough to hope that it will be to the International that people owe the peace."

26. *L'Humanité*, 3.i.19.

27. Loriot to Louis Bouët, 23.i.19. Kriegel collection.

28. L.-O. Frossard, *De Jaurès à Léon Blum* (1943), p. 34.

29. Pierre Renaudel, *L'Internationale à Berne* (1919), p. 134.

30. *L'Humanité*, 19.ii.19.

31. Comité pour la Reprise des Relations Internationales, *Programme (Congrès des 20, 21 et 22 avril 1919)* (1919), no pagination.

32. *Le Populaire*, 22.ii.19.

33. *L'Humanité*, 19.ii.19.

34. Carr, *Bolshevik Revolution*, III, 91–108.

35. Jane Degras, *The Communist International, 1919–1943, Documents* (London, 1956), I, 1.

36. *Ibid.*, p. 2.

37. *Ibid.*, p. 4.

38. *Pervyi Kongress Kommunisticheskogo Internatsionala, Protokoly zasedanii v Moskve so 2 po 19 Marta 1919 goda* (Petrograd, 1921), pp. 62, 64.

39. *Ibid.*, p. 150; Degras, I, 26.

40. *Pervyi Kongress*, p. 157.

41. Degras, I, 30.

42. *Ibid.*, pp. 44–45.

43. *Ibid.*, p. 3.

44. *Le Populaire*, 24.iii.19.

45. Loriot to Louis Bouët, 23.i.19. Kriegel collection.

46. See, for example, the interpellation of Cachin, Lafont, and Mayéras on March 24–25, 1919.

47. *Le Populaire,* 16.ii.19.

48. For the Black Sea mutinies, see M. Garçon, *Histoire de la justice sous la Troisième République,* 3 vols. (1957), III, 289–96, and André Marty, *La Révolte de la mer noire,* 4th ed. (1949).

49. *L'Humanité,* 30.iii.19.      50. Chastenet, *Années d'illusion,* p. 54.

51. *L'Humanité,* 31.iii.19.      52. *Le Temps,* 15.iv.19.

53. Frossard, *De Jaurès à Lénine* (1930), p. 28.

54. *L'Humanité,* 22.iv.19.      55. *Ibid.,* 24.iv.19.

56. *Ibid.*      57. *Le Temps,* 25.iv.19.

58. Paul Allard and Marcel Berger, *Les Dessous du Traité de Versailles* (1933), p. 31.

59. Marty, *Révolte de la mer noire,* p. 121. Marty spoke of a circulation of 300,000. He had reason to know better. A letter to Raymond Lefebvre in his archives mentions the figure of 8,000 in May 1918. Other accounts substantiate the popularity of *La Vague.* For instance, Daniel Halévy: Brizon's "violent little sheet, *La Vague,* has an audience. It has more than 15 subscribers in Ygrande, most of them veterans who suffered greatly and have not forgiven society for it." Halévy, *Visite aux paysans du Centre* (1921), p. 97.

60. *L'Avenir International,* Nov. 1918.

61. Loriot to Louis Bouët, 23.i.19. Kriegel collection.

62. Kriegel, I, 323.

63. *L'Avenir International,* Nov. 1918.

64. Quoted in Jean Maxe, *De Zimmerwald au bolchévisme* (1919), p. 119.

65. *Le Populaire,* 26.i.19.

66. *VO,* 30.iv.19.

67. Gérard Walter, *Histoire du Parti Communiste Français* (1948), p. 24.

68. Quoted from a police report in Kriegel, I, 325.

69. *Ibid.,* p. 313.

70. Interview with Boris Souvarine, 20.ii.61.

71. Cited from the circular "Le 16 avril la 'Vie Ouvrière' reparaîtra!" (16.iii.19).

72. *VO,* 30.iv.19.

73. Quoted from "Le 16 avril la 'Vie Ouvrière' reparaîtra!"

74. *VO,* 5.xi.19.

75. *VO,* 7.v.19.

76. CGT, *XIVᵉ Congrès,* p. 79.

77. Quoted in Edouard Dolléans, *Histoire du mouvement ouvrier,* 2 vols. (1946), II, 322.

78. *VO,* 7.v.19.

79. Quoted in Dolléans, II, 323.

80. Georges and Tintant, *Léon Jouhaux,* p. 363.

81. *L'Humanité,* 26.v.19.

82. *Union des Métaux,* June–July 1919. For a description of this strike, see CGT, *XIVᵉ Congrès,* pp. 90–114, and Picard, *Le Mouvement syndical,* pp. 208–9.

83. David J. Saposs, *The Labor Movement in Post-War France* (New York, 1931), p. 47.

84. *Ibid.*

85. *L'Humanité,* 4.vi.19.

86. *VO,* 11.vi.19.

87. Quoted in Degras, *The Communist International,* I, 28.

88. The history of this strike has yet to be written. For the details of the negotiations between the French and Italians, which took place at the beginning of June 1919, see

Donald Urquidi, "The Origins of the Italian Communist Party" (unpublished doctoral dissertation, Columbia University, 1962), p. 72.

89. CGT, *XIVᵉ Congrès*, pp. 116–19.

90. *VO*, 19.vii.19.

91. Georges and Tintant, *Léon Jouhaux*, p. 367, n. 3.

92. *Ibid.*, pp. 367–71.

93. *IC*, 1.viii.19, col. 469. The Italian Socialists found the CGT's "inexplicable and inexcusable defection" no less infuriating. *Avanti!*, 25.vii.19.

94. CGT, *XIVᵉ Congrès*, p. 28.

95. Monmousseau's reproach was typical of the minority: "Let those who have lost their faith, the skeptics, at least leave to those who still have hope in their hearts the task of educating their comrades; they should not dive in and engulf the working masses, the proletariat, in a wave of skepticism." *Ibid.*, p. 54.

96. Georges and Tintant, pp. 371–73.

97. Annie Kriegel has in her possession an unpublished manuscript, written by Louis Bouët, which describes the origins and objectives of the CSR at some length.

98. Pierre Monatte to Bouët, 1.xii.19. Kriegel collection.

99. Kriegel, I, 282–307.

100. *Le Titre Censuré!!!*, 21.vi.19.

101. *Ibid.*

102. *Le Communiste*, 1.xi.19.

103. *L'Internationale*, 28.vi.19.

104. *L'Humanité*, 8.iii.21.

105. Raymond Lefebvre, in his speech at the Second World Congress of the Comintern, referred to the Parti Communiste and the Fédération Communiste des Soviets as "tiny political organizations, with no influence on the masses, in which a few good militants are wasting their efforts.... Together the two groups have only a few dozen members." *Esquisse du mouvement communiste en France* (1921), p. 12.

106. *Clarté*, 11.x.19.

107. Barbusse, *Der Schimmer*, p. 88. See *Clarté*, 29.xi.19, for an interesting study of Bolshevism which emphasizes the syndicalist nature of the Russian Revolution.

108. For the history of the French group during 1918 and 1919, see L. M. Zak, "Deyatelnost Frantsuzskoi Kommunisticheskoi gruppy RKP (B) v 1918–1919 godakh," *Voprosy Istorii*, Feb. 1960, pp. 152–66, and Marcel Brody, "Les Groupes communistes français de Russie (1918–1921)," in Jacques Freymond, ed., *Contributions à l'histoire du Comintern* (Geneva, 1965), pp. 39–65.

109. Zak, "Deyatelnost," p. 157.

110. Victor Serge, *Mémoires d'un révolutionnaire, 1901–1941* (1951), p. 159.

111. For Lefebvre's background and development, consult my article "La Révolution ou la Mort: Raymond Lefebvre and the Formation of the French Communist Party," *International Review of Social History*, VII (1962), Part 2, pp. 177–202.

112. There are a number of interesting letters from Lefebvre to Henri Barbusse, bearing on the formation of both *Clarté* and ARAC, in the Marty Archives.

113. Henri Guilbeaux, *Du Kremlin au Cherche-Midi* (1933), pp. 141–42.

114. Lefebvre, *L'Internationale des Soviets* (1919), p. 5.

115. *Ibid.*, p. 6.

116. *Ibid.*, p. 11.

117. *Ibid.*, p. 12.

118. *Ibid.*, p. 14.

119. *JP*, 5.vi.17.

120. *La Vérité*, 5.vi.17. The full text of Lenin's letter is reproduced in *Polnoe sobranie sochinenii*, XXX, 261–72.

121. Boris Souvarine, *La Troisième Internationale* (1919), p. 12.

122. *Ibid.*, p. 22.

123. *Ibid.*, pp. 14–15.

124. In June 1919 Georges Leygues, then Minister of the Navy, defined Bolshevism as

"a poison that Germany planted in Russia to destroy her, to make a formidable enemy powerless. The poison has done its work." Edouard Bonnefous, *Histoire politique*, III, 10.

125. *Le Populaire*, 5.viii.19.

126. *Report on Labor and Socialism in France* (Washington, D.C., 1919), p. 67.

127. *L'Humanité*, 20.v.19.                    128. *Ibid.*, 28.vi.19.

129. *Ibid.*, 19.vii.19.                    130. *Ibid.*, 3.viii.19.

131. *Ibid.*, 30.viii.19.                    132. *Ibid.*, 11.ix.19.

133. *Ibid.*, 14.x.19.                    134. *Le Populaire*, 16.ix.19.

135. *JP*, 14.ix.19.

136. Joseph Paul-Boncour, *Entre deux guerres*, 3 vols. (1945), II, 18.

137. François Goguel, *La Politique des partis sous la IIIᵉ République*, 2 vols. (1946), II, 77–78.

138. *Le Temps*, 1.xi.19.

139. Bonnefous, *Histoire politique*, III, 63–64.

140. *L'Humanité*, 5.xi.19.

141. SFIO, *Congrès national* [Strasbourg, 1920], *Rapport du Secrétariat, La Vie du parti d'octobre 1918 à janvier 1920* (1920), pp. 50–61, has valuable information on the Socialist participation in the elections, as well as on other aspects of the party's life from the Armistice to the Congress of Strasbourg.

142. See Chambre des Députés, *Programmes, Professions de Foi et Engagements Electoraux de 1919*, No. 1431 (Annexe) (1920), especially pp. 777 and 798.

143. According to Daniel Renoult, in *L'Humanité*, 4.ix.23.

144. Peter Campbell, *French Electoral Systems* (London, 1958), p. 95.

145. SFIO, *Congrès national* [Strasbourg, 1920], *Rapport du Secrétariat*, pp. 34–35.

146. SFIO, *17ᵉ Congrès* [Strasbourg, 1920], pp. 184–85.

147. *L'Humanité*, 17.xi.19.

148. G. D. H. Cole, *Communism and Social Democracy* (London, 1958), Part I, pp. 321–22.

149. Quoted in Carr, *Bolshevik Revolution*, III, 167.

150. *Le Populaire*, 23.xii.19.

151. *Ibid.*, 28.xii.19. Longuet, however, stated the position of the Center in much less positive terms: "What we need to build is a new, more spacious, and better ventilated structure, which will be neither the Second, nor the Third, nor the Fourth International, but will grow out of the merger of all revolutionary elements and will simply be *the* International." *Ibid.*, 8.i.20.

152. *L'Humanité*, 30.i.20.                    153. *JP*, 1.i.20.

154. *IC*, Sept. 1919, col. 645.                    155. *VO*, 9.i.20.

156. *Le Populaire*, 10.i.20.

157. This letter was published by Souvarine in *BC*, 3.ii.21.

158. These motions were printed in *L'Humanité*, Feb. 4–6, 1920.

159. On February 10, 1920, Loriot wrote to Bouët: "I still don't think that we shall have a majority at Strasbourg, but the time is drawing near when the Socialist Party will once again be on the right track." Kriegel collection.

160. SFIO, *17ᵉ Congrès*, pp. 108–21.                    161. *Ibid.*, p. 467.

162. *Ibid.*, p. 256.                    163. *Ibid.*, pp. 348–53.

164. Leon Trotsky, *Terror and Communism* (Ann Arbor, Mich., 1961), p. 101.

165. SFIO, *17ᵉ Congrès*, p. 432.                    166. Frossard, *De Jaurès à Lénine*, p. 39.

167. SFIO, *17ᵉ Congrès*, p. 566.                    168. *Ibid.*, pp. 453, 468.

169. *Ibid.*, p. 566.                    170. *Ibid.*, p. 567.

171. "The Left has become a powerful faction, which, though it seems to count only a third of the party's members, has in fact a decisive influence on the general direction of

the Socialist movement, and is on the brink of winning acceptance for the doctrine of revolutionary Communism." Souvarine, "Après Strasbourg," *Le Phare*, 1.iv.20.

172. *Le Populaire*, 6.ii.20.

### Chapter five

Epigraph: *Der zweite Kongress der Kommunist. Internationale, Protokoll der Verhandlungen vom 19. Juli in Petrograd und vom 23. Juli bis 7. August 1920 in Moskau* (Hamburg, 1920), p. 239.

1. *L'Avenir Internationale*, Jan. 1920, p. 25.

2. Alfred Rosmer, *Moscou sous Lénine* (1953), pp. 69–70.

3. For Italy, see Donald W. Urquidi, "The Origins of the Italian Communist Party" (unpublished doctoral dissertation, Columbia University, 1962), pp. 72, 114. The Italians succeeded in establishing tentative communications with the Bolsheviks at the end of 1919. The German case was more complex. Soviet agents like Karl Radek and "Comrade Thomas" were active in Berlin, but because of the difficulty of getting messages through— and even more because of the uncertainty of the political situation—they were unable to act as spokesmen for the International's line. See "Le Récit du 'camarade Thomas,' " in Jacques Freymond, ed., *Contributions à l'histoire du Comintern* (Geneva, 1965), pp. 5–27, and Ruth Fischer, *Stalin and German Communism* (Cambridge, Mass., 1948).

4. Loriot, for instance, recounted that he had scanned Guilbeaux's telegram and had torn it up at the post office, not considering it of particular interest. (*L'Humanité*, 4.iii.21.) This may or may not be true, but it is not impossible.

5. Branko Lazitch, "Two Instruments of Control by the Comintern: The Delegates of the ECCI and the Party Representatives in Moscow" (unpublished ms.), p. 4.

6. For this question, see Kriegel, II, 564.

7. Interview with Alfred Rosmer, 13.ii.61, and Vladimir Diogott, *V "svobodnom" podpole: Vospominaniya o podpolnoi rabote za granitsei v 1919–1921 godakh* (Moscow, 1923), pp. 32–46.

8. *BC*, 18.iii.20.

9. *BC*, 29.ii.20.

10. Trotsky's article was published in *BC*, 3.vi.20.

11. *Le Phare*, 1.iv.20.

12. *VO*, 2.i.20.

13. Quoted in Edouard Bonnefous, *Histoire politique de la IIIᵉ République*, III (1959), 103–4.

14. On March 13, 1920, Monatte wrote to Trotsky: "The time when we were only a handful is now over, but all our scattered forces have yet to be drawn together. This will come about with the events that are almost upon us." Quoted in Kriegel, II, 569.

15. My account of the strikes of 1920 is based, to a large extent, on the research of Annie Kriegel, who has done an exhaustive study of these events. Kriegel, I, 357–547.

16. See Monmousseau's article in *VO*, 5.iii.20: "Une victoire?" Monmousseau asked. "Non! Une capitulation."

17. Quoted in Bonnefous, III, 119.

18. Kriegel, I, 414–15.

19. Quoted in *ibid.*, I, 417.

20. Bernard Georges and Denise Tintant, *Léon Jouhaux, cinquante ans de syndicalisme* (1962), pp. 379–81.

21. Kriegel, I, 437–39, and Eugen Weber, *Action Française: Royalism and Reaction in Twentieth-Century France* (Stanford, Calif., 1962), p. 130.

22. The Federal Council of the radical Teachers' Union was unable to guarantee the

participation of its members in a strike. "Not one union, not one militant, gave the federal bureau a firm commitment on the strike." Quoted in Max Ferré, *Histoire du mouvement syndicaliste révolutionnaire chez les instituteurs: Des origines à 1922* (1955), p. 233.

23. Georges and Tintant, *Léon Jouhaux*, p. 381.

24. Roger Picard, *Le Mouvement syndical pendant la guerre* (1927), p. 221.

25. Georges and Tintant, pp. 380–82.

26. See Kriegel, I, 461–75.

27. Quoted in Bonnefous, *Histoire politique*, III, 123.

28. Kriegel, I, 515.                                    29. Picard, p. 226.

30. Georges and Tintant, p. 407.                 31. *Ibid.*, pp. 384–88.

32. Pierre Monatte, *Trois scissions syndicales* (1958), p. 158.

33. *Le Temps* had commented on June 11, 1920: "What's beyond doubt is that foreign powers have tried to provoke a crisis that would endanger the economic recovery of France, and that Lenin's agents have sought to manipulate the organized proletariat in order to arouse it against the nation and make of it an instrument of universal revolution."

34. Interview with Boris Souvarine, 4.xii.60.

35. *JP*, 29.iv.20.

36. *L'Humanité*, 28.vi.20. Antonio Gramsci came to the same conclusion after the failure of the Turin sitdown strikes in August–September 1920. See Urquidi, "Origins of the Italian Communist Party," pp. 266–67.

37. *Report on Labor and Socialism in France* (Washington, D.C., 1919) gives a figure of 9,750,000 workers out of an active population of 21,000,000 (p. 69). This included 3,300,000 agricultural laborers.

38. Lenin, *"Left-Wing" Communism: An Infantile Disorder* (New York, 1934), pp. 72–74.

39. Edmund von Glaise-Horstenau, *The Collapse of the Austro-Hungarian Empire* (London, 1930), p. 16.

40. *L'Humanité*, 23.vi.20 and 17.ix.20, and Paul Faure, *La Scission socialiste en France et dans l'Internationale* (1921), p. 19.

41. My reconstruction of the Bolshevik view of France is based on a wide reading in Russian sources. Of these, the most useful were the following: Trotsky, *Kommunisticheskoe dvizhenie vo Frantsii* (Moscow, 1923); Lozovsky, *Rabochaya Frantsiya* (Moscow, 1923); Zinoviev, *Les Socialistes français et la guerre: Jaurès, Sembat, Guesde* (Petrograd, 1920); Lenin, *Polnoe sobranie sochinenii*; and Lenin and Zinoviev, *Contre le courant* (1927).

42. *IC*, 1.v.19, col. 39.

43. George Kennan, *Russia Leaves the War* (Princeton, N.J., 1956), p. 282. The French government openly defied Parliament on the question of the Russian intervention. On December 23, 1919, Clemenceau stated, in response to an interpellation by Barthou, that "Not only will we not go to war, we will not come to terms with the Soviet government." Then he went on to say that "we will continue to regard the Soviet government as the most odious and barbarous that has ever devastated any territory in the known world." (Bonnefous, *Histoire politique*, III, 82.) Clemenceau admitted that both France and England had spent great sums of money trying to destroy the Bolshevik government. France, he said, could not continue these expenses indefinitely. But "as long as Russia remains in its present state of anarchy, there can be no guarantee of peace in Europe. We have agreed on what I have called the policy of barbed-wire encirclement. We want to put a barbed-wire fence around Bolshevism to prevent it from launching an attack on civilized Europe." (*Ibid.*, p. 83.) This sums up very well the attitude of the Clemenceau

government toward Bolshevism. The policy followed by the Millerand government was similar. Millerand said that the French government had decided not to enter into relations with the Soviets. But he assured the Chamber "that the government was resolved not to interfere in the slightest with the internal development of the Russian people." (*Ibid.*, p. 131.) Nevertheless, in August 1920 the French government recognized General Wrangel, admitted to having given aid to White Russian generals in Siberia, and regarded the victory of the Poles over the Bolsheviks as its own triumph. (*Ibid.*, p. 158.) The Bolsheviks, in turn, recognized the French government as their chief enemy. See Trotsky, *My Life* (New York, 1930), pp. 344–45.

44. Lenin, *Polnoe sobranie sochinenii*, XXXIX, 179.

45. *IC*, 1.viii.19, col. 469.

46. *IC*, 1.vii.19, col. 345.

47. *IC*, Sept. 1919, col. 645; *IC*, Nov.–Dec. 1919, col. 1020.

48. Jane Degras, *The Communist International, 1919–1943, Documents* (London, 1956), I, 79.

49. *IC*, May 1920, col. 1654.

50. Degras, I, 93, 100, and 104.

51. Urquidi, "Origins of the Italian Communist Party," p. 187.

52. For an early statement of Lenin's attitude toward revolutionary syndicalism, see his article "Raznoglaciya v evropeiskom rabochem dvizhenii," *Polnoe sobranie sochinenii*, XX, 62–69.

53. Lenin, *"Left-Wing" Communism*, p. 55.

54. Trotsky, *Kommunisticheskoe dvizhenie*, p. 47.

55. David Cattell, "The Hungarian Revolution and the Reorganization of the Comintern," *The Journal of Central European Affairs*, XI (1951), 33. Lenin, who went over the Center's Strasbourg resolution word by word, concluded caustically that of its 143 lines only eight were "clear, precise, business-like, and to the point." *Polnoe sobranie sochinenii*, XL, 350.

56. See, for example, Cachin, Lafont, Mayéras, *Contre l'intervention en Russie: Discours prononcés à la Chambre des Députés les 24 et 25 mars 1919* (1919), p. 25.

57. Once more the description is by Frossard: *De Jaurès à Lénine* (1930), p. 45.

58. Frossard, *De Jaurès à Léon Blum* (1943), p. 11.

59. Frossard, *De Jaurès à Lénine*, pp. 235–44.

60. SFIO, *18ᵉ Congrès* [Tours, 1920], pp. 336–37.

61. Frossard, *De Jaurès à Lénine*, p. 49. From this point on, my account relies heavily upon Frossard's various memoirs. I am aware that Frossard's version of these events is open to dispute by men at all points on the political spectrum. In presenting himself as an inveterate double-dealer, Frossard himself has done much to discredit the historical value of his memoirs. Whenever possible I have checked Frossard's account against those of his contemporaries. Moreover, it should be noted that the first version of Frossard's memoirs, "Mon Journal de voyage en Russie," was not called into question by either Right, Center, or Left when it first appeared in December 1921. It goes without saying that if I had had access to the files of the Comintern and the memoirs of men like Zinoviev, Bukharin, and Cachin, the details, if not the broad outlines, of my account might have varied. Cachin kept a diary throughout his life, but its contents have not been made public by his heirs, and it is unlikely that they will be. Taking all this into consideration, I am convinced that the story which I present here is substantially correct.

62. Frossard, *De Jaurès à Lénine*, p. 54.

63. Humbert-Droz in *Le Phare*, Oct. 1920, p. 9.

64. Frossard, *De Jaurès à Lénine*, pp. 58–61.

65. *Ibid.,* pp. 254–67.

66. *Ibid.,* pp. 267–69, and Cachin, *Ecrits et Portraits* (1964), pp. 91–95.

67. *Ibid.,* p. 107.

68. Frossard, "Mon Journal de voyage en Russie" (1921). This is a collection of newspaper clippings from *L'Internationale* of December 1921. There is no pagination. So far as I know, the only copy is to be found in the Bibliothèque Nationale in Paris.

69. *L'Humanité,* 5.vii.20.

70. Frossard, *De Jaurès à Lénine,* pp. 272–77.

71. See Boris Sokolov, *Le Voyage de Cachin et de Frossard dans la Russie des Soviets* (1921).

72. Frossard, *De Jaurès à Lénine,* pp. 108–10. The telegram was published in *L'Humanité,* 21.vii.20.

73. *La Revue Communiste,* Mar. 1920, pp. 46–57.

74. Loriot to Vandeschamps, 28.vii.20. Kriegel collection.

75. E. H. Carr, *The Bolshevik Revolution, 1917–1923,* 3 vols. (New York, 1953), III, 188.

76. Quoted in Urquidi, "Origins of the Italian Communist Party," p. 196.

77. *Der zweite Kongress,* pp. 386–87.       78. *Ibid.,* p. 340.

79. Carr, *Bolshevik Revolution,* III, 197.       80. *Der zweite Kongress,* p. 244.

81. Rosmer, *Moscou sous Lénine,* pp. 103–4.

82. *Der zweite Kongress,* pp. 244–45.

83. *Ibid.,* p. 245.

84. *Ibid.,* p. 242.

85. Frossard, *De Jaurès à Lénine,* p. 132. The Russian reply is in *Der zweite Kongress,* pp. 281–303.

86. Frossard, *De Jaurès à Lénine,* pp. 131–35.

87. *Der zweite Kongress,* pp. 263–64.       88. *Ibid.,* p. 270.

89. *Ibid.,* p. 383.       90. *Ibid.,* pp. 383–84.

91. Urquidi, pp. 224–25, and Humbert-Droz in *Le Phare,* Oct. 1920, p. 9. This point, however, should not be overemphasized. The Bolsheviks, too, were still wary of the Center and wanted guarantees.

92. Frossard, *De Jaurès à Lénine,* pp. 136–40. Cachin's account in *Ecrits et Portraits* does not vary from Frossard's in any marked way.

93. *L'Humanité,* 14.viii.20.

94. Frossard, *De Jaurès à Lénine,* p. 152.

95. *L'Humanité,* 14.viii.20. The ensuing quotations are all taken from this source.

96. *Ibid.,* 15.viii.20.

97. *Ibid.,* 18.viii.20.

98. *Ibid.,* 6.ix.20.

99. Frossard, *De Jaurès à Lénine,* p. 162. According to Adrien Compère-Morel, Guesde used to like to repeat that "world history is not dependent solely on our will." (*Jules Guesde, le socialisme fait homme, 1845–1922,* 1937, p. 495.) In 1896 such determinism had had revolutionary implications; by 1920 it indicated a hostility to revolution.

100. Frossard, *De Jaurès à Lénine,* p. 162.       101. *L'Humanité,* 30.vii.20.

102. *Ibid.,* 3.viii.20.       103. *Ibid.,* 29.viii.20.

104. Frossard, *La Décomposition du Communisme* (n.d.), p. 13.

105. *L'Humanité,* 9.ix.20.       106. *Ibid.,* 10.ix.20.

107. *Ibid.*       108. *Le Populaire,* 2.ix.20.

109. *Ibid.,* 3.ix.20.       110. *Ibid.,* 10.ix.20 and 12.ix.20.

111. *L'Humanité,* 24.x.20.       112. *Ibid.,* 31.x.20.

113. *Ibid.,* 13.xi.20.       114. *Ibid.,* 30.ix.20.

115. *Ibid.*, 11.viii.20.
116. *Ibid.*, 17.viii.20.
117. *BC*, 22.vii.20.
118. *BC*, 5.viii.20.
119. *L'Humanité*, 3.viii.20.
120. See *BC*, 26.viii.20 and 10.ix.20.
121. *JP*, 4.ix.20.
122. Interview with Boris Souvarine, 4.xii.60, and *JP*, 3.vi.22.
123. Interview with Souvarine, 4.xii.60. Several "influential members of the Committee of the Third International" wrote to Serrati on October 13, 1920, to inform him that the Twenty-One Conditions would be "adapted to the circumstances in which our Party finds itself. The Executive Committee of Moscow, which has precisely foreseen exceptions in some cases, will understand that in the situation we find ourselves—and in which even you find yourselves—the immediate, strict, and integral application of the Twenty-One Conditions is impossible." Quoted in Urquidi, "Origins of the Italian Communist Party," p. 336.
124. Renoult's agreement with Zinoviev is reproduced in full by Humbert-Droz in *Le Phare*, Nov. 1920, p. 75.
125. Comité de la 3ᵉ Internationale, *La Résolution d'adhésion à la 3ᵉ Internationale* (1920); also to be found in *BC*, 4.xi.20.
126. *Le Communiste*, 4.vii.20. As early as May 1920, Emile Chauvelon, a leading anarchist spokesman, had warned that to try to combine Sovietism and parliamentarism was "not only absurd, but dangerous." There could be no compromise between the two, he insisted. *Le Soviet*, 9.v.20.
127. *Le Communiste*, 5.ix.20. This was the same Mauriskoff (Mauricius) who had attended the Second World Congress and been detained in Moscow. See note, p. 184 above.
128. This committee was formed on December 4, 1920. Its manifesto was published in *L'Humanité*, 6.xii.20.
129. See *JP*, 15.xi.20, for a report of a meeting of the Federation of the Seine at which Renoult read the agreement he had concluded with Zinoviev at Halle.
130. *Le Populaire*, 18.xi.20.
131. *Ibid.* and *L'Humanité*, 15.xi.20.
132. *BC*, quoted in *Le Populaire*, 2.xii.20.
133. *BC*, 2.xii.20.
134. SFIO, *18ᵉ Congrès*, pp. 580–85.
135. *Le Populaire*, 23.xi.20.
136. *Ibid.*, 11.xii.20.
137. For the details of Lefebvre's death and the controversy over his attitude toward the Soviet regime, see my article "La Révolution ou la mort," *International Review of Social History*, VII (1962), Part II, pp. 197–99. Annie Kriegel (II, 767–87) has added some interesting details to our knowledge of the circumstances surrounding the disappearance of Lefebvre, Lepetit, and Vergeat.
138. The quotation is from Longuet. *Le Populaire*, 14.xii.20.
139. Joseph Paul-Boncour, *Entre deux guerres*, 3 vols. (1945), II, 21–22.
140. SFIO, *18ᵉ Congrès*, p. 13.
141. *Ibid.*, p. 57.
142. *Ibid.*, p. 74.
143. *Ibid.*, pp. 177–78.
144. *Ibid.*, p. 274.
145. *Ibid.*, p. 391.
146. *Ibid.*, pp. 210–11.
147. *Ibid.*, pp. 189–91.
148. *Ibid.*, pp. 236–37.
149. *Ibid.*, p. 313.
150. *Ibid.*, p. 370.
151. *Ibid.*, pp. 341, 261, 381.
152. *Ibid.*, p. 481.
153. *Ibid.*, p. 482.
154. *Ibid.*, pp. 485–86.
155. *Ibid.*, p. 525.
156. I am paraphrasing one of the period's participants, Gaston Monmousseau; he is quoted in Val R. Lorwin, *The French Labor Movement* (Cambridge, Mass., 1954), pp. 51–52.
157. Urquidi, "Origins of the Italian Communist Party," p. 336.

Chapter six

Epigraph: *L'Humanité*, 27.iii.21.

1. For the March Action and the historiographical debates surrounding it, see Werner T. Angress, *Stillborn Revolution: The Communist Bid for Power in Germany, 1921–1923* (Princeton, N.J., 1963), pp. 105–96.

2. Trotsky's remark was made to André Morizet, *Chez Lénine et Trotski* (1922), pp. 108–9.

3. There is an account of the major European strikes during the years 1919–22 in *Ezhegodnik Kominterna* (Petrograd and Moscow, 1923).

4. Jacques Valdour, *Ouvriers parisiens d'après-guerre* (1921), especially p. 169. Valdour's book is the best source I know for the workers' state of mind after the failure of the general strike of May 1920. It is corroborated by other observers.

5. *Protokoll des Vierten Kongresses der Kommunistischen Internationale, Petrograd-Moskau, vom 5. November bis 5. Dezember, 1922* (Hamburg, 1923), p. 222.

6. Georg von Rauch, *A History of Soviet Russia* (New York, 1957), p. 130.

7. Robert Vincent Daniels, *The Conscience of a Revolution: Communist Opposition in Soviet Russia* (Cambridge, Mass., 1960), pp. 143–45.

8. Quoted in *ibid.*, p. 155.

9. E. H. Carr, *The Bolshevik Revolution, 1917–1923* (New York, 1953), III, 289, 303.

10. E. H. Carr, *Socialism in One Country, 1924–1926*, 3 vols. (London, 1958–64), I, 103–4, and Adam B. Ulam, *The Unfinished Revolution* (New York, 1960), p. 210. See Trotsky, *Terrorism and Communism* (Ann Arbor, Mich., 1961), p. 45, for a frank discussion of the Bolshevik atittude toward majorities.

11. Isaac Deutscher, *The Prophet Unarmed: Trotsky, 1921–1929* (New York, 1959), p. 15.

12. Daniels, *Conscience of a Revolution*, pp. 165–71.

13. *Le Libertaire*, 8.iv.21.

14. Edouard Herriot, *La Russie nouvelle* (1922), p. 65.

15. See, for example, Chicherin's message to Briand, published in *L'Humanité*, 15.iv.21, and André Morizet, *Chez Lénine et Trotski*, pp. 143–44 and 154–55.

16. *La Lutte de Classe*, 15.xi.22.

17. *L'Humanité*, 7.i.21.

18. SFIO, *18e Congrès* [Tours, 1920], p. 553.

19. L.-O. Frossard, *De Jaurès à Lénine* (1930), p. 199.

20. Alfred Rosmer, *Moscou sous Lénine* (1953), p. 242.

21. There is a short autobiographical sketch by Monatte in Jean Maitron, *Histoire du mouvement anarchiste en France*, 2d ed. (1955), p. 305.

22. Henry Torrès, *Pierre Laval* (New York, 1941), p. 16.

23. Frossard noted this in *De Jaurès à Lénine*, p. 186.

24. Kriegel, II, 847–55.

25. *Ibid.*, p. 827.

26. See Frossard's speech before the Federation of the Seine, in *L'Humanité*, 10.i.21.

27. Trotsky, *Kommunisticheskoe dvizhenie vo Frantsii* (Moscow, 1923), p. 32, and *IC*, Nov. 1920, cols. 2662–64.

28. *L'Humanité*, 12.i.21.

29. *Le Populaire*, 22.i.21.

30. For the details of this squabble, see *L'Humanité* and *Le Populaire*, especially the latter for 24.i.21.

31. *L'Humanité*, 20.ii.21. Souvarine told me in the course of an interview that *L'Humanité*'s account was pure invention.

32. Interview with Souvarine, 20.ii.61.

33. As Monmousseau put it: "The 'plot' refers either to the strike or to the Third International. If it's the strike, I should be the only one here. If it's the Third International, I'd like to know what I'm doing here, along with the others." *L'Humanité*, 3.iii.21.

34. *Ibid.*, 14.iii.21.

35. Edouard Bonnefous, *Histoire politique de la III<sup>e</sup> République*, III (1959), 230–37, and Angress, *Stillborn Revolution*, pp. 116–17.

36. *L'Internationale*, 21.iv.21.

37. According to Frossard, in *ibid.*, 8.v.21.

38. *L'Avant-Garde*, Apr. 15–30, 1921.

39. *L'Internationale*, 5.v.21.              40. *L'Humanité*, 27.iii.21.

41. *Ibid.*, May 17–18, 1921.               42. *Ibid.*, May 9–15, 1921.

43. *Ibid.*, 16.v.21.                        44. *Ibid.*, 17.v.21.

45. There is a copy of this motion in the Arbetarrörelsens Arkiv in Stockholm. Souvarine summarized it in *BC*, 10.xi.21, and dismissed it as "super-Bolshevist" and "inopportunist." According to his account, he received it in July and communicated it to the Executive Committee, which did not take it seriously. Paul Levi published it in *Unser Weg* in early November 1921.

46. *La Revue Communiste*, May 1921, p. 175, and *IC*, Mar. 1921, col. 3413.

47. *IC*, June 1921, col. 3960.

48. Carr, *Bolshevik Revolution*, III, 385.

49. *Ibid.*, p. 392.

50. Souvarine to Frossard, 23.vi.21, *L'Humanité*, 15.vii.21.

51. *Protokoll des III Kongresses*, pp. 607–9.

52. *IC*, Mar. 1921, col. 3794.

53. Rosmer, *Moscou sous Lénine*, pp. 178–79.

54. *Rapport du Secrétariat International* (1921?), p. 2. The document referred to is Loriot's report to the Congress of Marseille.

55. *Ibid.*, pp. 3–4.

56. *Ibid.*, p. 6.

57. *L'Internationale*, 14.vii.21; *BC*, 11.viii.21; and *Rapport du Secrétariat International*, p. 13.

58. Rosmer, *Moscou sous Lénine*, p. 179.

59. *L'Internationale*, 14.vii.21.

60. *BC*, 18.viii.21.

61. *La Revue Communiste*, Feb. 1922, pp. 25–26.

Chapter seven

Epigraph: *Clarté*, 4.xii.20.

1. *L'Internationale*, 5.ix.21.

2. For the resolutions on the French question passed after the Third Congress, see *L'Internationale*, 14.vii.21; *BC*, 11.viii.21; and *Rapport du Secrétariat International* (1921?), p. 13. Trotsky's letters to Monatte, Cachin, and Frossard can be found in *Kommunisticheskoe dvizhenie vo Frantsii* (Moscow, 1923) and in "Lettres du camarade Léon Trotsky à quelques camarades français, 1921–1922, à propos des problèmes du mouvement ouvrier français et du développement du parti," a collection to be found, so far as I know, only at the Bibliothèque Nationale.

3. "Lettres du camarade Trotsky," p. 8.

4. *Rapport du Secrétariat International*, p. 13.

5. *JP*, 18.ix.21.

6. *L'Internationale*, 6.vii.21.

7. *La Revue Communiste*, May 1921, p. 183.

8. *BC*, 20.i.21. The members of the Executive Committee of the Committee for the Third International elected May 13, 1921, were Boyet, Marcelle Brunet, Joseph Cartier, Clamamus, Fromentin, Victor Godonnèche, Marcel Hasfeld, Victor Hattenberger, Humbertdot, Kaufmann, Ker, Loriot, Monatte, Monmousseau, Pouthion, Rappoport, René Reynaud, Rochereuil, Souvarine, and Treint.

9. *BC*, 6.x.21.

10. Fernand Loriot, *Un An après Tours* (1922), p. 6. This pamphlet contains the speech given by Loriot before the Federation of the Seine on February 22, 1922, in which he attempted to explain the reasons for his resignation from the CD. It is an important source for the development of dissension within the leadership after the Third Congress.

11. *BC*, 15.ix.21.

12. A copy of Humbert-Droz's mandate, dated 27.ix.21 and signed by Zinoviev, is in the Humbert-Droz Archives at the International Institute of Social History in Amsterdam. The core of this very important collection of Comintern documents has recently been published by Humbert-Droz under the title *L'Oeil de Moscou à Paris* (1964). Microfilms of the original archives are available at the Hoover Institution and at Harvard University.

13. Interviews with Souvarine, 20.ii.61 and 4.xii.60.

14. Souvarine to CD, 28.ix.21. Rappoport Papers, International Institute of Social History, Amsterdam.

15. *JP*, 31.viii.21. See also *JP*, 29.ix.21.

16. *JP*, 9.x.21, 16.x.21, and 30.x.21.      17. *JP*, 4.xi.21.

18. Loriot, *Après Tours*, p. 9.      19. *Ibid.*, p. 10.

20. Frossard's resignation, dated 10.xi.21, read: "The Communist International feels that my position as General Secretary of the party is incompatible with my role as contributor to *Le Journal du Peuple*. Although my opinion differs from the International's, I yield to it in the name of discipline and submit herewith my resignation." *JP*, 24.xi.21.

21. See *JP*, 24.xi.21 and 15.xii.21.

22. *BC*, 15.xii.21.

23. Souvarine to Brécot (Monmousseau), dated Moscow, 13.xii.21. Rappoport Papers.

24. See Souvarine's article in *BC*, 25.viii.21, and Lozovsky, *BC*, 30.ix.21.

25. Lenin, *Polnoe sobranie sochinenii*, XV, 173–74.

26. *Comparative Labor Movements*, ed. Walter Galenson (New York, 1955), p. 481. The essay on Russia is by Isaac Deutscher.

27. *Ibid.*, pp. 508–14.

28. Trotsky, *Nouvelle Etape* (1922), pp. 126–28, and *Kommunisticheskoe dvizhenie*, pp. 51 and 80–82.

29. Alfred Rosmer to Annie Kriegel, 12.v.57. I am indebted to Mme. Kriegel for permitting me to read this letter.

30. Zinoviev, "Vers l'Internationale Syndicale Rouge: Message de l'Internationale Communiste aux syndicats de tous les pays" (1920). This circular emphasized that "The Red Unions must unite internationally and become an integral part (section) of the Communist International."

31. Comité de la 3e Internationale, *La Résolution d'Adhésion à la 3e Internationale* (1920), p. 4.

32. Loriot to Bouët, 15.xi.20.

33. CGT, *XVe Congrès confédéral tenu à Orléans du 27 septembre au 2 octobre 1920* (n.d.), pp. 405–6.

34. *Ibid.*, pp. 351–53.

35. "A Propos de la scission syndicale de 1921: Une Lettre de Georges Dumoulin," *Les Etudes Sociales et Syndicales*, Apr. 1955, pp. 15–16.

36. CGT, *XVᵉ Congrès*, pp. 405–6.

37. M. Isidure, in *Les Temps Nouveaux*, 15.x.20, pp. 2–3.

38. According to Vladimir Diogott, *V "svobodnom" podpole: Vospominaniya o podpolnoi rabote za granitsei v 1919–1921 godakh* (Moscow, 1923), pp. 32–46.

39. *VO*, 29.x.20. Monatte was writing under the pseudonym of Pierre Lemont.

40. See Humbert-Droz in *IC*, Dec. 1921, col. 4819, and Loriot in *BC*, 11.ix.21.

41. *BC*, 16.vi.21, and Frossard in *JP*, 14.v.21 and 19.vi.21. Renoult went so far as to write that "One would have to be mad to think that in a country like France, in the present conditions, the syndicalist organization could be subordinated to the political party." *L'Internationale*, 26.v.21.

42. *Protokoll des Vierten Kongresses der Kommunistischen Internationale, Petrograd-Moskau, vom 5. November bis 5. Dezember, 1922* (Hamburg, 1923), p. 830.

43. My account of the Profintern's Congress is based on John T. Murphy, *The "Reds" in Congress. Preliminary Report of the First World Congress of the Red International of Trade and Industrial Unions* (Manchester, 1921?), and Rosmer, *Moscou sous Lénine* (1953), pp. 191–92. The theses passed by the congress are reproduced in Jane Degras, *The Communist International, 1919–1943, Documents* (London, 1956), I, 274–81.

44. *L'Humanité*, 16.vii.21.

45. *VO*, 22.vii.21.

46. CGT, *XXIIᵉ Congrès national corporatif (XVIᵉ de la C.G.T.) tenu à Lille du 25 au 30 juillet 1921* (Villeneuve–St.-Georges, n.d.), pp. 17, 19–20.

47. Pierre Monatte, *Trois scissions syndicales* (1958), p. 152.

48. CGT, *XXIIᵉ Congrès national corporatif*, pp. 137, 148.

49. *L'Internationale*, 24.vii.21.

50. Mme. Kriegel has in her possession a manuscript by Louis Bouët describing the events leading up to the split of the CGT. My account owes a great deal to this invaluable source.

51. *JP*, 2.viii.21.  52. *BC*, 21.vii.21.

53. *L'Humanité*, 13.x.21.  54. *La Lutte de Classe*, 5.v.22.

55. *Lettres du camarade Trotsky*, pp. 3–6.  56. Guilbeaux in *BC*, 13.x.21.

57. His impressions are described in *IC*, Dec. 1921, cols. 4819–21.

58. *BC*, 6.x.21.

59. The thesis on the unions is printed in *BC*, 1.xi.21. But it must be supplemented by Dunois' articles, in *BC*, 20.x.21, and *L'Humanité*, 5.xi.21, which show him attempting to explain his policy and having a hard time of it.

60. *BC*, 1.xii.21.

61. *L'Humanité*, 1.xii.21.

62. These theses are reproduced in *BC*, 24.xi.21.

63. Loriot, *Après Tours*, p. 15.

64. Lengthy excerpts from the thesis and Lenin's comment are reproduced in Degras, *The Communist International*, I, 256–71.

65. The Loriot and Frossard projects are reproduced in *L'Humanité*, 12.xii.21.

66. *L'Humanité*, 12.xii.21.  67. *Ibid.*, 5.xii.21.

68. *Ibid.*, 12.xii.21.  69. *Ibid.*, 19.xii.21.

70. The message, signed by Humbert-Droz, was published in *L'Humanité*, 27.xii.21. It is included in Trotsky's *Kommunisticheskoe dvizhenie*, pp. 109–12.

71. *L'Humanité*, 27.xii.21. No stenographic report of this congress was ever published. *L'Humanité* therefore becomes the primary source for its proceedings.

72. A 27-page typewritten account of the sessions of this committee was drawn up by

Treint and circulated to the federations. *Le Populaire* then obtained a copy and published excerpts of it in installments during March 1922. The first installment appeared March 9. Rappoport's statement is from *Le Populaire*, 17.iii.21.

73. The motion on general policy is published in *L'Humanité*, 31.xii.21.

74. *Ibid.*

75. *Le Populaire*, 27.xii.21.

76. *Le Temps*, 27.xii.21.

77. Parti Communiste, *Un an d'action communiste: Rapport du secrétariat général présenté au 19ᵉ congrès national, 1ᵉʳ congrès* (1921), pp. 14–15, 29.

78. *Ibid.*, pp. 20, 24–25.

79. *L'Humanité*, 5.x.21.

80. These feelings are quite clearly hinted at in Rappoport's "Mémoires" (unpublished ms. in the Bibliothèque Nationale), pp. 246–47. According to this erudite Russian Marxist and Socialist elder statesman and philosopher, Souvarine tried to stir him up against Loriot and turned against him when this effort failed. Seizing the half-legal apparatus of the party, Souvarine became its dictator, "never listening to anyone, and blindly carrying out its orders in publishing, with its funds, *Le Bulletin Communiste*."

81. Frossard, "Socialisme et Syndicalisme: Discours prononcé au Congrès de la C.G.T. à Orléans, le 2 octobre 1920" (1920), pp. 19, 22–23.

82. *BC*, 3.ii.21.

83. *BC*, 5.v.21.

## Chapter eight

Epigraph: *La Revue Communiste*, Feb. 1922, p. 24.

1. *L'Humanité*, 9.i.22.

2. *BC*, 5.i.22. See also Loriot in *L'Humanité*, 2.i.22, and Dunois in *BC*, 12.i.22.

3. *L'Humanité*, 12.i.22.

4. PCF, *L'Action Communiste et la crise du parti: Rapport moral du Secrétariat général présenté au 20ᵉ Congrès national (2ᵉ Congrès du Parti Communiste)* (1922), pp. 33–35.

5. Two undated letters from Zinoviev to the CD of the PCF. In the second of these letters Zinoviev repeated: "Die Person Ihrer Vertreter bestimmen Sie." HDA.

6. Ruth Fischer, *Stalin and German Communism* (Cambridge, Mass., 1948), p. 171.

7. *Ibid.*, p. 180.

8. See Zinoviev, "Anciens Buts, nouvelles voies: De l'Unité du front ouvrier," *IC*, Dec. 1921, cols. 4664–73; the *BC*, 12.i.22, for Zinoviev's speech delivered before the Executive on December 4, 1921; and Jane Degras, *The Communist International, 1919–1943, Documents* (London, 1956), I, 307–16, for Zinoviev's theses on the united front.

9. Degras, I, 312.

10. *Ibid.*, pp. 315–16.

11. *IC*, Dec. 1921, col. 4684.

12. *Ibid.*, col. 4673.

13. *Le Populaire*, 13.iii.22.

14. *Ibid.*, 14.iii.22.

15. *L'Humanité*, 31.xii.22.

16. *BC*, 26.i.22.

17. *L'Humanité*, 23.i.22, 24.i.22.

18. *Ibid.*, 20.i.22.

19. See *La Vague*, Mar. 16–23, 1922, in which Brizon wrote: "C'est notre formule depuis la mal faite coupure de Tours. C'est l'union des petits contre les gros. C'est le tir à droite et non à gauche. C'est le Bloc des Rouges." See also *JP*, 28.i.22 and 21.ii.22.

20. *L'Internationale*, 22.i.22, and *L'Humanité*, 21.i.22.

21. *JP*, 26.i.22.

22. *L'Humanité*, 15.ii.22.

23. *BC*, 19.i.22, 26.i.22.

24. *L'Humanité*, 24.i.22.

25. *BC*, 2.iii.22.

26. *Compte Rendu de la conférence de l'Exécutif Elargi de l'Internationale Communiste, Moscou, 21 février–4 mars 1922* (1922), p. 62.

27. *Ibid.*, p. 56.    28. *Ibid.*, p. 78.

29. *Ibid.*, p. 87.    30. *Ibid.*, p. 109.

31. Trotsky, *Kommunisticheskoe dvizhenie vo Frantsii* (Moscow, 1923), pp. 124–25.

32. *Ibid.*, p. 144.

33. *Ibid.*, p. 147.

34. Treint's speech is printed in *BC*, 13.iv.22. The statement about the "volaille à plumer" was published in *L'Humanité* on May 7, 1922, and soon became identified with Treint.

35. PCF, *L'Action Communiste*, pp. 39–40.

36. Trotsky's speech is in *Kommunisticheskoe dvizhenie*, pp. 148–62. The resolution on the French question was printed in *L'Humanité*, 29.iii.22.

37. *Exécutif Elargi*, p. 225.    38. *L'Internationale*, 14.iii.22.

39. *L'Humanité*, 29.iii.22.    40. *Ibid.*, 6.iii.22.

41. *JP*, 3.iv.22. Commenting on the Berlin conference, Fabre wrote: "We have never, never been so completely justified." *JP*, 7.iv.22.

42. *JP*, 12.iv.22.

43. *L'Humanité*, 6.iv.22.

44. Trotsky, *Kommunisticheskoe dvizhenie*, p. 167.

45. For the proceedings of the conference, see *The Second and Third Internationals and the Vienna Union: Official Report of the Conference between the Executives, held at the Reichstag, Berlin, on the 2nd April, 1922, and following days* (London, n.d.).

46. PCF, *L'Action Communiste*, pp. 69–70, and Carr, *Bolshevik Revolution*, III, 407–12.

47. Quoted in Carr, III, 411.

48. *L'Humanité*, 14.iv.22.    49. *Ibid.*, 16.iv.22.

50. *Le Populaire*, 16.iv.22.    51. *Ibid.*, 2.v.22.

52. See Perceval's remarks, *L'Humanité*, 24.iv.22.

53. *Ibid.*, 24.iv.22.

54. *BC*, 8.vi.22.

55. *L'Humanité*, 7.v.22.

56. PCF, *L'Action Communiste*, p. 44, and *Bericht über die Tätigkeit des Präsidiums und der Exekutive der Kommunistischen Internationale für die Zeit vom 6. marz bis 11. juni 1922* (Hamburg, 1922), p. 33.

57. *Bericht*, pp. 33–35.    58. *Ibid.*, p. 37.

59. *Ibid.*, pp. 38–39.    60. *L'Humanité*, 1.vi.22.

61. *BC*, 17.viii.22, and *Bericht*, pp. 63–65. Trotsky's speech was also published in *Kommunisticheskoe dvizhenie*, pp. 180–204.

62. Trotsky, *Kommunisticheskoe dvizhenie*, p. 313.

63. *Ibid.*, p. 314.

64. "Lettres du camarade Léon Trotsky à quelques camarades français, 1921–1922, à propos des problèmes du mouvement ouvrier français et du développement du parti" (collection in the Bibliothèque Nationale), p. 19.

65. *Ibid.*, p. 29.

66. Humbert-Droz to the Presidium of the Comintern, 18.v.22; Rákosi to Humbert-Droz in Paris, 27.v.22. HDA.

67. Humbert-Droz to Presidium, 30.v.22. HDA.

68. *L'Humanité*, 1.vi.22.    69. *Bericht über die Tätigkeit*, pp. 80–84.

70. *Inprecorr*, 16.vi.22, p. 364.    71. *Bericht*, pp. 89–92.

72. *Ibid.,* pp. 93–94.

73. Trotsky, *Le Salut du Parti Communiste Français* (1922), p. 14. This is the complete French version of Trotsky's speech.

74. *Ibid.,* p. 25.                                   75. *Ibid.,* pp. 27–28.

76. *Ibid.,* p. 31.                                   77. *Ibid.,* p. 35.

78. *Bericht,* p. 108.                                79. *Ibid.,* p. 110.

80. *Ibid.,* p. 112.                                  81. *Ibid.,* p. 115.

82. *Ibid.*                                           83. *Ibid.,* p. 117.

84. *L'Humanité,* 2.vii.22.

85. PCF, *L'Action Communiste et la crise du parti,* p. 56.

86. *Ibid.,* p. 58.

## Chapter nine

1. Humbert-Droz to Presidium, 6.vii.22. HDA.

2. Leon Trotsky, *Le Salut du Parti Communiste Français* (1922), p. 34.

3. Lozovsky had written in September 1920: "The French Communists must make the takeover of the trade unions their principal task. It goes without saying that to leave the CGT is not only a crime, but a mistake." *BC,* 2.vi.21.

4. A. Lozovsky, *Rabochaya Frantsiya* (Moscow, 1923), pp. 56–57.

5. CGTU, *1er Congrès tenu à St.-Etienne du 25 juin au 1er juillet 1922* (n.d.), p. 200.

6. *Ibid.,* pp. 11–12.                                7. *Ibid.,* p. 6.

8. Lozovsky, p. 58.                                   9. *Ibid.,* p. 103.

10. *L'Humanité,* 28.vi.22.

11. Humbert-Droz to Presidium, 6.vii.22. HDA.

12. CGTU, *1er Congrès,* pp. 249, 251.

13. There is a copy of Lafont's circular in HDA.

14. *L'Humanité,* 2.vii.22.

15. Lozovsky, *Les Syndicats et la révolution* (1922), pp. 51–52.

16. Lozovsky recounts these events with obvious amusement in *Rabochaya Frantsiya,* pp. 96–99.

17. Humbert-Droz in a letter to a personal friend (not addressed), 2.ix.22, and Humbert-Droz to Zinoviev, 2.ix.22. HDA.

18. Souvarine to Presidium, 28.vi.22. HDA.

19. Humbert-Droz to Rosmer, 20.vii.22; Dunois to Humbert-Droz, 24.vii.22; and Rosmer to Humbert-Droz, 26.vii.22. HDA.

20. PCF, *L'Action Communiste et la crise du parti: Rapport moral du Secrétariat général présenté au 20e Congrès national (2e Congrès du Parti Communiste)* (1922), p. 63.

21. Zinoviev to Humbert-Droz, 4.vii.22. HDA. Zinoviev further developed his view of the crisis in the PCF in an article entitled "Birth of a Communist Party," which he wrote toward the end of July. In it Zinoviev pointed out that the Center of the French Party were not Centrists. The Centrists in France were actually Rightists. Once these men had been expelled, the existing majority would fuse with the Left to make a true Communist party. Frossard, Zinoviev recalled, said at the meeting of the Executive in June that he would not become the French Serrati. Perhaps. But everything we have seen of Daniel Renoult, Zinoviev continued, makes us fear that if he continues in his present way, he will play this role.

This article had its own history, which is revealing both of the state of relations between the Executive and the PCF at this time and of Zinoviev's enormous vanity. The article first appeared in *Inprecorr* on August 1, 1922. On August 12 Rákosi wrote Humbert-Droz and insisted that Zinoviev's article be published in the *Bulletin Communiste*. Souvarine picked it up from *Inprecorr* and published it on August 17. On August 29 Rákosi wrote once more and asked Humbert-Droz to see personally that the article was published in *L'Humanité*. "The matter involves a question of principle and must be settled once and for all." It was intolerable, he wrote, that *L'Humanité* published the anti-Communist articles of Heine and Méric and then sabotaged Zinoviev's articles. Three days later Rákosi wrote that the failure to print Zinoviev's piece was making a "very bad impression" here. The article was finally published in *L'Humanité* on an inside page on August 27, 1922. Humbert-Droz wrote to Zinoviev on September 2, 1922, and explained the whole affair. Souvarine had published the article in the *Bulletin Communiste* in order to embarrass Frossard. Frossard then saw no reason to publish it in *L'Humanité*. When Humbert-Droz asked him to publish it, he agreed immediately. Concluded Humbert-Droz: "After speaking to Labrousse, I am convinced that there was no deliberate attempt at sabotage, but simply the slowness, negligence, and lack of planning and organization that characterizes all the work of the party, and is unfortunately not confined to one faction." HDA.

22. The text of this resolution may be found in HDA.

23. *L'Humanité*, Aug. 13, 17, and 20, 1922.

24. Humbert-Droz to Zinoviev, 14.viii.22. HDA.

25. *L'Humanité*, Aug. 21, 22, and Sept. 4, 1922. For the two sets of statutes voted upon, see *L'Humanité*, 13.vii.22. The declaration of the Heine-Lavergne group, which had formed a Comité de Défense Communiste, is in HDA. The Federation of the Seine, it will be recalled, was the stronghold of the Parisian Ultra-Left. In April 1921 its members had approved a new set of statutes modeled after those of the Soviet Constitution. Every section (there were over a hundred) was represented on the Executive Committee, which met twice a month. A fourth of these delegates were replaced every four months. The statutes were designed in such a way that they deprived the Executive Committee of any power. Before policy could be made, or even administered, the sections had to be consulted. Federal congresses met every three months and absorbed all the energies of the Federation's members. Only two paid officials were maintained. *L'Internationale*, 26.vi.22, and *BC*, 15.vi.22. During the meetings of the Executive in June, Trotsky had aimed many of his sharpest barbs against the inappropriateness and absurdity of this form of organization for the chief federation of a party that was engaged in the process of trying to seize power. His letter to the Congress of the Seine is in *Kommunisticheskoe dvizhenie vo Frantsii* (Moscow, 1923), pp. 275–77.

26. *BC*, 24.viii.22.

27. Humbert-Droz to Zinoviev, 17.viii.22. HDA.

28. *L'Humanité*, 18.ix.22, 19.ix.22.

29. Humbert-Droz to Zinoviev, 17.ix.22. HDA.

30. *L'Humanité*, 28.ix.22.

31. Humbert-Droz to Zinoviev, 17.ix.22. HDA.

32. Humbert-Droz to Zinoviev, 14.viii.22. HDA.

33. *Ibid.*

34. Humbert-Droz to Zinoviev, 10.ix.22. HDA.

35. *L'Humanité*, 24.ix.22.

36. Humbert-Droz in a personal letter to a friend, 2.ix.22. HDA.

37. There is a good account of the strike in *Krasnyi Internatsional Profsoyuzov*, Sept. 1922, pp. 707–9.

38. Humbert-Droz to Zinoviev, 2.ix.22. HDA.

39. *The Times* (London), 30.viii.22.

40. Zinoviev to Humbert-Droz and Manuilsky, 20.ix.22. HDA.

41. Zinoviev to Manuilsky and Humbert-Droz, 20.ix.22. HDA.

42. *BC*, 5.x.22, 12.x.22.

43. Manuilsky to Humbert-Droz, 26.ix.22, and Humbert-Droz to Zinoviev, 5.x.22, HDA; *BC*, 5.x.22.

44. Humbert-Droz to Zinoviev, 5.x.22. HDA.

45. Frossard, *De Jaurès à Lénine* (1930), pp. 196–97.

46. The development of the negotiations is related in *L'Humanité*, 22.x.22, and from Frossard's point of view in *De Jaurès à Lénine*, pp. 196–97. The correspondence between the factions and the delegation of the International is in HDA.

47. Louise Bodin, *Le Drame politique du Congrès de Paris* (n.d.), pp. 7, 11. Since no stenographic record of this congress was ever published, the chief sources for its proceedings are Bodin's book and *L'Humanité*.

48. *L'Humanité*, 18.x.22.                    49. *Ibid.*, 19.x.22.

50. Bodin, *Le Drame*, p. 27.                51. *L'Humanité*, 19.x.22.

52. *Ibid.*, 20.x.22; Bodin, pp. 49–50.      53. *L'Humanité*, 20.x.22.

54. Bodin, p. 55.                             55. Dormoy in *L'Humanité*, 20.x.22.

56. *La Vague*, Oct. 26–Nov. 1, 1922.        57. *L'Humanité*, 20.x.22.

58. *Ibid.*, 21.x.22.

59. See Godonnèche's article in *La Lutte de Classe*, 30.x.22.

60. Frossard, *De Jaurès à Lénine*, pp. 198–99.

61. Ker to Humbert-Droz, 30.x.22. HDA.

62. *BC*, Jan. 11–18, 1923.

63. *Protokoll des Vierten Kongresses der Kommunistischen Internationale, Petrograd-Moskau, vom 5. November bis 5. Dezember, 1922* (Hamburg, 1923), pp. 40, 864.

64. *Ibid.*, pp. 39–40.

65. Trotsky to Zinoviev, 22.xi.22, with copies to Lenin, Radek, and Bukharin. Trotsky Archives, Harvard University, T759.

66. *Le Populaire*, 1.i.23, and interview with Humbert-Droz, 29.iv.61.

67. According to Alfred Rosmer.

68. *Inprecorr*, 23.viii.23.

69. *IV Congrès Communiste mondial: Résolutions* (1923), p. 26.

70. *Ibid.*, p. 28.                           71. *Ibid.*, p. 35.

72. *Ibid.*, p. 37.                           73. *Ibid.*, p. 40.

74. *Protokoll*, p. 868.

75. *Ibid.*, p. 853. The French version was published in *BC*, Jan. 11–18, 1923.

76. *Protokoll*, p. 877.

77. *Ibid.*, pp. 874–77. For an earlier clash between Jean and Trotsky at the congress, see p. 405 below.

78. *Protokoll*, pp. 878–80.

79. See, for example, p. 264 above.

80. *Ibid.*, p. 524.

81. E. H. Carr, *The Bolshevik Revolution, 1917–1923*, 3 vols. (New York, 1953), III, 460.

82. *Otchet ispolnitelnogo byuro Profinterna II Mezhdunarodnomu Kongressu Revoliutsionnykh Profsoyuzov iyul 1921–noyabr 1922* (Moscow, 1922), pp. 40–41.

83. CGTU, *Congrès national extraordinaire, 2ᵉ Congrès de la C.G.T.U. tenu à Bourges du 12 au 17 novembre 1923 et Conférence féminine du 11 novembre* (n.d.), p. 333.

84. *VO*, 27.x.22.

85. *VO*, 24.xi.22.

86. There is a brief but valuable sketch of Monmousseau in Kriegel, I, 414–16. For Sémard, see André Marty, *Pierre Sémard*, 4th ed. (1945).

87. *Krasnyi Internatsional Profsoyuzov*, Apr. 1924, pp. 293–94.

88. According to Humbert-Droz in conversation with the author, 29.iv.61, in Zurich.

89. There is an abridged account of the Second Congress of the Profintern in *La Lutte de Classe*, 30.xii.22, pp. 10–15.

90. *BC*, Jan. 11–18, 1923.

91. *La Lutte de Classe*, 30.xii.22.

92. *Krasnyi Internatsional Profsoyuzov*, Apr. 1924, p. 294.

93. Marguérite Rosmer to Humbert-Droz, 2.xi.22. HDA.

94. Trotsky to Zinoviev, 22.xi.22. Trotsky Archives, Harvard University, T759.

95. *Protokoll*, pp. 40, 985.

96. Interview with Humbert-Droz, 29.iv.61.

97. Interview with Alfred Rosmer, 13.ii.61.

98. Humbert-Droz to Zinoviev, Trotsky, and Kolarov, 30.xii.22. HDA.

99. *Cahiers Communistes*, 14.xii.22.

100. *Clarté*, 15.xi.22.

101. *L'Humanité*, 7.xii.22.

102. Humbert-Droz to Zinoviev, Trotsky, and Kolarov, 30.xii.22. HDA.

103. *Ibid.* and Rosmer, *Moscou sous Lénine* (1953), p. 246.

104. *L'Humanité*, 17.xii.22.

105. *Ibid.*

106. Interview with Rosmer, 13.ii.61.

107. For example, Dunois in *BC*, Jan. 11–18, 1923; Monatte in *La Révolution Prolétarienne*, Feb. 1925; and Rosmer, *Moscou sous Lénine*, p. 240.

108. Humbert-Droz to Zinoviev, Trotsky, and Kolarov, Jan. 9–11, 1923. HDA.

109. According to Mildred J. Headings, *French Freemasonry under the Third Republic* (Baltimore, Md., 1949), p. 75.

110. Humbert-Droz to Zinoviev, Trotsky, and Kolarov, Jan. 9–11, 1923; Sellier to Executive, 3.i.23; and interview with Humbert-Droz, 29.iv.61.

111. Copies of Frossard's letters of resignation are in HDA.

112. Frossard, *De Jaurès à Lénine*, p. 228.

113. *Kommunisticheskoe dvizhenie vo Frantsii*.

114. *Protokoll*, pp. 294–95.  115. *BC*, 27.vii.22.

116. *L'Humanité*, 4.vi.22.  117. *BC*, 17.viii.22.

118. *L'Humanité*, 16.vi.22.  119. *BC*, 22.vi.22.

120. *L'Action Communiste et la crise du parti*, pp. 101–2. Eberlein cited this same figure at the Fourth Congress. *Bulletin du IV Congrès de l'Internationale Communiste* (Moscow, 1922), November 23, 1922, p. 1. See also *BEIPI*, Mar. 1955, p. 24, which opts for 60,000, after analyzing the official figures.

121. *Le Populaire* noted on March 1, 1922, that the Communist candidate for the General Council of Sisteron (Basses-Alpes) presented himself as a Socialist, a Republican, and a freethinker. He did not mention Communism.

## Chapter ten

Epigraph: HDA.

1. *Inprecorr*, 16.vi.22.

2. Jane Degras, *The Communist International, 1919–1943, Documents* (London, 1956), I, 248.

3. Frossard, *La Décomposition du Communisme* (n.d.), pp. 90–94.

4. Humbert-Droz to Zinoviev, Trotsky, and Kolarov, Jan. 9–11, 1923. HDA.

5. *BC*, Jan. 11–18, 1923.    6. *BC*, 15.ii.23.

7. *BC*, 22.ii.23.    8. *BC*, 15.ii.23.

9. Humbert-Droz to Zinoviev, Trotsky, and Kolarov, 16.i.23. HDA.

10. Degras, *The Communist International*, I, 255.

11. *Ibid.*, p. 272.

12. *Protokoll des Vierten Kongresses der Kommunistischen Internationale, Petrograd-Moskau, vom 5. November bis 5. Dezember, 1922* (Hamburg, 1923), pp. 40, 864.

13. E. H. Carr, *The Bolshevik Revolution, 1917–1923* (New York, 1953), III, 454–55.

14. Degras, I, 431–33.

15. On February 2, 1923, Zinoviev wrote Humbert-Droz urging him to return to Paris as soon as possible: "One can say without exaggeration that the French section is now our most important section. To a certain extent, the fate of the Communist International rests in its hands." HDA. See also p. 303 above.

16. *Cour de Justice: Affaire Cachin, Monmousseau . . . et autres inculpés d'attentat contre la sûreté de l'Etat* (1923), p. 10. Paquereaux, unable to fulfill his mandate, was replaced by Ker.

17. *L'Humanité*, 4.i.23.

18. *Affaire Cachin*, p. 14.

19. *L'Humanité*, 10.i.23.

20. Maurice Laporte, *Les Mystères du Kremlin* (1928), pp. 125–26. Laporte was one of the principal leaders of the Federation of Young Communists at the time. For this reason his testimony is valuable, but it must be used with extreme caution because of his unfortunate predilection for exaggeration and sensationalism.

21. *Affaire Cachin*, pp. 16–17.

22. *Ibid.*, pp. 17–18.

23. *L'Humanité*, 8.i.23, 9.i.23.

24. The indictment against the arrested Communists claimed: "Since that time, the committee has undergone a change, and there are now departmental Action Committees throughout France." *Affaire Cachin*, p. 12.

25. *L'Humanité*, 14.i.23.

26. *Ibid.*, 26.i.23.

27. According to Lozovsky in *IC*, June 1923, pp. 10–11.

28. *BC*, 12.iv.23.

29. *Affaire Cachin*, pp. 1–2.

30. *L'Humanité*, 1.vi.23.

31. Humbert-Droz to Zinoviev, 14.vi.23. HDA.

32. *IC*, June 1923, p. 5.

33. Humbert-Droz to Zinoviev, 14.vi.23. HDA.

34. *IC*, June 1923, p. 5.

35. *L'Avant-Garde*, 1.xi.24.

36. Laporte, *Mystères du Kremlin*, p. 111. Laporte mentions the figure of a million francs. Vaillant-Couturier, Doriot, and Provost were in charge of this fund.

37. *Affaire Cachin*, p. 18.

38. *L'Avant-Garde*, May 1924. Vujović speaks of tens of thousands of pamphlets and millions of leaflets. *Internationale Presse-Korrespondenz*, 10.v.24, p. 11.

39. Henri Barbé, "Souvenirs de militant et de dirigeant communiste" (ms. at the Hoover Institution), pp. 19–33.

40. *Ibid.*, pp. 29–30. André Marty, *Le Procès de Mayence* (1924), p. 6, claimed that by April 20, 1923, 175 regiments and diverse units had put themselves into contact with the party.

41. Marty lists a number of cases of fraternization and insubordination and cites army documents to show the concern which the party's activities had occasioned in official quarters. *Ibid.,* pp. 8–15. See also André Ferrat, *Histoire du Parti Communiste Français* (1931), pp. 133–34.

42. Barbé, "Souvenirs de militant et de dirigeant communiste" (ms. at the Hoover Institution), pp. 26–28. Barbé found that his troops tended to break down into two groups: the Parisians and Bretons, on the one hand, and those from the occupied regions, on the other. The latter were hostile to the Germans. Vujović admitted that the Belgians "proved themselves especially impervious to our propaganda." *Internationale Presse-Korrespondenz,* 10.v.24, p. 11.

43. *La Révolution Prolétarienne,* July 1925, pp. 20–21.

44. For example, Dunois in *L'Humanité,* 2.i.23.

45. *BC,* 5.iv.23.

46. Humbert-Droz to Zinoviev, 13.iii.23. HDA.

47. Humbert-Droz to Zinoviev, Trotsky, and Kolarov, 16.i.23. HDA.

48. *L'Humanité,* 22.i.23.

49. *Ibid.,* 5.i.23.

50. According to Souvarine, Bukharin's speech at the Fourth Congress had caused a great deal of concern within the French delegation. To allay these fears, Souvarine brought home with him from Moscow a statement by Bukharin indicating that his speech expressed only his personal point of view, and had not been accepted or even discussed by the International. This statement was published in *L'Humanité* on January 17, 1923. Four days later, at the National Council, Souvarine emphasized that although he was willing to accept the idea of Soviet intervention in a counterrevolutionary country, the signing of a military alliance between a proletarian State and a bourgeois government was another matter. The problem, he concluded, would have to be discussed further. Kolarov, the International's delegate, did not insist. He was satisfied to observe that "one must applaud the Red Army enthusiastically for its contribution to world revolution, for being an admirable instrument of proletarian emancipation in the hands of the International." *L'Humanité,* 22.i.23.

On January 25 *L'Humanité* published a letter from Bukharin to Souvarine, in which the Bolshevik leader tried to clarify his position and put the fears of his French comrades to rest. The European and world revolution, he wrote, would not be achieved for decades. In the interim many proletarian States would be forced to sign alliances with oppressed or semi-oppressed bourgeois States. Each one of these agreements would have to be evaluated from the point of view of "the general interests of the world proletarian movement." It went without saying that agreements that would transform proletarian States into instruments of imperialism or instruments of oppression of other peoples would not be acceptable. It was the Communist International, Bukharin concluded, that would decide which agreements were permissible.

Apparently Bukharin's clarification was not sufficient for some of the French Communists, for Humbert-Droz himself felt called upon to spell out the Comintern's position with even greater clarity: "Pacifists we are; but we will be all the better pacifists to the extent that we get used to the idea of revolutionary violence and combat the false pacifism of the Social Democrats, which is nothing but a vulgar show, and the false pacifism of the Tolstoyans, which is a dangerous illusion." (*BC,* 12.iv.23.) The question had more than academic interest in view of the situation in the Ruhr and the ambivalence of Soviet policy toward Germany.

51. See Humbert-Droz to Cachin, 2.iv.23, and Humbert-Droz to Zinoviev and Trotsky, 3.iv.23. HDA.

52. *BC*, 29.iii.23.
53. Humbert-Droz to Zinoviev, 14.vi.23. HDA.
54. *Ibid.*                    55. *Ibid.*
56. HDA.                       57. *Ibid.*
58. *BC*, 12.vii.23.           59. *Ibid.*
60. SFIO, *11ᵉ Congrès*, pp. 95–113.        61. *L'Humanité*, 31.i.23, 18.ii.23.
62. *Ibid.*, Mar. 3, 4, and 5, 1923.        63. *BC*, 20.ix.23.
64. *Ibid.*, 22.iii.23.
65. Humbert-Droz to Zinoviev and Trotsky, 21.iv.23. HDA.
66. *L'Humanité*, 22.iii.23.
67. Humbert-Droz to Zinoviev, 13.iii.23. HDA.
68. Humbert-Droz to Cachin, 2.iv.23. HDA.
69. *BC*, 4.i.24.
70. Eugen Weber, *Action Française: Royalism and Reaction in Twentieth-Century France* (Stanford, Calif., 1962), p. 142.
71. Humbert-Droz to Zinoviev, 14.vi.23. HDA.
72. *L'Humanité*, June 3, 8, and 10, 1923.
73. *Ibid.*, 9.vi.23.
74. *Ibid.*, 24.vi.23.
75. Humbert-Droz to Zinoviev, 14.vi.23. HDA.
76. Trotsky, *Kommunisticheskoe dvizhenie vo Frantsii* (Moscow, 1923), pp. 142–43.
77. *Journal Officiel*, 15.vi.23.
78. *Ibid.*
79. Humbert-Droz to Zinoviev, 14.vi.23. HDA.
80. *L'Humanité*, 15.ix.23.
81. Humbert-Droz to Zinoviev, 29.ix.23. HDA.
82. Humbert-Droz to Zinoviev and Trotsky, 21.iv.23. HDA.
83. Humbert-Droz to Zinoviev, 29.ix.23. HDA.
84. The episode is recounted in Humbert-Droz to Zinoviev, 29.ix.23. HDA.
85. See n. 50 above.
86. Humbert-Droz to Zinoviev and Trotsky, 3.iv.23, HDA, and *L'Oeil de Moscou à Paris* (1964), p. 92.
87. Humbert-Droz to Zinoviev, 29.ix.23. HDA.
88. Humbert-Droz to Zinoviev, 13.iii.23. HDA.
89. Humbert-Droz to Zinoviev, 21.iv.23. HDA.
90. Humbert-Droz to Zinoviev, 29.ix.23. HDA.
91. *Inprecorr*, 22.vi.23, p. 439.
92. *Ibid.*
93. Humbert-Droz to Zinoviev, 14.vi.23 and 6.ix.23. HDA.
94. *L'Humanité*, 12.viii.23.
95. *Ibid.*, 22.viii.23.
96. For the details of this shift, see E. H. Carr, *The Interregnum, 1923–1924* (New York, 1954), pp. 174ff.
97. Quoted in Werner T. Angress, *Stillborn Revolution: The Communist Bid for Power in Germany, 1921–1923* (Princeton, N.J., 1963), p. 315.
98. Carr, *Interregnum*, p. 174.
99. *Ibid.*, p. 180.
100. For the application of the Schlageter line in Germany, see Angress, *Stillborn Revolution*, pp. 335–55.
101. Carr, *Interregnum*, p. 204, and Angress, pp. 378–406.
102. Ruth Fischer, *Stalin and German Communism* (Cambridge, Mass., 1948), p. 312.

103. Angress, p. 405.

104. In the case of Zinoviev, it was just the contrary. For the President of the Comintern, who was deeply involved in the Bulgarian disaster, now more than ever needed a revolutionary success to bolster his own position.

105. Humbert-Droz to Zinoviev, 5.x.23. HDA.

106. *BC*, 2.viii.23.

107. *Ibid.*, 16.viii.23.

108. *L'Humanité*, 11.ix.23.

109. See Grumbach's series "Réparations ou politique de guerre," in *Le Populaire*, Sept. 5, 7, 12, and 15, 1923.

110. *Le Populaire*, 28.ix.23.     111. *L'Humanité*, 17.ix.23.

112. HDA.     113. *Ibid.*

114. Humbert-Droz to Zinoviev, 5.x.23.

115. Rosmer, *Moscou sous Lénine* (1953), p. 276.

116. *L'Humanité*, 6.x.23.

117. *L'Avant-Garde*, Oct. 1–15, 1923, and *VO*, 5.x.23.

118. *VO*, 26.x.23.

119. Souvarine to Russian Opposition, Dec. 1927. Trotsky Archives, Harvard University, T1059.

120. Humbert-Droz to Zinoviev, 29.ix.23. HDA.

121. *L'Humanité*, 26.x.23.

122. Humbert-Droz to Zinoviev, 5.x.23. HDA.

123. *Congrès national extraordinaire: 2ᵉ Congrès de la C.G.T.U. tenu à Bourges*, p. 495; *Bulletin Bi-Mensuel de l'Internationale Syndicale Rouge*, 17.viii.23; and *VO*, 23.ii.23.

124. Humbert-Droz to Zinoviev, 15.x.23. HDA.

125. Humbert-Droz to Zinoviev, 5.x.23. HDA.

126. Humbert-Droz to Zinoviev, 22.x.23. HDA. The speakers of the CGTU met with the same indifference. *2ᵉ Congrès de la C.G.T.U.*, p. 392.

127. Rosmer, *Moscou sous Lénine*, p. 276.

128. Angress, *Stillborn Revolution*, pp. 440–42.

129. *Ibid.*, pp. 451–62.     130. *L'Humanité*, 24.x.23.

131. *Ibid.*, 26.x.23.     132. *Ibid.*, 12.xi.23.

133. Humbert-Droz to Zinoviev, 23.xi.23. HDA.

134. Humbert-Droz to Zinoviev, 8.xii.23.

135. Trotsky, *Kommunisticheskoe dvizhenie*, pp. 17–18. Monatte joined the party in the spring of 1923.

136. *VO*, 22.xii.22.     137. *2ᵉ Congrès de la C.G.T.U.*, p. 39.

138. *Ibid.*, pp. 334–35.     139. *Ibid.*, pp. 20–21.

140. *L'Humanité*, 30.vi.23.     141. *Ibid.*, 1.vii.23.

142. *VO*, 24.viii.23.

143. For the position of the minority, see *L'Humanité*, 8.vii.23, and *2ᵉ Congrès*, pp. 21–23.

144. *2ᵉ Congrès*, p. 74.     145. *Ibid.*, p. 46.

146. *Ibid.*, p. 376.     147. *VO*, 16.i.25.

148. Jean Montreuil, *Histoire du mouvement ouvrier en France, des origines à nos jours* (1948), p. 382.

149. *L'Humanité*, 16.x.23, and Humbert-Droz to Zinoviev, 22.x.23. HDA.

150. *BC*, 25.x.23.

151. Humbert-Droz to Zinoviev, 2.i.24. HDA.

152. *VO*, 4.i.24.

153. HDA.

154. 5.x.23. HDA.

155. Humbert-Droz to Zinoviev, 23.xi.23. HDA.

156. Humbert-Droz to Zinoviev, 8.xii.23. HDA.

157. Treint to the Executive, 14.xii.23. HDA.

158. Humbert-Droz to Zinoviev, 2.i.24. HDA.

159. *L'Humanité*, 3.i.24.                        160. Marcel Ollivier in *ibid.*, 10.i.24.

161. Paul Marion in *ibid.*, 3.i.24.              162. Maurice Boin in *ibid.*, 6.i.24.

163. *BC*, 4.i.24.

164. Humbert-Droz to Zinoviev, 2.i.24. HDA.

165. *L'Humanité*, 14.i.24.

166. *Internationale Presse-Korrespondenz*, 26.ii.24, p. 294.

167. *3e Congrès national tenu à Lyon les 20, 21, 22, 23 janvier 1924: Adresses et résolutions* (1924), p. 8. No stenographic account of this congress was ever published.

168. *Ibid.*, p. 10.                              169. *Ibid.*, p. 13.

170. *Ibid.*, p. 15.                              171. *L'Humanité*, 23.i.23.

172. *Ibid.*, 24.i.24.                            173. *Ibid.*, 26.i.24.

174. See *3e Congrès national* for the text of these resolutions.

175. *L'Humanité*, 26.i.24.

176. *BC*, 15.ii.24.

## Chapter eleven

Epigraph: *BC*, 29.iii.23.

1. Souvarine, *Staline* (1935), p. 342.

2. Robert Vincent Daniels, *The Conscience of the Revolution: Communist Opposition in Soviet Russia* (Cambridge, Mass., 1960), p. 154.

3. E. H. Carr, *Socialism in One Country, 1924–1926*, 3 vols. (London, 1958–64), I, 96, 100. This entire section owes a great deal to Professor Carr's brilliant study.

4. E. H. Carr, *The Bolshevik Revolution, 1917–1923*, 3 vols. (New York, 1953), II, 291.

5. Crane Brinton, *The Anatomy of Revolution*, rev. Vintage ed. (New York, 1957), p. 215.

6. Carr, *Socialism in One Country*, I, 130–31.

7. Trotsky, *Terror and Communism* (Ann Arbor, Mich., 1961), p. 98.

8. This was the central theme of Trotsky's speech at the Fourth World Congress. *Protokoll des Vierten Kongresses der Kommunistischen Internationale, Petrograd-Moskau, vom 5. November bis 5. Dezember, 1922* (Hamburg, 1923), p. 284.

9. *Ibid.*, pp. 317–18.

10. *Ibid.*, p. 222.

11. *Ibid.*, pp. 281–87.

12. In his letter to Souvarine in January 1923, Bukharin had spoken of the decades that would pass before the Revolution would triumph in Europe and throughout the world. See Chap. 10, n. 50.

13. Carr, *Socialism in One Country*, I, v–vi.

14. Daniels, *Conscience of the Revolution*, p. 176.

15. Rosmer, *Moscou sous Lénine* (1953), pp. 282–83, and Souvarine, *Staline*, p. 342.

16. Daniels, *Conscience*, p. 194.

17. Carr, *The Interregnum, 1923–1924* (New York, 1954), p. 368. Professor Carr has published a full translation of this document, pp. 367–73.

18. Trotsky, *Cours nouveau* (1924?), pp. 62–63.

19. *Protokoll des Vierten Kongresses*, p. 230.

20. Daniels, *Conscience*, p. 190.

21. Lenin's notes are translated and reproduced in full in Richard Pipes, *The Formation of the Soviet Union: Communism and Nationalism, 1917–1923* (Cambridge, Mass., 1954), p. 275.

22. Daniels, p. 182, and Isaac Deutscher, *The Prophet Unarmed: Trotsky, 1921–1929* (New York, 1959), p. 90.

23. As Lunacharsky pointed out in *Revolutionary Silhouettes*, Lenin was incapable of seeing things from the point of view of his adversary. Quoted in Max Eastman, *Since Lenin Died* (London, 1925), p. 134.

24. *Protokoll des Vierten Kongresses*, pp. 230–31.

25. *Ibid.*, p. 228; Pipes, *Formation of the Soviet Union*, pp. 273–74; and Daniels, p. 190.

26. Pipes, *Formation*, pp. 273–75.

27. For the relationship between Lenin and Stalin, see the discussion by Theodore H. Von Laue in *Why Lenin? Why Stalin?* (Philadelphia and New York, 1964), pp. 202–5.

28. Carr, *Interregnum*, pp. 342–43.

29. Deutscher, *Prophet Unarmed*, pp. 92–93.

30. Daniels, *Conscience*, p. 198.

31. *Ibid.*, pp. 211–12.

32. Eastman, *Since Lenin Died*, pp. 142–43.

33. For the response of the Politburo, see *ibid.*, pp. 143–45; the Platform of the 46 is reproduced and translated in Carr, *Interregnum*, pp. 367–73.

34. Quoted in Daniels, *Conscience*, p. 220.

35. Quoted in Carr, *Interregnum*, p. 309.

36. Daniels, *Conscience*, pp. 220–23, and Carr, *Interregnum*, p. 306.

37. Trotsky, *Cours nouveau*, p. 101.      38. *Ibid.*, p. 98.

39. *Ibid.*, p. 100.                          40. *Ibid.*, pp. 104–5.

41. Quoted in Carr, *Interregnum*, p. 316.      42. Quoted in *ibid.*, p. 317.

43. *Ibid.*, pp. 317–18.                      44. *Ibid.*, p. 326.

45. Quoted from Daniels, *Conscience*, p. 234.

46. Quoted in *ibid.*, p. 234.

47. Quoted in *ibid.*, p. 238.

48. Quoted in Deutscher, *Prophet Unarmed*, p. 139.

49. Quoted in Daniels, p. 240.

50. *Protokoll des Vierten Kongresses*, p. 859.

51. For the alignment of the Bolshevik leaders on the question of the German revolution, see Daniels, pp. 214–15, and Carr, *Interregnum*, pp. 201–3.

52. Werner T. Angress, *Stillborn Revolution: The Communist Bid for Power in Germany, 1921–1923* (Princeton, N.J., 1963), pp. 464–65, and Carr, *Interregnum*, p. 327.

53. Quoted in Angress, *Stillborn Revolution*, p. 463.

54. *Ibid.*, p. 462, and Carr, *Interregnum*, pp. 230–33.

55. Angress, p. 464.

56. Quoted in Carr, *Interregnum*, pp. 234–35.

57. Quoted in *ibid.*, p. 236.                58. *Ibid.*

59. *Ibid.*, p. 328.                          60. *Ibid.*, p. 329.

61. *Ibid.*, p. 238.                          62. Angress, pp. 471–73.

63. Carr, *Interregnum*, pp. 234–35, 240–41.

64. *BC*, 19.iv.23. Souvarine did not mention Zinoviev, whom he no doubt regarded as merely another talented mortal. In 1923 Souvarine had 29 articles in the *Bulletin Communiste*, Trotsky 24, and Zinoviev only 16.

65. *BC*, 6.ix.23.

66. In his preface to Trotsky's *Cours nouveau*, pp. 9–11.

67. *L'Humanité*, 20.iv.23.                68. *BC*, 6.xii.23.

69. *Ibid.*, 20.xii.23.                    70. *Ibid.*, 4.i.24.

71. Souvarine to Zinoviev, 6.i.24. Mentioned by Branko Lazitch in his essay, "Two Instruments of Control by the Comintern: The Delegates of the ECCI and the Party Representatives in Moscow," unpublished ms., p. 14.

72. According to Suzanne Girault at the Federal Assembly of the Seine, April 11, 1924; reported in *L'Humanité*, 13.iv.24.

73. *Ibid.*, 18.ii.24.

74. *BC*, 8.ii.24.

75. *BC*, 4.iv.24. So far as I know, Isaac Deutscher is mistaken when he writes (in *The Prophet Unarmed*, pp. 140–41) that the French CD had protested to Moscow against the defamation of Trotsky before the end of 1923. It is possible, however, that Souvarine had spoken to Zinoviev in his own name. Lazitch, "Two Instruments of Control," p. 14.

76. *BC*, 4.iv.24.

77. *Ibid.*, 7.iii.24.

78. For the origins of the letter, see Souvarine's statement at the Thirteenth Party Congress in Moscow: *Trinadtsatyi sezd Rossiskoi Kommunisticheskoi Partii (Bolshevikov)* (Moscow, 1924), p. 371. The letter is published in *BC*, 4.iv.24. Rosmer told me that he was not in favor of the approach of the open letter, but wrote it only when delegated by the CD. Interview, 2.xii.60.

79. *Trinadtsatyi sezd*, p. 371.         80. *L'Humanité*, 2.ii.24.

81. *Ibid.*, 9.ii.24.                     82. *BC*, 15.ii.24.

83. *L'Humanité*, 13.iii.24. The article was dated Feb. 14, from Moscow.

84. *BC*, 22.ii.24.                       85. *Ibid.*, 14.iii.24.

86. *Ibid.*, 21.iii.24.                   87. *Ibid.*, 28.iii.24.

88. According to Treint, in *Cahiers du Bolchévisme*, 28.xi.24, p. 74.

89. Souvarine mentioned such a motion of censure in *BC*, 7.iii.24. At that time he pointed out that he had published 22 articles for the majority and only five for the minority.

90. These theses were never made public, but Sellier discussed them in *BC*, 2.v.24.

91. *BC*, 4.iv.24.

92. *Ibid.*, 28.iii.24.

93. Interview with Rosmer, 13.ii.61.

94. Souvarine's theses are reproduced in *BC*, 11.iv.24.

95. Monatte insisted that his statement be published in the *Bulletin Communiste*. It was, in *BC*, 4.iv.24.

96. *BC*, 28.iii.24.

97. This letter is quoted *in extenso* by Lazitch, "Two Instruments of Control," p. 14.

98. *BC*, 4.iv.24.                         99. *Cours nouveau*, pp. 10–11.

100. *BC*, 4.iv.24.                        101. *L'Humanité*, 11.iv.24.

102. *Ibid.*, 4.iv.24.                     103. *Ibid.*, 13.iv.24.

104. Letter from a "Léon" to an unknown correspondent, Paris, 12.iv.24. Rappoport Papers. This account corresponds in most particulars with *L'Humanité*'s.

105. *BC*, 18.iv.24.

106. *Ibid.*, 11.iv.24.

107. See Dunois in *IC*, Feb.–Apr. 1924, p. 127. Monatte had written the same thing in his pamphlet *Les Commissions syndicales* (1923), p. 3, but at that time no one had thought to protest.

108. Their letters of resignation were published in *BC*, 23.v.24.

109. Interview with Rosmer, 13.ii.61.

110. See his articles in *BC*, 2.v.24, 9.v.24.

111. Rosmer, Monatte, and Delagarde, *Réponse du B.P. à la lettre de Monatte, Rosmer et Delagarde* (1924), p. 7, and *BC*, 9.v.24.

112. Dunois to Sellier, 8.iv.24. Monatte Archives. The letter was written and sent from Moscow.

113. *BC*, 2.v.24.

114. *Ibid.*, 23.v.24.

115. Florimond Bonte to Monatte, 28.iii.24. Monatte Archives. The letter was sent from Lille.

116. Maurice Thorez to Souvarine, 11.iv.24. *BEIPI*, May 1–15, 1950, p. 6.

117. Thorez to Souvarine, 2.v.24. *Ibid.*, p. 7.

118. Bruyère to Souvarine, 15.iv.24. Monatte Archives.

119. Louis Bouët to Monatte, 24.v.24. Monatte Archives.

120. *L'Humanité*, 17.xii.24.

121. SFIO, *3ᵉ Congrès* [1906], pp. 50–51.

122. See his articles in *La Vague*, Oct. 27–Nov. 3 and Nov. 17–24, 1923.

123. *Le Populaire*, 4.ii.24.

124. Such a circular is contained in the Arbetarrörelsens Arkiv in Stockholm.

125. See *Le Populaire* and *L'Humanité* for Mar. 1924. On March 26, *Le Populaire* ran a manifesto entitled: "Comment les Communistes, en divisant la classe ouvrière, font le jeu du Bloc National et de la réaction capitaliste." This was typical.

126. To the extent that Monmousseau wrote on May 16, 1924: "For the first time in the history of the working-class movement, a party freed of all careerists has run on a class program." *VO*.

127. *BC*, 25.iv.24.

128. *Le Temps*, 11.v.24.

129. *Le Populaire*, 24.v.24. To support his assertion, Zoretti pointed out that the total of votes (106,700) given to Alexandre Blanc, Celestin Philbois, Aussoleil, René Nicod, Georges Lévy, Marucci, and Maurel in 1919 had dropped by 30 per cent (to 77,200).

130. *BC*, 13.vi.24.

131. This motion was not reported in *L'Humanité*, but it was mentioned by Kleine. *L'Humanité*, 15.v.24.

132. *Ibid.* Thorez wrote Souvarine that his federation would probably pass this motion. He himself favored it. Thorez to Souvarine, 2.v.24; *BEIPI*, May 1–15, 1950, p. 7.

133. See the letter from Parreye, a member of the CD of the Federation of the Nord, to Monatte, May 19, 1924. Monatte Archives.

134. *Trinadtsatyi sezd*, p. 370. The telegram was published in *L'Humanité*, 20.v.24.

135. *L'Humanité*, 19.v.24.

136. *BC*, 6.vi.24.

137. *L'Humanité*, 3.vi.24.

138. Souvarine and Rosmer had already left Paris for Moscow.

139. *L'Humanité*, 2.vi.24.

140. Rosmer to Monatte, 6.vi.24. Monatte Archives.

141. Ruth Fischer, *Stalin and German Communism* (Cambridge, Mass., 1948), pp. 404–5.

142. *Vᵉ Congrès de l'Internationale Communiste (17 juin–8 juillet, 1924): Compte rendu analytique* (1924), pp. 8–9.

143. Barbé, "Souvenirs de militant et de dirigeant communiste" (ms. at the Hoover Institution), pp. 53–54.

144. Interview with Rosmer, 13.ii.61.

145. Fischer, *Stalin*, pp. 403–4.

146. *L'Humanité*, 22.iv.24.

147. *Vᵉ Congrès*, pp. 24–25.

148. *Ibid.*, p. 21.

149. *Ibid.*, p. 337.

150. *Ibid.*, pp. 23–24.

151. *Ibid.*, p. 48.

152. Fischer, *Stalin*, p. 403.

153. Barbé, "Souvenirs," p. 54.

154. *Ibid.*, pp. 53–54.

155. *Ibid.*, pp. 55–56.

156. *Ibid.*, p. 56.

157. *Vᵉ Congrès*, pp. 341–42.

158. My account of these discussions is based on a letter from Rosmer to Monatte, 18.vii.24. Monatte Archives.

159. *Vᵉ Congrès*, p. 464.

160. *Ibid.* This letter was written, and there is a copy of it in the archives of Humbert-Droz. However, I can find no evidence that it was ever published. Souvarine refused to attend the meeting, and learned of his expulsion the next day in *Pravda*.

161. Rosmer to Monatte, 18.vii.24. Monatte Archives.

162. *Ibid.*, 11.viii.24.

163. It was Zinoviev himself who revealed this embarrassing fact, in his report to the Fifth World Congress. *Vᵉ Congrès*, p. 48.

## Chapter twelve

Epigraph: *BC*, 22.viii.24.

1. According to E. H. Carr, Treint was the first Western Communist to use the phrase. *Socialism in One Country, 1924–1926*, 3 vols. (London, 1958–64), III, 92.

2. *Vᵉ Congrès de l'Internationale Communiste (17 juin–8 juillet, 1924): Compte rendu analytique* (1924), pp. 381–82.

3. *Inprecorr*, 22.i.25, p. 64.

4. *Exécutif Elargi de l'Internationale Communiste: Compte rendu analytique de la session du 21 mars au 6 avril 1925* (1925), p. 261.

5. *Inprecorr*, 16.x.24, p. 809.

6. *BC*, 22.viii.24.

7. The theory of the new organization was most fully developed by Roger Gaillard in his pamphlet *Les Cellules communistes d'usines* (1924), pp. 3–6.

8. *Les Questions d'organisation au Vᵉ Congrès de l'I.C.* (1925), p. 71.

9. *Inprecorr*, 27.ii.24, pp. 111–12. This resolution was not published in the *Bulletin Communiste* until April 4, 1924.

10. *L'Humanité*, 24.i.24.

11. *BC*, 4.iv.24.

12. See Gérard Walter, *Histoire du Parti Communiste Français* (1948), pp. 164–69.

13. The 27 regions are listed in *ibid.*, pp. 169–70.

14. They were discussed quite openly in the Comintern's first organizational conference, reported in *Inprecorr*, 30.iii.25.

15. In February 1925 the French Opposition wrote the Presidium, "Les cellules qu'on a voulu constituer vite et tout d'un coup existent bien sur le papier, mais leur existence réelle est morne." (Trotsky Archives, Harvard University, T849.) The Comintern's report for the year 1925–26 acknowledged that the majority of the PCF's cells had no active life. *Otchet ispolkoma Kominterna (aprel 1925–yanvar 1926)* (Moscow, Leningrad, 1926).

16. Maurice Duverger, *Political Parties* (New York, 1963 ed.), pp. 32–35, and Philip Williams, *Politics in Post-War France: Parties and the Constitution in the Fourth Republic* (New York, 1954), p. 48.

17. Again, precise figures are lacking, but the evidence seems to suggest that the party

became more proletarian. (André Ferrat, *Histoire du Parti Communiste Français, 1931,* p. 144.) Borkenau, for example, writing in 1939, was forced to admit that France was the one European country where the Communist Party was a truly working-class organization. *World Communism* (Ann Arbor, Mich., 1962), pp. 374, 397.

18. Charles A. Micaud, *Communism and the French Left* (New York, 1962), p. 83, and Duverger, *Political Parties,* pp. 124–32.

19. "Report on the incorporation of the Communist parliamentary Group into the Administrative Apparatus of the Party," dated May 18, 1924. There is a copy of this report in the Marty Archives.

20. These changes are described in the "Rapport moral du Secrétariat général," published as a special number in the *Cahiers du Bolchévisme,* 20.xii.24.

21. *Ibid.,* 15.x.25, p. 1963.

22. Barbé, "Souvenirs de militant et de dirigeant communiste" (ms. at the Hoover Institution), p. 74.

23. Charles Rappoport, "Mémoires" (unpublished ms. in the Bibliothèque Nationale), p. 261, and Souvarine to Russian Opposition, Dec. 1927. Trotsky Archives, T1059.

24. SFIO, *11e Congrès* [Amiens, 1914], pp. 44–45.

25. Souvarine to Russian Opposition, Dec. 1927. In this letter Souvarine gives the history of Russian aid to the PCF.

26. *L'Humanité,* 21.i.23.

27. Maurice Laporte gives various examples of this aid in *Les Mystères du Kremlin* (1928), pp. 98, 102, and 104. Barbé, whose knowledge of the inner workings of the party begins with 1922, speaks of a million francs per month for use in anti-militarist and anti-colonialist work ("Souvenirs," pp. 35–36); this is surely an exaggeration.

28. Rosmer, *Moscou sous Lénine* (1953), pp. 242–43, and Souvarine to Russian Opposition, Dec. 1927.

29. Humbert-Droz to Zinoviev, 12.ii.23. HDA.

30. Souvarine to Russian Opposition, Dec. 1927.

31. *Ibid.*

32. Rosmer to Monatte, 11.viii.24. (Monatte Archives.) Rosmer learned of the deficit through a meeting of the CD that he attended on August 6.

33. Laporte, *Mystères du Kremlin,* p. 91.

34. Souvarine to Russian Opposition, Dec. 1927.

35. Quoted in *ibid.*

36. Carr, *Socialism in One Country,* III, 564, 574. For the problem of the Profintern and trade union unity on a European scale, see *ibid.,* III, 525–97.

37. This was Jaurès's overriding interest. See Jean Bruhaut, "Zhan Zhores i kolonialnaya problema," *Frantsuzskii Ezhegodnik* (Moscow, 1959), pp. 408–26.

38. SFIO, *11e Congrès,* p. 20.

39. Quoted in Jane Degras, *The Communist International, 1919–1943: Documents* (London, 1956), I, 170.

40. *L'Humanité,* 7.i.21.

41. There is a copy of this memorandum in HDA.

42. BC, 14.xii.22.

43. *Protokoll des Vierten Kongresses der Kommunistischen Internationale, Petrograd-Moskau, vom 5. November bis 5. Dezember, 1922* (Hamburg, 1923), p. 870.

44. *IVe Congrès communiste mondial: Résolutions* (1923), p. 38.

45. BC, 13.vi.24.

46. PCF, *3e Congrès* [Lyon, 1924], pp. 66–75.

47. Carr, *Socialism in One Country,* III, 88.

48. *L'Humanité,* 11.ix.24.
49. Barbé, "Souvenirs," p. 80.
50. *L'Humanité,* 5.ii.25.
51. Barbé, "Souvenirs," p. 83.
52. There is an interesting account of this expedition in *ibid.,* pp. 84ff.
53. See Gordon Wright, *Rural Revolution in France: The Peasantry in the Twentieth Century* (Stanford, Calif., 1964), pp. 12–28.
54. *Polnoe sobranie sochinenii,* XLIV, 278.
55. Trotsky, *Kommunisticheskoe dvizhenie vo Frantsii* (Moscow, 1923), pp. 166–71.
56. They were the Seine-Inférieure, the Cher, and the Lot-et-Garonne. The Seine-et-Oise and Nord each elected three deputies.
57. Gordon Wright, "Communists and Peasantry in France," in Edward Mead Earle, ed., *Modern France* (Princeton, N.J., 1951), pp. 222–23.
58. According to Sémard. Quoted in Walter, *Histoire du Parti Communiste Français,* p. 158. Sémard cited the example of the Algerian federation, which had lost three-quarters of its members. This, he added, was not an isolated case. *Ibid.,* p. 160, n. 25.
59. *Cahiers du Bolchévisme,* 1.iii.25, p. 927.
60. Quoted in Wright, "Communists and Peasantry in France," p. 222.
61. Monatte to Parreye, 22.v.24. Monatte Archives.
62. Rosmer to Monatte, 11.viii.24. Monatte Archives.
63. *L'Humanité,* 23.ix.24, 24.ix.24.
64. According to an undated memoir in the Monatte Archives.
65. *L'Humanité,* 23.ix.24, 24.ix.24.
66. These letters are preserved in the Monatte Archives.
67. BP to Monatte, 24.ix.24. Monatte Archives.
68. *Cahiers du Bolchévisme,* 5.xii.24, p. 206.
69. The letter was published in *ibid.*
70. Chambelland, "Aux camarades de la section communiste de Juvisy." There is a copy of this undated communication in the Monatte Archives.
71. "Je suis exclus du Parti Communiste: Vive le parti." Letter from Edmond Guillou to the members of the PCF, 1.xii.24. Monatte Archives.
72. Rosmer to Sémard, 5.xi.24. Monatte Archives.
73. See Sémard's statement at the conference of federation secretaries, *L'Humanité,* 23.ix.24.
74. Carr, *Socialism in One Country,* II, 8–11.
75. *Ibid.,* p. 12.
76. *Inprecorr,* 15.xii.24, p. 968.
77. Carr, *Socialism in One Country,* II, 25–26.
78. "Rapport moral du Secrétariat général," *Cahiers du Bolchévisme,* 20.xii.24, p. 2.
79. *Ibid.,* 28.xi.24, p. 73.
80. For the theory and practice of Soviet foreign policy in this era, see Carr, *Socialism in One Country,* III, 21–69.
81. For the French recognition of the Soviet Union, see the articles by Stuart Schram in *Cahiers du Monde Russe et Soviétique,* Jan.–Mar. 1960, pp. 205–37, and July–Dec. 1960, pp. 584–629.
82. The reaction of the Right and the *bien pensant* public is described in Eugen Weber, *Action Française: Royalism and Reaction in Twentieth-Century France* (Stanford, Calif., 1962), pp. 154–56. See also *Le Temps,* Nov. 27, Dec. 3, and Dec. 5, 1924, which rediscovered "the Communist peril."
83. *L'Humanité,* 19.xii.24.
84. Weber, *Action Française,* p. 156.
85. According to an undated memoir in the Monatte Archives. This very interesting

document was designed to explain to critical comrades why Monatte and Rosmer had entered into open rebellion against the party leadership.

86. *Réponse du Bureau Politique à la lettre de Monatte, Rosmer et Delagarde aux membres du Parti Communiste* (1924).

87. Trotsky's speech was published in the *Cahiers du Bolchévisme,* 5.xii.24.

88. *L'Humanité,* 2.xii.24.

89. Frossard claimed that Communists had been ordered to return all copies of the Opposition's brochure to party headquarters—unread. *L'Oeuvre,* 2.xii.24.

90. *L'Humanité,* 7.xii.24.

91. Ferrat, *Histoire du Parti Communiste Français,* p. 144.

92. The Secretary's report at the end of 1924 implied that the reorganization had not yet been successfully extended beyond these areas. *Cahiers du Bolchévisme,* 20.xii.24, p. 4.

93. Weber, *Action Française,* p. 155.

94. Souvarine to Rosmer, Dec. 8–15, 1924. Monatte Archives.

95. *La Révolution Prolétarienne,* Mar. 1925, p. 24.

96. Published in *Inprecorr,* 15.i.25.

97. These theses are published in *Cahiers du Bolchévisme,* 9.i.25, pp. 555–58.

98. *Ibid.,* 1.v.25, p. 1144.

99. *Ibid.,* 15.iv.25, pp. 1061–62.

100. *L'Humanité,* 18.i.25. No stenographic account of this congress was ever published.

101. *Ibid.,* 19.i.25.

102. *Ibid.,* 20.i.25.

103. *La Révolution Prolétarienne,* Mar. 1925, p. 24.

104. *Ibid.,* Feb. 1925, p. 8.

105. A number of their letters are preserved in the Monatte Archives.

106. *Otchet ispolkoma Kominterna (aprel 1925–yanvar 1926).*

107. Dunois to Humbert-Droz, 9.ii.25. HDA.

108. There is a copy of this letter and others from the Opposition in the Trotsky Archives, T849.

109. Loriot to Zinoviev, 14.ii.25. Trotsky Archives, T850.

110. Pierre Pascal to Souvarine, 13.iv.25. Monatte Archives.

111. *Exécutif Elargi de l'Internationale Communiste: Compte rendu analytique de la session de 21 mars au 6 avril 1925,* p. 66.

112. Pascal to Souvarine, 13.iv.25. Monatte Archives.

113. *Exécutif Elargi,* p. 199.

114. Pascal to Rosmer, 12.iv.25. Monatte Archives.

115. *Cahiers du Bolchévisme,* 15.x.25, p. 1978.

116. Undated letter. Monatte Archives.

117. The letters of the French Opposition may be found in the Trotsky Archives, T854, T855, and T859. For Kleine, see *Cahiers du Bolchévisme,* 15.vi.25, pp. 1316–17, where he admits that the Right's criticisms would be valuable—if they were not made by the Right.

118. Herclet to Rosmer, 3.i.25. Monatte Archives.

119. Pascal to Rosmer, 12.iv.25. Monatte Archives.

120. Quoted by André Marty in his report on "Les Organisations et les cadres de renégats." Marty Archives.

121. *Staline* (1935). In English, *Stalin: A Political Survey of Bolshevism* (New York, 1939).

122. On Rosmer's Trotskyist activities, see Isaac Deutscher, *The Prophet Outcast* (London, 1963).

123. Rosmer, *Le Mouvement ouvrier pendant la guerre,* 2 vols. (1936–59).

124. *La Révolution Prolétarienne*, 25.xi.32, pp. 10–11.

125. Loriot's articles were later published in the form of a pamphlet, *Les Problèmes de la révolution russe* (1928).

126. Rappoport, "Mémoires," p. 307.

127. *Ibid.*, p. 310.

128. The description is Dunois', in a letter to Humbert-Droz, 9.ii.25. HDA.

129. Barbé, "Souvenirs," p. 51, and Branko Lazitch, "Two Instruments of Control by the Comintern" (unpublished ms.), p. 17.

130. Sémard, in *Dix années de lutte pour la révolution mondiale*, pp. 272–73.

131. According to Mahouy, *Contre le Courant*, 19.xii.27, p. 25.

132. For Thorez, see Wohl, "Thorez: Practitioner of the Popular Front," *Communist Affairs*, Sept.–Oct. 1963, pp. 21–26.

133. Barbé, "Souvenirs," p. 80.      134. Wohl, "Thorez," p. 24.

135. *Le Crapouillot*, Jan. 1962, p. 19.      136. Barbé, "Souvenirs," p. 19.

137. Raymond Aron's concept of "availability" would apply here. "Totalitarianism and Freedom," *Confluence*, II (June, 1953), 8–9, and William Kornhauser, *The Politics of Mass Society* (Glencoe, Ill., 1959), p. 223.

138. Barbé, "Souvenirs," p. 5.

139. Richard Crossman, ed., *The God That Failed*, Bantam ed. (New York, 1959), pp. 93–94.

## Conclusion

Epigraph: *Clarté*, 15.xi.22.

1. The Leninist interpretation can be found in André Ferrat, *Histoire du Parti Communiste Français* (1931); Gérard Walter, *Histoire du Parti Communiste Français* (1948); Jean Fréville, *Né du feu* (1960); S. Bantke, *Borba za sozdanie kommunisticheskoi partii Frantsii* (Moscow, 1936); and L. P. Kozhevnikova, *Rabochee i sotsialisticheskoe dvizhenie vo Frantsii v 1917–1920 g.g.* (Moscow, 1959). The left-wing point of view is presented in Alfred Rosmer, *Moscou sous Lénine* (1953); Fernand Loriot, *Les Problèmes de la révolution prolétarienne* (1928); Boris Souvarine, *Staline* (1935); and Pierre Monatte, *Trois scissions syndicales* (1958). For the Social Democratic version, see Frossard, *De Jaurès à Lénine* (1930); Daniel Ligou, *Histoire du socialisme en France, 1871–1961* (1962); and Léon Blum, *A l'échelle humaine* (1945).

2. George Lichtheim, *Marxism: An Historical and Critical Study* (New York, 1961), p. 280.

3. Michel Collinet, *Esprit du syndicalisme* (1951), pp. 12–13.

4. Letter of the French Opposition to the ECCI (Feb. 1925). Trotsky Archives, Harvard University, T849.

5. Michel Crozier, "La France, terre de commandement," *Esprit*, Dec. 1957, pp. 779–97.

6. Franz Borkenau, *World Communism* (Ann Arbor, Mich., 1962) and *European Communism* (London, 1951).

7. Borkenau, *World Communism*, pp. 22–26.

8. Various aspects of the liberal crisis are dealt with in Hannah Arendt, *The Origins of Totalitarianism* (New York, 1958); H. Stuart Hughes, *Consciousness and Society*, Vintage ed. (New York, 1961); Stanley Hoffmann *et al.*, *In Search of France* (Cambridge, Mass., 1963), pp. 1–117; Hajo Holborn, *The Political Collapse of Europe* (New York, 1958); Elie Halévy, *The Era of Tyrannies* (Garden City, N.Y., 1965); George Lichtheim, *Marxism*; George Dangerfield, *The Strange Death of Liberal England, 1910–1914* (New York,

1961); Theodore H. Von Laue, *Why Lenin? Why Stalin?* (Philadelphia and New York, 1964); and Barbara Tuchman, *The Proud Tower* (New York, 1965).

9. Hermann Hesse, *Demian* (Augsburg, 1964), pp. 176–77.

10. Eugen Weber, *The Nationalist Revival in France, 1905–1914* (Berkeley, Calif., 1959), especially pp. 150–51.

11. For the relationship between Russia's international position and her internal development, see Von Laue, *Why Lenin? Why Stalin?*, pp. 68–85.

12. George F. Kennan, *Russia and the West Under Lenin and Stalin* (Boston, 1960), pp. 18–32.

13. *L'Humanité,* 24.iv.19.

# Bibliographical Note

O glücklich, wer noch hoffen kann,
Aus diesem Meer des Irrtums aufzutauchen!
Was man nicht weiss, das eben brauchte man,
Und was man weiss, kann man nicht brauchen.
—*Goethe,* Faust, *Part I*

For all the call of scholarly precedent, it seems both unnecessary and unwise to burden this book with a long bibliography. My sources and annotations are in the references. When problems of interpretation and credibility have arisen (as in the case of Frossard's various memoirs), I have preferred to discuss them in their natural context. The reader who wants to pursue the subject further would do best to begin with Jean-Jacques Fiechter's list of sources on the pre-war SFIO in *Le Socialisme français: De l'affaire Dreyfus à la Grande Guerre* (Geneva, 1965), pp. 17–43; Annie Kriegel's thorough bibliography on the period 1914–20 in Volume II of *Aux origines du communisme français, 1914–1920: Contribution à l'histoire du mouvement ouvrier français* (1964); and Witold S. Sworakowski's checklist of Comintern materials and their locations, *The Communist International and its Front Organizations: A Research Guide and Checklist of Holdings in American and European Libraries* (Stanford, Calif., 1965). On the other hand, the time has not yet come for an extensive review of the literature on the origins and early development of French Communism; too little comment of value has been written, too much information of importance is becoming available, to make such an enterprise rewarding. What does seem worthwhile, however, is to situate my book in the geography of the literature, both past and future. The reader may find it useful to know where French Communist studies have been and where they are likely to be going. This Bibliographical Note will therefore fall somewhere between a review of the literature and a discussion of the major sources, followed by some suggestions for further study.

There has always been a great interest in the circumstances surrounding the emergence of the French Communist Party. Confronted with the impotence of their movement, working-class militants wanted to know why the splits of 1914–21 had taken place. Nor has there been a particular dearth of sources. While in the party, the founders talked quite openly of what they had in mind; once outside it, they talked even more. Since most of the men who founded the party either abandoned it or were expelled, the amount of inside information on the party's activities is considerable. It is thus surprising that the literature on the origins of French Communism is not better than it is. As recently as five years ago, one might have said with no fear of exaggeration that the history of the French working-class movement during the years 1914–24 had yet to be written. Nor was this state of affairs peculiar to the period; it reflected the generally low quality of working-class studies in France. Just as the SFIO had never fully experienced the Revisionist controversy, so had it never had an analyst of the caliber of Robert Michels.

Many reasons for the backwardness of working-class studies in France can be found. Until recently good statistics were hard to come by. Libraries were so badly organized that historians found it more convenient to work out of their own collections, with the result that books were seldom thoroughly researched. Most important, perhaps, the history of the working-class movement was written almost exclusively from within party and union ranks. This was in large part the fault of the professional historians. Convinced that "history" ended in 1848, they gladly yielded the ground to the polemicists.[a] These circumstances produced a strange type of history, composed of one part memory, one part rumor, one part newspaper clippings, and three parts political commitment.

One can forgive this literature its prejudices and its *partis pris;* what is more difficult to pardon is its drabness and its lack of insight. These latter, one suspects, were the product of an imperfectly digested Marxism. (It is just as possible, of course, that Marxism owed its popularity to an unwillingness to come to grips with real social and economic developments. Once armed with Marxist formulas, the author no longer had to think. The lack of sound economic training may indeed have been the central problem.) Whatever the cause, the consequences were disastrous. The working-class movement was viewed in isolation from the political culture and the national community. The direction of economic and social development, once taken for granted, was ignored. Events were presented as if they had no human or existential meaning. The Communists, it must be said, have raised these failings to the

---

[a] It must be admitted that the results were sometimes bad when academic historians did descend from their chairs to make pronouncements on contemporary history. We have seen Alphonse Aulard's misreading of the direction of the Russian Revolution of March 1917. (See p. 86 above.) Albert Mathiez, a temporary enthusiast of Communism, did little better. He compared the Bolsheviks to the Jacobins and thus contributed to the illusion that the Bolsheviks were carrying on the French Revolution.

level of an art. In their histories, the party wins even when it loses, just as their enemies lose even when they win. The political advantages of this approach may be considerable, but the literary costs are high. The "struggle for a progressive ideology" loses interest when one realizes its victory is inevitable. After five years of reading party documents, one ends by blaming the Communists not for distorting the history of their party but for making it so dull.

The literature on the making of French Communism may be divided into three periods, according to its focus: (1) 1905–14; (2) 1914–20; and (3) 1920–34. For views of the first period, one must turn to general histories of Socialism, Communism, anarchism, and syndicalism, and in a few instances to biographies. The relevant chapters in Paul Louis, *Histoire du socialisme en France*, 2d ed. (1950); Alexandre Zévaès, *Histoire du socialisme et du communisme en France de 1871 à 1947* (1947); and Marcel Prélot, *L'Evolution politique du socialisme français de 1789 à 1934* (1939), are still worth reading, while Jean Montreuil, *Histoire du mouvement ouvrier en France* (1946); Edouard Dolléans, *Histoire du mouvement ouvrier* (1946); and Jean Maitron, *Histoire du mouvement anarchiste en France, 1880–1914*, 2d ed. (1955), are useful for the development of syndicalism. Milorad M. Drachkovitch's study, *Les Socialismes français et allemand et le problème de la guerre, 1870–1914* (Geneva, 1953), is much more inclusive than its title indicates; in many respects, it is the best book on the development of French Socialism before the War. G. D. H. Cole, *The Second International, 1889–1914*, Part I (London, 1956), and Carl Landauer, *European Socialism*, 2 vols. (Berkeley, Calif., 1960), add a salutary European perspective. Cole is calm, learned, and sensible; Landauer is more venturous, more up-to-date, but also more often wrong.

Two new histories of Socialism by Daniel Ligou and Georges Lefranc have appeared in recent years. Though Ligou's *Histoire du socialisme en France, 1871-1961* (1961) is the more substantial and ambitious, Lefranc's *Le Mouvement socialiste sous la Troisième République* (1963) is the more interesting. It emphasizes the price of ideological inflexibility and points to the opportunities for State–working-class cooperation lost before 1914. Jean-Jacques Fiechter, *Le Socialisme français,* analyzes the SFIO's development in the decade and a half before the War. His book, though thoughtful, shows the need for more detailed studies in this area. It is for this reason that Claude Willard's account of the Guesdists, *Le Mouvement socialiste en France (1893–1905): Les Guesdistes* (1965), makes such an important contribution. Stronger on fact than analysis, Willard's heavily researched thesis has a great deal to say about the men who founded Socialism in France and the evolution of their ideas. Three recent biographies have also added to our knowledge of the period before 1914. Bernard Georges and Denise Tintant, in *Léon Jouhaux, cinquante ans de syndicalisme* (1962), have illuminated some of the forces undermining revolutionary syndicalism before the War, while Harvey Goldberg, *The Life of Jean*

*Jaurès* (Madison, Wis., 1962) has shown how circumstances pushed Jaurès toward the Left after 1905. B. W. Schaper's admiring study of Albert Thomas, *Albert Thomas: Trente années de réformisme social* (1960), by contrast, describes how one of Jaurès's most devoted disciples was increasingly attracted by reformism during the same decade. To my mind, the most stimulating work on this period has been done by Eugen Weber, *The Nationalist Revival in France, 1905–1914* (Berkeley, Calif., 1959); "Un Demi-Siècle de glissement à droite," *International Review of Social History,* Vol. V (1960), Part II, pp. 165–201; *Action Française: Royalism and Reaction in Twentieth-Century France* (Stanford, Calif., 1962); "France" in *The European Right,* edited with Hans Rogger (Berkeley, Calif., 1965), pp. 71–126. Though primarily interested in the origins of fascist movements, Weber has increasingly been led to emphasize the failure of the Left in explaining the success of the extreme Right in winning leaders and recruits. His work adds another dimension to our understanding of the Socialist crisis.

The greatest scholarly effort has borne on the period leading from the outbreak of the War to the splits of the SFIO and the CGT in 1920–21. The Right lost no time in making known its point of view. Writing in 1919, Jean Maxe, *De Zimmerwald au bolchévisme,* blamed the emergence of a Communist faction in France on the intrigues of revolution-mad Russians and the campaigns of pathologically unbalanced French intellectuals. Yet despite this unpromising perspective, his book is not devoid of information on the development of the Zimmerwald camp. The same cannot be said of J. Rocher's Communist interpretation, *Lénine et le mouvement zimmerwaldien en France* (1934). Rocher distorted the true relations between the Russian Socialists and the French Zimmerwaldians beyond all recognition, in trying to prove that Lenin had inspired and masterminded the French opposition to the War. The next Communist writer did better. S. Bantke's sturdy and well-documented volume on the period 1914–18, *Borba za sozdanie kommunisticheskoi partii Frantsii* (Moscow, 1936), though a far from balanced account, was a real contribution to the historiography of the Socialist split. Unfortunately, the author was unable to continue his work through the founding of the party, as he had originally planned.

All the above-mentioned works present a distorted picture of the Opposition. This is where Alfred Rosmer's two-volume work, *Le Mouvement ouvrier pendant la guerre* (1936–59) excels. Eschewing synthesis in favor of detailed factual reconstruction, Rosmer has described, almost month by month, the difficulties and confusion of the wartime Opposition up to the outbreak of the Russian Revolution. In explaining the dissension in working-class ranks, Rosmer emphasized the betrayal of the Socialist and syndicalist leaders. Merle Fainsod, *International Socialism and the World War* (Cambridge, Mass., 1935), on the other hand, approaching the subject from the point of view of the International as a whole, agreed with the Communists that the split had been implicit in prewar ideological differences. Franz Borkenau, *Der euro-päische Kommunismus: Seine Geschichte von 1917 bis zur Gegenwart* (Bern, 1952), pp. 72–100, also felt that ideological cleavages, though unreal, were im-portant; but when he came to sketching the background of the PCF in the emotion-charged atmosphere of the Cold War, he stressed the Machiavellian-ism of the Bolsheviks and the duplicity of Frossard and Cachin. His pages on the origins of the PCF are not among his best.

Some of the best work since the Second World War has been devoted to the study of the international situation within which the French working-class movement had to maneuver. Arno J. Mayer, *Political Origins of the New Diplomacy* (New Haven, Conn., 1959), has shown the impact of Wilson's and Lenin's diplomacy on the working-class organizations of the belligerent countries, while E. H. Carr, *The Bolshevik Revolution* (New York, 1953), Vol. III; James W. Hulse, *The Forming of the Communist International* (Stanford, Calif., 1964); and Donald W. Urquidi, "The Origins of the Italian Communist Party" (unpublished doctoral dissertation, Columbia University, 1962), have investigated the tension between Bolshevik principles and inter-national realities. The last two authors in particular have stressed the radical change in the Bolshevik strategy of world revolution that came in the spring of 1920. Postwar Soviet writers, on the contrary, have contributed little of value to the historiography of the period. L. P. Kozhevnikova, *Rabochee i sotsial-isticheskoe dvizhenie vo Frantsii v 1917–1920 g.g.* (Moscow, 1959), is mainly concerned to prove the power of the October Revolution; in her zeal to dis-tinguish heroes (those who embraced Bolshevism) from villains (those who opposed it), she seems blissfully unaware of the problems that exercise Western scholars.

The French meanwhile have continued to be fascinated by the splits of 1920–21. Jean Fréville, *Né du feu* (1960), greeted the fortieth anniversary of the PCF's founding with a well-documented and smartly written essay, which emphasizes—I think, quite properly—the impact of the War. Maurice Labi, *La Grande Division des travailleurs: Première scission de la C.G.T. 1914–1921* (1964), has given us an interesting volume on the schism of the CGT. His attractive, but not very convincing, conclusion is that the leaders of both the minority and the majority did not do all they might have to avoid the split. By far the best and most comprehensive book on the split of the French work-ing-class movement, however, is Annie Kriegel's *Aux origines du commu-nisme français* (1964). Mme. Kriegel was not satisfied with the tired Commu-nist saw that Communism had arisen because of its superior ideological pre-mises; nor was she any happier with the point of view, so dear to Cold War theorists, that Communism was a secular religion. Plunging into the study of the problem with boundless energy and a standard of evidence that French working-class history had never before seen, she concluded that Communism was "primarily a strategic concept, devised after the First World War, to carry out a proletarian revolution."

Little has been written on the period following the Congress of Tours. Having described the events leading to the split, Borkenau covered the party's subsequent development with a few quick and scornful strokes. Cole, quite properly, felt no need to dwell on it in a history of Socialist thought. The five general histories of the party have never quite known how to approach this confused period, and have leaped on as quickly as possible to more glorious and easily comprehensible events. Of these, André Ferrat's *Histoire du Parti Communiste Français* (1931), is still in most respects the best. Though full of distortions and omissions, it at least had the merit of describing the spirit in which the transformation of 1924–26 was carried out. Gérard Walter's *Histoire du Parti Communiste Français* (1948) is a paean to the inspired leadership of Maurice Thorez. Since Thorez played no role before 1924, the period is portrayed as one of stagnation and blackest night. Disgusted by the lack of information about the party's past, a group of anonymous Communist militants in 1960 began the publication of an *Histoire du Parti Communiste Français* that sought to re-establish the truth concealed by the leadership. Unfortunately, their desire to guarantee "la réalité des faits" did not make up for their ignorance of the party's origins and early development. The official party history, *Histoire du Parti Communiste Français (Manuel)* (1964), in its impatience to draw the lessons of the party's past, did little to rectify this situation. Only those individuals who happened to fit into the pattern that the team of authors were attempting to establish were mentioned; all others were consigned to the dustbin of history. Thus the role of Loriot and Souvarine in the founding of the party went undiscussed, while Treint was written off in a footnote as "one of the leaders of the French Communist Party at the time."

Jacques Fauvet's two-volume *Histoire du Parti Communiste Français* (1964–65) has helped to establish certain of the facts, but it has not done justice to the author's considerable analytical talents. In fact, all the histories suffer from the same defect: they take for granted what has to be explained. In the last two years, this period has at last begun to get the attention that it deserves. E. H. Carr has given a brief but accurate overview of the party's development in *Socialism in One Country, 1924–1926* (London, 1964), Vol. III, Part I, pp. 137–57, 348–66, based on research in the archives; David Caute, *Communism and the French Intellectuals, 1914–1960* (New York, 1964), has described the relations between the party and the intellectuals with verve and insight; and George Lichtheim, *Marxism in Modern France* (New York and London, 1966), has written intelligently about the party's adjustment to its non-revolutionary role. Their work, taken together with Mme. Kriegel's, suggests that the study of French Communism has finally come of age.

The recent interest in French Communism is, at least in part, a response to large reserves of unexploited material. In comparison with the sources for the early history of other Communist parties, those for the PCF are rather good. Stenographic accounts of party congresses and the main journals of party opinion are easily found (by those with access to Parisian libraries[b]), and there are several important collections of personal papers. What hiatuses there are are mostly due to the hazards of the German occupation or the carelessness of libraries, not to the secretiveness of Communists. The historian who plunges into this material, however, soon finds that it is highly selective. It generally tells you what party leaders said; it sometimes tells you what they did; seldom, though, does it tell you what they thought or how they got the ideas that they had. One finds oneself with a flood of information about the organization and almost nothing about the men who made it up. To learn the first name of an important party leader may take more time than to discover the truth about one of the party's so-called clandestine operations. The historian's greatest obstacle, though, is the layer of myths that overlies the party's past. Men are labeled—then forgotten. Facts are distorted and the distortions repeated until they attain the status of dogma. The historian must therefore be careful to scrutinize every personality and event with fresh eyes.

There are five major types of sources for the early history of French Communism: (1) party, union, and Comintern documents; (2) the press; (3) government documents; (4) private papers; and (5) personal accounts. Reports of party, union, and Comintern meetings are the single most important source for the period from 1914 to 1924. In general, these accounts are easily available; when they are lacking (as in the case of the wartime congresses of the SFIO or the Communist congresses of 1921, 1922, and 1923), one must have recourse to *L'Humanité,* which always recapitulated important meetings. Comintern documents present a special problem. Finding the definitive version of an important directive or discussion can be a Sisyphian task. Speeches on the French situation were sometimes published in *L'Humanité,* reprinted (in fuller form) in the *Bulletin Communiste,* issued in the form of a pamphlet, included in the record of the ECCI, and, in the case of Trotsky's speeches, reissued in the Russian edition of his writings on the Communist movement in France: *Kommunisticheskoe dvizhenie vo Frantsii* (Moscow, 1923). These documents are not only in different languages; they also vary in content. *Inprecorr* is an even more befuddling problem. Generally, the German edition was the most complete, but when looking for materials on France, one cannot be sure. Accounts of Comintern congresses also vary in content and in language. Some day no doubt a team of conscientious scholars will undertake a

[b] The two best libraries for the study of the early history of French Communism are the Bibliothèque Nationale and the Bibliothèque de Documentation Internationale Contemporaine. The newspapers and reviews that cannot be found in one can generally be found in the other. In the United States the Hoover Institution is unparalleled, both for the depth of its collection and for the helpfulness of its staff.

definitive edition of Comintern meetings; their task will not be an enviable one.

The press is an only slightly less important source for the making of French Communism. The development of the French working-class movement before 1914 can be followed in *L'Humanité, Le Socialiste, La Bataille Syndicaliste, La Guerre Sociale, L'Action Directe, Le Mouvement Socialiste, La Vie Ouvrière,* and the countless anarchist newspapers surrounding the SFIO and CGT. During the War the Opposition wrote throughout the spectrum of the working-class and left-leaning bourgeois press, sometimes even contributing to foreign-based papers and reviews. A Communist leader like Loriot, to give only one example, contributed to *L'Ecole de la Fédération, La Plèbe, Ce Qu'Il Faut Dire, La Nouvelle Internationale, Le Populaire, L'Humanité, La Vérité, Le Journal du Peuple, and La Vie Ouvrière.* After 1921 a certain tendency toward centralization set in, and the range of Communist opinion is represented by *L'Humanité, L'Internationale* (until 1922), the *Bulletin Communiste,* the *Internationale Communist, Inprecorr, Le Journal du Peuple, La Vague, La Vie Ouvrière,* and *La Lutte de Classe* (for the syndicalists), *L'Avant-Garde* (for the Jeunesses Communistes), and *Clarté* (for the intellectuals). After 1924 the situation again became complex. The *Bulletin Communiste* became the *Cahiers du Bolchévisme,* collaboration on *La Vie Ouvrière* was limited to the leadership of the CGTU, and the Opposition expressed itself through a variety of irregularly appearing journals, ranging from *La Révolution Prolétarienne* (Monatte, Rosmer, Louzon, Chambelland, Loriot) to the *Bulletin Communiste* (Souvarine) to *Contre le Courant* (Paz, Mahouy). Outside the Communist camp, *Le Temps* often ran penetrating articles on the development of the party, as did *Le Populaire,* which took a special delight in exposing the inconsistencies and internal quarrels of the Communists. *BEIPI,* which began publication in 1949, carried on this tradition, and though its interest was primarily the contemporary Communist world, its staff (Souvarine, Barbé, Pierre Célor, Claude Hormel, Branko Lazitch) was well equipped to make embarrassing references to the PCF's formative years.

Various types of government documents can also be of use to a historian of the working-class movement during the 1914–24 period. Parliamentary debates show Socialist and Communist leaders at grips with the political community, of which they were a part. Campaign statements filed with the government give some idea of the programs with which working-class candidates went to their electors. The records of political trials (like the "Trial of the Plot" in 1921) often yield insights into the clandestine operations of Communist leaders, as do foreign ministry documents, both French and foreign. The police report is another precious, though in my opinion somewhat overrated, source. This is not to say that working-class historians should not use them, but only that they should use them cautiously. In any case, owing to the so-called 50-year rule, the archives of the Sûreté Générale bearing on the period covered in this book will not be opened until 1971–75. Thus beginning in 1971 one can expect additional documentation and perhaps important revelations concerning the clandestine activities of the PCF in 1921–25.

The real strength of the sources on the early history of French Communism lies, however, in the large number of personal archives, many of which are just now becoming available for use by scholars. Some, of course, are more relevant than others, but all supply valuable pieces necessary for reconstructing the story of the PCF's origins and early years. The papers of Robert Grimm (International Institute for Social History, Amsterdam), Hjalmar Branting (Arbetarrörelsens Arkiv, Stockholm), and Camille Huysmans (Feltrinelli Institute, Milan), cast light on the development of the wartime Opposition. André Marty's archives (Institut Français d'Histoire Sociale, Paris, and the Hoover Institution, Stanford, California), contain letters bearing on the foundation of *Clarté*, the strikes of 1918–19, and the Black Sea mutinies. Charles Rappoport's papers (International Institute for Social History), though thin on the years after 1914, include a few items of interest on the campaign to take the SFIO into the Third International and the conflict over Souvarine in 1921. The importance of the archives of Jules Humbert-Droz (International Institute for Social History, Hoover Institution), has already been sufficiently stressed. Ranging in nature from the directives of the ECCI to the letters of individual Communist leaders like Treint and Cachin, the papers of the former Comintern agent in France offer a unique insight into the life of the PCF in 1922–23. Trotsky's archives (Houghton Library, Harvard University) are also richer for this topic than one might expect. Though weighted toward the affairs of the Russian party, they include some precious items on the Comintern's policy toward the PCF at the Fourth Congress, the finances of the party, and relations between the ECCI and the Opposition in 1925–26. Monatte's papers (Institut Français d'Histoire Sociale) are another mine of information, and are particularly strong on the crisis of 1924 and the development of the thinking of the Opposition. Like government documents, these materials have their dangers. Lacking the papers of Treint and Souvarine, the historian will inevitably see the crisis of 1922–23 through the eyes of Humbert-Droz. But the risks of distortion will diminish as more archives are opened.

Papers are useful; but by their very nature, they are highly concrete, fragmentary, and almost always lacking in perspective. For a more reflective and rounded picture of what happened and for sketches of personalities, the historian must turn to personal accounts. There are a few excellent memoirs touching on the origins of the PCF. Henri Barbé's unpublished autobiography, "Souvenirs de militant et de dirigeant communiste" (Hoover Institution), shows the importance of the youth movement and contains numerous vignettes of Young Communists who later became important Communist leaders. Frossard's memoirs, *De Jaurès à Lénine* (1930), *De Jaurès à Léon Blum* (1943), are invaluable sources for the attitude of the ex-Jauressians and Guesdists at grips with the new phenomenon of Communism. Rappoport's unpublished autobiography (Bibliothèque Nationale) also yields some interesting insights, though it is stronger on the prewar period. A. Lozovsky's *Rabochaya Frantsiya* (Moscow, 1923) gives a fascinating account of a Bolshevik leader's reaction to the complexities of the French working-class movement in 1922. No reading on this period was more delightful—or more instructive. Victor Serge's *Mémoires d'un révolutionnaire, 1901–1941* (1951) also contains some acute observations concerning the French working-class movement and French Communists in Russia. Vladimir Diogott, *V "svobodnom" podpole* (Moscow, 1923), has revealed some of the details of his trip to France in the spring of 1920, while Marcel Brody has published a personal account of the French group in Moscow during 1919–20 in *Contributions à l'histoire du Comintern,* ed. Jacques Freymond (Geneva, 1965). In general, though, the memoir situation is not good. Autobiographies are few, and when they do exist, as in the case of Rosmer, *Moscou sous Lénine* (1953) and Monatte, *Trois scissions syndicales* (1958), they seldom tell the historian the things he wants to know. Books like Henri Guilbeaux's *Du Kremlin au Cherche-Midi* (1933) and Maurice Laporte's *Les Mystères du Kremlin* (1928), moreover, must only be used with the greatest caution. Faced with this situation, the historian will inevitably turn to personal interviews (when possible) or novels (like Raymond Lefebvre's *Le Sacrifice d'Abraham,* 1919, and *L'Eponge du Vinaigre,* 1921), in an attempt to recapture something of the spirit of those days.

Historical studies tend to fluctuate between cycles of synthesis and cycles of research. Explanation, if it is daring, incites renewed research; research, in turn, if it is thorough, inspires further synthesis. My conviction is that French Communist studies are on the point of changing cycles. What is required now is less synthesis and more fact, a shift from the explanation of the whole to the detailed study of the part. For example, we need to know about the development of individual regions like the Nord and the Bouches-du-Rhône; only then will we understand the meaning of Communism as a national movement. We need to know the history of individual unions like the railway workers' or metallurgists' unions: what kind of people they attracted, how their leadership evolved, and to what extent union members were affected by union policy. We need studies of individual events like the occupation of the Ruhr and the Riff War, showing the relationship between the party and the national community. Most of all, we need biographies of individual Communist, Socialist, and union leaders, which will illuminate their personal development as well as their public role. The main thing is to recapture somehow the atmosphere—the veil of fears and frustrations, hopes and dreams, prejudices and certainties—within which the working-class leaders of the twenties lived their lives. Only then will we be on the road to understanding the Communist phenomenon.

# Index